Make Instruction Needs-Based

◆ Identify where your students are struggling and customize address their needs.

◆ Gauge how your entire class or individual students are doing by viewing the easy to use grade book.

◆ Ensure your students are getting the additional reinforcement and direction they need between class meetings.

Getting Started is as EASY as 1, 2, 3 . . . 4!

1. Sign Up

Instructors register with myBusinessCourse.com

2. Setup Your Course

Add your class details and additional materials.

3. Invite Your Students

Students register using your unique course code.

4. Manage Your Course

Study, test, and grade assignments. It's simple!

Provide Instruction and Practice 24/7

◆ Assign homework from your Cambridge Business Publishers textbook and have myBusinessCourse grade it for you automatically.

◆ With our eLectures, your students can revisit accounting topics as often as they like or until they master the topic.

◆ Guided Examples show students how to solve select problems.

◆ Make homework due before class to ensure students enter your classroom prepared.

◆ Upgrade to include the eBook and you have all the tools needed for an online course.

Want to learn more about myBusinessCourse?

Contact your sales representative or visit **www.mybusinesscourse.com**.

STUDENTS: Find your access code on the myBusinessCourse insert on the following pages. If you have a used copy of this textbook, you can purchase access online at **www.mybusinesscourse.com**.

Cambridge Business Publishers Series in Accounting

Financial Accounting

- **Financial Accounting for Undergraduates, 2e** by Ferris, Wallace, and Christensen
- **Financial Accounting, 4e** by Dyckman, Magee, and Pfeiffer
- **Financial Accounting for MBAs, 5e** by Easton, Wild, Halsey, and McAnally
- **Financial Accounting for Executives & MBAs, 3e** by Simko, Ferris, and Wallace
- **Cases in Financial Reporting, 7e** by Engel, Hirst, and McAnally

Managerial Accounting

- **Managerial Accounting, 6e** by Hartgraves & Morse
- **Cases in Managerial and Cost Accounting, 1e** by Allen, Brownlee, Haskins, and Lynch

Combined Financial & Managerial Accounting

- **Financial & Managerial Accounting for MBAs, 3e** by Easton, Halsey, McAnally, Hartgraves, and Morse

Intermediate Accounting

- **Cases in Financial Reporting, 7e** by Engel, Hirst, and McAnally

Cost Accounting

- **Cases in Managerial and Cost Accounting, 1e** by Allen, Brownlee, Haskins, and Lynch

Financial Statement Analysis & Valuation

- **Financial Statement Analysis & Valuation, 3e** by Easton, McAnally, Sommers, and Zhang
- **Cases in Financial Reporting, 7e** by Engel, Hirst, and McAnally

Advanced Accounting

- **Advanced Accounting, 2e** by Hamlen, Huefner, and Largay
- **Advanced Accounting, 2e** by Halsey & Hopkins

my BusinessCourse

FREE WITH NEW COPIES OF THIS TEXTBOOK

Scratch here for access code

U6Y9DjgG8mQpAfwE

Scratch here for access code

Start using my BusinessCourse Today: www.mybusinesscourse.com

my BusinessCourse is a web-based learning and assessment program intended to complement your textbook and faculty instruction.

Student Benefits
- eLectures
- Guided examples
- Immediate feedback with auto graded homework from the textbook
- Opportunities for additional practice and exam preparation
- Optional upgrade includes eBook

Instructor Benefits
- Easy-to-use course management system
- Homework automatically graded
- Provide students with additional help when you are not available
- Detailed diagnostic tools to assess class performance
- Resources for a complete online course

Interactive content that runs on any device.

Built for PCs, iPads, Laptops, Tablets, Smartphones

You can access my BusinessCourse 24/7 from any web-enabled device, including iPads, smartphones, laptops, and tablets.

Financial Accounting for Executives & MBAs

Third Edition

PAUL J. SIMKO
Darden School of Business
University of Virginia

KENNETH R. FERRIS
W.P. Carey School of Business
Arizona State University

JAMES S. WALLACE
The Peter F. Drucker and Masatoshi Ito
Graduate School of Management
Claremont Graduate University

Cambridge
BUSINESS PUBLISHERS

Photo Credits
Chapter 1: iStock Photo
Chapter 2: iStock Photo
Chapter 3: iStock Photo
Chapter 4: JAM Publications
Chapter 5: iStock Photo
Chapter 6: iStock Photo
Chapter 7: iStock Photo
Chapter 8: iStock Photo
Chapter 9: iStock Photo
Chapter 10: JAM Publications
Chapter 11: iStock Photo
Chapter 12: iStock Photo

FINANCIAL ACCOUNTING FOR EXECUTIVES & MBAs, Third Edition, by Paul Simko, Kenneth Ferris, and James Wallace

ISBN 978-1-61853-046-2

Bookstores & Faculty: to order this book, contact the company via email **customerservice@cambridgepub.com** or call 800-619-6473.

Students: to order this book, please visit the book's Website and order directly online.

Printed in the United States of America.
10 9 8 7 6 5 4 3 2 1

About the Authors

Paul J. Simko is Associate Dean of the MBA for Executives Program and Associate Professor of Business at the University of Virginia's Darden School. He received Bachelor of Science and Master in Accountancy degrees from the University of Florida, and a Ph.D. from the University of Texas at Austin. Professor Simko was previously on the faculty at Emory University, and has served as a visiting professor at Indiana, INSEAD, the Helsinki School of Economics, and the Indian School of Business. He was a Senior Analyst with Citicorp and is a Certified Public Accountant, and he remains a frequent consultant to government agencies and public and private corporations. Professor Simko has received numerous recognitions for his research and teaching. His research has appeared in such journals as *The Accounting Review*, *Journal of Accounting Research*, *Financial Analysts Journal*, and the *Stanford Journal of Law, Business and Finance*.

Kenneth R. Ferris is a Professor in the W.P. Carey School of Business at Arizona State University. He received a B.B.A. and an M.B.A. from The George Washington University and an M.A. and a Ph.D. from The Ohio State University. He previously served on the faculties of Northwestern University, The Claremont Graduate University, Southern Methodist University, and Thunderbird School of Global Management, In addition, he has taught at numerous academic institutions in Australia, Hong Kong, Japan, and New Zealand. Professor Ferris is the author or co-author of eleven books, over fifty academic and professional publications, and over eighty case studies. He previously served as a director of several NYSE listed companies and is active in executive education programs around the world.

James S. Wallace is an Associate Professor at The Peter F. Drucker and Masatoshi Ito Graduate School of Management at The Claremont Graduate University. He received his B.A. from the University of California, Santa Barbara, his M.B.A. from the University of California, Davis, and his Ph.D. from the University of Washington. Professor Wallace also holds a CPA certification from the state of California. He previously served on the faculty of the University of California, Irvine and has served as a visiting professor at the University of California, San Diego. Professor Wallace's work has appeared in leading academic journals including the *Journal of Accounting and Economics*, the *Journal of Corporate Finance*, and *Information Systems Research*, along with leading applied journals such as the *Journal of Applied Corporate Finance*, the *Journal of Accountancy*, *Issues in Accounting Education* and *Accounting Horizons*. Prior to his career in academics, Professor Wallace worked in public accounting and in industry with a Fortune 500 company. He has done consulting work with numerous companies in multiple industries.

Preface

WELCOME TO *FINANCIAL ACCOUNTING FOR EXECUTIVES & MBAS.*

If you have prior business experience, either working for a company or managing your own business, then you know firsthand that an understanding of financial accounting is essential to achieve your full potential on the job. Although business decisions certainly involve a careful analysis of non-financial factors, they also almost always require analysis of financial accounting information. Initiating a marketing campaign, restructuring a subsidiary, determining the sale price of a new product, or assessing whether to acquire another company (and at what price) are just a few of the business decisions that require an understanding of financial accounting. This textbook is written to facilitate that understanding and to facilitate the reader's personal goal of gaining a more complete understanding of financial accounting and its use in business decisions.

Target Audience

Financial Accounting for Executives & MBAs is written specifically for the Executive MBA and MBA markets. This concise text can be used in a wide variety of course formats, ranging from brief executive programs lasting only a few weekends to more traditional 15-week courses.

> "I've been teaching 10 years, and this is the BEST text I've seen for introducing financial accounting to a layperson. My major problem with texts has been that they are either too broad or too detailed. This book is the perfect mix of breadth and depth for a layperson, be they an executive who has had some exposure to accounting or a student who is just entering the study of accounting. This book is excellent."
>
> — **Catherine Eason,** *Queens University of Charlotte*

Book Organization

A succinct, flexible 12-chapter structure fits EMBA, full-time, part-time, and evening MBA programs. This book provides students with the tools and insights necessary to make informed business decisions ranging from performance evaluation to firm valuation. The chapters are organized around a decision-focused structure. The first four chapters introduce the basic financial statements and tools for financial analysis:

  I. The Foundations of Accounting and Financial Statement Analysis (Chapters 1–4)

The next seven chapters provide additional structure for this analysis, with each chapter including a section that discusses how the chapter's content should be analyzed and how that analysis will impact firm value:

 II. Operating Resources and Decisions (Chapters 5–6)
III. Investing Resources and Decisions (Chapters 7–8)
IV. Financing Resources and Decisions (Chapters 9–11)

The book concludes with an introduction to various methodologies to assess the value of a company:

 V. Equity Valuation (Chapter 12)

What is the Financial Statement Spreadsheet Approach to Illustrating Accounting Concepts?

The EMBA and MBA markets tend to be more analytical and decision-focused than the undergraduate market. Unlike undergraduate textbooks in accounting that use the classic debit and credit paradigm to explain key concepts, this textbook uses a financial statement spreadsheet approach to explain the fundamentals of financial accounting. Not only is this approach more user-friendly (because most managers routinely use spreadsheets in their daily professional lives), but it is also far less labor- and time-intensive than the classic debit/credit paradigm. The spreadsheet approach to recording transactions emphasizes user analysis and deemphasizes bookkeeping.

The financial statement spreadsheet approach builds upon the basic accounting equation to demonstrate how business events are processed and ultimately recorded. It will be appreciated by many executives and MBA students for its simplicity and intuitive appeal, as well as for its link back to how they likely see accounting information in their professional lives. That is, it presents a vertical format to the balance sheet equation, functionally following the form and presentation of the balance sheet most often observe in practice and annual reports. The format is also used to illustrate income statement accounts as inputs directly into the retained earnings account, reinforcing this important concept to students in a way that helps them more clearly understand the relation between the balance sheet and income statement. Below is an example of the financial statement spreadsheet approach used in the context of a long-term fixed asset acquisition and sale:

	Acquire Asset	Depreciate Asset	Sell Asset	End. Bal. (summary)	
Assets					
Cash.........................	(60,000)		15,000	(45,000)	
::					
Property, plant and equipment.....	60,000		(60,000)	—	
Accumulated depreciation		(50,000)	50,000	—	
Shareholders' Equity					
Retained earnings				(45,000)	
Depreciation expense..........		(50,000)			} Retained earnings = ($45,000)
Gain on sale			5,000		

Decision-Relevant Focus

A key skill set for all investment professionals, lenders, managers, analysts, and shareholders is the ability to use accounting information for decision-making purposes. In this book, we link the discussion of topics to the following two business decisions:

1. Should I extend credit, and at what terms, to this company?
2. Should I invest in this company, and if so, at what price?

Thus, the analysis of financial statements is a key organizational theme that extends throughout the book.

> "I believe that the concise and clear writing is a major strength of this book. The authors should also be complimented on being able to use a good number of examples while still keeping the chapters concise."
>
> — **Charles Leflar,** *University of Arkansas*

Grounded in the Context of Corporate Decisions

Accounting information is an integral part of decision making at every level in business. Consequently, the book's discussion of important accounting concepts is grounded in the context of actual corporate decisions. To this end, the book contains an abundance of excerpts and illustrations from actual corporate financial reports and disclosures that highlight the role and impact of accounting information, and financial statements specifically, in business decision making. Following is one example in the context of accounting for leases:

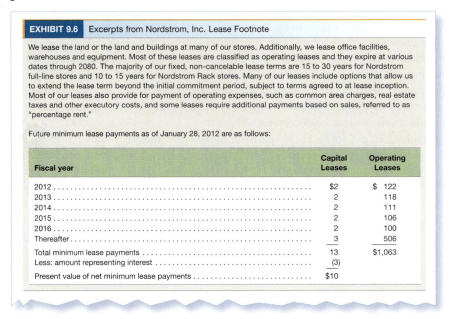

EXHIBIT 9.6 Excerpts from Nordstrom, Inc. Lease Footnote

We lease the land or the land and buildings at many of our stores. Additionally, we lease office facilities, warehouses and equipment. Most of these leases are classified as operating leases and they expire at various dates through 2080. The majority of our fixed, non-cancelable lease terms are 15 to 30 years for Nordstrom full-line stores and 10 to 15 years for Nordstrom Rack stores. Many of our leases include options that allow us to extend the lease term beyond the initial commitment period, subject to terms agreed to at lease inception. Most of our leases also provide for payment of operating expenses, such as common area charges, real estate taxes and other executory costs, and some leases require additional payments based on sales, referred to as "percentage rent."

Future minimum lease payments as of January 28, 2012 are as follows:

Fiscal year	Capital Leases	Operating Leases
2012	$2	$ 122
2013	2	118
2014	2	111
2015	2	106
2016	2	100
Thereafter	3	506
Total minimum lease payments	13	$1,063
Less: amount representing interest	(3)	
Present value of net minimum lease payments	$10	

Does the Book Reflect Contemporary Knowledge?

In our experience, EMBAs and MBAs frequently seem interested in exploring empirical questions such as: "How do the capital markets respond to accounting policy changes?" and "Which EPS measure—Basic EPS or Diluted EPS—is used by the capital market to value a company's stock?" Where appropriate, we have made reference to, and discussion of, the existing research in accounting and finance to address some of these empirically-based questions. By doing so, we enable the interested reader to further her/his knowledge of these questions.

Important Pedagogical Elements

The book applies several pedagogical elements to help readers further understand the ramifications of accounting for business.

Global Perspective boxed inserts emphasize the similarity of U.S. GAAP and IFRS, but they also identify key differences. Exposure to similarities and differences is important as the pressure mounts to harmonize accounting standards globally.

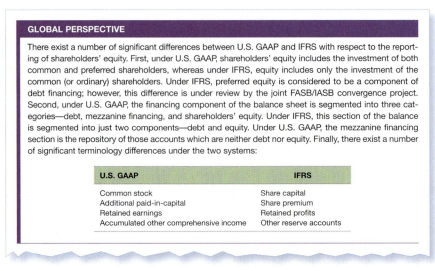

GLOBAL PERSPECTIVE

There exist a number of significant differences between U.S. GAAP and IFRS with respect to the reporting of shareholders' equity. First, under U.S. GAAP, shareholders' equity includes the investment of both common and preferred shareholders, whereas under IFRS, equity includes only the investment of the common (or ordinary) shareholders. Under IFRS, preferred equity is considered to be a component of debt financing; however, this difference is under review by the joint FASB/IASB convergence project. Second, under U.S. GAAP, the financing component of the balance sheet is segmented into three categories—debt, mezzanine financing, and shareholders' equity. Under IFRS, this section of the balance is segmented into just two components—debt and equity. Under U.S. GAAP, the mezzanine financing section is the repository of those accounts which are neither debt nor equity. Finally, there exist a number of significant terminology differences under the two systems:

U.S. GAAP	IFRS
Common stock	Share capital
Additional paid-in-capital	Share premium
Retained earnings	Retained profits
Accumulated other comprehensive income	Other reserve accounts

Ethics Perspective boxed inserts emphasize ethical decision making, as well as the importance of ethics in accounting. In today's environment post-implementation of Sarbanes-Oxley, this information is pertinent to business students and accounting students alike.

ETHICS PERSPECTIVE

Financial Statement Account Presentation at Groupon

Groupon was founded in 2008 and less than two years later was valued at over $1 billion. The business concept that bolstered this fast growth is simple but innovative. The company offers to consumers goods and services from select merchants at deep discounts. Consumers are contacted about the offers via email after becoming subscribers and providing Groupon with a personal profile, thus the offers can be tailored to specific geographic locations and personal preferences. Once each day for each market served (e.g., Richmond metropolitan), a Groupon offer is made to each subscriber. As an example, the subscriber might be offered a discounted entrance ticket and meal to the Colonial Downs Racetrack in Richmond for only $15. Typically this might cost around $30, but by offering the discount the racetrack hopes to pick up customers it would not otherwise get and help build a more permanent customer base. If a minimum number of pre-determined entrance tickets are sold then the deal becomes "live." This reduces both the risk to the retailer and enhances overall profits. Groupon and the retailer typically split the amount paid by the consumer, so in this example Groupon would net $7.50 for each offer sold, with the remainder going to Colonial Downs.

Groupon became a publicly traded company in October 2011 but the transition has not been without significant controversy. During the IPO process Groupon was forced to abandon a controversial metric it had been reporting, Adjusted Consolidated Segment Operating Income (ACSOI), wherein the company was treating marketing costs as assets. This treatment alone made Groupon appear to

---

Business Perspective boxed inserts illustrate key chapter topics using real-world examples and financial statements.

BUSINESS PERSPECTIVE

Airline Ticket Revenue Recognition at Delta Airlines

Delta Airlines is the largest airline in the world when measured by almost any metric: total revenue, fleet size, passenger miles flown, and number of passengers. The company is based in Atlanta, Georgia, the location of its primary hub, and it has helped make Atlanta's Hartsfield-Jackson International Airport the busiest in the world.

The sale of an airline ticket may seem straightforward from the consumer-perspective: buy a ticket, sometimes months in advance, then take the flight. But from Delta's perspective the sale involves other factors to consider regarding how much and when to record revenue. According to the company's footnotes to its financial statements, when tickets are sold a portion is initially recorded as a component of "air traffic liability," a current liability on the balance sheet (equivalent to deferred revenue or unearned revenue); and, if the passenger has a frequent flyer account, a portion is allocated to "frequent flyer deferred revenue." Delta's 2012 annual 10-K report filing with the U.S. Securities and Exchange Commission reports the amount of recognized revenue and deferred revenue for 2012 and 2011 was as follows:

	December 31	
	2012	2011
Income Statement		
Revenues	$36,670	$35,115
Balance Sheet (liabilities)		
Air traffic liability	$3,696	$ 3,480
Frequent flyer deferred revenue—current	1,806	1,849
Frequent flyer deferred revenue—noncurrent	2,628	2,700

These deferred revenue liability accounts are quite significant to Delta, approximating 22% and 23% of total revenues for 2012 and 2011, respectively.

Tax Perspective boxed inserts highlight select aspects of U.S. tax law and how they differ from generally accepted accounting principles. Executives and MBAs very often are interested in understanding how their decisions affect both financial accounting earnings and the cash flows related to the tax treatment of those same decisions. While this text is clearly focused on the former, high-level overviews of some key tax reporting differences are offered throughout the text. Below is an example related to investments:

TAX PERSPECTIVE

Investment Accounting Under U.S. Tax Law

The accounting for investments in other entities outlined in Chapter 8 highlights a diverse set of income measurement rules dependent on the level of ownership. In most respects the income measurement principles followed by the IRS are more straightforward than U.S. GAAP. Here we review some of the highlights.

Recall that under U.S. GAAP, some unrealized losses (gains) are included as income (i.e., trading securities); however, no such treatment is allowed for tax reporting. For investments, the IRS follows an "ability to pay" approach wherein gains or losses are not taxed as income until the asset is sold and the cash has been received by the selling company. Likewise equity income in affiliates is not taxable income as those earnings have been taxed once at the affiliate level and are not required to be taxed again at the investor level. Only at the point of sale is the gain or loss on the investment taxable, and then on an investment account value that has not been increased or decreased by the earnings of the affiliate.

Dividends received by a corporation are also treated differently for tax purposes relative to GAAP. Recall that the treatment of dividends varied under GAAP as follows: (i) if the investment was less than 20 percent ownership, dividends were treated as income, (ii) if the equity method applied, the

In Practice boxed inserts help bridge the gap between the classroom and what students encounter in the real world. "In Practice" illustrations document situations a reader is likely to encounter and present the choices that companies make in reporting financial results.

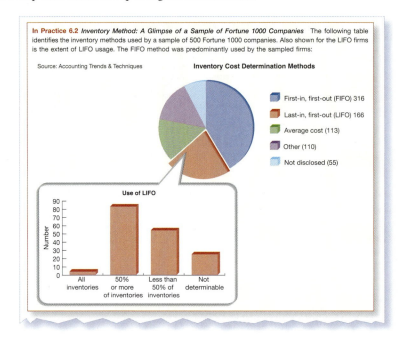

In Practice 6.2 *Inventory Method: A Glimpse of a Sample of Fortune 1000 Companies*   The following table identifies the inventory methods used by a sample of 500 Fortune 1000 companies. Also shown for the LIFO firms is the extent of LIFO usage. The FIFO method was predominantly used by the sampled firms:

Source: Accounting Trends & Techniques

Tools that Reinforce Reader Comprehension

Each chapter includes many tools that reinforce an understanding of the chapter contents. These tools include:

- **Review Problem**, with solution
- **Executive Summary**
- **Key Concepts and Terms**, with page references
- **Discussion Questions**
- **Exercises**
- **Problems**
- **Corporate Analysis**
- **Check figures** to accompany select exercises and problems, denoted by **CHECK FIGURE**

> "The discussion questions are great for an Executive MBA or MBA audience because they are targeted at a more sophisticated student than the typical introductory financial accounting text. They should help a professor stimulate interesting discussions in the classroom."
>
> — **Jeffrey Wong**, *University of Nevada, Reno*

Changes in the Third Edition

This edition of *Financial Accounting for Executives & MBAs* includes a number of important new features. These include:

- Paul Simko of University of Virginia's Darden School of Business has joined the author team.
- A (vertical) financial statement spreadsheet approach for analyzing transactions that reinforces the way in which students engage with financial statements in practice.

■ Extensive reference to recent accounting issues facing high profile companies such as **Apple**, **Groupon**, **American Airlines**, **Bank of America**, and **Under Armour**.

■ Tax perspectives boxes provide high-level contrasts between financial accounting rules and those that govern U.S. tax law.

■ Expanded discussion of relevant international accounting practices around the globe.

■ Many of the assignments have been revised and updated.

■ *myBusinessCourse*: This complete learning and assessment program is free with new copies of the textbook. *myBusinessCourse* includes a complete learning path for students. As the instructor, you can select assignments from the textbook or test bank and have students' responses automatically graded. You also have access to a robust grade book that provides many course management and diagnostic tools. Whether you teach a complete online course or just want to provide your students with additional resources to master the content, *myBusinessCourse* will prove to be an invaluable resource for you and your students.

■ The new edition features an exciting new full color design to engage students. The authors have used color as a pedagogical tool to highlight important points for students.

■ Appendix D covers the basic mechanics of accounting for those instructors that want to expose their students to the fundamentals of the debit-credit paradigm.

Companion Casebook for Case-Based Instruction

Cases in Financial Reporting, 7th edition by Ellen Engel (University of Chicago), D. Eric Hirst (University of Texas–Austin), and Mary Lea McAnally (Texas A&M University). This book comprises 27 cases and is a perfect companion book for faculty interested in exposing students to a wide range of real financial statements. The cases are current and cover companies from Canada, France, Austria, the Netherlands, the UK, India, as well as from the U.S. Many of the U.S. companies are major multinationals. Each case deals with a specific financial accounting topic within the context of one (or more) company's financial statements. Each case contains financial statement information and a set of directed questions pertaining to one or two specific financial accounting issues. This is a separate, saleable casebook (**ISBN 978-1-934319-79-6**). Contact your sales representative to receive a desk copy or email customerservice@cambridgepub.com.

SUPPLEMENTAL MATERIALS

For Instructors

Instructor's Manual: Written by the textbook authors, the *Instructor's Manual* provides suggestions for classroom use and suggested solutions for the end-of-chapter questions, exercises, and problems.

Test Bank: The *Test Bank* provides a full range of mechanical, analytical, and critical thinking problems for each chapter of the book.

PowerPoint Presentations: *PowerPoint* presentations illustrate chapter concepts and help formulate classroom lectures and presentations.

myBusinessCourse: A web-based learning and assessment program intended to complement your textbook and classroom instruction. This easy-to-use course management system grades homework automatically and provide students with additional help when you are not available. In addition, detailed diagnostic tools assess class and individual performance. *myBusinessCourse* is ideal for online courses or traditional face-to-face courses for which you want to offer students more resources to succeed. Assignments with the in the margin are available in *myBusinessCourse*.

For Students

Check Figures: Exercises and problems with check figures are identified with CHECK FIGURE in the margin. Check figures are located at the text Website.

BusinessCourse: A web-based learning and assessment program intended to complement your textbook and faculty instruction. This easy-to-use program grades homework automatically and provides you with additional help when your instructor is not available. Assignments with the ✔ in the margin are available in *myBusinessCourse*. Access is free with new copies of this textbook (look for page containing the access code towards the front of the book). If you buy a used copy of the book, you can purchase access at **www.mybusinesscourse.com**.

ACKNOWLEDGEMENTS

The development of this textbook and the accompanying instructor's manual has benefited from the assistance of Ms. Torrey Mann. Our special thanks for her help. We also thank George Werthman, Debbie McQuade, Terry McQuade, Rich Kolasa, Jill Fischer, Jocelyn Mousel, and the rest of the staff at Cambridge Business Publishers for their help. A special thank you to Eric Jourdan for his help checking the accuracy of our work. Professor Graeme Rankine made a significant academic contribution to the development of this book; and, our thanks are extended to him for his involvement. Finally, we extend our gratitude to the following colleagues, who provided detailed chapter feedback and insightful advice on the first and second editions:

Peter Aghimien, *University of Indiana-South Bend*
Robert Allen, *University of Utah*
Paul Bahnson, *Boise State University*
Jeff Brothers, *Regis University*
Marvin Bouillon, *Iowa State University*
Louis Braiotta, *SUNY-Binghamton*
Philip Brown, *Harding University*
Steve Buchheit, *Texas Tech University*
Thomas Buchman, *University of Colorado-Boulder*
James Cannon, *Iowa State University*
Jack Cathey, *University of North Carolina-Charlotte*
Robert Churchman, *Harding University*
Paul Clikeman, *University of Richmond*
Jane Cote, *Washington State University*
David Cottrell, *Brigham Young University*
Shirley J. Daniel, *University of Hawaii-Manoa*
Mark Dawkins, *University of Georgia*
Mark DeFond, *University of Southern California*
David Donnelly, *University of Missouri-Kansas City*
Catherine Eason, *Queens University*
Laurel Franzen, *University of Texas-Dallas*
George Geiss, *UCLA*
Julia Grant, *Case Western Reserve University*
Carla Hayn, *UCLA*
Michele C. Henderson, *Queens University*
Henry Huang, *Prairie View A&M University*
Gun Joh, *San Diego State University*
Jeff Jones, *Auburn University*
Richard C. Jones, *Hofstra University*
Thomas Kelley, *Seattle University*
Alison Kirby-Jones, *Boston University*
Mehmet Kocakulah, *University of Southern Indiana*

SP Kothari, *Massachusetts Institute of Technology*
Gopal Krishnan, *Lehigh University*
Claire Latham, *Washington State University*
Charles Leflar, *University of Arkansas*
David Lemoine, *Boston College*
Margarita Lenk, *Colorado State University*
Xu Li, *Lehigh University*
Robert Magee, *Northwestern University*
Michel Magnan, *Concordia University*
Ajay Maindiratta, *New York University*
Lorie Milam, *University of Texas-San Antonio*
Mark Myring, *Ball State University*
Sandeep Nabar, *Oklahoma State University*
Bruce Neumann, *University of Colorado-Denver*
Sarah Nutter, *George Mason University*
Leslie Oakes, *New Mexico State University*
Deborah Pavelka, *Roosevelt University*
Suresh Radhakrishnan, *University of Texas-Dallas*
Timothy Redmer, *Regent University*
Laura Rickett, *Kent State University*
Debra Salbador, *Virginia Tech University*
Elaine Sanders, *University of Texas-San Antonio*
Hadley Schaefer, *University of Florida*
Charles Stanley, *Baylor University*
Jan Taylor, *Sam Houston State University*
Thomas Tyson, *St. John Fisher College*
Mark Vargus, *University of Texas-Dallas*
Robert Walsh, *University of Dallas*
Charles Wasley, *University of Rochester*
Raymond Wilson, *Boston University*
Jeffrey A. Wong, *University of Nevada-Reno*
Lee Yao, *Loyola University-New Orleans*

Paul J. Simko
Kenneth R. Ferris
James S. Wallace
May 2013

Brief Contents

Table of Contents

CHAPTER 4

Using Financial Statements for Investing and Credit Decisions   118

CHAPTER 5

Operating Cycle, Revenue Recognition, and Receivable Valuation   154

CHAPTER 6

Operating Expenses, Inventory Valuation, and Accounts Payable   190

CHAPTER **7**

Long-Lived Fixed Assets, Intangible Assets, and Natural Resources 226

CHAPTER **8**

Investing In Other Entities 256

CHAPTER **9**

Debt Financing: Bonds, Notes, and Leases 298

When you complete this chapter you should be able to:

1. Explain how companies acquire capital from investors who purchase debt and equity securities to obtain an expected return commensurate with the risk they assume.

2. Describe the role of accounting rules in facilitating a properly functioning capital market.

3. Identify the basic financial statements—the income statement, the balance sheet, the statement of cash flow, and the statement of shareholders' equity.

4. Explain the conflicts of interest that can arise between executives, debtholders, and shareholders, and the costs associated with the divergent incentives that can arise when ownership and management of a company are separated.

The Economic Environment of Accounting Information

Amazon.com, Inc. was one of the first, and became perhaps the best known, internet-based reseller of retail goods. The company was one of the high-flying internet stocks that became a favorite of equity investors during the stock market bubble period of the late 1990s. Like many dot.com companies that lacked a history of proven earnings, investors began to question Amazon's business model following the U.S. stock market decline of 2001–2002. Investors also began questioning the way the stock market valued companies during this period of so-called "irrational exuberance." As a consequence, there eventually occurred a shift back to firm valuations based on such business fundamentals as strong operating earnings and a solid balance sheet.

Amazon.com was founded by Jeff Bezos in 1995 under the name Cadabra.com as an online bookstore to compete with traditional "brick-and-mortar" bookstores and mail-order catalogs. Bezos renamed the company "Amazon" after the world's largest river and took the company public in 1997. Like the South American river, Amazon.com was huge in scale, offering many times the selection of products of even its largest competitors. Amazon has since greatly expanded its product offerings to include DVDs, music CDs, computer software, video games, electronics, clothing, furniture, food, toys and much more. All of these offerings are designed to leverage the company's massive distribution network. As recent examples, with the launch of the *Kindle* in 2007 the company became the pioneer in the burgeoning e-book and e-reader markets. In 2011 Amazon entered the tablet computer market with the *Kindle Fire*, enabling it to further capitalize on the growth in electronic media.

From the start, Bezos believed in the long-term prospects for his company, although he did not expect the business to produce a profit for many years. As history has since demonstrated, Bezos' business strategy proved successful. Unlike many internet companies, Amazon grew at a steady pace and focused on such business fundamentals as revenue growth, cash flows, and attaining profitability. The bursting of the dot.com bubble in the early 2000s forced many e-companies out of business. Amazon, however, persevered and eventually reported its first profit in the fourth quarter of 2002. Amazon.com has continued to report profits every year since then, earning net income of $645 million in 2008, $902 million in 2009, $1,152 million in 2010, and $631 million in 2011. Despite its recent financial success, however, Amazon's cumulative profit only recently turned positive in 2008, largely as a consequence of its early history of operating losses. Today, Amazon.com trades on the NASDAQ stock exchange under the symbol AMZN and is a member of the prestigious Standard & Poor's 500 Index, an index of the shares of the 500 largest companies traded on U.S. stock exchanges.

In this chapter, we examine the financial statements of Amazon, as well as consider the generally accepted accounting principles that have been established to ensure a level of comparability among the many public companies, like Amazon, that produce financial statements for use by investors, lenders, and shareholders.

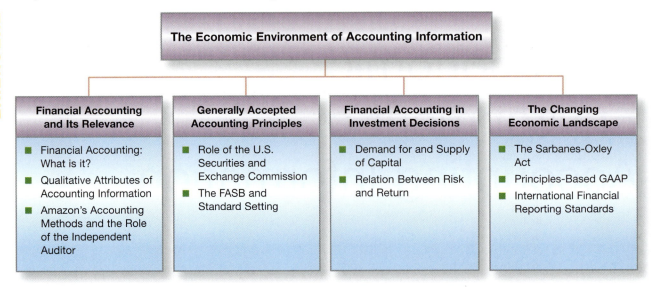

FINANCIAL ACCOUNTING AND ITS RELEVANCE

Most individuals are familiar with the game of baseball and its many rules. Most know, for instance, that according to the rules of the game, the team with the most runs scored at the completion of play is considered to be the winner. Of course the rules do much more than decide the measure by which we are able to determine which team won and which team lost; they also provide a framework within which to play the game and define how players should interact depending on their different roles. Imagine the chaos that might ensue if there were no mutually accepted rules for baseball. How would it be determined, for instance, if a base runner was out or was safe, if a pitch was a ball or a strike, and so on? Without an accepted set of rules governing the game, it would be impossible to play the sport and insure a consistent set of outcomes.

Keeping score with an accepted set of rules applies to more activities than just baseball; it also applies to running a business like **Amazon.com**. In fact, the similarities between baseball and financial accounting are probably closer than you might imagine. Understanding the "rules of the game" also helps us do more than simply declare the winner of a game or calculate the annual profit of a business; it enables us to keep track of various measures that can be used to determine the quality of a team's play or the quality of a business's operations. Our knowledge of the rules and how teams or businesses have performed in the past—for example, team batting averages, pitching records, and fielding percentages for baseball teams, and assorted financial ratios such as the return on assets, return on equity, or return on sales for a business—can, in turn, help us to predict how teams and businesses will perform in the future. This knowledge, as you will see in subsequent chapters, is invaluable when attempting to assess the value of a sports franchise or of a business enterprise.

Simply reading a rule book, however, may not be sufficient to obtain a complete understanding as to how a game is played and scored. It is also critical to understand the limitations regarding how the rules are applied, along with what is not covered by the rules. This caveat especially applies to financial accounting. Imagine the difficulty that would occur if each baseball team got to decide the distance from home plate to first base in its home stadium. Or imagine the confusion if, with the bases loaded, a team could choose which direction to run toward home plate, scoring either from first base or from third base. As we will see in the following chapters of this textbook, financial accounting permits considerable flexibility in determining the applicability of its "rules" to individual business enterprises. As a consequence, the rules governing financial accounting will be seen to involve considerable managerial judgment. In baseball, for example, while general guidelines exist as to whether a pitch should be called a ball or a strike, it is up to an umpire's judgment to make the exact call. In a similar fashion, while general accounting guidelines exist as to what is considered revenue for a business, financial accounting often requires that corporate managers exercise judgment in assessing just how much revenue a business earned in a given fiscal period. In addition to the obvious analytical challenges that can result from this flexibility in the application of the rules of the game, business analysis is also often hampered by a lack of certain key information. Many of the factors that are critical to a business's operating success, for example the quality of its workforce or a well-recognized brand name, are not measured and reported under current financial accounting rules.

Why Accounting Information Is Important

If you have prior business experience, either working for a company or managing your own business, then you have personal experience that a working knowledge of accounting is essential to do just about any job successfully. Although business decisions may involve a careful analysis of nonfinancial factors, they almost always involve a significant consideration of financial information. Initiating a multimillion-dollar marketing campaign, restructuring a subsidiary, acquiring another company, deciding on the sales price for a product—these are just some of the business decisions that require at least a basic knowledge of accounting. That's why, for instance, Anne Mulcahy, Chief Executive Officer of **Xerox Corporation** had to learn about accounting and finance when she took over at Xerox in 2001. As *Fortune* magazine explained,

> She knew she had to get to the bottom of Xerox's problems quickly. She cast about for someone, anyone, who could teach her Balance Sheet 101. The guy she found, Joe Mancini Jr., director of corporate financial analysis . . . became her tour guide in deciphering the company's $30 billion balance sheet. He taught her about debt structure, inventory trends, and the impact of taxes and currency moves so that she could understand what would generate cash and how each of her decisions would affect the balance sheet. (*Fortune*, June 9, 2003).

Executives, such as Anne Mulcahy, are also getting up to speed on accounting issues because now, more than ever, the post-Enron corporate environment in the United States puts these individuals at risk for civil and criminal lawsuits.[1] Under the **Sarbanes-Oxley Act**, passed into law by the United States Congress in 2002, the Chief Executive Officer (CEO) and Chief Financial Officer (CFO) of each company (foreign or domestic) with public debt or equity sold in the United States must certify in writing that the information contained in the company's publicly disseminated financial statements presents, in all material respects, the company's financial condition and results of operations. The Sarbanes-Oxley Act provides for both financial penalties (up to $5 million) and incarceration (up to 20 years) for executives who falsely certify their company's financial data.

In sum, a theme that will be repeated throughout this textbook is that accounting information is useful not only for keeping score of a business's past operating performance and financial health, but also for predicting its future performance and financial well-being, and ultimately, for helping to assess firm value. However, to be a good scorekeeper and a good analyst, and ultimately a great leader, one needs to know not only the rules of the game, but also how to interpret the data resulting from the application of the rules, the limitations of the rules, and when to make adjustments to the information to aid in its use for decision-making.

Financial Accounting: What Is It?

Financial accounting concerns the preparation and use of the accounting information provided in a company's financial statements. To appreciate the importance of financial accounting information one must first recognize the foundation for the need. At its most fundamental level, financial accounting is necessary from one overriding activity: capital has been exchanged with the intent of earning a return. As an organization grows, its need for outside sources of capital grows, often at an alarming pace. With this growth comes the demand by those willing to provide capital for some objective evidence of the company's ability to provide a return. Without financial accounting there would be no basis upon which to evaluate and monitor their investment. In other words, there would be no basis upon which one could keep "score."

The overarching objective of the financial accounting process is to provide a basis upon which to evaluate the financial position and performance of a company to those that have invested in that company, but for whom such information would not otherwise be available in a succinct, reliable and timely basis. By providing financial accounting information to the shareholders of a company, those who actually own the company through the shares they purchase, they can now adequately assess the risk and potential

---

[1] *The Wall Street Journal* (July 22, 2003) reported that 70 percent of the executives who took a test of basic accounting principles shortly after the passage of the Sarbanes-Oxley Act failed to earn a passing score. A survey of executives taken two years following the passage of the legislation indicates that executive understanding of accounting and finance issues has substantially improved since the legislation's enactment (*CFO Magazine*, May 2005).

returns related to their investments. Although shareholders are the primary user group for which the financial accounting process is centered, they are not the only group of stakeholders that have motivations for understanding the present and current prospects of a company. Bankers, a subset of the general investing group who loan money to a company for a fixed return, will want information about the financial status of the firm to help them assess their lending risk. Suppliers, competitors and customers all stand to be influenced in their own activities by the company's relative success or failure. Many governmental entities, such as the Federal Trade Commission, base regulatory decisions on information disclosed in annual reports. Public utilities, in fact, will frequently base their energy rates on the financial accounting based net income that it can generate. Taxing authorities, such as the IRS, will review financial accounting information in their reconciliations of taxable income. Labor unions might look to financial reporting performance to argue for greater benefits. Internally, the board of directors is known to use financial accounting information in decisions about dividend payments, compensation decisions, and other company policies. In sum, the financial accounting process provides information to a variety and diverse set of users, each with their own unique needs.

A financial accounting perspective can be distinguished from two other common processes that generate accounting information: managerial accounting and tax accounting. Unlike the external focus of financial accounting, **managerial accounting** focuses on the production of accounting information internal to a firm for deciding such operational questions as how much inventory to produce, what price to charge customers, and for measuring and rewarding the performance of a firm's employees. Managerial accounting information is rarely provided to anyone other than a firm's board of directors, managers, and employees, to avoid revealing proprietary information that might adversely affect a firm's competitive position. **Tax accounting** refers to the system of measurement used by tax authorities to determine the amount of taxes to levy on a company. Because this objective is quite distinct from that required by investors, these measurement rules can differ dramatically from financial accounting. The focus of this textbook is on financial accounting, and how financial advisors, investors, lenders, managers, and shareholders use this information for decision-making purposes. However, because tax accounting considerations often drive many real decisions faced by management, where appropriate throughout the text we highlight key high-level differences between financial and tax accounting.

Before getting into the details of how financial accounting information is prepared and analyzed, it is useful to first discuss the end result of the financial accounting process—the four primary financial statements. For the moment, don't worry about the numerous details that you will see, because these details will be explored in later chapters. Also don't worry about the numerous other supporting documents that often accompany the financial statements. Company financial reports include many items besides the basic financial statements, such as explanatory footnotes, a chairman's statement, and a management discussion and analysis of recent events and company performance. For simplicity, these latter items have been omitted from our discussion here as they will be considered in subsequent chapters.

To begin, it is useful to obtain a "big picture" view of a company by reading the introductory information about a company's business and its business strategy—that is, management's view of where the company is going based on the resources it has available (human, physical, and financial). Reading the financial statements will help you determine whether a company has the necessary financial resources, or can acquire them, to get where it wants to be.

Consider, for example, the corporate mission of Amazon.com:

> We seek to be Earth's most customer-centric company for four primary customer sets: consumers, sellers, enterprises, and content creators.

No small thinking here! Amazon truly aims to capture the world, virtually the entirety of the retail market space as their "customers"—buyers, sellers, and product developers. If Amazon can attract the millions of customers that the company has the capacity to handle, its future sales could be enormous.

Investment professionals who track the performance of companies like Amazon formalize sales and sales growth projections by gathering data regarding consumer demand, product shipments, product prices and sales discounts. These projections are integral to the analytical reports developed by investment professionals concerning a company's current financial health, and hence, its fair market value. Your review of Amazon's financial statements is likely to be enhanced by obtaining and reviewing a copy of a reputable analyst's report from any one of a variety of financial websites such as **Yahoo.com** or **MSN.com** or from a financial services company like **Merrill Lynch** or **Wells Fargo**. As to the stated mission that the company is "customer-centric" and that it meets the needs of four distinct sets of custom-

ers, you can verify for yourself whether it meets these objectives by logging on to Amazon's website (www.Amazon.com) if you haven't done so already.

The basic financial statements for Amazon.com, Inc.—the balance sheet, the income statement, and the statement of cash flow—are provided in Exhibits 1.1, 1.2, and 1.3. (A fourth financial statement, the statement of shareholders' equity, will be discussed later in this chapter.) The **balance sheet** in Exhibit 1.1 shows what resources the company currently has and who provided the financing to acquire the various resources—debtholders or shareholders. Specifically, Amazon's balance sheet reveals the amount and type of assets owned, the liabilities owed, and the shareholders' equity investment in the company. **Assets** refer to the resources of a company that are expected to provide future economic benefit. **Liabilities** represent the value of the company's obligations to repay monies loaned to it, to pay for goods or services received by it, or to fulfill commitments made by it. **Shareholders' equity**, the difference between a company's assets and liabilities, represents the shareholders' (owners') financial stake in a company. In essence, two investment constituencies provided the necessary financing for Amazon's assets—the shareholders who own the company as a consequence of their share purchases, and debtholders who have loaned money and other assets to the company. The basic accounting equation, Assets = Liabilities + Shareholders' equity, provides the foundation not for only the balance sheet, but more importantly for the entire methodology underpinning the recording of all

EXHIBIT 1.1	Consolidated Balance Sheet		
AMAZON.COM INC. **Consolidated Balance Sheet**			
		Year Ended December 31,	
($ millions)		**2011**	**2010**
Assets			
Current assets			
Cash and cash equivalents.		$5,269	$3,777
Marketable securities		4,307	4,985
Inventories		4,992	3,202
Accounts receivable, net and other		2,571	1,587
Deferred tax assets.		351	196
Total current assets.		17,490	13,747
Fixed assets, net		4,417	2,414
Deferred tax assets		28	22
Goodwill		1,955	1,349
Other assets.		1,388	1,265
Total assets		**$25,278**	**$18,797**
Liabilities and Stockholders' Equity			
Current liabilities			
Accounts payable.		$11,145	$ 8,051
Accrued expenses and other		3,751	2,321
Total current liabilities		14,896	10,372
Long-term debt		2,625	1,561
Stockholders' equity			
Common stock, $0.01 par value:			
Authorized shares— 5,000			
Issued shares—473 and 468			
Outstanding shares—455 and 451		5	5
Treasury stock, at cost		(877)	(600)
Additional paid-in-capital		6,990	6,325
Accumulated other comprehensive loss		(316)	(190)
Retained earnings.		1,955	1,324
Total stockholders' equity.		7,757	6,864
Total liabilities and stockholders' equity		**$25,278**	**$18,797**

accounting transactions. In various ways we will repeat this important facet of the balance sheet numerous times in the coming chapters.[2]

Amazon's balance sheet is based on this foundation. By the end of 2011, Amazon's balance sheet reveals that it had acquired over $25.278 billion in assets while the company's debt stood at $17.521 billion ($14.896 plus $2.625 billion). Notice that shareholders had a residual interest valued at $7.757 billion, and of that $1.955 billion has been earned and retained by the company. To evaluate how Amazon generates its earnings, we will need to explore the income statement, which we consider shortly.

> An alternative to the accrual basis of accounting is the **cash basis of accounting**. Under the cash basis, the financial effects of a business event are recorded in the financial statements *only* when the cash effect of the transaction occurs. Thus, a company records revenue from a sales transaction *only* after cash has been collected from the customer; similarly, expenses are recorded *only* when they are paid.

A few other features of Amazon's balance sheet are noteworthy at this point. The presence of various accounts on Amazon's balance sheet such as **accounts receivable**, the amount that Amazon expects to receive from its customers for prior online purchases, and **accounts payable**, the amount that Amazon expects to pay to its suppliers for prior credit purchases of inventory, indicates that this financial statement was prepared using the **accrual basis of accounting**. This approach requires Amazon to record the financial effects of a business transaction even though the timing of the cash effects of the event takes place at a different time. That is, Amazon records the revenue from each sales transaction when it occurs, regardless of whether the customer has paid for the ordered goods or not. Similarly, Amazon records the cost of doing business when such costs are incurred, regardless of whether those costs have yet to be paid. The balance sheets and income statements of most businesses are prepared using the accrual basis of accounting, as this approach is widely recognized as being superior to all other approaches for measuring the financial performance and health of a company. In fact, financial statements that follow U.S. GAAP must be prepared under the accrual basis.

Amazon's **income statement** in Exhibit 1.2 reports how much merchandise the company sold and how much profit, if any, it made from those sales. Amazon's consolidated statement of income reveals that the company's sales grew to over $48 billion by 2011. The "bottom line" of the income statement

EXHIBIT 1.2	Consolidated Income Statement			
AMAZON.COM INC.				
Consolidated Income Statement		**Year Ended December 31,**		
($ millions)		**2011**	**2010**	**2009**
Net product sales.		42,000	30,792	22,273
Net services sales		6,077	3,412	2,236
Total net sales		**48,077**	**34,204**	**24,509**
Operating expenses				
Cost of sales.		37,288	26,561	18,978
Fullfillment.		4,576	2,898	2,052
Marketing		1,630	1,029	680
Technology and content		2,909	1,734	1,240
General and administrative.		658	470	328
Other operating expense (income), net		154	106	102
Total operating expenses		47,215	32,798	23,380
Income from operations.		862	1,406	1,129
Interest income.		61	51	37
Interest expense.		(65)	(39)	(34)
Other income (expense), net		76	79	29
Total non-operating income (expense).		72	91	32
Income before income taxes		934	1,497	1,161
Provision for income taxes.		(291)	(352)	(253)
Equity-method investment activity, net of tax		(12)	7	(6)
Net income		**$ 631**	**$ 1,152**	**$ 902**

---

[2] Each transaction that is recorded must be done so such that the equation remains in balance. For this reason, the term "double-entry" accounting is often used to describe this method of recording transactions.

indicates that Amazon earned a profit in each of the three years covered by the income statements (2009 to 2011). But this is a relatively recent phenomenon. Prior to 2008, the company had racked up cumulative losses of just over $1.3 billion. In fact, a review of Amazon's historical financial statements (not presented here) reveals that from 1996 until 2002, Amazon failed to earn a profit in any of the six years since it became a public company! This history of operating losses during the early years of the company's existence explains the relatively modest size of retained earnings on the 2011 balance sheet.

To appreciate this, consider that both the balance sheet and income statement are prepared under an important tenet underlying the accrual basis of accounting—the **going concern assumption**. This notion specifies that the financial statements are prepared assuming that a business will continue operating in the future unless there is substantial evidence to the contrary. When a business has reached a steady state and is expected to continue operating in the future, investors tend to focus on revenues and net income from the income statement in order to forecast a firm's future operating performance. If, on the other hand, a business is expected to cease operations, investors are likely to focus their attention more closely on shareholders' equity on the balance sheet to determine what an investor might receive if, and when, the company is liquidated. Academic research consistent with the going concern assumption indicates that in setting share prices, investors place relatively more weight on shareholders' equity on the balance sheet when a business is facing financial distress than when a business is financially healthy.[3]

> Exhibit 1.2 presents Amazon's **consolidated income statement**. But just what was "consolidated" and what remains "unconsolidated"? Under the accounting rules of most countries, when one company obtains a majority of the voting shares of another company, the financial results of the two companies are combined and reported on a "consolidated" basis. Thus, in the case of Amazon, the consolidated income statement includes the complete financial results of Amazon's majority-owned subsidiaries, but only summary results of its subsidiaries in which its ownership interest is less than a majority. We will provide greater detail on this accounting treatment in Chapter 8.

Even though Amazon is currently highly profitable, you may have wondered how it can sustain multiple years of operating losses and still remain in business! The answers to these types of questions typically reside in a review of a company's statement of cash flow, to which we now turn.

Exhibit 1.3 presents Amazon's statement of cash flow. The **statement of cash flow** tells us how much cash Amazon.com generated from its core business operations or received from its shareholders and debtholders, and how much it spent to buy software and equipment. Investors are usually very interested in the statement of cash flow because it provides insight into a business beyond that provided by a balance sheet, which reflects a firm's current financial health,

> There exists substantial empirical evidence that investors who buy and sell shares use information about the past, especially financial statement information, to help make predictions about a company's future. Financial analysts, individual investors, bankers, and many other interested parties spend considerable time and resources predicting a company's future earnings and cash flows to help assess what a company's share price should currently be worth. We will have more to say about how to value a company's shares in Chapter 12; however, let it suffice for the moment that the value of a share of stock today is thought to be a function of a company's *future* earnings and cash flow.

or an income statement, which depicts a firm's recent operating performance. Amazon's statement of cash flow shows, for instance, that its operating activities generated $3.903 billion in cash in 2011 despite reporting net income of only $631 million. Amazon's total cash and cash equivalents increased by $1.492 billion in 2011, and the company's cash holdings on the balance sheet were in excess of $5.2 billion! Thus, Amazon has substantial cash on hand despite reporting many early years of operating losses on the income statement. These seemingly conflicting financial results are possible because of Amazon's use of the accrual basis of accounting in the preparation of its income statement and its balance sheet.

Without proper context, you might think that Amazon.com, which only began to earn an operating profit in 2003 and with liabilities representing nearly 70 percent of its assets, would have a share price that was floundering. Yet Exhibit 1.4 shows that Amazon's share price soared by over 17,000 percent since its initial public offering. The much broader Standard & Poor's 500 Index was relatively stable over the same period, returning a cumulative 75 percent. Amazon's share price at its initial public offering was just over $1.50 per share, but by March 2013, its share price was over $270 per share giving the company a market value of about $120 billion (shares outstanding × share price). This illustrates an important distinction between a company's financial statements and its share price—the former is concerned with the past while the latter is concerned with the future. Financial statements are a description of the historical financial performance of a company, whereas share prices reflect investor *expectations* regarding a firm's future financial health

---

[3] See M. Barth, W. Beaver and W. Landsman, "Relative Valuation Roles of Equity Book Value and Net Income as a Function of Financial Health," *Journal of Accounting and Economics* (February 1998).

| EXHIBIT 1.3 | Consolidated Statement of Cash Flow |

AMAZON.COM INC.
Consolidated Statement of Cash Flow

($ millions)	Year Ended December 31,		
	2011	2010	2009
Cash and cash equivalents, beginning of period	$3,777	$3,444	$2,769
Operating activities			
Net income	631	1,152	902
Adjustments to reconcile net income to net cash provided by operating activities:			
Depreciation of fixed assets, including internal-use software and website development, and other amortization	1,083	568	378
Stock-based compensation.	557	424	341
Other operating expenses (income), net	154	106	103
Losses (gains) on sales of marketable securities, net	(4)	(2)	(4)
Other expense (income), net	(56)	(79)	(15)
Deferred income taxes.	136	4	81
Excess tax benefits from stock-based compensation	(62)	(259)	(105)
Changes in operating assets and liabilities:			
Inventories	(1,777)	(1,019)	(531)
Accounts receivable, net and other.	(866)	(295)	(481)
Accounts payable	2,997	2,373	1,859
Accrued expenses and other.	1,067	740	300
Additions to unearned revenue	1,064	687	1,054
Amortization of previously unearned revenue	(1,021)	(905)	(589)
Net cash provided by operating activities	3,903	3,495	3,293
Investing activities			
Purchases of fixed assets, including internal-use software and website development.	(1,811)	(979)	(373)
Acquisitions, net of cash acquired, and other	(705)	(352)	(40)
Sales and maturities of marketable securities and other investments.	6,843	4,250	1,966
Purchases of marketable securities and other investments.	(6,257)	(6,279)	(3,890)
Net cash used in investing activities	(1,930)	(3,360)	(2,337)
Financing activities			
Excess tax benefits from stock-based compensation.	62	259	105
Common stock repurchased	(277)		
Proceeds from long-term debt and other.	177	143	87
Repayments of long-term debt, capital lease, and finance lease obligations	(444)	(221)	(472)
Net cash provided by (used in) financing activities	(482)	181	(280)
Foreign-currency effect on cash and cash equivalents	1	17	(1)
Net increase in cash and cash equivalents	1,492	333	675
Cash and cash equivalents, end of period.	$5,269	$3,777	$3,444

and performance. The fact that Amazon's market value is $120 billion versus a balance sheet value of just $7.757 billion for shareholders' equity suggests that the stock market is extremely optimistic that Amazon's future is going to be much brighter than its past.

Publicly listed companies in the United States are required to file a quarterly financial report (Form 10-Q) and an annual set of financial statements (Form 10-K) with the U.S. Securities and Exchange Commission. This information is also typically available on company websites, and is often mailed or e-mailed to shareholders and debtholders.

To summarize then, companies like Amazon.com who obtain capital from external sources such as debtholders and shareholders are expected to periodically provide these interested stakeholders with financial accounting information. This information includes an income statement, a balance sheet, and a statement of cash flow. The relation between these three financial statements is illustrated in Exhibit 1.5. A fourth statement—the statement of shareholders' equity—is also typically provided and is discussed in greater detail in Chapter 2.

From Exhibit 1.5 a number of important points can be made about the basic financial statements. First, a balance sheet is a description of a business's assets, liabilities, and shareholders' equity as of a particular

| EXHIBIT 1.4 | Stock Price Performance of Amazon.com: May 1997 (IPO) to March 2013 |

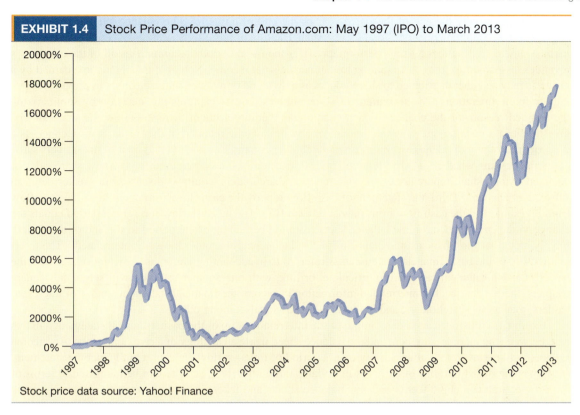

Stock price data source: Yahoo! Finance

| EXHIBIT 1.5 | Relation Among the Balance Sheet, Income Statement, and Statement of Cash Flow |

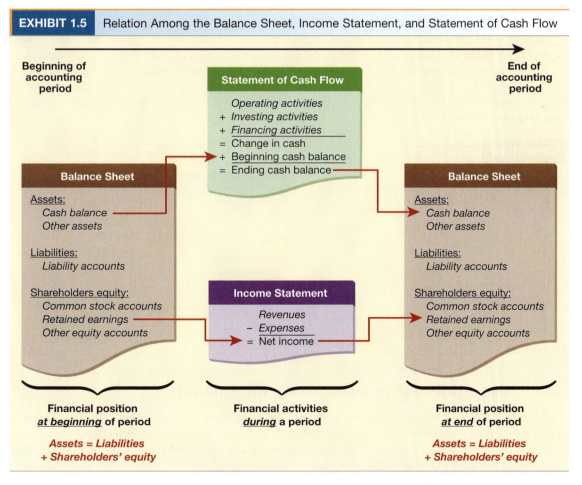

point in time, usually the end of the fiscal year or the end of a quarter. The balance sheet is represented by the basic accounting equation: Total assets equal Total liabilities plus Shareholders' equity. Second, the income statement describes a firm's performance over the fiscal period; it summarizes all of the company's revenues less expenses, the total equating to that period's net income. Note that the net income earned by a business may be either distributed to shareholders as a dividend or retained in the business to provide financing for future operations. The **statement of shareholders' equity** captures this decision by summarizing the detailed reason for the change in each shareholders' equity account. It reveals how the shareholders' investment in a business grew by the amount of any net income retained in the business or declined as a consequence of any dividend distributions to shareholders or any losses sustained by a business. This statement also reveals whether the shareholders' investment in a business increased by any new share sales or declined by any share repurchases. The statement of shareholders' equity is discussed in greater detail in subsequent chapters. Third, the statement of cash flow reports the cash flow from operations, the cash flow from investing, and the cash flow from financing for a firm. The net cash flow for a fiscal period equals the change in the cash account on the balance sheet from the beginning of the period to the end of the period. Finally, note that the financial statements are not independent, but rather they are interrelated. (The interrelationship of the basic financial statements is referred to in accounting jargon as "articulation;" that is, the basic financial statements are said to articulate, or link, with one another.) As you will see in subsequent chapters, there is unique, but interrelated information in each of the financial statements that is of interest to lenders, managers, shareholders, and investment professionals, among others.

Exhibit 1.6 illustrates another example of the interrelationship of the basic financial statements, in this case between the income statement and the balance sheet, using an analogy of a river and a lake. An income statement, like a river, measures activity over a period of time—a flow concept. On the income statement, activity is measured in terms of earnings in dollars, and with a river, activity can be measured in terms of the flow of water in cubic feet or meters. Balance sheets and lakes, in contrast, measure levels—a stock concept. Balance sheets measure the level of net assets and lakes can be measured as a level of water, both at a point in time. Just as a lake's level of water rises and falls because of the inflow and outflow of water from a river, the level of net assets on the balance sheet rises and falls as a consequence of the operating earnings or losses generated by a business and reported on its income statement. A similar analogy could be used between the cash balance on the balance sheet and the statement of cash flow. The cash account on the balance sheet reports the level of cash currently available to a business, whereas the statement of cash flow reports the inflows and outflows of cash that occurred over the fiscal period. To repeat, the balance sheet discloses the available "stocks" of various assets, while the income statement and the statement of cash flow reveal the various "flows" of those assets and claims on those assets.

EXHIBIT 1.6   Balance Sheets and Income Statements: "Stocks" and "Flows"

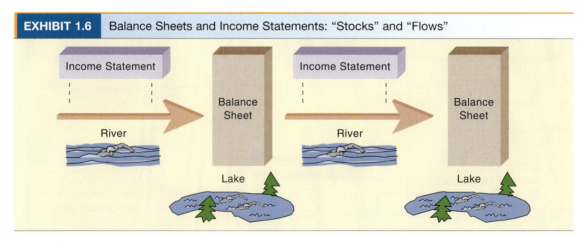

Qualitative Attributes of Accounting Information

It is generally agreed that accounting information is valuable because it contributes to the making of important economic decisions. For instance, managers often use accounting information to decide the price that they must charge for their company's products; bank credit analysts use accounting information to decide whether to extend a loan to a business; and, investors use accounting information to decide whether to invest in the shares of a company and at what price. Thus, accounting information is said to have **decision usefulness**.

There are two important attributes that underlie accounting information that help make it decision useful—relevance and faithful representation. **Relevance** refers to the capacity of accounting information to influence a decision. Relevant information is timely and possesses feedback value, predictive value, or both. Timeliness alone does not make accounting information relevant, but a lack of timeliness can render accounting information irrelevant. By preparing periodic financial statements it is possible for companies to provide analysts, managers, and investors with timely information. Feedback value pertains to decisions and actions already taken. Accounting information allows financial statement users to measure those actions and evaluate their success. Predictive value, on the other hand, suggests that accounting information helps financial statement users form predictions about future outcomes. Investment professionals and shareholders use the historical financial statements to help predict a firm's future operating performance, and hence, its market value.

> **In Practice 1.1** *Fiscal Year-End: A Glimpse of a Sample of Fortune 1000 Companies* The following table identifies the month selected as a firm's fiscal year-end based on a survey of 600 Fortune 1000 companies. As can be seen, December was selected by nearly two-thirds of the sampled firms, although every month is represented:
>
>
> Source: Accounting Trends & Techniques

The decision usefulness of accounting information is also influenced by the degree to which it faithfully represents events that occur during a period. **Faithful representation** refers to the fact that accounting information is, or should be, free from error or bias; accounting rules, therefore, tend to be written in such a way that the accounts are both objective and verifiable. This is a trade-off, however, and unfortunately the attributes of relevance and faithful representation are often in conflict with one another. As

> Because too much information can overwhelm financial statement users (i.e., the problem of "information overload"), **materiality** is a disclosure criterion used worldwide by companies to decide what, and how much, information to provide in their financial statements. Information that is immaterial is unlikely to be relevant to a decision maker. Although the definition of materiality varies from firm to firm, and often between external auditors, a common threshold for the income statement is five percent of revenues. Hence, any income statement item that equals or exceeds five percent of revenues presumably merits disclosure on a firm's income statement as such items are numerically large enough to potentially influence an investor's assessment of firm performance.

one example, the fair value of long-term fixed assets, while clearly relevant information, is typically not recorded under U.S. accounting rules because it cannot be objectively measured. And for those values that are recorded, a major role of the independent auditor, to which we now turn, is to review a company's publicly available accounting information to insure that it is largely error free.

Amazon's Accounting Methods and the Role of the Independent Auditor

By now, one question that you have probably considered about Amazon's financial statements is: Could the proper application of financial accounting by Amazon have led to accounting results computed in more than one way? The answer is yes. Nearly every country around the world maintains a set of formal accounting standards. In the U.S. these are Generally Accepted Accounting Principles—or GAAP—that provide guidance to companies regarding the preferred way to measure and report their performance. The confusing aspect about these standards, however, is their flexibility. For example, consider the depreciation on a building. Instead of having just one approach to calculate depreciation on a building, most countries allow for multiple methods, all of which are considered "generally accepted." As you will see in Chapter 7, just which depreciation method is selected can have a dramatic effect on a firm's reported performance.

Consider, for instance, the $4.992 billion reported by Amazon.com for inventory on its 2011 balance sheet in Exhibit 1.1. Was this the amount that Amazon paid for the inventory? Or, was it what the inventory could be sold for at the end of the year? Or, was it what the same inventory would cost to replace if it were purchased at the end of 2011? Companies provide details about their accounting methods and how the various accounts are measured in the **footnotes** to their financial statements. For example, the footnotes to Amazon's 2011 financial statements report that:

> Inventories, consisting of products available for sale, are primarily accounted for using the FIFO method, and are valued at the lower of cost or market value. This valuation requires us to *make judgments* (emphasis added), based on currently-available information, about the likely method of disposition, such as through sales to individual customers, returns to product vendors, or liquidations, and expected recoverable values of each disposition category.

There are several points to observe here. First, Amazon's financial statements are prepared by the company itself, raising the concern that the company might be tempted to boost its inventory value to make it appear that Amazon has more assets than it really does. Second, Amazon's top management and financial staff "make judgments" in deciding what inventory values to report. But since the financial statements provided by Amazon's management are potentially affected by these judgments, investors might skeptically discount the reported information and reduce their estimate of what the company is presumably worth. This issue is known as the **lemons problem**.[4]

One solution to the lemons problem is for a credible, independent party to provide a "warranty" as to the quality of the product offered. For example, in the used car market, an auto dealer might promise to take a vehicle back if the buyer experiences any problems. In the "accounting market," independent audit firms such as **Deloitte & Touche**, **Ernst & Young**, **KPMG**, and **PricewaterhouseCoopers** provide assurance of the faithful representation of the financial statements of the companies they audit in an **audit report** that accompanies the financial statements. Audit firms work hard to provide this assurance because errors in detecting defective financial statements can result in a significant loss of investor capital. A failure to adequately provide assurance can result in the loss of an audit firm's valuable reputation, and ultimately, as illustrated by the demise of **Arthur Andersen** in 2002, the collapse of an entire audit firm. Audit firms may also bear civil and criminal penalties from lawsuits brought by shareholders, debtholders, and/or governmental agencies like the U.S. Securities and Exchange Commission (SEC) if their work is found to be negligent.

The independent auditors' report by Ernst & Young for Amazon's financial statements is provided in Exhibit 1.7. Note first to whom the report is written—the directors and shareholders of Amazon. This is no accident, as it is to them that the financial reports are targeted and it is their capital at risk. The first paragraph of the report indicates that the scope of Ernst & Young's audit includes Amazon's balance sheet, income statement, statement of shareholders' equity, statement of cash flow, and other financial items. This paragraph also highlights the fact that the auditors' responsibility is only to provide an opinion, whereas the responsibility for the preparation of the statements themselves lies with Amazon's management. The second paragraph discloses that the audit firm's procedures used in the review of Amazon's financial data were in accordance with **generally accepted auditing standards** as prescribed by the Public Company Accounting Oversight Board, but that accepted auditing procedures do not consider every business transaction and instead rely only on a set of sampled transactions to form an opinion. An

In Practice 1.2 *Financial Statement Rounding: A Glimpse of a Sample of Fortune 1000 Companies* The following table identifies the degree of rounding in financial statements in a survey of 600 Fortune 1000 companies. Nearly all of the sampled firms rounded their reported numbers, with rounding to the nearest thousand dollars the most commonly used choice:

Source: Accounting Trends & Techniques

[4] G.A. Ackerlof, "The Market for Lemons: Quality Uncertainty and the Market Mechanism," *The Quarterly Journal of Economics*, (1970). In markets where buyers are uncertain about the quality of goods offered for sale, markets may break down because buyers reduce the price that they are willing to pay, causing sellers with high-quality products to withdraw from the market. The downward price spiral continues as products of continually decreasing quality become the only products available for sale, and eventually, market breakdowns can occur.

audit of a company like Amazon would be prohibitively expensive if every single business transaction was examined to reach an opinion.

| **EXHIBIT 1.7** | Independent Auditors' Report |

Report of Ernst & Young LLP, Independent Registered Public Accounting Firm

The Board of Directors and Shareholders
Amazon.com, Inc.

We have audited the accompanying consolidated balance sheets of Amazon.com, Inc. as of December 31, 2011 and 2010, and the related consolidated statements of operations, stockholders' equity, and cash flows for each of the three years in the period ended December 31, 2011. Our audits also included the financial statement schedule listed in the Index at Item 15(a)(2). These financial statements and schedule are the responsibility of the Company's management. Our responsibility is to express an opinion on these financial statements and schedule based on our audits.

We conducted our audits in accordance with the standards of the Public Company Accounting Oversight Board (United States). Those standards require that we plan and perform the audit to obtain reasonable assurance about whether the financial statements are free of material misstatement. An audit includes examining, on a test basis, evidence supporting the amounts and disclosures in the financial statements. An audit also includes assessing the accounting principles used and significant estimates made by management, as well as evaluating the overall financial statement presentation. We believe that our audits provide a reasonable basis for our opinion.

In our opinion, the financial statements referred to above present fairly, in all material respects, the consolidated financial position of Amazon.com, Inc. at December 31, 2011 and 2010, and the consolidated results of its operations and its cash flows for each of the three years in the period ended December 31, 2011, in conformity with U.S. generally accepted accounting principles. Also, in our opinion, the related financial statement schedule, when considered in relation to the basic financial statements taken as a whole, presents fairly in all material respects the information set forth therein.

We also have audited, in accordance with the standards of the Public Company Accounting Oversight Board (United States), Amazon.com, Inc.'s internal control over financial reporting as of December 31, 2011, based on criteria established in Internal Control—Integrated Framework issued by the Committee of Sponsoring Organizations of the Treadway Commission and our report dated January 31, 2012 expressed an unqualified opinion thereon.

/s/ Ernst & Young LLP
Seattle, Washington
January 31, 2012

The third paragraph provides Ernst & Young's opinion that Amazon has prepared its financial statements in accordance with generally accepted accounting principles and that there are no important (material) errors in representing the firm's accounting information. The final paragraph indicates that, in addition to its audit of the financial statements, Ernst & Young performed an audit of the effectiveness of Amazon's internal controls over its financial reporting.

Amazon's audit opinion refers to **generally accepted accounting principles**, or GAAP. But what principles are generally accepted, who accepted them, how did they get accepted, and why were they accepted?

GENERALLY ACCEPTED ACCOUNTING PRINCIPLES

Generally accepted accounting principles arose to benefit the capital market participants who use financial statements to evaluate a security's **expected return** and **risk**. The standardized conditions provided by the use of GAAP give market participants confidence that the investment decisions they make using accounting reports will be greatly enhanced by that information. In the United States, the ultimate power to set accounting standards rests with the U.S. Congress, which in 1934 established the **Securities and Exchange Commission (SEC)** by giving it the power to regulate securities markets and establish and enforce the accounting rules used by companies issuing those securities. At the time only state-by-state

The expected **return** on an investment refers to the expected income to be earned on the investment, whereas the **riskiness** of an investment refers to the uncertainty associated with the expected return. In general, risk and expected return are positively correlated; that is, investments with higher risk are generally expected to earn a higher rate of a return.

"blue sky"[5] laws existed that regulated disclosures made by firms offering public securities. The oversight role of the SEC is depicted in Exhibit 1.8. The stock market crash of 1929 and the Great Depression of the early 1930s brought turbulent times to the U.S. financial markets. The scandalous behavior of corporate executives in the downfall of some companies and the specter of ordinary citizens who had lost all of their savings were all that the U.S. Congress needed to step in and establish the SEC.

EXHIBIT 1.8   Economic Environment of Accounting Information

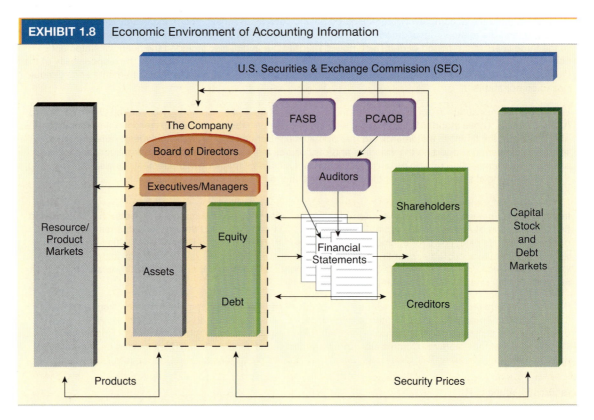

Similar events occurred again 70 years later. Calls for action in the aftermath of the **Enron**, **World-Com**, and **Global Crossing** debacles resulted in the passage of the Sarbanes-Oxley Act in 2002, bringing greater regulation of the accounting profession by a new organization called the **Public Company Accounting Oversight Board (PCAOB)**, which became responsible for overhauling auditing standards, inspecting accounting firms, and disciplining wayward auditors. The PCAOB supplanted a system of self-regulation in which accountants at the **American Institute of Certified Public Accountants (AICPA)** oversaw their peers.

Although the SEC has the final authority over the form and content of financial statements, it has delegated the responsibility for establishing U.S. GAAP to a private sector organization called the **Financial Accounting Standards Board (FASB)**. The FASB's position under the oversight of the SEC is depicted in Exhibit 1.8. The FASB was established in 1973 after the Accounting Principles Board (APB), the predecessor to the FASB, was discontinued. The APB was abandoned after losing public confidence and support for its role in setting accounting standards. The FASB is administered by the **Financial Accounting Foundation (FAF)**, whose trustees are drawn from several different groups including the American Accounting Association, the American Institute of Certified Public Accountants, the Association for Investment Management and Research, the Financial Executives Institute, and the Securities Industry Association.

---

[5] The term "blue sky" is commonly attributed to Supreme Court Justice McKenna who noted that many speculative schemes have "no more basis than so many feet of blue sky" (*Hall v. Geiger-Jones Co. 1917*). Others attribute the phrase to a Kansas legislator who observed that some investors in his state owned nothing more than a piece of the "blue sky." As of today, the authority of states to review the registration of securities offered nationally is limited by federal legislation.

The FASB has seven full-time members who must relinquish all ties to their former employers and accept no other paid employment during their five-year terms. Beginning in 2009, U.S. GAAP was streamlined into roughly 90 topics under the FASB's Codification Project. The FASB now updates and clarifies U.S. GAAP through the issuance of Accounting Standards Updates. The adoption of an Update requires the support of a simple majority of the board members.

The FASB accomplishes its mission through a comprehensive and independent process that includes wide participation from those who would be most affected by a proposed new rule. To the layperson, the notion that accounting rules generate heated debates is almost laughable. But in the late 1990s, the FASB issued a proposed accounting rule that required companies to charge the cost of executive stock options against corporate net earnings. Many technology companies feared that the decline in their reported income after implementation of this proposed accounting rule would cause their company's share price to materially decline. The debate over stock option accounting even reached the floor of the U.S. Congress. Senator Joseph Lieberman of Connecticut proposed a law prohibiting the SEC from requiring that executive stock options be expensed. The FASB, under intense political pressure, ultimately backed down, giving firms a choice of deducting the cost of stock options against net income or disclosing in their footnotes what a firm's net income would have been if the options had been charged against its income.

Stock option accounting resurfaced as a controversial topic in the aftermath of the Enron, WorldCom, and Global Crossing scandals as critics attributed the collapse of these companies, at least in part, to the incentive that option-holding executives had to drive share prices higher by inflating reported corporate earnings. Numerous companies began to voluntarily charge the cost of employee stock options against earnings while other companies (such as **Microsoft**) abandoned stock options in favor of other compensation arrangements. The FASB now requires that firms charge the expense of employee stock options against corporate earnings. (We will have more to say about employee stock options in Chapter 11.)

A more recent example of a hotly debated and controversial accounting topic relates to the required use of fair value accounting for most of a company's financial contracts. In 2006 the FASB implemented a standard (FAS 157) that clarified how and when to use fair values for these contracts, particularly those that were complex and those that did not have clearly defined inputs that could be used in the determination of fair values. The coincident timing of this rule could not have been worse, as just a year later the financial crisis began. At the same time many banks had to openly report the valuation of contracts such as **mortgage backed securities (MBS)** and **credit default swaps (CDS)**. The underlying problem many had with the accounting rules was that fair value could not be determined when financial markets were not functioning in an orderly manner. As homeowner defaults accelerated and the financial crisis picked up steam, the MBS and CDS paper was becoming "worthless", as there were no willing buyers of such contracts. Because the accounting required that these contracts be valued at prices between a willing buyer and willing seller, banks were technically deemed insolvent. The accounting rule itself was exacerbating the financial crisis.

The U.S. House Capital Markets Subcommittee, led by chairman Barney Frank of Massachusetts, demanded that the FASB modify fair value accounting rules in the face of financial crisis. In response, in early 2008 the FASB issued clarifying rules that now dictate how to apply fair value rules to illiquid markets. Interestingly, The Emergency Stabilization Act of 2008 also charged the SEC to conduct a detailed study of "mark-to-market" and its impact on financial institutions. The conclusion reached was that fair values are an important source of information to investors, and these rules did not play a meaningful role in bank failures during the crisis. We will have more to say about fair value accounting for financial contracts in Chapter 8.

As a concluding observation, it is helpful to understand that, in most countries, accounting standards are used only to prepare the financial statements distributed to such external parties as financial analysts, shareholders, and debtholders. It is rare that the same rules are used to prepare a company's income tax statements because income tax regulations are customarily set by elected legislators or governmental agencies, not accounting professionals. The internal financial statements used by managers to run a company may also differ from those statements issued to shareholders and debtholders. In short, it is not unusual for a company to maintain three (or more) sets of financial data—for managers, for the taxation authorities, and for analysts, shareholders, and debtholders. The focus of this textbook is on those financial statements prepared using GAAP for such external constituencies as financial advisors, lenders, investors, and shareholders. However, because of the importance of tax rules to managers and executives when they gauge the financial reporting effects of certain transactions, throughout the text we will highlight critical differences between financial reporting rules and tax rules.

GLOBAL PERSPECTIVE

Accounting standards have traditionally been established on a country-by-country basis. Unfortunately, this situation made the comparability and transparency of financial information across national borders difficult at best. To overcome the diversity in transnational GAAP, the **International Accounting Standards Board (IASB)** was established in 2001 to "harmonize" global accounting practice. The IASB replaced the International Accounting Standards Committee which had been established in 1973 with the goal of harmonizing world accounting standards. Many countries (Bulgaria, Estonia, Jamaica, New Zealand, Russia, Tanzania, and the Ukraine) have replaced their national GAAP with the **International Financial Reporting Standards (IFRS)** issued by the IASB. Beginning in 2005, the European Union (EU) required that all publicly-held companies in EU-member states and EU-applicant states use IFRS in their consolidated financial statements. Until recently, foreign companies that wanted to raise debt or equity capital in the U.S. were required to prepare their financial statements for U.S. investors using U.S. GAAP or, if their financial statements were prepared using some other form of GAAP, to present a reconciliation of their net income and shareholders' equity under the foreign GAAP and U.S. GAAP. In late 2007, however, the U.S. Securities and Exchange Commission voted to immediately allow foreign registrants to file their financial statements with the SEC using IFRS. If some other form of foreign GAAP is used, a reconciliation statement is still required. Many accounting and finance professionals hailed the SEC decision as the first step in a process that could later give U.S. companies the choice of filing their quarterly and annual financial data with the SEC using U.S. GAAP or IFRS. The decision was also seen as being a major step toward a unified set of global accounting practices that could be used worldwide. In 2008 the SEC issued a proposed roadmap for moving U.S. publicly traded companies toward using a uniform set of global accounting rules. The FASB and IASB have since expressed the joint commitment to improving U.S. GAAP and IFRS and achieving their convergence. The financial statements of LVMH Moet Hennessey-Louis Vuitton S.A. illustrating the use of IFRS are presented in Appendix C to this book.

(Note: For convenience, we use "IFRS" to refer to both the International Accounting Standards (IAS) issued by the International Accounting Standards Committee (IASC) and the International Financial Reporting Standards (IFRS) issued by the IASC's successor, the International Accounting Standards Board (IASB).)

ROLE OF FINANCIAL ACCOUNTING IN INVESTMENT DECISIONS: AN OVERVIEW

In very simplified terms, the lifetime profile of an individual consists of 12 to 16 years of education, 35 years of employment, and 15 to 20 years of retirement. During the first few years of employment, individuals spend most of their earnings acquiring assets like a car, a house, and taking the occasional vacation. After the basics are acquired, most individuals begin to consider the possibility that they will need substantial funds to maintain a lifestyle in retirement that they will have grown accustomed to in their working life. That means developing a retirement plan. The basic retirement plan consists of decisions about how long to work, the amount of funds to set aside over the employment period, and how to allocate those funds across different types of investments.

Individuals typically invest some of their retirement funds in the shares of companies or in a portfolio of companies to diversify their holdings. The old adage *Don't put all your eggs in one basket!* is good advice since a diversified portfolio reduces risk. Over the last decade, more and more individuals have begun simplifying the process of diversifying their equity investments by buying shares in mutual funds. By investing in a spectrum of companies, the value of mutual fund shares is not unduly influenced by the share price performance of a single company, but instead by the broad movement of stock prices in general. Stock market indices such as the Dow Jones Industrial Average (DJIA) and the Standard & Poor's 500 Index (S&P 500) are examples of indexes of a large portfolio of stocks that mutual funds often try to mimic.

Individuals also typically put a sizeable portion of their retirement funds in tax deferred, company-sponsored pension plans. Some individuals dislike risk so they put more of their funds in government debt securities that provide interest payments and repayment of principal. Securities issued by the United States government, and the governments of most other developed countries, are considered to be risk-free because of the very low probability that these entities will fail to pay the interest and principal on their debt securities.

The portfolio decisions of millions of individuals and businesses in allocating funds across different investment opportunities can be thought of as the **supply of capital**. At the same time, there are companies that have opportunities to invest in assets that far exceed their ability to generate the needed investment funds. These unfunded investment opportunities of millions of businesses can be thought of as the **demand for capital**. The **capital market**, on the other hand, can be thought of as the marketplace in which funds are traded between the suppliers of capital and those firms in search of capital. The financial statements provided by the multitude of firms seeking capital are used by the various suppliers of capital to evaluate the investment alternatives. Equilibrium prices for equity and debt securities result when millions of buyers and sellers agree to exchange capital on mutually acceptable terms.

Individual companies raise funds—that is, obtain capital—by issuing shares to shareholders and/or by borrowing from creditors such as financial institutions and bond investors. For shareholders, the return on their investment is derived from dividend payments and any appreciation (or depreciation) experienced from changes in a company's share price. In general, the return (r) for an equity security over a given period, such as a month or a year, is a function of its price at the end of the period (P_t), any dividends received during the period (D_t), and its price at the beginning of the period (P_{t-1}). That is,

> Companies "go public"—that is, sell ownership shares in the public capital market—as a means to gain access to capital to grow, to provide the original investors with "liquidity" (the ability to sell their ownership interests), and to have shares to be used to facilitate future mergers and acquisitions.

$$r_t = (P_t + D_t - P_{t-1})/P_{t-1}$$

For lenders, a return is generated by the interest payments paid by borrowers and the full and timely repayment of their initial capital investment.

In Practice 1.3 provides data on the average annual return for various types of securities sold in the United States over the 86-year period of 1926 to 2011. The In Practice also shows the standard deviation of the annual returns, a measure of the variation around the average return, which is often used as an indication of the riskiness of a given investment. According to the data, large company shares earned an average return of 9.8 percent per year compared to a return of 5.7 percent for long-term government bonds, but the standard deviation of the returns for large company stocks was much higher, 20.2 percent versus 9.7 percent. Small company shares have done even better than large company shares, having earned an average annual return of 11.9 percent, but the standard deviation of 32.3 percent is also considerably higher. The high standard deviation for small company shares means that the actual return in any year will vary considerably more than for large company shares. In short, when small company share prices fall (rise), they tend to fall (rise) farther than large company share prices; and thus, small company shares are considered to be a riskier investment than large company shares.

In Practice 1.3 *Average Annual Rate of Return by Type of Security: 1926–2011*

Security Classification	Average Return	Standard Deviation
Large company stocks....................	9.8%	20.2%
Small company stocks....................	11.9%	32.3%
Long-term corporate bonds...............	6.1%	8.7%
Long-term government bonds..............	5.7%	9.7%
U.S. Treasury bills......................	3.6%	3.1%
Inflation...............................	3.0%	4.4%

Source: Ibbotson Associates, Morningstar

The data in In Practice 1.3 indicate that investments in shares have provided higher average annual returns than investments in government bonds. If the standard deviation of the return is a reasonable measure of risk, the data indicate that shares have higher risk than government bonds, supporting the intuitive notion that higher returns come at the price of bearing higher risk. Investors in common shares can lose all of their investment whereas an investment in government bonds is considered to be risk-free (which means, an investor will receive all interest payments when due and will receive a full return of invested capital). The data also provide support for the notion that shareholders of large firms bear more risk than corporate bondholders since the standard deviation of corporate bonds is only 8.7 percent versus 20.2 percent for stocks. Yet, shareholders are compensated for this additional risk by earning higher returns, 9.8 percent versus 6.1 percent for bondholders.

What is the role of accounting information in the capital markets? For investors who follow an active investment strategy, one very important role for financial statement information is to provide better assessments of the expected return and risk of a firm's securities. This is called the **information role** of financial statements. In essence, financial statements help convey information about a firm's future prospects, namely its earnings power and expected persistence of earnings. Because stock prices correlate so strongly to these measures, any insights that can be gleaned from the trends, ratios, and accounts that embody the financial statements is of great value to these investors. However, for other investors who might follow a long-term buy-and-hold strategy, accounting information may have less value since these investors implicitly operate under the premise that security prices reflect all information that is publicly available. Many of these investors believe that it is not possible to find mispriced securities because capital markets quickly impound all financial information. A market in which security prices correctly reflect all publicly available information (for example, the information contained in financial statements) is referred to as an **efficient market**. But even though the market may indeed be efficient, on average, at the individual security level both anecdotal evidence and formal academic research refuting the market's efficiency abounds. One only need look to the size and growth of Wall Street's financial analyst community as testament to that fact. Opportunities to use historical financial statement information to enhance investment returns clearly exist.

Unlike those investing in stock, debtholders use financial statement and other accounting information for the sole purpose of assessing and monitoring financial risk—that is, the risk that a firm may not pay its debt service charges and principal payments on a timely basis. When debtholders determine that financial risk is high, they will demand commensurately higher returns (by charging higher interest rates) to compensate them for the additional risk assumed by lending to such a firm. They also frequently place formal restrictions on the dollar value and ratios derived from the financial statements, taking the form of contractually defined **debt covenants**.

CHANGING ECONOMIC LANDSCAPE

Enron, WorldCom, and Global Crossing are now household names synonymous with the most egregious corporate wrongdoing in the United States. These financial scandals brought about significant changes in U.S. corporate regulation. To demonstrate that it was responsive to the public's demand for action, numerous corporate executives and employees from Arthur Andersen, auditor for all three failed companies, were questioned on the floor of the U.S. Congress. In response to their findings, the U.S. Congress quickly enacted the Sarbanes-Oxley Act, establishing the Public Company Accounting Oversight Board to regulate the accounting profession.

Some observers believe, however, that the enacted changes didn't go to the root cause of the financial scandals, the seeds of which were sown in regulation changes made 30 years ago. They cite changes made in the 1970s to increase competition in audit markets by permitting accountants to advertise and solicit clients and to changes in the law that permitted auditors to be sued more easily for financial statement errors as causes of the "race to the bottom."[6] With decreasing fees from competition and increased legal costs, accounting firms introduced changes in auditing methodologies to reduce audit costs and lobbied for more precise standards to better defend themselves in lawsuits. Accounting firms also diversified into corporate consulting to reduce their dependence on auditing fees, the less profitable side of the business, and, by rewarding partners on the basis of client retention and new client acquisition, encouraged a compliant attitude to financial reporting disagreements. Observers also cite regulatory changes that abolished fixed brokerage commissions as another root-cause of the scandals. With the profitability of the securities business reduced, the research side of the securities industry focused more on pleasing clients that brought in underwriting and investment-banking business by releasing favorable earnings forecasts and recommendations. Thus, analysts lost their objectivity and failed to perform hard-nosed fundamental analysis that previously provided value to investors.[7]

Over the years, generally accepted accounting rules have become increasingly complicated, often requiring detailed manuals to guide companies in their implementation. The Sarbanes-Oxley Act of 2002 mandated, among other things, an investigation of the possibility of using "principles" rather than increasingly detailed "rules" as a basis for U.S. accounting standards. Whether principles become the guiding influence in setting future accounting standards remains to be seen.

---

[6] P.M. Healy and K.G. Palepu, "How the Quest for Efficiency Corroded the Market," *Harvard Business Review* (July 2003).
[7] Ibid.

What many now believe will drive the outcome of this debate is the potential wholesale replacement of U.S. GAAP by International Financial Reporting Standards (IFRS). In 2007, the U.S. SEC concluded that foreign registrants should be permitted to issue their financial reports to U.S. investors using IFRS without the need to perform a reconciliation to U.S. GAAP. There is strong sentiment that U.S. firms should also be given this option. The consensus among most in the U.S. financial community is not whether IFRS GAAP will be allowed, but whether IFRS will completely supplant U.S. GAAP or whether the two sets of accounting principles will coexist and firms will be permitted to elect to use either set of principles.

ETHICS PERSPECTIVE

There is an intense debate within the U.S. accounting standard-setting community as to whether accounting principles should be rules-based, as is the case with U.S. GAAP, or principles-based, as is the standard with international GAAP. The fundamental difference between these approaches is that principles-based accounting provides a conceptual basis for accountants to follow instead of a list of detailed rules. The landmark Sarbanes-Oxley legislation called for the U.S. Securities and Exchange Commission to study the adoption of principles-based standards for U.S. GAAP. The subsequent SEC staff report recommended that U.S. GAAP move toward a principles-based approach. In April 2003, the auditing firm of PricewaterhouseCoopers placed a full-page advertisement in the *Wall Street Journal*. Joining the debate over whether GAAP should be more principles—versus rules—based, the audit firm wrote: "Rules-based systems encourage creativity (and not the good kind) in financial reporting. They allow some to stretch the limits of what is permissible under the law, even though it may not be ethically or morally acceptable. A principles-based system requires companies to report, and auditors to audit, the substance or business purpose of transactions, not merely whether they can qualify as acceptable under incredibly complex or overly technical rules." The accounting firm advertisement further stated: "A rules-based system allows managers to ignore the substance and, instead ask, 'Where in the rules does it say I can't do this?'"

SEVEN ACCOUNTING MYTHS

It is rare that someone starting an introductory course in financial accounting begins the experience with a blank mental slate. Rather, most individuals bring with them a set of expectations. Almost everyone has had experience with some aspect of accounting, from balancing a checkbook or filling out a credit card application, to reading a set of financial statements. Through these experiences, and from discussions with others, a certain accounting mystery develops along with the formation of certain myths and misconceptions. It is the goal of this textbook to take you on a journey through the world of financial accounting, and along the way, attempt to solve many of the mysteries and debunk many of the myths and misconceptions.

The first two myths about accounting relate to the underlying rules that govern how accounting numbers are calculated and reported. This set of rules is known as **generally accepted accounting principles**, or GAAP. Perhaps the most widely held myth that we explore is the belief that:

1. Generally accepted accounting principles are a set of rigid rules that, if followed correctly, will lead to a unique, "correct" representation of the financial performance and health of a firm.

Closely related to myth number one is the belief that:

2. GAAP is created from a comprehensive analytical process, which is free from political influence.

The following four myths relate to the basic financial statements that are the output of the accounting process:

3. The basic financial statements, consisting of a balance sheet, an income statement, a statement of shareholders' equity, and a statement of cash flow, reflect a complete, accurate, and timely portrayal of the financial performance and well-being of a firm.

4. All of a firm's identifiable assets and liabilities appear on the balance sheet, and the difference between a firm's assets and its liabilities represents the value of the firm.

5. Each of the financial statements is independent, with each reflecting a different aspect of a firm's performance and financial health.

6. Cash flow is ultimately what matters to a firm and its investors; therefore, it is not really necessary to worry about the definition of earnings used in the preparation of the income statement. Rather, one need only consider the sources and uses of cash as reflected on a firm's statement of cash flow.

Lastly, and what we feel is perhaps the biggest myth of all is:

7. A knowledge of accounting is only necessary for someone who wants to be an accountant.

Some of the terminology from the above list of myths may be unfamiliar to you at this point. One thing that is certainly not a myth is that a major challenge associated with learning accounting is to simply understand all of the jargon. Perhaps we should have added an additional myth: Accounting is hard! While this is certainly a subjective assessment that each student will make, we believe that the approach followed in this textbook will go a long way to turning this challenge into a myth as well.

While most individuals reading this book do not plan to pursue a career in accounting, we believe that it is critical for anyone planning a career in management to understand the fundamentals of accounting, for it is the language of business. To use an analogy from sports, you don't have to be a great baseball player to enjoy the game of baseball. Stated alternatively, it is not critical to be trained as an accountant but you must understand how the game is played and scored.

Accounting, as noted above, has its own language. Two of the words that seem to strike fear into new accounting students are "debit" and "credit." Debits and credits represent a mechanism for accountants to record business transactions, in other words to keep score of the game. For those executives planning to continue their accounting studies to a more advanced level, we have included details on using debits and credits on the website (www.cambridgepub.com/faemba_3e) for this text. Sometimes, however, it is difficult to see the forest through all of the trees. Therefore, we utilize a spreadsheet approach to recording transactions within the chapters to explain the accounting process in a more straightforward, intuitive manner.

EXECUTIVE SUMMARY

In this chapter we considered the basic financial statements of Amazon.com, an online retailer of products. We examined how the financial statements can be used by debtholders and shareholders to predict the expected return and risk of individual securities. We also considered the role of the FASB, the IASB, and the SEC in setting accounting rules and the role of auditors in monitoring compliance with those rules.

As a validation of your understanding of the content of this chapter, you should now be able to:

- Understand that companies acquire capital from investors who purchase the debt and equity securities issued by such firms to obtain an expected return commensurate with the risk the investors assume.
- Understand the role of accounting rules in facilitating a properly functioning capital market.
- Identify the basic financial statements—the income statement, the balance sheet, the statement of shareholders' equity, and the statement of cash flow.
- Understand the conflicts of interest that may arise between the executives, shareholders, and debtholders of a corporation, and the costs associated with the divergent incentives that may arise when the ownership and management of a company are separated (see appendix).

In Chapter 2, we consider how the basic financial statements are developed from accounting events.

KEY CONCEPTS AND TERMS

Accounts payable, 8
Accounts receivable, 8
Accrual basis of accounting, 8
Agency costs, 24
American Institute of Certified
    Public Accountants, 16
Assets, 7, 25
Audit report, 14
Balance sheet, 7
Capital market, 19
Cash basis of accounting, 8

Comparability, 25
Comprehensive income, 25
Conservatism, 25
Consolidated income statement, 9
Contracting role, 24
Corporate charter, 23
Corporate governance, 23
Corporations, 23
Covenants, 24
Credit default swaps (CDS), 17
Debt covenants, 24

Decision usefulness, 12
Demand for capital, 19
Distributions to owners, 26
Economic entity, 25
Efficient market, 20
Equity, 25
Expected return, 15
Expenses, 25
Faithful representation, 13, 25
Financial accounting, 5
Financial Accounting Foundation, 16

APPENDIX 1A: Agency Costs and the Separation of Management and Capital Providers

Today, businesses are often organized as **corporations** owned by shareholders under the laws of the state or province in which a company is incorporated. State incorporation laws require a company to have a **corporate charter**—a set of bylaws governing the rights and responsibilities of the board of directors to a firm's shareholders and covering such topics as annual meetings, the election of directors, the type and quantity of shares to be sold, and shareholder voting rights. Shareholders usually delegate the task of running a business on their behalf to a board of directors who are elected by shareholders at the annual shareholders' meeting. The board of directors, on the other hand, has oversight responsibility for the company, but the day-to-day management of the firm is directed by the chief executive officer (CEO) who appoints the senior management team including the president, the chief operating officer (COO), and the chief financial officer (CFO). With the assistance of top management, the board of directors recommends a firm's independent auditors to shareholders. The shareholders vote on audit firm appointment (and reappointment) at the annual meeting. These arrangements are collectively referred to as a company's **corporate governance**, a topic much debated since the collapse of **Enron**, **WorldCom**, **Global Crossing**, and a host of other trouble-ridden firms.

A noteworthy characteristic of the corporate form of organization is the principle of **limited liability**, a feature that limits the liability of a business's shareholders for the debts incurred by the business. Thus, if a corporation's assets are insufficient to pay off a business's liabilities when they mature, the lenders are unable to satisfy their claims against the company by attempting to gain control of the personal assets of the company's shareholders.

BUSINESS PERSPECTIVE

The corporate form of business is one of the two primary organizational forms of companies. The other form is a partnership, also known as a sole proprietorship when there is only one partner. There are several key differences between these alternative organizational forms, the principal ones being limited liability, tax status, and ease of ownership transferability. The primary advantage of the corporate form of business is the limited liability provision in which shareholders are only liable for the debts of a business to the extent of their investment in the business. Partners in a partnership, in contrast, face joint and severable liability wherein each partner is liable for not only their own acts, but also for the acts of the other partners. In addition, a partner's liability is not limited to just his/her partnership investment, but liability extends to their personal assets as well. The limited liability attribute of corporations is essential to their ability to raise large amounts of capital because shareholders can invest in a corporation without risking their entire personal wealth. This attribute also facilitates the transferability of ownership interests in a corporation relative to a partnership.

Corporations are not without negatives, however, and the principal one is tax status. Corporations face a corporate income tax on their earnings, which may lead to a situation of "double taxation" when any previously taxed corporate income is taxed again to the shareholders when they receive a dividend distribution. Partnerships are not taxed separately; instead, the partnership income is taxed only once at the individual-partner level. In addition to these two primary organizational forms, several hybrid forms exist that have attributes of both corporations and partnerships. These hybrid forms include limited partnerships, limited liability partnerships, sub-chapter S corporations, and limited liability corporations.

The development of the concept of limited liability was significant because it enabled the ownership of a firm to be separated from the day-to-day management of the firm; and, consequently, permitted the segmentation of risk bearing by shareholders from the operational control of a business by its team of managers. Unfortunately, the separation of the ownership of a business from the management of a business often leads to a conflict of interest between the preferences of shareholders for greater wealth and the preferences of managers for increased leisure and on-the-job "perks" such as a company-financed jet. The separation of ownership and the provision of debt financing can also potentially create a conflict of interest between shareholders with preferences for higher-valued shares and debtholders with preferences for timely debt servicing and loan repayment. The costs associated with these divergent self-interests are referred to as **agency costs**.

Since conflicts of interest are likely to arise among the various constituencies that comprise a corporation (i.e., shareholders, managers, and creditors), the agency costs associated with these conflicts must be born by the company's shareholders by virtue of their ownership of the firm. Consequently, it is normally in the shareholders' interest to engage in various "monitoring" and "contracting" activities to help control or reduce these conflicts. For example, financial statement information is often used in employment contracts between managers and shareholders to measure, monitor, and control managerial behavior. This is referred to as the **contracting role** of accounting information.

Conflicts Between Managers and Shareholders

Since shareholders must bear the agency costs associated with the conflicting self-interests that result from the separation of management and ownership of a corporation, they are incentivized to develop contracts with corporate management that direct or control managerial behavior. For example, the shareholders of a business often develop and institute incentive contracts with a business's executives that tie an executive's compensation to the company's share price, via stock options or a restricted stock plan, or to the company's accounting earnings which have been shown to be correlated with a company's share price. Thus, incentive contracts work to align the financial interests of managers with those of a company's shareholders, thereby encouraging the managers to simultaneously work to maximize their own wealth as well as that of the shareholders. Amazon.com, for example, reported that the company granted bonus opportunities to various executive officers payable upon the achievement of *certain performance goals*. Undoubtedly, some of the performance goals were measured in terms of such accounting numbers as sales, cash flow or profits. By linking executive compensation to measurable accounting variables, management is more likely to take appropriate actions to see that the performance goals are met or exceeded, thereby increasing the wealth of the shareholders, and that of their own.

Conflicts Between Debtholders and Shareholders

When a company borrows funds, the terms of the loan agreement are formalized in a legal contract. Typically, these loan contracts contain provisions, called **covenants**, which restrict the actions of the borrower. For example, a common debt covenant limits the amount of dividends that can be paid to shareholders. Covenants are used by lenders to reduce financial risk and increase the likelihood that borrowers pay their interest and principal repayments in a timely manner.

Agency costs can also arise from conflicts between debtholders and shareholders. An extreme example of such behavior would occur in the case of a firm whose shareholders borrow a large amount of money from debtholders only to pay the borrowed funds out as a dividend. In effect, the shareholders redistribute the borrowed wealth from the debtholders to themselves, potentially leaving the debtholders with a worthless corporate shell and no resources to repay the loan. By virtue of their ownership of the firm, shareholders bear the agency costs of this conflict via higher interest rates because debtholders can anticipate these potentially unconstrained actions by shareholders. A solution to this conflict is for shareholders to agree to be bound by a legally enforceable loan contract containing provisions that restrict the shareholders' behavior. These contract provisions are called **debt covenants**, and may, for example, restrict the amount of dividends that may be paid.

To illustrate, the following disclosure related to the long-term debt that appeared on Amazon's 2008 balance sheet:

> The indenture governing the 4.75% Convertible Subordinated Notes contains certain affirmative covenants for us, including making principal and interest payments when due, maintaining our corporate existence and properties, and paying taxes and other claims in a timely manner. We were in compliance with these covenants through December 31, 2008.

Another example of a corporate action creating agency costs is the issuance of new debt with repayment priority over existing debt. In this situation, there is a redistribution of wealth from the initial debtholders to the shareholders. A solution to this conflict is for the shareholders to agree to a legally enforceable contract that limits the firm's ability to issue new debt with priority over the old debt. For example, Amazon's borrowing agreements in 2008 had covenants restricting the company's ability to borrow by requiring that the ratio of aggregate indebtedness divided by pre-tax operating earnings be less than 6 to 1. Under the terms of this covenant, Amazon was required to periodically provide debtholders with audited financial statements from which measures of aggregate indebtedness and pre-tax operating earnings could be taken and used to evaluate the firm's compliance with the covenant. How does this help Amazon? By agreeing to the restrictions imposed by the covenant, Amazon.com was able to obtain a loan that it might not otherwise gain access to.

APPENDIX 1B: Generally Accepted Accounting Principles: Purpose, Concepts, and Elements

Generally accepted accounting principles (GAAP) have as their purpose the measurement of economic activity by a business enterprise and the reporting of this activity in the form of financial statements, along with disclosures to aid users in the interpretation of the financial statements. The primary promulgator of U.S. GAAP is the Financial Accounting Standards Board (FASB). Prior to its codification project in 2009, the FASB issued a series of pronouncements, called Statements of Financial Accounting Concepts (SFAC), that served to create a foundation for U.S. GAAP.

The first SFAC identifies the three principal objectives of financial reporting: (1) the creation of information useful in making economic decisions; (2) providing information to aid in predicting cash flows; and (3) providing relevant information regarding a business's economic resources. These objectives facilitate the measurement and reporting of business activity during a **fiscal period** by an **economic entity** that is assumed to be a **going concern**. The economic entity assumption implies that the business activity to be measured can be identified with a particular unit of accountability and requires that the activity of the entity be assessed separately from the activities of its owners. It is further assumed that the entity will remain a going concern for the foreseeable future; in other words, that the enterprise will have a long life. Because the entity will exist for an extended period of time, it is necessary to segment its operational life into reporting periods, known as fiscal periods, so as to provide interested parties with timely, relevant information about its various activities. Public corporations that report to the Securities and Exchange Commission (SEC) file quarterly financial statements, called a 10-Q, and annual financial statements, called a 10-K. An additional **monetary unit** assumption implies that only those items that can be expressed in terms of a monetary unit, the U.S. dollar in the United States, are included in the financial statements. Because inflation is relatively mild in the United States, price-level changes are ignored and the U.S. dollar is assumed to remain stable over time.

The second SFAC discusses the qualities that make accounting information useful. The primary qualities are **relevance** and **faithful representation**. For information to be relevant, it should be timely and should either assist in predicting future cash flows or provide feedback value regarding past events. For information to be faithfully represented, it should be verifiable and faithfully represent the observed economic activity. Finally, information should also be comparable, consistent, and understandable. **Comparability** refers to comparisons made between different business entities, whereas consistency refers to comparisons made across time for a particular business entity.

The above qualities are subject to a **materiality** constraint. The materiality constraint is not explicitly defined and consequently requires some judgment in its application. In general, only economic events that are significant enough to affect a user's decisions are required to be accounted for in a manner consistent with GAAP.

Not all of these qualities are compatible, however; for example, there is often a conflict between relevance and faithful representation. When trade-offs between the qualities are necessary, GAAP tends to place more weight on the role of **conservatism**. Conservatism is a reaction to the uncertainty inherent in many financial events. Conservatism dictates that, when in doubt, the financial statements should understate assets, overstate liabilities, delay the recognition of revenues, and accelerate the recognition of expenses.

The third concept statement defines ten elements that form the basic building blocks of the financial statements. The first three elements relate to the balance sheet, which portrays an entity's net resources as of a particular point in time:

1. **Assets**—Probable future economic benefits obtained or controlled by a particular entity as a result of past transactions or events.
2. **Liabilities**—Probable future sacrifices of economic benefits arising from present obligations of a particular entity to transfer assets or provide services to other entities in the future as a result of past transactions.
3. **Equity** (net assets)—The residual interest in the assets that remain after deducting its liabilities.

The next five elements relate to the income statement, which measures an entity's performance over a given period of time:

4. **Revenues**—Inflows or other enhancements of assets of an entity or settlement of its liabilities (or a combination of both) from delivering or producing goods, rendering services, or carrying out other activities that constitute the entity's ongoing major and central purpose.
5. **Expenses**—Outflows or other using up of assets or incurrences of liabilities (or a combination of both) from delivering or producing goods, rendering services, or carrying out other activities that constitute the entity's ongoing major and central purpose.
6. **Gains**—Increases in equity (net assets) from peripheral or incidental transactions of an entity and from all other transactions and other events and circumstances affecting the entity except those that result from revenues or investments by owners.
7. **Losses**—decreases in equity (net assets) from peripheral or incidental transactions of an entity and from all other transactions and other events and circumstances affecting the entity except those that result from revenues or investments by owners.
8. **Comprehensive income**—The change in equity of a business enterprise during a period from transactions and other events and circumstances from sources other than investments by owners or distribution to owners.

The final two elements relate to transfers between a business enterprise and its owners:

9. **Investments by owners**—Increases in equity of a particular business enterprise resulting from transfers to it for the purpose of increasing ownership interests.
10. **Distributions to owners**—Decreases in the equity of a particular business enterprise resulting from transferring assets, rendering services, or incurring liabilities to owners.

QUESTIONS

Q1.1 **Financial Statement Data Users.** Financial statement data is utilized by a variety of user-groups to include a company's board of directors, bondholders, corporate employees and executives, customers, investment advisors, labor unions, loan officers and credit analysts, shareholders and suppliers. For each user-group, discuss how financial statement data might be used in their decision-making process.

Q1.2 **GAAP.** Discuss why generally accepted accounting principles are important to investors and to a properly functioning, efficient capital market. How do accounting rules help capital markets be (or become) "efficient"?

Q1.3 **Corporate Governance.** Discuss what "corporate governance" is and why it is important to shareholders.

Q1.4 **Risk, Return, and Accounting Information.** Discuss the relationship between investment risk and the expected rate of return on an investment. Explain why accounting information is useful in evaluating the risk/return trade-off inherent in all investments.

Q1.5 **Global GAAP.** Discuss the major impediments to the acceptance of a global set of generally accepted accounting principles. Prepare a list of those key impediments. Of the items on your list, which do you think will be the most difficult to overcome? Why? Why is having a global set of GAAP desirable?

Q1.6 **Asymmetric U.S. GAAP.** Under U.S. GAAP, long-lived assets such as real estate are carried on the balance sheet at the original purchase price of the asset. In the event that the value of a real estate asset becomes "impaired"—that is, the current value of the real estate falls below its original purchase price and is unlikely to recover the lost value in the foreseeable future—the asset's book value is written down to the lower current value and a loss is recorded on the firm's income statement. Under no circumstances, however, can a firm write up the value of its real estate assets in the event that current value exceeds original purchase price. Discuss whether U.S. GAAP should be changed to allow a symmetric treatment of asset value increases and decreases. What are the implications of this asymmetry in the accounting treatment of assets (such as real estate) for current U.S. financial statement users?

Q1.7 **Human Assets.** The balance sheet allegedly reports all of the assets of a business. But one of the most important assets of any business is its employees, and this asset is omitted from the balance sheet of every company in every country in the world. Thus, it can be concluded that the balance sheet of any company understates the true value of its assets. Discuss what types of companies and which industries are most likely to be impacted by this situation. Prepare a list of the companies that you feel are most adversely affected by this accounting practice. Why did you select these companies?

Q1.8 **Key Performance Indicators: Amazon.com.** Based upon your reading of the chapter, specifically a review of the financial statements of Amazon.com, identify five key indicators of performance (KPIs) for Amazon. com. Explain why you selected the five KPIs. Identify five KPIs that are not present in Amazon's financial statements but that you believe are important to consider when making a decision about whether to invest in Amazon.com.

Q1.9 **Audit Reports.** Review Amazon.com's audit report in Exhibit 1.7 and discuss what the report tells you about Amazon's financial statements. Is there anything in the audit report that causes you concern? Why or why not? According to the independent auditors, who has ultimate responsibility for the preparation of and fairness of the company's financial statements?

Q1.10 **Accounting Assumptions and Concepts.** Discuss the following accounting assumptions and concepts:
- Accrual basis of accounting
- Cash basis of accounting
- Going concern assumption
- Materiality concept
- Information role of accounting
- Contracting role of accounting

Why are the assumptions and concepts important?

Q1.11 **The Basic Financial Statements.** Describe or define the four basic financial statements:
- Income statement
- Balance sheet

- Statement of shareholders' equity
- Statement of cash flow

Discuss how the four statements are interconnected.

Q1.12   **Debt Covenants.** **American Airlines** has outstanding lines of credit and various loan agreements with a number of financial institutions. Under the terms of these debt contracts, American is required to (a) maintain a minimum balance of $1.25 billion of unrestricted cash and short-term investments, (b) maintain a ratio of operating cash flow to interest expense of at least 1.3 to 1.0, and (c) restrict any dividend payments to American shareholders to not more than 25 percent of net income. Discuss why American's lenders would impose these financial and operating restrictions on the airline. Discuss why American would agree to the restrictions.

Q1.13   **Debt Covenants.** **Titanium Metals Corporation** (TIMET) is one of the world's leading producers of titanium products. In November 2012, it was announced the company was being purchased by **Precision Castparts**, a diversified manufacturer of complex metal components and products. In TIMET's annual report, prior to its acquisition by Precision Castparts, the company disclosed the following:

> Under the terms of the company's U.S. asset-based revolving credit agreement, borrowings are limited to the lesser of $105 million or a formula-determined borrowing-base. . . . Borrowings are collateralized by substantially all of the company's U.S. assets.
>
> The U.S. credit agreement prohibits . . . the payment of dividends on the company's common stock . . . , limits additional indebtedness, requires compliance with certain financial covenants including a minimum net worth covenant and a fixed charge ratio covenant . . . .

Discuss why TIMET's U.S. lenders would impose such restrictions on the company. Discuss why TIMET would agree to such restrictions.

Q1.14   **(Appendix 1A) Separation of Ownership and Management.** Describe a conflict that may arise between the shareholders of a company and the managers of the company. Discuss what the shareholders might do to overcome that conflict and explain why you feel that your solution to the conflict would be effective.

Q1.15   **(Appendix 1A) Conflicts between Shareholders and Debtholders.** Describe a conflict that may arise between the shareholders of a company and the debtholders of the company. Discuss what the debtholders might do to resolve that conflict and explain why you feel that your solution to the conflict would be effective.

Q1.16   **The Going Concern Assumption.** **Ernst & Young, LLP** is the independent public accountant for **AMR Corporation**, the parent company of **American Airlines** and **American Eagle**. In 2002, Ernst & Young gave AMR a "clean opinion," indicating that its financial statements were fairly presented. In February 2013 AMR and **US Airways Group** announced the two companies would merge to form the largest airline in the world. In AMR's 2012 annual report, Ernst & Young gave AMR a "clean opinion," indicating that its financial statements were fairly presented. In the 2012 auditors' report for AMR, however, Ernst & Young notes:

> The accompanying consolidated financial statements have been prepared assuming that the Company will continue as a going concern. As discussed in Note 1 to the consolidated financial statements, the Company's bankruptcy filing raises substantial doubt about the Company's ability to continue as a going concern. Management's plans concerning these matters are described in Note 1. The consolidated financial statements do not include adjustments that might result from the outcome of this uncertainty.

Discuss why Ernst & Young would issue a "clean opinion" on the financial statements of AMR Corporation given its many doubts about the firm's ability to "continue as a going concern."

Q1.17   **Is the Sarbanes-Oxley Act Effective?** In 2006, *BusinessWeek* magazine (April 17, 2006) carried an opinion piece which questioned the effectiveness of the Sarbanes-Oxley Act of 2002. According to the author, Professor D. Moore, "key business failures that cost investors and employees tens of billions of dollars are all but sure to happen again. The calamitous scandals of Enron and many other companies were possible only because of breaches in a bulwark of our free market system—auditor independence." Professor Moore states that the Sarbanes-Oxley Act will be ineffective in preventing future corporate scandals because the act fails to address the real underlying problem, namely the lack of auditor objectivity. Do you agree with Professor Moore? If so, why? If not, why not?

Q1.18   **Should the Sarbanes-Oxley Act Be Revised?** In late 2006, *BusinessWeek* magazine (December 18, 2006) carried a report on the aftermath of the passage of the Sarbanes-Oxley Act. According to the piece, "the intentions were good, but in the two years since its passing, the Sarbanes-Oxley Act has collapsed into a glob of regulatory confusion costing U.S. businesses billions of dollars a year in compliance costs." The article further noted that "(T)he act never got the vetting it deserved because of the race to approve it after the **Enron** and **WorldCom** melt-downs. . ." Nevertheless, one direct consequence of the Act was that a record number of U.S.-listed firms—1,300 companies, or over 8 percent of the total—restated their earnings in 2005. Discuss whether the criticisms of the Act noted in the *BusinessWeek* article are justified given the large number of firms that found it necessary to restate their reported earnings following the passage of the Act.

Q1.19   **(Ethics Perspective) Rules-based Versus Principles-based Accounting.**   Do you believe that rules-based accounting leads to unethical managerial behavior? If so, why? Do you think that rules-based GAAP allows businesses to design their financial reporting so as to stay within the letter of the accounting standards even if they clearly violate the spirit of the standards?

Q1.20   **(Appendix 1B)**   Financial statements must contain objective and verifiable data if they are to be useful. Yet, many estimates and subjective assumptions are required to facilitate the preparation of these reports. Please reconcile these apparent inconsistencies in the preparation of the basic financial statements.

Q1.21   **(Appendix 1B)**   Much of the information contained in the balance sheet is reported on a historical cost basis. This means that such assets as land are reported at the amount that was originally paid for the item when purchased. Alternative possible reporting methods include current value, what a similar item would currently cost to acquire, and liquidation value, the amount an entity would receive if it was forced to sell the item. Discuss how the concepts of relevance, faithful representation, and going concern influence the choice of historical cost as a reporting method.

Assignments with the logo in the margin are available in BusinessCourse.
See the Preface of the book for details.
CHECK FIGURE indicates that check figures are available on the book's Website.

EXERCISES

 E1.22   **Account Identification.**   Presented below is a list of financial statement accounts. Using the letter A for assets, L for liabilities, SE for shareholders' equity, R for revenue, E for expenses, and NA for not applicable, identify (a) whether the listed accounts appear on the balance sheet (B/S) or income statement (I/S), and if so, (b) the nature of the account (A, L, SE, R, E, or NA).

1. Accounts receivable		9. Depreciation expense
2. Common stock		10. Accounts payable
3. Sales		11. Cash flow from operating activities
4. Land		12. Cash
5. Retained earnings		13. Cost of goods sold
6. Notes payable		14. Equipment
7. Dividends paid		15. Selling expense
8. Inventory		16. Interest income

E1.23   **The Balance Sheet Equation.**   The Arcadia Company reported the following financial results during its first two years of operations:

Year End	Assets	=	Liabilities	+	Shareholders' Equity
Year 1 . . .	$80,000	=	$60,000	+	$20,000
Year 2 . . .	70,000	=	40,000	+	30,000

Assuming that no dividends were declared and that no additional capital was invested in Year 2, determine Arcadia's net income (or loss) for Year 2.

CHECK FIGURE **E1.24**   **The Balance Sheet Equation.**   The Claremont Company reported the following financial results during its first two years of operations.

Year End	Assets	=	Liabilities	+	Shareholders' Equity
Year 1 . . .	$110,000	=	$60,000	+	$50,000
Year 2 . . .	125,000	=	80,000	+	45,000

Assuming that no dividends were declared and that no additional capital was invested in Year 2, determine the net income (loss) for the Claremont Company in Year 2.

E1.25 **Key Relations: Revenues, Expenses, Dividends, and Retained Earnings.** Compute the missing amounts (in millions) in the following table. (The balance in retained earnings at year-end 2012 was $2.2.) Comment on the firm's performance over the three-year period after calculating the level of expenses as a percentage of total revenues and net income as a percentage of total revenues. What advice would you give to this company in regards to its dividend policy?

	2010	2011	2012
Retained earnings (beginning)	$1.2	$ 2.0	?
Revenues	8.8	11.8	11.8
Expenses	7.4	?	11.0
Dividends	?	.6	.6

E1.26 **Key Relations: Revenues, Expenses, Dividends, and Retained Earnings.** Compute the missing amounts in the following table. (At the end of 2012, retained earnings had a balance of negative $2,086.) Comment on the company's performance over the three-year period after calculating the relationship of expenses as a percentage of revenues and net income as a percentage of revenues. Do you agree with the company's dividend policy? Why?

	2010	2011	2012
Retained earnings (beginning)	$(1,746.5)	$(1,830.5)	$(2,653.0)
Revenues	4,840.5	5,327.0	?
Expenses	?	5,628.0	5,425.0
Dividends	-0-	?	17.5

E1.27 **Financial Statement Results.** In its 2012 annual report to shareholders, **General Electric** reported the following financial results:

- Revenues increased from $147.3 billion to $147.4 billion.
- Net income decreased from $14.2 billion to $13.6 billion.
- Total assets decreased from $718.2 billion to $685.3 billion.
- Shareholders' equity increased from $116.4 billion to $123.0 billion.
- For the year, the cash flow from operating activities was $31.3 billion, the cash flow from investing activities was $11.3 billion, and the cash flow from financing activities was negative $51.1 million.

Discuss the possible explanations for the financial results of General Electric.

E1.28 **Financial Statement Results.** In its 2012 annual report to shareholders, **Johnson & Johnson**, a consumer-products company, reported the following financial results:

- Revenues increased from $65.0 billion to $67.2 billion.
- Net income increased from $9.7 billion to $10.9 billion.
- Total assets increased from $113.6 billion to $121.3 billion.
- Shareholders' equity increased from $57.1 billion to $64.8 billion.
- For the year, the cash flow from operating activities amounted to $15.4 billion, the cash flow from investing activities amounted to negative $4.5 billion, and the cash flow from financing activities amounted to negative $20.6 billion.

Discuss the possible explanations for the financial results of Johnson & Johnson.

E1.29 **Calculating Security Returns.** Presented below are the beginning-of-year common share price (P_{t-1}), the end-of-year common share price (P_t), and the annual dividend (D_t) for three competitors—**General Electric**, **Philips Electronics NV**, and **Siemens AG**.

	P_{t-1}	P_t	D_t
General Electric Co.	$32.01	$34.50	$0.86
Philips Electronics NV	72.52	72.90	1.28
Siemens AG	27.20	25.36	0.52

Calculate the annual return for each of the three individual securities. Which security provided the greatest return over the one-year period? What other information would you need to assess the return/risk trade-off on each of these individual securities?

PROBLEMS

CHECK FIGURE

P1.30   **Key Financial Statement Relations: Balance Sheet, Income Statement, and Statement of Cash Flow.**
Compute the missing amounts in the following financial statements. You may assume that accounts receivable
relate only to credit sales and that accounts payable relate only to credit purchases of inventory. There were no
sales of property and equipment during 2012 and any purchases of property and equipment were made using
cash. What is your assessment of the company's financial performance in 2012?

Balance Sheet at	December 31, 2011	December 31, 2012
Current assets		
Cash	$?	$ 25,000
Marketable securities	3,000	5,000
Accounts receivable	12,000	37,000
Merchandise inventory	52,000	23,000
Prepaid advertising	15,000	18,000
Total current assets	92,000	108,000
Property, plant and equipment (cost)	175,000	?
Accumulated depreciation	(35,000)	(63,000)
Land	15,000	?
Intangible assets	?	7,000
Total assets	$258,000	$342,000
Current liabilities		
Accounts payable	$ 12,000	$ 23,000
Wages payable	?	18,000
Interest payable	6,000	5,000
Dividends payable	3,000	?
Taxes payable	17,000	12,000
Total current liabilities	43,000	60,000
Long-term debt	?	86,000
Shareholders' equity		
Common stock	150,000	172,000
Retained earnings	23,000	32,000
Treasury stock	(10,000)	?
Total liabilities and shareholders' equity	$258,000	$342,000

Income Statement for Year Ending	December 31, 2012
Sales revenue	$?
Cost of sales	123,000
Gross profit	162,000
Expenses:	
Wages	15,000
Advertising	18,000
Depreciation	?
Amortization	4,000
Total expenses	65,000
Operating profit	97,000
Interest	?
Income (loss) before taxes	88,000
Tax expense	35,000
Net income	$ 53,000

Statement of Cash Flow for Year Ended	December 31, 2012
Cash flow from operating activities	
Cash collections from customers.........................	$ 260,000
Cash payments for:	
Inventory..	(83,000)
Wages...	(2,000)
Taxes	(40,000)
Interest	(10,000)
Advertising	?
Net cash provided by operations.....................	104,000
Cash flow from investing activities	
(Purchases) sale of property, plant and equipment	(111,000)
(Purchase) sale of marketable securities	?
(Purchase) sale of land...............................	11,000
Net cash provided by investing activities...................	(102,000)
Cash flow from financing activities	
Issuance (repayment) of long-term debt	34,000
Payment of dividend	(45,000)
Issuance (repurchase) of common stock....................	?
(Purchase) sale of treasury stock.......................	2,000
Net cash provided by financing activities..................	13,000
Change in cash.....................................	$?

P1.31 **Key Financial Statement Relations: Balance Sheet, Income Statement, and Statement of Cash Flow.** Compute the missing amounts in the following financial statements. You may assume that accounts receivable relate only to credit sales and that accounts payable relate only to credit purchases of inventory. There were no sales of property and equipment during 2012 and any purchases of property and equipment were made using cash. What is your assessment of the company's financial performance in 2012?

Balance Sheet at	December 31, 2011	December 31, 2012
Current assets		
Cash.....................................	$ 18,000	$?
Marketable securities....................	2,000	5,000
Accounts receivable.....................	8,000	10,000
Merchandise inventory...................	41,000	58,000
Prepaid advertising.....................	13,000	16,000
Total current assets	82,000	104,000
Property, plant and equipment (cost)........	?	201,000
Accumulated depreciation................	(41,000)	(52,000)
Land....................................	12,000	19,000
Intangible assets	12,000	?
Total assets.............................	$227,000	$282,000
Current liabilities		
Accounts payable........................	$ 18,000	$?
Wages payable..........................	15,000	18,000
Interest payable	?	6,000
Dividends payable	2,000	4,000
Taxes payable..........................	5,000	1,000
Total current liabilities...................	48,000	50,000
Long-term debt	46,000	?
Shareholders' equity		
Common stock..........................	121,000	160,000
Retained earnings	22,000	32,000
Treasury stock	?	(12,000)
Total liabilities and shareholders' equity......	$227,000	$282,000

Income Statement for Year Ending	December 31, 2012
Sales revenue...	$140,000
Cost of sales...	87,000
Gross profit...	53,000
Expenses	
Wages..	?
Advertising	5,000
Depreciation	?
Amortization	2,000
Total expenses	24,000
Operating profit	29,000
Interest	3,000
Income (loss) before taxes..............................	26,000
Tax expense	?
Net income...	$ 18,000

Statement of Cash Flow for Year Ended	December 31, 2012
Cash flow from operating activities	
Cash collections from customers.........................	$?
Cash payments for:	
Inventory..	(101,000)
Wages...	(3,000)
Taxes	(12,000)
Interest	(5,000)
Advertising	(8,000)
Net cash provided by operations........................	9,000
Cash flow from investing activities	
(Purchases) sale of property, plant and equipment	(39,000)
(Purchase) sale of marketable securities	(3,000)
(Purchase) sale of land.................................	?
Net cash provided by investing activities................	(49,000)
Cash flow from financing activities	
Issuance (repayment) of long-term debt	6,000
Payment of dividend	(6,000)
Issuance (repurchase) of common stock.................	39,000
(Purchase) sale of treasury stock.......................	(2,000)
Net cash provided by financing activities................	37,000
Net cash flow	$ (3,000)

CORPORATE ANALYSIS

CA1.32   **The Procter & Gamble Company.**   The 2012 annual report of **The Procter & Gamble Company (P&G)** is available at http://annualreport.pg.com/annualreport2012/index.shtml. After reviewing P&G's annual report, respond to the following questions:

a.   Prepare a list of some of the products produced by P&G. In what industry does P&G operate? Who are some of P&G's key competitors? (To identify the key competitors for P&G, you will need to access the Internet [e.g., http://finance.yahoo.com] or obtain a copy of a recent research report for P&G.)

b.   How much net income did P&G earn in 2010, 2011, and 2012? How much operating revenue did P&G report in 2010, 2011, and 2012? Are the trends in operating revenue and net income consistent and positive (i.e., increasing)?

c.   How much cash flow from operations was generated by P&G in 2010, 2011, and 2012? Is the trend in the cash flow from operations consistent with the trend in operating revenue and net income? Calculate the ratio of the cash flow from operations divided by net income for 2010, 2011, and 2012. (Note: The ratio of cash flow from operations divided by net income is called the "operating funds ratio.") What does this ratio tell you?

    d.   Calculate the ratio of total liabilities divided by total assets for 2011 and 2012. What does this ratio tell you? Is P&G principally debt-financed or principally equity-financed? Is the form of P&G's financing changing over time?

    e.   Consider the audit report for P&G. Who are P&G's auditors? What does P&G's audit report say about the firm's financial statements? Is there anything in P&G's audit report that causes you any concern? If so, what?

CA1.33 **Internet-based Analysis.** Consider a publicly held company whose products you are familiar with. Some examples might include:

Company	Product	Corporate Website
• Johnson & Johnson Company......	• Band-Aids	• www.jnj.com
• Microsoft Corporation.............	• Windows XP software	• www.microsoft.com
• Nokia Corporation	• Cellular phones	• www.nokia.com
• Intel Corporation	• Pentium processors	• www.intel.com
• Kimberly-Clark Corporation........	• Kleenex	• www.kimberly-clark.com

Access the company's public website and search for its most recent annual report. (Some companies will provide access to their financial data through an "investor relations" link, while others will provide a direct link to their "annual reports.") After locating your company's most recent annual report, open the file and review its contents. After reviewing the annual report for your selected company, prepare answers to the following questions:

    1. Prepare a list of the company's products.

    2. Identify which accounting firm audited the company's financial data. Briefly describe the contents of the audit report.

    3. How much net income did the company earn in each of the past two years?

    4. How much cash flow from operations did the company generate in each of the last two years?

    5. Explain why the amount of net income and the cash flow from operations differed.

    6. Comment on the company's performance and financial health over the last two years. Is the company's performance and financial health improving or declining? Why?

CA1.34 **IFRS Financial Statements.** The 2012 financial statements of **LVMH Moet Hennessey-Louis Vuitton S.A.** are presented in Appendix C at the end of this book. LVMH is a Paris-based holding company and one of the world's largest and best-known luxury goods companies. As a member-nation of the European Union, French companies are required to prepare their consolidated (group) financial statements using International Financial Reporting Standards (IFRS). After reviewing LVMH's consolidated balance sheet in Appendix C, prepare answers to the following questions:

    a.   Under U.S. GAAP, the balance sheet equation is defined as Assets = Liabilities + Shareholders' Equity. Describe how the balance sheet equation is defined under IFRS. Does the IFRS definition of the balance sheet equation change the informational content of the consolidated balance sheet?

    b.   Under U.S. GAAP, current assets and current liabilities are listed before noncurrent assets and noncurrent liabilities. Describe the listing sequence of LVMH's assets and liabilities. Does the listing sequence impact the informational content of the consolidated balance sheet?

    c.   Under U.S. GAAP, current assets are listed according to their expected liquidity, with the most liquid current assets listed first and the least liquid current assets listed last. How would you describe the listing sequence of current assets for LVMH?

    d.   Under U.S. GAAP, the balance sheet equation is defined as A = L + SE. LVMH replaces the label "shareholders' equity" with just "equity." What might explain this difference in labeling of this section of the consolidated balance sheet?

When you complete this chapter you should be able to:

1. Explain the accounting meaning behind the terms *asset*, *liability*, *shareholders' equity*, *revenue and expense*, and *matching*.

2. Apply the balance sheet equation in the preparation of financial statements from business events.

3. Apply selected financial ratios to evaluate a company's financial performance.

4. Understand the managerial motives for selecting between alternative accounting methods.

From Business Events to Financial Statements

Zynga Inc., headquartered in San Francisco, is a network game developer with some of the most widely used games in the world. The company's games can be found on most social networking sites and mobile platforms, such as **Facebook** and **Yahoo**, and are accessible on such devices as the iPad, the iPhone, and the Droid. As of January 2013, Zynga's games had over 302 million monthly active users, and its games were the most widely used on Facebook. The most popular (and most addictive) titles were *FarmVille*, *CityVille*, *Words with Friends*, and *Zynga Poker*. With all of the company's success, Zynga is relatively young, founded in 2007 by Marc Pincus.

ZYNGA

In July of 2011 Zynga filed a prospectus with the U.S. Securities and Exchange Commission (SEC) to raise approximately $1 billion in an initial public offering (IPO). One motive for the IPO was no doubt related to the desire to quickly raise large amounts of cash as a way to capitalize on the enormous growth potential of its products, both existing and proposed. The company issued 100 million shares valued at $10 per share, but this represented only 15 percent of the total outstanding shares. The total company, after the IPO, was valued at approximately $7 billion. Not bad for what was, a few years earlier, just an idea.

In the prospectus filed by the company, management provided three years of historical financial statements, figures that prior to that date had not before been previously published. From that data, numerous Wall Street analysts went to work forecasting the company's future prospects, beginning with forecasts of earnings and cash flows. Behind these calculations were full forecasts of Zynga's financial statements, direct from anticipated sales, costs, and investing and financing expectations.

The analyst forecasts were driven in large part by the financial prospects and product launches provided in various company disclosures. Zynga's topline was driven by two factors: the number of daily active users (DAUs) and the average amount that users pay per day to play the games. Forecasting growth expectations for sales was complicated by the fact that DAU levels for each game could erode quickly, so the company's total DAU count had to be supported by the release of even more popular titles even more frequently.

Unlike other blockbuster tech IPOs (e.g., **Netflix**), Zynga's IPO received only a lukewarm reception on Wall Street, perhaps due to these difficult-to-meet growth expectations or perhaps because the offering was too large and too many shares were made available to yield a boost in the stock.

In this and subsequent chapters, we will learn the techniques needed to understand how financial statements, and components in those statements such as earnings, cash flow, and net assets, can be derived from business events such as Zynga's stock issue and product sales. The balance sheet approach we take in this text provides a convenient way to record events in a format that facilitates the preparation and analysis of financial statements.

BALANCE SHEET EQUATION

Most individuals outside of the professional financial fields think of accounting as something that others do, or that others are responsible for, or that only others seem to understand. The truth is, however, that most of us apply the basic principles that comprise the framework of financial accounting in our everyday lives. When we balance our checkbook, decide whether to finance a new car purchase, or even think about what we might do with a raise, we are implicitly applying the principles that form the basis of financial accounting. Recognizing and appreciating this basic premise might save you some frustration when, later, you might be struggling with how a specific transaction is recorded in financial statements. As a means to introduce this notion, consider an event that almost all of us experience at some point in our lives—the process of securing a mortgage on a home.

The purchase of a personal residence is the single largest financial transaction entered into by most individuals. This purchase generally requires the individual to take out a loan, typically called a mortgage. Before lending any money, a financial institution will usually request certain information to assess whether an individual or a business represents a good credit risk. Exhibit 2.1 presents one of the forms that will need to be completed in order to have a loan application considered. If you have never completed one of these forms, now is a good time to try it out. As you review the form, pay close attention to its format, the level of detail requested, and some of the judgments that must be made by the preparer. You might consider the following questions: Why is this structure helpful to both the borrower and the lender? Why are certain categories required, while others are not? What estimates must be made, and what are the implications of providing estimates instead of precise values?

Let's focus on the left side of the form—your assets. The caption "cash or market value" indicates that the numbers that you are requested to insert should be your assets' current value. The top part of the form asks for the balance of your cash and checking/savings accounts, with the names and addresses of the institutions where you keep these accounts so that the lender can verify the reported amounts. The section below cash and checking/savings accounts asks for the value of all your stocks and bonds. To fill in this information, you will need to know the number of stocks and bonds that you own of each company and the current price for each security. If the stocks and bonds are traded on an exchange such as the New York Stock Exchange, the London Stock Exchange, or the Tokyo Stock Exchange, you can simply access a financial internet site to find the current price for each of the securities. Next, you will have to get the cash surrender value of any life insurance policies. If you have a life insurance policy, your insurance agent can provide that information.

The section below life insurance asks for the market value of any real estate owned, such as a rental house or a vacation home. Where do you get the market value for your real estate properties? It is harder to get this type of information because real estate does not have an actively traded market like the London, New York, or Tokyo Stock Exchanges. You will have to hire an appraiser who will estimate the value of your house by considering comparable properties—that is, houses with the same number of bedrooms,

EXHIBIT 2.1	A Typical Loan Application

VI. ASSETS AND LIABILITIES

This statement and any applicable supporting schedules may be completed jointly by both married and unmarried Co-borrowers if their assets and liabilities are sufficiently joined so that the Statement can be meaningfully and fairly presented on a combined basis; otherwise separate Statements and Schedules are required. If the Co-Borrower section was completed about a spouse, this Statement and supporting schedules must be completed about that spouse also.

Completed ☐ Jointly ☐ Not Jointly

ASSETS	Cash or Market Value	Liabilities and Pledged Assets. List the creditor's name, address and account number for all outstanding debts, including automobile loans, revolving charge accounts, real estate loans, alimony, child support, stock pledges, etc. Use continuation sheet, if necessary. Indicate by (*) those liabilities which will be satisfied upon sale of real estate owned or upon refinancing of the subject property.	Monthly Payt. & Mos. Left to Pay	Unpaid Balance
Description		**LIABILITIES**		
Cash deposit toward purchase held by:	$	Name and address of Company	$ Payt./Mos.	$
List checking and savings accounts below				
Name and address of Bank, S&L, or Credit Union				
		Acct. no.		
		Name and address of Company	$ Payt./Mos.	$
Acct. no.	$			
Name and address of Bank, S&L, or Credit Union				
		Acct. no.		
		Name and address of Company	$ Payt./Mos.	$
Acct. no.	$			
Name and address of Bank, S&L, or Credit Union				
		Acct. no.		
		Name and address of Company	$ Payt./Mos.	$
Acct. no.	$			
Name and address of Bank, S&L, or Credit Union				
		Acct. no.		
		Name and address of Company	$ Payt./Mos.	$
Acct. no.	$			
Stocks & Bonds (Company name/ number & description)	$			
		Acct. no.		
		Name and address of Company	$ Payt./Mos.	$
Life insurance net cash value				
Face amount: $	$			
Subtotal Liquid Assets	$			
Real estate owned (enter market value from schedule of real estate owned)	$	Acct. no.		
Vested interest in retirement fund	$	Name and address of Company	$ Payt./Mos.	$
Net worth of business(es) owned (attach financial statement)	$			
Automobiles owned (make and year)	$			
		Acct. no.		
		Alimony/Child Support/Separate Maintenance Payments Owed to:	$	
Other Assets (itemize)	$	Job Related Expense (child care, union dues, etc.)	$	
		Total Monthly Payments	$	
Total Assets a.	$	**Net Worth (a-b)** $	**Total Liabilities b.**	$

bathrooms, and in the same neighborhood. But determining the market value for your real estate holdings is considerably more subjective than coming up with a value for your stock or bond portfolio. If you hired three different appraisers, you would probably get three different estimates. After you have included any remaining assets that you own, such as a car or a business, you can then total them all up and put a number in the box for "Total Assets a."

Now turn to the far right column where you are asked to insert amounts for the unpaid balances on all of your outstanding loans, including credit cards, student loans, and real estate or automobile loans. For each of these loans you must also disclose the names and addresses of the people you owe money to so that the lender can verify your reported amounts. The sum of all of these items can be put in the box labeled "Total Liabilities b."

Finally, the form asks you to come up with your "Net Worth (a-b)." Thus, your **net worth** is simply the difference between your total assets and total liabilities. This is an important relationship so let's write it out:

$$A - L = NW$$

This expression says that your personal net worth (NW) is equal to the amount left over from your assets (A) after paying off all of your liabilities (L). Notice that this expression implicitly suggests that your creditors have first claim on your listed assets and you get what remains. Since the lenders have first claim, they are in a less risky position. As we observed in Chapter 1, there is a positive relationship between the amount of assumed risk and the expected return on an investment; that is, greater (less) assumed risk implies a higher (lower) expected return.

We can rearrange the relationship as follows:

$$A = L + NW$$

> In some countries, the balance sheet equation is formatted as:
> $$A - L = NW$$
> This format emphasizes the measurement of net worth. Regardless of which format is adopted, the information contained in a balance sheet is exactly the same.

This new expression is called the **balance sheet equation**. It shows that the total assets on the left side of that equation must exactly equal the sum of the claims on those assets on the right side. There are two types of claims—the lenders who have first claim on your assets—and you—the person who gets what is left over. It should now be clear why the balance sheet equation always balances—NW is just a balancing or plug figure! As you will see through numerous examples in this text, the balance sheet equation represents not only the basic structure of the balance sheet itself, but it also provides a basic structure that can be used at the individual transaction level. More on this later.

If we think about a company instead of an individual, shareholders (those that purchase ownership shares in the business) have the last claim on the corporate assets listed on the balance sheet. In the case of a business, the term NW can be replaced by the term SE, for shareholders' equity, to better represent this claim. The balance sheet equation that we will use to refer to a business is virtually identical to that of an individual:

$$A = L + SE$$

Refer back to the Amazon.com balance sheet that is presented in Exhibit 1.1 in Chapter 1. While the presentation and placement of the items in a loan application may be different, the similarities in the two documents should be readily apparent. The balance sheets are as of a specific reporting date in the life of the company. The list of accounts provided by Amazon are those relevant to that unique entity, and the sum of all the assets are equal to (*balanced with*) the sum of all the liability and stockholder equity claims. The balance sheet equation is represented in a different form by Amazon, which is typical of virtually all public company balance sheets, but you should clearly see the parallel with the formula listed above.

In a nutshell, the bottom half of the corporate balance sheet (i.e., the right side of the balance sheet equation), tells us that a business obtains cash and/or other assets (A) from shareholders by issuing shares (SE) and from lenders by promising to pay interest on any debt and repay any borrowed funds (L). As you will see in subsequent chapters, some companies borrow sparingly and thus are financed principally by shareholders. Other companies borrow extensively, and we will refer to these companies as being **leveraged**. The relative mix of funding from shareholders versus lenders is an important **financing decision** that can have a dramatic effect on a firm's financial performance.

The top half of the balance sheet (i.e., the left hand side of the balance sheet equation) shows how a business allocates its resources in various assets (A)—this is known as the **investment decision**. Who makes the investment decision? Technically, the shareholders have the right to make such decisions, but they usually delegate these decisions to a management team. Not surprisingly, shareholders are preoccupied with maintaining and growing their wealth; thus, they expect the management team to make investment decisions that increase SE over time.

Defining Some Accounting Terms

We have used the terms "asset," "liability," and "shareholders' equity" without precisely defining these terms. From the loan application shown in Exhibit 2.1, it is clear that assets include cash, stocks, bonds, and real estate, among other things. For now, we will define an **asset** as an economic resource that is expected to generate future benefits for a business. As we will see, assets may comprise a variety of economic resources to include those mentioned above, as well as inventory, property and equipment, and various intangible assets such as copyrights and patents, among others.

From the loan application shown in Exhibit 2.1, liabilities include car loans, credit card debt, student loans, and mortgages. But as you will soon see, a business's liabilities may include many types of obligations. For now, we define a **liability** simply as an obligation to make future payments. This definition implies that if a business is obliged to make payments in the future, then the obligation qualifies as a liability. In subsequent chapters, we will see that some liabilities that satisfy this definition need not be (and often are not) reported on the balance sheet. We will refer to these unreported obligations as **off-balance-sheet debt**. (Subsequent chapters will reveal that many of a firm's economic assets also fail to appear on the balance sheet!) Finally, we define **shareholders' equity** as the residual value of a business—that is, the value of any assets remaining after all liabilities have been satisfied. Shortly, we will see that shareholders' equity has two key components—the value of the shareholders' direct investment in a business, called **contributed capital** or **common stock (CS)**, and the amount of any profits retained in the business to support future operations, called **retained earnings (RE)**. Incorporating these two components of SE into the balance sheet equation yields the following:

$$A = L + (CS + RE)$$

PREPARING FINANCIAL STATEMENTS FROM BUSINESS EVENTS

Recording Transactions.   You may feel that there is little reason why you should be subjected to the rigors of learning how to record transactions since you probably have little, if any, desire to become an accountant. In fact, most executives and managers are apt to hire an accountant to perform these tasks. But having some knowledge of the recording process can be invaluable, and this can be illustrated by way of an analogy.

It is doubtful that the readers of this book will go on to a career in auto repair. Many readers, in fact, may never even look under the hood of a car. Each of you, however, likely drives a car; and, many of you likely have experienced mechanical problems at one time or another. It would certainly be helpful to the mechanic who will ultimately be responsible for repairing your car if you have the ability to provide detailed information regarding what is wrong. It could also prove financially beneficial if you have some understanding of what the mechanic plans to charge you for. You certainly do not want to be completely at his or her mercy. The same applies for business transactions. While you may not be responsible for the actual recording of a transaction, as a manager you may be responsible for the reported financial statements. At a minimum, you would want to understand the financial statement implications, both currently and in the future, of any transaction that affects your company. Wouldn't you want to be able to intelligently discuss with your accountant or controller what needs to be recorded and to also understand what should be recorded? A basic understanding of the recording process can give you this necessary competence.

Throughout this textbook, we illustrate two approaches to the recording of accounting information. First, in each chapter we utilize a vertical spreadsheet approach built upon the basic accounting equation of Assets equaling Liabilities and Shareholders' equity. The spreadsheet approach is appreciated by many readers for its simplicity; however, this is not the method used by accounting professionals. Many of you will find the spreadsheet approach more intuitive, and you will be heartened to know that this approach yields the exact same result as that used by accounting professionals.

An important feature of the spreadsheet approach is that its functionality follows exactly the form of balance sheets as observed in practice. Recall from Chapter 1 that we illustrated how the relation across the financial statements actually stems from providing greater detail about just one—the balance sheet. A comforting fact to always remember is that each and every business transaction recorded by the accounting process will have balance sheet implications. And because the balance sheet equation is by its very nature an identity, there exists a natural check to ensure you have evaluated a transaction that makes mechanical sense. The income statement, statement of cash flow, and statement of stockholders' equity become outputs from preparing a balance sheet from a set of transactions.

The second, more traditional approach to recording transactions is illustrated in an appendix at the end of the book, and represents how transactions are actually recorded by most accountants in practice. The recording is most often done by accounting software rather than by hand. This approach involves first recording transactions as journal entries, utilizing a double-entry system of debits and credits. These terms probably sound quite foreign, and rightly so. Unlike much in the natural sciences that is determined by nature, the accounting process of recording transactions is completely designed by man and is therefore somewhat arbitrary. The important thing, however, is that it works. And, not only does it work, but, as with the spreadsheet approach, it also has a built-in error detection mechanism. While many of the readers may struggle to understand the accounting process, most come to see this system as somewhat of an art form, poetic in its elegance.

To demonstrate how financial statements are prepared from accounting events, an illustration involving the hypothetical Russian River Valley Winery is presented. Our approach for organizing the firm's accounting data is a simple spreadsheet based on the balance sheet equation, $A = L + SE$, as follows:

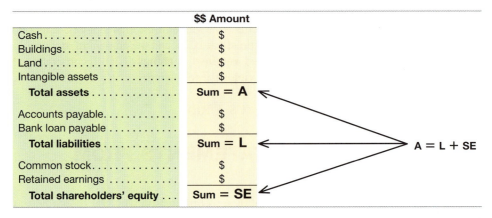

Because the balance sheet equation must always balance, we know that the value of the winery's assets on the top portion of the spreadsheet will always equal the value of the winery's liabilities plus its shareholders' equity on the bottom of the spreadsheet.

The Russian River Valley Winery

Matt and Kate Miller established the Russian River Valley Winery near Healdsburg, California. They owned a small parcel of farmland on which the winery would be operated. Kate further agreed to use her inheritance from her grandparents to construct buildings suitable for the new business.

Since Matt and Kate lacked sufficient land to grow their own grapes, they decided that the winery would purchase grapes from local growers. The wines would be aged in oak barrels, then bottled, corked, and held for a minimum of six months before sale.

Recognizing that the winery would need additional financial resources, Kate and Matt approached an old friend, Bob Buck, who worked as a loan officer at the Hap e-Loan Corporation. Via e-mail, Bob indicated that the business plan for the winery looked promising but that Hap e-Loan would need to review a comprehensive set of forecasted financial statements before the Miller's $4.8 million loan request would be considered. The loan agreement proposed a fixed interest rate of 6 percent per year on the outstanding loan balance and called for the borrowed amount to be repaid over 10 years in equal annual installments payable at the end of the year.

> One of the most important skills a manager can develop is the ability to prepare forward-looking financial forecasts. These forecasts are often prepared as pro forma financial statements. The terms *pro forma* and *forecasted* can be used interchangeably. Capital providers such as banks usually require such statements for new businesses in order to help determine whether the business represents a prudent investment. Pro forma financial statements are also very useful planning and budgeting tools.

Establishing the Business. On the basis of discussions with the company's legal advisors, Kate and Matt determined that the following events would likely occur during the start-up phase of the business:

1. Matt would receive four million shares of common stock, valued at $1 per share, in the Russian River Valley Winery, Inc., in exchange for contributing his land to the business. This transaction would increase the business's land (A) account by $4 million and increase the common stock (SE) account by $4 million.

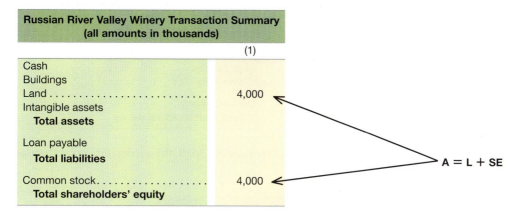

Russian River Valley Winery Transaction Summary (all amounts in thousands)	
	(1)
Cash	
Buildings	
Land	4,000
Intangible assets	
Total assets	
Loan payable	
Total liabilities	
Common stock.	4,000
Total shareholders' equity	

A = L + SE

2. Kate would receive two million shares of common stock in the winery for the buildings that she would finance with her inheritance. This would increase the winery's buildings (A) account by $2 million and increase the common stock (SE) account by $2 million.

Russian River Valley Winery Transaction Summary (all amounts in thousands)	
	(2)
Cash	
Buildings.	2,000
Land	
Intangible assets	
Total assets	
Loan payable	
Total liabilities	
Common stock.	2,000
Total shareholders' equity	

> Kate and Matt's transfer of the land and building to the corporation, along with the recording of common stock, reflects the **entity principle** of accounting. This principle stipulates that the financial affairs of a business must be maintained separate and distinct from the affairs of the owners of the business.

3. When the $4.8 million bank loan was approved and the cash disbursed to the Russian River Valley Winery, the cash (A) account would increase by $4.8 million and the bank loan payable (L) account would increase by $4.8 million.

Russian River Valley Winery Transaction Summary (all amounts in thousands)	
	(3)
Cash	4,800
Buildings	
Land	
Intangible assets	
Total assets	
Loan payable	4,800
Total liabilities	
Common stock	
Total shareholders' equity	

> Because the balance sheet measures account values as of a specific date, liabilities are recorded initially at the amount of principal owed. Under the **accrual** basis of accounting, any interest owed but not paid will be recorded as necessary at future balance sheet dates, with an appropriate charge to earnings (and retained earnings).

4. Kate and Matt concluded that since the Russian River Valley Winery was a new business venture, with no existing brand recognition or customer base, it would be wise to acquire an existing brand name from one of the established wine makers. After some research, they concluded that an established label would likely cost $100,000. This transaction would decrease the company's cash (A) account and increase its intangible assets by $100,000.

Most recorded assets such as buildings have an actual physical presence and are sometimes referred to as **tangible assets**. In addition, certain recorded assets lack a physical presence, but still provide future benefits to the organization. These **intangible assets** include such items as patents, copyrights, and brand names.

Russian River Valley Winery Transaction Summary (all amounts in thousands)	
	(4)
Cash...................	(100)
Buildings	
Land	
Intangible assets	100
Total assets	
Loan payable	
Total liabilities	
Common stock	
Total shareholders' equity	

Following the four pre-opening events identified by Kate and Matt, the winery's complete transaction summary would appear as follows:

Russian River Valley Winery Transaction Summary (all amounts in thousands)					
	(1)	(2)	(3)	(4)	Totals
Cash.......................			4,800	(100)	4,700
Buildings...................		2,000			2,000
Land......................	4,000				4,000
Intangible assets				100	100
Total assets					10,800
Loan payable			4,800		4,800
Total liabilities					4,800
Common stock..............	4,000	2,000			6,000
Total shareholders' equity ...					6,000

A = L + SE

Utilizing the column totals from the spreadsheet facilitates the construction of the winery's pre-opening balance sheet:

RUSSIAN RIVER VALLEY WINERY, INC. Pre-Opening Balance Sheet			
($ thousands)			
Assets		**Liabilities**	
Cash..................	$ 4,700	Loan payable	$ 4,800
Buildings...............	2,000		
Land..................	4,000	**Shareholders' equity**	
Intangible assets	100	Common stock..................	6,000
Total assets..............	$10,800	**Liabilities & shareholders' equity**	$10,800

As expected, the winery's pre-opening total assets of $10.8 million equal the sum of the winery's liabilities plus shareholders' equity of $10.8 million.

Projected Business Events

To comply with the bank's request for **forecasted financial statements**—that is, financial statements prepared on an "as if" basis using assumptions about what might happen in the future—Matt and Kate compiled a list of the important events that would likely occur during the first year of operations. These events appear below as business event numbers 1 through 14. Matt and Kate's analysis of how each of the events would affect the winery's balance sheet equation appear as bullet items. Observe that the analysis of each event leads to the identification of (at least) two financial effects on the balance sheet equation; and, that the financial effects of each transaction are recorded in the appropriate columns of the winery's spreadsheet. Further, notice in the Russian River Valley spreadsheet that after each event is analyzed, the balance sheet equation remains in balance, with total assets equal to the sum of total liabilities and shareholders' equity. To help understand how the balance sheet equation is affected by the various events, each asset account is labeled with an A, each liability account with an L, and each shareholders' equity account as SE. Finally, notice that the account balances from the winery's pre-opening balance sheet have been entered into the spreadsheet in the column labeled "beginning balance."

1. The winery would purchase $380,000 of inventory (grapes, corks, bottles, labels). All purchases would initially be on credit and would subsequently require payment within 30 days of the initial purchase transaction. It was estimated that the unpaid balance of this credit purchase would be $20,000 at the end of the year.

> In competitive business environments, it is often necessary to permit customers to buy goods and services on credit, allowing them to pay for the purchased goods over 30, 60, or even 90 days without incurring any interest charges. Extending credit to customers, however, carries a hidden cost to a business, called an **opportunity cost**. This opportunity cost is equal to a business's cost of borrowing over the time period during which the purchase price remains unpaid. We will have more to say about opportunity costs in Chapter 5. You may also want to read the appendix at the end of this book for insights about the time value of money.

Russian River Valley Winery Transaction Summary (all amounts in thousands)				
	Beg. Bal.	**(1a)**	**(1b)**	**Thru (1)**
Cash.	4,700		(360)	4,340
Inventory		380		380
Buildings.	2,000			2,000
Land	4,000			4,000
Intangible assets	100			100
Total assets	10,800			10,820
Accounts payable.		380	(360)	20
Loan payable	4,800			4,800
Total liabilities	4,800			4,820
Common stock.	6,000			6,000
Total shareholders' equity . . .	6,000			6,000

- In 1(a) the winery purchases inventory, but does not immediately pay for the inventory. Thus, inventory (A) increases by $380,000 and accounts payable (L)—that is, amounts owed by the winery to its suppliers—increases by $380,000.
- In 1(b) the winery pays $360,000 ($380,000 less $20,000) to its suppliers; thus, cash (A) decreases by $360,000 and accounts payable (L) decrease by $360,000.

2. The winery would spend $1.5 million in cash to acquire equipment to be used in crushing, separating, and fermenting the grape juice.

Russian River Valley Winery Transaction Summary (all amounts in thousands)			
	Thru (1)	**(2)**	**Thru (2)**
Cash.	4,340	(1,500)	2,840
Inventory.	380		380
Equipment		1,500	1,500
Buildings.	2,000		2,000
Land	4,000		4,000
Intangible assets	100		100
Total assets	10,820		10,820
Accounts payable.	20		20
Loan payable	4,800		4,800
Total liabilities	4,820		4,820
Common stock.	6,000		6,000
Total shareholders' equity . . .	6,000		6,000

- The winery increases the equipment (A) account by $1.5 million and decreases cash (A) by $1.5 million.

3. The winery would spend $2 million in cash to purchase oak aging barrels. The barrels would be considered a long-term investment in equipment because the barrels typically last five or more years.

Russian River Valley Winery Transaction Summary (all amounts in thousands)			
	Thru (2)	(3)	Thru (3)
Cash......................	2,840	(2,000)	840
Inventory..................	380		380
Equipment	1,500	2,000	3,500
Buildings..................	2,000		2,000
Land......................	4,000		4,000
Intangible assets	100		100
Total assets	**10,820**		**10,820**
Accounts payable............	20		20
Loan payable	4,800		4,800
Total liabilities	**4,820**		**4,820**
Common stock..............	6,000		6,000
Total shareholders' equity ...	**6,000**		**6,000**

Matt and Kate's analysis and recording of accounting events 2 and 3 reflects the **historical cost principle** of accounting, which stipulates that all assets should initially be recorded at their historical acquisition cost.

- The cash (A) account is reduced by $2 million and the equipment (A) account is increased by $2 million.

4. The Russian River Valley Winery would sell two types of wine—bulk wine and bottled wine. It was estimated that bulk wine sales would total 100,000 gallons at $15 per gallon, and bottled wine sales were estimated to be 50,000 bottles at $8 per bottle. About 20 percent of the sales would be immediately paid for in cash, with 80 percent of the sales on credit extended to customers with payment expected in 30 days after the sale transaction. Of that latter amount, $800,000 was expected to remain uncollected at year-end.

Russian River Valley Winery Transaction Summary (all amounts in thousands)				
	Thru (3)	(4a)	(4b)	Thru (4)
Cash........................	840	380	720	1,940
Accounts receivable..........		1,520	(720)	800
Inventory....................	380			380
Equipment	3,500			3,500
Buildings....................	2,000			2,000
Land.......................	4,000			4,000
Intangible assets	100			100
Total assets	**10,820**			**12,720**
Accounts payable............	20			20
Loan payable	4,800			4,800
Total liabilities	**4,820**			**4,820**
Common stock...............	6,000			6,000
Retained earnings	—			1,900
Revenues		1,900		
Total shareholders' equity ...	**6,000**			**7,900**

Revenues (R) are increases in shareholders' equity that result from providing goods and services to customers. Revenue is reported on the income statement when it has been earned—that is, when a company has provided substantially all of the goods or services it has promised to provide—and when the collectibility of the cash from the customer is reasonably assured. This important concept is known as the **revenue recognition principle**. Recognizing revenue is a wealth-increasing event for a business and its shareholders, and this is reflected by an increase in shareholders' equity (through the retained earnings account). In Chapter 5, we extend our discussion with examples of some revenue recognition issues.

- In 4(a), total sales are projected to be $1.9 million (100,000 gallons @ $15 plus 50,000 bottles @ $8). Of this total amount, the winery expects to collect $380,000 in cash (20 percent of $1.9 million) and will be owed the balance of $1.52 million by its customers. Thus, cash (A) is increased by $380,000, accounts receivable (A) is increased by $1.52 million, and shareholders' equity (specifically, revenue, an income statement component of retained earnings) is increased by $1.9 million. Accounts receivable represent amounts owed to the winery by its customers.

The relation between **revenues** and **expenses**, components of the income statement, and retained earnings, a component of the shareholders' equity section of the balance sheet, is illustrated below. As you will recall from Exhibits 1.5 and 1.6 in Chapter 1, the income statement articulates with the balance sheet through the retained earnings account. Revenues, which increase net income, also increase retained earnings, whereas expenses, which decrease net income, also decrease retained earnings. In this way, it may be helpful to you to think of the income statement as being completely reflected in the balance sheet through retained earnings. In our transaction summaries we represent this relation by including income statement accounts as subcomponents of retained earnings. Of course, the final balance sheet will report just the total retained earnings value. We further illustrate this articulation of the financial statements later in this chapter.

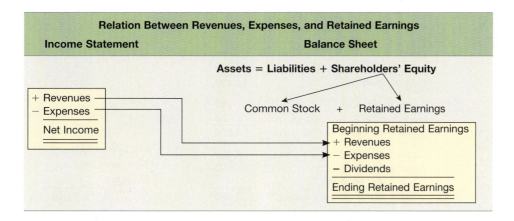

- In 4(b), customers are expected to owe the winery $800,000 at year-end; hence, they must have paid $720,000 in cash during the year. Thus, cash (A) is increased by $720,000 and accounts receivable (A) is decreased by $720,000.

5. Payroll expenses for employees were estimated to require cash payments of $100,000 during the year. Selling and administrative expenses of $300,000 were also expected to be paid.

Russian River Valley Winery Transaction Summary (all amounts in thousands)				
	Thru (4)	(5a)	(5b)	Thru (5)
Cash.........................	1,940	(100)	(300)	1,540
Accounts receivable...............	800			800
Inventory......................	380			380
Equipment	3,500			3,500
Buildings......................	2,000			2,000
Land	4,000			4,000
Intangible assets	100			100
Total assets..................	**12,720**			**12,320**
Accounts payable.................	20			20
Loan payable	4,800			4,800
Total liabilities................	**4,820**			**4,820**
Common stock...................	6,000			6,000
Retained earnings	1,900			1,500
Wages and salaries...........		(100)		
Selling and administrative			(300)	
Total shareholders' equity	**7,900**			**7,500**

- In 5(a), the winery pays $100,000 in cash for employee wage expense; thus, cash (A) decreases by $100,000 and shareholders' equity (specifically, expenses, a component of retained earnings) decreases by $100,000.

> Expenses (E) represent the using up of goods and services associated with the production of revenues by a business. Since expenses reduce assets, expenses are a wealth-reducing event. The cost of the goods and services consumed in generating revenues are said to be matched with the revenues they generate; as a consequence, a business is able to compare its accomplishments (revenue) with its effort (expenses). This important concept is known as the **matching concept** of accounting.

- In 5(b), the winery reduces cash (A) by $300,000 for the payment of selling and administrative expenses. Since these services are consumed in the process of generating revenues from wine sales, the cost of these used-up resources are matched with revenues, thus reducing retained earnings (SE) by $300,000.

6. The loan agreement will require payment of principal and interest at the end of the year.

Russian River Valley Winery Transaction Summary (all amounts in thousands)				
	Thru (5)	(6a)	(6b)	Thru (6)
Cash......................	1,540	(480)	(288)	772
Accounts receivable...........	800			800
Inventory....................	380			380
Equipment	3,500			3,500
Buildings...................	2,000			2,000
Land......................	4,000			4,000
Intangible assets	100			100
Total assets	**12,320**			**11,552**
Accounts payable.............	20			20
Loan payable	4,800	(480)		4,320
Total liabilities	**4,820**			**4,340**
Common stock..............	6,000			6,000
Retained earnings	1,500			1,212
Interest expense			(288)	
Total shareholders' equity ...	**7,500**			**7,212**

- In 6(a), cash (A) is reduced by $480,000, the first of 10 annual loan repayments ($4.8 million divided by 10), and the loan payable (L) account is reduced by the same amount.
- In 6(b), cash (A) is reduced by $288,000 (6 percent of $4.8 million) for the first year's interest payment. Interest is the cost of borrowing funds from a financial institution and is a financing expense of the business. Hence, retained earnings (SE) are also reduced by $288,000 as this business expense must be matched with the enterprise's revenues.
- We have separated transactions 6(a) and 6(b) for pedagogical reasons. However, in practice the payment of a loan would entail a single check that would be allocated across both principal and interest. Much like when an individual pays an auto loan or a home mortgage, the monthly check is written to cover a partial pay-down of the loan balance in addition to a monthly charge for interest.

7. The winery's policy was to order only as much inventory as would be needed for the current year's sales. Thus, it was estimated that the ending inventory would be zero.

Russian River Valley Winery Transaction Summary (all amounts in thousands)			
	Thru (6)	(7)	Thru (7)
Cash.......................	772		772
Accounts receivable..........	800		800
Inventory....................	380	(380)	—
Equipment	3,500		3,500
Buildings....................	2,000		2,000
Land......................	4,000		4,000
Intangible assets	100		100
Total assets	**11,552**		**11,172**
Accounts payable.............	20		20
Loan payable	4,320		4,320
Total liabilities	**4,340**		**4,340**
Common stock..............	6,000		6,000
Retained earnings	1,212		832
Cost of goods sold		(380)	
Total shareholders' equity ...	**7,212**		**6,832**

- The entire available inventory is assumed to have been used up in the production and sale of wine. Thus, inventory (A) decreases by $380,000, as does retained earnings (SE). The cost of inventory sold is an expense to be matched with revenues. Notice that inventory is first classified as an asset since it is assumed to provide future benefit to the enterprise in the form of future cash inflows. When the inventory is sold, and therefore used up, the asset is removed from the balance sheet and an expense, called cost of goods sold, is reported on the income statement, and ultimately as a reduction in shareholders' equity. This is another example of the matching concept in which the cost of goods sold (an expense account) is matched with the revenues from the sale of the goods, all recognized in the same accounting period. Without this alignment of expenses with revenues, the net income reported would be artificially skewed upwards in some periods and downwards in others. The matching principal helps ensure that net income represents the actual earning process within the proper accounting period.

Notice that if a business's inventory is overstated, the amount removed from inventory and transferred to cost of goods sold will be understated. This will result in net income, and retained earnings, being overstated. We will have more to say about the effects of inventory errors in Chapter 6.

8. Depreciation for the year was estimated as follows: $175,000 for equipment, based on an expected useful life of 20 years, and $50,000 for buildings, based on an expected useful life of 40 years.

Russian River Valley Winery Transaction Summary (all amounts in thousands)				
	Thru (7)	(8a)	(8b)	Thru (8)
Cash	772			772
Accounts receivable	800			800
Inventory	—			—
Equipment	3,500			3,500
Buildings	2,000			2,000
Accumulated depreciation		(175)	(50)	(225)
Land	4,000			4,000
Intangible assets	100			100
Total assets	**11,172**			**10,947**
Accounts payable	20			20
Loan payable	4,320			4,320
Total liabilities	**4,340**			**4,340**
Common stock	6,000			6,000
Retained earnings	832			607
Depreciation		(175)	(50)	
Total shareholders' equity . . .	**6,832**			**6,607**

- Depreciation refers to the systematic expensing of an asset as a consequence of the passage of time. Accountants often estimate the amount of depreciation to be taken on an asset by estimating the expected useful life of the asset and then allocating its cost equally across all

> Balance sheet accounts that are subtracted from other accounts (such as accumulated depreciation) are known as **contra-accounts (CA)**. The difference between the cost of an asset (e.g. equipment) and its accumulated depreciation is called the **net book value** of the asset. Other common contra-account examples include the allowance for uncollectible accounts and discounts on bonds payable.

years of the asset's expected useful life, a method called straight-line depreciation. In 8(a), the expected life of the equipment is 20 years so depreciation expense (E) is $175,000 ($3.5 million divided by 20 years). Hence, retained earnings (SE) are decreased by $175,000. Of course, the asset must also be decreased, but by convention, the equipment account is not decreased directly. Another account—called accumulated depreciation—is increased, and thus, reflects the negative $175,000. The accumulated depreciation account is then subtracted from the equipment account. We show an increase in accumulated depreciation as a negative number under the assets section of the spreadsheet. This is because accumulated depreciation is actually a contra-asset, where by convention it maintains a balance of the opposite sign as a regular asset. We will have much more to say about both depreciation expense and accumulated depreciation in Chapter 7. Another important point to note is that the purpose of depreciation is not to reduce the asset's book value in an attempt to equate its book value with its market value. Rather, the purpose of depreciation is to allocate the cost of the asset over time in an attempt to match the asset's cost with the revenue generated by the asset in each future period, an application of the matching concept.

- In 8(b), the depreciation expense associated with using the building for a year is estimated to be $50,000 ($2 million divided by 40 years); hence, retained earnings (SE) are decreased by $50,000. As in 8(a), accumulated depreciation (CA) is increased by $50,000 and deducted from the building account.

9. Kate and Matt decide that the acquired brand name of the business should be expensed over two years.

Russian River Valley Winery Transaction Summary (all amounts in thousands)			
	Thru (8)	(9)	Thru (9)
Cash	772		772
Accounts receivable	800		800
Inventory	—		—
Equipment	3,500		3,500
Buildings	2,000		2,000
Accumulated depreciation	(225)		(225)
Land	4,000		4,000
Intangible assets	100	(50)	50
Total assets	**10,947**		**10,897**
Accounts payable	20		20
Loan payable	4,320		4,320
Total liabilities	**4,340**		**4,340**
Common stock	6,000		6,000
Retained earnings	607		557
Amortization		(50)	
Total shareholders' equity . . .	**6,607**		**6,557**

- The write-off of the the purchased brand name, called amortization, is an expense of the business. Thus, the intangible asset account (A) is reduced by $50,000 ($100,000 divided by 2 years), as is retained earnings (SE). If Matt and Kate had estimated a five-year expected life for the brand name instead of just two years, the amortization expense would be only $20,000 per year ($100,000 divided by five years). Estimating the expected useful life of equipment, buildings, and such intangible assets as brand names is an important managerial activity. An incorrect estimate of an asset's expected useful life can have a dramatic positive (or negative) effect on a firm's reported performance. As you will see, many accounting numbers, like amortization expense, are just estimates, and as such, can be quite imprecise.

10. Matt and Kate issue 200,000 additional shares to an outside investor for $2 per share to finance future expansion plans.

Russian River Valley Winery Transaction Summary (all amounts in thousands)			
	Thru (9)	(10)	Thru (11)
Cash	772	400	1,172
Accounts receivable	800		800
Inventory	—		—
Equipment	3,500		3,500
Buildings	2,000		2,000
Accumulated depreciation	(225)		(225)
Land	4,000		4,000
Intangible assets	50		50
Total assets	**10,897**		**11,297**
Accounts payable	20		20
Loan payable	4,320		4,320
Total liabilities	**4,340**		**4,340**
Common stock	6,000	400	6,400
Retained earnings	557		557
Total shareholders' equity . . .	**6,557**		**6,957**

- The issuance of additional common shares increases common stock (SE) by $400,000 and increases cash (A) by the same amount. As a consequence of selling shares to the outside investor, Matt and Kate must now share control of the business and its profits with the investor who has become a co-owner of the winery. Kate and Matt must have forecasted that they would need the extra cash badly enough to relinquish some control of the business. If you look at the cash row you can see why—there is a large quantity of cash outflows.

11. Matt and Kate intend to buy grapes from the most respected local growers; and thus, they expect that their wines will be well received by their customers. As a consequence, Matt and Kate believe that their ownership shares in the business will be worth considerably more by the end of the year and that this should be reflected in the projected financial statements.

- The winery records no transaction for this information. Although a good business reputation is a valuable business asset, typically resulting in significant customer loyalty, higher sales revenue and increased profitability, an increase

> Brand names are not reported in the balance sheet unless purchased from other entities; in some countries (such as France), however, estimating the value of a brand name and placing that asset on the balance sheet is permitted.

in a company's market value as a consequence of this is never recorded in a business's financial statements. There are two reasons for this. First, there is no generally accepted approach to assessing the value of a business. Second, under U.S. GAAP, financial statements are premised on the historical cost concept discussed earlier, and not the fair value of a business's assets. **Zynga, Inc.**, introduced at the beginning of this chapter, is an example of a company with a brand that may be quite valuable but will not be recorded on the company's balance sheet.

12. Federal income taxes were estimated to be $240,000 with 60 percent being paid by year-end.

Russian River Valley Winery Transaction Summary (all amounts in thousands)			
	Thru (11)	(12)	Thru (12)
Cash	1,172	(144)	1,028
Accounts receivable	800		800
Inventory	—		—
Equipment	3,500		3,500
Buildings	2,000		2,000
Accumulated depreciation	(225)		(225)
Land	4,000		4,000
Intangible assets	50		50
Total assets	**11,297**		**11,153**
Accounts payable	20		20
Taxes payable		96	96
Loan payable	4,320		4,320
Total liabilities	**4,340**		**4,436**
Common stock	6,400		6,400
Retained earnings	557		317
Income taxes		(240)	
Total shareholders' equity	**6,957**		**6,717**

- Income taxes are a cost of doing business, and consequently, this expense must be matched with the winery's revenue; hence, retained earnings (SE) are reduced by $240,000. Since the winery expects to pay $144,000 (60 percent of $240,000), cash (A) is reduced by $144,000 and the remaining amount of $96,000 is still owed; thus, taxes payable (L) increase by $96,000.

13. On the last day of the year, Kate and Matt expect to acquire $60,000 of new grape inventory in anticipation of the following year's production. The purchase would be on credit, with payment terms of 30 days.

Russian River Valley Winery Transaction Summary (all amounts in thousands)			
	Thru (12)	(13)	Thru (13)
Cash......................	1,028		1,028
Accounts receivable...........	800		800
Inventory....................	—	60	60
Equipment	3,500		3,500
Buildings...................	2,000		2,000
Accumulated depreciation......	(225)		(225)
Land......................	4,000		4,000
Intangible assets	50		50
Total assets...............	**11,153**		**11,213**
Accounts payable............	20	60	80
Taxes payable...............	96		96
Loan payable	4,320		4,320
Total liabilities.............	**4,436**		**4,496**
Common stock...............	6,400		6,400
Retained earnings	317		317
Total shareholders' equity ...	**6,717**		**6,717**

- Inventory (A) increases by $60,000 and, since this purchase is not immediately paid for, accounts payable (L) increases by an equivalent amount.

14. Matt and Kate expect to declare and pay cash dividends of $260,000.
    - The dividend that Matt and Kate expect to pay is a distribution of the winery's earned profit; hence, it reduces cash (A) by $260,000 and retained earnings (SE) by $260,000. A dividend is considered to be a distribution of a business's earnings to its owners and not a cost of doing business; consequently, dividends are not considered in the calculation of net income on the income statement, although they are reflected in the calculation of retained earnings on the statement of shareholders' equity.

Russian River Valley Winery Transaction Summary (all amounts in thousands)			
	Thru (13)	(14)	Thru (14)
Cash......................	1,028	(260)	768
Accounts receivable...........	800		800
Inventory....................	60		60
Equipment	3,500		3,500
Buildings...................	2,000		2,000
Accumulated depreciation......	(225)		(225)
Land......................	4,000		4,000
Intangible assets	50		50
Total assets...............	**11,213**		**10,953**
Accounts payable............	80		80
Taxes payable...............	96		96
Loan payable	4,320		4,320
Total liabilities.............	**4,496**		**4,496**
Common stock...............	6,400		6,400
Retained earnings	317		57
Dividends		(260)	
Total shareholders' equity ...	**6,717**		**6,457**

Following the analysis of the 14 projected transactions identified by Kate and Matt, the winery's spreadsheet will appear as follows:

Russian River Valley Winery Transaction Summary
(all amounts in thousands)

	Beg. Bal.	(1a)	(1b)	(2)	(3)	(4a)	(4b)	(5a)	(5b)	(6a)	(6b)	(7)	(8a)	(8b)	(9)	(10)	(11)	(12)	(13)	(14)	End Bal.
Cash	4,700		(360)	(1,500)	(2,000)	380	720	(100)	(300)	(480)	(288)					400		(144)		(260)	768
Accounts receivable						1,520	(720)														800
Inventory		380										(380)							60		60
Equipment				1,500	2,000																3,500
Buildings	2,000																				2,000
Accumulated depreciation													(175)	(50)							(225)
Land	4,000																				4,000
Intangible assets	100														(50)						50
Total assets	**10,800**																				**10,953**
Accounts payable		380	(360)																60		80
Taxes payable																		96			96
Loan payable	4,800									(480)											4,320
Total liabilities	**4,800**																				**4,496**
Common stock	6,000															400					6,400
Retained earnings																					57
Revenues						1,900															
Cost of goods sold												(380)									
Wages and salaries								(100)													
Selling and administrative .									(300)												
Depreciation													(175)	(50)							
Amortization															(50)						
Interest expense											(288)										
Income taxes																		(240)			
Dividends																				(260)	
Total shareholders' equity . . .	**6,000**																				**6,457**

Income Statement accounts (bracket grouping Revenues through Dividends)

Preparing the Financial Statements

Since all of the projected financial events for the first year of operations for the winery have been analyzed and the financial effects entered into the spreadsheet, it is now possible to complete the spreadsheet by summing up the various values in each of the rows. These final balances are entered in the column labeled "ending balance." The completed spreadsheet for the Russian River Valley Winery thus becomes the basis for preparing the company's basic financial statements. The ending balance column of the spreadsheet, for example, provides the necessary inputs (the ending account balances) for the winery's balance sheet as of the end of the first year of operations, and this statement is presented in Exhibit 2.2.

Exhibit 2.2 reveals that the winery's total assets are projected to grow from $10.8 million at the beginning of the year to $10.953 million by year-end. By comparing the various account balances at the beginning of the year with those at the end of the year, it is possible to identify both the significance and the trends in each account. One of the objectives in reviewing a company's balance sheet is not only to understand what assets and liabilities a company has, but also how the changes in those accounts reflect the management of the business.

Russian River Valley's balance sheets in Exhibit 2.2 also provide information beyond just a listing of the company's assets, liabilities, shareholders' equity, and whether their balances changed over the fiscal period. The balance sheet provides information, for example, about when a business's noncash assets are likely to be converted into cash and when they are expected to be consumed as part of the business's regular operations, as well as information about when its liabilities are likely to require payment. This information is evident from the classification of the assets and liabilities into the categories of "current" and "noncurrent." (In accounting jargon, the balance sheet in Exhibit 2.2 is known as a classified balance sheet.) **Current assets** are those assets that are expected to be converted into cash or used to support operations during the next 12 months, while **noncurrent assets** are those assets expected

In Practice 2.1 *Balance Sheet Title: A Glimpse of a Sample of Fortune 1000 Companies*   The following table identifies the title used on the balance sheet by a sample of 600 Fortune 1000 companies. The title preferred by over 96 percent of the surveyed firms is "balance sheet:"

- Balance Sheet 96.1%
- Statement of Financial Position 3.7%
- Statement of Financial Condition 0.2%

Source: Accounting Trends & Techniques

EXHIBIT 2.2	Illustrative Balance Sheets

RUSSIAN RIVER VALLEY WINERY, INC.
Balance Sheets

($ thousands)	Pre-Opening	End of Year 1		Pre-Opening	End of Year 1
Assets			**Liabilities and shareholders' equity**		
Current assets			*Current liabilities*		
Cash.......................	$ 4,700	$ 768	Accounts payable.........	$ 0	$ 80
Accounts receivable...........	0	800	Taxes payable............	0	96
Inventory....................	0	60	Loan payable—current.....	0	480
Total current assets	4,700	1,628	Total current liabilities......	0	656
Noncurrent assets			*Noncurrent liabilities*		
Property, plant & equipment			Loan payable—noncurrent..	4,800	3,840
Equipment	0	3,500	**Total liabilities...........	4,800**	**4,496**
Buildings....................	2,000	2,000	*Shareholders' equity*		
Land.......................	4,000	4,000	Common stock...........	6,000	6,400
	6,000	9,500	Retained earnings	0	57
Accumulated depreciation	0	(225)	**Total shareholders' equity .**	**6,000**	**6,457**
Property, plant & equipment (net)..	6,000	9,275	**Total liabilities &**		
Intangible assets	100	50	**shareholders' equity......**	**$10,800**	**$10,953**
Total noncurrent assets	6,100	9,325			
Total assets.................	**$10,800**	**$10,953**			

to be available to support the continuing operations of a business for many years in the future. **Current liabilities** are those liabilities that are expected to require payment within the next 12 months, whereas **noncurrent liabilities** are obligations that are not expected to require payment for more than one year. The phrase "long-term" is often used instead of "noncurrent."

Notice in Exhibit 2.2 that since the second annual principal payment of $480,000 on the winery's outstanding bank loan is due within 12 months of the date when the balance sheet is prepared, this amount is reclassified from the noncurrent liabilities section of the balance sheet to the current liabilities section of the winery's balance sheet. This reclassification is important because it will enable anyone reviewing the balance sheet to fully understand just how much cash will be needed to satisfy the various claims against the business in the coming year.

Can other information be obtained from the Russian River Valley Winery spreadsheet? Recall that the retained earnings rows of the spreadsheet contained all of the revenue and expenses of the business. Thus, an income statement can be readily prepared from data contained in the retained earnings rows of the spreadsheet. The income statement for the first year of operations for the winery is presented in Exhibit 2.3.

Like the balance sheet, the Russian River Valley income statement provides a number of useful pieces of information. For instance, the income statement highlights several key measures of firm performance: revenues, gross profit, operating income, and net income. **Revenues** measure the inflow of cash and other assets (such as, accounts receivable) from a firm's primary business activity. **Gross profit**, on the other hand, measures the amount of cash and assets remaining after deducting the cost of sales, or what is often called the cost of goods sold. **Operating income** refers to a firm's net income before deducting such items as interest expense and income taxes; and, **net income** is the firm's bottom-line performance—the business's net income after all expenses are deducted, both operating and nonoperating, recurring and non-recurring.

Observe that the top section of the income statement, through operating income, reflects the results of the company's primary business activities—that is, the winery's core business of producing and selling wine, which is often referred to as its **recurring operations**. The section below operating income reflects the financing activities of the business and any non-recurring operations. The winery doesn't expect to have any non-recurring activities for the year but it does expect to have costs associated with financing its business, namely interest expense on the outstanding bank loan. The winery's net income of $317,000 is the "bottom line" profit available to shareholders. The management of a business must decide whether to reinvest these earnings in the business or to distribute them to shareholders as a dividend, and this

---

EXHIBIT 2.3 | An Illustrative Income Statement

RUSSIAN RIVER VALLEY WINERY, INC.
Income Statement

($ thousands)	Year 1
Revenues.	$1,900
Cost of goods sold.	380
Gross profit	1,520
Operating expenses	
Wages and salaries	100
Selling & administrative	300
Depreciation.	225
Amortization.	50
Total operating expenses	675
Operating income.	845
Interest expense.	288
Income before income taxes	557
Income taxes	240
Net income	$ 317

decision is reflected in the statement of shareholders' equity.

Recall from Chapter 1 that the remaining two financial statements relate directly to the activity captured in changes in balance sheet accounts. The statement of shareholders' equity reveals how the shareholders' direct investment in a business increased (decreased) due to the company's sale (repurchase) of its own common stock and how the retained earnings of a business were increased by net income and decreased by any net losses or dividends paid to shareholders. A statement of shareholders' equity for the Russian River Valley Winery is presented in Exhibit 2.4. Like the income state-

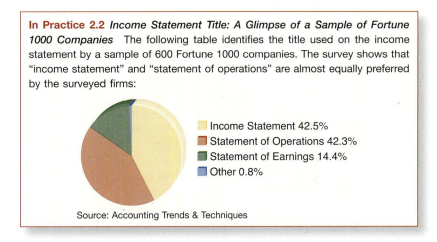

In Practice 2.2 *Income Statement Title: A Glimpse of a Sample of Fortune 1000 Companies*   The following table identifies the title used on the income statement by a sample of 600 Fortune 1000 companies. The survey shows that "income statement" and "statement of operations" are almost equally preferred by the surveyed firms:

- Income Statement 42.5%
- Statement of Operations 42.3%
- Statement of Earnings 14.4%
- Other 0.8%

Source: Accounting Trends & Techniques

ment, the information needed to prepare a statement of shareholders' equity is available from the shareholders' equity rows of the winery's spreadsheet. Exhibit 2.4 shows that the winery expects to begin the year with a zero balance in retained earnings but is expected to end the year with a balance of $57,000, and that the winery expects to begin the year with $6 million in common stock but is expected to end the year with a balance of $6.4 million. Notice how these figures reconcile with the data reported for retained earnings and common stock on the winery's balance sheet in Exhibit 2.2. In accounting jargon, we say that the data from the statement of shareholders' equity "articulate" with the data from the winery's balance sheet.

EXHIBIT 2.4 | An Illustrative Statement of Shareholders' Equity

RUSSIAN RIVER VALLEY WINERY, INC.
Statement of Shareholders' Equity

($ thousands)	Common Stock	Retained Earnings	Total
Balance at beginning of Year 1.	$6,000	$ 0	$6,000
Net income.		317	317
Dividends paid		(260)	(260)
Sale of common stock	400		400
Balance at end of Year 1	$6,400	$ 57	$6,457

In addition to generating profits, a business must make sure that its profits translate into cash so that cash is available to pay the business's expenses and obligations as they come due. The information about a company's available cash flow can be obtained from its final required financial statement, the statement of cash flow, which can be prepared from the cash inflows and outflows reported in the cash row of the completed spreadsheet. Exhibit 2.5 presents a statement of cash flow for the Russian River Valley Winery. Notice that all of the cash inflows and outflows from the cash row of the spreadsheet are included in this statement.

EXHIBIT 2.5	An Illustrative Statement of Cash Flow

RUSSIAN RIVER VALLEY WINERY, INC.
Statement of Cash Flow

($ thousands)	Year 1
Operating activities	
Cash receipts	
Cash sales	$ 380
Cash collections on account	720
Total cash receipts	1,100
Cash disbursements	
Cash payments for inventory	(360)
Cash payments for interest	(288)
Cash payments for wages & salaries	(100)
Cash payments for selling & administrative	(300)
Cash payments for taxes	(144)
Total cash disbursements	(1,192)
Cash flow from operations	**(92)**
Investing activities	
Purchases of property, plant & equipment	(3,500)
Cash flow from investing	**(3,500)**
Financing activities	
Sale of common stock	400
Repayment of loan	(480)
Payment of common stock dividends	(260)
Cash flow from financing	**(340)**
Change in cash	(3,932)
Cash balance, beginning of year	4,700
Cash balance, end of year	$ 768

The statement of cash flow classifies a business's cash flow into the three activity categories of operating, investing, and financing, which correspond to the main activities of any business. The **operating activities** section provides information about the day-to-day cash inflow and outflow from core business operations. The **investing activities** section contains information about the purchase and sale of long-term assets by the firm. This section provides insights about a company's investment strategy. Finally, the **financing activities** section provides information regarding how a business was financed during the period, for example whether the company raised cash from issuing debt or equity or used cash to repay debt or buy back its shares. This section provides insight about a firm's financing strategy. Notice that the cash dividend paid to shareholders is included in the financing section, yet the cash paid for interest on the bank loan is listed in the operating section. Under the accounting rules of most countries, interest expense is an operating cash outflow, whereas dividends are a financing cash outflow. Finally, notice that the "bottom line" of the statement of cash flow—the net cash flow for the period—equals the change in the cash account from a company's balance sheet. In the case of the Russian River Valley Winery, the change in cash as reported in Exhibit 2.5 is negative $3,932 ($768 − $4,700 = −$3,932). In essence, a statement of cash flow provides the detailed information to explain how and why the cash account on the balance sheet changed from the beginning of the fiscal period to the end. We will have more to say about the statement of cash flow in Chapter 3.

At this point, anyone reviewing the four financial statements can see a complete financial picture of how the business is anticipated to perform during the first year of operations. Kate and Matt are likely to be pleased with the projected net income of $317,000; however, they are also likely to be concerned about the large outflow of cash as shown on the statement of cash flow. Kate and Matt can explain most of the decrease in their cash balance as a necessary consequence of purchasing property, plant, and equipment, investments that are necessary for a young, growing company. They should be concerned, however, that they are also spending more cash on normal operating activities than they are taking in from these activities. As a consequence, Kate and Matt may wish to examine some alternative strategies for their business plan, such as the way that they price their products for sale or their policies regarding extending credit to, and collecting from, their customers.

Articulation of the Financial Statements

It should be apparent at this point that the basic financial statements of the Russian River Valley Winery are highly interconnected and are not independent from one another. In accounting parlance, we refer to this interconnectedness as **articulation**. Using the schematic from Exhibit 1-5 in Chapter 1, the articulation of the Russian River Valley Winery's basic financial statements can be illustrated as follows:

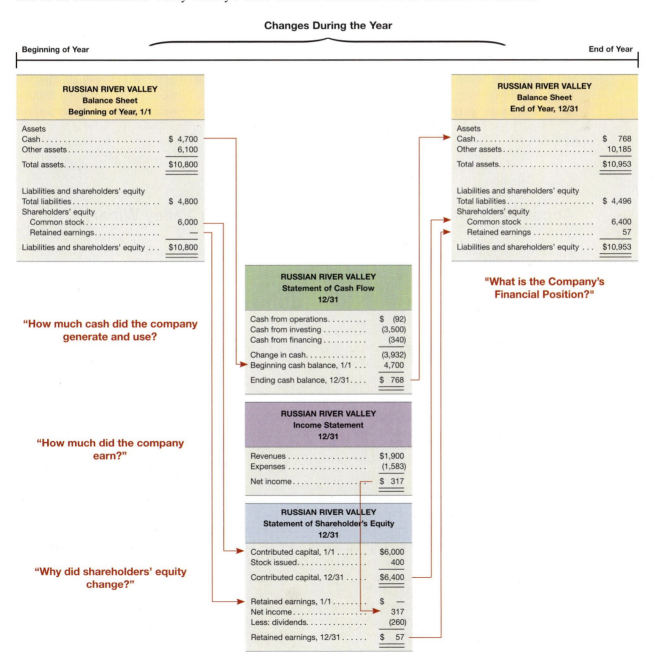

The divergent treatment of interest, the cost of debt financing, and dividends, the cost of equity financing, in the statement of cash flow is attributable to the fact that a statement of cash flow is prepared from the perspective of shareholders, reporting the residual cash flows from operations accruing to the owners after all expenses have been paid but *before* any cash distributions for dividends have been made.

As a review, notice that:

■ The change in the cash account (−$3,932) on the balance sheet from the beginning of the year to the end of the year equals the sum of the cash flow from operations (−$92), the cash flow from investing (−$3,500), and the cash flow from financing (−$340) on the statement of cash flow.

■ The change in retained earnings ($57) on the balance sheet equals the sum of the beginning balance ($0) in retained earnings plus net income ($317) from the income statement less any dividends (−$260) paid to shareholders.

■ The change in shareholders' equity ($457) on the balance sheet equals the change in retained earnings ($57) plus the change in common stock ($400) as reported on the statement of shareholders' equity.

Although the basic financial statements articulate with one another, they present different types of information about a business. The income statement, for example, describes a firm's operating performance for the current fiscal period, whereas the balance sheet describes the firm's financial condition as of the beginning or end of the fiscal period. The statement of shareholders' equity, on the other hand, describes how the shareholders' investment changed over the period, and the statement of cash flow explains why (and how) one very important business asset—cash—increased or decreased over the fiscal period. Like the income statement, the statement of cash flow also describes the firm's operating performance for the current period. The difference between these statements, however, relates to the definition of "firm operating performance." The income statement defines firm performance in terms of accrual net earnings whereas the statement of cash flow defines performance in terms of operating cash flow. Thus, although interconnected, the financial statements each depict a different aspect of a business's financial information. It is also important to note once again that the balance sheet is *at a period in time,* sometimes referred to as a snapshot. In contrast, the other statements are reported *for a period of time*, such as a year.

Accounting Policy Decisions at Russian River Valley Winery

While identifying the expected future events for the winery, Matt and Kate were required to implicitly make a number of accounting policy decisions that affected the forecasted financial statements of the winery, and thus, its likelihood of getting the bank loan. For example, by assuming that all of the $800,000 of outstanding accounts receivable at year-end was reasonably assured of collection, the winery's net income is potentially overstated. For most businesses, the existence of unpaid accounts receivable will usually mean that some future losses can be anticipated for uncollectible accounts. By not estimating what these losses might be, and by not matching those potential losses with the related operating revenue, Kate and Matt may have allowed the winery's projected performance for the first year of operations to be overstated.

Further, depreciation on the equipment and buildings was estimated by Matt and Kate based on expected useful lives of 20 and 40 years, respectively. If Kate and Matt overestimate the length of the useful lives of these assets, the annual depreciation expense on the income statement will be understated and projected net income overstated. Finally, the expected life chosen to amortize the purchased brand name was estimated to be two years. If Kate and Matt underestimate this expected life, the amortization expense will be overstated and the winery's net income understated.

These policy choices illustrate a little appreciated fact about accounting: Financial statements require managers to make many estimates and assumptions which may prove incorrect, and consequently, cause the financial statements to incorrectly characterize a company's performance. Because of the many estimates and assumptions inherent in preparing financial statements, it is wise to remember that accounting data, and hence, the financial statements themselves, are not precise descriptions of a business's financial performance.

To illustrate this point, consider the following statement from the **General Motors Corporation** 2012 annual report to shareholders:

The consolidated financial statements are prepared in conformity with U.S. GAAP, which require the use of estimates, judgments and assumptions . . . . we believe that the accounting estimates employed are appropriate and resulting balances are reasonable; however, due to inherent uncertainties in making estimates actual results could differ from the original estimates, requiring adjustments to these balances in future periods.

GLOBAL PERSPECTIVE

The mechanical preparation of financial statements around the world proceeds in exactly the same fashion. Not surprisingly, however, some differences in the actual format of the financial statements and in the labels used to describe various financial statement accounts do arise. For example, in North America, the labels "revenue" and "sales" are used to describe the value of the goods sold by a company as reported on its income statement. In the United Kingdom, however, the label "turnover" is used instead to represent the sales of a business. These labeling differences are superficial and in no way alter the content or purpose of the basic financial statements. In essence, worldwide, an income statement is an income statement; and, a balance sheet is a balance sheet!

EVALUATING BUSINESS PERFORMANCE AND MAKING FINANCIAL DECISIONS

Producing financial statements about a business is important, particularly if those statements are useful in decision-making. Matt and Kate would certainly be interested in using the financial statement information in Exhibits 2.2, 2.3, 2.4, and 2.5 to decide whether they should proceed with their proposed winery. Similarly, Bob Buck of Hap e-Loan Corporation will find the data in the forecasted financial statements invaluable in helping to decide whether lending money to Russian River Valley is a prudent idea. While a business's owners are primarily interested in the profitability of the business, a financial institution is primarily interested in assessing the financial risk that it will be exposed to when lending to a business.

But how can the financial statements help us learn about business profitability and the risks inherent in lending to a business? Stated alternatively, how can financial statements help us make investment and lending decisions?

Financial ratios are frequently used to evaluate firm performance. They permit valid comparisons of performance over time or between competitors. By dividing one accounting measure (such as, net income) by a second accounting measure (such as, net sales), the resulting ratio is standardized, thereby enabling an "apples-to-apples" comparison of firm performance.

Evaluating Firm Profitability

To evaluate the profitability of a business, it is often useful to consider various performance indicators from the financial statements. To illustrate, let's consider the most basic measure of firm performance—whether a business made a profit. The income statement in Exhibit 2.3 shows that net income for the Russian River Valley Winery is indeed expected to be positive—net income is projected to be $317,000 for its first year of operations. That's good news! But just looking at the absolute level of profits ignores how much investment it took to generate those profits. In addition, it is hard to compare the performance of firms of different sizes or of a company over time by just comparing the level of their profits. For example, one would certainly expect a firm such as **General Electric**, with over $670 billion in reported assets, to have a higher level of profit than a small winery. With far greater levels of sales and investments, it is only natural for General Electric to show a higher level of profit. Consequently, the use of financial ratios provides one approach to making useful comparisons of performance between firms of differing size and for a given firm over various time periods.

One profitability measure that considers relative firm size is the **return on sales** ratio (ROS), or net income divided by sales revenue:[1]

Ratio	Financial Variables	Computation	Result
Return on sales (ROS)	$\dfrac{\text{Net income}}{\text{Sales revenue}}$	$\dfrac{\$317}{\$1,900}$	16.7%

---

[1] Some investment professionals calculate the ROS ratio on an "unlevered" basis as follows:

$$\text{Unlevered ROS} = \frac{\text{Net income} + \text{Interest expense} \times (1 - \text{Tax rate})}{\text{Net sales}}$$

Unlevering the ROS ratio–that is, adding the interest expense paid by a company net of the tax benefit of the interest expense back to net income–creates a measure of net income as if the company were all equity financed. This alternative measure of ROS allows the analyst to focus on the efficacy of management's operating decisions independent of management's financing decisions. We will have more to say about unlevered ROS in Chapter 4.

The ROS ratio, which is also referred to as the **profit margin ratio**, for the Russian River Valley Winery is forecasted to be 16.7 percent, which indicates that for every dollar of sales revenue, the winery is expected to generate nearly 17 cents of bottom-line profit. You don't have to know much about wineries to recognize that a 16.7 percent return on sales is quite high. But to be certain, it would be wise to compare the Russian River Valley Winery's ROS against the ROS for other small wineries or against the average ROS for the wine industry. By making such inter-firm and industry comparisons, it is possible to more clearly benchmark the winery's performance and to determine how successfully the business is expected to perform.

Another measure of profitability that considers relative firm size is the **return on assets** (ROA) ratio, or net income plus after-tax interest expense divided by total assets:

Ratio	Financial Variables	Computation	Result
Return on assets (ROA)	$\dfrac{[\text{Net income} + \text{Interest expense} \times (1 - \text{Tax rate})]}{\text{Total assets}}$	$\dfrac{\$317 + \$288 \times [1 - (\$240/\$557)]}{\$10,953}$	4.4%

The return on assets ratio represents the amount of earnings available to a business's capital providers, to include both its lenders and its shareholders. Since lenders obtain their return in the form of interest payments, and since this expense is subtracted in the calculation of net income, it is necessary to add the interest expense back to net income to produce a measure of the total return available to a firm's capital providers. Interest expense, however, is tax deductible by the business, and therefore, effectively reduces a firm's total income tax expense. The positive impact of interest expense on a firm's income tax expense is referred to as a "tax shield." In order to correctly account for the **tax shield**, the amount of interest added back to net income should be reduced by the amount of the tax shield which is already reflected in a firm's income tax provision, and hence, in its net income. The income tax rate used in this calculation is the company's **effective tax rate**, or a firm's tax expense divided by its income before income taxes. Note that no such adjustment is needed for dividends paid to shareholders since dividends are not tax deductible and are not subtracted in the calculation of net income, and consequently, do not need to be added back.

Russian River Valley's expected ROA, also referred to as the **return on investment**, is 4.4 percent, indicating that it takes about $1 of assets to generate about four and a half cents of net income. Is that good? One benchmark—the six percent interest rate (but only 3.4 percent after considering the interest tax shield) to be charged by Hap e-Loan Corporation on the proposed bank loan—suggests that the winery's expected ROA is quite low. While the winery will earn slightly more than its 3.4 percent after-tax cost of borrowed funds, this is not a very large margin.[2] The low projected ROA for Russian River Valley may indicate several things—that the wine business is highly competitive, producing only marginal returns, or alternatively, that the winery's business model needs more work to enable the business to be more profitable.

From a shareholder perspective, the size of a business's profit relative to the shareholders' investment in the business is an important measure of profitability, and this can be evaluated by the **return on shareholders' equity** (ROE) ratio, or net income divided by shareholders' equity.[3] This ratio indicates how much profit was generated given the shareholders' investment in a business:

---

[2] Russian River Valley's after-tax cost of borrowed funds is calculated as follows:

$$\text{After-tax cost of borrowing} = \text{Before-tax cost of borrowing} \times (1 - \text{Tax rate})$$

In the case of Russian River Valley, the effective tax rate is 43 percent ($240/$557); hence, the after-tax cost of borrowing is:

$$3.4\% = 6.0\% \times (1 - .43)$$

[3] Many investment professionals define the return on shareholders' equity (ROE) ratio as:

$$\text{ROE} = \frac{\text{Net income} - \text{Preferred stock dividends}}{\text{Common shareholders' equity}}$$

This ratio definition reflects the widely held view that preferred stock is a quasi-form of debt, and hence, the cost of preferred stock (preferred stock dividends) should be subtracted from net income just as the cost of debt financing (interest expense) is subtracted from net income. Common shareholders' equity is then defined as total shareholders' equity less preferred stock equity. Since many firms do not issue preferred shares, the ROE ratio collapses to just net income divided by shareholders' equity. In addition, some ratios, like ROE, include a metric in the numerator that is measured over time (such as net income) and a metric in the denominator that is measured at a point in time (such as shareholders' equity). Because of this mismatch of the time dimension of a ratio's components, some analysts use averages, rather than ending balances, for the denominator of these ratios.

Ratio	Financial Variables	Computation	Result
Return on equity (ROE)	Net income / Shareholders' equity	$317 / $6,457	4.9%

The Russian River Valley Winery's expected ROE is 4.9 percent, which indicates that for every dollar of shareholders' equity invested in the winery, the business is expected to generate less than five cents of profit for its shareholders. This is a little higher than the after-tax 3.4 percent interest rate to be charged by Hap e-Loan Corporation on the bank loan, yet Matt and Kate bear much more risk than the lender. (Recall that assuming higher risk should result in higher returns.) We can tentatively conclude that this expected return is high enough to justify the investment that Kate and Matt will have to make. But, the two entrepreneurs will certainly want to focus on ways of improving the profitability of the business and its ROE.

Return on Equity Analysis

Investment professionals have devised an ingenious way of analyzing the profitability of a business by breaking the return on shareholders' equity (ROE) ratio into three component financial ratios—the return on sales, asset turnover, and financial leverage:

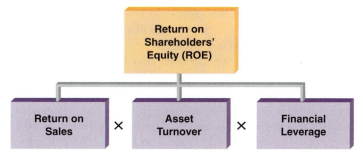

This paradigm reveals that there are four ways to improve a company's ROE, and hence, a firm's profitability: 1) improve a business's return on sales; 2) improve a business's asset turnover; 3) improve a business's use of financial leverage; or, 4) some combination of items 1, 2, and 3. **Asset turnover** is a measure of how effectively a business's assets are being used by the management team to generate sales revenue. This ratio is calculated as sales revenue divided by total assets. This metric is an important indicator of firm performance since the principal objective of any business is to generate income, and that is only possible after the business first generates sales revenue. **Financial leverage**, on the other hand, refers to the relative mix of debt versus equity financing used by a business and is calculated as total assets divided by shareholders' equity. For a firm that is all equity financed, the financial leverage ratio will equal one and will increase in value as debt financing is added. Since the after-tax interest rate on the winery's debt is only 3.4 percent, financing some of the Russian River Valley's assets with debt takes advantage of this cheaper source of financing.[4] We can apply ROE analysis to the winery's forecasted financial data as follows:

Financial leverage refers to the use of debt to finance a business's assets and/or its operations. The cost of debt financing is defined as the rate of interest specified in a debt contract. If a firm is able to earn a return on its borrowed assets greater than its after-tax cost of borrowing, the excess return accrues to the firm's shareholders. And, as a consequence, a company's ROE will exceed its ROA—for example, 4.9 percent versus 3.4 percent for the Russian River Valley Winery. Thus, when we observe that a firm's ROE exceeds its ROA, we can conclude that the firm has been able to successfully utilize financial leverage. When a firm is all equity financed, ROE and ROA will be equivalent.

Return on Equity	=	Return on Sales	×	Asset Turnover	×	Financial Leverage
Net income / Shareholders' equity	=	Net income / Sales revenue	×	Sales revenue / Total assets	×	Total assets / Shareholders' equity
$317 / $6,457	=	$317 / $1,900	×	$1,900 / $10,953	×	$10,953 / $6,457
4.9%	=	16.7%	×	0.173	×	1.70

[4] For all businesses, the cost of debt financing is cheaper than the cost of equity financing. Recall that since buying shares in a business is riskier than lending to a business, the returns expected by shareholders should be higher than the returns expected by lenders–lenders have first claim on the assets of a business and shareholders get what is left over.

The ROE analysis for the Russian River Valley Winery reveals why the winery's expected return on equity (4.9 percent) is low. Although the winery's expected ROS is a healthy 16.7 percent, Russian River Valley's expected asset turnover is only 0.173, which indicates that each dollar invested in the business's assets is expected to generate less than 18 cents in sales. Further, the winery has a financial leverage ratio of 1.70, indicating that the winery's assets are forecasted to be about 1.7 times the amount of shareholders' equity invested in the business. Put another way, the Russian River Valley Winery assets are financed with relatively more equity ($6,457) than debt ($4,496). Since the winery is able to earn a slightly higher return on its borrowed funds than the after-tax cost that the business will be charged for the use of these funds, the winery's expected ROE is enhanced by its use of financial leverage.

To enable us to benchmark the expected performance of the winery, Exhibit 2.6 presents an ROE analysis for ten wine companies over a recent five-year period. The data confirm the assessment that Russian River Valley has a low expected return on equity and asset turnover but a relatively high expected return on sales, as compared to the average of the other ten wineries. Observe, for instance, that while the expected ROS for Russian River Valley is 16.7 percent, it averages only about 6.3 percent for the ten wineries; and, while Russian River Valley's expected asset turnover is only 0.173, it averages 0.59 for the ten wineries, or more than three times higher than the turnover forecasted by the winery. This kind of information can be very useful to Kate and Matt in that it highlights the various financial strengths and weaknesses of their proposed business, and thus, highlights those areas in which Matt and Kate should try to improve their business plan. As ROE increases and decreases across accounting periods, this component analysis of ROE can also shed light on which aspect of the business might be contributing to the change. We will have more to say about ROE analysis in Chapter 4.

EXHIBIT 2.6 ROE Analysis: Median Values for 10 Firms in the Wine Industry

Return On Equity	=	Return On Sales	×	Asset Turnover	×	Financial Leverage
7.97%	=	6.28%	×	0.59	×	2.15

Source: *Compustat*

Evaluating Financial Risk

The concerns that the Russian River Valley Winery may have insufficient cash to pay its annual interest payments and repay the principal on its proposed bank loan on a timely basis are the types of financial risk that financial institutions must consider when lending to a business. Two financial ratios that assess this form of risk include the **long-term debt-to-equity ratio** and the **interest coverage ratio**:

Ratio	Financial Variables	Computation	Result
Long-term debt-to-equity	Long-term debt / Shareholders' equity	$4,320 / $6,457	0.67
Interest coverage	Operating income / Interest expense	$845 / $288	2.93

The long-term debt-to-equity ratio reveals the relative investment of long-term lenders versus that of the shareholders in the Russian River Valley Winery. A high debt-to-equity ratio, for example, indicates a financing strategy heavily dependent on borrowed versus shareholder-invested funds. The interest coverage ratio, on the other hand, reveals the extent to which current operating earnings "cover" current debt service charges (interest expense). A high interest coverage ratio, also referred to as the **times-interest-earned ratio**, indicates that a business has strong operating earnings (or low interest charges), and thus, has the capacity to take on additional debt and additional debt service costs, as well as to easily service its existing debt.

The Russian River Valley Winery's expected long-term debt-to-equity ratio is 0.67, indicating that its long-term debt of $4,320 ($3,840 + $480) is about two-thirds the amount of its shareholders' equity of $6,457. The winery's expected interest coverage ratio is 2.93, suggesting that the winery's operating income is projected to be almost three times the expected interest expense for the period. Both ratios indicate that there is a fair amount of cushion for the business's lenders. Overall, with a reasonable debt-to-equity ratio and interest coverage ratio, the winery should have a good chance of getting the proposed $4.8 million loan because it appears to have a good chance of paying both the annual interest charge and principal repayments in a timely manner.

MANAGERIAL DISCRETION AND ACCOUNTING METHODS

The balance sheet equation used for analyzing the various accounting events of a business can be helpful in understanding the accounting method choices that a company makes and how those choices affect a business's financial statements. To illustrate, we use the balance sheet equation to examine how B.J.'s Wholesale Club accounted for the membership fees it charges its customers and how America Online accounted for the cost of computer diskettes it used to attract new internet customers.

Operating Revenues at B.J.'s Wholesale Club

B.J.'s Wholesale Club Inc. is a wholesale membership club in the United States. Customers pay an annual fee of $50 for the right to shop at any of B.J.'s outlets, which offer its customers lower prices on goods that it buys in very large quantities. B.J.'s accounts for the $50 membership fee as operating revenue when it is received. To illustrate the financial effects associated with this practice, assume that a customer paid the $50 fee on July 1, halfway through B.J.'s fiscal year, which ends on December 31. B.J.'s would report the event by increasing cash (A) by $50 and increasing operating revenue and retained earnings (SE) by $50 (see Panel A, Exhibit 2.7).

EXHIBIT 2.7	B.J.'s: Accounting for Membership Fees		
Panel A			
	Cash	**Liabilities**	**Retained Earnings**
July 1	$50		$50
Ending Balance	$50		$50
Panel B			
	Cash	**Liabilities**	**Retained Earnings**
July 1	$50	$ 50	
December 31		$(25)	$25
Ending Balance	$50	$ 25	$25

B.J.'s accounting for membership fees, however, came under criticism from the U.S. Securities and Exchange Commission which required that the company abandon the practice and instead recognize the fee ratably over the 12-month membership period.[5] Under the new accounting policy, on July 1, B.J.'s would show an increase in cash of $50 and an increase in a liability account (called "unearned revenue") of $50 to recognize B.J.'s obligation to provide member services to its customer for the coming year (see Panel B). By December 31, B.J.'s has satisfied six months (or one-half) of its obligation and thus, would recognize $25 of operating revenues and a reduction in the liability for future services of $25. At the end of the year, B.J.'s has a remaining liability of $25 for services it has agreed to provide for the next six months.

Let's compare B.J.'s former accounting policy with its new policy by contrasting the account balances in Panels A and B in Exhibit 2.7. The former policy increases earnings by $25 for the year, reduces liabilities by $25, and increases shareholders' equity by $25. Thus, under the old policy, the performance of the company appears superior. Yet, the cash flows under both accounting policies are identical.

An astute observer might notice that with no new customers next year, the old accounting policy will result in zero earnings in Year Two. This observation highlights a fundamental difference between accrual accounting and cash accounting. Accrual accounting, with its adherence to revenue recognition

---

[5] Some investment professionals refer to B.J.'s original accounting treatment of its membership fees as **front-end loading of revenues**. Under this practice, the cash flows from the sale of a membership are immediately recognized as revenue even though some portion of the revenue may relate to services to be delivered in a future period.

and expense matching, creates timing differences between earnings recognition and cash flows. Over the two-year period, there will be no difference in cumulative net income; but, under B.J.'s new accounting policy, earnings will be $25 in the second year. Thus, the new policy shifts some revenues and earnings from the current year to the following year but does not change the total revenues or earnings over the two-year period. But suppose that there are more customers in each succeeding year—then current earnings will be higher under the old accounting policy than under the new accounting policy—and B.J.'s management team will appear to be doing a better job.

Operating Expenses at America Online

America Online (AOL) was a pioneer internet service provider that blanketed the United States with promotional materials (e.g., computer diskettes and CDs) to entice customers to sign up for the company's service. For accounting purposes, AOL accounted for the cost of these promotional materials as an asset on the balance sheet, called "deferred marketing costs," and expensed the resulting asset over a two-year period.[6] To see the effect of this accounting policy on AOL's balance sheet, assume that it costs $2 to produce and distribute each set of materials and that they are shipped on January 1. (AOL's fiscal year ends on December 31.) On January 1, AOL reduces cash (A) by $2 and increases intangible assets (A) by the same amount. On December 31, AOL expenses $1 by reducing intangible assets by $1 and reducing retained earnings (SE) by $1. These events are illustrated in Panel A of Exhibit 2.8.

EXHIBIT 2.8	AOL: Accounting for Advertising Costs		
Panel A			
	Cash	**Intangible Asset**	**Retained Earnings**
January 1	$(2.00)	$ 2.00	
December 31		$(1.00)	$(1.00)
Ending Balance	$(2.00)	$ 1.00	$(1.00)
Panel B			
	Cash	**Intangible Asset**	**Retained Earnings**
January 1	$(2.00)		$(2.00)
Ending Balance	$(2.00)		$(2.00)

After repeated criticism from Wall Street analysts regarding this policy, AOL switched to immediately expensing the cost of the promotional materials. Under immediate expensing, AOL would reduce cash (A) by $2 and reduce retained earnings (SE) by the same amount. The event would be recorded as shown in Panel B of Exhibit 2.8.

Contrasting the account balances from Panels A and B of Exhibit 2.8 reveals the effect of AOL's decision to change its accounting policy. Immediately expensing the cost of the promotional materials reduces assets on the balance sheet by $1 at December 31 and reduces earnings for the year by $1. Yet, there is no cash flow effect associated with the change since cash is initially reduced by $2 under both methods. Over a two-year period, there is no difference in AOL's performance under the two policies; however, under the old policy, net income is higher in Year One.

In both examples—B.J.'s and AOL—the selection of a firm's accounting policies can materially impact reported firm performance, in many instances making the operating performance look better than it really was. A theme throughout each of the following chapters is that informed financial statement users must look beyond the reported numbers and also consider the accounting policy choices made by a company's management. Evaluating a company's profits without knowledge of how that number is derived is like reporting the temperature on a given day without understanding what temperature scale was used—Celsius or Fahrenheit (32 degrees Fahrenheit is quite cold while 32 degrees Celsius is quite pleasant). As we will see from actual corporate examples, some managers will make

---

[6] Some investment professionals refer to AOL's treatment of deferred marketing costs as **rear-end loading of expenses**. Under this practice, the cash outflows for advertising and marketing are capitalized to the balance sheet as an asset even though some (or all) of the expenditure should be currently recognized on the income statement as an expense.

judicious accounting policy choices in an attempt to manage the level of reported firm performance, and consequently, to influence the perceived value of a firm.

ETHICS PERSPECTIVE

B.J.'s Wholesale Club Inc. and **America Online** represent two examples of how managers can use their discretion to manage the reported earnings of a firm. Much of this discretion is within the flexible guidelines that are part of the institutional setting of accounting; however, sometimes managers cross the line of acceptable accounting practice and engage in fraudulent reporting. Very often the line between the two is quite grey, where it is difficult to separate aggressive financial reporting from fraudulent financial reporting. In either case, it can be argued that the intent of some corporate managers is to deceive the investing public by misrepresenting a firm's financial performance.

In the post-**Enron** environment, and with the enactment of the Sarbanes-Oxley Act, many firms are proactively portraying themselves as being "ethical." Ethical behavior is, for example, part of the Corporate Social Responsibility movement. This behavior includes many dimensions, including the ethical treatment of employees and the environment, as well as ethical financial reporting. Academic research has found a positive correlation between a firm's reputation and its financial performance. Do you feel that strong ethics makes good business sense?

REVIEW PROBLEM

The Arcadia Company was founded by Thomas Smith and began operations in July 2012 as a neighborhood hardware store, selling branded lawn and garden supplies, household products, and small tools. The following transactions occurred during the second half of 2012:

1. Smith established The Arcadia Company by contributing $250,000 of his personal funds and receiving all of the company's capital stock in return for his equity investment.
2. The company purchased a small shop in a strip mall for $150,000 cash.
3. Needing working capital to purchase inventory, the company borrowed $120,000 cash from a local bank, using the recently purchased store as collateral for the loan. Interest on the loan was set at six percent per year, payable every six months. The loan could be repaid at any time, but full loan repayment was required within three years.
4. Smith used the entire loan amount of $120,000 to purchase inventory. In addition, he purchased $30,000 of inventory on credit. By the end of 2012, all but $6,000 of the credit purchase had been repaid.
5. Smith decided to use a simple rule-of-thumb for pricing his inventory for sale—all goods would be marked up 100 percent above their cost. By year-end, Smith noted that he had sold inventory with a cost basis of $80,000. All sales were for cash or on a debit/credit card.
6. Smith decided to depreciate his shop on a straight-line basis, using an expected useful life of 20 years.
7. During the latter half of 2012, Smith withdrew $20,000 in cash from the business as his salary.
8. Ignore all taxes when answering the following questions. Note: If treated as a corporation, the business would owe payroll taxes on the wages paid to the owner unless the money is paid as a dividend.

Required

1. Prepare a spreadsheet for The Arcadia Company using the balance sheet equation, reflecting the financial effects of the above transactions.
2. Prepare an income statement, balance sheet, and statement of cash flow for The Arcadia Company at the end of the first year of operations.
3. Compute for The Arcadia Company the following ratios; (1) Return on Sales, (2) Return on Assets, (3) Return on Equity.
4. Show that Return on Equity is equal to the multiplicative combination of Return on Sales, Asset Turnover, and Financial Leverage.

The solution is on pages 75–76

EXECUTIVE SUMMARY

In this chapter we examined the balance sheet equation and how financial statements are derived from a set of accounting events that affect a business. We also considered some of the estimates and assumptions inherent in the financial statement preparation process, observing that since estimates and assumptions can be incorrect, financial statements should never be considered to be a precise representation of a company's financial performance. Finally, we investigated how to use financial statement data to evaluate a business's operating performance and its financial risk.

As a validation of your understanding of the content of this chapter, you should now be able to:

- Explain the accounting meaning behind the terms asset, liability, shareholders' equity, revenue, expense, and matching.
- Prepare financial statements from accounting events.
- Use selected financial ratios to evaluate a company's financial performance.
- Use the balance sheet equation to understand the managerial motives for selecting between alternative accounting methods.

In the next chapter, we examine the various components of the income statement and also learn how to prepare a statement of cash flow from just an income statement and a set of balance sheets.

KEY CONCEPTS AND TERMS

Accrual, 41
Articulation, 55
Asset, 39
Asset turnover, 59
Balance sheet equation, 38
Common stock, 39
Contra-accounts, 47
Contributed capital, 39
Current assets, 51
Current liabilities, 52
Effective tax rate, 58
Entity principle, 41
Expenses, 45
Financial leverage, 59
Financial ratios, 57
Financing activities, 54
Financing decision, 38
Forecasted financial statements, 42

Front-end loading of revenues, 61
Gross profit, 52
Historical cost principle, 44
Intangible assets, 42
Interest coverage ratio, 60
Investing activities, 54
Investment decision, 38
Leveraged, 38
Liability, 39
Long-term debt-to-equity ratio, 60
Matching concept, 45
Net book value, 47
Net income, 52
Net worth, 38
Noncurrent assets, 51
Noncurrent liabilities, 52
Off-balance-sheet debt, 39
Operating activities, 54

Operating income, 52
Opportunity cost, 43
Profit margin ratio, 58
Rear-end loading of expenses, 62
Recurring operations, 52
Retained earnings, 39
Return on assets, 58
Return on investment, 58
Return on sales, 57
Return on shareholders' equity, 58
Revenue recognition principle, 44
Revenues, 45, 52
Shareholders' equity, 39
Tangible assets, 42
Tax shield, 58
Times-interest-earned ratio, 60

QUESTIONS

Q2.1   **Accounting Terminology.**   Describe or define the following terms:
- Asset
- Liability
- Shareholders' equity
- Revenue
- Expense

Discuss how the five terms relate to one another.

Q2.2   **Historical versus Forecasted Financial Statements.**   Discuss the difference between historical and forecasted (or pro forma) financial statements. How are these different sets of financial statements used by managers and shareholders for decision-making purposes?

Q2.3   **Accounting Principles.**   Consider the following accounting principles:
- Entity principle
- Revenue recognition principle
- Matching concept

Define these accounting principles. Discuss how these principles relate to one another.

Q2.4   **Balance Sheet Classifications.**   Most balance sheets are defined as "classified balance sheets" in that both the assets and liabilities are dichotomized into the categories of current and noncurrent. [Note: In those industries in which the business operating cycle is longer than one year (such as the wine industry, the real estate industry, the financial services industry), classified balance sheets are not required under U.S. GAAP.] Discuss how the balance sheet classifications of current versus noncurrent convey important information about a firm's financial condition to managers and shareholders.

Q2.5   **Key Performance Indicators: The Income Statement.**   Describe or define the following key performance indicators (KPIs) from the income statement:

- Operating revenue
- Gross profit
- Operating income
- Net income

Discuss how each of these measures depicts a firm's performance.

Q2.6   **Key Performance Indicators: The Statement of Cash Flow.**   Describe or define the following key performance indicators (KPIs) from the statement of cash flow:

- Cash flow from operating activities
- Cash flow from investing activities
- Cash flow from financing activities

Discuss how each of these measures conveys important information about firm performance to managers and shareholders.

Q2.7   **Return on Shareholders' Equity.**   The return on shareholders' equity ratio can be decomposed into three separate financial ratios—the return on sales, total asset turnover, and financial leverage. Define each of the ratios assuming the firm is all equity financed and discuss what actions a manager might take to increase a firm's return on shareholders' equity.

Q2.8   **Evaluating Financial Risk.**   Investment professionals use a variety of financial ratios to evaluate a company's financial risk. Two popular financial risk ratios include:

- Long-term debt to total assets ratio
- Interest coverage ratio

Define each ratio and discuss what actions a manager might take to reduce a firm's financial riskiness.

Q2.9   **Managing Operating Revenues.**   Some corporate executives have reportedly attempted to manage their firm's operating revenues through such actions as "front-end loading" or "rear-end loading" of operating revenues. Explain the concepts of front-end loading and rear-end loading of operating revenues. Discuss why some managers might undertake these actions. Discuss how you might be able to identify that a manager is managing a firm's operating revenues.

Q2.10   **Net Income, Cash Flow from Operations, and Dividend Policy.**   The Arizona Corporation reported positive net income but negative cash flow from operations. Further, despite the negative cash flow from operations, the company continued to pay its regular dividend on its common shares. Discuss why it is possible for a company to report positive net income when the cash flow from operations is negative. Do you agree with the firm's strategy of maintaining its regular dividend? Why or why not?

Q2.11   **Debt Covenants.**   **Bristol-Myers Squibb (BMS) Company** reports that it maintains a $2 billion, five-year revolving line of credit with a syndicate of lenders. The company disclosed in its annual report that:

> The availability of the line of credit is subject to the Company's ability . . . to meet certain conditions, including a financial covenant in which net debt-to-capital cannot exceed 50 percent.

Discuss why BMS would agree to the above financial covenant. Discuss why the syndicate of lenders would impose such a constraint on BMS. How would you calculate the "net debt-to-capital" ratio? What does the ratio reveal about a company?

Q2.12   **Managing Operating Expenses.**   Some corporate executives have reportedly attempted to manage their firm's operating expenses through such actions as "front-end loading" or "rear-end loading" of their operating expenses. Explain the concepts of front-end loading and rear-end loading of operating expenses. Discuss why some managers might undertake these actions. Discuss how you might be able to identify that a manager is managing a firm's operating expenses.

Q2.13   **Net Loss, Cash Flow from Operations, and Dividend Policy.**   The Phoenix Corporation reported a net loss but a positive cash flow from operations. Further, despite the net loss, the company continued to pay its regular dividend. Discuss why it is possible for a company to report a net loss while also reporting a positive cash flow from operations. Do you agree with the company's decision to continue the payment of its regular dividend? Why or why not?

Q2.14   **(Ethical Perspective) Corporate Social Responsibility and Ethics.**   In the post-**Enron** environment, and with the enactment of the Sarbanes-Oxley legislation, many firms are proactively portraying themselves as being "ethical." Ethical behavior is, for example, part of the Corporate Social Responsibility movement. This behavior includes many dimensions, from the ethical treatment of employees and the environment, to ethical financial reporting. Academic research has found a positive correlation between a firm's reputation and its financial performance. Why do you think that there is a positive correlation between ethical behavior and successful corporate financial performance?

Assignments with the ✓ logo in the margin are available in BusinessCourse.
See the Preface of the book for details.
CHECK FIGURE indicates that check figures are available on the book's Website.

EXERCISES

E2.15   **The Balance Sheet Equation.**   Fernandez & Co. experienced the following six events during the current year:

1.   The sale of common stock to investors for $5 million cash.
2.   The sale of a new bond issue to investors for $10 million cash.
3.   The purchase of $500,000 of inventory for cash.
4.   The purchase of $700,000 of equipment using bank financing.
5.   The payment of $100,000 cash for income taxes associated with last year's operations.
6.   The CFO determined that net income for the most recent month was $2 million.

Using the balance sheet equation as illustrated in this chapter, show how each of the above six events would affect the balance sheet of Fernandez & Co.

E2.16   **Account Classification.**   Presented below is a list of income statement and balance sheet accounts:

a. Interest expense
b. Land
c. Cost of goods sold
d. Intangible assets
e. Income tax expense
f. Inventory
g. Revenues
h. Accounts payable
i. Accounts receivable

j. Depreciation expense
k. Equipment
l. Loan payable
m. Wages and salaries expense
n. Buildings
o. Retained earnings
p. Selling and administrative expense
q. Amortization expense
r. Cash

For each account, indicate whether it would appear on the balance sheet (B/S) or the income statement (I/S). For those accounts appearing on the balance sheet, indicate whether the account is an asset (A), liability (L), or shareholders' equity (SE) account. For those accounts appearing on the income statement, indicate whether the account is a revenue (R) account or an expense (E) account.

E2.17   **Asset or Expense.**   The Rankine Corporation reported net income of $10 million in 2012, and it appears that net income for 2013 will be the same. During 2013, the company made the following expenditures:

1. $250,000 was spent to resurface the company parking lot. The resurfacing has to be done about every five years.
2. $500,000 was spent to upgrade the company's air filtration system in the plating department. The system worked satisfactorily, but the U.S. Department of Labor recently promulgated new rules (effective three years from today) that would have required the changes the company made voluntarily.
3. $900,000 was paid to a consultant for the design of a new manufacturing facility. The new plant was the dream of the prior CEO but had been shelved because the current CEO was uncertain about the firm's future.
4. $600,000 was spent on the development of a new inventory control system. The system was designed to allow salespeople in the field to electronically enter orders into the system so that they could be shipped the next day. The system appeared to be on track, but another $200,000 would have to be spent before it could be demonstrated that it would function as planned.

5. The company's Arizona plant was shut down for three months because of the slow economy. The company struggled to find ways to keep its employees busy so they could retain as many as possible. Some employees agreed to accept half pay while the company found maintenance work and training for the other employees. At the end of three months, about 85 percent of the workforce was still on the payroll when the company resumed normal production. The maintenance work done by the employees during this time cost about $1 million; the training cost the company another $800,000.

Indicate whether the above expenditures should be considered as an asset or as an expense. Be prepared to justify your answer.

E2.18 **The Statement of Cash Flow.**   The following cash flow information was taken from **The Johnson & Johnson Company (J&J)** annual report. Compute the missing values in the table (amounts are in millions). Based on this data, how does J&J finance its ongoing operations and asset purchases?

	Year 3	Year 2	Year 1
Cash, beginning balance	$ 9,013	$?	$ 3,171
Cash flow from operating activities	11,877	?	10,595
Cash flow from investing activities.	(279)	(2,347)	?
Cash flow from financing activities.	?	(5,148)	(3,863)
Cash, ending balance.	$16,055	$?	$ 5,377

E2.19 **The Statement of Cash Flow.**   The following cash flow information was taken from **The General Electric Company (GE)** annual report. Compute the missing values in the table (amounts are in millions). Based on this data, describe GE's cash flow performance for the three-year period. CHECK FIGURE

	Year 3	Year 2	Year 1
Cash, beginning balance	$?	$12,664	$?
Cash flow from operating activities	37,641	36,484	29,229
Cash flow from investing activities.	?	(38,414)	(21,843)
Cash flow from financing activities.	(6,119)	?	(3,632)
Cash, ending balance.	$11,801	$15,328	$?

E2.20 **Preparing the Basic Financial Statements.**   Marilyn Miller opened a floral shop using $5,000 of her own cash savings and with $15,000 in cash borrowed from her parents. She signed a lease on a small store for one year, agreeing to pay $350 per month in rent. During the first year of operations, Marilyn purchased fresh flowers from a local nursery for $2,500, paid $1,200 for utilities, and generated floral sales totaling $12,000. (Assume all transactions were cash transactions.) Marilyn was hoping to be able to repay her parents one-half of the borrowed money at the end of the first year of operations.

Prepare an income statement, balance sheet, and statement of cash flow for the floral shop. Can Marilyn achieve her goal of repaying one-half of the $15,000 loan at the end of the first year of operations?

E2.21 **Preparing Cash Flow Data.**   Marilyn Miller began the second year of her floral business with $12,000 in cash in her bank account. Using the information below, all of which occurred during Year 2, prepare a statement of cash flow for Marilyn. Evaluate her cash management strategy during Year 2. CHECK FIGURE

1. Sold an equity interest in the business for $13,000 cash.
2. Generated revenue from floral sales of $20,000, collecting all but $5,000.
3. Incurred operating expenses totaling $9,000, of which $2,000 remained unpaid at the end of Year 2.
4. Purchased new store equipment for $5,000, with a down payment of $2,500 cash and signing a note payable for $2,500.
5. Paid shareholders a cash dividend of $2,800.

PROBLEMS

P2.22 **Accounting Event Analysis and Financial Statement Preparation.**   Smith & Co. experienced the following six events in its first year of operations: CHECK FIGURE

1. Shareholders contributed $60,000 cash.
2. Purchased land for $40,000 cash.
3. Borrowed $18,000 in cash from a bank.

4. Provided services for $16,000, which will be paid to Smith & Co. next year.
5. Paid $11,000 cash for miscellaneous operating expenses.
6. Paid a $1,000 cash dividend to shareholders.

Required

Using the balance sheet equation as illustrated in this chapter, identify how each of the above six events affected the various accounts involved. Prepare an income statement, a statement of shareholders' equity, a balance sheet, and a statement of cash flow for the first year of operations. What is your assessment of the company's financial performance in its first year of operations?

 P2.23 **Accounting Event Analysis and Financial Statement Preparation.** Wilmot Real Estate Company experienced the following events during its first year of operations:

1. Received $50,000 in cash from investors as an equity investment.
2. Borrowed $40,000 in cash from a bank.
3. Purchased two parcels of land, each costing $15,000, for a total of $30,000 cash. The land was purchased for investment purposes.
4. Paid $10,000 cash to rent office equipment for the year.
5. Provided real estate appraisal services valued at $25,000, receiving $20,000 in cash and an account receivable for an additional $5,000.
6. Paid miscellaneous expenses totaling $11,000 in cash.
7. Sold one parcel of land, costing $15,000, for $22,000 cash.
8. Paid a $5,000 cash dividend to shareholders.

Required

Using the balance sheet equation as illustrated in this chapter, identify how each of the above events affect the balance sheet equation of A = L + SE. Prepare an income statement, a statement of shareholders' equity, a balance sheet, and a statement of cash flow for the first year of operations. Evaluate the company's financial performance during its first year of operations.

CHECK FIGURE **P2.24** **Accounting Event Analysis and the Balance Sheet.** Presented below are the balance sheet accounts of the Mayfair Company as of December 1, 2013. The accounts are listed in random order.

Machinery & equipment (net)	$15,000	Cash	$10,000
Accounts payable	10,000	Notes payable	9,500
Note receivable	2,000	Accounts receivable	15,000
Inventory	3,000	Goodwill	8,000
Bank loan	10,500	Additional paid-in capital	76,000
Building (net)	30,000	Land	40,000
Common stock ($1 par value)	5,000	Retained earnings	12,000

During the month of December 2013, the following events occurred:

1. Purchased inventory on credit that cost $3,000.
2. Issued common stock at par value in exchange for machinery and equipment valued at $12,000.
3. The building was appraised at a value of $45,000 by a certified real estate appraiser.
4. The note receivable of $2,000 was collected.
5. $8,000 cash was paid on the outstanding accounts payable.
6. Purchased land valued at $25,000, paying $3,000 in cash and signing a five-year note for the remaining amount.

Required

1. Prepare the balance sheet as of December 1, 2013, for the Mayfair Company.
2. Prepare a spreadsheet using the balance sheet equation as illustrated in this chapter for the December events.
3. Prepare the balance sheet as of December 31, 2013, for the Mayfair Company.
4. Evaluate the company's financial leverage at year-end 2013.

 P2.25 **Preparing a Balance Sheet.** The following financial information is known about **Pfizer, Inc.** (all amounts in millions):

  a. The balance of cash and cash equivalents was $2,247.
  b. Short-term investments have a fair market value of $19,979.
  c. Gross accounts receivable total $9,948, which includes $183 that is not expected to be collected.
  d. Inventory has a cost basis of $6,900 but a replacement cost of $6,709.
  e. Prepaid expenses total $3,196.
  f. Property, plant and equipment have a cost basis of $29,587, a current fair value of $42,500, and accumulated depreciation taken to date of $10,000.

g.   Intangible assets have a cost basis of $76,582 and accumulated amortization of $20,500.
h.   Accounts payable total $2,226; accrued expenses payable total $14,633; and, short-term borrowings total $11,589.
i.   Long-term debt totals $6,347, and post-retirement benefit obligations total $17,143.
j.   Shareholders' equity totals $65,627, composed of retained earnings of $37,608, other comprehensive income of $479, treasury stock of negative $39,767, and contributed capital of $67,307.

Required
Prepare a balance sheet for Pfizer, Inc. as of year-end. Evaluate Pfizer's financial risk.

P2.26   **Analysis of Financial Statement Data.**   The following data were taken from the financial statements of The Amphlett Corporation, which is all equity financed.

	2012	2013
Net sales.....................	$145,860	$161,585
Net income................	24,765	28,340
Total assets...............	171,225	192,440
Shareholders' equity	101,975	121,165

Required
1.   Calculate the following ratios for 2012 and 2013:
  a.   Return on equity
  b.   Return on assets
  c.   Return on sales
  d.   Total assets to shareholders' equity (financial leverage)
  e.   Total asset turnover
2.   Comment on the financial performance of The Amphlett Corporation based on your ratio calculations.

P2.27   **Analysis of Financial Statement Data.**   The following data were taken from the financial statements of The Mann Corporation, which is all equity financed.

	2012	2013
Net sales.....................	$1,300,000	$2,320,000
Net income................	100,000	220,000
Total assets...............	558,659	894,309
Shareholders' equity	303,030	371,622

Required
1.   Calculate the following ratios for 2012 and 2013:
  a.   Return on equity
  b.   Return on assets
  c.   Return on sales
  d.   Total assets to shareholders' equity (financial leverage)
  e.   Total asset turnover
2.   Comment on the financial performance of The Mann Corporation based on your ratio calculations.

P2.28   **Analyzing Financial Statement Information.**   The Thunderbird Corporation has applied to the Biltmore National Bank for a $100,000 loan to purchase new equipment for its manufacturing operations. As part of the loan application, the chief financial officer of Thunderbird submitted the following financial statement information:

	2013	2012
Balance sheet		
Current assets	$ 49,000	$ 42,000
Noncurrent assets	175,000	150,500
Total assets	224,000	192,500
Current liabilities	24,500	21,000
Noncurrent liabilities	91,000	73,500
Shareholders' equity	108,500	98,000

continued

continued from prior page

	2013	2012
Income statement		
Operating revenues	$122,500	$112,000
Operating expenses.	(80,500)	(91,000)
Net income.	$ 42,000	$ 21,000
Statement of cash flow		
Cash flow from operating activities	$ 52,500	$ 31,500
Cash flow from investing activities	(49,000)	(42,000)
Cash flow from financing activities	24,500	17,500
Change in cash	$ 28,000	$ 7,000

Required

Analyze the financial statement information of The Thunderbird Corporation and indicate whether you believe that the firm's loan application should be approved. And, if so, why?

P2.29 **The Operating Cycle and Financial Statements.** Presented below is the year-end 2012 balance sheet for The Little Corporation.

THE LITTLE CORPORATION
Balance Sheet
December 31, 2012

Assets			Liabilities & Shareholders' Equity	
Current			**Current liabilities**	
Cash.		$ 510,000	Accounts payable	$ 650,000
Accounts receivable (net). . . .		564,000	Wages payable	173,000
Inventory		720,000	Interest payable	56,000
Prepaid rent		222,000	Total current liabilities	879,000
Total current assets		2,016,000	**Noncurrent liabilities**	
Noncurrent			Bank loan.	450,000
Long-term investments		496,500	Bonds payable.	1,950,000
Equipment	$1,440,000		Total liabilities.	3,279,000
Less Accum. depreciation . . .	(288,000)	1,152,000	**Shareholders' equity**	
Machinery	2,850,000		Common stock	1,200,000
Less Accum. depreciation . . .	(712,500)		Retained earnings	1,548,000
		2,137,500	Total shareholders' equity	2,748,000
Intangible assets (net)		225,000	**Total liabilities &**	
Total assets		$6,027,000	**shareholders' equity**	$6,027,000

During 2013, the company entered into the following events:

1. Sales to customers totaled $2 million, of which $1.6 million were on credit and the remainder was cash sales. The cost of goods sold totaled $800,000.
2. Purchased $700,000 of inventory on credit.
3. Paid $620,000 cash to employees as wages. (This amount includes the wages payable at December 31, 2012.)
4. Collected $1.75 million cash from customers as payment on outstanding accounts receivable.
5. Paid $1.2 million cash to suppliers on outstanding accounts payable.
6. Sold machinery for $120,000 cash on January 1, 2013. The machinery had cost $370,000 and at the time of sale it had a net book value of $160,000.
7. Paid miscellaneous expenses totaling $98,000 cash.
8. Sold common stock for $450,000 cash.
9. Invested $200,000 of excess cash in short-term marketable securities.
10. Declared and paid a cash dividend of $100,000.

As part of the year-end audit, the internal audit staff identified the following additional information:

a. $180,000 of prepaid rent was consumed during the year.
b. The equipment had a useful life of 10 years and the machinery of 20 years. The company uses straight-line depreciation. (No depreciation should be recorded for machinery in Item 6 above.)

c. The intangible assets had a remaining useful life of 10 years.
d. Interest on the bank loan and bonds payable was 10 percent. During the year, interest payments totaling $260,000 had been paid in cash.

Required

1. Using the balance sheet equation as illustrated in this chapter, prepare a spreadsheet reflecting the events of The Little Corporation during 2013.
2. Prepare the income statement for 2013.
3. Prepare the statement of shareholders' equity, balance sheet, and statement of cash flow for 2013.
4. How has the company's use of leverage changed from 2012 to 2013?

P2.30 **Preparing Financial Statements from Accounting Events.** Photovoltaics, Inc. is an Arizona-based manufacturer and distributor of photovoltaic solar energy units. The company was founded in 2012 by Arthur Manelas and Harry Linn. Manelas, formerly a research scientist with NASA, had been operating a small photovoltaic manufacturing company in Massachusetts when Linn, a marketing consultant to industry and himself an owner of a solar energy company in Oregon, proposed the joint venture.

Convinced that excellent market opportunities for the solar arrays existed, Linn began preparing a prospectus that could be used to help raise capital to significantly expand Manelas's current operations. The two founders had located a manufacturing facility in Tucson, Arizona, that would cost approximately $8 million to acquire and equip with updated production equipment. Based on his prior experience, Linn knew that prospective venture capital investors would expect to see the following:

- A balance sheet identifying the company's assets and equities as they would appear at the start of operations.
- A pro forma income statement for the first year of operations.
- A pro forma balance sheet as it would appear at the end of the first year of operations.
- A pro forma statement of cash flow for the first year of operations.

In anticipation of preparing these reports, Linn collected the following information and arrived at the following projections for the first year of operations:

Data related to pre-opening events

1. Ten million shares of common stock (par value $1) were authorized for sale by the company's charter of incorporation. Manelas received 500,000 shares in exchange for the rights to the photovoltaic patent, and Linn received an equal number of shares after contributing $500,000 in personal funds to the firm.
2. Incorporation and attorney's fees (start-up costs) amounted to $27,000 and would be paid in cash. (Hint: Start-up costs are generally expensed as incurred.)
3. Sales of common stock to venture capitalists would total 2.5 million shares. A selling price of $3.25 per share was set, and transaction costs of 1.5 percent of the stock proceeds were projected (to be paid in cash). (Hint: Stock issuance fees are accounted for as a reduction to the Paid-in-Capital account.)
4. The $8 million purchase price of the manufacturing facility, paid in cash, was to be allocated as follows: building—$4.5 million; land—$750,000; and, equipment—$2.75 million. In addition, raw materials and partially completed solar units would be purchased on credit from Manelas's original manufacturing company at a cost of $1.3 million. A note, secured by the inventory itself and accruing interest at a rate of 10 percent per year on the unpaid balance, would be issued to Manelas.

Projected events

5. Revenues from the sale of solar arrays for the first year were projected to be $480,000, with 20 percent of this amount estimated to be uncollected at year-end. The company had decided to follow a particularly rigid credit-granting policy until operations were well established; hence, no provision for bad debts would be established because no uncollectible accounts were anticipated.
6. Cash purchases of inventory were estimated at $70,000; the cost of inventory sold was projected to be $215,000.
7. Insurance on the building, equipment, and inventory was expected to cost $2,700 per year.
8. Employee wages were estimated at $72,000; selling and administrative costs were projected at 2 percent of gross sales.
9. The useful life of the acquired assets were estimated as follows:

Building	20 years
Equipment	10 years

Linn decided to write the patent off over its remaining legal life of 17 years and to write off the start-up costs over five years.

10. Salaries to Linn and Manelas were set at $20,000 each for the first year.
11. Interest payments, but no principal repayments, would be made on the ten-percent notes issued to Manelas during the first year of operations.
12. Income taxes were estimated at 22 percent of pre-tax net income.
13. A cash dividend of $100,000 would be paid at the end of the first year to the equity investors.

Required
1. Using the balance sheet equation as illustrated in this chapter, prepare the following financial statements:
    a. Opening balance sheet as of the start of operations (i.e., after pre-opening events).
    b. Income statement for the first year.
    c. Balance sheet at the end of the first year.
    d. Statement of cash flow for the first year.
2. As a prospective investor in the company, what factors would you look for in the financial statements to help you decide whether to invest in the venture? Do you agree with the decision to pay a $100,000 cash dividend at the end of the first year of operations? Why?

P2.31   **Preparing Financial Statements from Accounting Events.** In January 2005, Susan and Clark Shipley, co-owners of Island Foods, Inc. began discussing the possibility of expanding their restaurant business from a single location in Glendale, Arizona, to two additional locations—one in Scottsdale and a second in Phoenix. Although the Glendale restaurant had only been open for about two years, it had attracted a loyal customer base from neighborhood businesses and schools. Despite the success of the Glendale restaurant in its first two years of operations, the Shipleys would still need to borrow money to finance the two new restaurants. Susan and Clark knew that they would be expected to present a set of recent financial statements as part of any loan proposal. So, the co-owners spent an afternoon compiling data regarding the key transactions of the two preceding years.

Background
In early 2003, Clark and Susan Shipley moved from the damp, gray environment of Seattle, Washington, to the dry, sunny climate of Phoenix, Arizona. After some reflection on their life in Seattle, as well as an analysis of the local business environment in the Phoenix area, they concluded that they would like to own and manage a restaurant. Glendale was Arizona's third largest city, but it was not noted for a plethora of eating establishments, and those that did exist were principally Italian, Mexican, or fast food. The Shipleys concluded that their restaurant would feature Japanese rice bowls and operate under the name "Island Teriyaki."

With that decision made, Clark and Susan began the long and difficult process of setting up their restaurant. In March 2003, they formed Island Foods, Inc. by contributing $10,000 in cash in exchange for all of the company's 1,000 shares of stock. Clark convinced his parents to loan the new venture $120,000 in cash, with principal payable at the rate of $12,000 per year over ten years and interest payable at a rate of 7.5 percent on the outstanding balance as of the beginning of the loan's year. The loan agreement was signed on March 31, 2003, and provided that both principal and interest would be paid only once a year on March 31.

During March, the Shipleys searched for a suitable location for the restaurant. Clark negotiated a lease for approximately 2,000 square feet of retail space at a rate of $1,400 per month. The lease agreement ran for five years, with an option to renew for five more years. The landlord agreed to give the Shipleys three months of free rent on the front end of the lease in order to help the new business survive the critical start-up period.

Also during the month of March, Clark arranged to buy a commercial refrigerator, range, and grill for $26,000 in cash, to be delivered and installed on March 31. Discussions with the seller indicated that the kitchen equipment should last for five years. Clark and Susan also purchased a computer system, with restaurant-specific software already installed, at a cost of $12,000 cash. While the system could last indefinitely, Susan suggested that it be depreciated over six years. Other purchases included food preparation equipment at a cost of $1,200 cash and various restaurant furniture and fixtures at a cost of $2,700 in cash; the equipment, furniture, and fixtures were expected to have a useful life of three years.

To enable the restaurant to be fully operational on April 1, the landlord allowed the Shipleys' carpenter, electrician, painters, and plumbers to begin renovations to the leased store on March 30 and 31. Working round-the-clock, the workers completed all necessary improvements and renovations to the leased space at a cost of $68,000 in cash. On March 31, the purchased kitchen equipment was delivered and "Island Teriyaki" opened for business as planned on April 1, 2003.

First Two Years of Operations
Although Susan and Clark had prepared a timely U.S. income tax return in April of 2004 (for 2003 income taxes), they had not bothered to prepare a full set of financial statements using the accrual method of accounting. Since Clark had "backed up" the hard drive on their computer system on a weekly basis, he had a CD containing all of the 2003 transactions and one of the 2004 transactions. Working from the CD, Clark generated

the necessary accounting information regarding the first two years of operations; he assembled the cash flow information in columnar form (see below) and relevant accrual information by each income statement account:

		2003	2004
•	**Revenues** In general, all restaurant sales were cash transactions; however, the Shipleys had developed a personal relationship with the general manager of one of Glendale's local businesses. As a courtesy to him, they had agreed to cater the company's New Year's Eve party each year and to bill the company directly. The billings totaled $3,000 in 2003 and $5,000 in 2004, and were paid by the company within 15 days of the following month.	$212,000	$327,000
•	**Expenses**		
○	**Food costs** Susan usually sat down once a week to write checks for any recent bills. Consequently, by year-end, only one week of food costs remained unpaid, totaling $9,000 in 2003 and $12,000 in 2004.	$60,000	$105,000
○	**Supply costs** Since payment on delivery was required for these miscellaneous restaurant supplies (such as ice, napkins, etc.), Susan usually paid this bill directly out of petty cash.	$4,800	$6,200
○	**Utility charges** At year-end one month's payment for electricity, telephone, and water remained due.	$8,000	$12,000
○	**Employee wages** Because Clark did much of the cooking himself while Susan worked on food and sauce preparation, the Shipleys were able to keep their labor costs fairly low. They also made a conscious decision to hire local high school and college students. At year-end, Clark determined that one week of wages, amounting to $1,100 in 2003 and $1,400 in 2004, were due to the employees.	$44,000	$76,000
○	**Licenses** Clark paid the one-time Glendale "new business license" fee at 9 a.m. on April 1, 2003, to enable the business to immediately begin operations.	$900	—
○	**Insurance** On April 1, 2003, the Shipleys purchased a three-year "all risks" insurance policy for $18,000 cash. The policy was very comprehensive, covering loss due to theft, fire, or storm damage, as well as such business-related risks as lawsuits arising from customer injury while on the restaurant premises.	$18,000	—
○	**Income taxes** For purposes of preparing the accrual financial statements, Clark and Susan decided to assume that income taxes would be paid on April 15 at a rate of 15 percent.	—	—
○	**Owner compensation** A review of the stored data revealed that the Shipleys had withdrawn $25,000 in cash for personal use in 2003 and $40,000 in 2004. For purposes of the loan proposal, Susan decided to treat these withdrawals as dividends.	$25,000	$40,000

Required

1. Prepare a balance sheet for Island Foods, Inc. as of March 31, 2003.
2. Prepare a balance sheet, income statement, and statement of cash flow as of December 31, 2003.
3. Prepare a balance sheet, income statement, and statement of cash flow as of December 31, 2004.
4. Calculate the following financial ratios for the restaurant for 2003 and 2004.

Probability	Solvency
• Return on sales	• Financial leverage
• Return on assets	• Long-term debt-to-equity
• Return on equity	• Interest coverage ratio
	Asset management
	• Total asset turnover

Would you extend a loan to the Shipleys in the amount of $200,000 in order to open two new restaurants?

CORPORATE ANALYSIS

CA2.32 **The Procter & Gamble Company.** The 2012 annual report of **The Procter & Gamble Company (P&G)** is available at http://annualreport.pg.com/annualreport2012/index.shtml. After reviewing P&G's annual report, respond to the following questions:

a.   P&G's net income increased each year from 2010 through 2012. Looking at the company's income statement, explain why P&G's net income decreased if its net sales increased over the same period. (To answer this question, divide each of P&G's expenses by net sales and consider the trend over the three-year period.)

b.   P&G's total assets decreased by approximately $6.11 billion from 2011 to 2012. Which assets principally accounted for this decline? (To answer this question, calculate each asset as a percentage of total assets and then compare between years.) Is this decline a problem? If so, why? If not, why not?

c.   Consider the change in P&G's total debt and total shareholders' equity from 2011 to 2012. Did the $6.11 billion decrease in its assets have an impact on debt? What was the impact on shareholders' equity? Calculate P&G's long-term debt-to-equity ratio and total debt to total assets ratio for both years as part of your analysis. What can you say about P&G's apparent financing strategy?

d.   Consider P&G's statement of cash flow. What were the five major cash outflows for the company in 2012? How did P&G finance these cash outflows?

e.   Compare P&G's dividend payments to its net income in 2011 and 2012. (Note: The ratio of dividends paid divided by net income is called the *dividend payout ratio*.) What percentage of net income does P&G pay to its shareholders? How does this payout percentage compare to P&G's competitors (such as Johnson & Johnson, Kimberly-Clark Corporation)? Do you agree with this dividend payment policy? What message does this policy convey to investors about the company's future growth potential?

CA2.33 **Internet-based Analysis.** Consider a publicly-held company whose products you are familiar with. Some examples might include:

Company	Product	Corporate Website
• **Johnson & Johnson Company**....	• Band-Aids	• www.jnj.com
• **Microsoft Corporation**..........	• Windows XP software	• www.microsoft.com
• **Nokia Corporation**	• Cellular phones	• www.nokia.com
• **Intel Corporation**	• Pentium processors	• www.intel.com
• **Kimberly-Clark Corporation**......	• Kleenex	• www.kimberly-clark.com

Access the company's public website and search for its most recent annual report. (Note: Some companies will provide access to their financial data through an "investor relations" link, while others will provide a direct link to their "annual reports.") After locating your company's most recent annual report, open the file and review its contents. After reviewing the annual report for your selected company, prepare answers to the following questions:

a.   Calculate the cost of goods sold, operating expenses, and net income as a percentage of net sales for the last two years. What is the trend in each of these percentages? Explain what might be driving the trend.

b.   Calculate the company's total liabilities as a percentage of total assets for the last two years. Did this percentage increase or decrease? Is the company principally debt-financed or equity-financed?

c.   Determine if the company paid dividends to its shareholders. (Hint: Look at the statement of shareholders' equity or the statement of cash flow.) If the company paid dividends, calculate the ratio of dividends paid divided by net income. (Note: This ratio is known as the dividend payout ratio.) What percentage of its net income did the company pay to its shareholders in each of the last two years?

d.   Review the company's statement of cash flow. Identify the major sources of financing used by the company in each of the last two years.

e. Review the company's "Summary of Significant Accounting Policies." Identify how the company recognizes revenue. Identify if the company uses any estimates in the preparation of its financial statement, and if so, prepare a list of the estimates used in its financial report.

SOLUTION TO REVIEW PROBLEM

Solution

THE ARCADIA COMPANY
Spreadsheet

	(1)	(2)	(3a)	(3b)*	(4a)	(4b)	(4c)	(5a)**	(5b)	(6)***	(7)	Balance Sheet
Cash.............	250,000	(150,000)	120,000	(3,600)	(120,000)		(24,000)	160,000			(20,000)	212,400
Inventory............					120,000	30,000			(80,000)			70,000
Buildings.............		150,000										150,000
Accumulated depreciation										(3,750)		(3,750)
Total assets												**428,650**
Accounts payable..........						30,000	(24,000)					6,000
Loan payable			120,000									120,000
Total liabilities...........												**126,000**
Capital stock	250,000											250,000
Retained earnings												52,650
Revenues								160,000				
Cost of goods sold									(80,000)			
Depreciation										(3,750)		
Wages and salaries											(20,000)	
Interest expense				(3,600)								
Total shareholders' equity ...												**302,650**

Income Statement accounts (Revenues, Cost of goods sold, Depreciation, Wages and salaries, Interest expense)

* ($120,000 × .06)/2 = $3,600
** $80,000 × 2 = $160,000
*** ($150,000/20)/2 = $3,750

THE ARCADIA COMPANY
Income Statement

Revenues	$160,000
Less: Cost of goods sold...........	80,000
Depreciation expense	3,750
Wages expense	20,000
Interest expense.............	3,600
Net income....................	$ 52,650

THE ARCADIA COMPANY
Balance Sheet

Assets		Liabilities	
Cash..................	$212,400	Accounts payable........	$ 6,000
Inventory..............	70,000	Loan payable	120,000
Total current assets	282,400	Total liabilities...........	126,000
Building	150,000	**Shareholders' equity**	
Less Accum. deprec.	(3,750)	Capital stock	250,000
	146,250	Retained earnings	52,650
		Total	302,650
		Total liabilities &	
Total assets............	$428,650	**shareholders' equity** ...	$428,650

THE ARCADIA COMPANY Statement of Cash Flow	
Operating Activities	
Cash sales	$ 160,000
Payments for inventory	(144,000)
Cash wages	(20,000)
Interest payment	(3,600)
Cash flow from operations.	(7,600)
Investing Activities	
Purchase of building	(150,000)
Cash flow from investing	(150,000)
Financing Activities	
Sale of capital stock	250,000
Bank loan.	120,000
Cash flow from financing	370,000
Cash, beginning	-0-
Cash, ending	212,400
Change in cash.	$212,400

3. ROS = 52,650 / 160,000 = 32.9%
    ROA = (52,650 + 3600) / 428,650 = 13.1%
    ROE = 52,650 / 302,650 = 17.4%

4. ROE = 52,650/160,000 × 160,000/428,650 × 428,650/302,650
         = 0.329 × 0.373 × 1.42 = 17.4%

When you complete this chapter you should be able to:

1. Interpret a statement of cash flow to explain a company's financing and investing strategies.

2. Prepare a statement of cash flow using the indirect method.

3. Interpret the components of net income to evaluate a company's sustainable earnings.

4. Explain the difference between EBITDA, free cash flow, and discretionary cash flow.

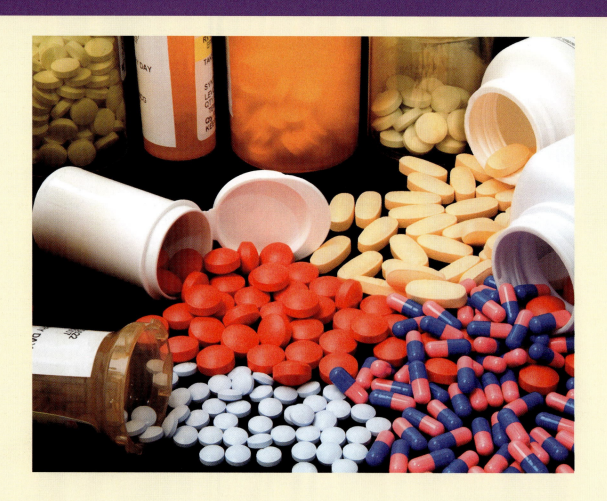

Measuring Performance: Cash Flow and Net Income

The **Bristol-Myers Squibb Company** was formed in 1989 with the merger of pharmaceutical companies Bristol-Myers Company and the Squibb Corporation. The company has as its mission "to discover, develop and deliver innovative medicines that help patients prevail over serious diseases." To that end, the company manufactures prescription pharmaceuticals in several therapeutic areas, including cancer (YERVOY), cardiovascular disease (PLAVIX), and diabetes (ONGLYZA). The company has long been rumored to be an acquisition target for other large pharmaceutical companies, such as **Novartis AG** and **Eli Lilly**.

BRISTOL-MYERS SQUIBB COMPANY

In 2002, Bristol-Myers Squibb agreed to pay $150 million to the U.S. Department of Justice and the U.S. Securities and Exchange Commission in settlement of a lawsuit alleging improper recording of $2.5 billion in revenue between 1999 and 2001. According to the government allegation, the company engaged in "channel stuffing" in order to report higher product sales on its income statement, presumably to meet Wall Street earnings' expectations. Channel stuffing refers to the practice of shipping unordered goods to retailers, usually with a guarantee to allow the retailers to return any unsold merchandise. When products are physically small but very expensive, like pharmaceuticals, this practice can lead to recording a boost to profits earlier than would otherwise occur, because the retailer would seldom return the goods.

Bristol-Myers Squibb apparently felt it was more important to report strong results on its income statement than it was to follow the "rules of the game." For those reading the financial statements, however, there was one telltale sign that something was suspect with the company's reported results: While the company was reporting inflated earnings on the unordered product it shipped to its customers, its operating cash flow failed to keep pace with the increase in sales. The end-user pharmacies had yet to pay for the unordered goods. So where would this information appear in the company's financial statements?

In addition to the income statement that included the inflated sales, Bristol-Myers Squibb was also required to provide a statement of cash flow to its shareholders. This statement includes a reconciliation of a firm's reported net income and its corresponding cash flow from operations. In 2001, the year prior to the alleged channel stuffing, Bristol-Myers reported net earnings in excess of $2 billion and cash flow from operations in excess of $5 billion. The company had in prior years consistently reported cash flow from operations that equaled or exceeded its reported net income. This changed in 2002, however, when the company reported net income in excess of $2 billion, but cash flow from operations of less than $1 billion. This shift in trend led the astute users of Bristol-Myers financial reports to search for the cause.

In this chapter, we examine how firm performance is measured. Both the income statement and the statement of cash flow contain important indicators of a company's operating performance. Public companies like Bristol-Myers Squibb are required to include both financial statements in their filings with the U.S. Securities and Exchange Commission and in their annual report to shareholders. To be fully informed, financial statement users must understand the information that each statement conveys about a company's operating performance.

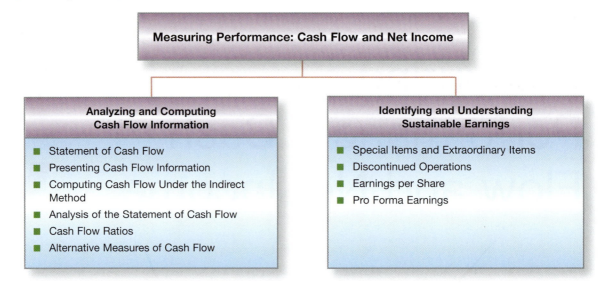

ANALYZING AND COMPUTING CASH FLOW INFORMATION

Recall from Chapter 2 that the accounting process can be thought of as beginning with one balance sheet and ending with another. The other financial statements, particularly the income statement, the statement of cash flow and the statement of shareholders' equity, are designed to summarize various aspects of a company's performance that occur *during* that period of time. In the minds of most investment professionals, lenders, and managers, the two most important measures of a firm's performance come directly from these two statements—its operating cash flow and its net income. In this chapter, we explore these two measures in greater detail, examining their similarities and differences, and how they are interrelated. We will see that the accrual accounting process imbeds estimates of future cash flow into current net income, and as a consequence, that current period net income is often a very good predictor of future operating cash flow.

We begin this chapter by considering the various ways that cash flow data can be presented. We then consider how cash flow information can be extracted from balance sheets and income statements. Finally, we consider the important concept of sustainable earnings and the various alternative measures of cash flow used by investment professionals.

Statement of Cash Flow

The purpose of the statement of cash flow is to provide a user of the financial statements with important information about how the company manages its cash. It does this by summarizing a firm's inflows and outflows of cash by segmenting into three activity categories:

- Cash flow from operating activities
- Cash flow from investing activities
- Cash flow from financing activities

These three categories represent the three key activities undertaken by all businesses—providing a good or service (operating activities), obtaining the assets necessary to provide a good or service (investing activities), and financing both the basic operations of a business and the investment in assets required to produce a product or provide a service (financing activities). Consider these three basic activities with a simple illustration of a pizza delivery business. Before the business can start delivering pizzas, it must first obtain the necessary funds to buy a delivery van. Taking out a loan at a bank is an example of a financing activity. When the borrowed cash is used to buy the van, this would represent an investing activity. Having purchased the van, the business can then begin using it to make deliveries and collecting cash from customers, an operating activity. Of course most businesses are not this simple, but no matter how complex a business becomes each of its financial statements can be reflected in these three activities.

Analyzing and understanding the contents of the statement of cash flow provide financial statement users with critical insights about a company's operating, investing, and financing strategies. Exhibit 3.1, for example, provides an illustration of a typical statement of cash flow. This exhibit reveals that the **cash flow from operations** represents the aggregate of the cash received from the sale of goods and services less the cash spent on operating expenses. The **cash flow from investing**, on the other hand, is the aggregate of the cash received from the sale of investments, property and equipment, and intangible assets less the cash spent to acquire these various types of assets. Finally, the **cash flow from financing** represents the aggregate of the cash received from the sale of debt and equity securities less the cash paid to retire debt, repurchase equity securities, or pay dividends to shareholders.

The statement of cash flow can be presented in two alternative formats—the direct and indirect method—to which we now turn.

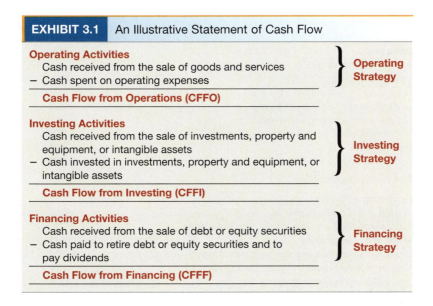

EXHIBIT 3.1 An Illustrative Statement of Cash Flow

Operating Activities
  Cash received from the sale of goods and services
 − Cash spent on operating expenses   } Operating Strategy
  Cash Flow from Operations (CFFO)

Investing Activities
  Cash received from the sale of investments, property and
  equipment, or intangible assets
 − Cash invested in investments, property and equipment, or
  intangible assets   } Investing Strategy
  Cash Flow from Investing (CFFI)

Financing Activities
  Cash received from the sale of debt or equity securities
 − Cash paid to retire debt or equity securities and to
  pay dividends   } Financing Strategy
  Cash Flow from Financing (CFFF)

Presenting Cash Flow Information

There are two formats available under GAAP to present the statement of cash flow—the direct method format and the indirect method format. Note that these approaches differ only in how the cash flow from operations detail is presented. The cash flow from investing and the cash flow from financing are identical under the two formats.

As we will see, because the indirect format provides information critical to understanding why net income differs from cash actually received, GAAP requires that firms choosing to use the direct method format also provide the indirect format as a supplemental disclosure. Therefore, the practical reality is that the vast majority of publicly held companies (about 99 percent) utilize solely the indirect method format. Because of this we will principally focus our discussion on this format. Appendix 3A at the end of this chapter illustrates how to construct a **direct method** statement of cash flow for those interested. You will see that under the direct method statement of cash flow, cash flow from operations is computed directly from the company's cash transactions, the critical difference between the two methods.

Under the **indirect method** a company computes its cash flow from operations by making various adjustments to convert its accrual-based net income to its cash flow from operations. While this at first may seem odd, the objective of this approach is to provide the user of the statement with critical information about why the firm's net income did or did not translate into cash generation. By starting with net income and ending with a cash flow figure, the detail in between is a valuable source of information for analysis. Exhibit 3.2 presents an indirect method statement of cash flow for **Texas Instruments, Inc. (TI)**.

Exhibit 3.2 reveals that TI's cash flow from operations begins with the company's 2011 net income of $2,236 million, and then reports the various adjustments needed to convert its net income under the accrual basis of accounting to its cash flow from operations of $3,256 million. Thus, these accrual accounting adjustments illustrate how it is possible for a company like TI to report cash flows from operating activities almost 50% larger than earnings. TI's statement of cash flow reveals that the largest positive adjustments to its net income from operations were depreciation expense ($904 million), stock-based compensation ($269 million), amortization of intangible assets ($111 million), and the change in accounts receivable ($112 million).

EXHIBIT 3.2	Illustration of the Indirect Method for Statement of Cash Flow

TEXAS INSTRUMENTS INC.
Consolidated Statement of Cash Flow

For Fiscal Years Ending December 31 [millions of dollars]	2011	2010	2009
Cash flow from operating activities			
Net income	$2,236	$3,228	$1,470
Adjustments to net income:			
Depreciation	904	865	877
Stock-based compensation	269	190	186
Amortization of acquisition-related intangibles.	111	48	48
Gain on sales of assets and divestiture	(5)	(144)	—
Deferred income taxes	(119)	(188)	146
Increase (decrease) from changes in:			
Accounts receivable	112	(231)	(364)
Inventories.	(17)	(304)	177
Prepaid expenses and other current assets	(29)	(8)	115
Accounts payable and accrued expenses	2	57	5
Accrued compensation.	(77)	246	(38)
Income taxes payable	(85)	(19)	87
Other	(46)	80	(66)
Net cash provided by operating activities	3,256	3,820	2,643
Cash flow from investing activities			
Additions to property, plant and equipment.	(816)	(1,199)	(753)
Proceeds from insurance recovery, asset sales and divestiture.	16	148	—
Purchases of short-term investments.	(3,653)	(2,510)	(2,273)
Sales, redemptions and maturities of short-term investments.	3,555	2,564	2,030
Purchases of long-term investments	(6)	(8)	(9)
Redemptions and sales of long-term investments.	157	147	64
Business acquisitions:			
Property, plant and equipment	(865)	(200)	(3)
Inventories.	(225)	(14)	(4)
Other.	(4,335)	15	(148)
Business acquisitions, net of cash acquired	(5,425)	(199)	(155)
Net cash used in investing activities.	(6,172)	(1,057)	(1,096)
Cash flow from financing activities			
Proceeds from issuance of long-term debt	4,697	—	—
Issuance costs for long-term debt	(12)	—	—
Repayment of commercial paper borrowings	(200)	—	—
Dividends paid	(644)	(592)	(567)
Sales and other common stock transactions.	690	407	109
Excess tax benefit from share-based payments	31	13	1
Stock repurchases	(1,973)	(2,454)	(954)
Net cash provided by (used in) financing activities.	2,589	(2,626)	(1,411)
Net (decrease) increase in cash and cash equivalents	(327)	137	136
Cash and cash equivalents at beginning of year	1,319	1,182	1,046
Cash and cash equivalents at end of year.	$ 992	$1,319	$1,182

TI's statement of cash flow also reveals the company's investing and financing strategies. In 2011, for example, the company used its available cash flow to acquire property, plant and equipment ($816 million), and a significant amount for various acquisitions of other businesses ($5,425 million). Financing for these capital investments came principally from the aforementioned cash generated from operations ($3,256 million) and the net issuance of long-term debt ($4,697 million). Interestingly the company was also an active buyer of its own stock in 2011, with stock repurchases totaling $1,973 million. Notice that the sum of TI's operating cash flow ($3,256 million) plus its financing cash flow ($2,589 million) was insufficient to cover its net capital investment of $6,172 million in 2011, forcing the company to draw down on its existing cash balance by a net $327 million.

Computing Cash Flow Under the Indirect Method

The statement of cash flow is a required corporate disclosure for public companies in their annual (10-K) and quarterly (10-Q) reports to shareholders filed with the U.S. Securities and Exchange Commission. There are many instances, however, where an important skill for investors, investment professionals, and managers to have is the ability to estimate a company's cash flow using only those statements that are more routinely available, namely income statements and balance sheets. (This skill is also important in the construction of forecasted financial statements, which are discussed in Chapters 4 and 12.)

In this section, we illustrate how to prepare an indirect method statement of cash flow using only two balance sheets and an income statement. To begin, it is important to revisit exactly what we are attempting to accomplish with the statement of cash flow. This statement details a firm's cash flow activity during a given fiscal period. It reveals how and why the cash balance on the balance sheet increased or decreased from the beginning of the period to the end of the period (i.e., the change in cash). The principal events that cause a firm's cash balance to change are summarized. These include the sale of goods, the purchase of inventory, the payment of operating expenses, the payment of dividends, the purchase or sale of property and equipment, and the sale or repurchase of stock, among other things. Importantly, you should recognize that all of the financial events that result in a change in a company's cash account are reported in some form on the firm's income statement or balance sheet. And, as a consequence, a statement of cash flow can be prepared using only a company's income statement and the changes in its balance sheet accounts. This can be seen by reference to the balance sheet equation:

$$\text{Assets (A)} = \text{Liabilities (L)} + \text{Shareholders' Equity (SE)} \qquad (1)$$

Separation and expansion of a firm's assets into its cash assets (Cash) and its noncash assets (NCA):

$$\text{Cash} + \text{NCA} = \text{L} + \text{SE} \qquad (2)$$

And, rewriting the balance sheet equation as the difference (Δ) between two balance sheets yields:

$$\Delta\text{Cash} + \Delta\text{NCA} = \Delta\text{L} + \Delta\text{SE} \qquad (3)$$

Finally, rearranging the components of the balance sheet equation shows that the change in cash, the ultimate objective of the statement of cash flow, can be computed from the change in all of the other balance sheet accounts:

$$\Delta\text{Cash} = \Delta\text{L} - \Delta\text{NCA} + \Delta\text{SE} \qquad (4)$$

Five Steps to Cash Flow.   Since you are already familiar with the financial affairs of the Russian River Valley Winery from Chapter 2, we will use this data for purposes of illustrating an approach for generating cash flow data from balance sheets and income statements. The process involves five steps, resulting in the preparation of an indirect method statement of cash flow. Our goal is to summarize the observed balance sheet change in cash for the company, a $3,942 decrease, using the required format under the indirect method. The approach we will use to get there, however, begins by focusing initially only on the balance sheet, and then proceeds to integrate a business's income statement through a series of systematic adjustments to a preliminary statement of cash flow derived solely from balance sheet data. Exhibit 3.3 presents the beginning of year (column 1) and end of year (column 2) balance sheets for the Russian River Valley Winery.

Step One: Calculate the change in all balance sheet accounts

Using just the beginning and ending balance sheets (see Columns 1 and 2 in Exhibit 3.3), calculate the change in each balance sheet account by subtracting the beginning balance sheet amount from the ending amount. The results of this step for Russian River Valley are presented in Column 3 of Exhibit 3.3. To simplify this step, the change in the property, plant, and equipment accounts are calculated as an aggregate amount after deducting any accumulated depreciation (on a net-of-accumulated-depreciation basis).

To verify the accuracy of the Step One calculations, simply compare the sum of the changes in the asset accounts ($153) to the sum of the changes in the liability and shareholders' equity accounts ($153). These totals must be equal. If the totals are not equal, it indicates the presence of a subtraction error that must be identified and corrected before progressing to Step Two.

Again to reemphasize, an important figure identified during Step One is the final result of the statement of cash flow, namely the change in the cash account. The bolded area in Exhibit 3.3 reveals that the cash account of the Russian River Valley Winery declined by $3,932 from the beginning of the year to the end of the year. Hence, all of the various cash inflows and outflows for the winery must aggregate to this figure.

EXHIBIT 3.3	Preparing a Statement of Cash Flow: The Indirect Method

RUSSIAN RIVER VALLEY WINERY, INC.
Balance Sheet

($ thousands)	(1) Beginning of Year 1	(2) End of Year 1	(3) Change For Year	(4) Cash Flow Classification
Current assets				
Cash.	**$ 4,700**	**$ 768**	**$(3,932)**	**Net cash flow**
Accounts receivable.	0	800	800	Operating
Inventory.	0	60	60	Operating
Total current assets	4,700	1,628		
Noncurrent assets				
Equipment	0	3,500		
Buildings.	2,000	2,000		
Land	4,000	4,000		
	6,000	9,500		
Accumulated depreciation	0	(225)		
Property, plant & equipment, net	6,000	9,275	3,275	Investing/Operating
Intangible assets, net	100	50	(50)	Investing/Operating
Total assets.	**$10,800**	**$10,953**	**$ 153**	
Current liabilities				
Accounts payable.	$ 0	$ 80	$ 80	Operating
Taxes payable.	0	96	96	Operating
Notes payable, current.	0	480	480	Financing
Total current liabilities.	0	656		
Notes payable, noncurrent.	4,800	3,840	(960)	Financing
Shareholders' equity				
Common stock, $1 par.	6,000	6,400	400	Financing
Retained earnings	0	57	57	Financing/Operating
Shareholders' equity	**6,000**	**6,457**		
Liabilities & shareholders' equity	**$10,800**	**$10,953**	**$ 153**	

Step Two: Classify each account into one of the three cash flow categories

This step involves identifying the appropriate cash-flow activity category—operating, investing, or financing—for each balance sheet account, and this is illustrated in Column 4 of Exhibit 3.3. Although measuring the change in the balance sheet accounts in Step 1 is straightforward, there can sometimes be confusion over the correct activity classification for some of the balance sheet accounts in Step 2. Learning the proper classifications often comes with some thought and some practice. Accounts receivable, inventory, accounts payable and taxes payable are all easily identified as operating activity items because they are associated with the day-to-day operations of a business. Changes in the notes payable (current and noncurrent) and common stock accounts, on the other hand, are clearly financing activity items because they are associated with raising capital to finance a business. Changes in net property, plant and equipment (PPE), however, can be both an investing activity item

---

In Practice 3.1 *Balance Sheet Caption: A Glimpse of a Sample of Fortune 1000 Companies*   The following table identifies the caption used by a sample of 600 Fortune 1000 companies on their balance sheets to describe the cash account. The overwhelming majority of firms utilize the caption "cash and cash equivalents."

Balance Sheet Captions	Number	Percentage
Cash	22	3.7
Cash and cash equivalents	528	88.0
Cash and equivalents.	34	5.6
Cash combined with marketable securities.	13	2.2
Other.	3	0.5
Total	600	100.0

Source: Accounting Trends & Techniques

and an operating activity item. Purchases and sales of PPE are associated with the capital investment needed to run a business, and thus, are an investing activity item; but, the depreciation expense associated with PPE is an operating activity item since the depreciation of PPE is deducted as an operating expense in the calculation of accrual net income. Similarly, changes in intangible assets can be both an investing activity item and an operating activity item because the acquisition or sale of intangibles is an investment in the business, whereas the amortization of intangibles is an operating expense deducted in the calculation of accrual net income, and hence, an operating activity item. Finally, changes in retained earnings can be both an operating activity item and a financing activity item because retained earnings is increased by net income, an operating activity item, but decreased by the payment of dividends, a transaction with shareholders that is classifiable as a financing activity item.

As a general rule, the following cash flow activity classifications apply, although exceptions will exist:

Balance Sheet Account	Cash Flow Activity Category
Current assets	Operating
Noncurrent assets	Investing/Operating
Current liabilities.	Operating
Noncurrent liabilities.	Financing
Capital stock	Financing
Retained earnings	Operating/Financing

Examples of exceptions to the above general activity classifications include the following:

■ Marketable securities, a current asset, are an investing activity item.

■ Current maturities of long-term debt, a current liability, are a financing activity item.

■ Employee pension obligations, a noncurrent liability, are an operating activity item.

Step Three: Prepare a preliminary statement of cash flow

Having completed Steps One and Two, you are now ready to build a preliminary statement of cash flow using the calculated increases or decreases in the various balance sheet accounts from Step One and the identified activity classifications from Step Two. The preliminary statement of cash flow for the Russian River Valley Winery, using the values from Column 3 of Exhibit 3.3 and the cash flow activity categories from Column 4, is presented in Exhibit 3.4.

EXHIBIT 3.4	An Illustration of a Preliminary Statement of Cash Flow: Balance Sheet Account Changes

RUSSIAN RIVER VALLEY WINERY, INC. Preliminary Statement of Cash Flow	
($ thousands)	Year 1
Operating activities	
Retained earnings	$ 57
Accounts receivable.	(800)
Inventory	(60)
Accounts payable	80
Taxes payable	96
Preliminary CFFO.	(627)
Investing activities	
Property, plant & equipment (net)	(3,275)
Intangible assets (net)	50
Preliminary CFFI.	(3,225)
Financing activities	
Notes payable, current.	480
Notes payable, noncurrent	(960)
Common stock	400
Preliminary CFFF	(80)
Change in cash (from balance sheet).	$(3,932)

Since a statement of cash flow measures the inflows and outflows of cash for a business, it is important to note that the sign of the asset account changes (but not the liabilities or shareholders' equity accounts) calculated in Step One must be reversed for purposes of preparing the preliminary statement of cash flow in Exhibit 3.4. This can be seen in equation (4) above in which the change in noncash assets has a negative sign. For instance, Exhibit 3.3 shows that the change in accounts receivable was an increase of $800, whereas the change in intangible assets was a decrease of $50. When preparing the indirect method cash flow statement, an $800 increase in accounts receivables represents a subtraction from net income (a cash outflow), and a decline in intangible assets of $50 represents an addition to net income (a cash inflow), to arrive at the cash flow from operations. To understand why an increase in accounts receivable must be subtracted from net income to arrive at operating cash flow, you first must recognize that net income is included in its entirety (i.e., $57 of retained earnings), but it doesn't all represent the actual cash received by the company. Assume that a $2,000 sale of inventory is paid for by the customer with $1,200 in cash and the remaining $800 recorded as an increase in accounts receivable. In this example, net income would have increased by $2,000 but cash by only $1,200. Therefore, net income, relative to cash, was overstated—we must therefore reduce net income by the $800 increase in accounts receivable to yield the correct cash flow from operations. Similar logic explains why it is necessary to add back the decrease in intangible assets to net income to arrive at the correct cash flow from operations. Intangible assets were reduced by amortizing the cost of the asset by $50. This $50 expense reduced net income; however, no cash outflow was involved. Therefore, it is necessary to add $50 back to net income to yield the correct change in cash. Hence, when preparing the preliminary statement of cash flow in Step Three, it is important to remember to reverse the sign of the change values for the asset accounts. This reversal in sign is unnecessary for the liability and shareholders' equity accounts as can be seen from equation (4) above.

Exhibit 3.4 presents the preliminary statement of cash flow for the Russian River Valley Winery. This preliminary statement suggests that the firm's cash flow from operating activities (CFFO) for the period was negative $627, the cash flow from investing activities (CFFI) was negative $3,225, and the cash flow from financing activities (CFFF) negative $80. As required, the cash inflows and outflows aggregate to the change in the cash account from the balance sheet of a decrease of $3,932.

Step Four: Integrate the income statement data

To this point we have used the balance sheet exclusively to provide the needed inputs to our statement of cash flow. For most businesses, however, cash flow will be generated by the firm's ongoing operations and not just by various events affecting the balance sheet accounts. Hence, it is now appropriate to introduce the operations-related data found on the winery's income statement (see Exhibit 3.5).

EXHIBIT 3.5	Income Statement

RUSSIAN RIVER VALLEY WINERY, INC.
Income Statement

($ thousands)	Year 1
Revenue	$1,900
Cost of goods sold	380
Gross profit	1,520
Operating expenses	
Wages & salaries	100
Selling, general & administrative	300
Depreciation	225
Amortization	50
Total operating expenses	675
Operating income	845
Interest expense	288
Income before income taxes	557
Income tax expense	240
Net income	$ 317

In this step, we will accomplish two important actions involving our preliminary statement of cash flow in Exhibit 3.4. First, we will replace the change in retained earnings from the balance sheet with net income from the income statement. In the event that the change in retained earnings does not equal net income, usually this difference represents cash dividends paid to shareholders. For the Russian River Valley Winery, net income is $317 and the change in retained earnings is $57. Thus, it is necessary to gross up the change in retained earnings by $260 to equal the current net income ($57 + $260 = $317) under the operating activities section; and, to keep the statement of cash flow in balance with the decrease in cash of $3,932, insert the cash outflow for dividends ($260) under the financing activities section.

Second, we will adjust Russian River Valley's net income for any **noncash expenses** such as the depreciation of plant and equipment and the amortization of intangibles that were deducted in the process of calculating the firm's accrual net income. These noncash expenses must be added back to net income in the operating activities section to correctly measure the firm's operating cash flow. Without such adjustments we would be understating actual operating cash flow. However, to keep the preliminary statement of cash flow in balance with the check figure of a decrease in cash of $3,932, it is also necessary to subtract equivalent amounts in the investing activities section, where the changes in PPE and intangibles currently reside.

> Depreciation expense and amortization expense are called **noncash expenses** because these expenses do not involve any current-period cash outflow. Depreciation expense, for example, represents the allocation of the purchase price of plant and equipment over the many periods that these assets produce revenues for a business. The matching concept requires that the cost of plant and equipment be matched with the revenues produced by these assets, and this is accomplished on the income statement by the inclusion of the periodic depreciation expense.

To summarize, the adjustments to the Russian River Valley Winery preliminary statement of cash flow in Exhibit 3.4 are as follows:

1. Net income of $317 replaces the change in retained earnings of $57 in the operating activities section. This action added $260 to the CFFO. To keep the statement of cash flow in balance with the check figure of negative $3,932 (the decrease in cash), it is necessary to subtract $260 elsewhere on the statement. Since retained earnings is calculated as follows:

> Retained earnings (beginning)
> + Net income for the period
> − Dividends paid
> ──────────────────────────
> Retained earnings (ending)

the outflow of $260 is reflected as a cash dividend paid to shareholders under the financing activities section.

2. Depreciation expense of $225, a noncash deduction from net income, is added back to net income to avoid understating the cash flow from operations. However, to keep the statement of cash flow in balance with the change in cash of negative $3,932, a similar amount must be subtracted from property and equipment under the investing activities section.

3. Amortization expense of $50, another noncash deduction from net income, is added back to net income to avoid understating the cash flow from operations. To insure that the statement is in balance with the check figure of negative $3,932, an equivalent amount is subtracted from intangible assets under the investing activities section.

The results of these adjustments are displayed in Exhibit 3.6, which presents the final statement of cash flow for the Russian River Valley Winery. Note that the winery's statement of cash flow remains in balance with the change in the cash account of negative $3,932 after the three adjustments. This result is possible because whatever amount was added to (or subtracted from) net income under the CFFO, an equal amount was subtracted from (or added to) CFFI or CFFF.

In Practice 3.2 *Method of Reporting the Cash Flow from Operations: A Glimpse of a Sample of Fortune 1000 Companies* The following table identifies the method of reporting the cash flow from operations as used by a sample of 600 Fortune 1000 companies. Over 98 percent of all companies surveyed used the indirect method:

Method of Reporting	Number	Percentage
Indirect method	592	98.7
Direct method.........	8	1.3
Total	600	100.0

Source: Accounting Trends & Techniques

EXHIBIT 3.6	Statement of Cash Flow: Indirect Method

RUSSIAN RIVER VALLEY WINERY, INC.
Statement of Cash Flow

($ thousands)	Year 1
Operating activities	
Net income	$ 317
Depreciation	225
Amortization	50
(Increase) in accounts receivable	(800)
(Increase) decrease in inventory	(60)
Increase (decrease) in accounts payable	80
Increase (decrease) in taxes payable	96
Cash flow from operations	**(92)**
Investing activities	
Purchase of property, plant & equipment	(3,500)
Cash flow from investing	**(3,500)**
Financing activities	
Sale of common stock	400
Payment of notes payable (current)	(480)
Payment of cash dividends	(260)
Cash flow from financing	**(340)**
Change in cash (on balance sheet)	**(3,932)**
Beg. cash	4,700
End. cash	$ 768

Step Five: Remove nonrecurring and/or nonoperating effects from net income

To provide the most useful cash flow data, a final step is required: Make any appropriate adjustments to the CFFO to calculate the recurring or sustainable CFFO. As noted above, the CFFO should include only the cash flow from operating activities. Recall also that the operating activities section of the indirect format of the statement of cash flow is a reconciliation of net income to CFFO. That is, the format requires the section begins with net income and ends with CFFO. Consequently, to calculate the CFFO of a business, it is necessary to review a company's income statement to identify and remove the financial effects of any nonoperating and/or nonrecurring transactions.[1]

To illustrate this point, assume that the Russian River Valley Winery sold property and equipment during the year at a loss of $25 and that the loss was included in its net income. This event is an investing activity and therefore properly belongs under CFFI. To correctly calculate the winery's CFFO, it is necessary to remove this loss from net income in the operating activity section and to add it to property and equipment under the investing activities section. These actions allow us to correctly measure the company's CFFO, as well as to correctly assess its cash flow for property and equipment. We will have more to say about this type of operating cash flow adjustment in subsequent chapters.

Exhibit 3.6 presents the final indirect method statement of cash flow for Russian River Valley and includes not only the adjustments from Step Four, but also, if needed, any adjustments to remove any nonoperating or nonrecurring gains and losses from the CFFO (Step 5). Russian River Valley's cash flow statement in Exhibit 3.6 using the indirect method reveals that the cash flow from operating activities is negative $92, the cash flow from investing activities is negative $3,500, and the cash flow from financing activities is negative $340. The resulting net cash flow of negative $3,932 exactly equals the decrease in cash on the balance sheet of $3,932, as required.

---

[1] An exception to this general rule is the treatment of interest expense, which many investment professionals view as a financing activity item. Interest payments are required to be included in CFFO (under U.S. GAAP). Another example of a noncash/nonoperating item that will need to be removed from net income when calculating the CFFO is any "income (loss) from equity investments." We will have more to say about this adjustment and the accounting for equity investments in Chapter 8.

The following illustration summarizes the five-step process to preparing an indirect method statement of cash flow:

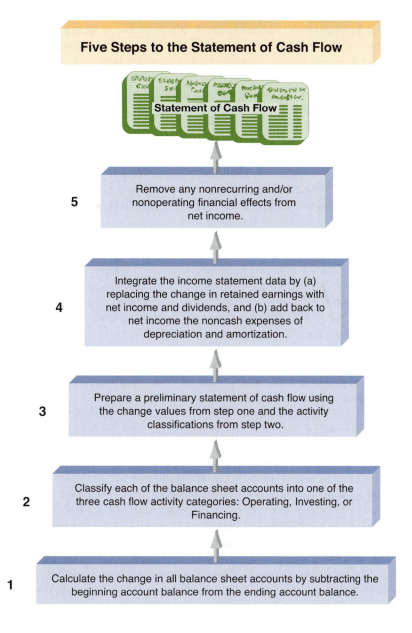

Five Steps to the Statement of Cash Flow

Statement of Cash Flow

5 — Remove any nonrecurring and/or nonoperating financial effects from net income.

4 — Integrate the income statement data by (a) replacing the change in retained earnings with net income and dividends, and (b) add back to net income the noncash expenses of depreciation and amortization.

3 — Prepare a preliminary statement of cash flow using the change values from step one and the activity classifications from step two.

2 — Classify each of the balance sheet accounts into one of the three cash flow activity categories: Operating, Investing, or Financing.

1 — Calculate the change in all balance sheet accounts by subtracting the beginning account balance from the ending account balance.

Analysis of the Statement of Cash Flow

Like the income statement, the statement of cash flow portrays another aspect of a business's performance over a period of time. The major difference between these two financial statements concerns how "performance" is defined. The income statement defines performance in terms of a business's accrual net income, where earned revenues are matched against the expenses associated with generating that revenue whether or not associated with cash. The statement of cash flow, by contrast, defines performance in terms of a business's actual operating cash flow, with the statement showing a company's sources and uses of cash. Rather than debating which statement is more important, it is better to understand what each statement tells us and how the statements complement each other.

As mentioned earlier in the chapter, the statement of cash flow can be prepared in two alternate formats, the indirect method as shown in Exhibit 3.6, and the direct method, as previously shown in Exhibit 2.5. Notice that each format provides identical totals for each of the three sections of the statement. The only difference between the two formats is in the presentation of the cash flow data in the operating activities section. As can be seen in Exhibit 2.5, the direct method format is prepared directly from the cash account and simply displays the sources and uses of operating cash flows. The indirect method, by contrast, comes to the same total operating cash flow in an indirect approach by starting with net income and then adjusting net income for the various noncash effects included in the measurement of net income under the accrual method. Net income, as we have seen, is computed by matching the earned revenues of a business, whether received in cash or not, with the related business expenses, regardless of whether those expenses have been paid in cash or not. Quite often, the revenues and expenses are recognized on a business's income statement in a different period than the corresponding cash inflow or outflow associated with those revenues and expenses. Consequently, it is necessary to adjust net income for these timing differences when calculating a business's operating cash flow using the indirect approach. For this reason the operating activities section of the statement of cash flow is often referred to as a "reconciliation between net income and changes in cash."

By partitioning a business's cash flow into the three categories of operating, investing, and financing activities, the statement of cash flow tells the reader much more than just how much its cash balance increased or decreased during the period; it also provides an explanation as to *why*. For instance, the statement of cash flow enables a financial statement user to understand whether a business's cash balance increased because the cash was earned from operations or because of an increase in bank borrowings. Similarly, statement users need to understand whether cash declined as a consequence of capital investments in new productive capacity or because the business is losing money from its operations. A review of each line in the statement of cash flow facilitates this type of understanding.

Most statement users agree that the most important component of the statement of cash flow is the cash flow from operating activities. This figure reflects the lifeblood of a company and is the principal source of financing for long-term survival. Regardless of the industry or life-stage of a business, it is always better for a company to generate a positive cash flow from operations. It should be noted, however, that many early-stage companies will show negative operating cash flow as a result of such normal business activities as building up inventory to service a growing customer base, or from significant research and development as it internally builds its product base.

While it is unambiguous that a business's cash flow from operating activities is better to be positive, the same cannot be said of the other two activity categories, investing and financing. A negative balance in the cash flow from investing activities, for example, will result when a firm spends more cash to purchase new equipment than it receives from the sale of old equipment. For many growth-oriented companies, a negative cash flow from investing activities is the norm, since investing in new productive capacity will ultimately result in future positive operating cash inflows. Most financial statement users expect to see a negative cash flow from investing activities since it indicates that a firm is maintaining itself as a going concern. In fact, a positive cash flow from investing activities may in some instances be a sign of concern since it may indicate that a business is liquidating its long-term, revenue-producing assets like plant and equipment.

Similar to the cash flows from investing activities, one cannot unambiguously say whether a positive or negative balance in financing activities is good or bad. A negative cash flow from financing activities will result when a company repays its loans and pays dividends to its shareholders, two activities that are usually considered positive by shareholders. A positive balance, on the other hand, could result from new business financing, perhaps from additional loans or the sale of capital stock. These activities may be necessary to finance new business growth, especially if a company's cash flow from operating activities is insufficient to finance this growth, which is often the case for early-stage companies.

As this discussion implies, the statement of cash flow provides a great deal of important information, but it also requires the user to have a solid understanding of what the statement is reporting. At the simplest level, the statement of cash flow merely tells the reader how much the company's cash balance changed during the period, reconciling the beginning and ending cash balances appearing on a company's balance sheet. At a more sophisticated level, the statement reveals just where a business's cash came from and how it was used. Such information is critical to those desiring to understand in greater detail how the company is being managed, and further, whether there are liquidity and solvency risks that might be of concern.

Exhibit 3.7 provides a summary of the typical sources and uses of cash in each of the three cash flow categories as a business progresses through its life cycle from a young start-up, through maturity, and later decline. As noted above, it is always the case that the cash flow from operating activities should be positive; however, for start-up companies, this is rarely the case. Likewise for start-up businesses, the cash flow from investing activities is often negative as the firm uses its available cash to invest in its future. As a firm matures, this category of cash flow tends to even out, as the firm's investing activities are generally for replacement of assets rather than growth. In the later, declining stage of a firm, the cash flow from investing may be positive as the firm sells off its assets as it exits certain markets. Finally, the cash flow from financing activities is likely to be positive for young companies as they require external financing to fund their growth. As the firm matures, its cash flow from financing tends to stabilize as the firm repays debt and begins paying dividends. Finally, in the declining stage, a firm is less likely to secure external financing and more likely to repay obligations or liquidate capital to retain its equity investors, leading to a negative cash flow from financing activities.

EXHIBIT 3.7	Cash Flow and a Company's Life Cycle		
Activity Section of the Statement of Cash Flow	**Life Cycle of the Firm**		
	Young/Start-Up	**Mature**	**Declining**
Operating	Likely negative	Likely positive	Uncertain
Investing.	Likely negative	Uncertain, but likely negative	Likely positive
Financing	Likely positive	Uncertain, but likely negative	Likely negative

The opening vignette to this chapter observed that an analysis of the statement of cash flow could have alerted a financial statement user about the problems at Bristol-Myers Squibb. The practice of "channel stuffing," in which large amounts of unordered goods are sent to retailers, is illustrated in the spreadsheet below. Assume for this illustration a company begins period 1 with a simple balance sheet consisting of only $1,000 of cash and $800 of inventory. Towards the end of period 1 the company ships those unordered products to a retailer, with an assumed selling price of $1,500, with later payment by the retailer in period 2.

	Beg. Bal.	(1)	(2)	Period 1	(3)	Period 2
Financial Statement Effects **Channel Stuffing**						
Cash.	1,000			1,000	1,500	2,500
Account Receivable		1,500		1,500	(1,500)	—
Inventory.	800		(800)	—		—
Total Assets	1,800			2,500		2,500
Total Liabilities	—			—		-
Common Stock	1,800			1,800		1,800
Retained Earnings				700		700
Sales		1,500				
Cost of Goods Sold			(800)			
Total Shareholders' Equity	—			2,500		2,500

(1) Record sales of product sent to retailer in period 1
(2) Remove inventory value of product sent to retailer in period 1
(3) Customer pays receivable during period 2

When a company "stuffs its sales channel," it recognizes revenue for the shipped-but-unordered inventory, which in turn leads to an increase in net earnings; however, as can be seen in the spreadsheet, this leads to an increase in accounts receivable during period 1 but not an increase in cash, unless and until the sales channel is able to absorb the additional product, sell the product to the end user, and make payment (period 2). These financial effects would be revealed in the operating activities section of the statement of cash flow as an unusual spike in earnings without the receipt of cash.

Cash Flow Ratios

Investment professionals frequently use components of the statement of cash flow to compute financial ratios that help highlight certain aspects of a firm's operating performance that might otherwise be obscured from financial statement users. For example, the **operating funds ratio** indicates the portion of a business's earnings supported by operating cash flow and is calculated as follows:

$$\text{Operating funds ratio} = \frac{\text{Cash flow from operations}}{\text{Net income}}$$

This ratio frequently approximates one for most firms, although during a period of business expansion (contraction), the ratio may decrease (increase) to less (more) than one. The operating funds ratio is not meaningful for the Russian River Valley Winery since cash flow from operations is negative; however, for Texas Instruments, the ratio is 1.46 (see exhibit 3.2), indicating that Texas Instruments' operating cash flows are much greater than its net income.

Another cash-flow-based ratio is the **operating cash flow to current liabilities ratio**, which is calculated as follows:

$$\text{Operating cash flow to current liabilities ratio} = \frac{\text{Cash flow from operations}}{\text{Current liabilities}}$$

This ratio provides insights about a firm's liquidity, specifically the extent to which a company's current obligations can be satisfied by its operating cash flow. This ratio highlights the fact that business liquidity is available not only from a firm's existing liquid assets and its ability to borrow or refinance, but also from its ongoing operations.

A final important cash-flow-based ratio is the **cash conversion ratio**, calculated as follows:

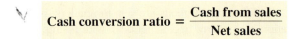

$$\text{Cash conversion ratio} = \frac{\text{Cash from sales}}{\text{Net sales}}$$

Cash from sales is calculated as net sales minus the increase in accounts receivable plus the increase in unearned (or deferred) revenue.

This ratio reveals the extent to which the sales reported on the income statement are converted into cash during the same accounting period. Like the operating funds ratio, this ratio typically approximates one, although smaller (or larger) ratio values are possible depending upon the growth (or decline) in a firm's accounts receivable and its deferred or unearned revenue. The cash conversion ratio for the Russian River Valley Winery is 0.58, indicating that the winery is projected to collect only $0.58 for each dollar of reported revenue during its first year of operations. (Can you verify the calculation of this ratio? Hint: Read Appendix 3A at the end of this chapter.)

Alternative Measures of Cash Flow

Although the statement of cash flow highlights the three cash flow measures of CFFO, CFFI, and CFFF, investment professionals often use other cash flow measures depending upon the purpose of their analysis. Three widely used alternatives are EBITDA, free cash flow, and discretionary cash flow.

EBITDA, or earnings before interest, taxes, depreciation and amortization (and other noncash charges, extraordinary items and nonrecurring charges), is often used as an alternative estimate of a firm's operating cash flow in those industries commonly identifiable as **capital intensive**—that is, in those industries characterized by large capital investments in property, plant and equipment and/or intangible assets. The financial statements of such firms typically include large noncash expenses for amortization and depreciation. As a consequence, the net income of companies in these industries may be substantially burdened by these charges, particularly as compared to companies in non-capital-intensive industries.

To make more effective performance comparisons between companies from different industries, and even within the same industry, some analysts rely on such metrics as EBITDA to level "the performance playing field." For example, to help analysts correctly evaluate the company's performance, **CSK Auto Corporation** reports both EBITDA and EBITDAR in its annual report. According to the company,

In Practice 3.3 *Average Dollar Amount of the Adjustments to Net Income when Computing the Cash Flow from Operations Using the Indirect Method Format.* The largest adjustment to net income is the depreciation and amortization expense, which averaged 83 percent of net income.

Operating activities (in millions)	
Net income.	$171.9
Depreciation and amortization	142.7
Gain on sale of assets	(12.8)
Earnings from subsidiaries.	(2.3)
Funds from operations—other	59.8
Increase in accounts receivable.	(28.8)
Increase in inventory	(56.8)
Increase in accounts payable.	18.4
Increase in taxes payable.	2.2
Sources of funds—other	16.9
Cash flow from operations.	$311.2

Source: Standard & Poor's Compustat, based on 6,316 firms reporting cash flow from operations.

> While EBITDA is not intended to represent cash flow from operations as defined by GAAP, it is included herein because we believe it is a meaningful measure which provides additional information with respect to our ability to meet our future debt service, capital expenditure and working capital requirements. EBITDAR, on the other hand, represents EBITDA plus operating lease rental expense. Because the proportion of stores leased versus owned varies among industry competitors, we believe that EBITDAR permits a meaningful comparison of operating performance among industry competitors. We lease substantially all of our stores.

EBITDA is thought to provide an easily calculated alternative to operating cash flow as both measures begin with net income and both measures adjust for the noncash operating expenses of depreciation and amortization.

Another cash flow measure, **free cash flow** (FCF), is often used by analysts to evaluate a company's cash-flow strength. For instance, **Acxiom Corporation**, a company that integrates data, services and technology, reported that it generated free cash flow of $190.9 million in fiscal 2009, compared to operating cash flow of $268.8 million. The company noted that

> . . . free cash flow provides investors with a useful alternative measure of operating performance by allowing an assessment of the amount of cash available for general corporate and strategic purposes after funding operating activities and capital expenditures, capitalized software expenses and deferred costs.

Stated differently, FCF is the amount of cash that could be "freely" distributed to the owners of the company, or used for general corporate purposes, without affecting the ongoing operations and required investments. FCF is an important performance reference point for many investment professionals because it is less subject to the accounting discretion and judgment that often characterizes accrual net income. Free cash flow is estimated as follows:

$$FCF = CFFO - CapEx$$

where CapEx is **capital expenditures**, the required reinvestment in the assets of a business necessary to enable the firm to maintain itself as a going concern.[2] It should be clear that a firm with strong free cash flow will carry a higher firm value than one with weak (or no) free cash flow. Some investment professionals incorporate the construct of free cash flow into a ratio called the free cash flow yield to facilitate interfirm comparisons of cash flow strength. A firm's **free cash flow yield** is defined as its free cash flow divided by its market capitalization (market price per share times the number of shares outstanding). Businesses with high free cash flow yields are frequently seen as attractive additions to a portfolio of investment securities. We will have more to say about FCF in Chapter 12.

While FCF addresses the issue of, "How much cash is available for general corporate use or distribution?" the concept of **discretionary cash flow** addresses the question, "How much internally-generated operating cash flow is available to permit a company's management to undertake a discretionary, value-creating action?" A business's discretionary cash flow (DisCF) is calculated as follows:

$$DisCF = CFFO - \text{Required debt payments} - \text{Dividend payments}$$

This expression reveals that DisCF is a company's internally-generated operating cash flow less any required payments to debtholders and any expected dividend payments to shareholders. Thus, DisCF is a measure of the excess internally-generated operating cash flow available to a business enterprise to undertake a discretionary project, for example investing in a new plant or acquiring a company. When DisCF is large, it indicates that a firm's internally-generated cash flow is strong relative to existing claims on those flows. When DisCF is small, it indicates that a firm will need additional external funding to

---

[2] A company's CapEx is frequently segmented into maintenance CapEx and incremental CapEx. Maintenance CapEx is the amount of capital investment required to leave a going concern as well off at the end of a fiscal period as it was at the start of the fiscal period. Maintenance CapEx is frequently estimated by the amount of depreciation expense taken in a given period. Incremental CapEx, on the other hand, is any capital investment in excess of maintenance CapEx and is usually associated with an expansion in the productive capacity of a business.

facilitate a plant expansion, merger or acquisition, or debt retirement. Some analysts look to a business's discretionary cash flow as another indication of a business's cash flow health.

GLOBAL PERSPECTIVE

Like U.S. GAAP, International Financial Reporting Standards (IFRS) require companies to report a statement of cash flow as one of the primary financial statements. The basic structure and objective of the statement is the same across the two reporting regimes, but a number of key differences do exist. First, IFRS allows companies to use either the direct or the indirect method of presentation. While this is true in the U.S. as well, GAAP requires firms using the direct method to also disclose as a supplement the indirect reconciliation of net income to cash from operations. No such requirement exists internationally. With respect to the format of the statement, under U.S. GAAP the statement of cash flow has three major activity categories—operating, investing, and financing—that reflect the three key activities that characterize all business enterprises. Under current IFRS, however, the cash flow statement is segmented into five activity categories: operating, investing, transactions relating to equity, financing, and the effect of exchange rate changes. While on the surface it may appear that the cash flow statement under IFRS, with its greater number of activities, is more encompassing than under U.S. GAAP, in reality the statements contain the same basic information since both must reconcile to the change in the cash account on the balance sheet.

Within these categories there are some classification differences as well. For instance, under GAAP interest paid and dividends received are treated as operating activities, while under IFRS the preparer has the choice of including these as either operating or financing. Taxes paid must be clearly delineated under IFRS (in the operating section), and is not so required in the U.S. The fifth IFRS section, the effect of exchange rate changes, is typically subsumed in the operating and investing activities under U.S. GAAP. Finally, even the definition of "cash" contains a subtle difference: IFRS requires bank overdrafts be treated as offsets to the cash balance and are thus treated as if they are simply negative cash, while under GAAP these are treated as loans in the financing section.

Despite these differences in format, the statement of cash flows following GAAP or IFRS look remarkably the same. There has been a recent push, however, to meet complete convergence. In 2010 the FASB and IASB jointly proposed a common presentation of the statement. The proposal called for the direct method of presentation for all firms, along with the current required indirect reconciliation following U.S. GAAP. There would be redefined categories: business operating, business investing, financing debt, financing equity, multi-category transactions, income taxes, and discontinued operations. While still in the proposal stage, if adopted these changes would have the clear benefit of standardizing what is currently a wide array of different formats currently in use.

IDENTIFYING AND UNDERSTANDING SUSTAINABLE EARNINGS

Market capitalization refers to a firm's current fair market value, calculated as its market price per share times the number of shares outstanding. A business's market capitalization reflects the capital market's outlook regarding the company's future operating performance and differs from a firm's book value (i.e., the value of its shareholders' equity), which is based on past performance and accounting measurement rules.

Net income, or net earnings, is the "bottom line" measure of firm performance. It is a measure that depends on accrual accounting procedures under the revenue recognition and expense matching policies selected by a firm's management. Generally, users of financial accounting information have historically emphasized the importance of accounting earnings because past accounting earnings have been found to be a good predictor of a firm's future operating cash flow. In Chapter 12, we will see that in earnings-based valuation models, the value of a company's share price largely depends on a firm's expected future earnings. Thus, an important role for historical accounting numbers is their use in forecasting a company's future earnings, and hence, a firm's value.

One of the determinants of the ability of historical earnings to predict future earnings is the extent to which earnings recur over time, or what is known as **earnings persistence**. Since the value of a share of stock today is a function of a firm's ability to consistently generate earnings year in and year out, the sustainability or persistence of a company's operating earnings is closely linked to its value. Sustainable earnings are also sometimes referred to as **permanent earnings**, whereas non-sustainable earnings are often referred to as

transitory earnings. In general, transitory earnings include such **single-period items** as extraordinary gains/ losses, special items, restructuring charges, changes in accounting principle, and discontinued operations.

To assist investors in their assessment of a company's sustainable earnings, and hence in assessing a firm's **intrinsic value**, companies are required under GAAP to classify income statement accounts in a manner that aids the user in assessing a firm's sustainable earnings. Exhibit 3.8 illustrates the basic format of the income statement for a hypothetical company, Savanna Company. Notice that the income statement is organized in such a way that items with greater persistence are reported higher in the income statement, whereas items considered more transitory are reported further down in the statement. Thus, accounts representing financial events that are both usual and frequent are reported first. *Usual* refers to whether an item is central to a firm's core operations, whereas **unusual items** display a high degree of abnormality and/or are unrelated, and/or only incidentally related to the ordinary and typical activities of the enterprise. *Frequent* refers to how often an item is expected to occur, with infrequent items not reasonably expected to recur in the foreseeable future.

> **Intrinsic value** refers to the underlying economic value of a business as a going concern; that is, the value that a business could be sold for in an efficient market.

Usual and frequent items typically consist of such income statement accounts as sales, cost of goods sold, and other operating expenses. Just below these usual and frequent items are items that are either unusual or infrequent, but not both. Examples of these special items include such financial events as asset write-downs and restructuring charges. While these items are not expected to occur regularly, they are not considered unusual in nature. Income statement accounts such as interest expense, interest income, and gains on sales of equipment are often frequently recurring items; however, they are not considered part of a firm's central operations and therefore are considered unusual. Each of the above items is reported as part of continuing operations and is shown before any tax expense. GAAP, however, requires two single-period items, or one-time events, to be reported on an after-tax basis. These two items, discontinued operations and extraordinary items, are each shown net of any applicable income taxes. Reporting these items on a net-of-tax basis allows the income tax expense reported on the income statement to reflect only the income taxes associated with a firm's continuing operations, consequently enabling financial statement users to more readily predict a firm's future expected effective income tax rate.

EXHIBIT 3.8	The Income Statement: Potential Transitory Earnings Items		

SAVANNA COMPANY Income Statement For Year Ended December 31		
Sales.		$500
Cost of goods sold.		200
Gross profit.		300
Operating expenses.	$200	
Special items.	50	250
Net operating income.		50
Other income and expense		
Interest income.	25	
Interest expense.	(35)	
Gain on sale of equipment.	15	5
Net income from continuing operations before tax		55
Income tax		20
Net income from continuing operations.		35
Gain (loss) on disposal of segment, net of tax		10
Net income before extraordinary item		45
Extraordinary gain (loss), net of tax		(15)
Net income		$ 30
Earnings per share (100 shares outstanding)		
Net income from continuing operations.		$ .35
Disposal of business segment		.10
Extraordinary item.		(.15)
Total earnings per share		$ .30

Special Items and Extraordinary Items

There is no generally accepted definition as to what constitutes a **special item**; therefore, there is some variation in what firms will classify as "special." Special items often include gains or losses that are outside a firm's normal operations. For example, litigation settlements, impairment charges for long-lived assets, and the gains or losses associated with the sale of property, plant and equipment are typically classified as special items. The income statements for **CSK Auto Corporation** presented in Exhibit 3.9 reveal several special items, including investigation and restatement costs of $12.348 million and securities class action settlement of $11.7 million in 2008, and a loss on debt retirement of $19.45 million in 2007.

A controversial type of special item that some companies include in their income statement involves **restructuring charges** associated with changing a business's operations. Restructuring—also sometimes referred to as right-sizing or down-sizing—usually involves employee layoffs, closing facilities, and changing the company's financial structure by paying down debt with the issuance of new equity. For example, in Exhibit 3.9, CSK Auto Corporation reports "store closing costs" in each year from 2006 to 2008 associated with the closure of CSK stores that overlapped with better-situated, acquired stores, and the operating losses of acquired automotive service centers that were closed.

EXHIBIT 3.9	An Illustration of Extraordinary and Special Items

CSK AUTO CORPORATION and Subsidiaries
Consolidated Statements of Operations

(in thousands except per share data)	February 3, 2008	February 4, 2007	January 29, 2006
Net sales.	$ 1,851,647	$ 1,907,776	$ 1,651,285
Cost of sales.	984,649	1,011,712	864,674
Gross profit.	866,998	896,064	786,611
Other costs & expenses:			
Operating & administrative	804,265	788,400	653,471
Investigation and restatement costs	12,348	25,739	—
Securities class action settlement	11,700	—	—
Store closing costs	1,983	1,487	2,903
Operating profit	36,702	80,438	130,237
Interest expense.	54,163	48,767	33,599
Loss on debt retirement.	—	19,450	1,600
Income (loss) before income taxes and cumulative effect of change in accounting principle.	(17,461)	12,221	95,038
Income tax expense (benefit)	(6,309)	4,991	37,248
Income (loss) before cumulative effect of change in accounting principle	(11,152)	7,230	57,790
Cumulative effect of change in accounting principle, net of tax	—	(966)	—
Net income (loss)	$ (11,152)	$ 6,264	$ 57,790
Basic earnings (loss) per share:			
Income (loss) before cumulative effect of change in accounting principle	$ (0.25)	$ 0.16	$ 1.30
Cumulative effect of change in accounting principle	—	(0.02)	—
Net income (loss) per share	$ (0.25)	$ 0.14	$ 1.30
Shares used in computing per share amounts.	43,971,417	43,876,533	44,465,409
Diluted earnings (loss) per share:			
Income (loss) before cumulative effect of change in accounting principle	$ (0.25)	$ 0.16	$ 1.29
Cumulative effect of change in accounting principle	—	(0.02)	—
Net income (loss) per share.	$ (0.25)	$ 0.14	$ 1.29
Shares used in computing per share amounts.	43,971,417	44,129,278	44,812,302

In recent years, there has been increasing criticism of companies that report annual restructuring charges because it is believed that these write-offs have become a device for managing earnings. For example, **Eastman Kodak Company** has taken "one-time restructuring charges" every year for twenty-one consecutive years, from 1992 to 2012. By taking recurring write-downs of property and equipment, management may attempt to convey the impression to investors, shareholders, and investment professionals that the resulting restructuring charges are one-time events—that is, that they are transitory in nature and consequently should be ignored for purposes of valuing the firm.[3] It should be observed, however, that these charges effectively reduce the regular depreciation expense on the income statement, and thus improve future operating income on an annual basis. Critics of this practice also note that restructuring charges are often taken in a "bad year" in which operating earnings are unusually weak. Lumping restructuring charges in years characterized by poor operating results to enhance the probability of improved performance in future years has become known as "**taking a bath**". Available evidence suggests that restructuring charges are often reversed in subsequent periods to enable a firm to beat analysts' earnings forecasts, to avoid reporting losses, or to avoid a decline in earnings from a prior year.[4]

Another one-time item is the additional income or charges that result from the implementation of a voluntary or mandatory **change in accounting principle**. Mandatory accounting changes occur when an accounting regulatory body, such as the FASB or IASB, changes the generally accepted accounting practice that is applicable to all audited companies. For example, in Exhibit 3.9, CSK Auto Corporation discloses that in 2007 it implemented a mandatory change in its method of accounting for share-based compensation. This accounting policy change resulted in a reduction in CSK's net income of $966,000, net of income tax savings.

A basic principle within U.S. GAAP is the **consistency principle**. Consistency requires that a firm use the same accounting measurement principles from one fiscal period to the next. This is not to be confused with uniformity, where all firms would need to report their financial results using the same set of principles and methods. Instead, consistency allows different firms to use different reporting methods; however, the same firm is expected to report its performance on a consistent basis from one year to the next. The consistent use of accounting policies enables financial statement users to make valid, and hence useful, comparisons of performance across multiple time periods. Voluntary accounting policy changes do occur, however, when the management of a company and its independent auditor decide that an alternative accounting method better reflects a firm's operations. Fortunately, voluntary changes in accounting methods don't happen very often—on average, less than two accounting policy changes per firm over a 20-year period. The capital market generally regards voluntary accounting policy changes suspiciously, often penalizing the share price of companies that make such changes. We will have more to say about voluntary accounting policy changes in Chapter 7.

As reflected in Exhibit 3.9, firms like CSK Auto Corporation were required in the past to separately show the cumulative financial effect of an accounting policy change, net of any income tax effect, as a separate line item on the income statement following the income from continuing operations. Under a current GAAP rule, however, the financial effect of a change in a company's accounting policies is now applied retrospectively to all prior periods to which the change can be estimated, with the financial effect of the change reported as an adjustment to retained earnings on the statement of shareholders' equity rather than on the income statement.

Extraordinary gains (losses) are gains (losses) that are both *unusual* and *infrequent* in nature. Extraordinary items are reported in the income statement *net* of any applicable income taxes and are reported after income from continuing operations—that is, the unusual and infrequent nature of these items is highlighted by prominently displaying them near the bottom of the income statement. Just what constitutes an extraordinary item, however, can be confusing. Consider, for example, a company whose uninsured building in California was destroyed in an earthquake. The firm would not be able to classify the loss as extraordinary because although the occurrence of earthquakes in California is infrequent, it would not be considered unusual since it is part of the business risk of operating in California. Extraordinary items include such items as a gain or loss resulting from a natural disaster when such events are unusual and infrequent (such as a hurricane) or a gain or loss resulting from new government regulations, such as an asset expropriation by a foreign government (e.g., Venezuela's 2007 expropriation of international oil company assets).

---

[3] **Eastman Kodak** filed for bankruptcy in 2012 as an attempt to survive a liquidity crisis after many years of declining film business sales. One might speculatively associate Kodak's frequent use of restructuring charges as indicative of its attempts to adapt to the fast changing photography industry.

[4] S.R. Moehrle, "Do Firms Use Restructuring Charge Reversals to Meet Earnings Targets?" *The Accounting Review* (April 2002).

Discontinued Operations

When a company discontinues a separately identifiable business unit, such as an existing division, to focus on other activities, it will generally incur costs to lay off employees, liquidate inventory, and shutter facilities. These costs and the profits (or losses) from operating the business unit until it can be disposed of are categorized as **discontinued operations** on the income statement. GAAP requires that companies separate the results of their continuing operations from their discontinued operations to facilitate shareholder assessment of sustainable earnings. As shown in Exhibit 3.10, **General Electric**'s income from discontinued operations, after applicable income taxes, totaled a loss of $873 million in 2010. This amount is further partitioned into two components—earnings from discontinued operations ($311 million) and a disposal loss on discontinued operations ($1,184 million). Whereas the first component represents the net operating income for the operations that will be discontinued for the period, the second component represents the difference between the proceeds from the sale and the depreciated cost of the net assets disposed of.

EXHIBIT 3.10	Illustration of Discontinued Operations

GENERAL ELECTRIC
Notes to the 2011 Financial Statements
Note 2. Assets and Liabilities of Businesses held for Sale and Discontinued Operations

Discontinued Operations

Discontinued operations primarily comprised BAC Credomatic GECF Inc. (BAC) (our Central American bank and card business), GE Money Japan (our Japanese personal loan business, Lake, and our Japanese mortgage and card businesses, excluding our investment in GE Nissen Credit Co., Ltd.), our U.S. mortgage business (WMC), our U.S. recreational vehicle and marine equipment financing business (Consumer RV Marine), Consumer Mexico, Consumer Singapore and our Consumer home lending operations in Australia and New Zealand (Australian Home Lending). Associated results of operations, financial position and cash flows are separately reported as discontinued operations for all periods presented.

Summarized financial information for discontinued operations is shown below.

(In millions)	2011	2010	2009
Operations			
Total revenues	$ 316	$ 2,035	$2,341
Earnings (loss) from discontinued operations, before income taxes	$ (30)	$ 215	$ 340
Benefit (provision) for income taxes	85	96	(18)
Earnings (loss) from discontinued operations, net of taxes	$55	$ 311	$ 322
Disposal			
Gain (loss) on disposal before income taxes	$(329)	$(1,420)	$ (196)
Benefit (provision) for income taxes	351	236	93
Gain (loss) on disposal, net of taxes	$ 22	$(1,184)	$ (103)
Earnings (loss) from discontinued operations, net of taxes[a]	$ 77	$ (873)	$ 219

[a] The sum of GE industrial earnings (loss) from discontinued operations, net of taxes, and GECS earnings (loss) from discontinued operations, net of taxes, is reported as GE earnings (loss) from discontinued operations, net of taxes, on the Statement of Earnings.

Earnings per Share

Since investors own shares whose prices are customarily quoted in terms of a price per share, public companies are required to provide earnings numbers that are scaled by the number of shares held by its shareholders. For example, **basic earnings per share** (EPS) is net income divided by the actual number of common shares outstanding—that is, the number of shares held by a company's shareholders. **Diluted earnings per share**, on the other hand, is basic earnings per share adjusted for the possibility that some existing claims against the business might be converted into additional shares of common stock, thus increasing the number of shares outstanding. Claims against a firm that can be satisfied by the issuance of additional shares of common stock are called **dilutive claims** because the issuance of shares to satisfy these claims will lower, or dilute, basic EPS. There are two adjustments to basic EPS for dilutive securities: (1) increasing the denominator shares outstanding for the additional shares, and (2) removing from net income in the numerator any earnings effects associated with those dilutive securities. Examples of dilutive claims include convertible bonds, employee stock options, and convertible preferred shares (which are discussed in Chapters 9 and 11, respectively).

Since **Kohl**'s diluted EPS in 2006 was $2.43 versus a basic EPS of $2.45 (see Business Perspective: Kohl's Corporation), the company must have had some dilutive claims outstanding. Does the capital market consider the impact of these dilutive claims by relying more heavily on diluted EPS than on basic EPS when assessing a company's intrinsic value? Available evidence that diluted EPS explains more of the variation in share prices than basic EPS does suggest that investors do indeed focus more closely on diluted EPS in setting share prices.[5] However, available evidence also suggests that alternative EPS measures that better capture the potential dilutive effect of employee stock options explain more of the variation in share prices than does even diluted EPS.[6] This is consistent with the notion that investors make additional adjustments to diluted EPS when assessing the performance of firms that issue employee stock options.

Pro Forma Earnings

In recent years, companies have begun reporting a variety of alternative measures of earnings that *exclude* certain expenses or write-offs, jokingly referred to by investment professionals as EBBS or "earnings before bad stuff." One such measure is **pro forma earnings**. While there is no generally accepted definition for the calculation of pro forma earnings, a commonly used calculation is net income before discontinued operations, restructuring charges, extraordinary and special items, and the effect of any mandatory or voluntary accounting policy changes.

Under the requirements of the Sarbanes-Oxley Act passed in 2002, companies that include a non-GAAP financial measure such as pro forma earnings with their audited financial statements must also provide the most directly comparable GAAP numbers. These firms must also provide a reconciliation between the two sets of numbers. For example, **Eastman Kodak Company** reported a loss of $0.04 per share for the last quarter of 2004 using GAAP. Yet, on a pro forma basis, Kodak announced "operational earnings" of $0.78 per share, a swing of $0.82 per share from GAAP EPS. Kodak's pro forma earnings, a figure tracked by analysts who follow the company, excluded such costs as the company's restructuring charges.

The divergence between the generally higher pro forma earnings and GAAP earnings has increased over time. In Practice 3.4 presents, for example, GAAP EPS and pro forma EPS for the fourth quarter of 2004 for a selection of S&P 500 companies. Unfortunately, the capital market's reliance on pro forma earnings as a performance metric has also increased as suggested by evidence that share prices track pro forma earnings more closely than GAAP earnings.[7] To ensure that investors consider GAAP EPS, the U.S. Securities and Exchange Commission adopted **Regulation G (Reg G)** in 2003, which requires that firms put GAAP-based earnings first in their public earnings announcements, as well as to reconcile any non-GAAP earnings numbers (e.g., pro forma earnings) with their GAAP-based earnings. The intent of Reg G is to insure transparency regarding the differences between GAAP earnings and any non-GAAP earnings reported by companies.

In Practice 3.4 *GAAP EPS versus Pro Forma EPS**

Company	4th Quarter 2004		
	GAAP EPS	Pro Forma EPS	Percentage Difference
Eastman Kodak.	$-0.04	$0.78	NM
Georgia-Pacific	0.06	0.51	750
Rowan	0.02	0.15	650
Ford Motor	0.05	0.28	460
Clorox	0.72	3.69	413
Genzyme.	−0.42	0.52	NM
Halliburton	−0.45	0.44	NM

*Source: *CFO Magazine*. NM = not meaningful.

---

[5] R. Jennings, M.J. LeClere and R.B. Thompson, "Evidence on the Usefulness of Alternative Earnings per Share Measures," *Financial Analysts Journal* (November/December 1997).

[6] J.E. Core, W.R. Guay and S.P. Kothari, "The Economic Dilution of Employee Stock Options: Diluted EPS for Valuation and Financial Reporting," *The Accounting Review* (July 2002).

[7] M.T. Bradshaw and R.G. Sloan, "GAAP versus The Street: An Empirical Assessment of Two Alternative Definitions of Earnings," *Journal of Accounting Research* (March 2002).

Kohl's Corporation: Operating versus Nonoperating Earnings

The income statement for **Kohl's Corporation** is presented below. Kohl's consolidated income statement discloses such operating expenses as the cost of merchandise sold, depreciation and amortization on property and equipment, and selling and administrative expenses (see bolded areas). Kohl's separates the results of its core retailing business from the financing of its business by reporting interest expense as a nonoperating item. It also separates the financial investing side of its business from its core business by reporting interest income on its investments and security holdings as a nonoperating item. The underlying logic of this distinction is that Kohl's could relatively quickly change the way it finances its business and/or liquidate its investments—hence these items are considered to be transitory—but that exiting its core retailing business would require a longer period of time.

KOHL'S CORPORATION
Consolidated Statements of Income

($ thousands, except per share data)	January 28, 2006	January 29, 2005 (Restated)	January 31, 2004 (Restated)
Net sales	$13,402,217	$11,700,619	$10,282,094
Cost of merchandise sold	**8,639,278**	**7,586,992**	**6,887,033**
Gross margin	4,762,939	4,113,627	3,395,061
Operating expenses			
Selling, general and administrative	**2,963,472**	**2,582,996**	**2,157,030**
Depreciation and amortization	**338,916**	**288,173**	**239,558**
Pre-opening expenses	**44,370**	**49,131**	**47,029**
Total operating expenses	3,346,758	2,920,300	2,443,617
Operating income	1,416,181	1,193,327	951,444
Other expense (income)			
Interest expense	**72,086**	**64,761**	**76,371**
Interest income	**(1,695)**	**(2,309)**	**(3,440)**
Income before income taxes	1,345,790	1,130,875	878,513
Provision for income taxes	503,830	427,474	332,050
Net income	$ 841,960	$ 703,401	$ 546,463
Net income per share			
Basic	$2.45	$2.06	$1.61
Diluted	$2.43	$2.04	$1.59

One of the potential problems associated with the corporate form of business is the agency costs that can result from the separation of the ownership of a corporation from those that manage the corporation. One mechanism used to mitigate these potential agency costs are employment compensation contracts. The theory underlying this mechanism is that if a compensation contract is properly structured, goal congruence between the manager and the corporation's shareholders will result. Thus, properly structured employment contracts provide performance incentives that result in larger amounts of compensation being paid when managers achieve better financial performance.

A potential unintended consequence of executive compensation contracts is that managers may also have an incentive to "cook the books" in order to report higher firm performance, and therefore, achieve higher personal compensation. In other words, rather than achieving goal congruence by working hard to sell more goods or to produce goods more efficiently, higher performance may be achieved through accounting trickery. Clearly, earnings management for purely personal gain can be argued to be an ethical breach of an executive's job.

REVIEW PROBLEM

The following balance sheet and income statement data were taken from the financial records of The Arcadia Company.

THE ARCADIA COMPANY Balance Sheets						
	2012	**2011**			**2012**	**2011**
Assets			**Liabilities & Shareholders' Equity**			
Cash..................	$ 30,000	$ 7,000	Accounts payable.........		$ 63,000	$ 65,500
Marketable securities......	60,000	67,500	Wages payable...........		47,500	37,000
Inventory...............	22,500	49,000	Total current liabilities......		110,500	102,500
Prepaid insurance........	4,500	6,000	Bank loan payable		85,000	83,000
Total current assets	117,000	129,500	Capital stock		75,000	75,000
Building (net).............	190,000	187,500	Retained earnings		36,500	56,500
Totals	$307,000	$317,000	Totals		$307,000	$317,000

THE ARCADIA COMPANY Income Statement For Year Ended December 31, 2012	
Revenues	$ 480,000
Less	
Cost of goods sold	320,000
Depreciation expense	28,500
Wage expense....................................	93,000
Insurance expense................................	46,000
Interest expense	10,500
Net loss	$ (18,000)

Required

Prepare an indirect method statement of cash flow for The Arcadia Company for 2012 and calculate the following cash flow ratios for 2012: (a) operating funds ratio; (b) operating cash flow to current liabilities ratio; (c) cash conversion ratio.

The solution is on page 117.

EXECUTIVE SUMMARY

In this chapter, we examined the components of a company's net income in an effort to identify its sustainable earnings. Sustainable earnings are those operating and nonoperating income flows that are expected to persist over many fiscal periods; they are the permanent earnings of a business. Sustainable earnings are important to managers and investors because they are a key determinant of firm value.

We also illustrated how a company's statement of cash flow can be prepared from its income statement and balance sheets. Finally, we examined the various alternative measures of cash flow that investors and investment professionals use to evaluate a firm's financial health: EBITDA, free cash flow, and discretionary cash flow.

As a validation of your understanding of the content of this chapter, you should now be able to:

■ Use a statement of cash flow to explain a business's financing and investing strategies.
■ Prepare a statement of cash flow using the indirect method.
■ Explain the difference between EBITDA, free cash flow, and discretionary cash flow.
■ Understand the components of net income to evaluate a company's sustainable earnings.

KEY CONCEPTS AND TERMS

APPENDIX 3A: Converting Indirect Method Cash Flows to Direct Method Cash Flows

Although it is quite straightforward to create a direct method statement of cash flow given access to a company's internal accounting records, such access is rarely available to anyone except a company's management team. The Russian River Valley cash flow statement that appears in Exhibit 2.5 in the previous chapter, for example, is simply a compilation of the cash inflows and outflows reported in the cash column from the Russian River Valley spreadsheet. All that is necessary is to pull the numbers directly off the spreadsheet and place them in the appropriate section of the cash flow statement. This is why, in fact, the direct method is referred to as "direct"—the cash flow from operations is taken directly from the company's accounting records rather than being indirectly computed from net income. Unfortunately, investors and lenders rarely have access to such proprietary internal data. Thus, it is necessary to be able to create direct method cash flow information using only such publicly available data as the indirect method statement of cash flow.

The process of converting an indirect method statement of cash flow to the direct method requires two steps. First, replace net income (the first line item under the operating activities section of the indirect method statement format) with the key line items appearing on a firm's income statement. For instance, Russian River Valley's income statement in Exhibit 3.5 contains the following key line items (in thousands):

Revenue	$1,900
Cost of goods sold	(380)
Operating expenses	(675)
Interest	(288)
Income taxes	(240)
Net income	$ 317

Thus, for the winery, we begin by replacing the net income of $317 under the operating activities section in Exhibit 3.6 with the five key income statement line items shown above, which aggregate to $317.

The second step involves adjusting the key income statement line items identified in Step One with the remaining line items from the operating activities section of the indirect method statement of cash flow. Using Russian River Valley's data in Exhibit 3.6, those adjustments would appear as follows:

Income Statement Line Items		Operating Activities Line Items	Direct Method Cash Flow	
Revenues	$1,900	Less $800 Accounts receivable	Cash collections from customers	$1,100
Cost of goods sold	(380)	Less $60 Inventory Add $80 Accounts payable	Cash paid for inventory	(360)
Operating expenses	(675)	Add $225 Depreciation Add $50 Amortization	Cash paid for operating expenses	(400)
Interest	(288)	(no adjustment required)	Cash paid for interest	(288)
Income taxes	(240)	Add $96 Taxes payable	Cash paid for income taxes	(144)
Net income	$ 317		Cash flow from operations	$ (92)

Exhibit 3A.1 presents the winery's direct method statement of cash flow after undertaking the above two steps. As expected, the direct method CFFO of negative $92 is exactly equivalent to the indirect method CFFO of negative $92 as reported in Exhibit 3.6. Note that the CFFI and CFFF are exactly the same in both Exhibit 3.6 and Exhibit 3A.1. The only difference between the two exhibits is the manner in which the CFFO is calculated. In Exhibit 3.6, the CFFO is calculated by beginning with net income and then adjusting for various noncash expenses (e.g., depreciation and amortization), as well as adjusting for the changes in the various working capital accounts (e.g., accounts receivable, inventory, accounts payable, and taxes payable). In Exhibit 3A.1, net income is replaced with the key income statement line items and the noncash expenses and working capital adjustments are disaggregated to the individual line items. But in each case, the CFFO total remains the same.

EXHIBIT 3A.1	Statement of Cash Flow: The Direct Method

RUSSIAN RIVER VALLEY WINERY, INC.
Statement of Cash Flow

($ thousands)	Year 1
Operating activities	
Cash from customer collections	$ 1,100
Cash paid for inventory	(360)
Cash paid for operating expenses	(400)
Cash paid for interest	(288)
Cash paid for income taxes	(144)
Cash flow from operations	**(92)**
Investing activities	
Purchase of property, plant & equipment	(3,500)
Cash flow from investing	**(3,500)**
Financing activities	
Sale of common stock	400
Payment of notes payable (current)	(480)
Payment of common stock dividends	(260)
Cash flow from financing	**(340)**
Net cash flow	(3,932)
Beginning cash	4,700
Ending cash	$ 768

QUESTIONS

Q3.1 **Building Shareholder Value.** Describe at least three ways that corporate managers can build shareholder value (increase their firm's share price). Rank-order the various managerial actions you identified according to their effectiveness in building shareholder value. Be prepared to justify your rank-ordering.

Q3.2 **Litigation, Reported Income, and Share Price.** In early 2006, Merck AG, a global pharmaceutical company, saw its share price decline dramatically after a jury in the United States found the company guilty of failing to warn consumers about safety issues surrounding one of the company's products, a painkilling drug called *Vioxx*. Although Merck was found not guilty in one case involving a plaintiff who died while taking the drug, the company was found guilty in a second case, with the court awarding the survivors of the deceased plaintiff $4.5 million in compensatory damages. At the time of the trial, over 5,000 separate *Vioxx*-related lawsuits had been filed against Merck. Discuss how Merck should disclose the $4.5 million lawsuit award in its 2006 annual report. How should Merck disclose the 5,000 pending lawsuits in its 2005 financial statements before the court case was decided against the company? How should Merck report the pending *Vioxx*-related lawsuits in its 2006 annual report?

Q3.3 **Basic versus Diluted Earnings per Share.** In its 2012 annual report, Merck & Co., Inc., reported that its basic earnings per share were $2.03 per share while its diluted earnings per share were $2.00 per share. Discuss the factors that might cause the number of shares used in the calculation of earnings per share to increase, and thus, cause diluted earnings per share (EPS) to be less than basic earnings per share. Which measure do you feel is more important to shareholders—basic EPS or diluted EPS? Why?

Q3.4 **Assessing the Quality of Reported Earnings Using Cash Flow Data.** Although much of the work of an equity analyst involves quantitative analysis, some analysts also engage in various qualitative analyses to help them assess the persistence of a firm's current earnings. Consider, for example, the case of **Blockbuster Entertainment Corporation**. In 1989, Lee J. Seidler, a senior analyst with Bear, Stearns & Co., issued a research report critical of Blockbuster's earnings. Mr. Seidler observed that although Blockbuster's 1988 net income was $15.5 million and its cash flow from operating activities $48.4 million, his review of the firm's cash flow data revealed that Blockbuster's purchases of new videocassette rental inventory had been classified as an "investing activity" rather than as an "operating activity" on the company's statement of cash flow. Presented below is selected financial statement information for Blockbuster:

(in millions)	1988	1987
Net income..	$15.5	$4.09
Cash flow from operations............................	48.3	10.3
Purchases of videocassette rental inventory..............	(51.3)	(14.3)

Discuss how the statement of cash flow can be used to help evaluate the quality of a company's reported earnings. Describe how Blockbuster's cash flow data can be used to illustrate this. Do you agree with Blockbuster's decision to classify its videocassette inventory purchases as an "investing activity"? Why or why not? How does Blockbuster's cash flow classification of its video inventory purchases affect its cash flow from operations?

Q3.5 **Earnings Announcements and Share Prices.** It is common to see share prices of a company increase with the announcement of good news from the company. It is also the case that record earnings qualify as very good news. The behavior of stock price increases with record earnings announcements is not always the case, however. For example, in January of 2013 **Apple Inc.**, the maker of the iPhone and Mac computers, announced record earnings of over $41.7 billion for 2012. Apple's stock dropped nearly 10 percent following the earnings announcement. Discuss why a record earnings announcement may lead to a share price increase, but may also lead to a share price decline as experienced by Apple.

Q3.6 **Managing Earnings.** Some members of the financial community allege that corporate managers "manage" their company's reported accounting results. Discuss the possible motivations behind this behavior. Can you envision a situation where a manager might manage a company's earnings downward? If so, why?

Q3.7 **Goodwill Impairment and Sustainable Earnings.** In 2002, the FASB concluded that the amortization of goodwill should no longer be required, and instead that goodwill be subject to an annual impairment test to verify that its value had not materially declined. If a decline in value is observed, the goodwill account is written down and an "impairment loss" is recorded on the income statement.

In a 2012 study of goodwill impairment, Duff & Phelps found that **Bank of America** and **AT&T** had among the highest impairment charges in 2011. Discuss how Bank of America and AT&T will account for the goodwill write-down in their financial statements. How will the impairment charge affect the firm's book value? How will the impairment charge impact the firm's sustainable earnings?

Q3.8 **Special Charges.** On September 11, 2001, two American Airlines aircraft were hijacked and destroyed in terrorist attacks on The World Trade Center in New York City and the Pentagon in northern Virginia. As a consequence of these actions, **AMR Corporation**, the parent company of American Airlines, concluded that its fleet of aircraft had become impaired, and consequently, took a special charge of $718 million against 2001 net income and an additional $1,466 million charge against 2002 net income.

Discuss how these special charges will be reflected in AMR's financial statements. Given the unusual circumstances associated with these charges, could they be considered extraordinary? Why or why not? Will these charges be included in the company's sustainable earnings? Why or why not?

Q3.9 **New Accounting Standard.** In 2002, following its adoption of a new accounting standard issued by the FASB for the impairment of goodwill accounting, **AMR Corporation**, the parent company of American Airlines, conducted an impairment test of its existing goodwill which had largely arisen in conjunction with American's acquisition of TWA in 2001. Based on this test, AMR Corporation concluded that its entire balance of $1.4 billion of goodwill had been impaired. Consequently, at year-end 2002, the company recorded a one-time, noncash charge to write off all of its goodwill. The charge-off of AMR's goodwill was reported as a "cumulative effect of accounting change" in the amount of $988 million, net of the related income tax effect of $412 million, on its consolidated statement of earnings.

Discuss AMR's treatment of its goodwill impairment charge. Do you agree with the disclosure adopted by the company? Why or why not? How will the impairment affect the firm's future sustainable earnings?

Q3.10 **Market Capitalization, Book Value, and Intrinsic Value.** Discuss the concepts of book value, intrinsic value, and market capitalization. Using a financial website such as **Yahoo.Finance** or **MSN.Money**, identify the market capitalization and book value of **The Procter & Gamble Company**. Calculate the difference between these values. Why do these measures differ in value?

Q3.11 **Accounting Statement Restatements.** According to *CFO Magazine* (April, 2006), the number of companies that issued corrections to their financial statements hit a new high in 2005. A total of 1,195 U.S. public companies, or about 8.5 percent of the total, filed financial statement restatements in 2005. That amount was approximately twice the total restatements (613) filed in 2004. The major types of accounting restatements for the period 2003 to 2005 were identified as follows:

Number of Restatements	2003	2004	2005
Lease accounting........................	23	22	249
Stock option accounting	30	39	71
Hedge accounting	13	25	57

Discuss why the number of financial statement restatements increased so dramatically from 2004 to 2005. Discuss how and why the capital markets respond to financial statement restatements.

Q3.12 **(Ethics Perspective) Earnings Management to Prevent Technical Defaults.** Earnings management may be used to avoid a technical default of a covenant under a loan agreement. Loan covenants are written into loan agreements in order to protect a lender from various actions that a borrower might undertake. These covenants often require attainment of certain target financial ratios calculated using reported GAAP numbers. Failing to achieve these minimum target ratios, and hence falling into technical default, can be very costly to a firm. Earnings management to prevent a technical default will likely save a corporation and its shareholders from experiencing a large loss in market value, without necessarily providing any direct personal benefit to the company's managers. Is earnings management to avoid a loan covenant violation an ethical breach by management?

Assignments with the ✔ logo in the margin are available in BusinessCourse.
See the Preface of the book for details.
CHECK FIGURE indicates that check figures are available on the book's Website.

EXERCISES

E3.13 **Classifying Accounting Events.** Presented below is a list of accounting events for the Longo Corporation. Classify each of the events as an operating (O) activity event, an investing (I) activity event, a financing (F) activity event, or as none-of-the-above (N).
   1. Sale of common stock for cash
   2. Collection of cash on accounts receivable
   3. Purchase of equipment for cash
   4. Sale of inventory on credit
   5. Borrowed cash from a bank
   6. Payment of a cash dividend
   7. Payment of utility expense using cash
   8. Purchase of land using bank financing
   9. Repurchase of previously issued stock using cash
   10. Cash payment of interest on a bank loan

E3.14 **Classifying Accounting Transactions.** Presented below is a list of accounting transactions for the Davis Company. Classify each of the transactions as an operating (O) activity transaction, an investing (I) activity transaction, a financing (F) activity transaction, or as none-of-the-above (N). **CHECK FIGURE**
   1. Purchase of machinery for cash
   2. Cash payment on loan principal
   3. Collection of cash on outstanding accounts receivable
   4. Payment of a stock dividend
   5. Sale of preferred stock for cash
   6. Prepaid the office rent for six months
   7. Cash payment of income tax expense
   8. Sale of land held as an investment for cash
   9. Declared (but did not pay) a cash dividend
   10. Purchased treasury stock using cash

E3.15 **Analyzing Cash Flow Data.** Presented below is cash flow information for two competitors—The Longo Corporation and The Davis Company (amounts in thousands):

| Company | Operating Profit | Cash Flow From | | |
		Operations	Investing	Financing
Longo Corporation..................	$(6,050)	$(1,320)	$ (693)	$ 415
Davis Company	(2,980)	(3,260)	1,502	1,809

Describe the cash management strategy of each company by identifying the key sources and uses of cash by each firm. Explain why the cash flow from operations of The Longo Corporation differs from the company's operating loss of $6,050. Calculate the change in the cash balance for The Davis Company.

E3.16 **Analyzing Cash Flow Data.** Presented below is cash flow information for two competitors—**Pfizer, Inc.**, and **The Johnson & Johnson Company** (amounts in millions):

| Company | Operating Profit | Cash Flow From | | |
		Operations	Investing	Financing
Pfizer, Inc.........................	$ 8,085	$14,733	$(5,072)	$(9,222)
Johnson & Johnson	10,411	11,877	(279)	(4,521)

Describe the cash management strategy of each company by identifying the key sources and uses of cash by each firm. Calculate the change in the cash balance for each firm. Explain why the cash flow from operations for Pfizer, Inc. of $14,733 is greater than its operating profit of $8,085.

 E3.17 **Calculating Earnings per Share.** During 2013, Mayfair Enterprises had the following securities outstanding:

1. 250,000 shares of common stock with an average market price of $25 per share.
2. 9.5% convertible preferred, which had been sold at its par value of $100. The preferred stock is convertible into three shares of common stock and 3,000 preferred shares are currently outstanding.

During 2013, Mayfair Enterprises earned net income after income taxes of $3.2 million. Calculate the (a) basic earnings per share and (b) diluted earnings per share for Mayfair Enterprises for 2013.

 E3.18 **Calculating Earnings per Share.** Little, Inc., reported earnings of $159,000 for 2013, and at the end of the year, had the following securities outstanding:

1. 60,000 shares of common stock. (The year-end share price was $25 per share.)
2. Employee stock options for the purchase of 8,000 common shares at an exercise price of $22 per share. (The options are fully vested.)

Calculate the (a) basic earnings per share and (b) diluted earnings per share for Little, Inc. for 2013.

 E3.19 **Permanent versus Transitory Earnings.** **Entrust, Inc.**, is a global provider of security software; it operates in one business segment involving the design, production, and sale of software products for securing digital identities and information. The consolidated statements of operations for a three-year period (all values in thousands) follows. On January 1, Year 1, the Entrust common shares traded at $10.40 per share; by year-end Year 3, the shares traded at $3.80 per share. The company's cash flow from operations was $(27,411), $(20,908), and $9,606, for Year 1, Year 2, and Year 3, respectively.

Calculate the sustainable earnings of Entrust, Inc., for each of the three years. Compare the company's reported net income (loss) with its sustainable earnings. Does Entrust's share price at year-end Year 3 reflect the firm's apparent turn-around? Why or why not?

ENTRUST, INC. Consolidated Statements of Operations			
Year Ended December 31 ($ thousands)	Year 3	Year 2	Year 1
Revenues			
Product	$29,295	$ 30,974	$ 44,734
Services and maintenance	61,662	56,920	58,013
Total revenues	90,957	87,894	102,747
Cost of Revenues			
Product	4,149	5,341	5,281
Services and maintenance	29,105	29,825	32,073
Amortization of purchased product rights	384	568	1,136
Total cost of revenues	33,638	35,734	38,490
Gross profit	57,319	52,160	64,257
Operating expenses			
Sales and marketing	26,322	34,985	44,128
Research and development	17,266	22,566	24,151
General and administrative	12,569	13,143	14,840
Impairment of purchased product rights	—	1,134	—
Restructuring charges and adjustments	—	13,623	(1,079)
Total operating expenses	56,157	85,451	82,040
Income (loss) from operations	1,162	(33,291)	(17,783)
Other income (expense)			
Interest income	1,281	1,680	3,346
Foreign exchange gain (loss)	429	(431)	(72)
Loss from equity investments	(1,111)	(603)	(602)
Realized loss on investments	—	—	(220)
Write-down of long-term strategic investments	—	(2,780)	(1,238)
Total other income (expense)	599	(2,134)	1,214
Income (loss) before income taxes and minority interest	1,761	(35,425)	(16,569)
Noncontrolling interest in subsidiary	4	—	—
Income (loss) before income taxes	1,765	(35,425)	(16,569)
Provision for income taxes	687	441	1,350
Net income (loss)	$ 1,078	$(35,866)	$(17,919)

E3.20 **(Appendix 3A) Converting Indirect Method Cash Flows to Direct Method Cash Flows.** The Miller Corporation disclosed the following statement of earnings in its 2013 annual report (amounts in thousands):

Earnings Statement	
	2013
Revenues	$1,430
Cost of goods sold	(500)
Gross margin	930
Selling, general and administrative expenses	(200)
Operating income	730
Unusual gain on sale of land	70
Net income	$ 800

In addition, the company reported the following data regarding its operating cash flow in its year-end statement of cash flow (amounts in thousands):

Statement of Cash Flow	
(Indirect Method)	**2013**
Operating activities	
Net income.	$800
Depreciation and amortization expense	260
Accounts receivable.	(150)
Inventory	(15)
Accounts payable	50
Gain on sale of land.	(70)
Cash flow from operating activities	$875

Using the above information for 2013, construct the Miller Corporation's cash flow from operating activities on a direct method basis.

 E3.21   **Measuring Sustainable Earnings.**   **Harnishfeger Corporation** was a mining machinery and equipment company based in Wisconsin. The company voluntarily changed its depreciation accounting policy from the accelerated method to the straight-line method. It disclosed the cumulative effect of this accounting policy change, equal to $11.005 million (net of applicable income taxes), in its financial statements. In addition, the company also voluntarily changed the estimated useful lives of certain of its U.S. plant and equipment. This estimate change increased its pretax reported profit by $3.2 million. The following are selected excerpts from the company's financial statements:

	(in thousands)
Income before income taxes, equity items, and cumulative	
effect of accounting method change.	$ 5,738
Provision for income taxes.	(2,425)
Income after taxes	3,313
Equity items	858
Cumulative effect of change in depreciation method	11,005
Net income.	$15,176

Calculate Harnishfeger's sustainable earnings. How would the capital market react to the company's decision to change its depreciation accounting policy and to change the estimated useful lives of its depreciable assets? Why?

PROBLEMS

 P3.22   **Statement of Cash Flow.**   Presented below are the financial statements for the Amphlett Corporation, as of year-end 2012 and 2013.

AMPHLETT CORPORATION Consolidated Balance Sheets		
As of Year-End ($ thousands)	**2013**	**2012**
Assets		
Current		
Cash.	$ 15,000	$ 90,000
Marketable securities.	200,000	—
Accounts receivable (net).	590,000	440,000
Inventory	600,000	615,000
Total current assets	1,405,000	1,145,000

continued

continued from previous page

AMPHLETT CORPORATION
Consolidated Balance Sheets

As of Year-End ($ thousands)	2013	2012
Noncurrent		
Long-term investments	310,000	390,000
Property & equipment	1,800,000	1,100,000
Less: Accumulated depreciation	(500,000)	(500,000)
Property & equipment (net)	1,300,000	600,000
Intangibles (net)	95,000	105,000
Total noncurrent assets	1,705,000	1,095,000
Total assets	$3,110,000	$2,240,000
Liabilities & Shareholders' Equity		
Accounts payable	$ 900,000	$ 850,000
Short-term bank debt	190,000	—
Total liabilities	1,090,000	850,000
Shareholders' equity		
Common stock, $10 par value	775,000	675,000
Additional paid-in-capital	380,000	300,000
Retained earnings	865,000	415,000
Total shareholders' equity	2,020,000	1,390,000
Total liabilities & shareholders' equity	$3,110,000	$2,240,000

AMPHLETT CORPORATION
Consolidated Income Statement

For Year Ended ($ thousands)	2013	2012
Revenues	$1,430,000	$1,200,000
Less: Cost of goods sold	500,000	420,000
Gross margin	930,000	780,000
Less: Selling, general & administrative expenses	150,000	120,000
Operating income	780,000	660,000
Gain on sale of investments	70,000	—
Net income before taxes	850,000	660,000
Less: Income taxes	50,000	11,000
Net income after taxes	$ 800,000	$ 649,000

The footnotes to the Amphlett Corporation's financial statements revealed the following additional information:

1. Property and equipment costing $450 million was sold for its book value of $200 million.
2. Long-term investments were sold for $150 million, which included a gain of $70 million.

Required

Using the above financial data for the Amphlett Corporation, prepare the firm's statement of cash flow for 2013 using the indirect method. What does the company's statement of cash flow reveal about the business's financial health?

P3.23   **Statement of Cash Flow.**   Presented below are the consolidated financial statements of The Mann Corporation as of year-end 2012 and 2013.

THE MANN CORPORATION Consolidated Balance Sheets		
As of Year-End ($ thousands)	2013	2012
Assets		
Current assets		
Cash.	$ 400,000	$ 250,000
Accounts receivable (net).	990,000	760,000
Inventory	710,000	400,000
Prepaid expenses	100,000	100,000
Total current assets	2,200,000	1,510,000
Investments in affiliate companies.	100,000	—
Property and equipment.	1,310,000	800,000
Less: Accumulated depreciation	(110,000)	(80,000)
Property & equipment (net).	1,200,000	720,000
Total assets.	$3,500,000	$2,230,000
Liabilities & Shareholders' Equity		
Current liabilities		
Accounts payable	$ 570,000	$ 500,000
Accrued expenses payable	200,000	220,000
Dividends payable	70,000	—
Total current liabilities.	840,000	720,000
Note payable—due in ten years.	500,000	—
Total liabilities.	1,340,000	720,000
Shareholders' equity		
Common stock ($5 par value)	300,000	200,000
Additional paid-in-capital.	1,200,000	1,160,000
Retained earnings	660,000	150,000
Total shareholders' equity	2,160,000	1,510,000
Total liabilities & shareholders' equity	$3,500,000	$2,230,000

THE MANN CORPORATION Consolidated Income Statement		
For Year Ended ($ thousands)	2013	2012
Sales.	$16,800,000	$12,000,000
Cost of goods sold.	14,000,000	10,400,000
Gross margin	2,800,000	1,600,000
Selling & administrative expenses	1,930,000	1,048,000
Depreciation expense.	30,000	20,000
Income tax expense.	240,000	152,000
Net Income.	$ 600,000	$ 380,000

Required

Using the above financial data, prepare the statement of cash flow for 2013 using the indirect method. What does the company's statement of cash flow reveal about the business's financial health?

P3.24   **Statement of Cash Flow.**   Presented below are the consolidated financial statements of Casual Clothing, Inc.

CASUAL CLOTHING INC. Consolidated Balance Sheet		
	12/31/13	**12/31/12**
Assets		
Current Assets		
Cash and cash equivalents	$ 8,794	$ 7,352
Merchandise inventory.	94,153	42,045
Accounts receivable (net).	25,700	17,800
Other current assets	35,103	25,393
Total current assets	163,750	92,590
Noncurrent Assets		
Buildings, furniture & equipment (net)	1,826,863	1,658,990
Land.	2,279,946	1,458,832
Construction-in-process	615,722	414,725
Intangibles (net)	9,780	6,700
Total assets.	$4,896,061	$3,631,837
Liabilities & Shareholders' Equity		
Current liabilities		
Notes payable	$ 779,904	$ 176,884
Current maturities of long-term debt.	250,000	350,000
Accounts payable	167,207	185,945
Accrued expenses & other liabilities	384,209	351,710
Income taxes payable	17,824	26,263
Total current liabilities.	1,599,144	1,090,802
Long-term liabilities		
Long-term debt	880,216	780,925
Total liabilities	2,479,360	1,871,727
Shareholders' equity		
Common stock ($.05 par value).	146,961	146,961
Additional paid-in-capital.	1,294,967	1,294,967
Retained earnings	974,773	318,182
Total shareholders' equity	2,416,701	1,760,110
Total liabilities & shareholders' equity	$4,896,061	$3,631,837

CASUAL CLOTHING, INC. Consolidated Statement of Earnings For Year Ended 12/31/13	
Net sales.	$13,673,460
Costs & expenses	
Costs of goods sold.	8,599,442
Operating expenses.	3,629,257
Interest expense (net).	62,876
	12,291,575
Earnings before income taxes	1,381,885
Income taxes	504,388
Net earnings.	$ 877,497

Note: In 2013, amortization expense for intangibles was $2,700 and depreciation expense for buildings, furniture & equipment was $123,000.

Required

Using the above financial data, prepare the statement of cash flow for 2013 for Casual Clothing, Inc. using the indirect method. What does the company's statement of cash flow reveal about the business's financial health?

P3.25 **Statement of Cash Flow.** The following financial data were taken from the Catalina Divers Supply Company for the year ended December 31, 2013.

CATALINA DIVERS SUPPLY COMPANY Balance Sheet Data		
	12/31/13	12/31/12
Assets		
Cash.	$ 12,000	$ 10,800
Accounts receivable (net).	22,400	18,000
Inventory	30,000	31,200
Prepaid rent	2,400	3,600
Total current assets	66,800	63,600
Equipment (net)	116,000	104,000
Total assets.	$182,800	$167,600
Liabilities & Shareholders' Equity		
Accounts payable	$ 22,400	$ 29,200
Wages payable	18,000	13,600
Interest payable	3,000	4,400
Deferred revenue	13,000	9,400
Total current liabilities.	56,400	56,600
Bank loan.	56,000	56,800
Total liabilities.	112,400	113,400
Capital stock	20,000	20,000
Retained earnings	50,400	34,200
Total shareholders' equity	70,400	54,200
Total liabilities & shareholders' equity	$182,800	$167,600

CATALINA DIVERS SUPPLY COMPANY Income Statement For the Year Ended December 31, 2013	
Revenues	$218,200
Cost of goods sold.	112,000
Gross margin	106,200
Wage expense	30,400
Rent expense	18,000
Interest expense.	5,800
Depreciation expense.	12,400
Loss on sale of equipment	8,400
Net income before income taxes	31,200
Income tax expense	8,800
Net income.	$ 22,400

Required

Using the above data, prepare the 2013 statement of cash flow for Catalina Divers Supply Company using the indirect method. What does the company's statement of cash flow reveal about the business's financial health?

P3.26   **Analyzing and Interpreting Cash Flow Data: A Growing Enterprise.**   Presented below are cash flow data for **L.A. Gear Inc.** During this period of time, the manufacturer of athletic shoes and sportswear experienced a 1200 percent growth in net income.

L.A. GEAR INC. **Statement of Cash Flow** **For Year Ended 12/31**			
(in thousands)	**Year 3**	**Year 2**	**Year 1**
Cash flow from operations			
Net income.	$55,059	$22,030	$ 4,371
Depreciation.	1,199	446	133
Noncash compensation to employees.	558	—	—
Increase in accounts receivable.	(51,223)	(34,378)	(12,410)
Increase in inventories	(72,960)	(50,743)	(1,990)
Increase in prepayments	(8,624)	(2,432)	(599)
Increase in accounts payable.	17,871	7,197	1,656
Increase (decrease) in other current liabilities	10,587	11,193	(537)
Cash flow from operations.	(47,533)	(46,687)	(9,376)
Cash flow from investing			
Sale of marketable securities.	—	—	5,661
Acquisition of property, plant & equipment.	(6,168)	(2,546)	(874)
Acquisition of other noncurrent assets.	(246)	(406)	(241)
Cash flow from investing	(6,414)	(2,952)	4,546
Cash flow from financing			
Increase (decrease) in short-term borrowing	(19,830)	50,104	4,566
Issue of common stock	69,925	495	—
Cash flow from financing.	50,095	50,599	4,566
Change in cash.	$ (3,852)	$ 960	$ (264)

Required

1. Explain why the cash flow from operations is negative.
2. How did the company finance its operations during the three-year period? Explain the logic of this strategy.
3. Depreciation expense as a percent of net income is only two to three percent during this period. What might explain this?

P3.27   **Analyzing and Interpreting Cash Flow Data: A Failing Enterprise.**   **L.A. Gear**, a manufacturer of sports shoes and sportswear, began operations in the early 1980s. By late 1996, however, the company was in bankruptcy. Following are cash flow data for the company for the period 1995–1996.

L.A. GEAR INC.		
Consolidated Statements of Cash Flow		
For Year Ended 12/31		
($ thousands)	1996	1995
Operating activities		
Net loss	$(61,689)	$(51,397)
Adjustments to reconcile net loss to net cash		
provided by (used in) operating activities		
Depreciation and amortization	4,555	7,266
Minority interest in net loss of joint venture	(6,986)	(1,324)
Loss on sale or abandonment of property and equipment . .	77	417
Increase in reserve for unused barter credits.	—	4,568
Write-off of goodwill.	8,324	1,012
Unrealized foreign exchange gain	—	(570)
(Increase) decrease, net of effects of acquisitions, in		
Accounts receivable, net	20,581	30,603
Inventories	18,095	6,100
Prepaid expenses & other current assets.	1,507	3,320
Other assets	(12)	1,624
Increase (decrease), net of effects of acquisitions, in		
Accounts payable & accrued liabilities.	16,166	(12,831)
Net cash provided by (used in) operating activities	618	(11,212)
Investing activities		
Capital expenditures	(710)	(3,256)
Net cash used in investing activities	(710)	(3,256)
Financing activities		
Costs related to issuance of Series B Shares	(661)	—
Net (repayments) borrowings under international		
credit facilities	(1,216)	622
Net cash (used in) provided by financing activities	(1,877)	622
Effect of exchange rate changes on cash & cash equivalents. . . .	252	92
Net (decrease) increase in cash & cash equivalents	(1,717)	(13,754)
Cash & cash equivalents at beginning of year.	35,956	49,710
Cash & cash equivalents at end of year.	$ 34,239	$ 35,956

Required

Explain how L.A. Gear generated cash to sustain its operations during the period prior to its bankruptcy filing. What other financing options were available to the company?

 P3.28 **Statement of Cash Flow: International.** Recent financial statements for **The Hoechst Group**, a German conglomerate with operations in agriculture, chemicals, pharmaceuticals, and veterinary products are presented as follows:

THE HOECHST GROUP
Consolidated Balance Sheet
(in millions of Euros)
For Year Ended 12/31

	Year 2	Year 1
Intangible assets	15,077	15,200
Property, plant & equipment	12,958	15,861
Investments	7,336	7,562
Noncurrent assets	35,371	38,623
Inventories	5,507	6,739
Receivables & prepaid items	14,630	14,908
Liquid assets	391	635
Current assets	20,528	22,282
Total assets	55,899	60,905
Equity of Hoechst AG stockholders	16,599	16,012
Minority interests	2,580	3,097
Stockholders' equity	19,179	19,109
Provisions for pensions & similar obligations	6,883	6,910
Other provisions	8,751	9,476
Provisions	15,634	16,386
Corporate debt	12,509	16,615
Liabilities & deferred income	8,577	8,795
Total stockholders' equity & liabilities	55,899	60,905

THE HOECHST GROUP
Consolidated Statement of Profit & Loss
(in millions of Euros)
For Year Ended 12/31

	Year 2	Year 1
Net sales	43,704	52,100
Cost of goods sold	(25,533)	(31,533)
Gross profit	18,171	20,567
Distribution & selling costs	(8,940)	(10,206)
Research & development costs	(3,820)	(3,990)
General & administrative costs	(2,680)	(2,808)
Other operating income	2,331	1,834
Other operating expense	(1,891)	(1,744)
Operating profit	3,171	3,653
Result on sale & transfer of business	64	304
Investment income, net	1,062	309
Interest expense, net	(1,037)	(1,019)
Other financial expense, net	(157)	(90)
Profit before taxes on income	3,103	3,157
Taxes on income	(944)	(1,383)
Income before minority interests	2,159	1,774
Minority interests	(264)	(431)
Net income	1,895	1,343

The following additional information was contained in the company's footnotes:

1. Depreciation expense of 2,190 in Year 2 was included in the cost of goods sold.
2. Amortization of intangible assets totaled 1,000 in Year 2 and was included in "General and Administrative Costs."

3. A gain on the sale of investments of 300 in Year 2 was included in "Investment income, net."
4. There were no sales or repurchases of Hoechst capital stock during Year 2.

Required

Prepare a statement of cash flow for The Hoechst Group for Year 2 using the indirect method. What does the company's statement of cash flow reveal about the business's financial health?

CORPORATE ANALYSIS

CA3.29   **The Procter & Gamble Company.**   The 2012 annual report of **The Procter & Gamble Company** (P&G) is available at http://annualreport.pg.com/annualreport2012/index.shtml. After reviewing P&G's annual report, respond to the following questions:

  a.   P&G's 2012 statement of cash flow is presented using the indirect method format. Calculate P&G's cash conversion ratio for 2012. What does the cash conversion ratio tell you about P&G's operating revenues? Is this good news or bad news? Why?
  b.   Calculate P&G's EBITDA, free cash flow, and discretionary cash flow for 2010, 2011, and 2012. What can you conclude about P&G's cash position from these measures?
  c.   Calculate P&G's sustainable earnings for 2010, 2011, and 2012. What can you conclude about the persistence of P&G's earnings?

CA3.30   **Internet-based Analysis.**   Consider a publicly-held company whose products you are familiar with. Some examples might include:

Company	Product	Corporate Website
• **Johnson & Johnson Company**.........	• Band-Aids	• www.jnj.com
• **Microsoft Corporation**...............	• Windows XP software	• www.microsoft.com
• **Nokia Corporation**..................	• Cellular phones	• www.nokia.com
• **Intel Corporation**....................	• Pentium processors	• www.intel.com
• **Kimberly-Clark Corporation**..........	• Kleenex	• www.kimberly-clark.com

Access the company's public website and search for its most recent annual report. (Note: Some companies will provide access to their financial data through an "investor relations" link, while others will provide a direct link to their "annual reports.") After locating your company's most recent annual report, open the file and review its contents. After reviewing the annual report for your selected company, prepare answers to the following questions:

  a.   Identify the company's basic and diluted earnings per share (EPS) for the past two years. Is there a difference between these EPS numbers? If so, what dilutive claims are responsible for the decline in basic earnings per share?
  b.   Review the company's income statement. Are there any extraordinary or special items, restructuring charges, changes in accounting principles, or discontinued operations in either of the last two years? If so, calculate the company's sustainable earnings for each year.
  c.   Consider the company's statement of cash flow. What format—indirect or direct—is used to present the cash flow from operations? Convert the company's cash flow from operations from the indirect (direct) format to the direct (indirect) format (see Appendix 3A).
  d.   Calculate the company's EBITDA, free cash flow, and discretionary cash flow for each of the past two years. Comment on the company's cash flow health.

CA3.31   **IFRS Financial Statements.**   The 2012 financial statements of **LVMH Moet Hennessey-Louis Vuitton S.A.** are presented in Appendix C of this book. LVMH is a Paris-based holding company and one of the world's largest and best-known luxury goods companies. As a member-nation of the European Union, French companies are required to prepare their consolidated (group) financial statements using International Financial Reporting Standards (IFRS). After reviewing LVMH's consolidated income statement and consolidated cash flow statement in Appendix C, prepare answers to the following questions:

  a.   What differences (if any) do you observe between the format of LVMH's consolidated income statement under IFRS and what you would expect to see if the company had been using U.S. GAAP to prepare its income statement?
  b.   What differences (if any) do you observe between the format of LVMH's consolidated cash flow statement under IFRS and the statement of cash flow for Texas Instruments presented in Exhibit 3.2?

SOLUTION TO REVIEW PROBLEM

Solution

THE ARCADIA COMPANY Statement of Cash Flow For Year Ended 12/31/12	
(Indirect Method)	
Operating activities	
Net loss	$(18,000)
Depreciation expense	28,500
Inventory	26,500
Prepaid insurance	1,500
Accounts payable	(2,500)
Wages payable	10,500
Cash flow from operations.	46,500
Investing activities	
Marketable securities.	7,500
Building, net.	(31,000)
Cash flow from investing	(23,500)
Financing activities	
Bank loan.	2,000
Dividends paid.	(2,000)
Cash flow from investing	-0-
Net increase in cash.	23,000
Cash, beginning of year	7,000
Cash, end of year.	$ 30,000
Change in cash (from balance sheet).	$ 23,000

Operating funds ratio = $46,500/$(18,000) = Not meaningful
Operating cash flow to current liabilities ratio = $46,500/$110,500 = 0.42
Cash conversion ratio = $480,000/$480,000 = 1.00

When you complete this chapter you should be able to:

1. Analyze financial statements to evaluate company profitability, asset management, and financial risk.

2. Construct pro forma financial statements to evaluate a company's ability to generate future earnings and cash flows.

3. Explain the return on equity model of financial analysis.

4. Describe the limitations of financial statement analysis.

Using Financial Statements for Investing and Credit Decisions

Under Armour, Inc. is a classic American success story. The company was founded in 1996 by Kevin Plank, a recent graduate and former football player at the University of Maryland. During his playing days Plank found one irritant hard to shake—the t-shirts under his pads became soaked and uncomfortable. He set out with the simple goal of making a better t-shirt, one that would keep perspiration off the body rather than absorb it, helping to regulate temperature, provide comfort, and ultimately help athletes perform at a higher level.

Starting from his grandmother's basement with $17,000 in sales in his first year, the company today has products sold around the globe with almost $2 billion in sales. Plank has kept the company to its founding core, operating much as it did at inception. There is a simple brand mission: "To make all athletes better through passion, design and the relentless pursuit of innovation." The company does this through the design, development, marketing, and distribution of apparel, shoes and accessories for most mainstream sports. The apparel offered by Under Amour is designed in three fit types: compression, fitted, and loose. These variations allow the clothing to be effective in various changing temperatures. Its most popular footwear products are for football, baseball, lacrosse, softball and soccer. The company's successful accessory categories are in these same sports.

Under Armour sells its products primarily through retail operations such as **Dick's Sporting Goods** and through contractual agreements with institutional athletic departments, sports leagues and professional teams. The company also sells directly to consumers through its website and stand-alone stores. Under Armour's recent success has been largely due to the energy and funds invested in building brand awareness. During 2011 the company's advertising expenditures topped $167.9 million. A number of high profile athletes have endorsement and sponsorship deals with the company, to include NFL quarterback Tom Brady, MLB baseball player Ryan Howard, and professional golfer Hunter Mahan.

While Under Armour has experienced phenomenal success over the last 15 years, it still operates on a much smaller scale than its primary competitor, **Nike**. As of December 2011 Nike was valued at about $38 billion, 12 times that of Under Armour. Product selection and brand awareness, particularly internationally, have been the primary drivers of the company's success and underlie its future prospects. In this chapter, we examine various financial statement analysis techniques that can be used to evaluate the profitability, asset management effectiveness, and financial risk of a company like Under Armour. The results of a historical financial analysis can then be used to help assess the fair value of a company's share price, either on a stand-alone basis or relative to a competitor like Nike.

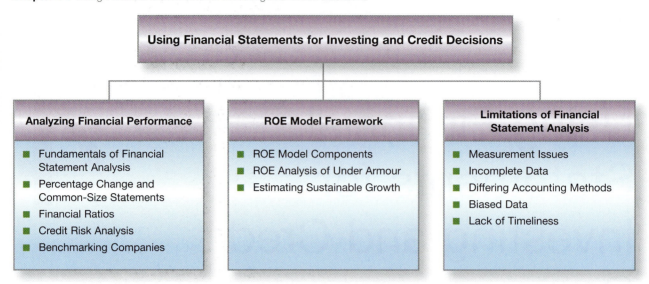

ANALYZING FINANCIAL PERFORMANCE

The financial statements of a company are perhaps the single most important source of information when making credit-granting and investment decisions. Credit-granting decisions involve a judgment about a firm's ability to make timely payments on existing or pending credit obligations. Investment decisions, on the other hand, involve determining an appropriate valuation for a security, often labeled "intrinsic value," based on a firm's ability to generate future payoffs such as earnings and/or cash flow.

Since credit and investment decisions are largely based on estimates of future revenues and expenses, as well as the assets and liabilities that help generate them, a thorough evaluation of a company's past financial performance can be a useful guide to predicting its future financial success. (A discussion of the development of forecasted financial statements is presented in Appendix 4B to this chapter.) In this section, the historical financial statements of **Under Armour, Inc.** are analyzed to illustrate how assessments of a company's recent and past profitability, asset management, and financial risk can be developed. These assessments can then be used to help forecast Under Armour's future performance, and hence, the company's fair market or intrinsic value.

Fundamentals of Financial Statement Analysis

Analysts and investors rely on a vast array of techniques to understand the financial performance and condition of companies. This collection includes methods for analyzing operating performance, financial condition, cash flow, liquidity and solvency, and capital structure and risk. Although there is no fixed set of these methods, and while individuals often rely upon their own personalized assessment tools, there is a core set of steps used by most when analyzing a company. In this chapter, we offer a general approach to financial statement analysis that will help answer the most fundamental questions regarding a company's operating performance and financial health.

To accomplish this, we perform an illustrative analysis of Under Armour, Inc., a successful apparel company profiled at the start of this chapter. We describe certain key ratios and techniques to illustrate how information can be extracted from financial statements. As we look at various metrics, remember that each is just one piece of a mosaic that an analyst is attempting to build regarding a company to form a realistic representation of its past performance and future prospects. A single piece of data or metric by itself does not tell us much. At the end of 2011, for instance, Under Armour had $175.4 million in cash and almost $97 million in net income. So what? These numbers seem large, but how large are they? Only when we understand how each piece of the analytical puzzle connects will we be able to answer that question. As they examine various ratios and

To evaluate a business's capital intensity, some investment professionals calculate a capital intensity ratio as follows:

$$\text{Capital intensity} = \frac{\text{Fixed assets} + \text{Intangible assets}}{\text{Total assets}}$$

A higher intensity ratio indicates higher levels of capital investment. Under Armour's capital intensity ratio for 2011 is 18 percent. Can you calculate the company's capital intensity ratio for 2010?

metrics, the analyst will be looking for certain key patterns and changes that will help reveal a company's underlying financial story.

The first and most basic technique of financial statement analysis is "ocular regression"—that is, examining a firm's financial statements to observe any trends in its account balances. This technique is also called **trend analysis** or **longitudinal analysis**. Under Armour's consolidated income statement in Exhibit 4.1 shows, for example, that the company grew rapidly over the period 2009 to 2011, with revenues increasing from $856.4 million in 2009 to over $1.4 billion in 2011 (see **bolded** areas in Exhibit 4.1), representing an annual growth rate of over 31 percent. This revenue growth also translated into increased profits, with net income more than doubling from $46.8 million in 2009 to $96.9 million in 2011.

EXHIBIT 4.1	Under Armour, Inc.: Consolidated Statement of Income		
$ In thousands, except per share amounts, for year ended December 31:	**2011**	**2010**	**2009**
Net revenues.	$1,472,684	$1,063,927	$856,411
Cost of goods sold.	759,848	533,420	446,286
Gross profit.	712,836	530,507	410,125
Selling, general and administrative	550,069	418,152	324,852
Income from operations	162,767	112,355	85,273
Interest expense, net	(3,841)	(2,258)	(2,344)
Other expense, net.	(2,064)	(1,178)	(511)
Income before income taxes	156,862	108,919	82,418
Provision for income taxes.	59,943	40,442	35,633
Net income	$ 96,919	$ 68,477	$ 46,785
Net income available per common share			
Basic.	$1.88	$1.35	$0.94
Diluted.	$1.85	$1.34	$0.92
Weighted average common shares outstanding			
Basic.	51,570	50,798	49,848
Diluted.	52,526	51,282	50,650

Under Armour's consolidated balance sheet in Exhibit 4.2 shows that the company's total assets grew from over $675.3 million in 2010 to over $919 million in 2011 (see **bolded** areas in Exhibit 4.2), with over three-quarters of the growth due to an increase in inventory and property and equipment ($109 million and $83 million, respectively). The increase in these accounts is consistent with the expansion of the company's customer base and the greater need for physical facilities to service an expanding customer base. Under Armour's balance sheet also reveals that inventory is the single largest asset account on the balance sheet, which is not surprising for a retailer. Under Armour is a **capital-intensive business**—that is, a business requiring large investments in short-term working capital directly tied to the customer (i.e., accounts receivable and inventories) as well as long-lived tangible assets needed to meet those needs (i.e. property and equipment).

Under Armour's balance sheet also reveals that the company is financed with relatively little debt—long-term debt plus the current portion of long-term debt totaled only $77.7 million versus $636.4 million of shareholders' equity in 2011. Consequently, it appears that while Under Armour's use of debt financing is increasing ($77.7 in 2011 versus $15.9 million in 2010), the company's management appears to have made a strategic decision to finance most of the company's growth using internally-generated operating cash flow and stock equity financing.

Under Armour's consolidated statement of cash flow in Exhibit 4.3 reveals that the company generated a positive cash flow from operations in all three years from 2009 to 2011 (see **bolded** areas in Exhibit 4.3). Although the company has been growing, Under Armour's cash flow from operations actually decreased to just $15.2 million in 2011, from over $119 million two years earlier. On the surface this may seem counter-intuitive, but one can note from the statement that the change in accounts receivable, inventories, and prepaid expenses are the main culprits (see the changes in 2011 reported on the statement of cash flow in the amounts of $33.9 million, $114.6 million, and $42.6 million). The high revenue growth that the company has been experiencing has been put to work in these working capital accounts, effectively consuming the company's operating cash through the funding of these short term assets. It should be apparent that the

EXHIBIT 4.2	Under Armour, Inc.: Consolidated Balance Sheets		
$ In thousands, except per share amounts, as of the year ended December 31:		**2011**	**2010**
Assets			
Current assets			
Cash and cash equivalents		$175,384	$203,870
Accounts receivable, net		134,043	102,034
Inventories		**324,409**	**215,355**
Prepaid expenses and other current assets		39,643	19,326
Deferred income taxes		16,184	15,265
Total current assets		689,663	555,850
Property and equipment, net		**159,135**	**76,127**
Intangible assets, net		5,535	3,914
Deferred income taxes		15,885	21,275
Other long term assets		48,992	18,212
Total assets		**$919,210**	**$675,378**
Liabilities and Stockholders' Equity			
Current liabilities			
Accounts payable		$100,527	$84,679
Accrued expenses		69,285	55,138
Current maturities of long term debt		**6,882**	**6,865**
Other current liabilities		6,913	2,465
Total current liabilities		183,607	149,147
Long term debt, net of current maturities		**70,842**	**9,077**
Other long term liabilities		28,329	20,188
Total liabilities		**282,778**	**178,412**
Stockholders' equity			
Class A Common Stock, $.0003 1/3 par value		13	13
Class B Convertible Common Stock, $.0003 1/3 par value		4	4
Additional paid-in capital		268,223	224,887
Retained earnings		366,164	270,021
Accumulated other comprehensive income		2,028	2,041
Total stockholders' equity		**636,432**	**496,966**
Total liabilities and stockholders' equity		**$919,210**	**$675,378**

company's increasing capital expenditures of $19.8 million to $56.2 million from 2009 to 2011 is also consistent with a company experiencing high growth, and one positioning itself for future growth.

In summary, a trend analysis of Under Armour's financial statements suggests that the following trends characterized the business over the three-year period of 2009 to 2011:

■ Under Armour's operating revenues grew substantially, and the company was able to turn this into even greater growth in bottom-line net income.

■ Under Armour's total assets increased due to substantial investments in such working capital assets as inventories and accounts receivable, as well as in such long-term tangible assets as property and equipment.

■ The company's cash from operations slowed even as the company itself expanded. The aforementioned expansion of the company's asset base was funded in part from this internally-generated cash flow and a modest increase in borrowing.

Percentage Change and Common-Size Financial Statements

A second widely used step in financial analysis requires a closer look at the relative size of the account balances on a company's financial statements so that they may be put into further historical perspective. Two complementary techniques are commonly used: (1) analyzing the growth in an account balance across time periods, and (2) analyzing the proportion of an account balance relative to other accounts.

EXHIBIT 4.3	Under Armour, Inc.: Consolidated Statements of Cash Flow		

$ In thousands, for year ended December 31:	2011	2010	2009
Cash flows from operating activities			
Net income	$ 96,919	$ 68,477	$ 46,785
Depreciation and amortization	36,301	31,321	28,249
Unrealized foreign currency exchange rate (gains) losses	4,027	1,280	(5,222)
Loss on disposal of property and equipment	36	44	37
Stock-based compensation	18,063	16,227	12,910
Gain on bargain purchase of corp. headquarters	(3,300)	—	—
Deferred income taxes	3,620	(10,337)	(5,212)
Changes in reserves and allowances	5,536	2,322	1,623
Changes in operating assets and liabilities			
Accounts receivable	**(33,923)**	(32,320)	3,792
Inventories	**(114,646)**	(65,239)	32,998
Prepaid expenses and other assets	**(42,633)**	(4,099)	1,870
Accounts payable	17,209	16,158	(4,386)
Accrued expenses and other liabilities	23,442	21,330	11,656
Income taxes payable and receivable.	4,567	4,950	(6,059)
Net cash provided by operating activities	**15,218**	**50,114**	**119,041**
Cash flows from investing activities			
Purchase of property and equipment	(56,228)	(30,182)	(19,845)
Purchase of corp. headquarters and related expenditures.	(23,164)	—	—
Purchase of long term investment	(3,862)	(11,125)	—
Purchases of other assets.	(1,153)	(478)	(35)
Change in restricted cash	(5,029)	—	—
Net cash used in investing activities	**(89,436)**	**(41,785)**	**(19,880)**
Cash flows from financing activities			
Proceeds from revolving credit facility	30,000	—	—
Payments on revolving credit facility.	(30,000)	—	(25,000)
Proceeds from term loan.	25,000	—	—
Proceeds from long term debt	5,644	5,262	7,649
Payments on long term debt.	(7,418)	(9,446)	(7,656)
Payments on capital lease obligations	—	(97)	(361)
Excess tax benefits from stock-based comp. arrangements	10,260	4,189	5,127
Proceeds from exercise of stock options and other	14,645	7,335	5,128
Payments of debt financing costs.	(2,324)	—	(1,354)
Net cash provided by (used in) financing activities.	**45,807**	**7,243**	**(16,467)**
Effect of exchange rate changes on cash and equivalents	(75)	1,001	2,561
Net increase (decrease) in cash and cash equivalents.	**(28,486)**	**16,573**	**85,255**
Cash and cash equivalents			
Beginning of year	203,870	187,297	102,042
End of year	$175,384	$203,870	$187,297
Non-cash financing and investing activities			
Debt assumed in connection with purchase of corporate			
headquarters.	$ 38,556	$ —	$ —
Other supplemental information			
Cash paid for income taxes	56,940	38,773	40,834
Cash paid for interest	2,305	992	1,273

Percentage change and **common-size financial statements**, respectively, are the labels given to these tools. View them for what they are—recasting dollar amounts contained in the original financial statements to an easy-to-interpret and more readily comparable set of financial relations. All accounts are expressed as either a growth variable or a relative proportion. Both of these perspectives together help highlight key financial activity, particularly the often subtle but important shifts in asset, liability, or expense mix.

A **percentage change income statement**, for example, shows how the revenue and expense accounts have grown or shrunk from period to period. A **common-size income statement**, on the other hand, shows

In highly competitive industries it is often necessary to offer customers the opportunity to buy a company's products on credit. To minimize the opportunity cost (the time value of money) associated with extending credit to customers, some businesses offer their customers an incentive for quick payment of credit purchases. Quick payment incentives typically take the form of a price reduction called a **sales discount**. Sales discounts are subtracted from gross revenues, and thus, represent a contra-revenue account. Another contra-revenue account is the **sales returns** account, which represents the value of goods allowed to be returned by customers who are dissatisfied with a product. We will have more to say about sales discounts and sales returns in Chapter 5.

all of the income statement items expressed as a percentage of net revenues for that same year. **Net revenues** are gross revenues less any **sales discounts** and/or **sales returns**. The advantages of these tools should be clear. Both statements would allow the financial statement user to readily compare the performance of firms of different size or to compare the performance of the same firm that grows or shrinks in size over time. As an example, one would naturally expect that as the dollar value of Under Armour's net sales revenue increases over time, so too would its cost of goods sold. Unfortunately, it is difficult to ascertain the relative rate of change in the cost of goods sold (or any other operating expense) just by examining the dollar-value of the account. Percentage change and common-size income statements make the analysis much simpler by highlighting whether, in what direction, and in percentage terms, how much each operating expense changed relative to a company's operating revenue. A percentage change and common-size income statement for Under Armour is presented in Exhibit 4.4. This data shows that all of Under Armour's major income statement accounts grew substantially in 2010 and 2011. For instance, 2011 saw a net revenue increase of 38.4 percent and a cost of goods sold increase of 42.4 percent (see **bolded** values in Exhibit 4.4). Thus, while growth is good, the fact that expenses grew faster than revenues implies the company would be earning less per dollar of sales in 2011 than it had in 2010. The common size income statement confirms this fact. Gross profit, the difference between net revenues and cost of sales, declined in 2011 to 48.4 percent from 49.9 percent in 2010. Note that one of Under Armour's largest percentage expense increases was for interest expense, 70.1 percent in 2011. While this does indicate an increase, on average, in the use of debt financing, and may seem a significant increase, the common-size income statement for 2011 also tells us that interest costs represent a paltry 0.3 percent of net revenues. Overall, Under Armour's **return on sales**, defined as net income divided by net sales, has been modestly improving to around 6.6 percent (see **bolded** area in Exhibit 4.4).

EXHIBIT 4.4	Under Armour, Inc.: Percentage Change and Common-Sized Income Statements					
		Percentage Change		**Common Size**		
		2011	**2010**	**2011**	**2010**	**2009**
Net revenues		38.4%	24.2%	100.0%	100.0%	100.0%
Cost of goods sold		42.4	19.5	51.6	50.1	52.1
Gross profit		34.4	29.4	**48.4**	49.9	47.9
Selling, general and administrative		31.5	28.7	37.4	39.3	37.9
Income from operations		44.9	31.8	11.1	10.6	10.0
Interest expense, net		**70.1**	(3.7)	**(0.3)**	(0.2)	(0.3)
Other expense, net		75.2	130.5	(0.1)	(0.1)	(0.1)
Income before income taxes		44.0	32.2	10.7	10.2	9.6
Provision for income taxes		48.2	13.5	4.1	3.8	4.2
Net income		**41.5%**	**46.4%**	**6.6%**	**6.4%**	**5.5%**

Percentage change and common-size balance sheets for Under Armour are presented in Exhibit 4.5. As with the income statement, percentage changes are computed by comparing the current year account balance with those from the prior year. A **common-size balance sheet**, similar to that of the income statement, shows all of the balance sheet accounts expressed in terms of a single common denominator, a given year's total assets. A review of Exhibit 4.5 reveals that Under Armour's two largest assets in 2011 were cash and inventories, representing 19.1 and 35.3 percent of the company's total assets for that year, respectively (see **bolded** area in Exhibit 4.5). Relative to 2010, however, cash declined substantially from 30.2 percent for that year, or a 14.0 percent total decline. Consistent with the trend analysis of Under Armour's financial statements, the common-size balance sheet highlights the fact that Under Armour has relatively little long-term debt on its balance sheet—long-term debt plus the current portion of long-term debt is just 8.5 percent of total assets while shareholders' equity is over 69 percent of total assets. But consistent with the higher interest costs referenced in Exhibit 4.4, debt use increased during 2011; in 2010, total long-term debt was just 2.4 percent of total assets. Overall, this finding reinforces the prior observation that Under Armour is principally equity financed.

| EXHIBIT 4.5 | Under Armour, Inc.: Percentage Change and Common-Sized Balance Sheets |

	% Change	Common Size	
	2011	2011	2010
Assets			
Current assets			
Cash and cash equivalents	(14.0)	19.1	30.2
Accounts receivable, net	31.4	14.6	15.1
Inventories	50.6	35.3	31.9
Prepaid expenses and other current assets	105.1	4.3	2.9
Deferred income taxes	6.0	1.8	2.3
Total current assets	24.1	75.0	82.3
Property and equipment, net	109.0	17.3	11.3
Intangible assets, net	41.4	0.6	0.6
Deferred income taxes	(25.3)	1.7	3.2
Other long term assets	169.0	5.3	2.7
Total assets	36.1	100.0	100.0
Liabilities and Stockholders' Equity			
Current liabilities			
Accounts payable	18.7	10.9	12.5
Accrued expenses	25.7	7.5	8.2
Current maturities of long term debt	0.2	0.7	1.0
Other current liabilities	180.4	0.8	0.4
Total current liabilities	23.1	20.0	22.1
Long term debt, net of current maturities	680.5	7.7	1.3
Other long term liabilities	40.3	3.1	3.0
Total liabilities	58.5	30.8	26.4
Stockholders' equity			
Class A Common Stock	—	0.0	0.0
Class B Convertible Common Stock	—	0.0	0.0
Additional paid-in capital	19.3	29.2	33.3
Retained earnings	35.6	39.8	40.0
Accumulated other comprehensive income	(0.6)	0.2	0.3
Total stockholders' equity	28.1	69.2	73.6
Total liabilities and stockholders' equity	36.1	100.0	100.0

Financial Ratios

Another technique for analyzing a company's financial performance is the calculation of **ratios** of relevant accounting variables—that is, dividing (or standardizing) one accounting measure by another economically relevant measure. A company may, for instance, report a numerically large net income, but the reason for the firm's success in generating a large net income may simply be a function of its size and not that the business is well run. To address this analytical issue, it is useful to compute such ratios as the return on assets (ROA), which provides an assessment of whether net income is large relative to a firm's size, as defined by its investment in assets. Financial ratios enable financial statement users to make valid comparisons of firm operating performance, over time for the same firm and between comparable companies.

When analyzing a firm's financial health, investment professionals, lenders, managers, and shareholders are usually interested in gaining insights about a firm's profitability, asset management, and financial risk. **Profitability** refers to how much income was generated by a business, particularly relative to the amount of total assets invested in the business or relative to the amount of assets specifically invested by a company's shareholders. **Asset management**, on the other hand, refers to how effectively the invested assets were used in the business by the company's management team. Finally, **financial risk** refers to a firm's ability to repay its borrowings in a timely manner and may be evaluated both in terms of a firm's short-term debt repayment capability and its long-term debt repayment capacity. **Liquidity** refers to the ability of a company to generate cash and is often considered a good indication of a company's ability to pay its outstanding *short-term* obligations. Short-term sources of liquidity include existing current assets, ongoing operations, and available lines of credit. **Solvency**, on the other hand, generally refers to the ability of a company to repay its outstanding *long-term* obligations. Liquidity and solvency are related concepts since a company must have sufficient liquidity to remain solvent. Firms that borrow extensively are said to be highly leveraged and carry greater financial risk; they are also said to be less solvent. **Leverage** refers to the use of borrowed funds to finance operations and/or asset purchases. Solvency and leverage are inversely related—that is, all else equal, a highly leveraged firm is less solvent than a firm that uses little or no debt to finance its business.

Some of the financial ratios that are commonly calculated by investment professionals, lenders, and managers are presented and explained in Exhibit 4.6. The application and interpretation of these ratios can be illustrated using the financial data of Under Armour, to which we now turn.

EXHIBIT 4.6 Key Financial Ratios

Ratio	Definition	Explanation
Profitability		
• Return on shareholders' equity (ROE)	$\dfrac{\text{Net income} - \text{Preferred stock dividends}}{\text{Shareholders' equity}}$	Rate of return generated by a business for its common shareholders.
• Return on assets (ROA)	$\dfrac{\text{Net income} + [\text{Interest expense}\,(1 - \text{Tax rate})]}{\text{Total assets}}$	Rate of return generated on a company's investment in assets from all sources.
• Return on sales (ROS)	$\dfrac{\text{Net income}}{\text{Net sales}}$	Percentage of net income remaining from a dollar of sales after subtracting all expenses. Often this ratio is referred to as "net profit margin".
• Gross profit margin ratio	$\dfrac{(\text{Net sales} - \text{Cost of goods sold})}{\text{Net sales}}$	Percentage of income generated from sales after deducting the cost of goods sold.
Asset Management		
• Receivable turnover	$\dfrac{\text{Net sales}}{\text{Accounts receivable}}$	Number of sales/collection cycles experienced by a firm.
• Receivable collection period	$\dfrac{365}{(\text{Net sales}/\text{Accounts receivable})}$	Number of days required, on average, to collect an outstanding account receivable.
• Inventory turnover	$\dfrac{\text{Cost of goods sold}}{\text{Inventory}}$	Number of production/sales cycles experienced by a firm.
• Inventory-on-hand period	$\dfrac{365}{(\text{Cost of goods sold}/\text{Inventory})}$	Number of days, on average, required to sell the inventory currently on hand.
• Asset turnover	$\dfrac{\text{Net sales}}{\text{Total assets}}$	Amount of sales generated from each dollar invested in assets.
Liquidity		
• Cash and marketable securities to total assets	$\dfrac{(\text{Cash} + \text{Marketable securities})}{\text{Total assets}}$	Percentage of total assets held as highly liquid assets.
• Quick ratio	$\dfrac{(\text{Cash} + \text{Marketable securities} + \text{Accounts receivable})}{\text{Current liabilities}}$	Amount of liquid assets available to pay short-term liabilities.
• Current ratio	$\dfrac{\text{Current assets}}{\text{Current liabilities}}$	Amount of current assets available to service current liabilities.
• Accounts payable turnover	$\dfrac{\text{Cost of goods sold}}{\text{Accounts payable}}$	Number of account payment cycles experienced by a firm.
• Days' payable period	$\dfrac{365}{\text{Cost of goods sold}/\text{Accounts payable}}$	Number of days, on average, required to pay an outstanding account payable.'
Solvency		
• Long-term debt to total assets	$\dfrac{(\text{Long-term debt} + \text{Current portion of long-term debt})}{\text{Total assets}}$	Percentage of total assets provided by creditors.
• Long-term debt to shareholders' equity	$\dfrac{(\text{Long-term debt} + \text{Current portion of long-term debt})}{\text{Shareholders' equity}}$	Relative investment of long-term creditors versus shareholders in a business.
• Interest coverage ratio	$\dfrac{\text{Net income before taxes} + \text{Interest expense}}{\text{Interest expense}}$	Extent to which current operating income covers current debt service charges.

Financial ratios assessing the profitability, asset management, liquidity and solvency for Under Armour are shown in Exhibit 4.7. You may wish to replicate these calculations using Under Armour's financial statements in Exhibits 4.1, 4.2, 4.3, and the ratio definitions in Exhibit 4.6.

EXHIBIT 4.7	Financial Ratios: Under Armour, Inc.		
Fiscal Year Ending		**2011**	**2010**
Ratio			
Profitability			
Gross profit margin ratio.		48.4%	49.9%
Return on sales (ROS)		6.6%	6.4%
Return on assets (ROA)		10.8%	10.3%
Return on equity (ROE).		15.2%	13.8%
Asset Management			
Receivable turnover (# times).		11.0	10.4
Receivable collection in days.		33.2	35.0
Inventory turnover (# times)		2.3	2.5
Inventory-on-hand in days		155.8	147.4
Asset turnover		1.6	1.6
Liquidity			
Cash & marketable securities to total assets.		0.19	0.30
Quick ratio		1.69	2.05
Current ratio		3.76	3.73
Accounts payable turnover (# times)		7.56	6.30
Days' payable in days		48.29	57.94
Solvency			
Long-term debt to total assets.		8.5%	2.4%
Long-term debt to shareholders' equity.		12.2%	3.2%
Interest coverage ratio (# times).		41.8	49.2

There is no generally accepted definition for most of the financial ratios presented in Exhibit 4.6, and consequently, the ratios may be calculated in a variety of ways. For example, to calculate the return on assets ratio, some analysts use an average of the beginning and ending total assets as the denominator, while others use only the ending or beginning balance of total assets. This is done to match the numerator (i.e. net income), which is computed over a period of time, with the denominator (i.e. total assets), which is computed at a point in time. In general, unless there has been a large movement in the level of the denominator over the time period being analyzed, the definition used to define a ratio's calculation won't make much difference when ranking companies from best to worst. What is important is to define ratios consistently over time and between companies so that any performance comparisons are "apples to apples" and not "apples to oranges."

With respect to corporate profitability, Under Armour's cost of goods sold increased slightly relative to net sales over the two-year period 2010 to 2011 (see Exhibit 4.4), causing the company to suffer a small decrease in its **gross profit margin ratio** from 49.9 percent of net revenues in 2010 to 48.4 percent in 2011. However, Under Armour generated a slightly improved **return on sales** (ROS) of 6.6 percent in 2011, up from 6.4 percent in 2010.[1] This means that for every dollar of sales in 2011, Under Armour earned 6.6 cents after subtracting all expenses. An ROS of this magnitude may seem low, although it should be noted that the apparel industry is extremely competitive, requiring significant manufacturing and marketing expenditures. Under Armour's **return on assets** (ROA) of 10.8 percent in 2011 was also up from the company's 2010 level of 10.3 percent. The company's **return on equity** (ROE) followed a similar pattern, increasing to 15.2 percent in 2011 from 13.8 percent a year earlier, more than 4.4 percentage points over its 2011 ROA and 5.5 percentage points above its cost of equity. (See Appendix 4C for a discussion of how to calculate a company's cost of equity financing.)

---

[1] Many investment professionals use an alternative calculation of the return of sales (ROS) ratio, called the unlevered ROS ratio, calculated as follows:

$$\text{Unlevered ROS} = \frac{\text{Net income} + \text{Interest}\,(1 - \text{tax rate})}{\text{Net sales}}$$

The unlevered ROS ratio enables the analyst to evaluate the effectiveness of a company's operating strategy independent of its financing strategy; that is, unlevering ROS restates a firm's net income as if the firm were all equity financed. A discussion of unlevering ratios is presented in Appendix 4A to this chapter.

One measure of how well a company utilizes its borrowed funds involves a comparison of the company's ROE with its ROA. Since the ROA represents the return to all capital contributors while ROE is the return to just the company's shareholders, an ROE in excess of ROA indicates that a firm is earning more on its borrowed funds than its cost to borrow those funds. For example, if a firm borrows funds at an interest rate of five percent and subsequently earns eight percent from the use of those funds, the excess earnings accrue to the company's shareholders. Since Under Armour reported an ROE that was 4.4 percentage points greater than its ROA, the company can be described as being able to effectively utilize financial leverage. We will discuss **financial leverage** in greater detail shortly.

With respect to asset management, Under Armour's **inventory-on-hand** period—that is, the average number of days that a business's inventory remains on hand before being sold—indicates that Under Armour keeps high amounts of inventory on hand (i.e., 155.8 days in 2011). This ratio indicates a very slow moving inventory that may carry with it inventory holding and storage costs as well as obsolescence risk, and is consistent with the high inventory levels observed in our review of the company's balance sheet. The **receivable collection period**—that is, the average number of days that customers take to pay their bills—is a much more reasonable 33.2 days in 2011 (about one month). The company's **asset turnover** ratio indicates that, in both 2010 and 2011, every dollar invested in the business's assets generated $1.60 in sales. All else equal, the stability of this ratio indicates that as Under Armour has grown in size, it has not become more efficient at converting assets used in the business into sales to its customers.

GLOBAL PERSPECTIVE

Financial statement analysis is executed, worldwide, in exactly the same fashion. Common-size financial statements and financial ratios, for example, are currency-neutral and can be effectively utilized anywhere in the world. Not all ratios are relevant, however, in all countries. For example, in lesser-developed countries, which lack the infrastructure to support a credit system, ratios involving accounts receivables (such as receivable turnover and the receivable collection period) or accounts payable (such as accounts payable turnover and the days' payable period) are likely to be not as relevant for purposes of financial statement analysis.

Our review thus far of Under Armour indicates that inventory purchases and sales are critical operational drivers for the company. Ultimately purchases and sales of inventory must result in cash generation, and therefore analysts often combine the inventory-on-hand period with the receivable collection period to estimate the length of a company's **cash collection period**. This measure identifies the amount of time, on average, needed from the outlay of cash for inventory, through the sale of that inventory, until the ultimate collection of cash from the sale. In other words, the cash collection period represents the cash-to-cash cycle of a business. Since companies often acquire inventory on credit, without the necessity of paying interest on the credit purchase, an amount representing the average time taken to pay a company's accounts payable is often subtracted when estimating the cash collection period. The number of days needed to pay a firm's accounts payable is calculated as 365/(cost of goods sold/accounts payable) and is referred to as the **days' payable period**. Thus, a firm's cash collection period can be estimated as follows:

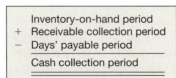

In the case of Under Armour, the cash collection period for 2011 was 140.7 days (33.2 days + 155.8 days − 48.3 days). Since Under Armour's business is inventory intensive and its inventory turnover very slow, the company is less able to finance its business operating cycle using interest-free trade credit from its suppliers. This business attribute may significantly impact Under Armour's profitability from year-to-year, as not only does the company bear certain inventory holding costs, but it is not able to leverage its suppliers to help finance that inventory. It is worth noting that accounts payable represent interest-free loans provided by one business to another business, and as such, need to be carefully monitored and managed through such financial indicators as the cash collection period and the days' payable period. It is also noteworthy that such interest-free debt as accounts payable are considered separately from a business's interest-bearing debt—its bank loans, bonds, and notes payable—when performing credit risk analysis, the focus of the next section.

The financial ratios in Exhibit 4.7 also indicate that Under Armour is relatively liquid—that is, it has liquid resources in the form of current assets to pay its current obligations as they come due. Under Armour's **current ratio**—the ratio of current assets to current liabilities—is well above one in both years. Hence, if all of the company's current assets were converted to cash, there would be sufficient cash to pay off all of Under Armour's current obligations. The **quick ratio**, which excludes Under Armour's potentially illiquid inventory, is 1.7 in 2011 and indicates that Under Armour's highly **liquid assets**, such as cash, marketable securities, and accounts receivable, are 1.7 times as large as the total of the obligations due within one year. Use of these ratios to analyze liquidity implicitly assumes that these assets can be converted into cash at a rate sufficient to match the timing of when the current obligations become due. Investment professionals often couple their analysis of the current and quick ratios with additional ratios such as the receivable collection period and the inventory-on- hand period, which indicate how quickly cash can be generated. Even though the cash collection period of 140 days for Under Armour may appear to be slow, the reality is that the company has solid liquidity in the short term, especially when coupled with its positive operating cash flow. Because of its liquid position and its high growth prospects, the relatively slow cash collection period for Under Armour is not as much of a concern as it otherwise might be.

> A company's **liquid assets** include cash, cash equivalents, marketable securities and accounts receivable, but exclude inventory and prepaid expenses, which are often illiquid. **Cash equivalents** are very short-term (90 days or less) investments in highly liquid, risk-free certificates of deposit or government securities.

Credit Risk Analysis

Current shareholders, investment advisors, and top management are vitally interested in a company's profitability and asset management because these factors are closely linked to future increases and decreases in a company's share price. Lenders, on the other hand, are less interested in these factors because creditors generally don't share in the upside potential of a firm when its share price appreciates. Creditors are more concerned with downside risk—that is, not getting paid the interest and principal they were promised. But what factors affect credit risk?

In general, the more indebtedness a firm has, the more likely it is that an unforeseen decline in sales and/or an increase in expenses will reduce a firm's capacity to meet its loan servicing commitments. The ratios of long-term debt, including the current portion of long-term debt, to total assets and to shareholders' equity are two ratios that measure the relative amount of a company's outstanding debt, and thus, its solvency. Similarly, the more operating income a company generates relative to the amount of its annual interest expense—the **interest coverage ratio**—the more likely it is that a company will be able to make timely interest payments from operating cash flow.

At the end of 2011, Under Armour's long-term debt was only 12.2 percent of its outstanding shareholders' equity. Further, Under Armour's interest coverage ratio—the ratio of operating income to interest expense—was a massive 41.8 times in 2011 and 49.2 times in 2010, respectively. On both counts, Under Armour's ability to take on additional debt with little risk to its lenders seems substantial. That puts the company in an excellent position to negotiate favorable credit terms such as a large loan with a low interest rate. With the company's strong historical operating cash flow averaging about $61 million per year over the period 2009-2011, the company should have little difficulty paying its interest charges or principal payments in a timely manner.

But how can you be sure that Under Armour has reported all of its outstanding debt on its balance sheet? Following the Enron Corporation scandal, it is likely that many more investors will carefully read the footnotes that accompany a company's financial statements, and in the case of Under Armour, such **due diligence** would be revealing. Under Armour's footnotes indicate that the company leases a number of its store locations through operating leases. Under an **operating lease** agreement, the value of the leased asset and the related lease liability do **not** appear on the company's balance sheet. Under Armour's footnotes reveal that the company has minimum future lease payments under operating leases of $185.2 million due over the next ten years. That means that Under Armour's debt ratios measured

> Because of complex accounting standards, some obligations (such as operating leases) do not appear on the face of the balance sheet, and thus, understate a firm's true debt position. These unreported liabilities are often referred to as **off-balance-sheet liabilities** and are described in detail in Chapters 9 and 10.

using only the debt listed on Under Armour's balance sheet *understate* the total level of corporate debt! Even if those **off-balance-sheet liabilities** were considered, however, Under Armour appears to be an excellent credit risk.

Benchmarking: Comparisons with Similar Companies

Assessing the significance of financial ratios can be substantially enhanced by comparing a company's financial ratios with those of competing companies in the same industry or the same line of business. This process is called **benchmarking** or **cross-sectional analysis**. Under Armour is classified as being in **Standard Industrial Code (SIC)** 2300 —The Apparel/Accessories Industry. Nike is a direct competitor to Under Armour and also operates in this industry. The company's trademark "swoosh" is an easily recognized logo across the globe, and Nike has translated this advantage into over $24 billion in annual sales. Shoe sales represent about 56 percent of this total, but the company has a diversified athletic product line across multiple apparel categories.

A Standard Industrial Classification (SIC) code is a categorization tool for all industries and services. The code itself is a unique number that corresponds to a text definition of a given industry. SIC codes are reported by companies on tax returns, U.S. Census Bureau reports, and other government filings.

Comparison ratios for Under Armour and Nike are reported in Exhibit 4.8. First observe that Nike has a fiscal year ending in the month of May, five months after Under Armour's fiscal year end of December. While the values used in both sets of ratios are still measured on an annual basis for both companies, the analyst should be aware that there is a five month lag between the two, during which time economic and market conditions may differ. Our comparisons for each company will be made with respect to their most recent year.

EXHIBIT 4.8	Financial Ratios: Under Armour versus Nike				
		Under Armour Year Ended Dec. 31		Nike Year Ended May 31	
Fiscal Year Ending		**2011**	**2010**	**2012**	**2011**
Profitability					
Gross profit margin ratio.		48.4%	49.9%	43.4%	45.6%
Return on sales (ROS)		6.6%	6.4%	9.2%	10.2%
Return on assets (ROA)		10.8%	10.3%	14.4%	14.2%
Return on equity (ROE).		15.2%	13.8%	21.4%	21.7%
Asset Management					
Receivable collection in days.		33.2	35.0	49.6	54.9
Inventory-on-hand in days.		155.8	147.4	89.5	87.3
Asset turnover		1.6	1.6	1.6	1.4
Liquidity					
Quick ratio		1.69	2.05	1.82	1.94
Current ratio.		3.76	3.73	2.98	2.85
Days' payable in days		48.29	57.94	42.44	47.22
Solvency					
Long-term debt to total assets.		8.5%	2.4%	1.8%	3.2%
Long-term debt to shareholders' equity.		12.2%	3.2%	2.7%	4.8%

With regard to firm profitability, Nike reported a lower gross profit margin, 43.4 percent versus Under Armour's 48.4 percent, but had a return on sales over two percentage points higher than Under Armour's—9.2 percent versus 6.6 percent. This suggests that Nike does a better job than Under Armour in controlling its overall total costs, but Under Armour has a lower relative cost of sales. This latter difference may be due in part to the company's product mix and pricing, as well as where their products are sold. Compared to Nike, Under Amour currently has a greater proportion of its sales in the U.S. and a much lower overall proportion of shoe sales. Depending on the pricing and manufacturing costs associated with these items in these markets, differences in gross margins do not come as a surprise. Nike's return on assets of 14.4 percent was also higher than Under Armour's ROA of 10.8 percent, with the same relation found for return on equity—21.4 percent versus 15.2 percent. Overall, it is difficult to avoid the conclusion that Nike is more profitable than Under Armour.

In terms of asset management, Nike holds significantly less inventory than Under Armour—89.5 days versus 155.8 days for Under Armour—which may reflect the different supply chain arrangements between the two companies, different strategies for product flexibility, or even possibly the effect of different inventory valuation methods (a topic that will be considered in Chapter 6). The two companies have similar asset turnover ratios at 1.6 each. In terms of liquidity, no conclusions can be reached other than Nike is carrying slightly less current assets (i.e., likely lower inventory levels), although both companies would be considered highly liquid as current ratios are strong. Quick ratios for each company also exceed 1.5, indicating highly liquid assets that can easily cover all liabilities that will come due in the next year. On both measures of solvency evaluated, it is apparent that Nike carries a much lower level of long-term debt – 2.7 percent of equity versus 12.2 percent for Under Armour. However, given that both companies have overall little debt, coupled with the strong profitability measures of each, there appears to be a low likelihood of either company being unable to meet its debt service obligations. Even with this said, however, one could reasonably conclude that Under Armour has a slightly higher degree of financial risk than Nike.

To summarize, although Under Armour is profitable, Nike overall has been able to generate higher levels of profitability while at the same time taking on lower levels of leverage. Both companies arguably produced strong levels of profitability during an otherwise sluggish worldwide economy during this time period.

In Practice 4.1 *Financial Ratio Benchmarks by Industry*   The following table presents industry median benchmarks for a set of selected financial ratios:

Industry	ROE	ROA	ROS	A/R Turnover	Inventory Turnover	Current Ratio	Debt-to-Equity
Agriculture Crops	10.2	4.4	2.8	12.3	9.3	1.6	72.6
Oil Gas Extraction.	14.4	6.9	7.3	5.4	34.2	1.4	82.1
Food, Kindred Product.	11.2	5.0	2.5	13.3	13.0	1.7	105.3
Apparel Related Products	10.9	5.1	2.5	9.6	7.8	2.4	74.8
Printing, Publishing	15.0	5.9	3.2	8.5	26.7	1.9	95.1
Rubber & Plastics.	12.7	5.5	2.6	8.0	10.3	2.1	96.7
Fabricated Metal Products. . . .	14.6	6.7	3.3	8.0	11.1	2.2	85.3
Electrical Equipment	9.2	4.3	2.9	6.9	7.2	2.6	57.5
Trucking & Warehousing.	19.9	7.4	2.6	10.5	168.4	1.7	121.7
Transportation Services	21.9	8.1	2.0	9.8	43.3	1.5	138.3
Communication	8.3	1.8	1.9	8.9	36.7	1.4	95.2
Wholesale Trade.	12.9	5.2	1.9	9.6	8.5	1.9	113.8
Eating Drinking Places	13.6	6.2	2.9	82.9	83.8	1.0	102.9
Miscellaneous Retail Stores . . .	8.8	4.1	1.5	22.7	8.2	2.1	80.9
Real Estate	13.2	4.3	7.1	20.2	20.5	1.9	86.7
Personal Services.	10.7	5.6	2.9	11.5	38.2	1.7	97.3
Misc. Business Services.	17.6	7.0	3.0	7.6	37.0	1.7	93.9
Health Services	9.1	4.4	3.7	7.7	60.4	2.0	83.8
Educational Services	6.9	3.6	5.0	16.7	163.1	2.1	68.2

Source: Dunn & Bradstreet Industry Norms & Key Business Ratios

---

ROE MODEL FRAMEWORK

The Return on Equity (ROE) Model introduced in Chapter 2 actually encompasses a second model known as the DuPont Model. The DuPont Model was developed by the controllers' department of the DuPont Chemical Company in the 1960s as a means to evaluate the performance of the company's many operating divisions and division-level managers. Under the DuPont Model, divisional performance is evaluated in terms of the return on assets (ROA), which can be shown to be a function of the return on sales (ROS) and total asset turnover (AT). The DuPont Model does not include a component for financial leverage since most division-level managers have no control over how their division is financed. Consequently, as the level of financial analysis or performance evaluation shifts from a division to an entire company, it is important to move from the DuPont Model, which ignores leverage, to the ROE model, which includes leverage. The cornerstone of the ROE Model is the return on equity and reveals that a firm's ROE can be decomposed into the three component ratios of return on sales, asset turnover, and financial leverage:[2]

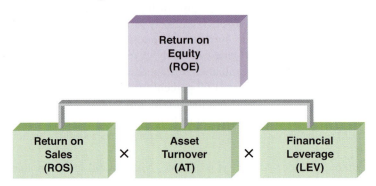

The framework shows that, all else equal, a business can increase its return on equity by increasing one or more of the following factors:

■ Return on sales (such as by increasing the price of products sold and/or by reducing operating expenses).

■ Asset turnover (such as by using the key operating assets of accounts receivables, inventory and property and equipment more efficiently, for example by generating the same volume of sales with a smaller investment in these assets or generating greater sales volume with the same level of investment in these assets).

■ Financial leverage (such as by financing the business with debt to leverage the use of high-return assets with a lower after-tax cost of funds).

Data for computing an ROE analysis for Under Armour, Inc. is presented in Exhibit 4.9. In 2011, Under Armour's ROE rose to just over 15 percent, although in 2007 the company's ROE was at a high of 18.7 percent (see **bolded** area in Exhibit 4.9). As mentioned above, it is reasonable to conclude that based on the recent level of its ROE, Under Armour is a profitable company.

EXHIBIT 4.9	ROE Model Analysis: Under Armour, Inc.				
($ thousands)	2011	2010	2009	2008	2007
Financial statement values					
Total revenue	$1,472,684	$1,063,927	$856,411	$725,244	$606,561
Net income	96,919	68,477	46,785	38,229	52,558
Total assets	919,210	675,378	545,588	487,555	390,613
Shareholders' equity	636,432	496,966	399,997	331,097	280,485
ROE analysis					
ROE (NI/Shareholders' equity)	**15.2%**	**13.8%**	**11.7%**	**11.5%**	**18.7%**
=					
ROS (NI/Revenues)	6.6%	6.4%	5.5%	5.3%	8.7%
× AT (Revenues/Total assets)	1.60	1.58	1.57	1.49	1.55
× LEV (Total assets/ SE)	1.44	1.36	1.36	1.47	1.39

But just what factors contributed to the decline in Under Armour's ROE to its current level from its high in 2007? The decline was due entirely to a drop in ROS from 8.7 percent in 2007 to 6.6 percent in 2011. Both asset turnover and financial leverage increased slightly over this same time period, changes that would have enhanced, not reduced, ROE. Thus we can conclude that in 2011, relative to 2007, Under Armour is not controlling it costs per dollar of sales as well as it previously had.

---

[2] Appendix 4A to this chapter presents a reformulation of the ROE Model using unlevered ratios.

In summary, Under Armour experienced a substantial decline in its ROE from 2007 to 2008, but an increasing trend since 2008. Despite that initial decline, the company's share price increased almost 150 percent over the five year period ending December 31, 2011, largely due to its steady and profitable growth and bright prospects to gain further market share. Over the five year period the company has generally maintained a stable asset turnover, ranging within just a few points from its 2011 level of 1.6. Financial leverage has also remained stable, even given the modest increase in debt. The changes in Under Armour's ROE appear largely attributable to management's more recent efforts to effectively control costs while sales are growing. While Under Armour is able to earn returns well above its cost of borrowing, management has been reluctant to utilize more than a minimum amount of leverage. The fact that Under Armour's return on assets of 10.8 percent in 2011 likely far exceeds its after-tax cost of borrowing suggests that the firm is foregoing the opportunity to maximize shareholder value by growing the company through additional leverage.

Estimating Sustainable Growth

Sales growth is one of the key factors of interest to all financial statement users, in part because of the high correlation between sales growth and growth in share price. Many investment professionals believe, for example, that the key driver of share price is the rate of growth in business revenue. In the case of Under Armour, Exhibit 4.1 revealed that revenues grew from $856 million in 2009 to over $1.47 billion in 2011, an average annual growth rate of over 31 percent. But revenue growth comes at a cost, namely the related growth in a firm's investment in such operating assets as accounts receivable, inventory, and property, plant and equipment. This was particularly the case with Under Armour and its recent spike in inventory. And, an increase in a firm's investment in operating assets presents a secondary problem—the need to finance the required investment in new operating assets.

As previously discussed, firms may finance their asset purchases with debt, new equity, or with internally-generated funds. In general, financing new capital investments with the sale of equity is the least desirable financing option as equity is the most expensive form of financing. (See Appendix 4C for a discussion of how to estimate a firm's cost of equity.) Hence, financing a firm's growth in operating assets with debt and/or internally generated funds are the options preferred by most managers.

Although sales growth is desirable, excessively rapid growth can strain the financial resources of a business, even to the point of destroying a business by inducing bankruptcy. To help managers avoid this situation, investment professionals have developed an approach to estimate a firm's maximum desired rate of growth, called the **sustainable growth rate** (SGR), which is calculated as follows:

$$\text{Sustainable growth rate} = \text{Return on equity} \times \text{Dividend retention rate}$$

The **dividend retention rate** (DRR) is equal to the percentage of net income **not** paid to shareholders in the form of dividends, and consequently, which is retained in a business.[3] Thus, a business's SGR is the rate of return on shareholders' equity available to be reinvested in the business. Since a firm's ROE can be decomposed into its three component ratios of return on sales (ROS), asset turnover (AT), and financial leverage (LEV), we can identify the key drivers of a firm's SGR as follows:

$$\text{SGR} = \text{ROS} \times \text{AT} \times \text{LEV} \times \text{DRR}$$

Thus, a firm can increase its SGR by increasing any of its key components—the return on sales, total asset turnover, financial leverage, or the dividend retention rate.

To illustrate the use of SGR, let's apply the concept to Under Armour. To help you understand the concept of SGR, consider two extremes: a company that pays all of its earnings to shareholders as dividends (DDR = 0 percent), and a company that pays none of its earnings as dividends (DDR = 100 percent). For the former, the SGR is zero (ROE × 0%), because none of the returns on equity are reinvested in the business. Consequently, any sales growth experienced during the year that yielded earnings would

---

[3] The dividend payout ratio (discussed in Chapter 11) is the percentage of net income paid out to shareholders in the form of dividends (Dividends paid/Net income). Thus, the dividend retention ratio can be calculated as 1 minus the dividend payout ratio. The dividend retention ratio is also sometimes referred to as the "plow-back percentage."

not be sustainable to future periods, all else equal. The company that retains all of its earnings, by way of contrast, would have an SGR equal to its ROE, and would therefore be expected to be able to sustain its sales growth at a rate equivalent to its ROE. That is, a company that earns 10 percent and retains all of its earnings would be expected to sustain a 10 percent rate of growth. Under Armour, like many companies, does not pay a dividend, and thus the dividend retention rate for the period 2008 through 2011 would be 100 percent. Exhibit 4.10 reports Under Armour's ROE for this period and illustrates the SGR calculation:

EXHIBIT 4.10	Sales Growth, ROE and SGR: Under Armour 2008-2011			
	2011	**2010**	**2009**	**2008**
Sales Growth.	38.4%	24.2%	18.1%	19.6%
ROE	15.2%	13.8%	11.7%	11.5%
× DDR	100.0%	100.0%	100.0%	100.0%
= SGR	15.2%	13.8%	11.7%	11.5%
Sales Growth less SGR	23.2%	10.4%	6.4%	8.1%

For each year presented the sales growth for Under Armour exceeded its SGR, reaching a peak difference of 23.2 percent in 2011. These results indicate that Under Armour's high growth strategy is on a collision course with its financing strategy—that is, the company's past rate of growth is not sustainable given its current financial structure. The company's ROE generation would have to be much higher to sustain it present rate of sales growth.

LIMITATIONS OF FINANCIAL STATEMENT ANALYSIS

It is important to understand not only what can be learned about a company by using the financial statement analysis techniques illustrated in this chapter, but also to understand that there are limitations to these techniques. One limitation is the ratios themselves. There is no GAAP that prescribes which ratios should be used in any given analysis, nor even how the ratios that are used should be calculated. As such, it is critical that a manager or an investment professional either compute the ratios directly or be sure to learn how any provided ratio has been computed. For example, it is entirely possible to obtain the same ratio, such as the return on assets, from two different data sources that have calculated them differently. Without knowing this, it is possible to make incorrect inferences when comparing the performance of different companies.

Just knowing how a ratio has been computed, however, does not insure the validity of the analysis. It is also quite possible that the numbers from which a ratio is calculated contain problems. Some of the potential problems that may exist with the underlying financial statement data include:

1. **Measurement concerns.** Arguably, the most relevant method of measurement for a company's assets and liabilities is their market value. After all, for valuation purposes you would expect to pay what something is currently worth, not what it was worth at some point in the past. Unfortunately, market values are often much more subjective than what accounting standard setters consider acceptable for use in the basic financial statements, and therefore, the more reliable historical cost concept pervades financial statement measurement. Thus, while the price paid for land in Manhattan, New York, forty years ago may be a reliable number, it is not terribly relevant to today's valuation of a business operating in New York City.

2. **Incomplete data.** Although the historical cost concept does help insure that the reported financial statement numbers are reliable, the relevance of many of the reported assets and liabilities values on the balance sheet are lessened, and many are not even reported at all. One accounting construct that impedes the relevance of financial statement data is that of conservatism. **Conservatism** dictates that, when in doubt, a company should report its accounts such that assets are understated, liabilities are overstated, the recognition of losses are accelerated, while the recognition of gains are delayed. Many important assets such as a company's trained workforce, management talent, internal processes, and brand go unreported on the balance sheet. For example, while GAAP requires the firm to record salary expense, no effort is made to record the value of those employees. In addition, money spent on public relations and advertising to enhance a company's brand image, or research and development expenditures to create future products, are expensed as incurred even though these expenditures arguably generate

future benefits for a business. Conservatism dictates that these items not be capitalized as assets on the balance sheet because their future value is uncertain and because they cannot be reliably measured. In an apparent contradiction to conservatism, some liabilities are also excluded from the balance sheet. These so called off-balance-sheet liabilities include some leases and certain contingencies.

3. **Differing accounting methods.** GAAP is not a one-size-fits-all set of rules. Instead, management is allowed significant flexibility in choosing the accounting methods that are used to report a firm's performance. Choices among alternative depreciation methods, alternative inventory cost flow assumptions, and alternative revenue recognition approaches are but a small sample of the policy choices that can dramatically alter reported income in any given year. This flexibility creates difficulties when performing benchmarking if the comparison companies use different accounting methods.

4. **Biased data.** GAAP allows not only the flexibility to choose different accounting methods, but also significant discretion in the various accrual estimates used in the preparation of the income statement and the balance sheet. A partial list of estimates that impact reported earnings includes estimates for uncollectible accounts, warranty expense, and sales returns, along with estimates for such things as asset write-downs, pension expense, and asset lives. Because many employment contracts are written using reported accounting numbers, managers often have a perverse incentive to bias the estimates used in financial statements as a means to favorably influence the outcome of such contracts.

5. **Lack of timeliness.** The expression "old news is no news" was probably not written about accounting data, but it certainly applies to some extent. Security markets react nearly instantly to any news deemed valuation-relevant. Certainly company performance is valuation-relevant; however, the performance reported in a company's financial statements is not timely. The annual 10-K report containing a company's financial statements, for example, is often filed with the U.S. Securities and Exchange Commission over two months after a company's fiscal year-end. As a consequence, much of the information contained in the report is already known by the time the 10-K becomes public information. Further, the accounting reports are, by definition, backward-looking reports, reporting on what has already occurred. Investment professionals, in contrast, want timely information that helps them predict what the future holds.

ETHICS PERSPECTIVE

Financial analysts are one of the primary user-groups of the financial information considered in this chapter. There are two principal types of financial analysts—buy-side analysts and sell-side analysts. **Buy-side analysts** work primarily for investment management companies such as Fidelity Investments or The Vanguard Group. The job of these analysts is to provide unbiased research that helps the portfolio managers of these mutual fund companies select securities for inclusion in their mutual fund portfolios. A second type of analyst, the **sell-side analyst**, works primarily for large financial services/investment banking companies such as Merrill Lynch or Morgan Stanley. Unlike buy-side analysts who do their research for a company's internal use, sell-side analysts provide their research for sale and use by their company's customers.

It has been argued that sell-side analysts are sometimes put under unreasonable pressure to be less than completely objective in their recommendations. Several apparent lapses in ethical behavior by sell-side analysts have come to light in recent years, eventually leading to mandated changes prescribed in the Sarbanes-Oxley Act. The purpose of these changes was to eliminate many of the conflicts of interest that sell-side analysts were exposed to and included:

■ A prohibition of the solicitation of investment banking business by sell-side analysts.

■ The creation of separate organizational structures for sell-side analysts and investment bankers.

■ Restrictions placed on the interactions between, and contact with, sell-side analysts and investment bankers.

■ Imposition of policies designed to prevent investment bankers from influencing the content of analysts' research reports.

■ Creation of analyst compensation packages in which a significant portion of a sell-side analyst's compensation is linked to the quality and accuracy of the analyst's research.

REVIEW PROBLEM

The following balance sheet and income statement data were taken from the financial records of The Dana Point Company:

THE DANA POINT COMPANY Balance Sheets					
	2013	**2012**		**2013**	**2012**
Assets			**Liabilities & Shareholders' Equity**		
Cash................	$ 7,000	$ 30,000	Accounts payable........	$ 65,500	$ 63,000
Accounts receivable.....	67,500	60,000	Wages payable..........	37,000	47,500
Inventory..............	49,000	22,500	Total current liabilities.....	102,500	110,500
Prepaid insurance.......	6,000	4,500	Bank loan payable	83,000	85,000
Total current assets	129,500	117,000	Capital stock	75,000	75,000
Building (net)..........	187,500	190,000	Retained earnings	56,500	36,500
Total	$317,000	$307,000	Total	$317,000	$307,000

THE DANA POINT COMPANY Income Statements		
	2013	**2012**
Revenues	$480,000	$430,000
Less: Cost of goods sold	250,000	240,000
Gross margin	230,000	190,000
Less: Depreciation expense...........................	22,000	22,000
Wage expense	90,000	86,000
Insurance expense	16,000	16,000
Interest expense	6,600	6,800
Net income before taxes	95,400	59,200
Less: Tax expense (30%)	28,600	17,800
Net income...	$ 66,800	$ 41,400

Required

1. Calculate the following ratios for The Dana Point Company for 2012 and 2013:

    *   Return on equity
    *   Return on sales
    *   Total asset turnover
    *   Financial leverage
    *   Receivable collection period
    *   Inventory-on-hand period
    *   Days payable period

    *   Long-term debt to total assets
    *   Long-term debt to equity
    *   Interest coverage
    *   Quick ratio
    *   Current ratio
    *   Gross profit margin

2. Comment on the trends in profitability, asset management, and financial risk for The Dana Point Company from 2012 to 2013.

The solution is on page 153.

EXECUTIVE SUMMARY

In this chapter, we considered a variety of financial analysis techniques: ocular regression (or trend analysis), common-size financial statements, and financial ratios. These analytical techniques are used to gain an understanding of a company's historical financial performance. The performance areas of interest include profitability, asset management, and financial risk. As a validation of your understanding of the content of this chapter, you should now be able to:

- Analyze a company's financial statements to evaluate its profitability, asset management, and financial risk.
- Construct pro forma income statements, balance sheets, and statements of cash flow. (See Appendix 4B.)
- Explain the Return on Equity model of financial analysis.
- Understand the limitations of financial statement analysis.

KEY CONCEPTS AND TERMS

APPENDIX 4A: Unlevering Financial Ratios

In Chapter 4, the return on equity (ROE) model was introduced as an approach to organize the analysis of a company's financial performance and health. The ROE of a company was shown to be composed of three component ratios, as follows:

$$\textbf{Return on equity} = \textbf{Return on sales} \times \textbf{Asset turnover} \times \textbf{Financial leverage}$$

Further, since the return on assets (ROA) ratio was revealed to be a function of the return on sales (ROS) ratio and asset turnover (AT), the ROE ratio could also be expressed as:

$$\textbf{Return on equity} = \textbf{Return on assets} \times \textbf{Financial leverage}$$

Because ROA is a measure of the return generated by a business's total investment in assets, to include those assets contributed by shareholders as well as those assets loaned to the business by its creditors, many investment professionals "unlever" the ROA ratio by adding the current-period interest expense paid to creditors back to the business's net income. Unlevering the ROA ratio grosses up net income for a business's cost of debt, yielding a measure of net income before any returns are distributed to either debtholders or shareholders. The resultant unlevered ROA is calculated as follows:

$$\textbf{Return on assets} = \frac{[\textbf{Net income} + \textbf{Interest} \, (1 - \textbf{Tax rate})]}{\textbf{Total assets}}$$

The interest expense added back to net income is multiplied by (1 − Tax rate), or one minus a firm's effective tax rate (Income tax expense/Net income before taxes). As a consequence, the amount of the interest expense added back to net income is reduced by the income tax savings associated with the tax deductibility of interest expense. These tax savings are referred to as the interest tax shield and must be removed to avoid double-counting their positive impact on net income (it is already reflected in the provision for income taxes used in the calculation of net income).

Some investment professionals believe that a similar unlevering adjustment should be made to the ROS ratio, as follows:

$$\textbf{Return on sales} = \frac{[\textbf{Net income} + \textbf{Interest} \, (1 - \textbf{Tax rate})]}{\textbf{Net sales}}$$

Unlevering ROS allows the financial analyst to focus on the effectiveness of a company's operating decisions, independent of the effectiveness of its financing decisions. Incorporating the unlevered ROS ratio into the calculation of ROA yields the following formulation:

$$\begin{array}{ccc} \text{Unlevered return} & = & \text{Unlevered return} \times \text{Total asset} \\ \text{on assets} & & \text{on sales} \quad \text{turnover} \end{array}$$

$$\text{ROA} = \frac{[\text{Net income} + \text{Interest}\,(1 - \text{Tax rate})]}{\text{Net sales}} \times \frac{\text{Net sales}}{\text{Total assets}}$$

$$= \frac{[\text{Net income} + \text{Interest}\,(1 - \text{Tax rate})]}{\text{Total assets}}$$

Unlevering ROS also facilitates a reformulation of the ROE Model, as follows:[4]

$$\textbf{ROE} = \frac{\textbf{Unlevered}}{\textbf{ROS}} \times \frac{\textbf{Asset}}{\textbf{turnover}} \times \frac{\textbf{Financial}}{\textbf{leverage}} \times \frac{\textbf{Common equity share}}{\textbf{of operating earnings}}$$

where the **common equity share of operating earnings** (CSOE) is defined as:

$$\text{CSOE} = \frac{\text{Net income}}{\text{Net income} + \text{Interest}\,(1 - \text{Tax rate})}$$

and represents the portion of a company's operating earnings allocable to the common shareholders. Incorporating CSOE into the ROE model yields the following:

$$\text{ROE} = \frac{\text{Net income} + \text{Interest}\,(1 - \text{Tax rate})}{\text{Net sales}} \times \frac{\text{Net sales}}{\text{Total assets}} \times \frac{\text{Total assets}}{\text{Shareholders' equity}} \times \frac{\text{Net income}}{\text{Net income} + \text{Interest}\,(1 - \text{Tax rate})}$$

When a company is all (or substantially) equity financed, the unlevered ROA and ROS ratios collapse to their familiar levered form, as does the ROE Model:

$$\textbf{Return on equity} = \textbf{Return on sales} \times \textbf{Total asset turnover} \times \textbf{Financial leverage}$$

APPENDIX 4B: Pro Forma Financial Statements

Lenders, managers, investment professionals, and shareholders are often interested in how a firm might perform in the future under various economic scenarios. For example, lenders might be interested in assessing whether Under Armour's business can generate sufficient cash in the future to make the principal payments on a proposed bank loan. But how can you forecast the future, and especially, how can you forecast a firm's ability to repay debt? The past is often an excellent guide to the future because many financial variables remain relatively constant from one year to the next and many financial variables maintain a relatively stable relationship with sales or total assets over time.

Forecasted financial statements are called **pro forma statements**—that is, financial statements prepared on an "as if" basis using assumptions about what might happen in the future. Excel™ spreadsheets are handy devices for preparing pro forma financial statements because it is possible to build a spreadsheet in such a manner as to easily change the underlying assumptions to see what will happen under alternative operating scenarios.

The process of preparing pro forma financial statements typically involves five steps:

1. Forecast sales, cost of goods sold, gross profit, and other operating expenses on the income statement, and the cash balance on the balance sheet.
2. Forecast accounts receivables, inventory, accounts payable, property and equipment, long-term debt, and short-term loans payable on the balance sheet.
3. Forecast depreciation expense and interest expense on the income statement.
4. Forecast any remaining items on the income statement, expected dividend payments, and then, the statement of shareholders' equity and the balance sheet.
5. Prepare the pro forma statement of cash flow from the forecasted income statement and forecasted balance sheets using the indirect method format.

When developing pro forma data, it is often the case that a plug figure will be needed to balance the pro forma balance sheet. If a plug figure is needed to balance the asset side of the pro forma balance sheet, most investment professionals use the current asset account "marketable securities" as their plug figure. When a firm is producing excess cash flow from its operations, that excess will usually be invested in short-term marketable securities to enable the firm to earn a higher rate of return than would be possible if the excess funds were invested in a lower-yielding cash account. Similarly, when additional cash is needed to support operations, the first source of that cash is likely to be the liquidation of any available short-term marketable securities. If, on the other hand, a plug figure is needed to balance the liability side of the

---

[4] The development of the ROE Model using unlevered ratios is generally attributed to C. Stickney and T. Selling, "The Effects of Business Environment and Strategy on a Firm's Rate of Return on Assets," *Financial Analysts' Journal* (1989).

pro forma balance sheet, most professionals use a short-term interest-bearing line of credit as the plug. A short-term line of credit is used as a plug figure because this form of financing is cheaper than financing with long-term debt, which of course, is cheaper than financing with equity, and therefore, likely to be the first choice of new financing by management.

The principal challenge to preparing pro forma statements is to determine how to forecast each of the income statement and balance sheet accounts. (It is unnecessary to forecast the pro forma statement of cash flow because the data for this statement can be indirectly derived from the pro forma income statements and balance sheets using the process described in Chapter 3.) The first account to be forecasted is revenue on the income statement, and this forecast is usually arrived at after a careful assessment of the expected external demand for a company's products. Most expenses on the income statement can be forecasted by reference to the common-size income statement percentages generated while developing the historical financial statement analysis of a company's past performance. Some expenses, however, must be forecasted by reference to items on the pro forma balance sheet. For example, depreciation expense is a function of a company's past and current investment in property, plant and equipment. Similarly, interest expense is a function of a company's past and current borrowings. And, income tax expense is a function of a firm's pre-tax net income and its expected effective tax rate. To forecast these expenses using historical common-size income statement percentages would mistakenly link the change in these expenses to the change in revenues.

On the balance sheet, many accounts are forecasted by reference to ratios that link the balance sheet account to a firm's operations. For example, here is a list of typical balance sheet accounts and the ratios that are commonly used to forecast them once a pro forma income statement has been prepared:

Balance Sheet Account	Ratio
Accounts receivable........	Receivable turnover
Inventory.................	Inventory turnover
Fixed assets.............	Fixed asset turnover
Total assets..............	Total asset turnover
Accounts payable.........	Accounts payable turnover

For many income statement and balance sheet accounts that are immaterial in amount, investment professionals often forecast the account balance as a constant on grounds of immateriality. And, in the case of some balance sheet accounts (such as the cumulative foreign currency translation adjustment), whose future value is not readily forecasted, the investment professional will often merely assume a constant future value. The key to well-constructed pro forma financial statements is to thoughtfully forecast the key income statement accounts (such as operating revenue and expenses) and the key balance sheet accounts (such as operating assets and liabilities).

It is important to recognize that forecasting income statements and balance sheets is not a hard-and-fast science. There are many different approaches used by investment professionals, and for this reason, forecasting is referred to as "an art and not a science." We will have more to say about developing and using pro forma financial statements in Chapter 12.

APPENDIX 4C: Calculating the Cost of Equity Financing

Shareholders buy shares in a company because they expect a return, either in the form of dividends or in the form of share price appreciation, or both. Since shareholders assume more risk than creditors, they are entitled to a higher rate of return. But how can the rate of return expected by shareholders be estimated? Stated alternatively, how can we calculate the expected **cost of equity financing** for a company?

A widely accepted approach to estimating the cost of equity financing—that is, the rate of return expected by shareholders—is through the **capital asset pricing model**, or CAPM.[5] The CAPM posits that there is a linear relationship between a company's systematic risk (β) and the expected return required by investors (r_e). The model states that if investors can earn the risk-free rate of return (r_f) by investing in government securities, then the expected return on a risky investment (such as common stock) should equal the risk-free rate of return plus an incremental return proportional to the company's risk. The incremental return associated with investing in equity securities versus risk-free securities is called the **equity risk premium**. The formula for the CAPM is given as follows:

$$r_e = r_f + \beta \times (\text{Equity risk premium})$$

where

r_e = Cost of equity financing.

r_f = Risk-free rate of return, often proxied by the current yield to maturity of the U.S. ten-year Treasury bond.

β = Measure of the systematic risk of a business, proxied by a firm's equity **beta** (available from any financial internet website).

[5] W.F. Sharpe, "Capital Asset Prices: A Theory of Market Equilibrium," *Journal of Finance*, 1964.

The equity risk premium is estimated as follows:

$$\text{Equity risk premium} = r_m - r_f$$

where

r_m = Market rate of return for a diversified portfolio of equity securities, often proxied by the rate of return on the Standard & Poor's 500 Index.

The equity risk premium expected by investors on a diversified portfolio of equity securities is often assumed to be 7.0 percent, which is the average risk premium observed in the U.S. capital market over the past 85 years.

To illustrate the use of the CAPM, assume that our goal is to estimate the cost of equity financing for Under Armour. Yahoo!Finance reports Under Armour's beta (β) to be 1.10, suggesting that if the U.S. stock market increases by $1, Under Armour's share price will increase by $1.10; that is, there is a strong positive correlation between movements of the U.S. equity market and Under Armour's share price. Beta is a reflection of the **systematic risk** associated with a company's share price. Systematic risk is the risk that a company's share price will fall (rise) in some proportion to a fall (rise) in the overall stock market—that is, a rising tide lifts all ships. **Non-systematic risk** is the risk that a company's share price will fall (rise) as a consequence of firm-specific and industry-specific information. Thus, Under Armour's share price will fall (rise) as a consequence of overall market movements (systematic risk) or as a consequence of new information about the company's performance or about the apparel industry in general (non-systematic risk).

If the current yield on the U.S. ten-year Treasury bill is assumed to be 2 percent, and if we assume that the equity risk premium—that is, the incremental risk of investing in equity securities rather than in risk-free government bonds—is 7.0 percent, Under Armour's cost of equity can be estimated using the CAPM as follows:

$$r_e = 2.0\% + 1.10 \times (7.0\%) = 9.70\%$$

As a basis of comparison, if Under Armour had been a less well established company (more risky), investors would have expected a higher rate of return on their investment. Private equity investors, for example, who invest in nonpublic companies often expect a 20 to 40 percent return on their investments because these investments are less liquid than investments in publicly-traded companies like Under Armour—a reduced ability to sell shares (lower liquidity) implies higher risk for an investor. Similarly, venture capital investors who invest in high-risk new business ventures expect returns ranging from 40 to 100 percent, or more. As previously noted, the assumption of greater risk is typically associated with an expectation of higher returns.

In Chapter 4, our ratio analysis of Under Armour revealed that the company's return on equity (ROE) was a healthy 15.2 percent in 2011. Thus, Under Armour is able to earn a return on its equity that exceeds the cost of its equity funds (15.2% − 9.7% = 5.5%), and as a consequence, Under Armour is presently able to build value for its shareholders.

QUESTIONS

Q4.1 **Using Financial Ratios to Evaluate Firm Performance.** Financial statement analysis is a process whereby the basic financial statements are reviewed and evaluated to assess a firm's financial health and/or performance. Calculating financial ratios is an integral part of financial statement analysis. Discuss what a ratio is and why the use of ratios is helpful in assessing firm performance and financial condition.

Q4.2 **Using Financial Leverage Effectively.** Many corporations finance at least a part of their operations and asset purchases using debt, principally because the cost of debt financing is cheaper than equity financing. Moreover, some firms are able to use leverage more effectively than others—that is, the returns to shareholders as a result of financing with debt are higher for some firms than for other firms. Using the ROE model, discuss when the use of financial leverage is most effective and least effective. When should a firm stop using debt to finance its operations or asset purchases?

Q4.3 **Calculating the Return on Shareholders' Equity.** When calculating a firm's return on shareholders' equity (ROE), some investment professionals modify the ROE ratio by subtracting any dividends paid by the firm to its preferred stock shareholders as follows:

$$\text{Return on shareholders' equity} = \frac{(\text{Net income} - \text{Preferred stock dividends})}{(\text{Total shareholders' equity} - \text{Preferred stock equity})}$$

This modified ROE ratio is often referred to as the "return on common equity," or ROCE. Discuss why and when ROCE might be a superior assessment of a firm's return on equity.

Q4.4   **Unlevering the Return on Assets.**   When calculating a firm's return on total assets (ROA) ratio, some investment professionals modify the ROA ratio by adding back the interest expense paid by a firm to its creditors, on a net-of-taxes basis, as follows:

$$\text{Return on assets} = \frac{[\text{Net income} + i(1 - \text{Tax rate})]}{\text{Total assets}}$$

where i is the actual interest expense paid by a firm and the tax rate is a firm's "effective tax rate" (income tax expense divided by pre-tax net income). Adjusting net income for the interest expense paid by a firm is called "unlevering net income" because the adjustment yields a measure of net income as if the firm were all equity financed (with no debt financing). Discuss when and why unlevering ROA might produce a more useful measure of the return on assets of a firm.

Q4.5   **Evaluating a Firm's Liquidity and Solvency.**   The Manhattan Company has $265 million in assets, $90 million in current liabilities, $135 million in noncurrent liabilities, and $40 million in shareholders' equity. Of the company's $85 million in current assets, the company's cash and cash equivalents total $23 million, accounts receivable total $24.5 million, inventory totals $26.4 million, and other current assets total $11.1 million. Is the Manhattan Company solvent? Why or why not? Is the company liquid? Why or why not?

Q4.6   **Evaluating Capital Intensity.**   Presented below are selected financial data (in millions) for **Bristol-Myers Squibb**, **Coca-Cola Enterprises**, and the **General Electric Company**. Calculate the capital intensity ratio for each of the three firms and discuss the relative capital intensity of the firms. Why is it important or useful to know the relative capital intensity of a company?

	Fixed Assets	Intangible Assets	Total Assets
Bristol-Myers Squibb	$ 5,693	$ 6,744	$ 28,138
Coca-Cola Enterprises	6,560	15,394	25,357
General Electric Company	67,528	81,726	673,342

Q4.7   **Identifying the Unknown Companies.**   Presented below are common-sized income statement data for three well-known companies representing three different industries (pharmaceutical, beverage, and diversified):

- **Bristol-Myers Squibb**
- **Coca-Cola Enterprises**
- **General Electric Company**

Identify which of the three companies goes with each of the common-size data profiles. Discuss the rationale for your choice.

	Company 1	Company 2	Company 3
Common-size income statement			
Net sales.	100.0%	100.0%	100.0%
Cost of goods sold.	30.9	44.3	59.8
Marketing, selling & admin.	22.6	13.0	32.6
Research & development	18.3	6.0	—
Other expenses	12.6	26.0	4.9
Net income.	15.6%	10.7%	2.7%

Q4.8   **Evaluating the Return on Assets.**   Presented below are selected financial data for two competitors. Discuss why the return on assets increased for Company A but decreased for Company B.

	Return on Assets		Return on Sales		Total Asset Turnover	
	Year 1	Year 2	Year 1	Year 2	Year 1	Year 2
Company A.	7.9%	10.7%	12.3%	15.6%	.637	.683
Company B	9.2	6.9	21.6	15.7	.427	.436

Q4.9   **Evaluating the Return on Assets.**   Presented below are selected financial data for two competitors. Discuss why the return on assets increased for each firm.

	Return on Assets		Return on Sales		Total Asset Turnover	
	Year 1	Year 2	Year 1	Year 2	Year 1	Year 2
Company C	16.0%	17.9%	18.0%	20.6%	0.89	0.87
Company D	31.2	42.7	24.6	31.2	1.27	1.37

Q4.10   **Evaluating the Return on Equity.**   Presented below are selected financial data for two competitors. Discuss why the return on equity decreased for each firm.

	Return on Equity		Return on Sales		Total Asset Turnover		Financial Leverage	
	Year 1	Year 2	Year 1	Year 2	Year 1	Year 2	Year 1	Year 2
Company X.........	15.2%	15.0%	30.6%	27.3%	0.073	0.089	6.8	6.2
Company Y.........	11.1	9.1	3.4	2.8	0.67	0.74	4.92	4.40

Q4.11   **(Ethics Perspective) Ethics and Financial Analysts.**   Explain why a sell-side analyst might be less objective than a buy-side analyst in his/her research reports. If an analyst is working for **Merrill Lynch**, where should the analyst's loyalties lie—with Merrill Lynch, with the companies that the analyst reviews and evaluates, or with the clients who purchase the analyst's research?

Assignments with the logo in the margin are available in BusinessCourse.
See the Preface of the book for details.
CHECK FIGURE indicates that check figures are available on the book's Website.

EXERCISES

 E4.12   **Analyzing Financial Statement Data.**   Presented below are summary financial data from the **Bristol-Myers Squibb** annual report. Using the ratio definitions from Exhibit 4.6, calculate the following ratios: return on equity, return on assets (levered), return on sales (levered), total asset turnover, and financial leverage. (Assume that the company is all equity financed.) Does the company appear to be a good investment? Why or why not?

(amounts in millions)	Year 1	Year 2
Balance sheet		
Total assets	$30,435	$28,138
Shareholders' equity	10,202	11,208
Income statement		
Net sales	$19,380	$19,207
Net income..	2,388	3,000

CHECK FIGURE **E4.13**   **Analyzing Financial Statement Data.**   Presented below are summary financial data from the **Pfizer, Inc.**, annual report. Using the ratio definitions from Exhibit 4.6, calculate the following ratios: return on equity, return on assets (levered), return on sales (levered), total asset turnover, and financial leverage. (Assume that the company is all equity financed.) Does the company appear to be a good investment? Why or why not?

(amounts in millions)	Year 1	Year 2
Balance sheet		
Total assets	$123,078	$117,565
Shareholders' equity	68,278	65,627
Income statement		
Net sales	$ 52,516	$ 51,298
Net income.	11,361	8,085

E4.14 **Analyzing the Return on Equity.**   Presented below are summary financial data from the **Johnson & Johnson Company** annual report. Using the ratio definitions from Exhibit 4.6, calculate the following ratios: return on equity, return on assets (levered), return on sales (levered), total asset turnover, and financial leverage. (Assume that the company is all equity financed.) Does the company appear to be a good investment? Why or why not?

(amounts in millions)	Year 1	Year 2
Balance sheet		
Total assets	$53,317	$58,025
Shareholders' equity	31,813	37,871
Income statement		
Net sales	$47,348	$50,514
Net income.	8,509	10,411

E4.15 **Analyzing Financial Risk.**   Presented below are summary financial data from the **Bristol-Myers Squibb** annual report. Using the ratio definitions from Exhibit 4.6, calculate the following liquidity and solvency ratios: cash and marketable securities to total assets, quick ratio, current ratio, long-term debt to total assets, long-term debt to shareholders' equity, and the interest coverage ratio. Evaluate Bristol-Myers' liquidity and solvency.

(amounts in millions)	Year 1	Year 2
Balance sheet		
Cash and cash equivalents	$ 3,680	$ 3,050
Marketable securities.	3,794	2,749
Accounts receivable (net).	4,373	3,378
Total current assets	14,801	12,283
Total assets	30,435	28,138
Current liabilities	9,843	6,890
Current portion of long-term debt	1,883	231
Long-term debt	8,463	8,364
Shareholders' equity	10,202	11,208
Income statement		
Interest expense	$ 310	$ 349
Net income before taxes	4,418	4,516

E4.16 **Analyzing Financial Risk.**   Presented below are summary financial data from the **General Electric Company** annual report. Using the ratio definitions from Exhibit 4.6, calculate the following liquidity and solvency ratios: cash and marketable securities to total assets, quick ratio, current ratio, long-term debt to total assets, long-term debt to shareholders' equity, and the interest coverage ratio. Evaluate General Electric's liquidity and solvency.

CHECK FIGURE

(amounts in millions)	Year 1	Year 2
Balance sheet		
Cash and cash equivalents	$ 12,152	$ 9,011
Marketable securities.	56,923	53,144
Accounts receivable (net).	14,233	14,851
Total current assets	93,086	87,480
Total assets	750,507	673,342
Current liabilities	200,137	204,927
Current portion of long-term debt	157,195	158,156
Long-term debt	207,871	212,281
Shareholders' equity	110,821	109,354
Income statement		
Interest expense	$ 11,656	$ 15,187
Net income before taxes	19,771	22,129

E4.17   **Analyzing Financial Risk.**   Presented below are summary financial data from the **Coca-Cola Enterprises, Inc.,** annual report. Using the ratio definitions from Exhibit 4.6, calculate the following liquidity and solvency ratios: cash and marketable securities to total assets, quick ratio, current ratio, long-term debt to total assets, long-term debt to shareholders' equity, and the interest coverage ratio. Evaluate the company's liquidity and solvency.

(amounts in millions)	Year 1	Year 2
Balance sheet		
Cash and cash equivalents	$ 155	$ 107
Marketable securities.	–0–	–0–
Accounts receivable (net).	1,884	1,802
Total current assets	3,371	3,395
Total assets	26,461	25,357
Current liabilities	3,451	3,846
Current portion of long-term debt	607	944
Long-term debt	10,523	9,165
Shareholders' equity	5,378	5,643
Income statement		
Interest expense	$ 619	$ 633
Net income before taxes	818	790

E4.18   **Analyzing Asset Management Effectiveness.**   Presented below are selected financial data from the **Bristol-Myers Squibb** annual report. Using the ratio definitions from Exhibit 4.6, calculate the following ratios: accounts receivable turnover, receivable collection period, inventory turnover, and the inventory-on-hand period. Evaluate Bristol-Myers' receivable and inventory asset management effectiveness.

(amounts in millions)	Year 1	Year 2
Balance sheet		
Accounts receivable (net).	$ 4,373	$ 3,378
Inventory	1,830	2,060
Income statement		
Net sales	$19,380	$19,207
Cost of goods sold	5,989	5,928

CHECK FIGURE   **E4.19**   **Analyzing Asset Management Effectiveness.**   Presented below are selected financial data from the **Coca-Cola Enterprises, Inc.,** annual report. Using the ratio definitions from Exhibit 4.6, calculate the following ratios: accounts receivable turnover, receivable collection period, inventory turnover, and the inventory-on-hand period. Evaluate Coca-Cola Enterprise's receivable and inventory asset management effectiveness.

(amounts in millions)	Year 1	Year 2
Balance sheet		
Accounts receivable (net).	$ 1,884	$ 1,802
Inventory	763	786
Income statement		
Net sales	$18,158	$18,706
Cost of goods sold	10,771	11,185

E4.20   **Debt Covenants and Financial Analysis.**   During 2013, The Mann Corporation borrowed $500,000 from The Biltmore National Bank. The loan agreement included a debt covenant restricting the company's level of debt relative to shareholders' equity. The covenant specified that Mann's long-term debt to equity ratio could not exceed 1-to-1 at any time during the loan period. The Mann Corporation's 2013 year-end balance sheet appeared as follows:

	2013
Total assets.	$2,001,600
Current liabilities.	$ 542,100
Long-term debt	625,500
Shareholders' equity	834,000
	$2,001,600

Calculate The Mann Corporation's long-term debt to equity ratio at year-end 2013. What is the company's maximum borrowing capability at year-end 2013 without violating the long-term debt to equity covenant of the existing loan agreement? What is the maximum dividend that the company can pay at year-end without violating the debt covenant? If the company pays a cash dividend of $100,000 at year-end 2013, what is the company's maximum borrowing capability without violating the debt covenant?

E4.21   **Estimating Sustainable Growth.**   The following information is taken from **Procter & Gamble**'s 2012 annual report:

(in millions)	2012	2011	2010
Income statement			
Net sales	$83,680	$81,104	$77,567
Net earnings	10,756	11,797	12,736
Balance sheet			
Shareholders' equity	63,439	67,640	
Statement of cash flow			
Dividends to shareholders	6,139	5,767	5,458

Calculate the company's actual and sustainable rate of growth in sales. How do the two growth rates compare? What advice would you give to P&G's management on the basis of these two rates of growth?

E4.22   **Estimating Sustainable Growth.**   The following information is taken from the **Fossil, Inc.**, 2012 annual report:

(in thousands)	2012	2011	2010
Income statement			
Net sales	$2,857,508	$2,567,302	$2,030,690
Net earnings	343,401	294,702	255,205
Balance sheet			
Shareholders' equity	1,233,535	1,105,929	1,044,118
Statement of cash flow			
Dividends to shareholders	0	0	0

Calculate Fossil's actual and sustainable rate of growth in sales. How do the two rates of growth compare? What advice would you give to Fossil's management on the basis of these rates of growth?

PROBLEMS

P4.23   **Analyzing Financial Statements.**   Presented below are selected financial data from the annual report of the **Bristol-Myers Squibb Company**:

(amounts in millions)	Year 1	Year 2
Balance sheet		
Cash and cash equivalents	$ 3,680	$ 3,050
Marketable securities	3,794	2,749
Accounts receivable (net)	4,373	3,378
Inventory	1,830	2,060
Other current assets	1,124	1,046
Total current assets	14,801	12,283
Total assets	30,435	28,138
Current liabilities	9,843	6,890
Noncurrent liabilities	10,390	10,040
Shareholders' equity	10,202	11,208
Income statement		
Net sales	19,380	19,207
Cost of goods sold	5,989	5,928
Interest expense	310	349
Net income	2,388	3,000

Required

Using the ratio definitions from Exhibit 4.6, calculate the financial ratios for Bristol-Myers Squibb and determine whether the company is a good investment. Assume an effective tax rate of 30 percent.

P4.24 **Analyzing Financial Data: Trend Analysis.** Presented below is selected financial data for **Apple Inc.**, for the five-year period 2008 to 2012.

(in millions)	2012	2011	2010	2009	2008
Net sales.	$156,508	$108,249	$65,225	$42,905	$37,491
Net income.	41,733	25,922	14,013	8,235	6,119
Cash dividends declared per share	2.65	0	0	0	0
Total assets.	176,064	116,370	75,183	47,501	36,171
Total long-term obligations.	16,664	10,100	5,531	3,502	1,745
Total shareholders' equity	118,210	76,615	47,791	31,640	22,297
Total cash, cash equivalents, and					
marketable securities	121,251	81,570	51,011	33,992	24,490

Required

1. Comment on why the growth rate of net income could be greater than the growth rate in net sales.
2. Comment on the company's use of long-term obligation as a form of financing over the five-year period.
3. Comment on the company's total asset turnover.
4. The company declared its first dividend in 2012. Do you agree with this decision? Why?

CHECK
FIGURE

P4.25 **Financial Statement Analysis and Debt Covenants.** Wilmot Real Estate Co. had the following balance sheet at year-end 2012:

WILMOT REAL ESTATE CO.
Balance Sheet
Year-end 2012

Assets		**Liabilities and Shareholders' Equity**	
Current assets	$ 60,000	Current liabilities.	$ 45,000
Real estate investments.	250,000	Long-term liabilities	150,000
Other noncurrent assets.	25,000	Shareholders' equity	140,000
Total assets.	$335,000	Total liabilities & shareholders' equity	$335,000

In early 2013, the company took out a $200,000 two-year bank loan to finance new real estate investments. The loan specified that Wilmot must maintain a current ratio of at least 2-to-1 at all times during the loan period. Failure to satisfy this debt covenant would represent a "technical default" of the loan agreement, enabling the bank to demand immediate repayment of the outstanding loan balance and any accrued interest.

During 2013, Wilmot experienced the following events:

1. Generated $750,000 in revenues, of which $700,000 was collected by year-end 2009.
2. Incurred $650,000 in expenses, of which $575,000 was paid in cash.

Required

1. Prepare a balance sheet at year-end 2013 assuming that Wilmot invested the maximum allowable amount of the bank loan in new real estate investments in early 2013.
2. Evaluate Wilmot's compliance with the current ratio debt covenant assuming (a) the bank loan is included in current liabilities and (b) the bank loan is included in long-term liabilities.
3. Calculate the maximum dividend that Wilmot can distribute to its shareholders in 2013 assuming the bank loan is included in long-term liabilities.

P4.26 **Financial Statement Analysis Using the ROE Model: International.** Presented below are the consolidated balance sheets and income statements for the **Tesco, PLC**, the world's third largest retailer, for the years 2012 and 2011. Tesco is based in the United Kingdom.

TESCO, PLC Group Income Statement For the years ended February 2012 and 2011	2012	2011
Continuing operations:		
Revenue	64,539	60,455
Cost of sales	(59,278)	(55,330)
Gross profit	5,261	5,125
Administrative expenses	(1,652)	(1,640)
Profit on property-related items	376	432
Operating profit	3,985	3,917
Share of post-tax profits of joint ventures and associates	91	57
Finance income	176	150
Finance costs	(417)	(483)
Profit before tax	3,835	3,641
Taxation	(879)	(864)
Profit for the year from continuing operations	2,956	2,777
Discontinued operations:		
Loss for the year from discontinued operations	(142)	(106)
Profit for the year	2,814	2,671
Attributed to:		
Owners of the parent	2,806	2,655
Non-controlling interests	8	16
	2,814	2,671

TESCO, PLC Group Balance Sheet As of February 25, 2012 and February 26, 2011	2012	2011
Non-current assets		
Goodwill and other intangible assets	4,618	4,338
Property, plant, ad equipment	25,710	24,398
Investment property	1,991	1,863
Investment in joint ventures and associates	423	316
Other investments	1,526	938
Loans and advances to customers	1,901	2,127
Derivative financial instruments	1,726	1,139
Deferred tax assets	23	48
	37,918	35,167
Current assets		
Inventories	3,598	3,162
Trade and other receivables	2,657	2,330
Loans and advances to customers	2,502	2,514
Derivative financial instruments	41	148
Current tax assets	7	4
Short-term investments	1,243	1,022
Cash and cash equivalents	2,305	2,428
	12,353	11,608
Assets of the disposal group and non-current assets classified as held for sale	510	431
	12,863	12,039

continued

continued from previous page

TESCO, PLC
Group Balance Sheet
As of February 25, 2012 and February 26, 2011

	2012	2011
Current liabilities		
Trade and other payables	(11,234)	(10,484)
Financial liabilities:		
Borrowings	(1,838)	(1,386)
Derivative financial instruments and other liabilities	(128)	(255)
Customer deposits and deposits by banks	(5,465)	(5,110)
Current tax liabilities	(416)	(432)
Provisions	(99)	(64)
	(19,180)	(17,731)
Liabilities of the disposal group classified as held for sale	(69)	0
Net current liabilities	(6,386)	(5,692)
Non-current liabilities		
Financial liabilities:		
Borrowings	(9,911)	(9,689)
Derivative financial instruments and other liabilities	(688)	(600)
Post-employment benefit obligations	(1,872)	(1,356)
Deferred tax liabilities	(1,160)	(1,094)
Provisions	(100)	(113)
	(13,731)	(12,852)
Net assets	**17,801**	**16,623**
Equity		
Share capital	402	402
Share premium	4,964	4,896
Other reserves	40	40
Retained earnings	12,369	11,197
Equity attributable to owners of the parent	17,775	16,535
Non-controlling interests	26	88
Total equity	**17,801**	**16,623**

Required

1. Calculate the following ratios for Tesco:

   a. Return on equity
   b. Return on assets
   c. Return on sales
   d. Financial leverage
   e. Total debt to equity ratio
   f. Long-term debt to equity ratio
   g. Current ratio
   h. Quick ratio

   i. Interest coverage ratio
   j. Accounts payable turnover
   k. Accounts receivable turnover
   l. Inventory turnover
   m. Fixed asset turnover
   n. Total asset turnover
   o. Common-size income statements
   p. Common-size balance sheets

2. Comment on the company's performance in 2012 relative to 2011.

P4.27 **(Appendix 4B) Pro Forma Financial Statements.** Handy Dan, Inc., operates warehouse-style stores, selling a variety of home building products and lawn and garden supplies. Presented below are Handy Dan's historical financial statements for Year 1 and Year 2:

HANDY DAN, INC.
Statement of Income

(amounts in millions)	Year 2
Sales	$980
Cost of goods sold	727
Gross profit	253
Depreciation expense	8
Other operating expenses	217
Operating income	28
Interest expense	21
Income before taxes	7
Income tax expense	2
Net income	$ 5

HANDY DAN, INC.
Balance Sheets

(amounts in millions)	Year 1	Year 2		Year 1	Year 2
Assets			**Equities**		
Cash	$ 10	$ 14	Accounts payable	$ 74	$104
Accounts receivable (net)	27	38	Short-term loans payable	10	29
Inventory	153	214	Long-term debt	207	289
Total current assets	190	266	Total liabilities	291	422
Property & equipment (cost)	199	279	Contributed capital	50	62
Accumulated depreciation	(9)	(17)	Retained earnings	39	44
	190	262	Total shareholders' equity	89	106
Total assets	$380	$528	Total liabilities & shareholders' equity	$380	$528

HANDY DAN, INC.
Statement of Retained Earnings

(amounts in millions)	Year 2
Retained earnings (Year 1)	$39
Add: Net income	5
Less: Dividends	0
Retained earnings (Year 2)	$44

HANDY DAN, INC. Statement of Cash Flow	
(amounts in millions)	Year 2
Operations	
Net income.	$ 5
Depreciation expense	8
Accounts receivable (net).	(11)
Inventory	(61)
Accounts payable	30
Cash flow from operations.	(29)
Investing activities	
Purchase of property & equipment	(80)
Cash flow from investing	(80)
Financing activities	
Short-term borrowing	19
Long-term borrowing.	82
Stock sales	12
Dividend payment	0
Cash flow from financing.	113
Change in cash.	4
Beg. cash	10
End. cash	$ 14

Required

Using the following set of assumptions, prepare pro forma financial statements for Handy Dan, Inc. for Year 3:

- Sales are projected to grow by 40 percent.
- Cash is expected to increase at the same rate as sales.
- Assume the following ratios to forecast the identified accounts:

Account	Financial Ratio	
Accounts receivable.	Receivable turnover	= 25.9x
Inventory.	Inventory turnover	= 3.39x
Property & equipment	Fixed asset turnover	= 3.52x
Cost of goods sold.	Gross profit margin percentage	= 25.9%
Operating expenses.	Operating expenses ÷ sales	= 22.1%
Accounts payable.	Payable turnover	= 7.55x

- Depreciation expense is based on a 30-year expected life with no salvage value; any property and equipment acquired during the year is depreciated for only one-half year.
- Interest expense is based on a six percent short-term cost of debt and eight percent long-term cost of debt; only one-half year of interest is charged on loans taken out during the year.
- Effective income tax rate is 33.33 percent.
- The mix of short-term loans payable, long-term debt and contributed capital is set to satisfy an existing debt covenant that requires the company to maintain a current ratio of 2.0 (or greater) and a total debt-to-total assets ratio of 80 percent (or less).

Discuss the expected profitability and operating cash flow of Handy Dan in Year 3.

P4.28 **Benchmarking Firm Performance.**   Presented below are profitability ratios for three competitors: **Bristol-Myers Squibb** (BMY), **Pfizer, Inc.** (PFE), and the **Johnson & Johnson Company** (JNJ):

2012	BMY	PFE	JNJ
Return on equity (ROE)............................	14.39%	17.93%	16.74%
Return on assets (ROA)	5.46%	7.80%	8.94%
Return on sales (ROS)	11.12%	24.70%	16.14%
Total asset turnover	0.49	0.32	0.55
Price-to-earnings multiple	27.85x	12.80x	17.63x

Required

Compare the relative profitability of the three firms. Which one appears most profitable? Which one would you prefer to add to a portfolio of securities? Why?

P4.29 **Evaluating Financial Performance.**   Presented below are selected financial statement data for three global energy firms:

(amounts in millions)	Chevron Texaco Corporation	Conoco Phillips Corporation	Marathon Oil Corporation
Balance sheet			
Total assets	$ 93,036	$ 91,756	$ 20,733
Short-term debt...........................	816	632	16
Long-term debt	10,217	14,370	4,057
Total debt.................................	47,806	49,033	12,622
Shareholders' equity	45,230	42,723	8,111
Income statement			
Revenues.................................	$155,300	$135,076	$ 49,598
Net income...............................	13,328	8,129	1,261
Cash flow from operations	14,690	11,959	3,730
Ratios			
Receivable collection period	29.2 days	14.7 days	23.2 days
Inventory-on-hand period	10.4 days	13.7 days	18.2 days
Long-term debt to total assets	11.0%	26.0%	24.0%
Return on assets	14.3%	8.8%	5.4%
Return on equity	29.5%	19.0%	15.5%

Required

1. Compare the three firms in terms of their size and their financing strategy.
2. Evaluate the performance of the three firms. Was performance linked to firm size?

P4.30 **(Appendix 4A) Calculating ROE using Unlevered Financial Ratios.**   Presented below are summary financial data from the 2013 annual report of The William Likert Company. Using the ratio definitions from Appendix 4A, calculate the following financial ratios: unlevered return on sales, total asset turnover, financial leverage, and common equity share of operating earnings. Evaluate the trend in the company's return on equity. Assume an effective income tax rate of 30 percent.

(amounts in thousands)	2013	2012
Balance sheet		
Total assets	$28,138	$30,435
Shareholders' equity	11,208	10,202
Income statement		
Net sales	26,000	28,000
Interest expense	349	310
Net income after taxes.............................	4,516	4,418

P4.31 **(Appendix 4C) Calculating the Cost of Equity.** The following information is available for The Philippi Winery Company, Inc.

	2013	2012	2011
Beta	0.80	0.75	0.70
Risk-free rate of return	5.50	5.25	5.00
Equity risk premium	7.50	7.30	7.00

Calculate the company's cost of equity capital for 2013, 2012, and 2011 using the Capital Asset Pricing Model discussed in Appendix 4C. Discuss the trend in the company's beta and its cost of equity.

CORPORATE ANALYSIS

CA4.32 **The Procter & Gamble Company.** The 2012 annual report of **The Procter & Gamble Company** (P&G) is available at http://annualreport.pg.com/annualreport2012/index.shtml. After reviewing P&G's annual report, respond to the following questions:

a. Prepare common-size income statements for the period 2010 through 2012. What major trends can you identify from this data?

b. Prepare common-size balance sheets for 2011 and 2012. What major trends can you identify from this data?

c. Calculate the following ratios for P&G for 2011 and 2012:
   - Return on shareholders' equity
   - Return on assets
   - Return on sales
   - Gross profit margin ratio
   - Receivable turnover
   - Receivable collection period
   - Inventory turnover
   - Inventory-on-hand period
   - Total asset turnover
   - Quick ratio
   - Current ratio
   - Long-term debt to total assets
   - Interest coverage ratio
   - Financial leverage ratio

   What major trends can you identify from this data?

d. Develop an overall assessment of the financial performance of P&G for the period 2010 through 2012.

CA4.33 **Internet-based Analysis.** Consider a publicly held company whose products you are familiar with. Some examples might include:

Company	Product	Corporate Website
• **Johnson & Johnson Company**	• Band-Aids	• www.jnj.com
• **Microsoft Corporation**	• Windows XP software	• www.microsoft.com
• **Nokia Corporation**	• Cellular phones	• www.nokia.com
• **Intel Corporation**	• Pentium processors	• www.intel.com
• **Kimberly-Clark Corporation**	• Kleenex	• www.kimberly-clark.com

Access the company's public website and search for its most recent annual report. (Note: Some companies will provide access to their financial data through an "investor relations" link, while others will provide a direct link to their "annual reports.") After locating your company's most recent annual report, open the file and review its contents. After reviewing the annual report for your selected company, prepare answers to the following questions:

a. Prepare common-size income statements and common-size balance sheets for the past two years. What significant trends can you identify from these common-size statements?

b. Calculate the following ratios for the past two years. (Note: Use the ratio definitions in Exhibit 4.6.)

Gross profit margin ratio	Cash and marketable securities to total assets
Return on sales	Quick ratio
Return on assets	Current ratio
Return on equity	Accounts payable turnover
Receivable turnover	Days' payable period
Receivable collection period	Long-term debt to total assets
Inventory turnover	Long-term debt to shareholders' equity
Inventory-on-hand period	Interest coverage ratio
Asset turnover	

What significant trends in the company's profitability, asset management, liquidity, or solvency can you identify from your calculations?

c. Identify several key competitors of your selected company. Go to Yahoo.Finance.com and benchmark your company against its key competitors on the following metrics:

Market capitalization	Return on assets
Return on sales	Return on equity

d. Review the company's long-term debt footnotes. Is the company subject to any debt covenants? If so, what are the covenants and is the company currently in compliance with the covenant(s)?

SOLUTION TO REVIEW PROBLEM

Solution

1. Ratio Analysis

	2013	2012
Return on equity	50.8%	37.1%
Return on sales	13.9%	9.6%
Total asset turnover	1.51	1.40
Financial leverage	2.41	2.75
Receivable collection period	51.3 days	50.9 days
Inventory-on-hand period	71.5 days	34.2 days
Accounts payable period	95.6 days	95.8 days
Long-term to total assets	26.2%	27.7%
Long-term debt to equity	63.1%	76.2%
Interest coverage	15.5	9.7
Quick ratio	0.7	0.8
Current ratio	1.3	1.1
Gross profit margin	47.9%	44.2%

2. The profitability of The Dana Point Company is up dramatically from 2012 to 2013, as revealed by the trend in the return on equity and return on sales ratios. The gross profit margin increase suggests that the company was able to realize some economies of scale over this same period. Overall, the company's asset management was up from 2012 to 2013, as revealed by the trend in the total asset turnover ratio, despite a small increase in the receivable collection period and a larger increase in the inventory-on-hand period. The cash collection cycle grew dramatically, however, from minus 10.7 days in 2012 to over 27 days in 2013 (a swing of over 37 days). The financial riskiness of the company improved from 2012 to 2013, as indicated by a decline in the use of financial leverage (see the financial leverage and the long-term to equity ratios). This improvement is also reflected in an improving interest coverage ratio and current ratio.

When you complete this chapter you should be able to:

1. Explain how retail, service, and manufacturing companies recognize their operating revenue.
2. Describe how revenue is recognized under the completed contract and percentage of completion methods.
3. Explain how accounts receivable are valued and how the allowance for uncollectible accounts and bad debt expense are estimated.
4. Describe why the effective management of accounts receivable is important for a business.

Operating Cycle, Revenue Recognition, and Receivable Valuation

5

EMBRAER S.A.

Embraer, S.A. otherwise known by its parent holding company name, **Empresa Brasileira de Aeronáutica S.A.**, was created in 1969 as a Brazilian state-owned enterprise. In its initial years the company produced a variety or small aircraft for the Brazilian air force and small commercial airlines. By the mid-1980s it had shifted to larger aircraft and the Brazilian government sought to fully privatize the company. Embraer was soon acquired by a Brazilian bank holding company and two private pension funds who listed the company on the Sao Paulo and NYSE stock exchanges (tickers EMBR3 and ERJ). Embraer has been a solidly performing international aircraft manufacturer ever since. As of 2012 Embraer manufactured a variety of regional and business jets, including its popular ERJ-190 and 195 models, and two small-cabin jets introduced in 2009—the Phenom 100 and 300.

Embraer's total sales for fiscal year 2012 topped $6 billion for the first time. But what constitutes a "sale" at Embraer? Is it as simple as just making and selling a plane? An analysis of Embraer accounting policies reveals that it sells its aircraft under a number of different arrangements, and each has its own unique impact on Embraer's revenue account. For straightforward commercial or executive aircraft sales, revenue is recognized when delivery is made and all benefits and risk of ownership are transferred to the buyer. In contrast, in cases where all of the company's contractual obligations have not been met, the value of pending obligations is recorded in unearned income. Military aircraft sales are typically arranged through long-term development contracts with Brazilian and foreign governments. Revenue on these contracts is realized under the percentage of completion method. Embraer also delivered aircraft under leasing arrangements, typically meaning that rental income was recorded under the straight line method over the lease period (i.e., and operating lease contract). Finally, many sales contained multiple-element arrangements, wherein training, technical assistance, spare parts and others concessions were included in the aircraft purchase price.

A review of the company's balance sheet also provides interesting insights into Embraer's sales activities. The following select accounts are particularly relevant:

(in millions)	2012	2011
Assets		
Trade accounts receivables, net	$ 539.1	$ 506.0
Customer and commercial financing	109.6	102.2
Collateralized accounts receivable	426.0	487.6
Liabilities		
Advances from customers	1,002.4	1,070.1
Unearned income	241.9	215.1

Each of these balance sheet accounts relate directly to the revenue recognition policies being applied by the management at Embraer. In this chapter, we explore the important accounting concept of revenue recognition and its influence on the balance sheet accounts.

EXECUTIVE OUTLINE

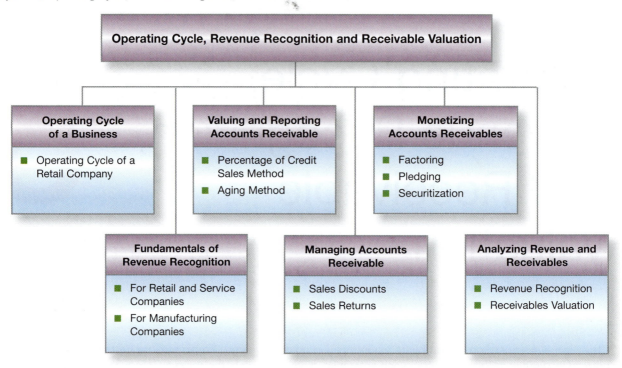

OPERATING CYCLE OF A BUSINESS

Almost all companies have an identifiable cycle of activities that reflect the ongoing operations of the business. This repetitive cycle of events is commonly referred to as the **operating cycle** of the business. Exhibit 5.1 presents, for example, the operating cycle of a typical retail operation. It reveals that retail companies buy inventory ready for sale to their customers, then sell the inventory, and finally, collect cash following the sales transaction.

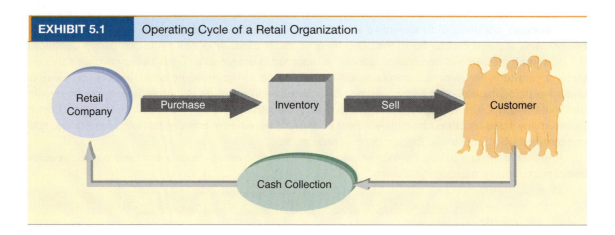

EXHIBIT 5.1   Operating Cycle of a Retail Organization

Illustrative of these events are the operating cycles of **Wal-Mart** and **Ford**, both international retail businesses.[1] Wal-Mart, for example, uses its operating resources to buy inventory for sale to its customers; but, because the products it sells are relatively inexpensive, and because its business strategy is to be a low-cost, low-profit margin, but high-volume business, almost all of Wal-Mart's sales transactions

---

[1] Ford Corporation is, technically, a manufacturing company; however, the company maintains a network of dealers that specialize in the sale and maintenance of Ford products. We are referring here to that retail network of dealers.

are in cash or using a debit/credit card. In short, Wal-Mart does not generally extend credit to its customers.[2] Ford, on the other hand, operates in the highly competitive automotive industry and sells an expensive product to its customers, most of whom could not afford to buy that product for cash. Thus, Ford, through its financing subsidiary, arranges for most of its customers to purchase on credit. As these examples reveal, depending upon the relative cost of a product, the financial capability of the customer, and the competitiveness of a given business environment, a company may (or may not) sell its products or services to its customers on credit.

In this chapter we explore the various ways that businesses recognize their operating revenues, and if they extend credit to their customers, we review the accounting rules, the risks, and the attendant costs associated with this important business practice.

FUNDAMENTALS OF REVENUE RECOGNITION

Revenue refers to the inflow of assets (such as cash, accounts receivable, or bartered assets) to a business that occurs as a direct consequence of providing goods or services to customers. In Chapter 2, the topic of revenue recognition was introduced. At that time, we said that revenue could be **recognized**— that is, revenue could be reported on the income statement as having been earned—at the point in time at which a company provides goods or services to its customers, and when collectability of any unpaid cash from the customer is reasonably assured.

Recognizing revenue is a significant economic event for a business. It signifies that the business has successfully performed its primary activity of selling a product or providing a service. In the view of most investment professionals, recognizing revenue is the most important event affecting a business since it indicates the market's acceptance of the firm's product or service. Since revenue recognition increases shareholders' wealth, it is also considered to be the primary driver of firm share price, and thus, the key driver of firm value.

When revenue is recognized and then matched with the expenses incurred to produce the revenue, net income (loss) results. In Chapter 2, the financial data of the Russian River Valley Winery was used to illustrate how financial statements could be produced from a series of economic events and transactions. In that illustration, the winery recognized revenue from the sale of its wine at the time that its wines were sold to the company's customers (when legal ownership of the wine passed from the winery to the customer). But there were other points in time where it could be argued that the winery might have recognized its revenue, for example, when the wine was delivered if delivery occurred after the sale, or at the point of cash collection if customers were allowed to purchase the wine on credit. The question then is: What criteria should be used to determine the timing and amount of revenue recognition? The answer can have a significant impact on a firm's reported results.

In essence, the key business conditions that must be satisfied before a firm may recognize revenue include: (1) the revenue must be earned; and (2) the revenue must be **realized** or **realizable**. The first condition refers to the fact that the company must satisfy its obligations to a customer under the terms of the sales agreement. If the revenue relates to a service, then this typically means that the service has been performed. If the revenue relates to a product, then this typically means that ownership right (e.g., title) of the product has passed to the customer. The second condition refers to the fact that the company has been paid or can reasonably expect to be paid. In other words, there must be the expectation that the sale will ultimately result in the customer fulfilling his or her responsibility. While these conditions may seem relatively clear cut, inaccurate revenue recognition is by far the leading cause for U.S. Securities and Exchange Commission (SEC) enforcement actions against U.S. exchange-listed companies. The revenue recognition inaccuracies range from differences of opinion regarding the application of revenue recognition rules to outright fraud. We will have more to say about this problem later in this chapter.

The large number of inaccurate, usually aggressive or premature, revenue recognition practices adopted by firms led the SEC to issue explicit guidance regarding the recognition of revenue in Staff

---

[2] Wal-Mart does carry some receivables on its balance sheet. These primarily relate to amounts due from (i) insurance companies from pharmacy sales, (ii) suppliers for marketing and incentive programs, and (iii) certain real estate transactions.

Accounting Bulletin (SAB) 101 (see Appendix 5A). According to SAB 101, the following criteria must be satisfied before revenue can be recognized by a business:

- Persuasive evidence of a sales arrangement must exist;
- Delivery of the product or service must occur;
- The seller's price to the buyer is fixed or determinable; and
- Collectibility of any unpaid cash is reasonably assured.

Notice that Embraer's revenue recognition criteria described in the vignette at the start of this chapter closely mirrors the criteria required by SAB 101.

Unfortunately, numerous grey areas arise within the interpretation of exactly when to recognize revenue. A partial list of the controversial issues includes: (1) what constitutes persuasive evidence of a sales arrangement; (2) consignment sales; (3) a right-of-product-return policy exists; (4) the product is complete and paid for but not yet delivered; (5) the seller receives nonrefundable fees; (6) the seller acts as a middleman between the retailer and the customer; and, (7) the sale involves a barter transaction. Appendix 5A to this chapter provides an analysis of these controversial issues.

To illustrate just a few of these controversies, Exhibit 5.2 depicts six possible points in time when revenue might be recognized by a business enterprise. Moving from right to left, these points represent a continuum of increasing risk that the amount of revenue recognized will subsequently prove to be in error. For instance, if revenue is recognized before production of a product even begins (see the far left end of the continuum), there is a much higher probability that the amount of recorded revenue will not actually be earned or realized. Many events may occur before the product is ultimately produced, sold, and delivered to the final consumer that could change its final selling price, and thus, the appropriate amount of revenue to be recognized.

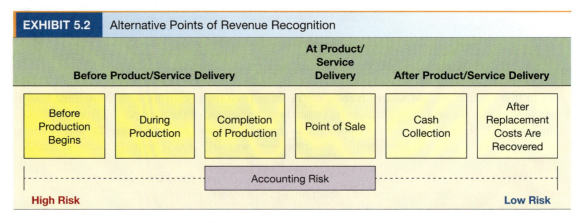

EXHIBIT 5.2 Alternative Points of Revenue Recognition

To help you see the intuition behind the revenue recognition criteria, consider the case of a jewelry manufacturer that uses diamonds and gold in its finished products. If the jeweler were to recognize revenue for a ring that has not even been produced, the jeweler would have to be very certain that the price of diamonds and gold would not change, that the cost of labor would remain stable, and that the ring would be sufficiently attractive so that there would be no trouble finding a buyer at the planned selling price. But one or all of these assumptions is likely to be false, and hence, revenue (and net income) would be potentially overstated, and very likely incorrectly reported. Thus, the left-most point on the risk spectrum—before production begins—is too early to recognize revenue even if the company has a guaranteed purchase commitment from a customer at a specified purchase price (such as a signed purchase contract). The company has yet to *earn* the revenue and, therefore, cannot recognize the revenue.

The second point, when the company is actively producing inventory for sale, indicates that the risk of being able to produce the product has been at least partially resolved. The risks that remain, however, include finding a buyer for the product at the anticipated selling price and collecting the full purchase price in cash, among others.

At the third point production of the product is complete, and thus, the risk of production has been eliminated; but, the risk that remains is that a buyer will need to be found who is willing to pay the specified selling price. If a purchase order from a customer is received, this would indicate that the customer is convinced of the product's value, and thus, it may seem that revenue recognition could be justified. This is not the case, however, since the earnings process has not been completed. Until delivery takes place and the risks of ownership transfer to the buyer, revenue cannot be recognized.

At the fourth point, the point of sale, all of the risks of successful production have been resolved and a final consumer has been identified. At this point, the principal remaining risks are that of cash collection, assuming that a business allows its customers to buy its goods and services on credit, and the risk of customer dissatisfaction, assuming that a business offers its customers the opportunity to return unwanted or defective goods. For these businesses, there is the risk that some customers will be unable or unwilling to pay for previously purchased goods and services, as well as the risk that some products will be returned. While the point of delivery is the customary point at which revenue is properly recognized, questions remain as to whether the revenue has been earned and whether collection is reasonably assured. If a right-of-return policy exists or if collection is not assured, it is premature to recognize the entire revenue amount. In such cases, companies must establish certain allowances or reserves to provide for the contingency that the product will be returned or will not be paid for. We illustrate such reserves later in the chapter.

At the fifth point, the point of cash collection, all revenue realization risks have been eliminated except for product-return risk. The product has been successfully produced; a final customer has been identified; and, the expected cash has been received. The remaining risks at this stage involve customer dissatisfaction and inflation. In the case of customer dissatisfaction, if a business maintains a policy of allowing customers to return unwanted and/or defective products, the risk of product return will persist until any product-return-guarantee period has expired. With respect to inflation, a business must be able to generate sufficient cash flow from its sales to replace its sold inventory; otherwise, it will be unable to survive in the long-term. In most situations, this business risk is unavoidable and is simply a matter of degree; however, a carefully constructed product pricing policy, which links retail prices to expected rates of inflation, can successfully manage inflation risk.

At the right-most final point, recognizing revenue after product replacement costs have been recovered, there are no revenue realization risks remaining unless the company's product-return-guarantee period has not yet expired. Also, at this point, all business risks have been successfully encountered. But, is it necessary for a business to wait until this point in time is reached before recognizing its revenue? Definitely not. Generally accepted accounting practice around the world provides considerable flexibility to companies to select the point of revenue recognition that makes the most economic sense for a given business model. This flexibility is possible because the accrual accounting system has built-in mechanisms that allow the measurement and reporting of any remaining revenue realization risks (such as bad debts, sales returns, etc.). Thus, it is possible to recognize revenue at a point in time with some remaining revenue risk so long as these risks are estimable and reported in the financial statements.

Revenue Recognition by Retail and Service Companies

Most retail businesses buy goods completely manufactured and ready for sale to the final consumer, whereas service companies provide a service to the final customer. For these businesses, the selection of a revenue recognition method is usually limited to the following two options:

- Point of sale or completion of service
- Point of cash collection

Global retail companies like **Wal-Mart** typically recognize revenue at the point of sale (which coincides with product delivery) because they rarely grant credit to their customers. Wal-Mart customers pay with cash, debit card, credit card, or by writing a check. For those retail businesses or service companies, such as the accounting firm **Ernst and Young**, that do grant credit to their customers, point of sale is still the most common method of revenue recognition *unless* there is significant doubt regarding the debt-paying ability of a customer. When account payment is uncertain, companies may instead choose to recognize revenue at the point of cash collection, or what is commonly called the **installment method**.

Under the installment method of revenue recognition, revenue is recognized only to the extent of any cash received. For instance, if a used car dealer sells an automobile to a customer with poor credit (who is unable to obtain bank financing for the purchase), the dealer may choose to recognize the revenue from the transaction on an installment basis. To illustrate, assume that the dealer sold a car for $15,000 that had a cost basis to the dealer of $12,000. Under the terms of the purchase agreement, the customer made an initial down payment of $1,500 (ten percent of the purchase price) and signed a promissory **note receivable** requiring nine additional monthly payments of $1,500.

> **Accounts receivable** refer to short-term (usually 30, 60, or 90 days in duration) credit arrangements that are typically interest-free. **Notes receivable**, on the other hand, refer to credit that is longer term (perhaps as long as three to five years) for large amounts, and consequently, is likely to involve interest charges.

Under the installment method, the car dealer will recognize only the initial down payment of $1,500 as revenue and record cost of goods sold of $1,200 (ten percent of $12,000). As each monthly payment is received, the dealer will recognize $1,500 in revenue and $1,200 in cost of goods sold, yielding a profit of $3,000 ($15,000 − $12,000) after all cash payments have been received. Since receipt of the entire $15,000 is in doubt because of the customer's poor credit history, the dealer appropriately only recognizes revenues and costs to the extent of the cash received. Note however, because the dealer effectively helped financed the customer's purchase over a nine-month period, there is a hidden **opportunity cost** to the dealer because of the time value of money. (If you are unclear about the time value of money, please read Appendix A at the end of this textbook.) If the dealer has a cost of borrowing of, say, one percent per month, the opportunity cost to the dealer implicit in the transaction would be $651, calculated as follows:

Deferred payments made by customer	$13,500
Less: Present value of 9 payments of $1,500 @ 1%: $1,500 × 8.566	(12,849)
Opportunity cost	$ 651

Thus, the dealer's real economic profit is only $2,349 ($3,000 − $651). To recover such opportunity costs, businesses that sell their product on credit over extended periods (such as greater than 90 days) often charge their customers interest on any unpaid balances. We will have more to say about the concept of opportunity costs in Chapter 9.

Revenue Recognition by Manufacturing Companies

Manufacturing companies take one or more raw materials and produce a product. To allow these companies to focus on the task of producing a product, most manufacturers do not sell directly to the final consumer of their products but rather sell to retailers who specialize in product distribution. For example, General Motors manufactures cars and trucks but does not sell these products directly to the final consumer. Instead, GM sells its cars and trucks to a network of dealers who specialize in retailing to consumers.

For most manufacturers, revenue recognition will occur at the point of product delivery or the point of cash collection if collection is uncertain. In some industries, manufacturers produce goods under contract when production may span several fiscal periods. In these situations, special rules apply that allow revenue recognition either during production or after production when the product is complete. Companies that manufacture a product under contract include such firms as Boeing, one of the world's leading manufacturers of commercial aircraft, and General Dynamics Corporation, one of the world's leading manufacturers of aerospace and defense systems. Since the cost of the products sold by these companies is quite large, they begin the manufacture of a product only after a purchase contract has been signed by the customer and a deposit customarily paid, principally to help minimize their business risk.

To illustrate the financial effects of alternative revenue recognition approaches for long-term manufacturing contracts, we will consider a contract signed by ProFlight Inc., a manufacturer of private corporate jets. For simplicity we will assume that immediately before the contract signing, the balance sheet of ProFlight consisted of only $4 million in cash and common stock. In 2011, the company signed a contract to build five jets over a two-year period for TransGlobal Airlines. Under the contract, ProFlight will receive total revenues of $10 million and anticipates that its cost to build the planes will equal $8 million, yielding a gross profit of $2 million. Data regarding the contract is presented in Exhibit 5.3.

EXHIBIT 5.3	Revenue Recognition by a Company Manufacturing under Contract		
	2011	**2012**	**2013**
Percentage of Work Completed	**20%**	**80%**	
Costs incurred	$2,000,000	$6,000,000	—
Progress billings	1,000,000	9,000,000	—
Cash collected	500,000	4,500,000	$5,000,000

Exhibit 5.3 reveals that in 2011, ProFlight completed 20 percent of the work required under the contract, sent an invoice for $1 million to TransGlobal, and received a payment of $500,000. In 2012, ProFlight completed the remaining 80 percent of the project on budget at $8 million in total costs, deliv-

ered the five planes, sent an invoice for the remaining $9 million to TransGlobal, and received a $4.5 million payment. In early 2013, after completing flight testing of the aircraft, TransGlobal remitted the final $5 million in cash to ProFlight.

Revenue Recognition During Production.

If ProFlight recognizes revenue as production of the planes proceeds, it will recognize revenue on the basis of the percentage of work actually completed each period. According to Exhibit 5.3, ProFlight completed 20 percent of the work in 2011 and the remaining 80 percent in 2012. This would suggest that ProFlight should recognize $2 million as revenue (20 percent of $10 million) in 2011 and $8 million as revenue (80 percent of $10 million) in 2012. This method of revenue recognition is commonly referred to as the **percentage of completion method**—that is, revenue is recognized in proportion to the amount of work actually completed each fiscal period.[3]

The spreadsheet below summarizes the transactions for 2011 and the ending balance sheet for that year. ProFlight records revenues of $2 million in 2011 and costs of production of $1.6 million (20 percent of $8 million). Of the $2 million in revenue, only $1 million is actually billed to the customer; the remaining $1 million is accounted for as an **unbilled account receivable**. (An unbilled account receivable is an internal billing for revenue which, for contractual reasons, is not sent to a customer for payment.) During 2011, ProFlight collected $500,000 on account and acquired $2 million in production materials which it paid for at year-end. The remaining $400,000 in production material not recognized as a cost of production on the income statement is carried on ProFlight's balance sheet as an asset, called production-in-progress.

ProFlight Inc. Transaction Summary—Year 2011							
Percent of Completion Method							
(in $ thousands)	**2011 Beginning Balance Sheet**	**Contract Signing (no entry)**	**Acquire Production Items on Credit**	**Bill Customer**	**Collect Cash**	**Record Production Costs**	**Pay Suppliers**	**2011 Ending Balance Sheet**
Assets								
Cash.	4,000				500		−2,000	2,500
Accounts receivable.				1,000	−500			500
Production-in-progress			2,000			−1,600		400
Unbilled accounts receivable.				1,000				1,000
Total assets.	**4,000**							**4,400**
Liabilities and Shareholders' Equity								
Accounts payable.			2,000				−2,000	0
Total liabilities.	**0**							**0**
Common stock.	4,000							4,000
Retained earnings								400
Revenue					2,000			
Cost of production						−1,600		
Total liabilities and shareholders' equity.	**4,000**							**4,400**

In 2012, ProFlight records the remaining $8 million in revenue, collects $4.5 million in cash, and records $6.4 million in production costs (80 percent of $8 million). In 2013, ProFlight collects the remaining $5 million in cash. The transaction summary for 2012 and 2013 is provided below. Note that at the end of the contract, total earnings of $2 million has been recorded, allocated in total as $400,000 in 2011 and $1.6 million in 2012, consistent with the percentage of work completed in those years.

One of the challenges to effectively implementing the percentage of completion method is estimating the amount of work actually completed in a given fiscal period. A frequently utilized approach is to

---

[3] Note that it is most common for companies to recognize revenue in proportion to the work completed, but the actual allocation can be based on any reasonable method. These might include costs incurred, certain milestones (fuselage completed, wings attached, etc.) or even units of production. There is an underlying requirement though that the recognition of both revenue and profits be related to the work performed.

compare the actual costs incurred to the total budgeted costs. This method can be effective when project costs can be forecasted with relative certainty. When there exists uncertainty regarding the costs to complete a project, alternative estimation techniques may be required, for example using work completion estimates provided by engineering consultants. Of course, utilizing work completion estimates based on uncertain cost estimates may cause the forecasted level of revenues in a given period to be too high or too low, and consequently, overstate or understate firm performance.

ProFlight Inc. Transaction Summary—Years 2012 and 2013
Percent of Completion Method

(in $ thousands)	2011 Ending Balances	Acquire Production Items on Credit	Bill Customer	Collect Cash	Record Production Costs	Pay Suppliers	2012 Ending Balances	Collect Cash	2013 Ending Balances
Assets									
Cash..........................	2,500			4,500		−6,000	1,000	5,000	6,000
Accounts receivable..............	500		9,000	−4,500			5,000	−5,000	0
Production-in-progress	400	6,000			−6,400		0		0
Unbilled accounts receivable.......	1,000		−1,000				0		0
Total assets....................	**4,400**						**6,000**		**6,000**
Liabilities and Shareholders' Equity									
Accounts payable................	0	6,000				−6,000			
Total liabilities.................	**0**						**0**		**0**
Common stock..................	4,000						4,000		4,000
Retained earnings	400						2,000		2,000
Revenue				8,000					
Cost of production					−6,400				
Total liabilities and shareholders' equity...........	**4,400**						**6,000**		**6,000**

Revenue Recognition at the Completion of Production.
If ProFlight recognizes its revenue, costs of production, and hence gross profit when the project is complete, no revenues or expenses will be reported on the income statement until 2012. (ProFlight will consider the contract to be satisfied upon delivery of the planes at the end of 2012; TransGlobal Airlines, however, might consider the contract to be complete after successful flight testing of the aircraft in 2013.)

Since no revenue is recognized in 2011, the $1 million billed to TransGlobal in 2011 will be accounted for as **deferred revenue**, a liability account on ProFlight's balance sheet. The deferred revenue account has a meaning just as it sounds, revenue whose recognition on the income statement has been deferred to the future until other criteria have been met. In this case the relevant criteria is the completion of the project. When the project is complete at the end of 2012, the deferred revenue will then be considered earned, and the balance in the deferred revenue account will be transferred to the revenue account on the income statement (and retained earnings on the balance sheet). Similarly, the $2 million spent on production costs in 2011 will be accounted for as **production-in-progress**, an asset account on ProFlight's balance sheet until the project is complete, at which time the balance in the production-in-progress account is transferred to the cost-of-production account on the income statement. As a consequence, no profit is recognized in 2011 and instead is deferred until 2012 when all work is completed. This method of revenue recognition is called the **completed contract method**, and the events using this revenue recognition approach are presented in ProFlight's transaction summary that follows. For consistency with the above example we again separate the transactions into those for 2011 and those for 2012–13. For 2011:

In Practice 5.1 *Revenue Recognition Method: A Glimpse of a Sample of Fortune 1000 Companies* The following table identifies the method used by a sample of 83 Fortune 1000 companies to account for revenue under long-term contracts. Over 64 percent of the firms surveyed used the percentage of completion method:

Accounting Method	Number	Percentage
Percentage of completion	43	51.8
Units of delivery	32	38.6
Completed contract........................	8	9.6
Total	83	100.0

Source: Accounting Trends & Techniques

	ProFlight Inc. Transaction Summary—Year 2011 Completed Contract Method						
(in $ thousands)	2011 Beginning Balance Sheet	Contract Signing (no entry)	Acquire Production Items on Credit	Bill Customer	Collect Cash	Pay Suppliers	2011 Ending Balance Sheet
Assets							
Cash..	4,000				500	−2,000	2,500
Accounts receivable............................				1,000	−500		500
Production-in-progress			2,000				2,000
Total assets.................................	4,000						5,000
Liabilities and Shareholders' Equity							
Accounts payable..............................			2,000			−2,000	0
Deferred revenue				1,000			1,000
Total liabilities...............................	0						1,000
Common stock................................	4,000						4,000
Total liabilities and shareholders' equity	4,000						5,000

BUSINESS PERSPECTIVE

Microsoft Corporation is the world's largest software developer. Its products include operating systems for personal computers, servers, mobile phones, and other devices. The company also designs and sells hardware including the Xbox 360 gaming and entertainment console. According to Microsoft's 2012 annual report, the company's revenues grew from $69.9 billion in 2011 to $73.7 billion in 2012, an annual growth rate of just over 5 percent. According to Microsoft's footnotes to its financial statements:

> Software revenue recognition requires judgment, including whether a software arrangement includes multiple elements, and if so, whether vendor-specific objective evidence ("VSOE") of fair value exists for those elements. A portion of revenue may be recorded as **unearned** (emphasis added) due to undelivered elements. Changes to the elements in a software arrangement, the ability to identify VSOE for those elements, and the fair value of the respective elements could materially impact the amount of earned and unearned revenue.

Microsoft's 2012 balance sheet disclosed the following amounts for its unearned revenue:

(in millions)	2012	2011
Short-term unearned revenue	$18,653	$15,722
Long-term unearned revenue...	1,406	1,398
Total unearned revenue	$20,059	$17,120

Although consistent with generally accepted accounting principles, many investment professionals view Microsoft's practice of deferring the recognition of a portion of the revenue from its retail products and OEM-licensed products as a form of **rear-end loading** of revenues. Rear-end loading of revenues—that is, postponing the income statement recognition of certain revenues until a later fiscal period—reduces the total level of revenues currently recognized, and thus, reduces currently reported operating income.

Analysts critical of Microsoft's revenue reporting argue that the practice creates an **earnings reserve** on the company's balance sheet, enabling the firm to manage its reported earnings and consistently meet or exceed Wall Street's earnings' expectations. Microsoft has met or exceeded the Street's annual earnings' expectations for 23 consecutive years. Wall Street pundits also note that the practice of revenue deferral enables Microsoft to appear less profitable, and hence, less monopolistic—an important feature as the company appeals the anti-competitiveness ruling brought against it in 2004 and again in 2006 by the European Union Committee on Competition.

And the summary transactions for 2012 and 2013:

ProFlight Inc. Transaction Summary—Years 2012 and 2013
Completed Contract Method

(in $ thousands)	2011 Ending Balances	Acquire Production Items on Credit	Bill Customer	Collect Cash	Pay Suppliers	Recognize Revenue	Record Cost of Production	2012 Ending Balances	Collect Cash	2013 Ending Balances
Assets										
Cash	2,500			4,500	−6,000			1,000	5,000	6,000
Accounts receivable	500		9,000	−4,500				5,000	−5,000	0
Production-in-progress . . .	2,000	6,000					−8,000	0		0
Total assets	**5,000**							**6,000**		**6,000**
Liabilities and Shareholders' Equity										
Accounts payable	0	6,000			−6,000			0		0
Deferred revenue	1,000		9,000			−10,000		0		0
Total liabilities	**1,000**							**0**		**0**
Common stock	4,000							4,000		4,000
Retained earnings								2,000		2,000
Revenue						10,000				
Cost of production							−8,000			
Total liabilities and shareholders' equity . . .	**4,000**							**6,000**		**6,000**

A Comparison of Performance: Percentage of Completion and Completed Contract.

Exhibit 5.4 presents a comparison of gross profit for ProFlight under the two alternative revenue recognition methods. The results are equal, in total, however the percentage of completion method spreads the gross profit between 2011 and 2012, whereas the completed contract method recognizes all the gross profit in the year of completion.

EXHIBIT 5.4	Comparison of Gross Profit under Percentage of Completion and Completed Contract Revenue Recognition			
		2011	**2012**	**2013**
Percentage of completion		$400	$1,600	$0
Completed contract		0	2,000	0

GLOBAL PERSPECTIVE

There are many similarities between U.S. GAAP and IFRS in regards to revenue recognition, but there are also several significant differences. For example, U.S. GAAP requires that a product or service be delivered before revenue may be recognized, whereas IFRS allows a business to recognize revenue if a firm commitment to provide goods or services in the future at a fixed price exists, the revenue and costs can be reliably measured, and significant risks and rewards of ownership are transferred to the customer. In essence, IFRS allows future commitments to be recognized (under certain conditions) that would not be permitted under U.S. GAAP. Another important difference is that IFRS does not permit the use of the completed contract method, whereas under U.S. GAAP a company may elect to use either the completed contract or percentage-of-completion method.

VALUING AND REPORTING ACCOUNTS RECEIVABLE

Companies extend credit to current and potential customers as a means to attract an additional source of profit. This decision is not made lightly by management, and granting credit to customers makes sense only when the expected profit from these incremental sales exceed the costs associated with extending the credit—specifically, when the incremental profit from the sale is enough to offset both the opportunity cost of delaying the receipt of cash (the time value of money) and the risk that some customer accounts will not be collected.[4] Credit sales are commonly short-term and, therefore, do not carry an interest charge. The accounting process, therefore, does not reflect the opportunity cost related to the time value of money for receivables. The accounting for uncollectible accounts, however, is not ignored and, in fact, is a necessity if the financial statements are to be a useful representation of company performance.

To help you understand why accounting for uncollectible receivables operates as it does, recall the following basics of how receivables are established in the first place. When a sale is made on credit and meets the criteria for revenue recognition, the revenue recorded on the income statement (and likewise the retained earnings on the balance sheet) will be balanced with an increase to the accounts receivable account. The account therefore reflects the expectation of receiving cash at a later date for a sale made at an earlier date. A problem arises though: when the credit sale is recorded there may be an overstatement of the actual receivables balance that will be received by the company if some accounts are not paid by the customer. The accounting process, therefore, requires that we record receivables at **net realizable value**, an amount that reflects the expected net collectability of the total accounts receivable balance.

Company management knows that some customers will not pay for sales made on credit but they just don't know which ones. If they did, they would certainly avoid extending credit to these customers! Companies can reduce, but not eliminate, this risk by acquiring information about their customers from credit information intermediaries such as **Dun and Bradstreet**. For a fee, Dun and Bradstreet will supply information about a customer's past credit history and will use credit scoring techniques to predict the likelihood that a customer will pay for goods and services on a timely basis.

Despite the fact that a company might not know by the end of a fiscal period with certainty how much of its receivables balance will be paid, and likewise what its credit losses associated with its current period's revenue will be, the *matching principle* nonetheless requires that an estimate of these losses be made to facilitate a full matching of revenue and expenses on the income statement. Furthermore, the *conservatism principle* requires that accounts receivable on the balance sheet not be overstated relative to what will ultimately be collected in cash. There are a variety of methods available to help businesses estimate their expected credit losses. The two most widely used methods are the **percentage-of-credit-sales method** and the **aging method**.[5] We discuss each in turn.

Percentage-of-Credit-Sales Method

Under the percentage-of-credit-sales method, a business estimates its expected future credit losses as a function of the relationship between its historical credit losses and its historical credit sales. The percentage of historical credit losses divided by historical credit sales is multiplied with current period credit sales to estimate a business's expected future credit losses. The principal limitations of this approach are that it fails to capture the changing payment patterns of customers in a timely manner and it lacks the estimation precision provided by the aging method.

To demonstrate the percentage-of-credit-sales method, assume that the Savanna Company recognized $600,000 of credit sales during the current fiscal period. Further, assume that Savanna's management has determined from prior experience that approximately three percent of all credit sales eventually must be written off due to collection failure. Since bad debts resulting from collection failure are a cost of doing business, it is necessary to match this expense with current period revenue. Consequently, Savanna will recognize a bad debt expense in the amount of $18,000 (3 percent of $600,000) on its income statement in the current period. Savanna will also establish a contra-account—the **Allowance for Uncollectible Accounts**—on its balance sheet to reflect the amount of the outstanding receivables that are not expected to be collected. We will discuss this contra-account more fully shortly; but, what is important to note is that Savanna's management recorded their estimate of the expected bad debt expense in the current period rather than waiting until a future period at which time they will know with certainty which receivables are uncollectible and should be written off.

---

[4] Most businesses extend interest-free trade credit to their customers who are also businesses (i.e., a B2B transaction) while rarely extending trade credit to their customers who are not businesses (i.e., a B2C transaction).

[5] A third approach is the **direct write-off method**, in which no estimate of credit losses is matched with current revenue. Instead, the actual accounts receivable write-off is reported on the income statement as a bad debt expense in the period in which non-collectibility is confirmed. Assuming materiality, the direct write-off method is not allowable under GAAP because it fails to match the cost of extending credit to customers in the same period in which the corresponding revenue is recognized.

Savanna Company Transaction Summary
Percentage-of-Credit-Sales Method

	Sell Goods on Credit	Estimate 3% of Credit Sales Uncollectible	Subtotals
Assets			
: :			
Accounts receivable....................................	600,000		600,000
Less: Allowance for uncollectible accounts..................		−18,000	−18,000
Accounts receivable, net			582,000
Shareholders' Equity			
: :			
Retained earnings			582,000
Revenue	600,000		
Bad debt expense...................................		−18,000	

Aging Method

A more refined approach to credit loss estimation, and consequently, the most widely used approach, is the aging method. Under the aging method, a business first categorizes its outstanding accounts receivable according to how much time has elapsed since the credit sale took place. Then, using historical customer payment data to estimate the probability of nonpayment, the estimates are multiplied by the outstanding receivable age category balance to arrive at the expected credit loss. You should readily see that an aging approach has the distinct advantage of evaluating an entire receivables balance based on an objective measure—the time elapsed since payment. In this way the reported net realizable value of the accounts receivables account will reflect the increasing uncertainty of collectability that comes with older accounts.

To illustrate this method, consider the following scenario. Pan American Enterprises Inc. sells its internationally recognized wine on credit to bars and restaurants throughout the United States. The company's credit terms require customers to pay their bills within 30 days of a transaction. The chief financial officer (CFO) of Pan American is concerned about the possibility of bad debts arising when customers fail to pay for previously purchased inventory. The CFO realizes that bad debts may occur, but offering the company's customers credit has generated much higher sales and profit levels.

Exhibit 5.5 shows that credit sales for Pan American Enterprises were $3.2 million in 2012, of which Pan American collected $2.85 million in cash. In Pan American's accounting, this information is reported as an increase in retained earnings (via revenue) and an increase in accounts receivable in the amount of $3.2 million, and an increase in cash and a decrease in accounts receivable in the amount of $2.85 million.

EXHIBIT 5.5	**Pan American Enterprises, Inc.—Credit Sales and Write-offs**		
Year	**Credit Sales**	**Accounts Receivable (year-end)**	**Write-Off**
2012	$3,200,000	$350,000	—
2013	5,300,000	800,000	$11,500

Even if Pan American Enterprises screens its customers carefully, it is unlikely that the entire $350,000 of outstanding accounts receivable at year-end 2012 will be collected. Further, prior to the preparation of an income statement for 2012, the matching concept requires that the cost of extending credit to its customers—that is, the **bad debt expense**—be estimated and matched with the sales revenue for 2012.

Many companies consider receivables over 120 days old to be worthless, and consequently, remove these receivables from the balance sheet to avoid overstating the realizable value of accounts receivable. Worthless receivables are usually turned over to a collection agency to pursue collection.

Airline Ticket Revenue Recognition at Delta Airlines

Delta Airlines is the largest airline in the world when measured by almost any metric: total revenue, fleet size, passenger miles flown, and number of passengers. The company is based in Atlanta, Georgia, the location of its primary hub, and it has helped make Atlanta's Hartsfield-Jackson International Airport the busiest in the world.

The sale of an airline ticket may seem straightforward from the consumer-perspective: buy a ticket, sometimes months in advance, then take the flight. But from Delta's perspective the sale involves other factors to consider regarding how much and when to record revenue. According to the company's footnotes to its financial statements, when tickets are sold a portion is initially recorded as a component of "air traffic liability," a current liability on the balance sheet (equivalent to deferred revenue or unearned revenue); and, if the passenger has a frequent flyer account, a portion is allocated to "frequent flyer deferred revenue." Delta's 2012 annual 10-K report filing with the U.S. Securities and Exchange Commission reports the amount of recognized revenue and deferred revenue for 2012 and 2011 was as follows:

	December 31	
	2012	**2011**
Income Statement		
Revenues	$36,670	$35,115
Balance Sheet (liabilities)		
Air traffic liability	$3,696	$ 3,480
Frequent flyer deferred revenue—current.	1,806	1,849
Frequent flyer deferred revenue—noncurrent.	2,628	2,700

These deferred revenue liability accounts are quite significant to Delta, approximating 22% and 23% of total revenues for 2012 and 2011, respectively.

The accounting for airline tickets in this way follows straight from the economics of what has been sold, and more specifically from the expectation of when Delta will meet its obligation to fly the passenger on the plane. Revenue recognition guidelines under SAB No. 101 require that any revenue must be earned before it can be recognized. Since Delta does not earn its revenue until it has provided air transportation to its customers, it appropriately defers the recognition of its revenue until the time of flight service. The air traffic liability account reflects this obligation.

The allocation of a portion of the ticket to deferred revenue for frequent flyer miles, however, recognizes that there is an additional obligation attached to each ticket sold. Delta must award a passenger ticket when the miles are used, thus in effect the passenger is purchasing a portion of a future flight. Delta must, therefore, estimate the value of each frequent flyer mile sold. The language used to describe this process in Delta's 2012 10-K was:

Mileage credits are a separate unit of accounting as they can be redeemed by customers in future periods for air travel on Delta and participating airlines, membership in our Sky Club and other program awards. .... We defer revenue from the mileage credit component of passenger ticket sales and recognize it as passenger revenue when miles are redeemed and services are provided. We record the portion of the passenger ticket sales for air transportation in air traffic liability and recognize these amounts in passenger revenue when we provide transportation or when the ticket expires unused.... we value each deliverable on a standalone basis. Our estimate of the standalone selling price of a mileage credit is based on an analysis of our sales of mileage credits to other airlines and customers and is re-evaluated at least annually.

To estimate Pan American's bad debt expense using the aging method, an aging schedule of Pan American's accounts receivable is prepared and is presented in Exhibit 5.6. For convenience, we show the aging schedules for both the years 2012 and 2013. This exhibit shows that, at year-end 2012, $145,000 in receivables have been outstanding for less than 30 days, $100,000 outstanding for 31 to 60 days, $70,000 for 61 to 90 days, $20,000 for 91 to 120 days, and $15,000 for over 120 days.

An analysis of Pan American's past customer payment experience is then used to estimate the amount that will be uncollected from each category. As shown in Exhibit 5.6, the CFO's analysis of prior credit customer payment behavior found that 0.5 percent of accounts 30 days or less fail to pay, one percent of accounts that are 31 to 60 days old fail to pay, and that as much at 20 percent of accounts outstanding for more than 120 days end up in default. The total amount that is not expected to be collected is the sum of the amounts in each category times the percentage estimated to be uncollectible. For example, $725 (0.5 percent times $145,000) of the less than 30-days accounts is expected to be uncollectible. For the total outstanding receivable balance of $350,000 as of year-end 2012, $10,925 is expected to be uncollectible.

EXHIBIT 5.6	Aging of Accounts Receivable—Pan American Enterprises				
		December 31, 2012		December 31, 2013	
Period Outstanding	Estimated Uncollectible Percentage	Outstanding Receivable Balance	Estimated Bad Debt	Outstanding Receivable Balance	Estimated Bad Debt
30 days or less	0.5%	$145,000	$ 725	$400,000	$ 2,000
31–60 days	1.0%	100,000	1,000	200,000	2,000
61–90 days	6.0%	70,000	4,200	100,000	6,000
91–120 days	10.0%	20,000	2,000	75,000	7,500
More than 120 days	20.0%	15,000	3,000	25,000	5,000
Total		$350,000	$10,925	$800,000	$22,500

To record the results of the aging analysis, Pan American will establish a contra-account—the **Allowance for Uncollectible Accounts**—on its balance sheet to reflect the amount of the outstanding receivables that are not expected to be collected. The allowance for uncollectible accounts is a reserve for future expected losses resulting from uncollectible credit sales. Despite the fact that the future losses cannot be known with certainty at year-end, the matching concept nonetheless requires that an attempt be made to estimate those losses, recognizing that the estimate may prove incorrect as additional information is obtained. Thus, $10,925 will be the balance in the allowance for uncollectible accounts and this contra-account is subtracted from the total outstanding receivable balance on Pan American's balance sheet to arrive at the **net realizable value** ($350,000 − $10,925 = $339,075) of the outstanding accounts receivable. It is the net realizable value of Pan American's accounts receivable that will be included in the firm's total assets.

Because 2012 was Pan American Enterprises' first year of operations, the beginning balance in the allowance account is $0. Thus, $10,925 is the amount necessary to bring the allowance account to the required amount of $10,925, and hence, it is also the amount of the bad debt expense reported on Pan American's income statement for the period. In the following transaction summary, the bad debt expense reduces retained earnings by $10,925 and the allowance for uncollectible accounts decreases assets by the same amount. Since the allowance account is an offset to the accounts receivable account, this transaction effectively reduces the net balance of accounts receivable. Under this approach, total "gross" accounts receivable are not reduced directly because the allowance account is just an estimate of Pan American's expected future credit losses. Reporting the accounts in this way thus tells the user of Pan American's balance sheet two important pieces of information: (i) how much is owed to the company in total ($350,000), and (ii) how much is the estimate of what won't be collected ($10,925).

Pan American Enterprises Transaction Summary—2012 Aging Method	Sell Goods on Credit	Collect Cash from Customers	Recognize Bad Debt Expense	Subtotals
Assets				
Cash.......................................		2,850,000		2,850,000
Accounts receivable............................	3,200,000	−2,850,000		350,000
Less: Allowance for uncollectible accounts.............			−10,925	−10,925
Total assets......................................				**3,189,075**
Shareholders' Equity				
: :				
Retained earnings				3,189,075
Revenue	3,200,000			
Bad debt expense.............................			−10,925	
Total shareholders' equity......................				**3,189,075**

Pan American's abbreviated income statement for 2012 discloses sales revenue, less the bad debt expense, of $3,189,075 (see Exhibit 5.7, Panel A), and Pan American's balance sheet at December 31, 2012, reflects an accounts receivable balance, net of the allowance for uncollectible accounts, of $339,075, representing the net cash that Pan American expects to collect from its credit customers (see Exhibit 5.7, Panel B).

EXHIBIT 5.7	Selected Financial Data

Panel A

PAN AMERICAN ENTERPRISES INC. Income Statement (abbreviated)	2012
Sales revenue...	$3,200,000
Less: Bad debt expense.................................	10,925
Net income...	$3,189,075

Panel B

PAN AMERICAN ENTERPRISES INC. Balance Sheet (accounts receivable accounts)	2012
Accounts receivable.....................................	$ 350,000
Less: Allowance for uncollectible accounts.................	10,925
Accounts receivable, net.................................	$ 339,075

In early 2013, Pan American Enterprises received information from a number of its credit customers that they would be unable to pay their outstanding unpaid bills. As a consequence, Pan American's CFO immediately wrote off the identified uncollectible accounts receivable, which totaled $11,500. In the accounting transaction summary provided below, the **write-off of uncollectible accounts** is executed by reducing accounts receivable by $11,500 and adjusting the allowance for uncollectible accounts for an equivalent amount. To see why the transaction takes this form consider the following. Recall that the allowance account represents a reserve for expected future losses from uncollectible credit sales. When Pan American received information about actual customers and the expected credit losses were no longer uncertain, the reserve is no longer needed, nor should the amounts be included in accounts receivable if they will not ever be paid. Thus the CFO immediately removed both the uncollectible receivables from the balance in accounts receivable and an equivalent amount from the reserve for such losses. Note however, that in this particular case Pan American had underestimated its actual 2012 credit losses by $575 ($11,500 − $10,925). The accounting process will correct for this understatement of the 2012

In Practice 5.2 *Balance Sheet Caption: A Glimpse of a Sample of Fortune 1000 Companies* The following table identifies the caption used by a sample of 600 Fortune 1000 companies on their balance sheets to describe the allowance for uncollectible accounts:

Doubtful Account Captions	Number	Percentage
Allowance for doubtful accounts	325	54.2
Allowance.	141	23.5
Allowance for uncollectible accounts.	25	4.2
Allowance for losses.	13	2.1
Reserve for doubtful accounts.	17	2.8
Other.	4	0.7
Receivables shown net	23	3.8
No reference to doubtful accounts.	52	8.7
Total	600	100.0

Source: Accounting Trends & Techniques

bad debt expense in its 2013 financial statements. Notice also that the actual write-off of $11,500 in accounts receivable in 2012 is simply a housekeeping adjustment. No expense is recognized at this time as the expense had already been recognized at the time that the initial reserve estimate was made (at year-end 2012). In addition, the net accounts receivable balance remains unchanged as an equal amount is removed both from accounts receivable and from the allowance for uncollectible accounts. With this in mind, below is a summary of how the contra-asset allowance for uncollectibles account will always operate (note the amounts in blue are reported as part of the balance sheet, and the amount in red reported on the income statement):

The Allowance for Uncollectible Accounts		
	$ Amount	**Notes**
	Beginning Balance	The balance sheet amount to start a period
less:	Write-offs of uncollectible accounts	Off-set against accounts receivable; no expense charge
plus:	**Bad debt expense**	The amount expensed on the income statement; typically a period-end adjustment
	Ending Balance	The balance sheet amount that ends a period

According to Exhibit 5.5, Pan American Enterprises generated credit sales of $5.3 million during 2013 and received cash payments from customers totaling $4,838,500. At the 2013 year-end, the outstanding balance in accounts receivable for the company totaled $800,000. The aging schedule (see Exhibit 5.6) revealed that Pan American could suffer bad debt losses of as much as $22,500 on this $800,000 receivables balance. However, given that the credit losses for 2012 had been understated by $575, Pan American will need to correct this in 2013 by increasing the allowance for uncollectible accounts and the bad debts expense by a total of $23,075 ($22,500 + $575).

Pan American Enterprises Transaction Summary—2013 Aging Method						
(in $ thousands)	2012 Ending Account Values	Write-off Accounts Receivable	Sell Goods on Credit	Collect Cash from Customers	Recognize Bad Debt Expense	2013 Ending Account Values
Assets						
Cash.	2,850,000			4,838,500		7,688,500
Accounts receivable.	350,000	−11,500	5,300,000	−4,838,500		800,000
Less: Allowance for uncollectible accounts . . .	−10,925	11,500			−23,075	−22,500
Total assets	**3,189,075**					**8,466,000**
Shareholders' Equity						
: :						
Retained earnings	3,189,075					8,466,000
Revenue			5,300,000			
Bad debt expense.					−23,075	
Total shareholders' equity	**3,189,075**					**8,466,000**

A summary reconciliation of Pan American's allowance for uncollectible accounts for 2012 and 2013 is as follows:

Pan American Enterprises Summary of Allowance for Uncollectible Accounts Aging Method		
	2012	2013
Allowance for uncollectible accounts, beginning balance.	$ —	$10,925
Less: Write-offs of accounts receivable during the period.	—	(11,500)
Unadusted balance	—	(575)
Plus: Bad debt expense adjustment (to the income statement)	10,925	23,075
Allowance for uncollectible accounts, ending balance	**$10,925**	**$22,500**

Pan American's abbreviated income statement for 2013, presented in Exhibit 5.8 (Panel A), shows sales revenue, less the bad debt expense, of $5,276,925, while Pan American's balance sheet (Panel B) shows net receivables at December 31, 2013, of $777,500. The company's use of the aging method insures that a full matching of revenue and expenses, including an estimate of the bad debt expense, occurs on the company's income statement, and that the expected realizable value of the outstanding accounts receivable is correctly reflected on the company's balance sheet.

EXHIBIT 5.8	Selected Financial Data

Panel A

PAN AMERICAN ENTERPRISES INC.
Income Statement (abbreviated)

	2013
Sales revenue.	$5,300,000
Less: Bad debt expense.	23,075
Net income.	$5,276,925

Panel B

PAN AMERICAN ENTERPRISES INC.
Balance Sheet (accounts receivable accounts)

	2013
Accounts receivable.	$ 800,000
Less: Allowance for uncollectible accounts	22,500
Accounts receivable, net	$ 777,500

MANAGING A COMPANY'S INVESTMENT IN RECEIVABLES

When a company extends credit to its customers by permitting them to buy goods and services on credit, the company is, in effect, making an investment in accounts receivable. Like any investment, an investment in accounts receivable should generate returns to the company that are sufficiently large to justify the risks associated with the investment—that is, the gross profit resulting from the incremental credit sales must exceed the cost of extending credit. The principal costs of extending credit to customers include the cost of the goods or services if a customer fails to pay for their credit purchases and/or the time value of money (the opportunity cost) when a customer takes a long time to pay.

Sales Discounts

By extending credit to customers, a company is effectively lending to its customers on an interest-free basis for the period of time that the account receivable is outstanding. To maximize the return on a company's investment in accounts receivable, and thus, the firm's overall profitability, it is important to keep the duration of these interest-free loans as short as possible. One way that companies attempt to manage account receivable **duration** is by giving customers an incentive to pay quickly. That incentive usually takes the form of a price discount. For instance, some companies offer their customers **credit terms** or **trade terms** of 2/10, n/30. The term "2/10" indicates that if customers pay their bill within ten days of purchase, they will be given a two percent reduction in the gross purchase price of the purchased items. The term "n/30"—pronounced "net 30"—indicates that if the customer fails to take advantage of the quick-payment incentive, the full purchase price is expected within 30 days of the sales transaction. The specific credit terms used by a company are usually dictated by the competitive conditions that characterize a given industry. Thus, in less competitive industries, terms of 2/10, n/30 are common, whereas in highly competitive industries, more generous trade terms of 3/10, n/90 may be required.

When a customer takes advantage of a quick-pay incentive, this price reduction is called a **sales discount** and is reported on the income statement as a deduction from gross revenue. The resulting amount is called **net revenue** or net sales. In accounting terminology, the sales discount account is a contra-revenue account.

To illustrate, consider a credit sale of $1,000 with trade terms of 2/10, n/30. For a customer who pays her bill in full within the ten-day period, the final purchase price will be reduced to $980 ($1,000 less two percent of $1,000). This is shown in the summary below. In contrast, a customer who pays after the ten-day "quick pay" window has expired will be expected to pay the full $1,000, and payment is expected not later than 30 days after the original sale transaction.

(in $ thousands)	Sell Goods on Credit	Cash Collections	Subtotals
Assets			
Cash.		980	980
Accounts receivable.	1,000	−1,000	0
Shareholders' Equity			
Retained earnings			980
Revenue	1,000		
Less: Sales discounts		−20	

When customers fail to take advantage of existing quick-pay incentives, the seller is faced with another dilemma: The longer a receivable remains unpaid, the lower the real profit on the sale because of the time value of money. Thus, well-managed companies usually pay considerable attention to their **receivable collection period** to help monitor this potential problem area. As discussed in Chapter 4, the receivable collection period is calculated as follows:

$$\text{Receivable collection period} = \frac{365 \text{ days}}{\text{Net sales/Account receivable balance}}$$

To illustrate the use of this financial ratio, consider the following data for the **Flow International Corp.**, a U.S. technology company that provides water jet cutting and surface preparation solutions:

(in thousands of dollars)	2012	2011
Net sales.	$253,768	$216,524
Accounts receivable (net).	$ 46,830	$ 47,082
Receivable collection period	$\frac{365}{(253,768/46,830)} = 67.4$ days	$\frac{365}{(216,524/47,082)} = 79.4$ days

The data suggest that the average credit customer for Flow International took from 79.4 days to 67.4 days to pay for their credit purchases in 2011 and 2012, respectively. Even with this improvement, if Flow International's credit terms are 2/10, n/60, then some of its customers have greatly exceeded the company's payment terms. How would Flow International benefit if the average payment period were reduced to 50 days? With an average payment period of 50 days and the same level of revenue, Flow International would have reported outstanding receivables of only $29,661 and $34,763 at year-end 2011 and 2012, respectively:

(in thousands of dollars)	2012	2011
Revised receivable balance	$\frac{50 \times \$253,768}{365} = \$34,763$	$\frac{50 \times \$216,524}{365} = \$29,661$
Increase in cash	$46,830 − $34,763 = **$12,067**	$47,082 − $29,661 = **$17,421**

The reduction in Flow International's outstanding accounts receivable balance and the associated reduction in the receivable collection period would have resulted in an increase in the company's operating cash balance by $17.421 million in 2011 or $12.067 million in 2012. What could Flow International do with the extra cash? Some possibilities would be to pay down interest-bearing debt, increase dividends, or invest in new operating assets.

TAX PERSPECTIVE

Revenue Recognition and Accounts Receivable

Throughout this chapter we have discussed how managers of firms should determine the proper period in which to recognize revenues under GAAP, and when those revenues are made by granting credit how GAAP requires the recording of reserves for expected uncollectible accounts. The treatment of these issues from the perspective of U.S. tax authorities can differ substantially. With respect to revenue, while GAAP requires that SAB 101 criteria be applied in the determination of revenue recognition, the IRS follows a modified framework labeled the "all events" test when determining how much and when to record these amounts. Under the assumption that the contractual amount from the sale of a service or product can be determined with reasonable accuracy, the all-events test is met on the earliest of one of three dates: (1) when the company completes the task required to earn the income, (2) when the payment of the task is due from the customer, or (3) when the business receives payment for the task. Note that with respect to this latter date, GAAP would require the recording of a liability (deferred revenue) until SAB 101 criteria are met. Tax authorities also allow for such deferral, but only under special elections made by the company when its tax return is filed. Executives and managers are encouraged to investigate and review these special circumstances carefully, as accelerating revenue recognition could materially affect the timing of tax cash outflows.

Receivables accounting is another area wherein there are stark differences between the tax and GAAP treatment of expense measurement. As we have seen GAAP is rooted in the concept of allowing for estimates of uncollectibles within a period, without specific knowledge of which customer account may in fact be the one that is ultimately not collected. The IRS gives no such leeway. Only when a specific account is deemed uncollectible can it be written off and charged against income. Thus, it is the write-off transaction that becomes expensed under tax law, not the bad debt expense estimate illustrated throughout this chapter. Here would be an example of IRS tax accounting rules biasing against potentially understating income, and putting in place less room for judgment and more certainty to deductions included on a tax return.

Sales Returns

Many companies allow their customers to return unwanted and/or defective products for a cash or credit refund or for store credit. Like uncollectibles, the amount of customer returns may not be known with certainty until well after the completion of a fiscal period. To insure that a business's revenue is not overstated, managers must estimate the expected future customer returns at the end of each fiscal period before an income statement can be prepared. Customer returns are typically estimated on the basis of recent historical business experience.

The amount of any expected sales returns is reported in a contra-revenue account, the **sales returns** account, on the income statement as well as in a contra-asset account on the balance sheet, called the **allowance for sales returns**, if the original sale was on credit. Like the allowance for uncollectible accounts, the allowance for sale returns is a reserve for future losses associated with product returns and is subtracted from the balance in accounts receivable to arrive at the net realizable value of accounts receivable.

Sales returns can be a serious problem in some businesses. The most effective way to manage this problem is through a program of continuous quality control of manufacturing processes to insure the production of high-quality goods, as well as a diligent assessment of customer needs and preferences to insure that a company's products are meeting or exceeding customer needs and expectations.

MONETIZING ACCOUNTS RECEIVABLE TO MANAGE OPERATING CASH FLOW

Monetizing is the process of converting a noncash asset into cash. In the case of accounts and notes receivable, these assets may be converted into cash by selling or factoring, by borrowing against the value of the asset (pledging), or by securitization through the creation of an SPE or SPV.

In addition to collecting accounts receivable as a means to generate operating cash, a business can also sell its receivables to an outside buyer, use the receivables as collateral in a borrowing arrangement, or securitize its receivables. Collectively, these actions are referred to as "monetizing" a company's accounts receivable. Each of these cash-management options is considered below.

Factoring

The process of selling accounts and notes receivable is called **factoring**. Many financial institutions have divisions devoted exclusively to buying accounts and notes receivable from businesses that need cash quickly and are unable to wait for customer payment on outstanding credit transactions. Factors convert a business's receivables into cash at their face value less a service charge and a charge for the time value of money. Because factoring represents a form of an asset sale, accounts receivable are removed from the books, the cash received is recorded, and the difference charged against income as fees on the transaction. The service charge for factoring varies considerably depending upon the degree of collection risk assumed by the factor. Receivables that are sold **with recourse** means that if a factor is unable to collect on a particular account or note receivable, the factor has the right to return the uncollectible receivable to the seller and recover its money directly from the seller. In this case, the factor assumes no collection risk, and thus, the factor's service fee is likely to be low, ranging, for example, from five to ten percent of the face value of the sold receivables.[6]

When receivables are sold **without recourse**, the factor assumes all risk of collection and thus will charge a considerably higher fee (such as 12 to 15 percent or more) to compensate for the potential loss associated with any uncollectible receivables. When accounts and notes receivable are sold without recourse, the factor is unable to recover any uncollected amounts from the seller. To help estimate the extent of the assumed collection risk, factors frequently ask companies that sell their receivables to provide them with a copy of their aging schedule.

Because factoring is an expensive financing option for most businesses, it is only used when less expensive options are unavailable (such as pledging, described below). For instance, a business with a 15 percent gross profit margin that sells its receivables to a factor charging a 10 percent service fee (sold with recourse) would see its profit margin on these credit sales decline by 67 percent!

Pledging

Another way that businesses can use their accounts and notes receivable to expedite operating cash inflows is to use the receivables as collateral to obtain bank financing, usually in the form of working capital financing. Although the business typically retains ownership of its pledged receivables, as well as the responsibility and risk of collecting the receivables, the cash flow from account and note collection is usually "pledged" to pay the principal and debt service charges associated with such a loan. **Pledging** receivables is a common form of financing for most businesses because it is a lower-cost option than factoring.

Securitization

A third approach to monetize accounts and notes receivable is to sell the receivables to a private legal entity created by a company for the exclusive purpose of buying its receivables. Entities established for this purpose are called **special purpose entities (SPEs)** or **special purpose vehicles (SPVs)**.

---

[6] The company selling a receivable with recourse also must record a "recourse liability" account for the expected amount that will not be collected, adding to the net cost of the factoring transaction.

For example, **General Motors (GM) Corporation** disclosed in its 2011 annual report the following:

> GM Financial finances its loan and lease origination volume through the use of credit facilities and securitization trusts that issue asset-backed securities to investors. GM Financial retains a residual interest in these entities and is not required to provide any additional financial support to its sponsored credit facilities and securitization SPEs. The SPEs are considered VIEs because they do not have sufficient equity at risk and are consolidated because GM Financial has the power over those activities that most significantly affect the economic performance of the SPEs.

In essence, an SPE or SPV acts like a company-owned factor. The SPE borrows money from investors or from a financial services company and then uses the borrowed funds to buy accounts and notes receivable from its parent company. The advantage of **securitization** over pledging is that the parent company does not increase its leverage. Because of complex accounting rules, the borrowings of an SPE or SPV remain off-balance-sheet to its parent company. The advantage of securitization over external factoring is that the cost of factoring to a company-sponsored SPE is less than would normally be incurred when selling receivables to an independent, unaffiliated factor. We will have more to say about SPEs and SPVs, as well as **variable interest entities (VIEs)**, in Chapter 8.

ANALYZING OPERATING REVENUE AND RECEIVABLES

Because security prices are sensitive to earnings' news, some managers resort to the use of questionable accounting practices as a means to favorably impact their firm's share price. Two common approaches used by some managers to manage their company's reported earnings involve overestimating the amount of earned revenue and underestimating the amount of expected credit losses on accounts and notes receivable.

Revenue Recognition Policy

In the case of revenue, it is not uncommon to find that some companies have recognized revenue on the income statement before it is appropriate—that is, before goods or services have been delivered to the customer and/or when cash collection is doubtful. Recognizing revenue prematurely is often referred to as front-end loading. Consider, for example, the case of **MicroStrategy, Inc.** MicroStategy is a publicly-traded provider of business intelligence software ("data-mining" software) that enables firms to analyze their proprietary data to reveal trends about their business, and consequently, manage themselves more effectively. In early 2000, the shares of MicroStrategy traded at $333 per share, but fell to $140 per share in mid-March 2000 after announcing that the company would restate its operating results for 1999 and 2000 to comply with new SEC accounting guidelines on revenue reporting (see Appendix 5A to this chapter). MicroStrategy had reported its revenue for software service contracts at the time the contracts were signed, even though the contracts provided for services to be delivered over many future fiscal periods. In essence, the company front-loaded revenue that should have been deferred until the future services were actually delivered to the customer. The company originally reported 1999 earnings of $0.16 per share, but the firm's EPS were subsequently restated to a loss of $0.44 per share. By April 2000, MicroStrategy's share price had fallen to $33 per share, a decline of 90 percent.

While it is far more common to observe aggressive or premature revenue recognition, some firms actually attempt to delay the recognition of some of their company's revenue flows (see the "Microsoft Corporation" Business Perspective earlier in this chapter). Investment professionals frequently assume that a company that delays the recognition of some of its revenue, or what is often referred to as "rear-end loading" of revenue, is attempting to create a revenue reserve on the balance sheet (ie. the Deferred Revenue account) to enable the firm to more readily meet or exceed future Wall Street earnings' expectations. To help evaluate whether a firm is engaging in either front-end loading or the rear-end loading of revenues, some investment professionals calculate a financial ratio called the cash *conversion ratio*, defined as cash sales divided by accrual sales (see Chapter 3). When the cash conversion ratio gets significantly below (above) one, it may indicate the presence of front-end (rear-end) loading of revenue.

Receivable Valuation Policy

In the case of receivable valuation, some managers intentionally understate the cash collection risk associated with their accounts and notes receivable as a means to minimize the bad debts expense and, in so doing, boost the level of currently reported earnings. Consider, for example, the case of **Fairfield Communities, Inc.**, a U.S.-based developer of time-share resorts. Fairfield sells the annual right to vacation at any of the company's resorts for the duration of a buyer's lifetime. The purchase price is typically financed with a down payment of 15 percent and a seven-year, non-recourse note receivable for the balance. An analysis of Fairfield's allowance for uncollectible accounts revealed that Fairfield's expected credit losses amounted to only 4.7 percent of time-share revenue, as contrasted with the industry average of seven to nine percent. Some investment professionals alleged that Fairfield understated its expected credit losses on its notes receivable as a means to "pump up" its earnings by understating the allowance for uncollectible accounts, and hence, understating its bad debt expense on the income statement.

In a more recent similar situation, in 2012 large Wall Street banks were accused of using available discretion in determining their balances in the allowance for uncollectible accounts to help significantly bolster quarterly earnings. In the third quarter of 2012 alone, **Citigroup, Inc.** cut $1.7 billion from its $27.6 billion allowance for uncollectibles account, and **Bank of America** cut $1.9 billion from its $30 billion allowance. At Citigroup, Inc. this change led to all of the company's third quarter profit. While management of these banks might justify the changes in the allowance for uncollectible accounts on the basis of an improving economy, and thus less of a need for large reserves, critics argued that during that same quarter economic indicators were pointing to rising delinquencies in most consumer credit categories, most notably home mortgages in which Citigroup, Inc. and Bank of America were significantly exposed.

To help evaluate whether a company is managing its bad debt expense as a means to positively impact its current net earnings, some investment professionals calculate the average percentage of total receivables the company estimates will not be collected. This calculation takes the form of the ratio of the allowance for uncollectible accounts divided by gross accounts receivable. Below is a summary of the calculation of this ratio for Citigroup over the five quarters ending with the 2012 third quarter:

Citigroup, Inc.: Percentage Expected Uncollectible Loans			
Quarter (in billions)	**(1)** Total Gross Loans Outstanding	**(2)** Allowance for Uncollectible Loans	**(2)/(1)** % Estimated Uncollectible
3rd Qtr. 2011.	$637.24	$32.05	5.03%
4th Qtr. 2011.	647.24	30.12	4.65%
1st Qtr. 2012.	648.02	29.02	4.48%
2nd Qtr. 2012	654.97	27.61	4.22%
3rd Qtr. 2012.	658.42	25.92	3.94%

In the case of Citigroup, the ratio of uncollectible accounts to gross loans outstanding had dramatically improved, to 3.94 percent in the 2012 third quarter from 5.03 percent a year earlier. While this may seem like a small percentage change, note that a 1% shift downward in this ratio on Citigroup's approximately $650 billion loan portfolio, translates into $6.5 billion of pretax profit in the form of lower bad debt expense. Because of the magnitude of these changes, most investment professionals viewed Citigroup's decline in its allowance for uncollectible accounts, and the corresponding decline in bad debt expense and increase in pretax net income, very suspiciously.

Financial Statement Account Presentation at Groupon

Groupon was founded in 2008 and less than two years later was valued at over $1 billion. The business concept that bolstered this fast growth is simple but innovative. The company offers to consumers goods and services from select merchants at deep discounts. Consumers are contacted about the offers via email after becoming subscribers and providing Groupon with a personal profile, thus the offers can be tailored to specific geographic locations and personal preferences. Once each day for each market served (e.g., Richmond metropolitan), a Groupon offer is made to each subscriber. As an example, the subscriber might be offered a discounted entrance ticket and meal to the Colonial Downs Racetrack in Richmond for only $15. Typically this might cost around $30, but by offering the discount the racetrack hopes to pick up customers it would not otherwise get and help build a more permanent customer base. If a minimum number of pre-determined entrance tickets are sold then the deal becomes "live." This reduces both the risk to the retailer and enhances overall profits. Groupon and the retailer typically split the amount paid by the consumer, so in this example Groupon would net $7.50 for each offer sold, with the remainder going to Colonial Downs.

Groupon became a publicly traded company in October 2011 but the transition has not been without significant controversy. During the IPO process Groupon was forced to abandon a controversial metric it had been reporting, Adjusted Consolidated Segment Operating Income (ACSOI), wherein the company was treating marketing costs as assets. This treatment alone made Groupon appear to be reporting a profit, when in fact GAAP earnings were just below break-even when marketing costs were properly characterized as an expense. There was more, however, particularly as it related to revenue recognition. The company was applying a "gross" presentation for earned revenue rather than a "net" presentation. This means in the above example for Colonial Downs, for each purchase by the consumer Groupon would record $15 of revenue and a corresponding $7.50 cost (i.e., the amount received by the end retailer), rather than just a single value of $7.50 net. This alone did not inflate net income per se, but it did have the effect of making the company appear stronger, larger, and more successful than it may have otherwise appeared. Revenue appeared twice as high. Because Groupon never took title to the goods sold, bore no risk of loss, and was simply acting as a middle-man to help move a retailer's product, the treatment of all amounts sold as revenue to Groupon was clearly an aggressive stance. In late 2011, Groupon was forced to restate it prior financial statements for this accounting treatment. The impact on many important metrics was significant:

■ The average revenue per subscriber and customer was cut in half,
■ Marketing expense as a percent of revenue shot up, exceeding 90% for 2010,
■ Net profit margins (net income divided by sales) was dramatically worse, and
■ Year-to-year revenue growth appeared much slower.

Since its IPO Groupon's company value has been on a steady decline, from about $12 billion at the IPO date to just over $3 billion as of early 2013. Many experts question its ongoing viability because its business model has not been the boon to the retailers originally sought. Repeat business has been lower than expected. The questionable accounting practices employed by management have certainly not helped. Like many companies before, it seems Groupon management had chosen to take the aggressive approach when faced with accounting judgments, but unfortunately causing reputational damage that will be difficult for many investors to forget.

REVIEW PROBLEM

The Arcadia Company bid on a multiyear contract to construct the new hockey arena for the Phoenix Coyotes. The contract required that construction begin not later than January 1, 2011, and be completed not later than December 31, 2013. Arcadia won the contract with a bid of $720 million. During the three-year period 2011 to 2013, the company incurred the following construction costs:

	Construction Costs	Percentage of Project Completed
2011	$144 million	30%
2012	144 million	30
2013	192 million	40
Total	$480 million	100%

Under the terms of the contract, The Arcadia Company was entitled to bill the city of Glendale, Arizona, for 25 percent of the total bid ($180 million) upon completion of 30 percent of the planned project. Thus, at the end of 2011, and again at the end of 2012, Arcadia sent progress billings to, and was paid by, the City of Glendale in the amount of $180 million. At the end of 2013, after receiving all necessary occupancy approvals, The Arcadia Company billed the City of Glendale for the remaining $360 million.

Required

Prepare income statements for The Arcadia Company for 2011, 2012, and 2013 assuming that the company recognizes revenue from the Coyote arena contract (*a*) on the cash basis, (*b*) on the completed contract basis, and (*c*) on the percentage-of-completion basis.

The solution is on page 189.

EXECUTIVE SUMMARY

This chapter investigated the important concepts of revenue recognition and receivable valuation. We saw that depending upon the particular business circumstances encountered, a company could recognize its operating revenue at the point of sale and delivery, during the production process, at the end of the production process, or at the point of cash collection if collection was in doubt. We also saw that when businesses allow their customers to buy their products on credit, certain additional costs are likely to be encountered, specifically the opportunity cost of not immediately collecting the promised cash and the potential losses when an account is uncollectible. Approaches to manage these costs were discussed; in addition, approaches to monetize a firm's accounts and notes receivable were considered.

As a validation of your understanding of the content of this chapter, you should now be able to:

- Explain how service, retail, and manufacturing companies recognize their operating revenue.
- Explain how revenue is recognized under the completed contract and percentage of completion methods.
- Explain how accounts receivables are valued and how the allowance for uncollectible accounts and bad debt expense are estimated.
- Explain why the effective management of accounts receivable is important for a business.

In Chapter 6, we examine various inventory valuation approaches used by companies to measure the cost of their products sold and the inventory remaining on hand.

KEY CONCEPTS AND TERMS

Accounts receivable, 159
Aging method, 165
Allowance for sales returns, 173
Allowance for Uncollectible
    Accounts, 165, 168
Bad debt expense, 166
Completed contract method, 162

Credit terms, 171
Deferred revenue, 162
Direct write-off method, 165
Duration, 171
Earnings reserve, 163
Factoring, 174
Installment method, 159

Net realizable value, 165, 168
Net revenue, 172
Note receivable, 159
Notes receivable, 159
Operating cycle, 156
Opportunity cost, 160

APPENDIX 5A: Revenue Recognition: SAB No. 101

Although the general criteria regarding revenue recognition is quite straightforward—the revenue must be earned and the collection of cash realized or realizable—revenue recognition issues dominate SEC enforcement actions involving exchange-traded companies. SEC Staff Accounting Bulletin (SAB) No. 101 on revenue recognition in financial statements was written to provide guidance for those situations in which a straightforward interpretation was not obvious. Below are key questions and answers extracted from SAB No. 101.[7]

General Guidance on Revenue Recognition

Revenue should not be recognized until it is realized or realizable and earned. Revenue is generally realized or realizable and earned when all of the following criteria are met:

- Persuasive evidence of a sales arrangement exists.
- Delivery has occurred or services have been rendered.
- The seller's price to the buyer is fixed or determinable; and,
- Cash collectibility is reasonably assured.

Persuasive Evidence of a Sales Arrangement

Facts: Company A has product available to ship to Company B prior to the end of the period. It is customary for Company A to enter into a written sales agreement that requires the signature of the buyer company. Company B places a verbal order stating that it is highly likely that the contract will be approved one week after the end of the fiscal period. Company A ships the goods and Company B received the goods prior to the end of the period.

Question and Response: May Company A recognize revenue in the current period? It would not be appropriate to recognize revenue until the signed sales agreement is received since this is the general business practice of Company A. The signed agreement represents persuasive evidence of an agreement.

Facts: Company A enters into an arrangement with Customer B to deliver products to Customer B on a consignment basis. Title does not pass from Company A to Customer B until Customer B consumes the product. Company A delivers the product to Customer B under the terms of the arrangement.

Question and Response: May Company A recognize revenue upon delivery of its product to Customer B? No, consignment arrangements do not qualify for revenue recognition until a sale occurs. Revenue recognition is not appropriate since Company A retains the risks and rewards of ownership and title did not pass to Customer B.

  Another characteristic in a transaction that will likely preclude revenue recognition, even if title has passed, is if the buyer has a right of product return. In general, under this set of circumstances, revenue recognition will be precluded until the right-of-return period has expired.

Delivery and Performance

Facts: Company A receives a purchase order for products it has in stock; however, the customer is unable to take delivery at this time.

Question and Response: Can Company A recognize revenue if it either segregates the inventory in its own warehouse or ships to a third-party warehouse if Company A retains title to the product? Generally, no; delivery is not considered to have taken place until the customer has taken title and assumed the risks and rewards of ownership. This interpretation includes layaway sales where a seller takes a nonrefundable deposit and holds the merchandise for later pickup by the customer. Further, revenue should not be recognized, even after delivery, if uncertainty exists regarding customer acceptance. Uncertainty exists, for example, if the customer has the right to test the product or require additional services subsequent to delivery.

---

[7] For further discussion on revenue recognition and SAB No. 101 see "The Right Way to Recognize Revenue" by Phillips, Luehlfing and Daily published in the June 2001 issue of the Journal of Accountancy. This article can be found online at www.journalofaccountancy.com/Issues/2001/Jun/TheRightWayToRecognizeRevenue

Facts: Companies often require up-front, nonrefundable fees from its customers. Examples include a lifetime membership fee in a health club or an activation fee by a wireless telephone provider.

Question and Response: When should the revenue related to nonrefundable, up-front fees be recognized? Deferral of revenue recognition is appropriate unless the up-front fee is in exchange for delivered products or the performance of services that represent the culmination of a separate earnings process. Health club membership fees or activation fees by wireless telephone providers generally do not qualify for immediate revenue recognition.

Fixed or Determinable Sales Price

Facts: Company B is a discount retailer that generates revenue from annual membership fees it charges customers to shop at its stores and from the sale of products at a discount price to those customers. The membership arrangements with retail customers require the customer to pay the entire membership fee at the start of the arrangement. The customer has the unilateral right to cancel the arrangement at any time during its term and receive a full refund of the initial fee.

Question and Response: May Company B recognize revenue for the membership at the beginning of the membership period? No; the earnings process is not complete, and the ability of the member to receive a refund raises an uncertainty as to whether the fee is fixed or determinable. A company's contracts may include provisions for the customer to cancel or terminate early. In addition, side agreements may be present providing additional rights for the customer. Provisions of this type raise questions as to whether the sales price is fixed or determinable. The sales price is neither fixed nor determinable until cancellation privileges expire. If the cancellation privilege expires ratably over a stated time period, the sales price is considered to become determinable ratably over the stated period.

Other Issues

Facts: Company A operates an internet site from which it sells the products of other companies. Company A receives orders, processes credit card payments, and passes the order to Company B which possesses the product. Company B then ships the product to the ultimate customer. The product is sold for $175, of which Company A retains a $25 commission.

Question and Response: Should Company A report revenue on a gross basis as $175 with a corresponding $150 cost of sales or report revenue on a net basis of $25? Company A should report revenue on a net basis unless it takes title to the product and assumes the risks and rewards of ownership.

QUESTIONS

Q5.1 **Revenue Recognition Criteria.** **MicroStrategy, Inc.**, is a software company that sells its services to other companies under multiyear contracts (on average for three years). The contracts call for a minimum fee, paid monthly, and additional fees when the services provided exceed certain levels. The chief operating officer (COO) of MicroStrategy is uncertain when the most appropriate time is to recognize the revenue from such contracts: (*a*) at the time of contract signing; (*b*) monthly, when billings are sent to customers; or (*c*), when the contract is complete and all services have been rendered. Discuss the criteria that should be considered in reaching this accounting policy decision. What would you recommend to MicroStrategy's COO?

Q5.2 **The Materiality Concept.** The materiality concept is a financial statement disclosure guideline used by most businesses to help determine when a particular account balance or economic event should be separately disclosed in a firm's financial statements. Unfortunately, there are no generally accepted guidelines for determining when an amount is material. Assume that you are the chief operating officer of a company generating $100 million in revenue, $10 million in net income, and $150 million in total assets. Discuss the materiality standard that you believe would be appropriate for such a business. Be prepared to justify your decision.

Q5.3 **Accrual Accounting, Accounts Receivable, and Cash Flow.** A well-known poem about accounting was written by H.S. Bailey, Jr. and published in 1975 in Publishers Weekly:

> *Though my bottom line is black, I am flat upon my back.*
> *My cash flows out and customers pay slow.*
> *The growth of my receivables is almost unbelievable.*
> *The result is certain—unremitting woe!*
> *And I hear the banker utter an ominous low mutter—"Watch cash flow."*

Discuss the message that Mr. Bailey was trying to convey through this poem.

Q5.4   **Revenue Recognition, the Matching Principle, and the Bad Debt Expense.**   **Urcarco, Inc.,** was a publicly held used-car dealer that had defined its market niche as customers with a low or no credit rating. In some years, Urcarco's repossession rate had run as high as 40 percent of all vehicles sold. Discuss how Urcarco should recognize revenue from vehicle sales and how it should estimate its bad debt expense.

Q5.5   **Revenue Recognition in the Air Transportation Industry.**   **U.S. Airways** recognizes revenue from airline ticket sales when a customer takes a flight or not later than one year from the date of sale (flight coupons have a useful life of one year from the date of purchase). Discuss the alternative revenue recognition policy options available to U.S. Airways.

Q5.6   **Managing Earnings and the Bad Debt Expense.**   **Total Networks, Inc.,** reported gross accounts receivable of $1.2 billion in 2008 and an allowance for doubtful accounts of $300 million. In 2009, the company's gross accounts receivable declined slightly to $1.1 billion and its allowance for doubtful accounts likewise declined to $150 million. Calculate the ratio of the allowance for doubtful accounts divided by gross accounts receivable for 2008 and 2009. Discuss how Total Networks, Inc., might be managing its earnings.

Q5.7   **Sales Channel Stuffing.**   On April 14, 2006, *The Wall Street Journal* carried an article headlined "Research in Motion Skeptics Pipe Up." The article concerned **Research in Motion Ltd.** (RIM), the manufacturer of the Blackberry. One week earlier, RIM had disappointed investors with a weaker-than-expected revenue forecast for the current quarter. In the one-week period following the revenue announcement, RIM's share price declined 9.5 percent.

      The Wall Street Journal article expressed new concerns about RIM's financial performance. RIM generates revenue two ways:

1.   70 percent of its revenue comes from sales of the Blackberry device; and,
2.   30 percent of its revenue comes from the sale of subscriptions to the wireless network that supports the Blackberry.

Of concern to Wall Street analysts was the fact that a widening gap was beginning to build between the number of new Blackberry network subscribers and the number of Blackberry devices shipped to retailers. In the latest reporting period, RIM reportedly shipped 1.12 million Blackberries, while new network subscribers totaled only 625,000, a difference of about 495,000. According to the company, the "gap" between units shipped and new network subscribers for the prior three quarters, respectively, was 475,000, 335,000, and 248,000.

      Discuss whether RIM is engaging in "channel stuffing." (Note: Channel stuffing refers to the practice of shipping unwanted and unsolicited goods to retailers, usually with a guarantee to allow the return of any unsold goods.) Why is channel stuffing of concern to analysts and investors?

Q5.8   **Sales Forecasts and Share Prices.**   In early 2006, the **Bausch & Lomb Company** halted shipments of its ReNu contact lens product and recalled from retailers any unsold containers of its contact lens solution. The contact lens cleaning solution had been linked to an increasing number of serious eye infections caused by a fungus. ReNu products generated about $45 million in 2005 sales for Bausch & Lomb, but analysts predicted a wider decline in sales in related products as well. For 2006, equity analysts predicted that the company might lose $75 million to $100 million in lens-solution sales, or about 4.6 percent of the firm's total projected sales for 2006. Shares of Bausch & Lomb declined over $8 per share, or 15 percent, in response to the product recall.

      Discuss the relationship between revenue forecasts and security prices. Did the capital market overreact to the Bausch & Lomb news about ReNu?

Q5.9   **Revenue Recognition by Software Companies.**   **Microsoft, Inc.,** recognizes revenue from its licensed software products at the "time of sale" or "time of installation." Despite receiving such revenue in cash, Microsoft defers the recognition of a portion of its software revenue. The deferred portion represents the value of any future software upgrades that might be distributed free of charge, as well as the value of any technical support services provided free of charge during the software warranty period. Discuss Microsoft's revenue recognition policy. Do you agree with Microsoft's policy choice? Discuss the company's possible motivation for adopting this revenue recognition approach.

Q5.10   **Revenue Recognition by Aircraft Manufacturers.**   **Airbus** and **Boeing** are the world's two largest manufacturers of commercial and military aircraft. Each company requires a deposit of as much as $100 million per aircraft prior to the start of construction of an airplane, which may take as long as nine months to complete. Airbus and Boeing also receive periodic progress payments from their customers as certain aircraft construction milestones are met. Typically, ten percent of an airplane's purchase price is withheld by the buyer until flight testing is complete and title of the aircraft is transferred to the buyer. The average cost of a commercial aircraft is approximately $350 million. Discuss the possible approaches to revenue recognition that Boeing and Airbus might adopt. Which approach do you prefer? Why?

Q5.11   **Ethics and the Tone at the Top.**   Discuss what is meant by the "tone at the top" and why it is important. Further, discuss whether you feel it is ethical to be a whistle-blower.

Assignments with the ✔ logo in the margin are available in BusinessCourse.
See the Preface of the book for details.
CHECK FIGURE indicates that check figures are available on the book's Website.

EXERCISES

E5.12   **Revenue Recognition Policy Decisions.**   Consider the following independent situations:

1. An international health club sells lifetime memberships costing $1,500 which allow the purchaser unlimited use of any of the club's 300 facilities around the world. The initiation fee may be paid in 36 monthly installments, with a two percent interest charge on any unpaid balance.

2. Global Motors, Inc., has always offered a limited, 36-month warranty on its cars and trucks, but to counter the significant competition in the industry, the company has come to the conclusion that it must do something more. With that in mind, the company developed a new warranty program: For a $1,500 payment at the time of purchase, a customer can buy a seven-year warranty that will cover replacement of almost all parts and labor. The purchased warranty expires at the end of seven years or when the customer sells the vehicle, whichever occurs first.

3. Arcadia Promotions Inc. sells coupon books that give the holder a ten percent discount at any of 50 participating merchants. The buyer of the coupon book pays $25 for the book but can realize up to $500 in savings. Arcadia convinces merchants to participate in the program at no cost, arguing that participation will build customer traffic and will create the opportunity for repeat business from the coupon book-holders.

4. Luxury Furniture Inc. sells household furniture under installment purchase contracts. The contracts usually carry interest rates of 16 percent or more a year. When the company accumulates $500,000 of contracts with at least a year or more to go, it sells the contracts to a finance company on a nonrecourse basis. Luxury Furniture continues to service the contracts and is paid a service fee. If a contract is uncollectible, Luxury Furniture turns it over to a collection agency and has no further responsibility for it. In January, Luxury sold contracts with a face value of $1 million and received $1.06 million in cash from the finance company.

5. Community News, Inc., prints and distributes a weekly newspaper throughout the city. Local stores order a certain number of the papers each week and pay for them on delivery. Community News always takes back any unsold papers and gives the merchant a credit toward future purchases.

For each of these situations, describe the revenue recognition policy that you believe that the company should follow, explaining the basis for your recommendation.

E5.13   **Revenue Recognition.**   The Longo Corporation contracted with The Davis Company to manufacture various metal component parts that would be assembled by Longo before resale to Longo's customers. Longo placed its most recent order with Davis for 10,000 parts in December 2009. Because of existing work commitments, however, Davis indicated that work on the Longo order could not commence until January 2010, with an expected delivery date of February 2010. Davis provides its customers with trade credit terms of 2/10, n/30, and thus, didn't expect to be paid the contract price of $100,000 by Longo until March 2010.

In which month should Davis Company recognize the $100,000 in revenue from the Longo order? Why?

CHECK FIGURE **E5.14**   **Analyzing Accounts Receivable.**   The following information is taken from the annual report of **The Lincoln Electric Company**.

Balance Sheet	Year 1	Year 2
Accounts receivable, net of the allowance for uncollectible accounts of $2,460 and $2,700, respectively........................	$79,500	$75,390

Calculate the ratio of the allowance for uncollectible accounts divided by gross accounts receivable for Year 1 and Year 2. Did this ratio increase from Year 1 to Year 2? If so, what does that indicate? The bad debt expense on Lincoln Electric's income statement did not equal $2,700. What might explain this?

 E5.15   **Analyzing Accounts Receivable.**   The following information is taken from the annual report of the Couche Corporation.

Balance Sheet	Year 1	Year 2
Accounts receivable, net of the allowance for uncollectible accounts of $4,500 and $4,100, respectively........................	$125,650	$132,500

Calculate the ratio of the allowance for uncollectible accounts divided by gross accounts receivable. Did this ratio decrease from Year 1 to Year 2? If so, what does that indicate? The bad debt expense on the Couche Corporation's earnings statement did not equal $4,100. What might explain this?

E5.16   Accounting for Quick-Pay Incentives. Charles Smith, Inc., is a manufacturer of small office equipment. Smith transacts most of its business on credit and offers its customers credit terms of 2/10, n/30. On July 1, Smith shipped an order valued at $120,000 to a customer and shipped a second order valued at $80,000 to another customer on July 10. Payment was received on the July 1st order on July 6, but payment on the July 10th order was not received until August 15. Calculate total sales, the sales discount, and net sales for Charles Smith, Inc., for July. Why do companies like Smith, Inc., offer sales discounts to their customers? Why are sales discounts valuable to the customers of Smith, Inc.?

E5.17   Preparing an Aging Schedule. M. Beall Inc. uses the aging method to estimate the company's bad debt expense. Mike Beall, the president of the company, collected information about the company's outstanding accounts receivable and their probability of collection:

Account Age	Amount	Probability of Non-Collection
0–30 days	$725,000	0.5%
31–60 days	275,000	1.5
61–90 days	170,000	2.5
91–120 days	100,000	4.0
Over 120 days	40,000	20.0

Calculate the expected bad debt expense for M. Beall, Inc., the total balance in accounts receivable, and the net realizable value of the company's accounts receivable. Assume that M. Beall Inc. adopts a policy of writing off as worthless all unpaid accounts receivable over 120 days old. How will implementation of this policy impact the net realizable value of the company's accounts receivable? Why?

E5.18   Analyzing Accounts Receivable. The following information is taken from the annual report of **Coca-Cola Enterprises, Inc.**:

CHECK FIGURE

(amounts in millions)	Year 1	Year 2
Net sales	$18,158	$18,706
Accounts receivable (net)	1,884	1,802

Calculate the receivable turnover ratio and the receivable collection period for Year 1 to Year 2. How much additional cash flow from operations could Coca-Cola Enterprises generate in Year 2 if it could reduce its receivable collection period to just 30 days?

E5.19   Analyzing Accounts Receivable. The following information is taken from the annual report of The Mann Corporation:

(all amounts in millions)	Year 1	Year 2
Net sales	$26,258	$25,649
Accounts receivable (net)	4,684	4,883

Calculate the receivable turnover ratio and the receivable collection period for Year 1 to Year 2. How much additional cash flow from operations could The Mann Corporation generate in Year 2 if it could reduce its receivable collection period to 60 days?

E5.20   Revenue Policy Change: Software Service Contracts. **CA Technologies**, is a software company that designs, develops, installs, and services business software for manufacturing companies. Typically, CA Technologies provides its services over a multiyear period. Following the release of SAB 101, the company changed its method of recognizing revenue under its multiyear service contracts. Originally, CA Technologies recognized all contract revenue at the time that a contract was signed; however, consistent with SAB 101, the company decided to recognize contract revenue on a prorata basis over the life of each multiyear contract.

1. How will the change in revenue recognition policy affect the following items on the financial statements of CA Technologies?
   - *a.* Revenue
   - *b.* Total assets
   - *c.* Cash flow from operations
   - *d.* Total liabilities
2. Do you agree with the policy change implemented by Computer Associates? Why?

PROBLEMS

 CHECK FIGURE

P5.21 **Installment Basis versus Point-of-Sale Revenue Recognition.** The Apollo Company is a catalogue-based retailer. The following describes Apollo's operations:

	Year 1	Year 2
Sales (all on account)..	$400,000	$600,000
Cash collections from customers		
On Year 1 sales...	180,000	220,000
On Year 2 sales...	—	240,000
Cash purchases of merchandise inventory	360,000	480,000
Merchandise inventory-on-hand (year-end)................................	120,000	228,000
Operating expenses (other than inventory)	64,000	88,000

Required

1. Prepare an income statement for each year assuming that Apollo recognizes revenue using the point-of-sale method and assuming that all operating expenses are paid in cash.
2. Prepare an income statement for each year assuming that Apollo recognizes revenue using the installment method and assuming that all operating expenses are paid in cash.

 P5.22 **Revenue Recognition.** At the beginning of 2012, John Cornell decided to quit his job as a construction company supervisor and formed his own residential housing construction company. When he resigned, he had a contract to build a custom home at a price of $400,000. The full price was payable in cash when the house was completed.

By year-end 2012, Cornell's new company Luxury Homes, Inc. had spent $50,000 for labor, $107,740 for materials, and $3,800 in miscellaneous expenses in connection with the construction of the new home. Cornell estimated that the project was 70 percent complete at year-end. In addition, construction materials on hand at year-end 2012 had cost $2,600.

During the year, Luxury Homes, Inc., had also purchased a small house for $95,000, spent $32,000 fixing it up, and then sold it on November 1, 2012, for $175,000. The buyer paid $25,000 down and signed a note for the remainder of the balance due. The note called for interest payments only at a rate of 12 percent per year, with a lump-sum payment for the outstanding balance payable at the end of 2011. John's wife, Karen, kept the accounting records for Luxury Homes, Inc., and on December 31, she prepared the following statement:

LUXURY HOMES, INC. Where We Stand at Year-End			
Assets		**Debts and Owners' Capital**	
Cash..........................	$ 21,000	Accounts payable..................	$ 44,600
Materials......................	2,600	Owners' investment	242,540
Renovation contract receivable	150,000	Sale of renovated house.............	175,000
Construction in progress	161,540		
Cost of renovated house	127,000		
Total assets......................	$462,140	Total debts & owners' capital.........	$462,140

After reviewing the statement, John and Karen got into a discussion concerning the level of revenue the company had earned during the year. John argued that all of the revenue from the sale of the renovated home, along with 70 percent of the expected revenue from the new construction contract, had been earned. Karen, on the other hand, maintained that the revenue on the renovation project should be recognized only to the extent of the cash actually collected and that no revenue should be recognized on the new home construction until it was completed and available for occupancy. John and Karen agreed that there were four possible alternative approaches to measuring the company's revenue:

1. Report the entire amount of renovation revenue and a proportionate amount of the new construction contract revenue.
2. Report the entire amount of renovation revenue but none of the new construction contract revenue.
3. Report the renovation revenue in proportion to the amount of cash received and the new construction contract revenue in proportion to the amount of work completed.
4. Report the renovation revenue in proportion to the amount of cash received but none of the new construction contract revenue.

Required

Prepare the balance sheets and income statements that would result under each of the four approaches. Which set of statements do you believe best reflects the results of Luxury Homes, Inc. for 2012? Why?

P5.23   Completed Contract Method versus Percentage-of-Completion Method.   The Miller Company won a contract to build a shopping center at a price of $240 million. The following schedule details the estimated and actual costs of construction and the actual cash collections under the contract:

 ✔ CHECK FIGURE

	Estimated (Actual) Costs of Construction	Cash Collections From Customer
Year 1	$ 40,000,000	$ 48,000,000
Year 2	60,000,000	60,000,000
Year 3	70,000,000	60,000,000
Year 4	30,000,000	72,000,000
	$200,000,000	$240,000,000

Required

1. Prepare an income statement for the Miller Company for each year assuming that the company recognizes revenue under the completed contract method.
2. Prepare an income statement for the Miller Company for each year assuming that the company recognizes revenue under the percentage-of-completion method.
3. Which set of income statements best reflects the actual performance of the Miller Company? Why?

P5.24   Revenue Recognition under Long-Term Construction Contracts.   In June 2010, Biltmore Construction Company (BCC) was hired by the City of Phoenix, Arizona, to assist in constructing its new Trade Center complex. The construction agreement called for work to begin no later than August 2010 and required Biltmore to construct the concrete frame for the complex. Under the terms of the three-year contract, BCC was to receive a total of $10 million in cash payments from the City of Phoenix, to be paid as follows: 25 percent when the project was 30 percent complete, 25 percent when the project was 60 percent complete, and the remaining 50 percent, when the project was fully complete. The contract required that BCC's completion estimates be certified by an independent engineering consultant *before* any cash progress payments would be made.

In preparing its bid, Biltmore estimated that the total cost to complete the project would be $8.3 million, assuming no cost overruns. During the first year of the contract, BCC incurred actual costs of $2.49 million, and on June 30, 2011, the engineering firm of J. Graham & Associates determined that the project had attained a 30 percent completion level. (BCC's fiscal year ran from July 1 to June 30.) In the following year, BCC incurred actual costs of $3.1 million, and on June, 30, 2012, the firm of J. Graham & Associates determined that the project had attained at least a 60 percent completion level. By May 2013, BCC had completed the remainder of the project. Actual costs incurred during the year to June 30, 2013, amounted to $3.11 million. The firm received a certification for the fully completed work.

Required

1. Assuming that BCC had no other sources of revenue or expenses, determine the level of profits to be reported for the years ended June 30, 2011, 2012, and 2013, using the following revenue recognition methods:
    a. Percentage of completion
    b. Completed contract
    c. Cash basis
2. Which set of results best reflect the economic performance of the company over the period 2011–2013? Why?

P5.25 **Revenue Recognition: R & D Company.** Wind Technology, Inc., is an independent research laboratory that undertakes contractual research for a variety of corporate and governmental clients. In January 2010, scientists at Wind Technology began work on a number of projects involving wind-power generation. During 2010, costs incurred in these efforts amounted to $363,000. In May 2011, promising results emerged and were reported to the U.S. Department of Energy. Development costs incurred in 2011 through the end of May totaled $204,000.

At this point, Wind Technology tried to secure a government contract to support the remainder of the research effort. The Department of Energy (DOE) was reluctant to commit substantial sums until further tests had been completed. Nonetheless, to ensure that it retained access to the new technology, the DOE gave Wind Technology a seed grant of $50,000 to help support continuation of the studies. This grant carried a stipulation that the DOE would retain the right to acquire the results, patents, and copyrights from the research any time on or before December 31, 2012, for $2.4 million.

Further testing proved favorable, although additional development costs incurred in 2011 amounted to $325,000 and to $210,000 in 2012. On December 28, 2012, the DOE exercised its right and agreed to purchase the results, patents, and copyrights from the lab. As previously agreed, the DOE paid Wind Technology $300,000 immediately, with the remainder of the contract price payable in seven equal annual installments beginning on December 31, 2013, through December 31, 2019. On March 1, 2013, Wind Technology delivered all scientific and legal documents, test results, and samples to the DOE offices in Washington, D.C.

Required

Evaluate the facts and determine when Wind Technology, Inc., should recognize the various revenue streams associated with its work on this project: (*a*) the $2.4 million contract proceeds; (*b*) the $50,000 seed grant; and (*c*) the interest implicit in the seven-year deferred payment (assume a discount rate of ten percent).

P5.26 **Aging of Accounts Receivable.** The Miller Company's accounts receivable reveal the following balances by age category:

Age of Account	Receivable Balance
0–30 days	$ 800,000
31–60 days	180,000
61–90 days	80,000
91–120 days	40,000
	$1,100,000

The allowance for uncollectible accounts has an existing positive balance of $34,200. The company's internal auditors suggest that the following percentages be used to estimate the amount of outstanding receivables that will eventually prove to be uncollectible.

0-30 days	0.5%
31-60 days	1.0
61-90 days	10.0
91-120 days	70.0

Required

1. Calculate the projected new balance for (*a*) the allowance for uncollectible accounts and (*b*) the bad debts expense.
2. Why is there an existing balance of $34,200 in the allowance for uncollectible accounts? What could be inferred if the existing balance in the allowance for uncollectible accounts was a negative balance of $34,200?

P5.27 **Accounts Receivable Analysis.** Kate Miller owned a dance studio in Los Angles, California. Students could buy access to the dance classes by paying a monthly fee. Unfortunately, many of Kate's students were struggling actors and actresses who lacked the ability to pay their bills in a timely manner. And, although the students were expected to pay for classes in advance, Kate had begun offering credit to many of her students to grow her business. This, however, had put Kate in a serious liquidity problem as revealed by the growing balance in the studio's outstanding accounts receivable:

Age Classification	Accounts Receivable Outstanding Balance	Historical Estimate of Non-Collection
0–30 days.....................................	$44,000	4%
31–60 days....................................	31,000	8
61–90 days....................................	22,000	12
91–120 days...................................	13,000	14
121–150 days..................................	9,000	20
> 150 days	5,000	50

Kate's accountant, Matt Thomas, had tried to help her get a handle on the studio's accounts receivable problem, but to little avail. One trick he had successfully used in the past to make Kate realize the seriousness of the problem was to overestimate the extent of Kate's bad debt problem; consequently, there currently existed a balance in the allowance for uncollectible accounts totaling $2,700.

Required

1. The first step to help get Kate's business back on track is to write off all receivables having a very low probability of collection (those accounts over 150 days). What balance sheet accounts will be affected, and in what amount, when Matt executes this action?
2. Prepare an aging of Kate's remaining accounts receivable. What balance should be in the Allowance for Uncollectible Accounts account?
3. Kate is in need of an immediate cash infusion and Matt has advised her to sell some of her receivables. A local bank has offered her two alternatives:
   a. Factor $40,000 of "current" receivables (0–30 days old) on a nonrecourse basis at a flat fee of eleven percent of the value of the receivables sold.
   b. Factor $40,000 of "current" receivables on a recourse basis at a flat fee of six percent of the value of the receivables sold.
   Which option should Kate choose? Why?

P5.28 **Factoring versus Pledging of Accounts Receivable.** Global Markets, Inc. was experiencing a shortage of cash. Consequently, the President was considering two options to provide an immediate inflow of cash. The first option was to obtain a 60-day loan from a local bank using its outstanding receivables as collateral. Under the loan agreement, Global Markets would be charged 13 percent annual interest on the outstanding loan and would pledge receivables equal to 122 percent of the loan amount (a loan-to-value ratio of 82 percent). The second option was to sell $2 million of the company's accounts receivable on a nonrecourse basis. The factoring cost would amount to 15.5 percent of the value of the factored receivables.

Required
Compare the cost under each financing option. Which option is best for the company? Why?

P5.29 **Improving Cash Flow through Receivable Management.** UTStarcom, Inc. designs, manufactures, and sells telecommunication equipment, and provides services associated with their installation, operation, and maintenance in China, India, Korea, and Vietnam. During 2005, the company's share price traded as high as $23 per share; but, in January, 2005, the company disclosed that it would file its Form 10-K with the U.S. Securities and Exchange Commission late due to material internal control problems identified by its independent auditor, PricewaterhouseCoopers. One of the identified concerns related to the company's recording of revenue and the related accounts receivable. In response, the company's share price sank to $6 per share. Following are selected financial data from UTStarcom's 2004 annual report:

	2004	2003
Net sales..	$2.56 billion	$1.78 billion
Accounts receivable (net)..	0.81 billion	0.37 billion

Required

1. Calculate UTStarcom's receivable collection period for 2003 and 2004. Is the company's receivable management decreasing in quality, improving, or about the same?
2. If the company could improve its receivable collection period to the industry average of 60 days, how much additional cash flow from accounts receivable would have been generated in 2003 and 2004?

CORPORATE ANALYSIS

CA5.30 **The Procter & Gamble Company.** The 2012 annual report of the Procter & Gamble Company (P&G) is available at http://annualreport.pg.com/annualreport2012/index.shtml. After reviewing P&G's annual report, respond to the following questions:

  a. When does P&G recognize revenue from its product sales?
  b. In the Management Discussion and Analysis section, the company highlights its financial targets (strategic focus). What percentage sales growth is targeted by the company? P&G's revenue growth over the past five years averages 2.4%. Assuming that this trend continues, what level of sales might the company achieve in 2013? What was the company's growth in sales in 2011 and 2012? Do the new sales targets indicate that sales growth is increasing or decreasing?
  c. When does P&G recognize its sales discounts and sales product returns?
  d. Calculate P&G's receivable turnover ratio and receivable collection period for 2011 and 2012. Are these ratios improving?
  e. Assume that P&G's allowance for uncollectible accounts was $180 million at year-end 2011 and $205 million at year-end 2012. Calculate the ratio of the allowance for uncollectible accounts to gross accounts receivable for 2011 and 2012. Did this ratio improve? If so, what does that indicate?
  f. Using your forecast of net sales for 2013 from question (b), and your 2012 receivable turnover ratio from question (d), forecast the balance of accounts receivable for 2013 (assuming that receivable turnover remains the same from 2012 to 2013).

CA5.31 **Internet-based Analysis.** Consider a publicly held company whose products you are familiar with. Some examples might include:

Company	Product	Corporate Website
• Johnson & Johnson Company....	• Band-Aids	• www.jnj.com
• Microsoft Corporation...........	• Windows XP software	• www.microsoft.com
• Nokia Corporation..............	• Cellular phones	• www.nokia.com
• Intel Corporation	• Pentium processors	• www.intel.com
• Kimberly-Clark Corporation......	• Kleenex	• www.kimberly-clark.com

Access the company's public website and search for its most recent annual report. (Some companies will provide access to their financial data through an "investor relations" link, while others will provide a direct link to their "annual reports.") After locating your company's most recent annual report, open the file and review its contents. After reviewing the annual report for your selected company, prepare answers to the following questions:

  a. Identify whether the company is a retailer, a manufacturer, or a service provider.
  b. Review the company's "Summary of Significant Accounting Principles." When does the company recognize its operating revenue? Can you identify an alternative method to recognize its operating revenue? If so, describe the alternative approach.
  c. Review the company's balance sheet and related footnotes. Identify the gross accounts receivable and the allowance for uncollectible accounts for each of the last two years. Calculate the ratio of the allowance for uncollectible accounts divided by the gross accounts receivable for each of the last two years. Is this ratio increasing or decreasing? Why?
  d. Calculate the company's receivable turnover and receivable collection period for each of the last two years. Is the receivable collection period increasing or decreasing? What might explain this increase or decrease?
  e. Calculate the company's cash collections from sales for each of the last two years. Using this calculation, compute the company's cash conversion ratio (cash from sales divided by net sales). Is the cash conversion ratio increasing or decreasing? Is the cash conversion ratio at an acceptable level? Note that cash from sales is calculated as net sales plus/minus the change in accounts receivable plus/minus the change in unearned (or deferred) revenue. See Chapter 3.

CA5.32 **IFRS Financial Statements.** The 2012 financial statements of **LVMH Moet Hennessey-Louis Vuitton S.A.** are presented in Appendix C of this book. LVMH is a Paris-based holding company and one of the world's largest and best-known luxury goods companies. As a member-nation of the European Union, French companies are required to prepare their consolidated (group) financial statements using International Financial Reporting Standards (IFRS). Under IFRS, as is the case under U.S. GAAP, companies are required to disclose their accounting policies. In LVMH's Notes to the Consolidated Financial Statements (not presented in Appendix C), the company discloses its revenue recognition policy:

> Revenue mainly comprises retail sales within the Group's store network and sales through distributors. Sales made in stores owned by third parties are treated as retail transactions if the risks and rewards of ownership of the inventories are retained by the Group.
>
> Direct sales to customers are made through retail stores . . . (and) are recognized at the time of purchase by retail customers.
>
> Wholesale sales through distributors . . . (are recognized) when title transfers to third-party customers, generally on shipment.

Consider the following questions:

a. Describe LVMH's revenue recognition policy.
b. Contrast LVMH's revenue recognition policy with the policy that you would expect a retailer to use under U.S. GAAP.

SOLUTION TO REVIEW PROBLEM

Solution

a. Cash basis:

(in millions)	2011	2012	2013	Total
Revenue	$180	$180	$360	$720
Less: Construction costs	144	144	192	480
Net income.	$ 36	$ 36	$168	$240

b. Completed contract basis:

(in millions)	2011	2012	2013	Total
Revenue	$ 0	$ 0	$720	$720
Less: Construction costs	0	0	480	480
Net income.	$ 0	$ 0	$240	$240

c. Percentage-of-completion basis:

(in millions)	2011	2012	2013	Total
Revenue	$216[1]	$216[1]	$288[2]	$720
Less: Construction costs	144	144	192	480
Net income.	$ 72	$ 72	$ 96	$240

[1] $720 million × 30% = $216 million.
[2] $720 million × 40% = $288 million.

When you complete this chapter, you should be able to:

1. Describe how the initial cost of inventory is determined.

2. Explain how inventory is valued using FIFO, LIFO, and the weighted-average cost method and how the resulting cost of goods sold is matched with revenue.

3. Describe the conditions under which the lower-of-cost-or-market method must be used to value ending inventory and how this method affects reported net income.

4. Explain the LIFO reserve and how a LIFO-inventory liquidation can increase a company's gross profit and net income.

5. Describe how accounts payable are valued and how the payment of these payables can be managed to positively impact a firm's operating cash flow.

Operating Expenses, Inventory Valuation, and Accounts Payable

Ford Motor Company is the world's fifth largest automaker by sales, and second in the U.S. Founded in 1903 by Henry Ford and based in Dearborn, Michigan, Ford manufactures its cars and trucks on six continents under the primary brands of Ford and Lincoln. The company owns a small stake in the Mazda brand, but recently streamlined its business by selling the Volvo brand in 2010, the Jaguar and Land Rover brands in 2008, and discontinuing the Mercury line in 2011.

FORD MOTOR COMPANY

Ford is considered to be a capital-intensive company with a capital intensity ratio of 0.13—that is, the company's investment in property, plant and equipment and intangible assets represents 13 percent of total assets. Besides its significant investment in property, plant and equipment, Ford maintains a sizeable investment in inventory to service its worldwide network of dealers. Ford's investment in inventory represented approximately 3.5 percent of total assets in 2011 and 2010. A major challenge for Ford's management team is to keep its investment in inventory as low as possible without damaging its ability to effectively service its worldwide dealer network.

According to the company's 2011 annual report, Ford's investments in inventory totaled $5.9 billion in both 2011 and 2010. The company's inventory turnover for these same fiscal years was 17.7 in 2010 and improved to 19.2 in 2011. Ford's inventory-on-hand period was 21 days in 2010 and improved to 19 days in 2011. By way of comparison, the average inventory turnover for the automobile industry in 2011 was only 9.3, representing an inventory-on-hand period of over 39 days. For **Toyota**, the recognized leader in efficiency in the industry, 2011 inventory turnover was 10.5, representing an inventory-on-hand period of over 34 days. The year 2011 was a difficult one for the auto industry as the continuing worldwide economic slump impacted auto sales in almost every country, making it difficult for even efficiency experts like Toyota to quickly move inventory.

In this chapter, we investigate the important accounting principle of matching and examine the various ways that companies like Ford can match the cost of manufacturing their inventory with the revenue produced when the inventory is sold. In the case of Ford, the company used the last-in, first-out (LIFO) method to account for 32 percent of its worldwide inventory and the first-in, first-out (FIFO) method to account for the remaining 68 percent.

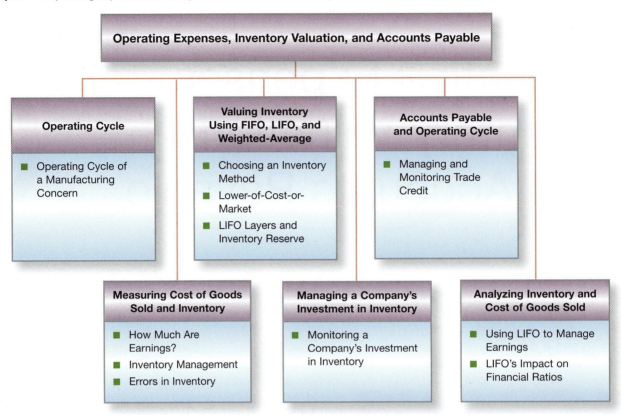

OPERATING CYCLE OF A MANUFACTURER

Most businesses have an identifiable cycle of activities that reflect the day-to-day operations of the business. This cycle is known as its **operating cycle**. Exhibit 6.1, for instance, presents the operating cycle of a typical manufacturing company. In Chapter 5, we illustrated the operating cycle for a retail company (see Exhibit 5.1). In the case of a retailer, the business acquires inventory ready for sale and then sells the inventory to its customers. Initially, the inventory is carried as an asset on the retailer's balance sheet, but upon its sale, the cost of the inventory is transferred from the balance sheet to cost of goods sold on the income statement, to be matched with the operating revenue produced by the sale. The inventory is subsequently replaced by cash, or an account receivable if sold on credit, on the balance sheet.

In the case of a manufacturing firm, the operating cycle is more complex. A manufacturing company begins its operating cycle with the purchase of **raw material**, which then enters its production process. During the production process, the raw material is altered by the production-line workers and manufacturing equipment, yielding what is known as **work-in-process inventory**. When the production process is complete, the ready-for-sale inventory is called **finished goods inventory**. As in the case of a retail company, the manufacturer's finished goods inventory (as well as its raw material and work–in–process inventory) is considered to be an asset on the balance sheet. Upon the sale of the finished goods inventory, the cost of the sold inventory is transferred to cost of goods sold on the income statement and replaced by cash or accounts receivable on the balance sheet.

Although retailers and manufacturers have clear differences in how they acquire inventory and get it ready for sale, an important commonality does exist in what amounts can be initially capitalized to the balance sheet as inventory. The fundamental rule-of-thumb is any cost necessary to get the inventory ready for sale should be capitalized. For retailers, this is the purchase price plus such other costs as taxes and shipping costs borne by the company. For manufacturers, the application of this concept is much more complex. Consider the three stages of inventory represented above: raw materials, work-in-process, and finished goods. These themselves entail the acquisition of component parts (i.e. including raw materials) and the physical act of creating the final product (i.e., the work-in-process stage). Costs such as labor, depreciation on manufacturing equipment, and factory rent are all "necessary" to get the inventory ready for sale, and thus these costs become part of the inventory value recorded on the balance sheet. While the estimation of these amounts is a topic covered in depth with the study of *managerial* accounting, it is important to know how many different types of costs might be included in inventory when analyzing a company's financial reports.

In this chapter, we will focus on the operating cycle of two companies—Home Heating Oil Inc. and the Arizona Ice Cream Company Inc. We will see that one of the key **operating expenses** for each of these enterprises is cost of goods sold. In subsequent chapters, we will further consider some of the other typical operating expenses of such businesses—depreciation expense, employee compensation expense, interest expense, and income tax expense, among others.

| **EXHIBIT 6.1** | Typical Business Operating Cycle of a Manufacturing Company |

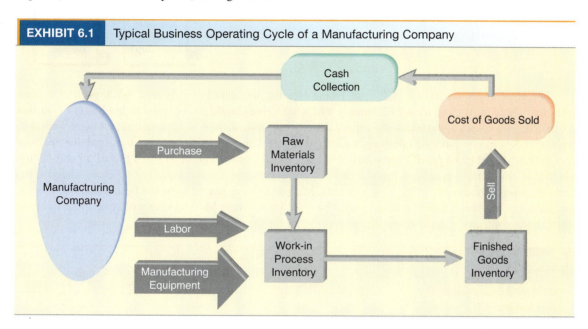

MEASURING COST OF GOODS SOLD AND ENDING INVENTORY

Inventory values on the balance sheet are charged to earnings in the period in which the inventory is sold. This is an example of the "matching" concept at work, wherein the effort (i.e. expense) is recorded in the same period during which any benefit is received by the company (i.e., revenue), We first introduced the matching concept in Chapter 1 When dealing with inventory, the charge matched against revenues is most commonly labeled "cost of goods sold"; and like its name suggests, what this account represents is the cost of the inventory that was sold to customers. This may sound simple enough on the surface, but in reality the measurement of cost of goods sold, and by default the value of inventory that remains on the balance sheet, is subject to numerous measurement issues. Consider the very frequent case when actual inventory items that a company owns for resale are physically identical, but the amounts that are recorded on the balance sheet varies greatly simply because of the timing of when they were purchased or manufactured. On the date one item is sold, how much is the value that needs to be recorded as the cost of that item? The revenue side is easy enough, the price paid by the consumer. But the cost of goods sold side must often be determined by assumption because the inventory records can contain many different cost values. Below we illustrate this point with a simple case illustration.

Case Illustration: How Much are Earnings?

Home Heating Oil Inc. purchases heating oil from a major oil company and then resells and delivers the oil to its retail customers. The company began its first month of operations by acquiring one barrel of heating oil at a cost of $10 on January 1. It purchased another barrel of oil on January 12 for $16. On January 20, Home Heating sold one barrel for $25, by which time the wholesale price of heating oil had risen to $22 per barrel. This sequence of events is shown on the following timeline:

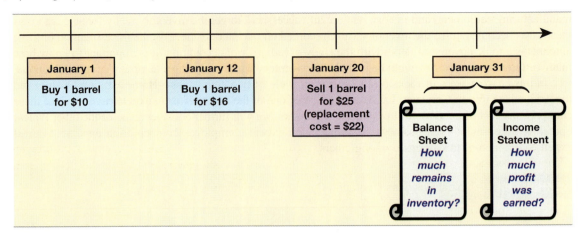

The chief executive officer (CEO) of Home Heating wondered exactly how much profit the company had made during the month of January and what value should be assigned to the barrel of oil that remained in inventory at the end of the month. After some review, the CEO concluded that there were four possible ways to compute the company's earnings and to value its ending inventory. Applying the four methods produced gross profit for the business that ranged from a high of $15 to a low of $3 and ending inventory valuations that ranged from $22 to $10 per barrel (see Exhibit 6.2). The CEO wondered if the company could choose any of the four methods. Method Four appeared to be the best choice for income tax purposes because taxable earnings would be only $3, whereas Method One would be more likely to impress the company's shareholders because earnings for the month would be $15.

EXHIBIT 6.2	Alternative Inventory Valuation Methods: Home Heating Oil Inc.			
	Method 1	**Method 2**	**Method 3**	**Method 4**
Income Statement				
Revenue	$25	$25	$25	$25
Cost of goods sold.	10	16	13	22
Gross profit.	$15	$ 9	$12	$ 3
Balance Sheet				
Inventory.	$16	$10	$13	$22
Summary of key inventory accounts:				
Cost of goods sold (on the income statement)	$10	$16	$13	$22
Inventory (on the balance sheet)	16	10	13	22
Total	**$26**	**$26**	**$26**	**$44**

To the CEO, the answer seemed clear: Use Method Four on the company's income tax return and Method One in the annual report to shareholders. That way Home Heating would pay low income taxes but report high earnings to its shareholders! The last idea sounded particularly appealing to the CEO whose year-end bonus was linked to reported earnings, and consequently, his personal income would be positively impacted.

Fortunately, Home Heating's chief financial officer (CFO) set the CEO straight about the constraints the company faced when selecting an inventory valuation method for the company's income tax return and when selecting a method for use in its audited financial reports to shareholders. Although Methods One, Two, and Three are acceptable under generally accepted accounting practice (GAAP) in the United States, Method Four is not. Method Four—using the replacement cost to value inventory—could be used in some countries including Mexico, Australia, and the United Kingdom, but it was not allowable GAAP in the United States.[1]

---

[1] A key reporting convention followed under U.S. GAAP, and the GAAP of many other countries, is the **historical cost convention**, which stipulates that all assets be initially valued at their original or historical cost. Methods One, Two, and Three are consistent with this convention, whereas Method Four, which relies on the inventory's _future_ replacement cost, is not. In addition, an inherent problem with Method Four, as can readily be seen, is that the total inventory purchases of $26 are not perfectly captured across the cost of goods sold and inventory accounts, and would necessitate recording a holding gain to increase the inventory balance to the replacement cost of $22.

The CFO informed Home Heating's CEO that Method One was known as **FIFO**—first-in, first-out—and as the name suggests, this approach assumes that the first units purchased are the first units sold, so Home Heating's cost of goods sold for January would be $10. The units remaining on hand are the units purchased more recently so the company's ending inventory would be $16, the cost of the last unit purchased on January 12. Method Two was known as **LIFO**—last-in, first-out. This method assumes that the units purchased most recently, the $16 unit purchased on January 12, are the first units sold. Hence, the unit in ending inventory would be the $10 unit purchased on January 1. Use of the LIFO method would result in reduced income taxes but there was a hitch—in the United States, the Internal Revenue Service requires businesses that use LIFO for income tax purposes to also use LIFO in the preparation of their audited financial reports to shareholders. This is known as the **LIFO conformity rule**. The CFO noted that this requirement would put a crimp in the CEO's desire to pay low taxes *and* report high earnings to shareholders. He would have to choose! LIFO also appeared to have the undesirable effect of reporting a low value for ending inventory ($10) on the balance sheet—a value that was considerably less than it would cost ($22) the business to buy a similar unit at the end of the month. Method Three, the **average cost method**, caused the unit sold and the unit in inventory to both be valued at $13, the average of the $10 and $16 purchase prices. Method Four, the **replacement cost method**, valued both the unit sold and the unit on hand at the inventory's replacement cost of $22.

> The **weighted-average cost method** differs from the average cost method in that each inventory price is weighted by the quantity of units purchased at a given price, whereas the average cost method calculates a simple average of the various inventory purchase prices without regard to the quantities purchased. The weighted-average cost method is widely regarded as being informationally superior to the average cost method, and consequently, is used by most firms not electing to adopt FIFO or LIFO. The weighted-average cost method is often simply referred to as the "average cost method" in many corporate financial reports.

Home Heating's CFO also informed the CEO that there was another option available to the company—the specific identification method. Under the specific identification method, if the CEO could identify exactly which barrel of heating oil was sold on January 20—the barrel purchased on January 1 or the barrel purchased on January 12—then the actual price of the identified barrel would be charged to cost of goods sold and the cost basis of the remaining barrel would also be known. Not surprisingly, the CEO could not clearly identify which barrel of oil was purchased on which date since the barrels were identical in appearance, content, and quality. Observing that the specific identification method was impractical for some companies, this option was discarded by both the CEO and CFO.

> The **specific identification method** tends to be used by manufacturers (such as Boeing) that produce a limited number of high-value products. For companies that produce in large volume, the additional record-keeping costs associated with this method are rarely justified.

After much debate, the CEO selected LIFO as the company's inventory valuation method. He decided that he would explain to shareholders that the operating cash flow saved by using LIFO for income tax purposes would enable the firm to pay more dividends, make additional investments in long-term assets, and reduce debt. That should keep the shareholders happy enough to pay him a large bonus!

Inventory Management Systems

In addition to selecting an inventory valuation method, one of the decisions that must be made by a company like Home Heating Oil Inc. is the type of inventory management system that will be used to keep track of the inventory purchased, sold, and on hand. The choice involves two types of systems—periodic and perpetual.

As the name implies, a **periodic system** periodically updates such information as the cost and quantity of inventory on hand, but only when new goods are purchased and when a physical count of the on-hand inventory is undertaken. A periodic system presumes that management does not need minute-by-minute (or even daily) information regarding the quantity of inventory on hand or its cost. The deficiency of this system is that reliable information about a company's inventory available for sale is only periodically available. For this reason, it is rarely used by well-run businesses because knowing how much inventory is available for sale is important for managers who try to provide the best possible service to their customers.

A **perpetual system**, on the other hand, updates a firm's inventory data after every purchase *and* every sale, providing a constant source of reliable information about the cost and quantity of goods available for sale. Perpetual systems are informationally superior to periodic inventory systems, but they are also more costly. In today's competitive marketplace, however, even small companies can realize the benefits of a perpetual system given the low cost of inventory management software.

A good way to understand the strengths and weaknesses of each inventory management system is by considering some illustrative inventory data. Assume that Home Heating Oil Inc. experienced the following events:

January 1	Purchased 100 barrels of oil at $10 per barrel, for a total expenditure of $1,000.
January 3	Sold 50 barrels at $15 per barrel, for a total sale of $750.
January 15	Purchased 100 barrels at $13 per barrel, for a total expenditure of $1,300.
January 20	Sold 125 barrels at $15 per barrel, for a total sale of $1,875.
January 30	Physically counted the available inventory, determining that 25 barrels were on hand.

Under a periodic system, the managers of Home Heating would not know exactly how many barrels of oil were on hand and available for sale until January 30, following a physical count of the inventory. Although a periodic system does capture information concerning units purchased, it does not record the cost of the sold units until a physical count of the inventory on hand verifies the quantity actually available. Thus, a periodic system records the quantities added to inventory on January 1 and January 15, but does **not** record the quantities removed from inventory on January 3 and January 20 until a physical count is executed on January 30. Hence, if an additional order for 30 barrels had been received on January 22 for delivery on January 25, Home Heating's managers would not have had the necessary information from reference to the financial statement ledgers to know whether the company could satisfy the order because the inventory accounts had not been updated.

Under a perpetual system, however, the quantity of on-hand inventory is updated after every purchase and sale transaction. Thus, the system constantly provides current information about the quantity and cost of goods available for sale. Under a perpetual system, if an additional order for 30 barrels were received on January 22, Home Heating's manager could easily access the inventory management system to verify that the quantity on hand was insufficient to service the order. In this case, Home Heating's managers would find that there were only 25 barrels on hand, and thus, that five more barrels would first need to be ordered.

The Inventory Count

Even though a perpetual system provides up-to-the-minute information regarding inventory quantities, it is still important for a company to periodically physically count its inventory on hand. Almost all types of inventory are subject to damage, deterioration, and theft, and a physical count is the best way to identify the existence and magnitude of these problems.[2] In fact, GAAP requires that a physical inventory count by taken at least once a year so as to ensure the integrity of the inventory balances recorded on the financial statements. A physical inventory count serves as the basis to determine the quantity and value of ending inventory, along with the cost of goods sold for firms utilizing a periodic inventory system. In addition, the inventory count serves as a confirmation of the ending inventory balance for firms employing a perpetual inventory system. If the inventory value computed from the physical count differs from the inventory records maintained under the perpetual system, the company will adjust its records to match the physical count.

It should be noted that any amount needed to adjust ending inventory will affect not only inventory on the balance sheet but also cost of goods sold, and therefore net income on the income statement. Consider the case of the Home Store Company, a retail hardware store. Home Store maintains a perpetual inventory system and shows an ending inventory balance of $2,550 as of December 31. A physical count of the inventory on December 31, however, reveals that the actual inventory on hand is only $2,325, perhaps due to inventory breakage or theft. To recognize the inventory loss, it is necessary to enter a charge of $225 to cost of goods sold and a reduction of $225 to inventory (see the company's spreadsheet below). Note that this adjustment affects not only income in the current year—a reduction of $225—but will also affect earnings and inventory in the following year. This results because the ending inventory of $2,325 in the current year becomes the beginning inventory in the following year.

---

[2] Retailer's like **Dillard's, Nordstrom's**, and **Wal-Mart** typically do a physical count of their merchandise inventory at least once a year, and more commonly, twice a year. To avoid interrupting normal daily sales activities, physical counts are usually executed at night, after store closing hours.

Home Store Company Spreadsheet			
	Balance Before Count	Inventory Count Adjustment	Ending Balance
Assets			—
Inventory.	2,550	(225)	2,325
Shareholders' Equity			
Retained earnings:			
Cost of goods sold		(225)	(225)

The adjustments to cost of goods sold and inventory can be best understood by considering the following basic computation of cost of goods sold. This representation describing the relation between ending inventory, purchases, and cost of goods sold, is also useful when analyzing the balances in inventory accounts. The partition of inventory expenditures between the inventory account and the cost of goods sold is as follows:

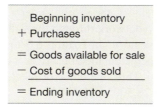

Beginning inventory
+ Purchases
_____
= Goods available for sale
− Cost of goods sold
_____
= Ending inventory

As can be seen from this basic formula, goods available for sale are partitioned into either ending inventory, an asset on the balance sheet, or cost of goods sold, an expense on the income statement. If the ending inventory balance is erroneously too high (low), then cost of goods sold will be erroneously too low (high). Further, ending inventory in one year becomes the beginning inventory for the next year. Since goods available for sale includes beginning inventory, any error in the previous year would be carried forward and would result in an error in cost of goods sold of equal magnitude, but opposite direction, the following year. For these reasons, periodic and accurate physical counts of inventory are an essential part of the financial accounting process.

VALUING INVENTORY USING FIFO, LIFO, AND WEIGHTED-AVERAGE—A CLOSER LOOK

The choice of inventory valuation method can yield vastly different amounts on the income statement and balance sheet, even though economically a company and its physical inventory are not any different regardless of the method chosen. From both a management and financial analysis perspective it is important to understand the mechanical differences that exist between these methods even though computers (or accountants) will keep track of the calculations. To illustrate these mechanics, we use a new set of facts.

Arizona Ice Cream Company (AICC) sells ice cream in large order sizes in Phoenix, Arizona. The current year is the company's first year of operations. The retail sales price of a ten-gallon bucket of ice cream is $20. The company has a sophisticated bar code scanner system that enables the company to operate a perpetual inventory system in each of its ten retail outlets. When ice cream is sold to a customer at one of its stores, the

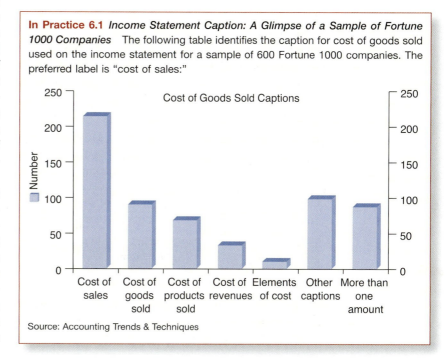

In Practice 6.1 *Income Statement Caption: A Glimpse of a Sample of Fortune 1000 Companies* The following table identifies the caption for cost of goods sold used on the income statement for a sample of 600 Fortune 1000 companies. The preferred label is "cost of sales:"

Cost of Goods Sold Captions

Source: Accounting Trends & Techniques

inventory system automatically updates the company's inventory records. It also sends a purchase order to a supplier when inventories fall to predetermined levels. The system records the cost of goods sold based on the specific inventory method the company uses, although AICC has not decided whether to use FIFO, LIFO, or the weighted-average cost method.

During the year, AICC made purchases of ice cream on September 5, October 22, November 15, and December 30 at prices that ranged from $10 to $15 per bucket. AICC purchased a total of 10,000 buckets of ice cream at an aggregate cost of $128,500. AICC also sold inventory on September 20, November 4, December 22, and December 31. Total sales amounted to $160,000 (8,000 buckets at $20 per bucket). The crucial financial accounting questions then become: How much profit did AICC make on its sales? And what was the value of its ending inventory? What you should understand before these questions are answered is that the inventory balance on the balance sheet is based on the 2,000 buckets remaining on hand and the cost of goods sold on the income statement is based on 8,000 buckets actually sold. The values that are assigned to these accounts reflect the decision that management must make when selecting an inventory accounting method. Under each possible method, there is a presumptive matching of cost of goods sold with revenue, but the profits determined under each approach are quite different.

If AICC uses FIFO to value its inventory, the results under a perpetual system would appear as presented in Exhibit 6.3. (We suggest that you work through the values in the columns labeled "FIFO Cost of Goods Sold" and "FIFO Ending Inventory" in Exhibit 6.3 to insure that you understand how these values are calculated.) Using the FIFO perpetual method, AICC's cost of goods sold is $98,500, and gross profit is $61,500 ($160,000 − $98,500). Thus, the value of the 2,000 buckets of ice cream remaining in inventory for future sale is $30,000 ($128,500 − $98,500).

EXHIBIT 6.3	Valuing Inventory and Cost of Goods Sold using FIFO					
Date	Purchases (# buckets)	Purchase Price (per bucket)	Total Cost	Sales (# buckets)	FIFO Cost of Goods Sold	FIFO Ending Inventory
Sep 5	1,000	$10	$ 10,000			1,000 @ $10
Sep 20 ...				800	800 @ $10 $ 8,000	200 @ $10
Oct 22....	2,500	12	30,000			200 @ $10
						2,500 @ $12
Nov 4				2,600	200 @ $10 30,800	100 @ $12
					2,400 @ $12	
Nov 15 ...	4,500	13	58,500			100 @ $12
						4,500 @ $13
Dec 22 ...				3,400	100 @ $12 44,100	1,200 @ $13
					3,300 @ $13	
Dec 30 ...	2,000	15	30,000			1,200 @ $13
						2,000 @ $15
Dec 31 ...				1,200	1,200 @ $13 15,600	2,000 @ $15
Total.....	**10,000**		**$128,500**	**8,000**	**$98,500**	**$30,000**

If, on the other hand, AICC uses LIFO, the results under a perpetual system would appear as presented in Exhibit 6.4. Under the LIFO perpetual method, AICC's cost of goods sold is $101,200, and gross profit is $58,800 ($160,000 − $101,200). The value of the 2,000 buckets of ice cream remaining in inventory for future sale is $27,300 ($128,500 − $101,200).

The operating revenue that AICC would recognize from selling 8,000 buckets at $20 per bucket is $160,000 regardless of whether the company uses FIFO or LIFO. However, the cost of goods sold under FIFO and LIFO varies ($98,500 versus $101,200, respectively) as a consequence of the different inventory cost flow assumptions that characterize FIFO and LIFO. As a result, AICC's gross profit varies under the different inventory methods, as follows:

Income Statement Summary		
	FIFO	LIFO
Revenue..	$160,000	$160,000
Cost of goods sold.......................................	(98,500)	(101,200)
Gross profit...	$ 61,500	$ 58,800

EXHIBIT 6.4	Valuing Inventory and Cost of Goods Sold using LIFO

Date	Purchases (# buckets)	Purchase Price (per bucket)	Total Cost	Sales (# buckets)	LIFO Cost of Goods Sold		LIFO Ending Inventory
Sep 5	1,000	$10	$ 10,000				1,000 @ $10
Sep 20 . . .				800	800 @ $10	$ 8,000	200 @ $10
Oct 22. . . .	2,500	12	30,000				2,500 @ $12 200 @ $10
Nov 4				2,600	2,500 @ $12 100 @ $10	31,000	100 @ $10
Nov 15 . . .	4,500	13	58,500				4,500 @ $13 100 @ $10
Dec 22 . . .				3,400	3,400 @ $13	44,200	1,100 @ $13 100 @ $10
Dec 30 . . .	2,000	15	30,000				2,000 @ $15 1,100 @ $13 100 @ $10
Dec 31 . . .				1,200	1,200 @ $15	18,000	800 @ $15 1,100 @ $13 100 @ $10
Total.	**10,000**		**$128,500**	**8,000**		**$101,200**	**$27,300**

Similarly, even though the quantity of inventory on hand for AICC is the same at the end of the year (2,000 buckets), the reported value of the ending inventory under FIFO versus LIFO varies ($30,000 and $27,300, respectively):

Balance Sheet Summary				
	Units	FIFO $	LIFO $	Difference
Beginning inventory	0	$ 0	$ 0	$ 0
Purchases.	10,000	128,500	128,500	0
Available for sale	10,000	128,500	128,500	0
Cost of goods sold.	(8,000)	(98,500)	(101,200)	(2,700)
Ending inventory.	2,000	$ 30,000	$ 27,300	$2,700

The gross profit for Arizona Ice Cream Company is highest under FIFO and lowest under LIFO. This outcome will occur when the cost of inventory is increasing. In this instance, the cost of AICC's inventory purchases increased from $10 to $12 to $13 per bucket, and finally to $15 per bucket. If, on the other hand, inventory costs are decreasing, LIFO will yield the highest gross profit and FIFO the lowest. If prices are perfectly stable, there will be no difference in the cost of goods sold or ending inventory under any of the methods.

But what if AICC decided to use the weighted-average cost method instead?[3] The results for the weighted-average cost method under a perpetual system are presented in Exhibit 6.5. Under this approach, AICC's cost of goods sold is $100,018, about midway between the cost of goods sold under FIFO and LIFO. The value of AICC's ending inventory is $28,482, again about midway between the value of ending inventory under FIFO and ending inventory under LIFO. Finally, gross profit is $59,982, about midway between FIFO gross profit of $61,500 and LIFO gross profit of $58,800. (Were you able to verify each of these figures by working through the two right-most columns of Exhibits 6.3, 6.4,

---

[3] The CEO and CFO decided that use of the specific identification method by Arizona Ice Cream Company, Inc., was not practical since the appearance, content, and quality of the buckets of ice cream were indistinguishable, and in any case, the additional record-keeping cost associated with the specific identification method did not appear justified.

and 6.5?) In essence, while FIFO and LIFO yield values representing the ends of a continuum, the weighted-average cost method yields results that fall somewhere within that continuum.[4]

EXHIBIT 6.5		Valuing Inventory and Cost of Goods Sold using Weighted-Average					
Date	Purchases (# buckets)	Purchase Price (per bucket)	Total Cost	Sales (# buckets)	Weighted-Average Cost of Goods Sold		Weighted-Average Ending Inventory
Sep 5	1,000	$10	$ 10,000				1,000 @ $10
Sep 20 ...				800	800 @ $10	$ 8,000	200 @ $10
Oct 22....	2,500	$12	30,000				2,700 @ $11.852*
Nov 4				2,600	2,600 @ $11.852	30,815	100 @ $11.852
Nov 15 ...	4,500	$13	58,500				4,600 @ $12.975**
Dec 22 ...				3,400	3,400 @ $12.975	44,115	1,200 @ $12.975
Dec 30 ...	2,000	$15	30,000				3,200 @ $14.241***
Dec 31 ...				1,200	1,200 @ $14.241	17,088	2,000 @ $14.241
Total.....	10,000		$128,500	8,000		$100,018	$28,482

* [(200 × $10) + (2,500 × $12)]/2,700 = $11.852
** [(100 × $11.852) + (4,500 × $13)]/4,600 = $12.975
*** [(1,200 × $12.975) + (2,000 × $15)]/3,200 = $14.241

Choosing an Inventory Method

With the diversity of cost of goods sold and ending inventory values provided under FIFO, LIFO, and the weighted-average cost method, how do managers decide which method is "best" for their company? In many cases, the inventory method decision is driven by the prevailing industry standard. For instance, the industry standard in the United States' automobile industry is LIFO; and thus, investment professionals expect to observe car and truck manufacturers using this inventory valuation method. If they observed otherwise, it might be a "red flag" raising concern about a company's reported financial results.

In some companies, the inventory method decision is linked to the physical flow of inventory through the business. Companies that supply perishable food products to hotels and restaurants, for example, frequently use FIFO. It is noteworthy, however, that it is not a requirement that the selected inventory method reflect the actual flow of goods through a business. A supermarket selling perishable food products can use LIFO or the weighted-average cost method even though store managers encourage customers to buy on a FIFO basis to minimize losses associated with food spoilage. The prevailing economic environment is also a contributing factor to the inventory method decision. In inflationary environments, LIFO is preferred over FIFO because it more effectively matches inflated selling prices with inflated inventory costs. Finally, for some firms, the inventory method selection is driven by a desire to report higher (or lower) earnings. For companies desiring to report the highest level of reported income, the FIFO method is often selected, at least when inventory costs are increasing. On the other hand, for firms desiring to constrain the level of reported (or taxable) earnings, the LIFO method is often adopted.

Once a company has selected a particular inventory valuation method, does the company have to use that same method for all of its inventories? No. Companies that manufacture and/or sell multiple products may choose to use LIFO for one product, FIFO for another, and weighted-average for a third, although this is rarely done. Recall that at the beginning of this chapter, Ford Motor Company disclosed that it used LIFO to account for 32 percent of its worldwide inventories, with the remainder accounted for

An important principle of accounting is the **consistency principle**, which stipulates that whenever possible, a business should utilize a consistent set of accounting policies from one fiscal period to the next. When companies change their accounting policies (such as a LIFO to FIFO switch), the analysis of financial statements is adversely impacted because a change in accounting policy is likely to induce variance in the reported accounting numbers unrelated to a firm's actual performance. For this reason, voluntary corporate accounting policy changes are widely regarded as a "red flag" by investment professionals.

---

[4] Worth noting is that as a company ages, weighted-average more closely approximates FIFO inventory balances rather than LIFO inventory balances. The reason for this is that LIFO inventory will always contain values from the first inventory units acquired, while FIFO by definition eliminates those units first. Thus, as long as a company acquires and sells its inventory at a reasonable pace, the weighted average methodology will place less weight on very old purchases, and more weight on more recent purchases, resulting in a closer approximation to FIFO relative to LIFO.

using FIFO. Can a company change its method of inventory valuation? Under certain circumstances, yes, they can. GAAP provides companies with considerable flexibility. Not only can a company choose between different inventory valuation methods (FIFO, LIFO, specific identification, and weighted-average cost), but GAAP permits a LIFO company, for example, to switch to FIFO. Companies are encouraged, however, to be consistent from year to year in the accounting methods they apply in their financial reporting. Companies are allowed to switch methods if they can justify why a switch will provide a more meaningful financial statement presentation. Changing inventory valuation methods, however, is often viewed as a "red flag" by investment professionals who worry that such voluntary accounting policy changes may be motivated more by a desire to manage earnings than to use the most appropriate accounting method. In addition, the Internal Revenue Service, under Revenue procedure 92–20, requires taxpayers who have changed from LIFO to another method to wait five years before readopting LIFO unless extraordinary circumstances can be shown.

In Practice 6.2 *Inventory Method: A Glimpse of a Sample of Fortune 1000 Companies*   The following table identifies the inventory methods used by a sample of 500 Fortune 1000 companies. Also shown for the LIFO firms is the extent of LIFO usage. The FIFO method was predominantly used by the sampled firms:

Source: Accounting Trends & Techniques

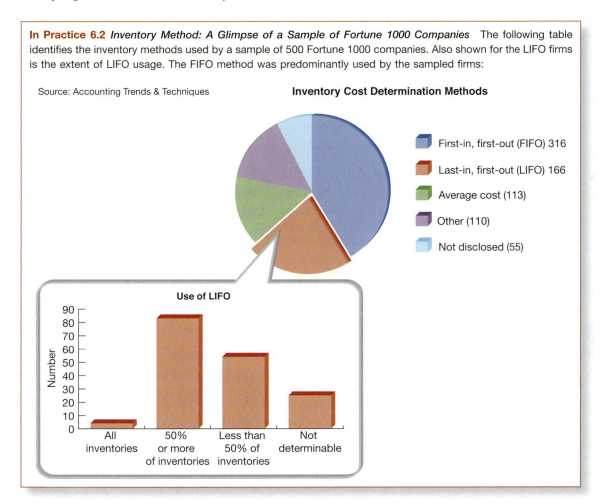

Inventory Cost Determination Methods

- First-in, first-out (FIFO) 316
- Last-in, first-out (LIFO) 166
- Average cost (113)
- Other (110)
- Not disclosed (55)

Use of LIFO

Lower-of-Cost-or-Market (LCM)

Under U.S. GAAP and IFRS, companies are required to ensure that the value of ending inventory carried on the balance sheet is recorded at an amount that does not exceed its current replacement cost. This reflects the desire to ensure that asset values are never overstated (although they are sometimes understated, for example as a consequence of the use of the historical cost convention). Under this practice, if the current replacement cost of inventory is less than its recorded book value, the company must write the value of its inventory down to its lower replacement cost. If, however, the replacement cost is higher than its recorded book value, the inventory is not written up to the higher value but remains valued at its cost. This convention is called the **lower-of-cost-or-market (LCM) method** and is an excellent illustration

> The LCM method reflects the **conservatism principle** of accounting, namely that losses should be recognized as soon as they are identified (even if unrealized), whereas gains should be recognized only after they are realized.

of the general conservative bias of financial accounting—losses on inventory are recognized immediately, even if the inventory is unsold, but gains are not. The practice of using the LCM method has a long history in the United States. In its 1921 annual report, General Motors announced that the company had written down its inventory to $98 million. By way of contrast, General Motors's 2011 ending inventory was valued at over $14 billion.

To illustrate the application of the LCM method, assume that AICC's CFO determined that the replacement cost of the company's ice cream was $14 per bucket at year-end. With 2,000 buckets in inventory, the replacement cost of AICC's inventory at December 31 would be $28,000 ($14 × 2,000). If AICC used FIFO, the LCM convention would require the company to write its ending inventory down by $2,000 ($30,000 less $28,000). No write-down would be required if AICC used LIFO because its ending inventory would be stated at its LIFO cost of $27,300, which is lower than its replacement cost of $28,000. AICC's application of LCM under FIFO is demonstrated as follows:

Arizona Ice Cream Company Spreadsheet			
	Balance Before Count	**LCM Adjustment**	**End. Bal.**
Assets			—
Inventory...............................	30,000	(2,000)	28,000
Shareholders' Equity			
Retained Earnings:			
Cost of Goods Sold		(2,000)	(2,000)

When an end-of-period write-down of inventory is necessary, as illustrated above, the adjustment is usually recorded as a component of cost of goods sold on the income statement; that is, both inventory and retained earnings are reduced by the amount of the LCM write-down, with the charge to retained earnings recorded as costs of goods sold on the income statement. If the amount of the write-down is material in amount, however, it may be necessary to disclose the inventory write-down on the income statement as a separate line item (such as "loss on inventory write-down") so as to inform a user of the financial statements about all relevant detail pertaining to inventory-related charges.

TAX PERSPECTIVE

Inventory Accounting Under U.S. Tax Law

Inventory accounting rules specified by the U.S. Internal Revenue Service generally follow the same fundamental principles as U.S. GAAP but with two important exceptions. First, like U.S. GAAP, the amounts included in inventory for tax purposes must comprise all costs necessary to get the inventory ready for sale, and these costs generally may not be expensed until the inventory is sold. Uniform cost capitalization rules (UNICAP) under the Internal Revenue Code, however, provide for an expanded definition of which costs must be capitalized. Specifically, UNICAP requires that costs incurred that are not directly tied to production but that provide support for the production process, such as purchasing costs, technology, and general administrative costs, must be capitalized as inventory. As a consequence, the deferral of these additional costs to inventory delays the cash inflow from the tax deductibility of those costs.

Second, consistent with U.S. GAAP, a cost flow method must be determined and consistently applied for tax purposes. Valid methods include LIFO, FIFO, average cost and specific identification. The incentives with respect to the tax method choice, however, are almost always focused on minimizing current taxes due. Therefore, LIFO tends to be the preferred method for tax purposes as the expense deduction for cost of goods sold will typically be higher, and therefore, taxable income lower.

When inventory costs are rising, as is usually the case, management would obtain the optimal outcome by choosing FIFO for financial reporting (higher income) and LIFO for tax reporting (lower income). Refering back to exhibits 6.3 and 6.4, notice the difference between the cost of goods sold reported by AICC under LIFO versus FIFO. LIFO was $2,700 higher, which would result in a lower tax bill. Recognizing the implicit motivation most managers would have to choose LIFO over FIFO, tax authorities require that companies use LIFO as a chosen tax method only if they also do so for financial reporting purposes. This requirement is called the **LIFO conformity rule**, and it has significantly limited the use of LIFO for tax purposes.

One consequence of the LCM method is that while the immediate financial statement effect of an inventory write-down is to reduce current earnings by the amount of the inventory write-down, the effect in the future may be inflated earnings. For example, if AICC maintains its selling price of $20 per bucket, the LCM adjustment will lower current profit by $2,000, but raise future profit by the same amount when the inventory on hand is ultimately sold. In effect, the LCM method may shift the profit on some sales from one period to the next.

Inventory Accounting Under International Reporting Standards

The accounting for inventory under U.S. GAAP and IFRS differs in three significant ways. First and most important, IFRS does not permit the use of the LIFO method. The very old values of inventory resulting from LIFO accounting are perceived to reduce the relevance of the balance sheet to such a degree that under IFRS the method is deemed invalid. In Practice 6.2 reveals, however, that a significant percentage of companies in the United States use LIFO to account for at least a portion of their inventories. This means that analysts making comparisons of a U.S. company to one following IFRS would need to pay particularly close attention to the inventory method used. Further complicating the analysis is that the restriction of LIFO under IFRS puts companies desiring to switch to IFRS in a potentially unfavorable tax position. Given the LIFO conformity rule in the U.S., if a company were not to use LIFO for financial accounting purposes, the tax authorities would then require a switch to FIFO, potentially resulting in a significant tax increase.

A second critical inventory accounting difference between U.S. GAAP and IFRS relates to the method choice when there are various inventory product lines used by a company. Under U.S. GAAP a company may use multiple inventory methods to value inventory, regardless of the type of inventory under consideration. Under IFRS, however, a single inventory method must be used for inventory that is similar in nature or use. This does not preclude the use of multiple methods by an IFRS company, but only when the inventory is of a sufficiently different type. Finally, lower-of-cost-or-market (LCM) differs between the two systems. Under U.S. GAAP, "market" for purposes of applying LCM is generally defined as the inventory's net replacement value. Under IFRS, "market" is defined as the inventory's net realizable value which often approximates fair market value. Also, while U.S. GAAP only allows inventory to be written down under LCM when the inventory's replacement cost falls below its recorded cost, IFRS permits inventory to be written back up to the amount of the original write-down. Any write up in value above the book value of inventory is also added to a shareholders' equity account called the revaluation reserve. In essence, LCM under U.S. GAAP is a "one-way street," but under IFRS, it is a "two-way street" wherein both inventory value declines and (reversing) increases may be recognized.

Beyond the codified requirements under IFRS, in some countries the inventory method decision is further constrained by the allowable generally accepted business practices. For instance, the operating environment faced by a business frequently drives the inventory method decision. In Japan, for example, auto and truck manufacturers use FIFO because this industry has been able to implement just-in-time (JIT) inventory management techniques. For companies able to operate in a "lean manufacturing" environment, the inventory method decision has little impact on reported results because the required investment in inventory is kept to a minimum. In countries whose economies are characterized by high rates of inflation, several variants of LIFO may also be GAAP: **HIFO, highest-in, first-out**, and **NIFO, next-in, first-out**. Neither HIFO nor NIFO is acceptable under U.S. GAAP.

LIFO Layers and the LIFO Inventory Reserve

As noted above, the value of AICC's ending inventory is highest under FIFO and lowest under LIFO because the cost of inventory purchases is increasing. Comparing the calculated cost basis of AICC's ending inventory on December 31 under the two methods reveals the following:

LIFO Ending Inventory	FIFO Ending Inventory
100 @ $10	
1,100 @ $13	
800 @ $15	2,000 @ $15
$27,300	$30,000

These figures illustrate that the entire FIFO ending inventory is valued at the most recent purchase price of $15 per bucket, whereas less than half of the LIFO inventory is valued at $15 per bucket. The LIFO ending inventory reflects a blend of purchase prices—100 buckets at $10, 1,100 buckets at $13, and 800 buckets at $15. These differing prices are referred to as **LIFO layers** and AICC has three such layers. Since the LIFO method assumes that the most recently purchased inventory is the first inventory to be sold, it is not unusual for a company like AICC to have multiple LIFO layers, often reflecting prices from several prior fiscal periods. As a consequence, when inflation is present, the value of ending inventory under LIFO may be much lower than its current replacement cost or its FIFO cost. For this reason many users of financial statements consider FIFO to yield more relevant inventory values on the balance sheet than LIFO.

Concerned that the LIFO method may produce misleading ending inventory values—that is, that the ending inventory (and hence, current assets) under LIFO may be materially undervalued relative to its current replacement value, and consequently, that comparability with non-LIFO firms may be impaired—accounting standard-setters require that companies using LIFO disclose the value of the **inventory reserve**, often called the **LIFO reserve**, in their footnotes. The inventory reserve is a measure of the difference ($2,700) between the FIFO cost of ending inventory ($30,000) and the LIFO cost of its ending inventory ($27,300). The disclosure of the inventory reserve in a company's footnotes is important because it enables financial statement users to use that value to determine a more current value of LIFO ending inventory by simply adding the value of the reserve ($2,700) to the value of the reported LIFO ending inventory. Notice that adding the inventory reserve to the value of LIFO ending inventory effectively restates the value of the ending inventory from the LIFO method to the FIFO method.

Disclosure of the inventory reserve is significant because it enables investment professionals to restate AICC's gross profit under LIFO ($58,800) to estimate what gross profit would have been had FIFO ($61,500) been used instead. The inventory reserve is a cumulative measure of the difference between the LIFO cost of ending inventory and the FIFO cost of ending inventory. This amount may accumulate over multiple periods as prices rise and as a company maintains certain minimum quantities of inventory on hand to service the needs of its customers. It is possible to disaggregate this accumulated amount on a period-by-period basis by calculating the change in the reserve from one period to the next. The change in the value of the inventory reserve from one fiscal period to the next is a good estimate of the difference between LIFO cost of goods sold and FIFO cost of goods sold on a period-by-period basis. Thus, adding the **change in the inventory reserve** to the LIFO gross profit yields an estimate of FIFO gross profit:[5]

Gross profit under LIFO	$58,800
Add: increase in inventory reserve ($2,700 − $0)	2,700
Gross profit under FIFO	$61,500

The restatement of the balance sheet and income statement amounts reported under LIFO to their as-if estimates under FIFO can be summarized with the following two formulas:

LIFO Inventory + LIFO Reserve = FIFO Inventory

LIFO Cost of Goods Sold − Change in LIFO Reserve = FIFO Cost of Goods Sold

Following is an excerpt of the inventory footnote disclosure for heavy equipment manufacturer **Caterpillar Inc.** that includes information about the company's LIFO reserve. Note in the first paragraph that the company indicates that for the year 2011 about 65 percent of its total inventory was valued using LIFO. This implies the remaining 35 percent was based on some other method (i.e FIFO or average cost), a feature not unusual for companies with multiple types of inventory. The 2011 LIFO reserve for Caterpillar was $2.422 billion dollars, a decline from previous years' values of $2.575 billion and $3.022 billion.

---

[5] If the inventory reserve decreases (increases) during the period, it is necessary to subtract (add) the decrease (increase) from the LIFO gross profit to compute FIFO gross profit.

> *Summary of Significant Accounting Policies*: **Caterpillar 2011 Annual Report**
> Inventories are stated at the lower of cost or market. Cost is principally determined using the last-in, first-out (LIFO) method. The value of inventories on the LIFO basis represented about 65% of total inventories at December 31, 2011, and about 70% of total inventories at December 31, 2010 and 2009.
> If the FIFO (first-in, first-out) method had been in use, inventories would have been $2,422 million, $2,575 million and $3,022 million higher than reported at December 31, 2011, 2010 and 2009, respectively.

To illustrate the potential differences in magnitude of ending inventory values that can result under LIFO, In Practice 6.3 presents 2011 inventory data for the eleven U.S. companies having the largest LIFO inventory reserves. Consider again, for example, Caterpillar Inc. (see **bolded** area in In Practice 6.3). This company's ending inventory is valued at $14.544 billion under LIFO. Under FIFO, this same inventory would be valued at $16.966 billion ($14.544 billion + $2.422 billion). Given Caterpillar's LIFO inventory reserve at the beginning of the period was $2.575 billion, the change in the reserve for the period of $153 million suggests that the company's FIFO earnings before income taxes would have been $6.548 billion ($6.701 billion less $153 million), as compared to $6.701 billion under LIFO. Additionally, since Caterpillar used LIFO for income tax purposes, we can infer that the company has deferred approximately $847.7 million in income taxes, assuming a 35 percent effective tax rate ($2.422 billion × 35% = $847.7 billion). Although Caterpillar may ultimately pay these income taxes at some point in the future, in the interim, the U.S. government has effectively provided the company with $847.7 million in interest-free financing.

As a concluding point, it is worth noting that eight of the eleven companies in In Practice 6.3 come from the energy sector. While this clustering may seem surprising, what this simply indicates is that oil prices have been rising significantly over the past decade along with increasing physical inventory volumes maintained by these companies to service the ever growing worldwide demand for energy products.

In Practice 6.3 *Eleven U.S. Companies with the Largest Inventory Reserves (in millions of dollars)*

	Ending Inventory	Cost of Goods Sold	Earnings Before Income Taxes	LIFO Reserve	LIFO Reserve/ Ending Inventory
ExxonMobil Corp.	$15,024	$346,775	$73,257	$25,600	170.4%
Chevron Corp.	5,543	179,115	47,634	9,025	162.8%
Phillips 66	3,466	177,242	6,624	8,600	248.1%
ConocoPhillips	4,631	200,990	23,001	8,400	181.4%
Valero Energy Corp.	5,623	119,726	3,322	6,800	120.9%
Marathon Petroleum	3,320	67,903	3,719	5,015	151.1%
Sunoco Inc.	587	43,234	(2,404)	2,920	497.4%
Caterpillar Inc.	**14,544**	**43,578**	**6,701**	**2,422**	**16.7%**
Tesoro Corp	1,763	28,300	905	1,700	96.4%
Walgreen Co.	8,044	50,603	4,294	1,587	19.7%
Deere & Co.	4,371	21,721	4,231	1,486	34.0%

Source: Standard and Poor's Compustat. Based on data for fiscal year 2011.

Liquidating LIFO Layers

Most companies have a number of operating objectives that they strive to meet. For example, a common corporate goal is to maximize shareholder wealth (maximize share price) while being a good member of the local community. Achieving these goals may involve trying to produce the highest-quality product or service at the lowest price, being attentive to customer needs, providing a healthy work environment for employees, being environmentally friendly, and trying to save on income taxes. Another goal may be to meet profit expectations as set by the board of directors, by Wall Street financial analysts, or by institutional investors.

Sometimes it is impossible to meet internal or external earnings expectations by increasing sales, and thus, managers may look for other ways to increase net income (such as cutting costs). One temporary profit-enhancing approach used by some managers of LIFO-accounted companies is the liquidation of LIFO layers. Liquidating a LIFO layer has the effect of lowering the reported cost of goods sold, and hence, raising gross profit because a lower cost of inventory is effectively matched with revenue.

BUSINESS PERSPECTIVE

Caterpillar Inc. (CAT) discloses the following information about inventories in its 2011 annual report:

7. Inventories

Inventories (principally using the LIFO method) are comprised of the following:

	December 31,		
(Millions of dollars)	2011	2010	2009
Raw materials..	$ 3,872	$2,766	$1,979
Work-in-process.......................................	2,845	1,483	656
Finished goods..	7,570	5,098	3,465
Supplies	257	240	260
Total inventories	$14,544	$9,587	$6,360

We had long-term material purchase obligations of approximately $1,628 million at December 31, 2011.

During 2009 inventory quantities were reduced. This reduction resulted in a liquidation of LIFO inventory layers carried at lower costs prevailing in prior years as compared with current costs. In 2009, the effect of this reduction of inventory decreased Cost of goods sold in Statement 1 by approximately $300 million and increased Profit by approximately $240 million or $0.39 per share. There were no significant LIFO liquidations during 2011 or 2010.

Footnote #7 for Caterpillar summarizes the components for the company's inventory by stage of production. Over half of total inventory is complete and ready for sale (i.e. "finished goods"), but notice there are significant portions of inventory in stages of production not yet ready for sale. The company notes that 2009 profits were aided by $240 million (after tax) from a reduction of inventory quantities and resulting LIFO liquidation. Recall from Exhibit 6.6 Caterpillar chose to disclose its LIFO reserve in its *Summary of Significant Accounting Policies*, and that in total the amount for 2009 was over $3 billion. Thus, while the $0.39 per share boost to 2009 profits was likely material, the potential for even greater liquidations existed.

To illustrate this phenomenon, consider again the case of the Arizona Ice Cream Company. AICC's LIFO layers consist of the following:

LIFO Layers

100 Buckets at $10 per Bucket

1,100 Buckets at $13 per Bucket

800 Buckets at $15 per Bucket

AICC's managers could decide to temporarily cease replacing its inventory when units are sold and instead liquidate its current inventory. At the current retail price of $20 per bucket, AICC's gross margin on its 800 buckets costing $15 is $5 per bucket. But AICC's gross margin increases to $7 per bucket if the 1,100 buckets costing $13 are sold, and its gross margin increases to $10 per bucket if the 100 buckets costing $10 are sold.

In essence, by liquidating the LIFO layers that have a lower cost basis, AICC is able to lower its cost of goods sold, and consequently, boost its gross profit and net income. It is important to observe, however, that these LIFO price-layer liquidations produce what is commonly called **phantom profit** because although gross profit is increased, cash flow is not. (Remember that AICC's selling price remains constant at $20 per bucket.) In fact, the operating cash flow from LIFO price-layer liquidations is actually reduced as a consequence of the additional income taxes that must be paid on the phantom profits generated by these sales.

To illustrate the phenomenon of the phantom profit associated with a LIFO-price-layer liquidation, consider the data presented in In Practice 6.4. This exhibit presents inventory reserve data for 34 companies, all of which lost money. Consider, for example, **Rite Aid Corporation**, which reported a loss of almost $400 million before extraordinary items (see **bolded** area of the In Practice 6.4). Notice also that Rite Aid reported a LIFO inventory reserve of over $875 million. If Rite Aid's managers had chosen to liquidate the various LIFO layers reflected in its inventory reserve of $875 million, it could have substantially reduced or eliminated its loss for the year.

The 34 firms listed in the In Practice 6.4 illustration all used LIFO (at least for some inventories), and reported negative earnings before extraordinary items. All of these firms could have reduced the size of their reported loss by liquidating their inventory reserves but most chose not to do so. Can you think of any reason why these companies chose to behave this way? If you thought about income taxes, you are probably correct. Liquidating the inventory reserve would create additional profits, which in turn would have reduced the companies' reported losses, and hence, reduced the tax benefit provided by their operating loss carryback and/or carryforward.

In Practice 6.4 *Inventory Reserve Data*

($ millions)	Ending Inventory	Earnings Before Income Taxes	LIFO Reserve
AK Steel Holding Corp.	$ 418.700	$ (254.100)	$ 524.000
American Biltrite Inc.	39.460	(1.467)	4.000
Books-A-Million Inc..	201.283	(5.638)	4.017
Castle (AM) & Co..	272.039	(2.886)	138.882
Chiquita Brands Intl. Inc.	238.279	(25.364)	45.000
Commercial Metals	908.338	(110.100)	307.300
Continental Materials Corp.	17.397	(3.032)	5.783
Courier Corp.	39.353	(0.942)	5.300
Donnelley (RR) & Sons Co..	510.900	(237.400)	96.400
Farmer Bros Co..	79.759	(63.484)	69.565
Federal Screw Works	10.518	(2.378)	1.154
Fortune Brands Home & Secur	336.300	(43.600)	26.400
Gencor Industries Inc.	17.328	(2.534)	4.435
Huttig Building Products Inc..	44.800	(13.000)	9.600
Imperial Sugar Co..	70.589	(58.889)	24.200
ITT Corp.	254.000	(318.000)	8.000
Katy Industries Inc..	17.262	(9.365)	4.499
Lee Enterprises Inc.	7.388	(167.760)	3.895
Louisiana-Pacific Corp.	163.600	(211.000)	0.100
New York Times Co.-CL A	21.087	(3.718)	5.000
Owens-Illinois Inc.	1,012.000	(406.000)	49.000
Rite Aid Corp.	**3,158.145**	**(545.582)**	**875.012**
Ryerson Holding Corp..	732.400	(19.800)	29.000
Sears Holdings Corp..	8,407.000	(1,751.000)	70.000
Stanadyne Corp.	41.984	(8.816)	0.106
Sunoco Inc.	587.000	(2,404.000)	2,920.000
Supervalu Inc..	2,150.000	(1,028.000)	342.000
Trex Co. Inc..	28.896	(14.193)	28.218
United Refining Co.	171.880	(11.027)	92.059
Valspar Corp.	336.750	(103.150)	91.379
Vulcan Materials Co..	327.657	(153.740)	140.335
Wausau Paper Corp.	107.057	(33.538)	55.754
Whirlpool Corp.	2,354.000	(28.000)	203.000
Zale Corp..	$ 720.782	$ (110.490)	$ 35.900

Source: Standard and Poors Compustat. Based on data for fiscal year 2011.

MANAGING A COMPANY'S INVESTMENT IN INVENTORIES

When a business holds large quantities of inventory to service its customers' needs, the business is required to invest its cash not only to purchase and/or manufacture the inventory, but also for warehousing and insurance on the inventory. To help minimize these costs, some businesses have devised methods for reducing the quantity of inventory that they must maintain to support their customers' purchases. For example, supply-chain management techniques integrate a company's information system with those of its suppliers so that inventory can be delivered just-in-time, or JIT. JIT inventory delivery helps reduce a company's investment in the quantity of inventory on hand, along with the related costs of warehousing and insurance.

For those businesses unable to use JIT techniques, the investment in inventory must be carefully monitored to avoid overstocking and damaging profits. One method used by investment professionals to assess how effectively a company is managing its investment in inventory is the **inventory-on-hand period** (365 days/[cost of goods sold/cost of inventory on hand]), which measures the average number of days required to sell the existing on-hand inventory.[6] This ratio is one of many useful measures of a firm's liquidity, as well as a firm's effectiveness in controlling its investment in inventory.

To illustrate the positive impact of JIT on inventory costs and the use of the inventory-on-hand ratio as an inventory quantity monitoring tool, consider the historical data for **Dell Computer** provided in Exhibit 6.6. Beginning in 1996, Dell began introducing JIT techniques into its operations and was able to reduce its inventory-on-hand period from 37 days in 1996 to only 15 days in 1997. Dell continued to refine its inventory management practices, and as a consequence, reduced its inventory-on-hand period to less than four days by 2002. If Dell had not introduced JIT into its operating system, the company would have required an investment in inventory-on-hand in 2003 of nearly $3 billion (based on the 1996 inventory-on-hand ratio of 37 days) versus the $306 million actually on hand at the beginning of 2003. The opportunity cost savings created by Dell by using JIT are enormous! Assuming a cost of inventory financing of only five percent, Dell saved over $130 million in inventory financing costs in 2003 alone.

EXHIBIT 6.6	Illustration of the Effects of Just-in-Time Inventory Management

DELL COMPUTER CORPORATION
Fiscal Year Ending

($ in millions)	1/30/94	1/29/95	1/28/96	2/2/97	2/1/98	1/29/99	1/28/00	2/2/01	2/1/02	1/31/03
Net sales	$2,873	$3,475	$5,296	$7,759	$12,327	$18,243	$25,265	$31,888	$31,168	$35,404
Cost of goods sold	2,440	2,737	4,229	6,093	9,605	14,137	20,047	25,445	25,661	29,055
Sales growth		21.0%	52.4%	46.5%	58.9%	48.0%	38.5%	26.2%	(2.3%)	13.6%
Inventories	$ 220	$ 293	$ 429	$ 251	$ 233	$ 273	$ 391	$ 400	$ 278	$ 306
Total assets	1,140	1,594	2,148	2,993	4,268	6,877	11,471	13,670	13,535	15,470
Inventory-on-hand period (in days)	32.95	39.07	37.03	15.04	8.85	7.05	7.12	5.74	3.95	3.84

ACCOUNTS PAYABLE AND A COMPANY'S OPERATING CYCLE

Because of competitive market conditions, most businesses permit their customers to buy goods and services on credit. As a consequence, the sale of inventory is usually accompanied by the creation of an account (or note) receivable by the seller and an account (or note) payable by the purchaser.

In Chapter 5, we observed that most businesses try to constrain the amount of time that their customers take to pay their bills by offering quick-pay incentives. Credit terms such as "2/10, n/30" indicate that if a buyer pays a bill within ten days of the original transaction date, they will receive a two percent reduction in the purchase price; but, if payment is not made within the ten-day quick-pay window, then full payment is expected within 30 days of the transaction. As a practical matter, taking advantage of such price discounts can be very valuable to a buyer. A two percent price discount, when annualized, is equivalent to an opportunity cost of 36 percent (365/20 × 0.02). Thus, a customer would be better off obtaining

---

[6] The inventory-on-hand period is often referred to as days inventory turnover.

bank financing at interest rates exceeding 25 percent to take advantage of such price discounts. But what happens if a customer's payment is not received within 30 days of the transaction date?

Failure to pay an outstanding accounts payable within the allotted period indicates that a buyer has violated the implied credit agreement with the seller and is in technical default. At this point most sellers start contacting their custom-

> Businesses grant credit to other businesses who are their customers, although they rarely grant credit to individuals who are the final consumer of their products or services. In this latter case, payment by cash, check, or debit/credit card is normally expected when the product or service is provided. When credit is extended to a business customer, **accounts payable** refers to relatively immaterial, short-term, non-interest-bearing credit balances. When the credit period exceeds 90 days or the amount involved is material, it is usually represented by an interest-bearing debt contract called a **note payable**.

ers by mail, e-mail, or by telephone, suggesting that payment is required. And, in some cases, the seller may begin charging interest on the unpaid account payable balance.

Some customers intentionally violate the credit terms of their suppliers as a way to preserve their operating cash, particularly if there are no interest charges for doing so. In essence, these customers look to the credit provided by their suppliers as a source of interest-free financing for their own operations. One measure of the extent to which a firm utilizes this form of vendor financing is the **days' payable period**. This ratio indicates the average number of days that a company normally takes to pay its outstanding accounts payable:

$$\text{Days' payable period} = \frac{365}{[\text{Cost of goods sold/Accounts payable}]}$$

Some companies use the days' payable period as a component of their credit-granting review process. Customers that have historically taken a long time to pay for their credit purchases may be poor future credit risks. Comparing a customer's historical days' payable period with a seller's credit terms provides an easy approach to identify whether a customer is likely to pay for its credit purchases in a timely manner.

ANALYZING INVENTORY AND COST OF GOODS SOLD

In this chapter, we examined the various ways that businesses calculate their cost of goods sold and the value of their ending inventory. We learned that many U.S. public companies elect to use the LIFO method for this purpose. Since LIFO results in a lower taxable net income when input costs are rising, as compared to FIFO and weighted-average cost, we can speculate that the widespread usage of LIFO is linked to the income-tax sheltering afforded by the method, along with the U.S. Department of Treasury's LIFO conformity rule.

Despite LIFO's tax advantage, and the related positive impact on firm operating cash flow, some investment professionals charge that the method has a "dark side." For instance, some professionals allege that, as a consequence of LIFO's tax advantage, the method creates a "hidden earnings reserve" on the balance sheet in the form of undervalued ending inventory. The value of that earnings reserve on a pretax basis is, of course, the value of the LIFO inventory reserve that must be disclosed in the footnotes to the financial statements. Some investment professionals allege that LIFO-accounted firms can draw down on their LIFO reserve when additional income is needed to meet Wall Street earnings' expectations. While this is all true, it must be remembered that when a firm liquidates its LIFO earnings reserve—that is, when a firm liquidates its LIFO layers—the amount of the LIFO liquidation profits must be disclosed in the footnotes to the financial statements. So, it is a simple matter for a professional, as part of his or her due diligence review, to read the inventory footnote, determine the amount of LIFO liquidation profit, and restate a firm's net income as if the liquidation had not occurred.

LIFO liquidation profits are often derisively referred to as phantom profit because such profits do not result in a corresponding increase in a firm's cash flow from operations. In fact, a firm that liquidates its LIFO inventory reserve will reduce its operating cash flow as a consequence of the additional income taxes due on the LIFO liquidation profits.

Another LIFO-related concern expressed by some investment professionals is that the method causes distortions in many of the popular financial ratios used to evaluate firm performance. For example, the LIFO method causes cost of goods sold to be overstated and the value of ending inventory to be understated relative to a FIFO-accounted firm, assuming increasing inventory costs. And, as a consequence, a firm's inventory turnover ratio will be overstated and the inventory-on-hand period understated. Similarly, since net income under LIFO will be lower than net income under FIFO, some professionals worry that the return on sales, the return on assets, and the return on equity will be artificially misstated. Fortunately, using the techniques discussed in this chapter, it is possible to restate a firm's cost of goods sold and its pretax net income on the income statement and the ending inventory on the balance sheet to their approximate values as-if FIFO had been used instead of LIFO. By making these financial statement restatements, it is possible to develop restated financial ratios that will facilitate interfirm comparisons of performance.

ETHICS PERSPECTIVE

One of the distinguishing characteristics of a profession is a code of ethics that its members are required to follow. The accounting profession is no exception. In order to be granted a certified public accounting (CPA) certificate it is necessary to not only pass a competency exam but also an ethics exam. One reason for this requirement may be the public trust that is associated with membership in a profession and the fact that it is often difficult for a consumer to judge the quality of the service provided. This is certainly true regarding an audit, and is likely true regarding such services as tax planning and investing. Ultimately, the public's belief in how competently and ethically a profession performs will determine its ability to dictate how it does business. Prior to the **Enron** and **WorldCom** scandals, the accounting profession was largely self-policed by an internal organization, the American Institute of Certified Public Accountants (AICPA), which monitored the quality of the work of its members. Because of the profession's loss of credibility as a result of these corporate audit failures, the profession is now subject to oversight by the Public Company Accounting Oversight Board (PCAOB), a governmental organization.

REVIEW PROBLEM

Part A.

The Walgreen Company is the United States' largest drugstore chain, operating over 4,500 retail outlets in the United States and Puerto Rico. According to Walgreen's 2012 annual report, the company values its inventory using the lower of last-in, first-out (LIFO) cost or market basis. The company footnotes also disclose that:

> Inventories are valued on a lower of last-in, first-out (LIFO) cost or market basis. At August 31, 2012 and 2011, inventories would have been greater by $1,897 million and $1,587 million, respectively, if they had been valued on a lower of first-in, first-out (FIFO) cost or market basis. As a result of declining inventory levels, the fiscal 2012 LIFO provision was reduced by $268 million of LIFO liquidation. Inventory includes product costs, inbound freight, warehousing costs and vendor allowances not classified as a reduction of advertising expense.

Thus, Walgreen's inventory reserve as of year-end 2012 and 2011 was $1,897 million and $1,587 million, respectively, and the change in the company's inventory reserve from 2011 to 2012 was $310 million ($1,897 − $1,587). The income statements and balance sheets for Walgreen's are produced below:

REVIEW PROBLEM EXHIBIT   Financial Statement Disclosures: Walgreen Company

Panel A. Consolidated Statement of Earnings (in millions)	2012	2011	2010
Net sales.	$71,633	$72,184	$67,420
Costs and deductions			
Cost of sales.	(51,291)	(51,692)	(48,444)
Selling, occupancy and administration	(16,878)	(16,561)	(15,518)
Interest income (expense)	(88)	(71)	(85)
Other income		434	
Earnings before income tax provision	$ 3,376	$ 4,294	$ 3,373
Income tax provision	(1,249)	(1,580)	(1,282)
Net earnings.	$ 2,127	$ 2,714	$ 2,091

continued

REVIEW PROBLEM EXHIBIT	Financial Statement Disclosures: Walgreen Company		
Panel B. Consolidated Balance Sheets (in millions)		**2004**	**2003**
Cash and cash equivalents		$ 1,297	$ 1,556
Accounts receivable, net		2,167	2,497
Inventories		**7,036**	**8,044**
Other current assets		260	225
Total current assets		$10,760	$12,322
Property and equipment, at cost, less accumulated			
depreciation and amortization		12,038	11,526
Other noncurrent assets		10,664	3,606
Total assets		$33,462	$27,454
Trade accounts payable		$ 4,384	$ 4,810
Accrued expenses and other liabilities		4,338	3,088
Income taxes			185
Total current liabilities		$ 8,722	$ 8,083
Deferred income taxes		$ 545	$ 343
Other noncurrent liabilities		5,959	4,181
Total noncurrent liabilities		$ 6,504	$ 4,524
Shareholders' equity			
Common stock, $.078125 par value; authorized 3.2 billion shares, issued			
1,025,400,000 in 2004 and 1,024,908,276 in 2003		$ 80	$ 80
Paid-in capital		936	834
Employee stock loan receivable		(19)	(34)
Retained earnings		20,156	18,877
Accumulated other comprehensive income		68	16
Treasury stock at cost, 2,107,263 shares in 2004		(2,985)	(4,926)
Total shareholders' equity		$18,236	$14,847
Total liabilities and shareholders' equity		$33,462	$27,454

Required

1. What would Walgreen's earnings before income tax provision have been (in millions) at year-end 2012 if the Walgreen Company had used FIFO to value its inventory?
2. What would Walgreen's disclose on its balance sheet at year-end 2012 as the value of its inventory (in millions) if the company had used FIFO instead of LIFO?
3. How much did the Walgreen Company save in income taxes (in millions) in 2012 by using LIFO to value its inventory?
4. What was Walgreen's inventory-on-hand period for 2012? 2011?
5. Would Walgreen's inventory-on-hand period change if the company had used FIFO to value its inventory instead of LIFO?
6. What was Walgreen's days' payable period ratio for 2012? 2011?

Part B.

The Arcadia Company is uncertain whether it should utilize the first-in, first-out (FIFO) method or the last-in, first-out (LIFO) method to account for its inventory. The company's controller decided that she would compare the financial results under the two approaches as a way to reach a decision regarding which method to adopt. Data for the first two months of operations were as follows:

		Units	Unit Cost	Total
January				
Beginning inventory		6,000	$2.00	$ 12,000
Purchases:	Jan. 5	10,300	2.00	20,600
	Jan. 20	29,300	2.10	61,530
				$ 94,130
Sales:	Jan. 25	38,400		

continued

	Units	Unit Cost	Total
February			
Beginning inventory	7,200		
Purchases: Feb. 8	28,200	2.20	$ 62,040
Feb. 23	15,300	2.60	39,780
			$101,820
Sales: Feb. 27	40,700		
Ending inventory.	10,000		

Required

a. Calculate the cost of goods sold for January and February for The Arcadia Company using both FIFO and LIFO.

b. Assume that revenue for the two-month period totaled $300,000. What inventory valuation method would you recommend that the company adopt? Why?

The solution is on pages 224–225.

EXECUTIVE SUMMARY

This chapter examined the important accounting issue of how to match operating revenue and operating expenses—specifically, how to match the cost of goods and services sold with the revenue produced by the sale of those goods and services. A number of inventory costing methods were considered—FIFO, LIFO, and the weighted-average cost method. Just which method a company adopts was shown to have a dramatic effect on reported gross profit and net income. Finally, the chapter illustrated that the choice of an inventory costing method was often linked to income tax and income reporting considerations.

As a validation of your understanding of the content of this chapter, you should now be able to:

■ Explain how inventory is valued using FIFO, LIFO, and the weighted-average cost method and how the resulting cost of goods sold is matched with revenue.

■ Explain why the lower-of-cost-or-market method is sometimes used to value ending inventory and how this method affects reported net income.

■ Explain what the inventory reserve is and how a LIFO inventory liquidation may artificially increase a company's gross and net profit.

■ Explain how accounts payable are valued and how the payment of these payables can be managed to positively impact a firm's operating cash flow.

In Chapter 7, our investigation of the matching concept continues; however, in the next chapter, the focus shifts to matching the cost of such long-lived assets as plant and equipment, intangible assets, and natural resources with the operating revenue produced by these assets.

KEY CONCEPTS AND TERMS

Accounts payable, 209
Average cost method, 195
Change in the inventory reserve, 204
Conservatism principle, 201
Consistency principle, 200
Days' payable period, 209
Finished goods inventory, 192
First-in, first-out (FIFO), 195
Highest-in, first-out (HIFO), 203
Historical cost convention, 194

Inventory-on-hand period, 208
Inventory reserve, 204
Last-in, first-out (LIFO), 195
LIFO conformity rule, 195, 202
LIFO price layers, 204
LIFO reserve, 204
Lower-of-cost-or-market (LCM) method, 201
Next-in, first-out (NIFO), 203
Note payable, 209

Operating cycle, 192
Operating expenses, 193
Periodic system, 195
Perpetual system, 195
Phantom profit, 207
Raw material, 192
Replacement cost method, 195
Specific identification method, 195
Weighted-average cost method, 195
Work-in-process inventory, 192

QUESTIONS

Q6.1   **Consistency Principle.**   The consistency principle stipulates that when a company begins using a given inventory valuation method (FIFO, LIFO, or the weighted-average cost method), the company should continue to use that method to prepare its financial statements until such time as its senior management, with concurrence from the firm's independent auditors, conclude that another method would more fairly present the company's financial condition and performance. Discuss why the consistency principle is important to investors and shareholders. If a company changes its method of accounting for its inventory, how will that change be disclosed in its financial statements?

Q6.2   **Physical Inventory Counts.**   Although physically counting a business's inventory is integral to the periodic system of inventory recordkeeping, it is not an explicit component of the perpetual system. Nonetheless, most well-run businesses do annually (and sometimes, semiannually) conduct a physical count of their inventory. Discuss why physically counting a company's inventory is considered to be "best practice" regardless of which inventory recordkeeping system is utilized.

Q6.3   **Inventory Valuation Method Changes and Share Prices.**   Voluntary accounting policy changes are said to be "unintended signals" about the financial health and future prospects of a firm from management to a firm's shareholders. Discuss how and why you would expect the capital markets to react to news that a company was voluntarily changing its inventory valuation policy from (a) LIFO to FIFO and from (b) FIFO to LIFO.

Q6.4   **Lower-of-Cost-or-Market Method.**   The lower-of-cost-or-market method (LCM) is often referred to as a "one-way street" because under LCM, ending inventory values may be written down to a lower replacement value but are never written up when the expected replacement cost exceeds the inventory cost basis. What accounting principle is reflected in the application of LCM? What accounting principle is violated by the application of LCM? Discuss whether you think that LCM should be modified to become a "two-way street," allowing both inventory value write-ups and write-downs.

Q6.5   **Earnings Management and Inventory Valuation.**   Investment professionals frequently develop concerns that earnings management may be present when they observe that a firm has voluntarily changed its inventory valuation policy from LIFO to FIFO. Similar concerns arise when the capital market discovers that a firm using LIFO is liquidating its inventory price layers. Discuss why these two financial statement disclosures might indicate the presence of earnings management. Discuss when these disclosures might *not* indicate the presence of earnings management.

Q6.6   **LIFO Inventory Reserve.**   The LIFO inventory reserve is a measure disclosed in a company's footnotes and reveals the difference between the current value of a company's ending inventory and the LIFO value of its ending inventory. Discuss why and how this measure is useful to shareholders and investment professionals as they evaluate the financial condition and performance of a company that uses LIFO inventory valuation.

Q6.7   **LIFO and Earnings Management.**   Some investment professionals refer to LIFO inventory valuation as an "earnings management" tool, suggesting that LIFO allows a company to create a hidden earnings reserve on a company's balance sheet, to be used in later periods to help meet Wall Street earnings expectations. Discuss why this assertion might be true and how to measure the size of a company's "hidden LIFO earnings reserve."

Q6.8   **Inventory Valuation Policy Change.**   **Riverwood International Corporation**, a leading provider of paperboard, announced the following:

> During the fourth quarter, the Company changed its inventory valuation method from the last-in, first-out method to the first-in, first-out (FIFO) method as the Company determined that over time, FIFO more closely matches the Company's revenues with its costs.

Discuss why, and under what conditions, FIFO might enable Riverwood International to "more closely match" its costs with its revenue.

Q6.9   **LIFO Layer Liquidations.**   **Alleghany Technologies Incorporated** disclosed in its annual report that:

> . . . inventory usage resulted in liquidations of LIFO inventory quantities. These inventories were carried at differing costs prevailing in prior years as compared with the cost of current manufacturing cost and purchases. The effect of these LIFO liquidations was to increase cost of sales by $1.5 million in 2012, increase cost of sales by $0.1 million in 2011 and decrease cost of sales by $1.8 million in 2010.

Discuss why a liquidation of LIFO inventory quantities would reduce a company's cost of goods sold. Does this event indicate that a firm is attempting to manage its earnings? Why or why not?

Q6.10   **Inventory Write-Down.**   *The Financial Times* reported that **Delphi, Inc.**, a manufacturer of automotive parts, would take a $100 million write-down of its inventory to reflect reduced demand for some of its products. The write-down was part of the company's efforts to restructure its money-losing operations. Discuss what accounting principle is being followed by Delphi when it implements the inventory write-down. Discuss how the write-down will affect the company's financial statements. Discuss how the write-down will affect the company's inventory turnover ratio and its inventory-on-hand period. Could an inventory write-down be used to manage earnings? If so, how?

Q6.11   **(Ethics Perspective) Code of Ethics.**   It has been argued that to be classified as a professional one must offer services to the public rather than simply be an employee of an organization. As such, most employees of an organization, including accountants that are not CPAs, are not subject to their profession's ethical code of conduct. We have seen, however, that serious breaches of the public trust can result from the unethical conduct of some of these "professional" employees. Examples of such breaches include faulty construction in the city of Boston "Big Dig" and the scandal involving back-dated employee stock options. Do you feel that professionals working for an organization should be bound by the same code of ethical conduct as their colleagues that serve the public directly?

Assignments with the ✔ logo in the margin are available in BusinessCourse.
See the Preface of the book for details.
CHECK FIGURE indicates that check figures are available on the book's Website.

EXERCISES

E6.12   **Compute the Missing Inventory Values.**   The following information was disclosed in the 2012 annual report of The Arcadia Company.

	2012	2011	2010
Beginning inventory	$?	$?	$11,560
Purchase of inventory.	45,850	?	42,640
Inventory available for sale.	?	?	54,200
Ending inventory.	?	9,655	?
Cost of goods sold.	13,600	42,480	43,715

Fill in the missing values.

CHECK
FIGURE   **E6.13**   **Calculating FIFO Inventory Values.**   The Mann Corporation began operations in 2011. Information relating to the company's purchases of inventory and sales of products for 2011 and 2012 is presented below.

2011			
January 1	Purchase	200 units	@ $10 per unit
April 1	Sold	120 units	@ $25 per unit
July 1	Purchase	100 units	@ $14 per unit
September 1	Sold	130 units	@ $25 per unit

2012			
January 1	Purchase	100 units	@ $16 per unit
April 1	Sold	80 units	@ $30 per unit
July 1	Purchase	100 units	@ $18 per unit
September 1	Sold	100 units	@ $35 per unit

Calculate the FIFO cost of goods sold and ending inventory for 2011 and 2012 assuming use of (*a*) the periodic method and (*b*) the perpetual method.

E6.14   **Calculating LIFO Inventory Values.**   The Mann Corporation began operations in 2011. Information relating to the company's purchases of inventory and sales of products for 2011 and 2012 is presented below.

2011			
February 1	Purchase	200 units	@ $10 per unit
May 1	Sold	120 units	@ $25 per unit
August 1	Purchase	100 units	@ $14 per unit
October 1	Sold	130 units	@ $25 per unit

2012			
February 1	Purchase	100 units	@ $16 per unit
May 1	Sold	80 units	@ $30 per unit
August 1	Purchase	100 units	@ $18 per unit
October 1	Sold	100 units	@ $35 per unit

Calculate the LIFO cost of goods sold and ending inventory for 2011 and 2012 assuming use of (*a*) the periodic method and (*b*) the perpetual method.

E6.15   **Calculating Weighted-Average Cost Inventory Values.**   The Mann Corporation began operations in 2011. Information relating to the company's purchases of inventory and sales of products for 2011 and 2012 is presented below.

2011			
March 1	Purchase	200 units	@ $10 per unit
June 1	Sold	120 units	@ $25 per unit
September 1	Purchase	100 units	@ $14 per unit
November 1	Sold	130 units	@ $25 per unit

2012			
March 1	Purchase	100 units	@ $16 per unit
June 1	Sold	80 units	@ $30 per unit
September 1	Purchase	100 units	@ $18 per unit
November 1	Sold	100 units	@ $35 per unit

Calculate the weighted-average cost of goods sold and ending inventory for 2011 and 2012 assuming use of (*a*) the periodic method and (*b*) the perpetual method.

E6.16   **FIFO versus LIFO: Ratio Analysis.**   Presented below is financial data for two companies that are identical in every respect except that Company X uses the FIFO method to value its inventory and Company Z uses the LIFO method to value its inventory. Using this data, calculate the following ratios: return on sales, inventory turnover, inventory-on-hand period, and current ratio. Which of the two companies is the better investment opportunity? Why?

	Company X	Company Z
Sales.	$100,000	$100,000
Cost of goods sold.	47,500	56,400
Net income.	29,000	18,600
Inventory.	19,000	8,600
Current assets	64,000	53,600
Current liabilities.	21,000	21,000

E6.17   **Inventory Management.**   The following financial information is taken from the annual report of **Intel Corporation**:   **CHECK FIGURE**

(amounts in millions)	Year 2	Year 1
Net revenues	$38,826	$34,209
Cost of goods sold.	15,777	14,463
Ending inventories	3,126	2,621

Using the above data, calculate the company's inventory turnover, inventory-on-hand period, and gross profit percentage for Year 1 and Year 2. Is the company's inventory management improving? Intel uses FIFO to value its inventory. Would these ratios look better if the company used LIFO instead? Why?

E6.18   **LIFO to FIFO Change.**   At year end, **Riverwood International Corporation** announced that it would change its inventory valuation method from last-in, first-out (LIFO) to first-in, first-out (FIFO). The company also disclosed that the inventory valuation policy change would have a "positive impact on gross profit by $12.6 million." Presented below is Riverwood International's originally reported (using LIFO) financial results for the year.

(in thousands)	For the year
Net sales.	$298,731
Gross profit.	49,766
Income from operations	10,201

Describe the financial effects of this policy change on the company's income statement, balance sheet, and statement of cash flow. Does the inventory method change materially impact the company's reported income from operations?

E6.19   **Ratio Analysis: Alternative Inventory Valuation Methods.**   Exhibits 6.3, 6.4, and 6.5 in Chapter 6 present the financial results of the Arizona Ice Cream Company, Inc., using FIFO, LIFO, and the weighted-average cost method, respectively. Using this data, complete the following table for the company:

	FIFO	LIFO	Wt. Average
Inventory turnover	_____	_____	_____
Inventory-on-hand period.	_____	_____	_____
Gross margin percentage.	_____	_____	_____

Under which inventory valuation method does the company's performance appear most favorable? Using which inventory valuation method does the company's performance appear least favorable?

E6.20   **LIFO Reserve: Restating Financial Statements.**   The following information is taken from the annual report of the **Walgreen Company**:

(in millions)	Year 2	Year 1
Cost of goods sold.	$30,414	$27,310
Net income before tax	2,456	2,160
Ending inventory.	5,593	4,739
Inventory reserve	804	736

The Walgreen Company uses LIFO to value its inventory. Restate the company's financial results for Year 2 assuming the use of the FIFO method. Assume an effective tax rate of 30 percent. Which method—FIFO or LIFO—should Walgreen use to report its financial results to its shareholders? Why?

✔ E6.21   **Calculating the Days' Payable Period.**   The following information is taken from the annual report of **Coca-Cola Enterprises, Inc.**:

(amounts in millions)	Year 2	Year 1
Net revenue	$18,706	$18,158
Cost of goods sold.	11,185	10,771
Inventories	786	763
Accounts payable.	2,639	2,708

Using this information, calculate the accounts payable turnover ratio and the days' payable period for Year 1 and Year 2. Is Coca-Cola Enterprises taking longer to pay its accounts payable to its suppliers? Do the ratios indicate that the company's credit risk is increasing? Why or why not?

E6.22   **LIFO Layer Liquidations and Net Income.**   The following information is taken from the annual report of The Claremont Corporation:

(in millions)	Year 2	Year 1
Net income before tax	$360	$20

The company uses the LIFO method to value its inventory. In addition, the footnotes to the company's annual report revealed that, during Year 2 and Year 1, inventory usage resulted in liquidations of LIFO inventory quantities, and the effect of these liquidations was to reduce the cost of goods sold by $28 million and $6 million in Year 2 and Year 1, respectively. Calculate the company's net income before tax assuming that the LIFO inventory liquidations had not occurred. Discuss why the incremental profit from a LIFO-layer liquidation is often referred to as "phantom profit."

PROBLEMS

P6.23   **Calculating the Value of Ending Inventory and Cost of Goods Sold: Periodic Method.**   **Keystone Consolidated, Inc.** is a leading manufacturer of steel products. The following inventory data relates to the firm's production during the first quarter of 2010:

Date of Purchase	Tons of Raw Steel Purchased	Purchase Price per Ton	Total Cost
Jan. 1	500	$40	$20,000
Jan. 15	700	35	24,500
Feb. 7	200	33	6,600
Feb. 21	450	30	13,500
March 15	350	42	14,700
	2,200		$79,300

At the end of the first quarter of 2010, Keystone's internal auditors determined that 1,700 tons of raw steel had been processed and sold.

Required
1. Calculate the cost of steel processed and sold during the quarter under each of the following methods, assuming use of a periodic inventory management system:
    a. FIFO
    b. LIFO
    c. Weighted-average
2. Assume that the replacement cost per ton is $39 at the end of the quarter. What amount should Keystone's ending inventory be valued at on its March 31 balance sheet under each of the following methods?
    a. FIFO
    b. LIFO
    c. Weighted-average
3. Which method—FIFO, LIFO, or the weighted-average cost method—should Keystone use for reporting its financial results to its shareholders? Why? How does this decision constrain the company's method choice for income tax reporting?

P6.24   **Calculating the Value of Ending Inventory and Cost of Goods Sold: Perpetual Method.**   Consider the following inventory data for the first two months of the year for CompX International:

	Total Units	Unit Cost	Total Cost
Beginning inventory on hand			
January 1	60,000	$2.00	$120,000
Purchases during month			
January 5	103,600	2.00	207,200
January 20	293,900	2.10	617,190
	457,500		$944,390
Sales of inventory			
January 25	383,900		
Beginning inventory at			
February 1	73,600		
Purchases during month			
February 8	282,200	2.20	620,840
February 23	153,500	2.60	399,100
	509,300		
Sales of inventory			
February 27	407,600		
Ending Inventory	101,700		

Required

1. Calculate the cost of goods sold and ending inventory for January and February under each of the following methods, assuming use of a perpetual inventory management system:
   a.   FIFO
   b.   LIFO
   c.   Weighted-average
2. Assume that the replacement cost of CompX International's ending inventory is $2.05 per unit on January 30 and $2.35 per unit on February 28. Calculate the value of the ending inventory for January and February under each of the following methods:
   a.   FIFO
   b.   LIFO
   c.   Weighted-average
3. Which method—FIFO, LIFO, or the weighted-average cost method—should CompX International use when reporting its financial results to its shareholders? Why? How does this decision constrain the company's method selection for income tax reporting?

P6.25   **Calculating the Value of Ending Inventory and Cost of Goods Sold: Lower-of-Cost-or-Market Method.** The following inventory data is taken from the financial records of Fernandez, Inc., a personal computer software manufacturer.

	No. of Units	Unit Cost	Total Cost
Beginning inventory (Jan. 1)	160,000	$1.00	$160,000
Purchases: May 5	60,000	1.50	90,000
Sept. 3	60,000	2.00	120,000
Total available for sale	280,000		$370,000
Less: Sales*	250,000		?
Ending inventory (Dec. 31)	30,000		?
Expected replacement cost per unit		1.40	

*Sales for the year	No. of Units Sold
Feb 3	120,000
Jun. 30	30,000
Oct. 5	100,000
	250,000

Required

1. Complete the following table.

	Method	Periodic		Perpetual	
		Ending Inventory	Cost of Goods Sold	Ending Inventory	Cost of Goods Sold
a.	FIFO	_____	_____	_____	_____
b.	LIFO	_____	_____	_____	_____
c.	Weighted-average	_____	_____	_____	_____

2. Which inventory method would you recommend that Fernandez, Inc., use for income tax purposes? Why?
3. Which method would you recommend that Fernandez, Inc., use for accounting purposes if the company operates in a highly inflationary environment? Why?
4. Which method would you recommend that Fernandez, Inc., use for accounting purposes if the company operates in a deflationary environment? Why?

P6.26 **Restating Inventory Values Using the LIFO Inventory Reserve.** Presented below are the condensed financial statements of Global Enterprises, Inc. The company's inventory is valued using LIFO. The company's footnotes reveal that the LIFO reserve was as follows.

Year	LIFO Reserve (in thousands)
Year 1	$2,266
Year 2	2,152

Also, the footnotes indicate that net reductions in inventory levels resulted in a liquidation of LIFO layers amounting to $163,000 in Year 1 and $114,000 in Year 2.

GLOBAL ENTERPRISES, INC.
Condensed Balance Sheet

($ thousands)	Year 1	Year 2
Assets		
Quick assets	$ 7,327	$ 7,754
Inventory	3,029	3,158
Total current assets	10,356	10,912
Noncurrent assets	11,259	12,376
Total assets	$21,615	$23,288
Liabilities and Shareholders' equity		
Current liabilities	$ 8,153	$ 8,688
Long-term liabilities	3,099	3,162
Total liabilities....................................	11,252	11,850
Shareholders' equity	10,363	11,438
Total liabilities and shareholders' equity	$21,615	$23,288

GLOBAL ENTERPRISES, INC.
Condensed Income Statement

($ thousands)	Year 1	Year 2
Sales of products	$26,500	$26,797
Cost of goods sold................................	(24,095)	(24,248)
Other income	312	450
Income taxes	(900)	(975)
Net earnings.....................................	$ 1,817	$ 2,024

Required:
1. Restate the company's financial statements for Year 2 assuming the use of FIFO instead of LIFO.
2. Compare the tax consequences of using LIFO versus FIFO in Year 2, and for all prior years. (Assume an effective tax rate of 33 percent.)
3. Which method—FIFO or LIFO—should Global Enterprises use for reporting its financial results to shareholders? Why?

CHECK FIGURE

P6.27 **Restating Inventory Values Using the LIFO Inventory Reserve: International.** **BASF, Inc.** is an international manufacturer of chemical and derivative products, headquartered in Germany. The company is best known for its advertising slogan: "We don't make a lot of the products that you buy, we make a lot of the products that you buy better!" Presented below is selected information from BASF's recent annual report.

BASF, INC. Condensed Balance Sheet						
(millions of Euros)						
Assets	**Year 2**	**Year 1**	**Liabilities & Shareholders' Equity**	**Year 2**	**Year 1**
Inventory.............	€ 6,500	€ 6,200	Liabilities...............	€25,270	€24,520
Other current assets......	13,560	13,900	Capital stock	7,460	7,180
Noncurrent assets	20,300	18,900	Retained earnings	7,630	7,300
Total	€40,360	€39,000	Total	€40,360	€39,000

BASF, INC. Condensed Statement of Earnings		
(millions of Euros)	**Year 2**	**Year 1**
Revenues	€40,570	€41,900
Cost of goods sold.....................................	27,650	28,240
Gross profit...	12,920	13,660
Other expenses	11,760	12,425
Income taxes	300	620
Net earnings..	€ 860	€ 615

The footnotes to the company's financial statements revealed that BASF values most of its inventory using LIFO. The LIFO reserve was approximately €600 million and €300 million, respectively, at year-end Year 2 and Year 1.

Required
1. If BASF had used FIFO instead of LIFO to value its inventory, what value would have been reported for Year 2 for the following accounts?
   a. Ending inventory   c. Net income before tax
   b. Cost of goods sold   d. Retained earnings
2. How much additional income tax would the company have paid if it had used FIFO instead of LIFO to value its inventory?

 P6.28 **Inventory Valuation and Earnings.** Dominick Portet Wines Inc. began operations to import fine wines from Australia to the United States. Sales and purchase information is provided below.

	Year 1	**Year 2**	**Year 3**
Sales......................	170 units	220 units	300 units
Purchases.................	250 units @ $10 each	200 units @ $8 each	? units @ $15 each
LIFO ending inventory	80 units @ $10	60 units @ $10	

Assume that Portet Wines uses the LIFO method of inventory valuation. The purchase amount for Year 3 has been left blank because Portet Wines has not yet decided the total number of units to purchase during the year. (Assume that all sales occur on the last day of the year, after all purchases for the year have been made. The company's year-end is December 31.)

Required

1. How many units should be purchased in Year 3 if the firm's objective is to maximize reported income for the year?
2. Compute the cost of goods sold for Year 3 assuming the number of units computed in (1) is purchased.
3. How many units should be purchased in Year 3 if the firm's objective is to minimize income taxes for the year?
4. Compute the cost of goods sold for Year 3 assuming the number of units computed in (3) is purchased.
5. Assume Portet Wines uses FIFO instead of LIFO and the company purchased just enough units to meet sales demand. What would the cost of goods sold be in Year 3? Assume that FIFO ending inventory is equal to 80 units at $10 in Year 1 and 60 units at $8 in Year 2.

P6.29 **Inventory Valuation and Earnings.**   Santiago, Inc., began operations as an importer of fine Chilean wine to the United States. Sales and purchase information is provided below.

CHECK FIGURE

	Year 1	Year 2	Year 3
Sales....................	250 units	140 units	300 units
Purchases................	300 units @ $10 each	200 units @ $15 each	? units @ $20 each
Ending Inventory	50 units @ $10 each	50 units @ $10 each	
		60 units @ $15 each	

Santiago, Inc., uses the LIFO method of inventory valuation. The purchase amount for Year 3 has been left blank because the company has not yet decided the total number of units to purchase during the year. (Assume that all sales occur on the last day of the year, after all purchases for the year have been made. The company's year-end is December 31.)

Required

1. How many units should be purchased in Year 3 if the firm's objective is to minimize income taxes for the year?
2. Compute the cost of goods sold for Year 3 assuming that the number of units computed in (1) is purchased.
3. How many units should be purchased in Year 3 if the firm's objective is to maximize reported income for the year?
4. Compute the cost of goods sold for Year 3 assuming that the number of units computed in (3) is purchased.

P6.30 **FIFO versus LIFO: Ratio Analysis.**   Presented below are the financial statements of two companies that are identical in every respect except the method of valuing their inventories. The method of valuing inventory is LIFO for the LIFO Company and FIFO for the FIFO Company.

Comparative Income Statements	FIFO Company	LIFO Company
Sales......................................	$20,000,000	$20,000,000
Less: Cost of goods sold	9,200,000	11,280,000
Gross profit...............................	10,800,000	8,720,000
Less: Operating expenses	(5,000,000)	(5,000,000)
Net income before tax	$ 5,800,000	$ 3,720,000

Comparative Balance Sheets	FIFO Company	LIFO Company
Assets		
Cash......................................	$ 3,000,000	$ 3,000,000
Receivables	6,000,000	6,000,000
Inventory.................................	3,800,000	1,720,000
Total current assets	12,800,000	10,720,000
Total noncurrent (net)	20,000,000	20,000,000
Total	$32,800,000	$30,720,000
Liabilities and Equities		
Current liabilities.........................	$ 4,200,000	$ 4,200,000
Noncurrent liabilities......................	9,000,000	9,000,000
Total liabilities...........................	13,200,000	13,200,000
Total shareholders' equity	19,600,000	17,520,000
Total	$32,800,000	$30,720,000

Required

Using the two sets of financial statements, calculate the following ratios for each firm:

1. Current ratio
2. Inventory turnover ratio
3. Inventory-on-hand period
4. Return on total assets
5. Total debt to total assets
6. Long-term debt to shareholders' equity
7. Gross margin ratio
8. Return on sales
9. Return on shareholders' equity
10. Earnings per share (assume 2 million shares outstanding)

Based on the above ratios, which company represents the better investment opportunity? The better acquisition opportunity? The better lending opportunity? Why?

P6.31 **Evaluating Firm Performance using FIFO and LIFO.** **Costco Wholesale Corporation** operates membership warehouses. As of November 2012 Costco operated 617, with 447 in the United States. In addition, the store sells merchandise through its website costco.com. Using selected parts of Costco Corp.'s. 2012 10-K report, answer the questions below. (The year 2012 refers to the year ending September 2, 2012. The effective tax rate is 36.1 percent.)

Required

1. Was 2012 a good year or a bad year for Costco Corporation? Why?
2. Costco Corporation accounts for its U.S. inventory and the related cost of goods sold using the last-in, first-out (LIFO) method. Inventory is stated at the lower of LIFO cost or market. The cumulative LIFO inventory reserve was $108 million and $87 million at year-end 2012 and 2011, respectively. Estimate the income before income taxes in 2012 assuming the company used FIFO to value its inventory.

COSTCO WHOLESALE CORPORATION		
Consolidated Balance Sheets		
(in millions)	2012	2011
Assets		
Current assets		
Cash and cash equivalents............................	$ 3,528	$ 4,009
Short-term investments	1,326	1,604
Receivables, net....................................	1,026	965
Inventory...	7,096	6,638
Other current assets................................	550	490
Total current assets..............................	13,526	13,706
Property, plant, and equipment, net....................	12,961	12,432
Other assets......................................	653	623
Total assets.....................................	$27,140	$26,761
Liabilities		
Current liabilities		
Accounts payable..................................	$ 7,303	$ 6,544
Current portion of long-term debt	1	900
Other current liabilities	4,956	4,606
Total current liabilities	12,260	12,050
Long-term debt	1,381	1,253
Other liabilities	981	885
Total liabilities	14,622	14,188
Equity		
Common stock....................................	2	2
Additional paid-in capital	4,369	4,516
Accumulated other comprehensive income................	156	373
Retained earnings	7,834	7,111
Noncontrolling interests	157	571
Total equity	12,518	12,573
Total liabilities and equity...........................	$27,140	$26,761

continued

COSTCO WHOLESALE CORPORATION Consolidated Balance Sheets		
(in millions)	2012	2011
Total revenue	$99,137	$88,915
Operating expenses		
Merchandise costs	86,823	77,739
Selling, general, and administrative	9,518	8,691
Other.......................................	37	46
Operating income	2,759	2,439
Other income (expense)		
Interest expense.....................................	(95)	(116)
Other income	103	60
Income before income taxes	2,767	2,383
Provision for income taxes............................	1,000	841
Net income including noncontrolling interests..............	1,767	1,542
Net income attributable to noncontrolling interests..........	(58)	(80)
Net income attributable to Costco......................	$ 1,709	$ 1,462

CORPORATE ANALYSIS

CA6.32 **The Procter & Gamble Company.** The 2012 annual report of the **Procter & Gamble Company** (P&G) is available at http://annualreport.pg.com/annualreport2012/index.shtml. After reviewing P&G's annual report, respond to the following questions:

a. How does P&G value its inventory? What costs does P&G include in its cost of products sold? Do you agree with these policy decisions? How much of P&G's total assets are represented by its inventory?

b. Calculate P&G's inventory turnover ratio, inventory-on-hand period, accounts payable turnover ratio, and days' payable period for 2011 and 2012. What can you conclude from these ratios?

c. Assume that P&G needs to maintain an inventory of about $6.7 billion in 2013, the gross margin percentage remains the same as in 2012, and that in 2013, the company is able to raise its inventory turnover rate to 7.0 times. How much would their gross margin increase as a result of the improvement in the inventory turnover?

CA6.33 **Internet-Based Analysis.** Consider a publicly held company whose products you are familiar with. Some examples might include:

Company	Product	Corporate Website
• Johnson & Johnson Company....	• Band-Aids	• www.jnj.com
• Microsoft Corporation...........	• Windows XP software	• www.microsoft.com
• Nokia Corporation	• Cellular phones	• www.nokia.com
• Intel Corporation	• Pentium processors	• www.intel.com
• Kimberly-Clark Corporation......	• Kleenex	• www.kimberly-clark.com

Access the company's public website and search for its most recent annual report. (Some companies will provide access to their financial data through an "investor relations" link, while others will provide a direct link to their "annual reports.") After locating your company's most recent annual report, open the file and review its contents. After reviewing the annual report for your selected company, prepare answers to the following questions.

a. What method does the company use to account for its inventory? Do you agree with the company's selection of its inventory valuation method? Calculate the inventory as a percentage of total assets. Did the percentage increase or decrease over the last two years?

b. Calculate the inventory turnover ratio and the inventory-on-hand period for each of the last two years. Is the inventory-on-hand period increasing or decreasing? What might explain the change in the inventory-on-hand period?

c. Calculate the days' payable period for each of the last two years. Is the company paying its accounts payable faster or slower? What might explain this change?

CA6.34 **IFRS Financial Statements.** The 2012 financial statements of **LVMH Moet Hennessey-Louis Vuitton S.A.** are presented in Appendix C of this book. LVMH is a Paris-based holding company and one of the world's largest and best-known luxury goods companies. As a member-nation of the European Union, French companies are required to prepare their consolidated (group) financial statements using International Financial Reporting Standards (IFRS). In LVMH's Notes to the Consolidated Financial Statements (not presented in Appendix C), the company discloses its inventory policy:

> Inventories are valued using the weighted average cost or FIFO methods. Inventories other than wine produced by the Group are recorded at the lower of cost (excluding interest expense) and net realizable value; cost comprises manufacturing cost (finished goods) or purchase price, plus incidental costs (raw materials, merchandise). Provisions for impairment of inventories are chiefly recognized . . . because of product obsolescence (date of expiry, end of season or collection, etc.) or lack of sales prospects.

Consider the following questions:

a. If LVMH followed U.S. GAAP, what inventory valuation method would you expect the company to use? Why?

b. Where would you expect to find the provision for inventory impairment in the company's financial statements?

SOLUTION TO REVIEW PROBLEM

Solution Part A.

1. LIFO earnings before income tax provision (see Panel A of Review Problem Exhibit) $3,376
   Add: Change in inventory reserve (as reported in Walgreen's footnote disclosures) 310
   Earnings before income tax provision assuming use of FIFO $3,686

2. Inventory (see Panel B of Review Problem Exhibit) $7,036
   Add: Inventory reserve 310
   Inventory assuming use of FIFO. $7,346

3. Walgreen's effective tax rate for 2012: $1,249 ÷ $3,376 = 37.0%
   Inventory reserve data
   Inventory reserve (2012) $1,897
   Less: Inventory reserve (2011) .... (1,857)
   Change in the reserve. .... $ 310

   Income tax savings in 2012: $310 × 37.0% = $114.7 million

4. $$\text{LIFO Inventory-on-hand period} = \frac{365}{\text{Cost of sales/Inventory}}$$

   2012: $\dfrac{365}{(\$51,291/\$7,036)} = 50.1 \text{ days}$

   2011: $\dfrac{365}{(\$51,692/\$8,044)} = 56.8 \text{ days}$

5. FIFO Inventory-on-hand period for 2004

$$\frac{365}{[(\$51,291 + \$310)/(\$7,036 + \$1,897)]} = 63.2 \text{ days}$$

6. Days payable period ratio $= \dfrac{365}{\text{Cost of sales/Accounts payable}}$

2012: $\dfrac{365}{(\$51,291/\$4,384)} = 31.2 \text{ days}$

2011: $\dfrac{365}{(\$51,692/\$4,810)} = 34.0 \text{ days}$

Solution Part B.

a. Cost of goods sold:

					Costs of Goods Sold
FIFO					
January	6,000 units	@	$2.00		$12,000
	10,300 units	@	2.00		20,600
	22,100 units	@	2.10		46,410
					$79,010
February	7,200 units	@	$2.10		15,120
	28,200 units	@	2.20		62,040
	5,300 units	@	2.60		13,780
Total					$169,950
LIFO					
January	29,300 units	@	$2.10		$ 61,530
	9,100 units		2.00		18,200
					79,730
February	15,300 units	@	$2.60		39,780
	25,400 units	@	2.20		55,880
Total					$175,390

b. If the goal of the management of The Arcadia Company is to report the highest gross profit, the company should adopt the FIFO method:

	FIFO	LIFO
Revenues	$300,000	$300,000
Less: Cost of goods sold	(169,950)	(175,390)
Gross profit	$130,050	$124,610

If, however, the goal of the management of The Arcadia Company is to report the lowest gross profit, perhaps to minimize taxable net income, the company should adopt the LIFO method.

When you complete this chapter you should be able to:

1. Explain how the acquisition cost of a long-lived asset is determined, and describe how the accounting treatment for ongoing costs related to these assets can differ.

2. Describe why the matching of depreciation, depletion, and amortization expense with operating revenue is important.

3. Explain how depreciation is calculated using straight-line, double-declining-balance, and the units-of-production methods.

4. Define what an asset impairment is and how impairments are reflected in financial statements.

Long-Lived Fixed Assets, Intangible Assets, and Natural Resources

Green Mountain Coffee Roasters, Inc. (GMCR) is a specialty coffee company based in Waterbury, Vermont. The company participates in a variety of beverage related businesses, including sourcing, producing, and selling over 200 varieties of coffee, cocoa, and teas. Many of its products come in single serving portion packs, although it also sells coffee in traditional packaging, whole bean and ground. GMCR sells its products primarily in North America through general retailers, restaurants, office coffee distributors, and directly to consumers through the internet. The company also manufactures gourmet single-cup brewing systems and brewing equipment. The company was founded in 1981 as a small café and by any measure has been a phenomenal success—by 2011 annual sales exceeded $2.6 billion.

GREEN MOUNTAIN COFFEE ROASTERS, INC.

But by early 2012 the luster had begun to wear off the GMCR story. On May 3, coincident with another solid quarter of earnings, the company forecast modestly slower growth and that day the stock shed almost 50 percent of its value. Compounding the problems caused by lofty growth expectations, some investors had become skeptical that the company was achieving past earnings targets by classifying some of its costs as capitalized assets, rather than immediately expensing them. One particularly vocal skeptic was David Einhorn, a hedge fund manager at Greenlight Capital.

In an October 2011 presentation at the Value Investing Conference in New York City, cynically titled "GAAP-uccino", Einhorn laid out what he thought were questionable capital expenditure forecasts for the company. His analysis showed that the historic change in K-cup unit sales did not correspond to the change in capital expenditures. He estimated that over half of the company's 2011 expenditures for long-term assets were unexplainable, arguing that as the company grew it should have achieved more scale with that growth. Capital expenditures for long-term fixed assets should have shown a company becoming more efficient, not less efficient. A New York Times article further questioned GMCR's announced capital expenditures of $175 million, versus analyst estimates of less than half that amount.

GMCR's responses to these inquiries, whether well-founded or not, were simply that the company adhered to required accounting standards and principles for its capital expenditures. The claims against the company, however, highlight the importance of accounting for long-term assets and the potential attention on these capital investments for many interested investors. In this chapter we explore these issues. We investigate the acquisition, use, and accounting for investments in long-lived fixed assets, intangible assets, and natural resources. We will see that the key issues surrounding these assets are (1) how to match their acquisition cost with the revenue generated by their use, and (2) the continuing asset value that should be reported on a company's balance sheet.

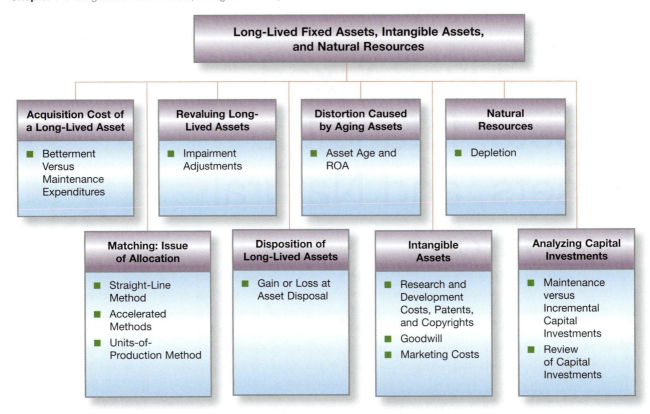

ACQUISITION COST OF A LONG-LIVED ASSET

When an asset is initially acquired by a business, it is generally accepted accounting practice globally to **capitalize** the acquisition cost of the asset—that is, to place the value of the asset on the company's balance sheet at the asset's acquisition cost. This accepted practice reflects the historical cost principle discussed in Chapter 2. Frequently, the **acquisition cost** includes more than just its listed purchase price; it also includes any sales tax on the purchase price, transportation costs from the seller to the buyer's location, as well as a number of ancillary costs. As a general rule, all expenditures necessary to purchase an asset, transport the asset to the buyer's place of business, and place the asset into a revenue-producing state should be capitalized to the balance sheet as part of an asset's total acquisition cost. For example, if installation of an asset requires modification of the buyer's facilities (such as the installation of higher voltage electrical wiring or reinforced flooring), these costs should be capitalized to the balance sheet because without these expenditures the asset would not reach a revenue-producing state. While this accounting treatment might seem straightforward, many expenditures are less clear. For instance, if the use of an acquired asset requires special employee training, these costs may be capitalized to the balance sheet as part of the asset's acquisition cost because without them the asset would not be operational.

Some businesses self-construct the assets they utilize in their business. For example, automotive and truck manufacturers typically "retool" their production lines every three to five years. Retoolings often coincide with the introduction of a new model or the redesign of existing models. The cost of retooling is quite expensive, frequently involving billions of dollars. Rather than outsource these production-line changes, the automotive companies often undertake the retooling themselves. Consequently, the costs incurred during the retooling process are capitalized to the automotive company's balance sheet as a component of the plant and equipment account. Included in the amount capitalized would be any and all costs related to the retooling, such as wages paid to workers and depreciation on equipment and tools used in the retooling process.

The interest charges on any borrowed funds used to finance the retooling can also appropriately be capitalized to the balance sheet as part of the production-line cost during the period of retooling. However, once the retooling process is complete, the interest charges (and all other costs) may no longer be capitalized as part of the cost of the asset, and instead, must thereafter be expensed. When borrowing costs are capitalized, it is accepted practice to disclose the amount of the **capitalized interest** charges in the company's footnotes. Many investment professionals question the economic rationale behind the practice of capitalizing interest charges, preferring to see all financing costs expensed in the fiscal period in which they are incurred (recognizing the income statement deduction in the same fiscal period as the cost is incurred). Disclosure of the amount of capitalized interest costs in the footnotes to the financial statements enables these professionals to restate a company's financial statements as if the interest charges had been expensed, rather than capitalized.

Betterment Versus Maintenance Expenditures

After an asset has been placed in service, it is not uncommon to incur expenditures related to the asset's continued use. Just as with expenditures related to the initial acquisition of an asset, the financial reporting decision for expenditures made after the asset has been placed in service similarly relates to whether they are expensed immediately or capitalized to the balance sheet. Some post-acquisition expenditures involve routine maintenance of the asset (such as an oil change on a company truck) that is necessary to obtain the normal productive output from the asset. As a consequence, routine **maintenance expenditures** are expensed on the income statement in the fiscal period in which they are incurred. Other expenditures may be nonroutine, however, and consequently, may be more appropriately accounted for by capitalizing them to the balance sheet as part of the cost of an asset. For example, a factory with an expected useful life of 50 years may require a new roof every twenty years. The cost of replacing the factory roof is not a maintenance expense, but instead, is typically considered to be a **betterment** or improvement.

So how does one determine whether an expenditure is a betterment or maintenance? Betterment expenditures are frequently material in amount and either (1) extend the productive life of an asset, (2) improve the quality and/or quantity of an asset's output, or (3) reduce the operating expenses associated with the asset. As a consequence, betterments are capitalized to the balance sheet, to be depreciated over the asset's remaining expected useful life. Those expenditures that do not meet one of the above conditions are more appropriately classified and expensed as a maintenance expenditure.

The identification of just which expenditures are maintenance expenditures versus those that are betterment expendiures is often quite ambiguous. Since this accounting decision can have a significant impact on a business's current earnings, these decisions should be carefully reviewed by a firm's CFO in conjunction with its independent auditor. As with most financial reporting decisions, the earnings impact

---

BUSINESS PERSPECTIVE

Capitalizing Versus Expensing at WorldCom

WorldCom Inc. was a discount long-distance telephone service provider founded in 1995 with the merger of Williams Telecommunications Group Inc. and LDDS Inc. By 2002, WorldCom had become the United States' second largest long-distance telephone company through more than 60 mergers and acquisitions. In 2003, a U.S. Securities and Exchange Commission complaint alleged that World-Com changed its accounting for the cost of landlines leased from such companies as **AT&T** and **SBC**, among others. Originally, the line costs—that is, the charges paid by WorldCom for access to other telephone company networks—were expensed to match the company's operating expenses with its operating revenue. However, beginning in 2000, WorldCom began inappropriately capitalizing these costs to its corporate balance sheet as an asset. An investigation by WorldCom's auditors **KPMG** revealed that as much as $7 billion in line costs may have been inappropriately capitalized to enable the struggling company to report positive earnings. The accounting change was masterminded to buoy WorldCom's sagging share price. In July 2002, WorldCom filed for bankruptcy, the largest in U.S. corporate history. In March 2005, former WorldCom CEO Bernard Ebbers was convicted of conspiracy to commit fraud by falsifying WorldCom's financial results, securities fraud by misleading investors and the public about WorldCom's true financial condition, and making false filings with the U.S. Securities and Exchange Commission that misrepresented WorldCom's financial position. In late 2005, Mr. Ebbers was sentenced to 25 years in prison; he began serving his prison sentence in September 2006.

Could an astute financial analyst have identified the pending WorldCom disaster? It is very likely that a rigorous financial analysis and review of WorldCom's financial statements would have provided analysts with "red flags" regarding the company's financial problems. For instance, WorldCom's **fixed asset turnover ratio**—that is, its net sales divided by net fixed assets—declined over the period 2000 to 2002 from 0.31 to a mere 0.19, a drop of nearly 40 percent, as the amount of capitalized landline costs increased. A decline of this magnitude should have raised concern among the investment professionals that followed the company.

of the treatment of an expenditure as maintenance versus a betterment is a matter of timing. Betterment expenditures capitalized to the balance sheet do not immediately reduce current earnings but will reduce future earnings through increased depreciation expense. Maintenance expenditures that are expensed immediately, on the other hand, reduce current pretax profit. Managers who are compensated on the basis of reported earnings, or those otherwise pressured to meet short-term earnings expectations, often prefer to capitalize as many expenditures as can be justified to avoid the adverse effect on net income (and their compensation) caused by immediately expensing such outlays.

MATCHING: THE ALLOCATION OF COSTS TO FUTURE PERIODS

Once the capitalized cost of a long-lived asset has been determined, the next accounting issue to be confronted is how best to allocate that cost over the asset's expected productive life. First, be aware that there are a variety of different terms used to describe the allocation of capitalized costs to future periods. The process of allocating the capitalized cost of a fixed asset over its expected useful life is commonly referred to as **depreciation**, whereas the process of allocating the acquisition cost of an intangible asset over its productive life is called **amortization**. **Depletion**, on the other hand, refers to the allocation of the acquisition and development costs of a natural resource over its expected productive life. **Fixed assets** include such tangible assets as property, plant and equipment, whereas **intangible assets** include goodwill, the intellectual property represented by copyrights and patents, and other contract rights. **Natural resources** include such assets as standing timber, oil and gas reserves, iron ore, coal and gold mines.

The significance of the allocation process for long-lived assets arises as a consequence of the matching concept—that is, the desire within a given accounting period to match a company's operating revenues with **all** of the costs incurred to generate that revenue. Long-lived assets, by their nature, have the capacity to generate operating revenue over many years, and consequently, it is necessary to arrive at a logical and systematic way to distribute the capitalized value of these assets against the future revenue generated by their use.

For most long-lived fixed assets, it is difficult to know with certainty in what amount, or when, an asset's future revenue stream is going to occur since operating revenue is dependent on so many externalities such as product demand, competition, changing customer tastes, and innovation, among others. Consequently, given the ambiguity surrounding the revenue streams associated with such assets, the accounting community has developed a number of "logical and systematic" allocation schemes that have become accepted as GAAP. In the case of fixed assets, these generally accepted allocation approaches include:

- Straight-line method
- Accelerated methods
  - Double-declining balance
- Production-based methods
  - Units-of-production

In the case of intangible assets, amortization using the straight-line method is almost universally practiced worldwide. And, in the case of natural resources, the use of the units-of-production depletion approach is considered to be "best practice." Below we provide further detail on the application of each of these methods.

Straight-Line Method

As its name implies, the **straight-line method** of depreciation (and amortization) allocates the capitalized cost of an asset equally over an asset's expected productive life. The amount of expense each period is determined using the following formula:

$$\text{Operating expense for the period} = \frac{1}{n}(\text{Acquisition cost} - \text{Residual value})$$

where n equals the asset's expected useful life in months or in years. The **useful life** of an asset is the length of time that the asset is expected to be productive (i.e., produce revenue) for the company. This length of time is generally shorter than the actual physical life of the asset. For example, a computer may have a ten-year physical life; however, the useful life for accounting purposes is likely to be much shorter, perhaps only four years or less, because of technological improvements in the area of information technology. The estimated amount that an asset could be sold for at the end of its useful life is called the asset's **residual value**, scrap value, or salvage value. The residual value is important not only because of its inclusion in the straight-line expensing formula, but also because it represents a minimum balance sheet value for the asset at all times. That is, the asset value should not be depreciated or amortized below the residual value, as that amount represents the expected value that can be obtained by the company at the asset's ultimate disposition.

As an example, if the asset to be depreciated is a truck having an expected useful life of five years, costing $30,000, and with an expected residual value of $4,000 at the end of its five-year useful life, the annual straight-line depreciation charge would be $5,200 (1/5[30,000 − 4,000]). Thus, in each of the asset's five years, a constant amount ($5,200) would be matched against the revenue produced by the truck. An implicit assumption underpinning the straight-line method is that an asset's productive capacity is approximately equal during each period of its useful life. Over the expected five-year useful life of the truck, the depreciation charges will aggregate to $26,000 (five years × $5,200 per year), representing the **depreciable cost** of the asset. The residual value of the asset ($4,000) should not be depreciated since this is the expected value that the asset can be sold for when retired from use.

How is depreciation calculated when an asset is acquired partway through a fiscal period? In recognition of the reality that depreciation expense is just an estimate of the value of an asset that is consumed or used up in a given fiscal period, most companies employ a practice known as the **half-year convention**. Under this convention, no matter when an asset is acquired during a fiscal year, only one-half year of depreciation expense is taken in the first year of use. An alternative application of the half-year convention used by some companies is that when an asset is acquired during the first six months of the year, the asset is assumed to have been acquired on the first day of the year and thus a full year of depreciation expense is taken. For assets acquired anytime during the second six months of the fiscal year, only one-half year of the first year's depreciation expense is taken.

When a company records its depreciation expense for the period, retained earnings is reduced by the amount of the expense and an equivalent amount is subtracted from the book value of the asset. However, in the case of long-term fixed assets, instead of reducing the original asset account directly, the current depreciation charge is placed in a contra-asset account called **accumulated depreciation**, which is then subtracted from the asset account. With the use of this account two important pieces of information are retained on the balance sheet: (1) the original cost of the asset and (2) the accumulated depreciation on the asset taken to date. The difference in these two amounts, the asset's remaining **net book value** ($24,800), is calculated as the acquisition cost ($30,000) minus the accumulated depreciation ($5,200) to date. In the case of the truck, this information is illustrated below for the first year of depreciation taken on the truck.

	Acquire Asset	Depreciate Asset	End. Bal. (Summary)	
Assets				
Cash.	(30,000)		(30,000)	
::				
Property, plant and equipment.	30,000		30,000	} Net book value = $24,800
Accumulated depreciation		(5,200)	(5,200)	
Shareholders' Equity				
Retained earnings			(5,200)	} Retained earnings = ($5,200)
Depreciation expense.		(5,200)		

As noted above the convention of using the accumulated depreciation account to record the depreciation taken on an asset stems from a desire to preserve an asset's original acquisition cost while also disclosing its current book value. Comparing an asset's acquisition cost to its book value reveals the relative age of an asset and consequently, how soon the asset will need to be replaced. For example, the ratio of book value to acquisition cost for our $30,000 truck after one year of use yields a ratio of 83 percent ($24,800/$30,000), suggesting that only 17 percent of the asset has been consumed to date, and thus, that the asset will not need to be replaced for some years in the future. Knowing the relative age of a business's assets is useful as managers and investment professionals try to forecast a company's future cash flow needs.

Accelerated Methods

Accelerated depreciation methods refer to allocation methods that cause an asset to be expensed at a rate faster early in its useful life, then at a slower rate later in its life. The **double-declining-balance** method is an accelerated method, yielding the fastest write-off of any generally accepted depreciation method. Under this approach, the annual depreciation expense is calculated as follows:

> The **double-declining-balance** (DDB) method is part of a family of declining-balance depreciation methods. The depreciation rate for DDB is 2/n, where n is the asset's expected useful life. But other rates are also permissible (such as 1.5/n, 1.25/n, etc.) so long as they do not exceed the DDB rate of 2/n.

$$\text{Operating expense for the period} = \frac{2}{n}(\text{Net book value})$$

where n equals the asset's expected useful life in months or in years.

In the case of the truck with a five-year life, costing $30,000, and with a residual value of $4,000, double-declining depreciation would be calculated as follows:

	Depreciation Expense	Double-Declining-Balance Calculations	End of Period Book Value
Year 1	$12,000	2/5 × ($30,000)	$18,000
Year 2	7,200	2/5 × ($30,000 − $12,000)	10,800
Year 3	4,320	2/5 × ($30,000 − $12,000 − $7,200)	6,480
Year 4	1,240	1/2 × ($26,000 − $23,520)	5,240
Year 5	1,240	1/2 × ($26,000 − $23,520)	4,000
	$26,000		

A close inspection of the truck's depreciation expense each year reveals that the double-declining-balance depreciation formula was not strictly applied in years 4 and 5. This departure in not unusual and was required because the formula depreciates the truck so rapidly that by the end of Year 3, the remaining book value is only $6,480. Continuing to mechanically apply the formula would cause the truck to be depreciated below its expected residual value of $4,000. Consequently, at this point, the convention typically applied is that the declining-balance formula is abandoned, and thereafter, a straight-line approach is utilized for the remaining costs to be depreciated. As of year 4 these amount to $2,480 ($6,480 − $4,000), and they are thus spread equally over the remaining two years of the truck's useful life ($2,480/ 2 years = $1,240).

Exhibit 7.1 provides a graphical comparison of the annual depreciation expense taken for the truck under the two distinct methods. From the graph you can readily see why one is labeled "straight-line" and the other "accelerated." Important to emphasize again is that the total depreciation taken under both methods across the five years is $26,000. What differs is the timing of the allocation across periods.[1]

It is noteworthy that all generally accepted depreciation methods incorporate an asset's expected residual value in the calculation of the annual (or periodic) depreciation expense except the double-declining-balance method. The declining-balance method does not consider an asset's expected residual value except as a lower bound of total depreciation taken. In those situations when applying the method

---

[1] A second, but less widely used, accelerated depreciation method is the **sum-of-the-years' digits method**. The sum-of-the-years' digits (SYD) may be calculated as follows: SYD = n(n + 1)/2, where n is the asset's expected useful life. For an asset costing $30,000, with a useful life of five years (SYD = 15) and residual value of $4,000, the depreciation expense under this method would be calculated as follows:

	Depreciation Expense	Calculation
Year 1	$ 8,667	5/15 × ($30,000 − $4,000)
Year 2	6,933	4/15 × ($30,000 − $4,000)
Year 3	5,200	3/15 × ($30,000 − $4,000)
Year 4	3,467	2/15 × ($30,000 − $4,000)
Year 5	1,733	1/15 × ($30,000 − $4,000)
	$26,000	

would cause the total depreciation expense taken on an asset to exceed its depreciable cost base, an adjustment to the depreciation formula will be necessary, typically to cap the depreciation expense taken so as not to allow the asset's net book value to drop below its residual value.

EXHIBIT 7.1	Comparison of Double-Declining-Balance Versus Straight-Line

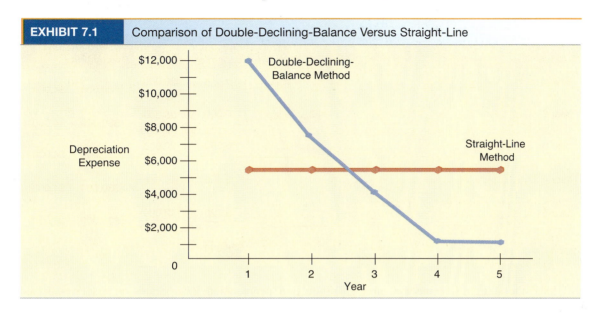

Units-of-Production Method

For some assets, calculating depreciation as a function of time (such as straight-line) may not be relevant since the expected useful life of certain assets is more closely linked to their actual usage than the passage of time. For example, some equipment manufacturers have determined that their products have a reasonably well-defined useful life as measured by the number of machine-hours they are likely to run or the number of units they are likely to produce. For instance, the manufacturer of our truck costing $30,000 may believe that, based upon engineering statistics and actual utilization data, the truck's useful life is best defined in terms of expected miles to be driven (such as most truck leases are defined in terms of a maximum allowable mileage). Application of a straight-line or double declining balance method potentially would result in depreciation patterns unrelated to the earnings power of the truck. Under these circumstances, the use of an output-based allocation method, such as the units-of-production method, may yield superior matching results.

Under the **units-of-production method**, the periodic depreciation charge is calculated as follows:

In Practice 7.1 *Depreciation Method: A Glimpse of a Sample of Fortune 1000 Companies* The following table identifies the depreciation method used by a sample of 600 *Fortune 1000* companies. Over 98 percent of the surveyed firms reported using the straight-line method for some or all of their depreciable assets:

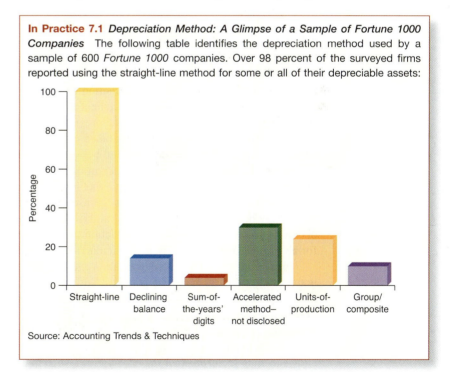

Source: Accounting Trends & Techniques

$$\text{Operating expense for the period} = \frac{\text{Output consumed this period}}{\text{Total estimated lifetime output}} \times (\text{Aquisition cost} - \text{Residual value})$$

As an illustration, if the truck is expected to be driven an aggregate 100,000 miles before replacement, and the actual mileage driven is 28,000 miles in Year 1, 25,000 miles in Year 2, 20,000 miles in Year 3, and 15,000 and 12,000 miles in Years 4 and 5, respectively, the units-of-production depreciation would be calculated as follows:

	Depreciation Expense	Units-of-Production Calculation
Year 1	$ 7,280	$\frac{28,000}{100,000} \times (\$30,000 - \$4,000)$
Year 2	6,500	$\frac{25,000}{100,000} \times (\$30,000 - \$4,000)$
Year 3	5,200	$\frac{20,000}{100,000} \times (\$30,000 - \$4,000)$
Year 4	3,900	$\frac{15,000}{100,000} \times (\$30,000 - \$4,000)$
Year 5	3,120	$\frac{12,000}{100,000} \times (\$30,000 - \$4,000)$
	$26,000	

Like the straight-line method, units-of-production depreciation incorporates an asset's expected residual value, and consequently, the formula only allocates the truck's depreciable cost of $26,000 ($30,000 − $4,000) over its expected five- year life. The advantage of this method should be clear, however, in that the depreciation pattern is directly aligned to usage of the truck rather than its age.

Choosing a Depreciation Method

The process of allocating the cost of an asset over its useful life is done solely for the purpose of matching the acquisition cost of the asset with the revenue generated by the asset's use. The purpose is not to align the asset's balance sheet value—its book value—with the actual market value of the asset. It will only be by coincidence that an asset's book value will ever equal the market value of the asset at any time other than the point of initial purchase. It should also be noted that accumulated depreciation is nothing more than a running total offset to the acquisition cost of the asset. This account does not represent a fund of money that can be used for asset replacement as is sometimes thought by those who lack an understanding of accounting. In your review of each depreciation method illustrated above, be sure to observe that each resulted in the same total depreciation taken over the asset's useful life—only the amount of the periodic depreciation charge, the timing, differed between the methods.

Given the variety of depreciation approaches that are considered acceptable under GAAP, how does the management of a company choose a method to depreciate its assets? Further complicating the answer to this question is that GAAP permits the use of a combination of depreciation methods—that is, some assets may be depreciated using the straight-line method while others may be depreciated using double-declining-balance or the units-of-production method—although most companies tend to use one approach for all of their depreciable assets, particularly for publicly disclosed financial statements.

In the United States, the depreciation method most commonly used in audited financial statements is the straight-line method. The popularity of the straight-line method in the United States appears linked to several considerations. First, for capital-intensive companies, depreciation expense is one of the largest operating expenses (if not the largest) deducted against operating revenue. The straight-line method holds that expense stable, thereby enabling management to know with certainty a significant component of the operating expenses that they will need to cover each fiscal period. Some managers feel that this knowledge allows them to focus on other important issues when making operating decisions. Second, some investment professionals allege that companies attempt to "smooth" their reported earnings on the presumption that earnings stability is highly valued by the capital market (smooth earnings represent certainty, and hence, less risk). The straight-line method is thought to facilitate **income smoothing** because it provides a stable level of depreciation deductions over the life of an asset. Finally, relative to the accelerated methods, the straight-line method provides smaller depreciation deductions against operating revenues, especially in the early years of an asset's life (see Exhibit 7.1). As companies grow and continue to add to their fixed asset bases, these differences will get increasingly exaggerated. For management concerned about reporting the highest possible earnings, the straight-line method tends to facilitate this financial reporting objective.

Related to the choice of depreciation method is the estimation of other assumptions embedded within the methods. Just as the choice of straight-line or accelerated methods can influence earnings, so too can estimates of an asset's useful life and residual value. An accurate assessment of these two inputs at the date of acquisition is very difficult. But both must be made based on the best known facts and circumstances at the time the asset is placed in service. If managers were to assume a longer useful life, then the result would be a lower depreciation expense than otherwise would be reported. A higher residual value would result in a similar effect. GAAP provides no definitive guidelines for estimating the useful life and residual value of an asset, other than that these amounts should approximate the expected revenue generating life of the asset and its expected recoverable value at the end of that life, respectively. As with all accounting judgments made by management, these choices should be made consistently and conservatively, with appropriate levels of oversight and review.

TAX PERSPECTIVE

Long-Term Assets Under U.S. Tax Law

Because long-term fixed assets are a significant part of nearly every business, managers and executives should be aware of certain important differences between the accounting required under U.S. GAAP and the rules that govern the tax treatment for those same assets. Here we provide a brief overview of some of the highlights.

Recall that a number of accounting issues were identified with regard to determining the amount of depreciation to be recorded on a company's income statement, and relatedly, the book value to be recorded on a company's balance sheet. These issues include the amount to be capitalized to the asset account and the choices surrounding the depreciation/amortization method for an asset (i.e., the asset's residual value and the asset's expected useful life). For U.S. income tax purposes, depreciation and amortization rules are generally more restrictive in choice. But the rate at which an item is allowed to be expensed is generally quite generous. This can be traced directly to economic stimulus considerations—the quicker a company can write-off a long-term fixed asset, the more likely the asset will be replaced with another.

Regarding the amount to be capitalized as an asset, U.S. tax authorities generally apply the same criteria as U.S. GAAP. All payments necessary to get an asset to its intended use, including its purchase price, sales tax, and shipping charges, are considered part of an asset's acquisition cost. Subsequent payments made for items other than routine maintenance that improve an asset's functionality, its profitability, or extend its useful life, would also be capitalized.

After the amount to be capitalized is determined, companies must follow a depreciation system called the **modified accelerated cost recovery system** (MACRS), a system that specifies the method and the rate at which various assets must be depreciated for tax purposes. The MACRS system provides for deductions that approximate the charges experienced under an accelerated method but with some qualifications. For tangible real property (i.e., buildings and real estate) and all intangibles, MACRS requires the use of the straight-line method. For all other tangible property, a manager can choose either an accelerated depreciation method (e.g., double declining balance) or straight-line.* Unlike U.S. GAAP where a manager is expected to consistently apply a depreciation method for assets of similar use, under tax law a company may elect either an accelerated or straight-line method for the tangible assets placed in service during a given year. Thus, the selected tax depreciation method may vary from year to year, forming the basis for effective tax planning.

The most significant difference between U.S. GAAP and tax accounting relates to the useful life restrictions placed on assets. Under GAAP, an asset's useful life is determined by management, whereas under tax accounting, it is predetermined by the IRS. Tables exist that categorize each asset type and give little room for deviation. Machinery and equipment, for instance, have a useful life for tax purposes of seven years. By way of contrast, under U.S. GAAP, managers may choose an expected life longer or even shorter than that used for tax purposes. As another example, under IRS rules, real property such as residential apartments or office buildings have lives ranging from 27.5 to 39 years, whereas for U.S. GAAP purposes, management may select a useful life longer or shorter than these periods.

* Because the former provides greater tax savings earlier, the accelerated method is virtually always selected. But, note that if expected tax rates for a company are lower in the earlier years of an asset's life, then a straight-line method may be preferred.

Accounting Policy Changes

Under the GAAP of most countries, companies are permitted to change the estimated useful life of a depreciable asset, its expected residual value, or the particular depreciation method in use. Frequent accounting policy changes, however, are normally not observed because it is well known that investment professionals regard any type of voluntary accounting policy change suspiciously, possibly indicating an attempt by management to "manage" reported earnings through the accounting policy change. Empirical evidence indicates that when a company's earnings increase as a consequence of an accounting policy change (such as a switch from double-declining-balance depreciation to straight-line depreciation), a firm's share price will tend to fall as the capital market speculates that such a change may forebode adverse future corporate news.[2] In essence, the capital market appears to "second-guess" the motivation behind voluntary corporate accounting policy changes. If the policy change results in an increase in accounting earnings, the market appears to infer that management is attempting to cover up poor expected future operating performance. If, on the other hand, an accounting policy change results in a decrease in accounting earnings, the market appears to infer that the firm's operating performance is expected to exceed management's projections, and consequently, the policy change is intended to "bank" some of the excess earnings for use in future periods (creating an earnings reserve to help meet future earnings' expectations).

There are three types of **accounting policy changes** permitted under GAAP: entity, estimate, and method. An **entity change** occurs when a company acquires, merges with, or divests itself of another company, such as a subsidiary or division. In this case, the consolidated reporting entity is changed, and consequently, changes in the reported consolidated financial results are clearly imminent. To help financial statement users understand the effects of an entity change, companies are required to include pro forma financial data in their annual report—that is, data "as if" the entity change had not occurred—to enable statement users to evaluate the consolidated entity's performance independent of the entity change. The presentation of such pro forma information is normally required for only one year following an entity change.

An **estimate change**, on the other hand, is a change in an existing accounting estimate used by a firm in the preparation of its financial statements. Common financial statement estimates include the estimated bad debt expense, estimated sales returns, the estimate of an asset's residual value, and the estimated useful life of an asset. When a firm changes one of its estimates, the financial impact of the estimate change on the firm's net earnings must be disclosed in the company's footnotes. Consider, for example, the case of **Valley National Gas, Inc.** The company changed its estimate of the remaining expected useful life of its plant and equipment from 12 to 30 years. The change had the effect of reducing the company's annual depreciation expense by $2.3 million and increasing the company's net income after tax by $1.3 million. The change in accounting estimate raised Valley National's earnings per share by $0.14 per share, or approximately 80 percent.

Estimate changes like Valley National's expected useful life change are executed on a **prospective basis**; that is, no attempt is made to restate the historical financial statements of the company for the financial effects of the change. For example, if after two years of depreciating a truck costing $30,000, with a residual value of $4,000 and expected useful life of five years using the straight-line method, it is determined that the truck will last eight years in total, no change would be required to the depreciation expense taken in years one and two. Those amounts would remain at $5,200 each year, or $10,400 for both years combined. Instead, the remaining depreciable cost of the truck of $15,600 ($26,000 − $10,400) will be spread over the new remaining expected useful life of six years (8 years − 2 years). Consequently, the new depreciation expense will be $2,600 per year ($15,600/6 years), as compared to the original annual depreciation expense of $5,200. After 8 years, the total depreciation taken would amount to $26,000 as required.

Finally, a **method change** occurs when, for instance, a firm changes its revenue recognition policy from completed contract to percentage-of-completion or when a company switches its inventory valuation approach from LIFO to FIFO. Unlike estimate changes which are executed on a **prospective basis**, accounting method changes are generally reported on a **retrospective basis**. Under retrospective restatement, a firm recalculates each affected account balance under the

> **Voluntary accounting policy changes** are characterized by some investment professionals as an "unintended signal" from the management of a company to the capital market regarding the company's future operating prospects. This characterization of accounting policy changes reflects what has become known as **signaling theory**.

---

[2] D. Dharam and B. Lev, "The Valuation of Consequences of Accounting Changes: A Multi-Year Examination," *Journal of Accounting, Auditing and Finance* (1993).

BUSINESS PERSPECTIVE

Long-Lived Fixed Asset Disclosures

Financial statement disclosures of the **H.J. Heinz Company** for its fixed assets are presented below. The data reveals that Heinz uses the straight-line method to depreciate these assets (see footnote information). Since land is generally not depreciated, the depreciation expense of $295.718 million reported in Heinz's 2012 consolidated financial statements relates only to the company's buildings and equipment. Is it possible to estimate the average age of Heinz's buildings and equipment and their expected useful lives?

The aggregate cost of Heinz's depreciable assets in 2012 is $5.185 billion ($1.009 billion + $4.176 billion). Since the company uses the straight-line method, if we assume a zero residual value, the expected useful life of these assets can be estimated by dividing their aggregate cost by the depreciation for 2012 ($5.185 billion/$295.718 million), yielding an average expected useful life of approximately 17.5 years. With respect to the remaining useful life of the company's buildings and equipment, dividing the accumulated depreciation balance at year-end 2012 by the assets' aggregate capitalized cost ($2.782 billion/$5.185 billion) indicates that approximately 53.7 percent of the assets' expected useful lives have been used up, leaving 46.3 percent, or approximately 8.1 years (46.3 percent $\times$ 17.5 years), of remaining useful life. Thus, we can conclude that at the current rate of depreciation, Heinz will not need to replace these long-lived productive assets for about eight years.

H.J. HEINZ COMPANY Consolidated Balance Sheet		
(in thousands)	**2012**	**2011**
Property, plant and equipment		
Land	$ 81,185	$ 85,457
Buildings and leasehold improvements	1,009,379	1,019,311
Equipment, furniture and other.	4,175,997	4,119,947
	5,266,561	5,224,715
Less: Accumulated depreciation	2,782,423	2,719,632
Total property, plant and equipment, net	$2,484,138	$2,505,083

Consolidated Statement of Cash Flow		
(in thousands)		
Operating activities section:		
Depreciation	$295,718	$255,227
Investing activities section:		
Capital expenditures.	(418,734)	(335,646)
Proceeds from disposals of property, plant and equipment.	9,817	13,158

Footnote Disclosure (Note #1):

Land, buildings and equipment are recorded at cost. For financial reporting purposes, depreciation is provided on the straight-line method over the estimated useful lives of the assets, which generally have the following ranges: buildings—40 years or less, machinery and equipment—15 years or less, computer software—3 to 7 years, and leasehold improvements—over the life of the lease, not to exceed 15 years. Accelerated depreciation methods are generally used for income tax purposes. Expenditures for new facilities and improvements that substantially extend the capacity or useful life of an asset are capitalized. Ordinary repairs and maintenance are expensed as incurred. When property is retired or otherwise disposed, the cost and related accumulated depreciation are removed from the accounts and any related gains or losses are included in income. The Company reviews property, plant and equipment, whenever circumstances change such that the recorded value of an asset may not be recoverable. Factors that may affect recoverability include changes in planned use of the asset and the closing of facilities. The Company's impairment review is based on an undiscounted cash flow analysis at the lowest level for which identifiable cash flows exist and are largely independent. When the carrying value of the asset exceeds the future undiscounted cash flows, an impairment is indicated and the asset is written down to its fair value.

new accounting policy for each affected fiscal period. Since it is impractical and expensive to issue restated financial statements for all prior periods impacted by a method change, the restated results are reported only for those fiscal years included in the latest annual report. A lump-sum restatement to reflect the prior-period financial effect of the method change, called the **cumulative prior period effect of an accounting policy change**, is then made to beginning retained earnings in the statement of shareholders' equity. The retrospective approach is not required when it is impracticable, as is sometimes the case in accounting policy changes from FIFO to LIFO or when the policy change involves the depreciation, amortization, or depletion of long-lived, non-financial assets. In this latter case, the policy change is accounted for as "a change in accounting estimate due to a change in accounting principle" using the prospective approach.

As noted previously, accounting estimate and method changes are viewed skeptically by the capital market. Available empirical evidence, for example, suggests that a company's share price will tend to fall when a firm changes from an income-reducing method to an income-enhancing method (such as a switch from double-declining-balance depreciation to straight-line depreciation). Similarly, when a firm changes from an income-enhancing method to an income-reducing method (such as a FIFO to LIFO change), the company's share price will tend to increase.

REVALUING LONG-LIVED ASSETS

Two constructs that underpin the accounting frameworks of most developed countries are the **historical cost concept** and **conservatism**. The former stipulates that the assets of a business should initially be valued at their prior acquisition cost, and the latter that the expected losses of a business should be recorded as soon as they are identified, while expected gains should not be recorded until they are actually realized. As a consequence of these concepts, accepted accounting practice in the United States, for example, requires downward revaluations of all assets (such as the lower-of-cost-or-market rule for inventory) whereas upward asset revaluations are only selectively permitted. As will be seen in Chapter 8, marketable securities are often carried at their current market value, and thus, may be revalued upward or downward to reflect changes in their fair market value. But, this asset group is an exception to the general rule under U.S. GAAP.

In the U.S. long-lived assets may only be written down in value. and this may occur in two situations. First, downward value adjustments are periodically recorded as depreciation expense to reflect the consumption of a long-lived asset associated with the ongoing operations of a business. Second, when the future earnings capacity of an asset declines unrelated to the depreciation process, the diminishment in value is recorded in the firm's income statement as an **impairment loss**. A depreciable long-lived asset is said to be "impaired" when the undiscounted sum of the future cash flow it is expected to help generate is less than the recorded balance sheet net book value. For assets subject to amortization, such as many intangibles, the relevant test for impairment is a comparison of the net book value to the asset's market value. In both cases, the write-down for impairment is made to the estimated market value of the asset, with a loss recorded on that period's income statement.

Often impairments occur when consumer demand for a product declines and the revenue-producing capacity of the long-lived assets used to produce the product, such as plant and equipment, cannot be utilized in the production of some alternative product. Consider the case of **AMR Corporation**, the parent company of American Airlines and American Eagle Airlines. Following the aircraft hijacking associated with the September 11, 2001, New York City terrorist attacks, AMR determined that the revenue-producing capacity of its fleet of aircraft had been impaired as consumer and business air travel declined significantly. Lacking an ability to convert its fleet of commercial aircraft to alternative revenue-producing activities, AMR took a $1.24 billion impairment charge at year-end 2001 and a second impairment charge of $0.46 billion at year-end 2002.

The use of annual asset revaluations in the U.K. and elsewhere reflects the commitment of standard-setters in these countries to the **market-value model of accounting**, in which all assets and liabilities are valued at their fair market value on the balance sheet.

In some countries, such as the United Kingdom, Australia, and New Zealand, when an asset appreciates in value, it is permissible to revalue the asset upward to reflect its appreciation in value. These upward revaluations may be executed annually and are reported in the financial statements by increasing the appreciated asset's balance sheet value and by increasing a shareholders' equity account called the **asset revaluation reserve** for the amount of the appreciation in asset value. The asset revaluation reserve is analogous to the "Unrealized gain/loss on available-for-sale securities" account found under U.S. GAAP that will be discussed in Chapter 8. These accounts represent unrealized wealth changes for a business and are reported as part of shareholders' equity on the balance sheet of the business because the wealth change has not yet been realized.

SALE OR RETIREMENT OF LONG-LIVED ASSETS

When long-lived assets are first acquired, they are recorded at their acquisition cost following the historical cost convention. These assets are then depreciated over their expected useful lives in order to properly match those past expenditures with the revenue that they contribute to a business. When an asset is eventually sold or retired, it is necessary to remove the asset's remaining book value from the company's books. Any difference between the proceeds from the sale of an asset and the remaining book value of the asset is recorded as a gain if the proceeds exceed the book value, or as a loss if the proceeds are less than the book value. To illustrate, assume that Savanna Corporation sells a truck and receives $15,000. Further, assume that the truck was originally purchased for $60,000 and has accumulated depreciation to date of $50,000. Since the proceeds of $15,000 exceed the asset's remaining book value of $10,000 ($60,000 − $50,000), Savanna will record a $5,000 gain on the sale. This is shown in spreadsheet format below. Observe that not only is the original cost of the asset removed from the balance sheet at the time of sale but so too is any accumulated depreciation related to the asset sold. These amounts are replaced with the cash received, and the net difference reflected as a gain to income (and retained earnings).

	Acquire Asset	Depreciate Asset	Sell Asset	End. Bal. (summary)	
Assets					
Cash........................	(60,000)		15,000	(45,000)	
::					
Property, plant and equipment.....	60,000		(60,000)	—	
Accumulated depreciation........		(50,000)	50,000	—	
Shareholders' Equity					
Retained earnings				(45,000)	
Depreciation expense..........		(50,000)			} Retained earnings = ($45,000)
Gain on sale			5,000		

There are a few other noteworthy points regarding the sale or retirement of a long-lived asset. First, in the case of an asset retirement, the accounting treatment is the same as if the asset were sold, but at a sales price of zero. Because nothing was received, the book value becomes the amount of loss recorded on the transaction. Second, when an asset is sold, the depreciation and amortization up to the sales date must be recorded. This has the effect of properly categorizing the use of the asset for a portion of the period it was in use, and to also not understate the gain or overstate the loss on the sale itself. Finally, remember that any gains and losses are reported on the income statement on a net basis because this activity is usually peripheral to the company's primary business operations. In other words, the company does not report cash received from an asset sale as revenue or the book value of the asset sold as an expense, but rather reports only a single number for income statement reporting purposes.

DISTORTION CAUSED BY AGING ASSETS

Since the book value of a long-lived asset declines as the asset ages, a reduction in book value can cause a distortion in some financial ratios when they are compared across time for a given company. For example, in cases when the productivity of an asset does not vary much during its early life, the return on assets (ROA) ratio will increase simply because the denominator of the ratio—total assets—decreases over time.

To illustrate, assume that Savanna Corporation purchases a single asset for $1,100,000 that is estimated to have a ten-year life and a salvage value of $100,000. Further assume that Savanna reports constant net income of $120,000 per year, including the annual $100,000 depreciation expense on its only asset. The return on assets ratio, defined as net income divided by ending total assets, will be 12 percent for the first year ($120,000/$1,000,000). After six years, however, the book value of the asset will have declined to $500,000 and Savanna's ROA will have climbed to 24 percent, twice as high as the first year. Recall that net income has remained constant and Savanna is still operating with the same asset. The doubling of

Savanna's ROA is simply a function of the reduction in book value resulting from the annual depreciation charge on the asset. Results such as this can provide perverse incentives to managers, preventing them from making needed capital investments to replace their aging assets. The following table illustrates how the aging of long-lived assets can distort such important performance metrics as Savanna's ROA ratio:

	Acquisition Cost	Year 1	Year 2	Year 3	Year 4	Year 5	Year 6
Book value	$1,100,000	$1,000,000	$900,000	$800,000	$700,000	$600,000	$500,000
Depreciation		100,000	100,000	100,000	100,000	100,000	100,000
Net income		120,000	120,000	120,000	120,000	120,000	120,000
ROA		12%	13%	15%	17%	20%	24%
Asset age (in years)		1	2	3	4	5	6

INTANGIBLE ASSETS

Intangible assets refer to those long-lived revenue-producing assets that lack physical substance. Over the last several decades, as the U.S. economy has shifted toward a much more technology-based economy and less so manufacturing-based, intangible assets have become a more significant part of company's balance sheets. Examples of common intangible assets include the intellectual property rights associated with copyrights and patents, goodwill associated with merger and acquisition transactions, and, under some circumstances, research and development costs and marketing costs.

Research and Development Costs, Patents, and Copyrights

The accounting treatment of research and development (R&D) costs is globally quite diverse. Under U.S. GAAP, all R&D is expensed when incurred. Under IFRS accounting, however, research costs are expensed, whereas development costs may be capitalized (i.e., recorded initially as an asset) when a commercially viable output is evident and market demand for the product is likely. Under Brazilian GAAP, on the other hand, all R&D is capitalized.

The conservative treatment of R&D under U.S. GAAP stems from the high degree of uncertainty regarding whether the expenditure will result in future cash inflows. Because this link cannot be directly established, conservatism requires that R&D expenditures be immediately expensed. This causes several notable problems for public companies with active R&D programs. In the pharmaceutical industry, for example, although billions of dollars may be spent on the development of a new drug, almost none of the massive R&D expenditure associated with new drug discoveries is capitalized to pharmaceutical company balance sheets since most (if not all) of the costs have been previously expensed as R&D. This accounting treatment results in very high profit margins when the drug is ultimately produced and sold, because most of the associated costs were expensed in prior periods. Using any given year of data, therefore, it is difficult to assess the true underlying profitability of a drug over its entire lifecycle. In contrast, when a drug company purchases the patent rights to a new drug from another company, that cost of the purchased patent is capitalized to the acquirer's balance sheet and subsequently amortized over the drug's expected useful life, but not in excess of the patent's remaining legal life. Amortization of copyrights, patents, and capitalized R&D universally follows the straight-line method.

Exceptions to the general practice of expensing all R&D under U.S. GAAP exist in the computer software industry for subsequent generations of a software program (such as Microsoft Vista) and in the oil and gas industry for exploration and development costs. The cost of second-and third-generation software enhancements and natural resource exploration/development costs may be capitalized to corporate balance sheets.

Goodwill

The concept of **goodwill** may mean different things in different parts of the world. In France, for instance, goodwill may refer to a firm's positive corporate image as evidenced by how desirable the firm's products are perceived to be by consumers (a positive brand image). As a consequence, under French GAAP, companies may capitalize internally generated goodwill on the balance sheet as an asset, along with an increase in a parallel shareholders' equity account called the asset revaluation reserve. In the United States and most

Intangible Asset Disclosures

Presented below are the income statement disclosures of the **Bristol-Myers Squibb Company (BMS)** for its intangible assets. Consistent with U.S. GAAP, BMS expenses its research and development costs, amounting to over $4 billion in 2011, on its income statement (see **bolded** area). As a consequence, the cost of any internally developed pharmaceutical products does not appear on BMS's balance sheet. However, for those drug-related intangible assets purchased from other pharmaceutical or biotechnology companies, the cost of the acquired asset less any amortization taken to date is capitalized on BMS's balance sheet. BMS's footnotes (not presented) reveal that the company amortizes its intangible assets on a straight-line basis over their expected useful lives, ranging from three to 17 years. In short, BMS's investment in pharmaceutical assets is materially understated on its balance sheet as only those drug-related intangible assets purchased from other entities are reported on its balance sheet under U.S. GAAP.

Intangible Asset Disclosures: BRISTOL-MYERS SQUIBB COMPANY Consolidated Statement of Earnings			
	Year Ended December 31,		
	2011	2010	2009
Net sales.	$21,244	$19,484	$18,808
Cost of products sold.	5,598	5,277	5,140
Marketing, selling and administrative.	4,203	3,686	3,946
Advertising and product promotion	957	977	1,136
Research and development.	**3,839**	**3,566**	**3,647**
Provision for restructuring	116	113	136
Litigation expense, net.	—	(19)	132
Equity in net income of affiliates.	(281)	(313)	(550)
Other (income)/expense.	(169)	126	(381)
Total expenses	14,263	13,413	13,206
Earnings from continuing operations before income taxes	6,981	6,071	5,602
Provision for income taxes.	1,721	1,558	1,182
Net earnings from continuing operations.	5,260	4,513	4,420
Discontinued operations:			
Earnings, net of taxes.	—	—	285
Gain on disposal, net of taxes	—	—	7,157
Net earnings from discontinued operations.	—	—	7,442
Net earnings	**$ 5,260**	**$ 4,513**	**$11,862**
Net earnings attributable to noncontrolling interest.	$ 1,551	$ 1,411	$ 1,250
Net earnings attributable to Bristol-Myers Squibb Company	3,709	3,102	10,612

other developed countries, however, goodwill only arises as a consequence of a merger or acquisition. When one corporate entity acquires a second corporate entity at a price exceeding the acquiree's fair market value of identifiable net assets, the excess of the total consideration paid over the acquiree's fair market value of net assets is capitalized to the acquiror's consolidated balance sheet as goodwill. (**Negative goodwill**, which is rare, arises when a firm acquires another corporate entity for less than the acquiree's reported book value. When negative goodwill occurs, it is recognized as extraordinary income on the acquiror's income statement.)

Acquisition goodwill is not subject to amortization, but instead, is evaluated annually for any impairment or diminishment in value. In the event of an impairment, a reduction in the goodwill account is recorded along with an "impairment loss" on the income statement. For example, as a consequence of the terrorist attacks of September 11, 2001, AMR Corporation determined that its entire $1.4 billion of goodwill relating to prior acquisitions had been impaired. Consequently, in 2002, AMR recorded a one-time, noncash goodwill impairment charge against net earnings of $988 million, net of tax benefits of $363 million, to write off all of the company's goodwill associated with prior acquisitions. We will have more to say about the measurement and initial recording of goodwill in Chapter 8.

The process to evaluate capitalized goodwill for value impairment under U.S. GAAP is a two-step procedure. In the first step, the amount of goodwill associated with each prior corporate acquisition is first identified. The current fair market value of the previously acquired corporate entity is then calculated and compared to the investor's book value of the acquired entity. In the event that the acquired entity's book value exceeds its current market value, preliminary evidence exists that a goodwill impairment has occurred. In the second step, the investor company estimates the value of the goodwill associated with each prior acquisition as if the acquired entity were acquired at its current market value. Any goodwill is then written down and a loss recorded if the new market value is less than the goodwill's book value. As a consequence of the two-step procedure followed to evaluate the current value of goodwill, goodwill impairment write-downs are rare and are likely to occur only in those cases in which an acquisition was materially overpriced or when an extraordinary externality impacts a business (such as AMR and the terrorist attack of 2001).

Marketing Costs

As a general rule, advertising and marketing costs are expensed when incurred under U.S. GAAP and IFRS. Similar to R&D accounting in the U.S., the conservative treatment of these operating expenditures stems from an inability to determine whether an advertising campaign has been successful, and if so, an inability to predict when the resulting increase in product sales associated with the advertising will occur. Thus, lacking reliable information about "when" and "how much," U.S. GAAP and the GAAP of most other countries recommend, but do not require, that advertising and marketing costs be expensed against operating revenue in the period in which the costs are incurred.

Occasionally, exceptions to this generally accepted practice may arise. Consider, for example, the case of **HCI Direct Inc.** HCI was engaged in the direct mail and internet marketing, manufacturing and distribution of hosiery products in Canada, the United States, and the United Kingdom. HCI capitalized its cost of soliciting customers to its balance sheet as an asset called "deferred customer acquisition costs." By year-end 2000, HCI had deferred customer acquisition costs totaling $47.5 million on its balance sheet, representing approximately 34 percent of its total assets. Including HCI's marketing expenditures in its income statement as an operating expense would have caused the company to report a loss of $54.3 million. In 2002, HCI filed for bankruptcy. In essence, the capitalization of its marketing costs allowed HCI to maintain a façade of corporate viability until 2002.

NATURAL RESOURCES

Natural resources include such assets as standing timber, oil and gas reserves, and iron ore, coal, gold, silver, and uranium mines. When these assets are purchased from other natural resource companies, they are reported on the balance sheet at their acquisition cost. Alternatively, when these assets are internally developed by a resource company, two valuation approaches are available: the **full cost method** and the **successful efforts method**. Under the full cost method, all costs associated with the exploration for, and development of, natural resource assets are capitalized to the natural resource account on the balance sheet. Under this method, even the costs of unsuccessful exploration activities are capitalized to the balance sheet under the philosophy that the identification of new natural resource reserves is a speculative activity involving some inherent failure. In contrast, under the successful efforts method, only the costs associated with successful exploration and development activity are capitalized to the balance sheet. The cost of any unsuccessful activity is immediately expensed against net income.

Both the full cost and the successful efforts methods are generally accepted, and thus, both are available for use by managers of natural resource companies. In practice, however, only small resource companies tend to use the full cost method, whereas larger companies tend to utilize the successful efforts method. Can you think of a reason why small firms would prefer to use the full cost method?[3]

To illustrate the difference between these two approaches, consider the case of an energy company involved in the exploration and development of oil and gas wells. Assume that the energy company owns the rights to explore for oil and gas on a given site and anticipates drilling four exploratory wells at a cost

---

[3] If you thought about the adverse effect on net income associated with the successful efforts method, you are correct. Small firms have difficulty raising exploration and development capital, and this fund-raising is made more difficult when a firm reports little or no earnings. The full cost method capitalizes all exploration and development costs, making it more likely that a small firm will be able to report positive earnings, thus increasing its chances of raising future exploration capital.

of $1 million each. The company's exploration program yielded three successful wells and one unsuccessful (or "dry") well. Under the full cost method, the entire $4 million spent on drilling the four exploratory wells would be capitalized to the company's balance sheet, whereas under the successful efforts method, only $3 million, representing the cost of the three successful wells, may be capitalized. The $1 million cost associated with the unsuccessful well would be expensed on the income statement.

For those amounts capitalized to the company's balance sheet, GAAP requires that those amounts be depleted over the resource's expected useful life. Unlike depreciation, there is only one generally accepted depletion approach, the units-of-production method. This method is procedurally equivalent to the units-of-production depreciation method utilized by some companies. Under this method, the first step is to estimate the number of units—barrels of oil, tons of ore, board feet of timber—likely to be produced by a well, mine, or tract of timber. Next, a depletion rate per unit is determined by dividing the capitalized resource cost by the asset's expected total output in barrels, tons, or board feet. For example, if the estimated number of tons of ore to be extracted from a mine is two million and the mine's original cost, less estimated residual value, is $10 million, the depletion rate per ton of extracted ore would be $5.00 ($10 million/2 million tons). If, during the first year of operations, 20,000 tons of ore are extracted, the depletion expense on the annual income statement would be $100,000 ($5 × 20,000 tons), and the book value of the mine on the balance sheet would be $9.9 million ($10 million − $100,000).

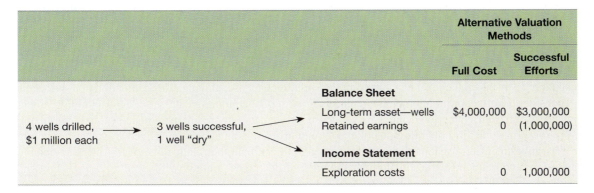

		Alternative Valuation Methods	
		Full Cost	**Successful Efforts**
4 wells drilled, $1 million each → 3 wells successful, 1 well "dry"	**Balance Sheet**		
	Long-term asset—wells	$4,000,000	$3,000,000
	Retained earnings	0	(1,000,000)
	Income Statement		
	Exploration costs	0	1,000,000

LONG-TERM FIXED ASSET ACCOUNTING UNDER INTERNATIONAL FINANCIAL REPORTING STANDARDS

The accounting for property, plant and equipment (PP&E) under U.S. GAAP and International Financial Reporting Standards (IFRS) differs in two significant ways. First, under U.S. GAAP, while PP&E must be written down if an asset's value becomes impaired, the balance sheet value of these assets may not be written up if their value appreciates above recorded book value. The test for impairment requires comparing the undiscounted cash flows generated (or saved) by the PP&E against its book value. Under IFRS, however, the book value of PP&E may be both written down and, if an election is made, written up. The test for impairment is more closely aligned with assessing the recoverable value of the PP&E against its book value rather than a focus on undiscounted cash flows. Allowing the write-up of PP&E reflects the IFRS's generally stronger grounding in the tenets of fair value accounting. A second important difference with U.S. GAAP is that IFRS permits the interest cost incurred during the construction of PP&E to be either capitalized to the balance sheet or expensed on the income statement. In the U.S. there is no such choice, as it is required that interest cost on self-constructed PP&E be capitalized and then subsequently depreciated. This latter IFRS/U.S. GAAP difference, among others, as of early 2013 is under review by the joint FASB/IASB convergence project.

The factors that influence depreciation method choice also frequently differ. For example, in Germany and Japan, income tax authorities consider the reported financial accounting book values in their calculations of a taxable base, causing most public companies to prefer accelerated methods for financial statement purposes. While in the United States it is necessary for public companies to maintain multiple sets of financial data (such as one set of accounting data for managers, one set for shareholders, and one set for taxation purposes), the governments of Germany and Japan use the audited financial reports distributed to shareholders as the basis for assessing income taxes. Thus, managers in these countries face a dilemma: Use straight-line depreciation to report higher profits to shareholders and pay higher income taxes, or use an accelerated method to reduce the tax burden but show lower profits to shareholders. Managers facing this dilemma tend to prefer the preservation of their operating cash flow by using accelerated depreciation methods that lower earnings, and hence, lower income tax payments.

The accounting for intangibles also differs internationally from U.S. GAAP. For instance, intangibles cannot be recognized under IFRS unless they meet the criteria of an asset, whether purchased or not. This means that all expenditures for such items as research or employee training are not capitalized. While this may seem more restrictive, differences appear the other way as well. Development costs, costs that in the U.S. sometimes are considered part of research and development, are capitalized under IFRS if economic benefits are expected to flow from the expenditures. With only a few exceptions, in the U.S. development costs are expensed immediately as part of research and development.

ANALYZING CAPITAL INVESTMENTS

The accrual basis of accounting is one of the principal constructs underlying the financial statements of going-concern businesses. For these companies, investment professionals, lenders, and shareholders expect to see recurring investments in new property, plant and equipment (PP&E) and intangible assets. If these types of capital investments were not routinely observed, there would exist concern regarding the sustainability of a firm's cash flow and operating earnings. The amount of a company's capital investment is readily identifiable from the investing activities section of the statement of cash flow. These cash outflows are usually segmented by financial statement users into two categories—maintenance capital expenditures, which are intended to maintain a business's existing productive capacity, and incremental capital expenditures, which are designed to increase a business's productive capacity. To help assess the relative amount of each type of capital investment, investment professionals usually estimate the amount of maintenance capital investment by the level of the current depreciation expense, although this estimation approach fails to consider the effect of inflation on the replacement cost of such long-lived assets. Any capital investment in excess of the current period depreciation expense is assumed to represent incremental capital investment.

For firms that do not follow a policy of regularly replacing their long-lived, revenue-producing assets, investment professionals require an approach to estimate the relative age of a firm's depreciable assets, and consequently, to estimate how soon a significant cash outlay will be required to finance the replacement of these assets. In this situation, the ratio of accumulated depreciation divided by gross property, plant and equipment is a good indicator of the percentage of a firm's capital assets that have been consumed by operations to date. Subtracting the percentage of consumed capital assets from 100 percent yields the relative percentage of the assets' remaining productive life. Finally, multiplying the percentage of estimated remaining useful life times the average life expectancy of a firm's capital assets yields an estimate of the number of years before a major capital asset refinancing will be required. See the H.J. Heinz Business Perspective discussion earlier in this chapter for an example calculation of this estimate.

$$\text{Estimated number of years remaining} = \left[100 - \left(\frac{\text{Accumulated depreciation}}{\text{Gross PPE}}\right)\right] \times \text{Average life expectancy}$$

Estimating the amount and timing of any major capital investments is important when estimating firm value. As we will see in Chapter 12, the calculation of firm value assumes regular capital asset replacement.

When conducting a due diligence review of the financial statement disclosures associated with a firm's capital investments, important issues to consider include not only the age of the existing capital investments, how soon the existing assets will need to be replaced, and whether a company follows a program of regular asset replacement, but it should also include a consideration of the following questions:

- What depreciation accounting policy has the company chosen to depreciate its capital assets (straight-line or double-declining balance) and is the method consistent with the industry standard? If not, what rationale does the firm offer for its use of the selected method?

- Has the company changed any of its depreciation or amortization policy components (such as the method of depreciation or amortization, the estimate of expected useful life, or the expected residual value), and if so, what explanation did the company offer for the policy change? Did the policy change bring the firm's accounting procedures more (or less) into compliance with the industry norm?

■ For companies that engage in significant research and development expenditures (such as pharmaceutical and technology companies), does the company have any unreported capital investments in such intangible assets as patents and copyrights?

■ Is the company capitalizing any expenditures that would more properly be accounted for as an operating expense, and if so, should the financial statements be restated for these amounts?

■ Is the company taking regular capital investment write-downs as "restructuring costs," perhaps to lower the annual depreciation expense and positively impact firm value?

■ Is the company capitalizing significant amounts of interest costs associated with the self-construction of capital assets? And if so, is a financial statement restatement appropriate to facilitate firm benchmarking?

The answers to most of the above questions provide financial statement users with evidence regarding the quality of a firm's earnings and assets—an important investigative topic when evaluating firm value. A firm that undertakes regular capital investment write-downs as a means to lower its recurring depreciation charge, or what has become known as "taking a bath," is generally considered by investment professionals to have a lower quality of earnings and assets than a firm that does not resort to such discretionary accounting (see In Practice 3.4 on page 99). Similarly, a company that does not inappropriately capitalize its operating expenses to the balance sheet as a capital investment is considered to have a higher quality of earnings and assets than a company that does (see the WorldCom Inc. Business Perspective on page 229). Where sufficient information exists regarding the financial statement impact of these discretionary accounting policy decisions—for example, the amount of capitalized interest is reported in the footnotes to the financial statements—it is possible for financial statement users to undertake a financial restatement to compensate for any questionable accounting policy decisions. Otherwise, financial statement users will need to consider alternative approaches to account for these risks when developing an assessment of firm value (such as increasing the discount rate used to discount a firm's future operating cash flows).

ETHICS PERSPECTIVE

Publicly-listed companies are under constant pressure to meet the earnings expectations of Wall Street analysts. It is often argued that this pressure induces some managers to focus too much attention on short-term corporate profitability. Many accounting policy choices can be made to enhance short-term profits at the expense of future profits. One such choice is the estimate of an asset's expected useful life. The longer the estimated useful life, the lower the current year depreciation, and hence, the higher current year profits will be. A longer estimated useful life, however, also means that the total depreciable cost of the asset will be spread over a greater number of years, thereby increasing future profits as well. Given the significant impact of this and other accounting estimates on reported corporate earnings, an integral part of the annual audit process for a firm involves a review of these estimates by a firm's independent auditor.

REVIEW PROBLEM

The Arcadia Company is contemplating a large capital investment of $32 million in new production-line equipment, which is expected to have a useful life of six years and a residual value of $2 million at retirement. The company's controller is uncertain whether the equipment should be depreciated using the straight-line method or the double-declining-balance method. The CEO suggested that a decision be made only after comparing the financial effects of the two methods.

Required

a. Prepare a depreciation schedule for The Arcadia Company for the new equipment assuming (1) use of the straight-line method and (2) use of the double-declining-balance method.

b. The Arcadia Company's net income exclusive of depreciation expense is expected to be $6 million each year for the next six years. Which depreciation method would you recommend to the CEO? Why?

The solution is on page 254.

EXECUTIVE SUMMARY

This chapter investigated the accounting for long-lived fixed, intangible, and natural resource assets. Various depreciation methods used to match the cost of these long-lived assets with the operating revenue they produce were explored: straight-line, double-declining-balance, and units-of-production. In addition, the issues of amortization of intangible assets and depletion of natural resources were examined. Finally, the accounting for asset sales, asset impairments and asset revaluations was also investigated.

As a validation of your understanding of the content of this chapter, you should now be able to:

■ Explain how the acquisition cost of a long-lived asset is determined.
■ Explain why the matching of depreciation, depletion, and amortization expense with operating revenue is important.
■ Explain how depreciation is calculated using the straight-line method, the units-of-production method, and the double-declining-balance method.
■ Explain what an asset impairment is and how such impairments are reflected in corporate financial statements.

In the next chapter, the accounting for intercorporate investments is considered, to include the equity method and consolidation accounting.

KEY CONCEPTS AND TERMS

Accelerated depreciation methods, 232
Accounting policy changes, 236
Accumulated depreciation, 231
Acquisition cost, 228
Amortization, 230
Asset revaluation reserve, 238
Betterment, 229
Capitalize, 228
Capitalized interest, 228
Conservatism, 238
Cumulative prior period effect of an accounting policy change, 238
Depletion, 230
Depreciable cost, 231
Depreciation, 230

Double-declining-balance, 232
Entity change, 236
Estimate change, 236
Fixed assets, 230
Fixed asset turnover ratio, 229
Full cost method, 242
Goodwill, 240
Half-year convention, 231
Historical cost concept, 238
Impairment loss, 238
Income smoothing, 234
Intangible assets, 230
Maintenance expenditures, 229
Market-value model of accounting, 238
Method change, 236

Modified accelerated cost recovery system, 235
Natural resources, 230
Negative goodwill, 241
Net book value, 231
Prospective basis, 236
Residual value, 231
Retrospective basis, 236
Signaling theory, 236
Straight-line method, 230
Successful efforts method, 242
Sum-of-the-years' digits method, 232
Units-of-production method, 233
Useful life, 230
Voluntary accounting policy changes, 236

QUESTIONS

Q7.1 **Brand Names. Williams-Sonoma, Inc.,** is a specialty retailer of products for the home. The retail segment of the company's business sells products through its retail concepts: Williams-Sonoma, Pottery Barn, Pottery Barn Kids, PBteen, West Elm, and Rejuvenation. The direct-to-customer segment sells similar products through its direct-mail catalogs and e-commerce websites. Williams-Sonoma stores offer a wide selection of culinary and serving equipment, including cookware, cookbooks, cutlery, informal dinnerware, glassware, and table linens. In addition, these stores carry a variety of quality foods, including a line of Williams-Sonoma food products, such as gourmet coffees and pasta sauces. The Williams-Sonoma brand name is well known in the United States. Discuss why the company doesn't report its brand name as an asset on its balance sheet. Is the company's brand name reflected anywhere in its financial statements?

Q7.2 **Depreciation, Depletion, and Amortization: The Matching Concept.** Depreciation, depletion, and amortization are allocation processes that distribute the acquisition cost of an asset to the many periods of the asset's expected useful life. Discuss how these processes reflect the matching principle and why they are important to the measurement of corporate profitability.

Q7.3 **Advertising Costs: Capitalize or Expense?** **The Johnson & Johnson Company** discloses in its annual report that "costs associated with advertising are expensed in the year incurred and are included in selling, marketing and administrative expenses" on the income statement. Discuss why the expensing of advertising costs is considered to be "best practice." Can an argument be made that advertising costs should be capitalized?

Q7.4 **Revaluation of Long-lived Assets.** The Thunderbird Corporation was founded in 1947 on a decommissioned military installation that had been purchased from the U.S. government for a price of $1. Today, that same land carries a fair market value of $70 million. Consistent with the historical cost principle, The Thunderbird Corporation continues to value the land at its original purchase price of $1 plus the cost of any improvements (such as roadways, lights, and drainage). Discuss the financial statement problems created by the historical cost principle for entities like The Thunderbird Corporation that have significant investments in long-lived appreciating assets (such as land). Should these companies be allowed to revalue these assets? Why? How would a land revaluation be reflected in the financial statements?

Q7.5 **Capitalization of Interest Costs and Earnings Quality.** Under U.S. GAAP, a company may capitalize any interest costs associated with borrowings used in the self-construction of a business asset. Any capitalized interest is added to the cost basis of the asset and then depreciated over the expected useful life of the asset. Some investment professionals question the appropriateness of interest capitalization, observing that the interest costs associated with general corporate borrowings are expensed when paid and are not capitalized. These professionals allege that interest capitalization is a form of rear-end loading of expenses, and when material in amount, draws into question the quality of a firm's reported earnings. Discuss the validity of these arguments.

Q7.6 **Changing Depreciation Methods.** **The Tomoegawa Paper Company Ltd.** (TPC) is a well-known public company headquartered in Tokyo, Japan. In TPC's annual report, the company revealed that it had changed its method of depreciating its fixed assets from the straight-line method to the declining-balance method. Discuss the various financial effects of this accounting policy change on TPC's financial statements. Why do you think the company made this voluntary accounting policy change?

Q7.7 **Changing the Estimated Useful Life of a Long-lived Asset.** **McCormick & Company** revealed in its annual report that it had changed the estimated useful life of certain capitalized software costs from five to eight years. Discuss the effect of this accounting policy change on the company's financial statements. How would you expect the capital markets to react to this voluntary accounting policy change?

Q7.8 **Exploration and Development Costs in the Natural Resource Industry.** Under U.S. GAAP, research and development costs are expensed as incurred; however, in the natural resource industry, the cost of finding and developing natural resources may be capitalized to the balance sheet under the full cost and successful efforts methods. Are these methods inconsistent with the general treatment of research and development costs under U.S. GAAP? If so, why? What explanation can you offer for this inconsistency in accounting treatment of similar outlays under U.S. GAAP?

Q7.9 **Asset Impairments.** Under U.S. GAAP, an asset that is "impaired" should be written down in value, with an equivalent loss taken on the income statement. Discuss how you would determine whether an asset's value was impaired or not.

Q7.10 **Capitalized Interest and Cash Flow.** Under U.S. GAAP, the interest cost associated with borrowings used in the self-construction of a business asset may be capitalized to the balance sheet as part of the self-constructed asset's cost basis. As a consequence, the cash outflows for capitalized interest reported as part of the cash flow from investing on the statement of cash flow. The interest cost associated with general corporate borrowings, however, is reported on the income statement, and thus, as part of the cash flow from operations. Discuss whether the practice of interest capitalization misstates a company's cash flow from operations.

Q7.11 **Depreciation, Depletion, Amortization, and Cash Flow.** Users of financial statements often describe depreciation expense, depletion expense, and amortization expense as "sources of operating cash flows." Discuss the accuracy of this assertion.

Q7.12 **R&D Failure and Share Prices.** On December 2, 2006, **Pfizer Inc.** announced that it was immediately discontinuing clinical trials of its Torcetrapib drug. Recent clinical results showed that patients taking the drug suffered a higher incident of heart attacks than patients taking a placebo. Pfizer reported that it had spent over $1 billion on the development of the drug, which had been expected to be a "blockbuster" for the pharmaceutical company. Pfizer's share price fell 11 percent, or nearly $2.90 per share, following the announcement. Discuss the financial statement impact of the announcement to discontinue clinical trials for Torcetrapib. Discuss why Pfizer's share price declined by 11 percent following the announcement. Discuss the impact of this decision on Pfizer's financial statements.

Q7.13 **(Ethics Perspective) Depreciation Policy Choices to Manage Short-term Profits.** Do you feel that there are any ethical issues involved when management decides to extend the depreciable life of its long-lived assets in order to increase the firm's current net income to a level that meets analysts' expectations?

Assignments with the logo in the margin are available in BusinessCourse.
See the Preface of the book for details.
CHECK FIGURE indicates that check figures are available on the book's Website.

EXERCISES

CHECK FIGURE ✓

E7.14   **Determining the Cost of an Asset.**   Omar Corporation paid $200,000 for a tract of land that had an old gas station on it. The gas station was demolished at a cost of $20,000 and a new warehouse was constructed on the site at a cost of $550,000. In addition, several other costs were incurred:

Legal fees (associated with the purchase of the land)	$35,000
Architect fees (associated with the new warehouse)	42,000
Interest on the construction loan (for the new warehouse)	18,000

What value should be assigned to (a) the tract of land and (b) the new warehouse? Why?

E7.15   **Determining the Cost of an Asset.**   Keystone, Inc., replaced its truck-and-dolley system of moving inventory around its plant with a computer-controlled conveyor system. The costs associated with this equipment replacement were as follows:

Purchase price of conveyor system	$1,200,000
Book value of truck-and-dolley system	40,000
Installation cost of new conveyor system	75,000

The truck-and-dolley system was sold for scrap for $60,000. What value should be capitalized to the balance sheet of Keystone, Inc., as the cost basis of the new conveyor system? Why?

E7.16   **Calculating Repair and Maintenance Expense.**   The Camelback Cement Company made the following expenditures relating to its plant and equipment:

- Overhauled several machines at an aggregate cost of $175,000 to improve the efficiency of the equipment over its remaining useful life.
- Replaced a broken driveshaft on a forklift at a cost of $30,000.
- Completed regularly scheduled repairs at a cost of $75,000.
- Installed a foam roof on the plant over the existing, but leaking, flat-rolled roof at a cost of $200,000.

What amount should be expensed as repairs and maintenance? Why?

✓ **E7.17**   **Computing Depreciation Expense.**   Equipment costing $290,000, with an expected scrap value of $30,000 and an estimated useful life of five years, was purchased on January 1, 2012. Calculate the depreciation expense for years 2012 to 2016 using (a) the straight-line method and (b) the double-declining-balance method. Which method would you prefer to use for (a) income tax purposes and (b) financial reporting purposes? Why?

✓ **E7.18**   **Full Cost versus Successful Efforts Method.**   During 2012, The Alberta Oil & Gas Company began an exploration project in Montana. The company had paid $500,000 for the drilling rights on a tract of 500 acres of land. The company then spent another $40,000 building roads and containment ponds. The project called for eight exploratory wells to be drilled at an expected cost of $100,000 per well. The first six wells drilled were found to be "dry" (lacking commercially viable quantities of oil or gas); however, both the seventh and eighth wells drilled contained commercially viable quantities of oil condensate. Consequently, two additional development wells were drilled at a cost of $120,000 per well. Calculate the capitalized cost of Alberta's oil reserves under (a) the full cost method and (b) the successful efforts method. Which method should the company adopt for income tax reporting purposes? Which method should the company use when reporting its financial results to its shareholders? Why?

✓ **E7.19**   **Calculating Accelerated Depreciation.**   Equipment costing $640,000, with an expected useful life of twelve years and an expected salvage value of $20,000, was purchased at the beginning of the year. Calculate the depreciation expense for the first five years using (a) the sum-of-the-years' digits method and (b) the double-declining-balance method. Which method would you prefer to use for (a) income tax purposes and (b) financial reporting purposes? Why?

✓ **E7.20**   **Calculating Units-of-Production Depreciation.**   Swift Trucking Company purchased a long-haul tractor-trailer for $400,000 at the beginning of the year. The expected useful life of the tractor-trailer rig was eight years or 500,000 miles. Salvage value was estimated to be $40,000. During the first five years of use, the rig logged the following usage in miles:

Year 1	80,000 miles
Year 2	75,000 miles
Year 3	80,000 miles
Year 4	76,000 miles
Year 5	60,000 miles
Total	371,000 miles

Calculate the depreciation expense to be taken on the tractor-trailer for each year using (a) the units-of-production method and (b) the straight-line method. Which method gives you higher total depreciation charges over the five-year period?

E7.21 **Analyzing Noncurrent Asset Disclosures.**   The following are financial data taken from the annual report of Pfizer, Inc:

CHECK FIGURE

(amounts in millions)	Year 1	Year 2
Net sales.	$51,298	$52,516
Gross property, plant and equipment.	26,617	26,919
Accumulated depreciation	(9,527)	(8,534)
Intangible assets (net).	27,786	33,251

Calculate the following ratios for Year 1 and Year 2: intangible asset turnover, fixed asset turnover, accumulated depreciation divided by gross fixed assets. What do the trends in these ratios reveal about Pfizer?

E7.22 **Calculating the Depletion Expense.**   Herberger Oil & Gas Company paid $10 million for the drilling rights to a 1,000 acre tract of land near Midland, Texas. On the basis of several exploratory wells that had cost an aggregate of $400,000 to drill, petroleum engineers estimated that the tract of land might contain as much as 500,000 barrels of oil. Four additional development wells were drilled at a cost of approximately $200,000 each. Calculate the depletion expense for the first year assuming that 100,000 barrels are extracted. Calculate the depletion expense for the second year assuming that 150,000 barrels are extracted. What is the cost basis of the remaining reserves at the end of the second year?

E7.23 **Intangible Assets.**   Intelligencia Inc. was incorporated as a research and development company in the biotechnology industry. The company incurred the following costs relating to various intangible assets:

1. The company incurred $125,000 in organization costs associated with its incorporation.
2. During the year, the company completed work on a research project and filed for a patent. The research work had cost $450,000 and the patent filing cost $30,000.
3. Shortly after receiving the patent, it was challenged in court by another biotechnology company. Intelligencia won the case, protecting its patent, but incurred legal fees of $200,000.
4. The company purchased a patent from another biotechnology company for $700,000. Unfortunately, this patent was also challenged in court and Intelligencia lost the case, incurring legal fees of $175,000.

Should the above costs be capitalized to the balance sheet as an intangible asset or expensed on the income statement? Why or why not?

E7.24 **Changing the Estimated Life of a Depreciable Asset.**   At the beginning of the year, The Claremont Company purchased a 100-ton press for $750,000. The equipment had an estimated useful life of ten years and a salvage value of $30,000. The company decided to depreciate this equipment using the straight-line method. After eight years of trouble-free use, The Claremont Company concluded that it would be able to utilize the equipment for up to a total of 14 years; and consequently, at the end of year eight, changed its estimate of the equipment's expected life to 14 years, adding four more years to the asset's remaining useful life. Calculate the depreciation expense on the equipment in years eight and nine.

CHECK FIGURE

PROBLEMS

P7.25 **Calculating Depreciation.**   The Miller Company purchased a new headquarters building on January 1 at a cost of $40 million. The building is expected to last 20 years, at which time its residual value is expected to be $5 million.

Required

Calculate the depreciation expense for each of the first three years on the new headquarters building using each of the following methods:

1. Straight-line
2. Double-declining-balance

Does the selection of a depreciation method affect a company's cash flow from operations? In what ways?

 P7.26 **Capitalize versus Expense.** On September 1, 2003, reported that **China Unicom**, a leading Chinese telecom company, had capitalized to its balance sheet the cost of customer handset subsidies (the difference between the cost of the handset and the price charged to retain customers). Observers suggested that the subsidies should have been charged against income at the time the customer purchased the handset rather than capitalized to the company's balance sheet.

Required

If China Unicom switched from capitalizing and amortizing handset subsidies to immediately expensing them (for reporting to shareholders only), indicate how the following financial statement items would be affected:

1. Operating expenses   4. Liabilities
2. Assets   5. Operating revenue
3. Cash flow from operations

P7.27 **Intangible Assets.** Global Music Enterprises, Inc., had a balance sheet loaded with intangible assets—copyrights on music, goodwill from various prior acquisitions, and internet customer lists purchased from other online music retailers. During the year, several accounting policy decisions were required regarding various intangible asset-related expenditures.

Required

What accounting policy should be adopted for the following expenditures? Why?

1. Legal fees incurred while successfully defending a copyrighted song.
2. Advertising costs intended to create customer goodwill.
3. Purchase of online customer lists from Amazon.com.
4. Legal fees incurred to successfully defend Global's CEO from a sexual harassment lawsuit.
5. Legal fees incurred to unsuccessfully defend a copyrighted song and lyrics.

P7.28 **Betterment versus Maintenance Expenditures.** During the year, Graham International made the following expenditures relating to plant, machinery, and equipment:

- Completed regularly scheduled repairs at a cost of $250,000.
- Overhauled several stamping machines at a cost of $500,000 to improve production efficiency.
- Replaced a broken cooling pump on a 100-ton press at a cost of $25,000.

Required

Identify which expenditures should be expensed as a maintenance expense or capitalized as a betterment outlay.

CHECK FIGURE **P7.29** **Depletion Expense.** In 2011, Ottawa Oil Corporation paid $40 million for a partial interest in a Canadian oil field with proven reserves. The company's share of the future production was capped at eight million barrels.

Required

1. Assuming that the oil field attains its expected future output, calculate Ottawa's depletion charge per barrel.
2. If in 2012, Ottawa's share of the field's total production amounts to two million barrels, what is the firm's depletion expense for 2012?
3. Go to the following Internet website www.irs.gov and locate Publication 535 "Business Expenses." Section 9 of this publication is entitled "Depletion." Read this section to determine how oil and gas companies in the United States calculate their depletion expense for U.S. income tax purposes. How does this tax practice compare to U.S. GAAP?

 P7.30 **Estimating Depreciation Expense and Book Value.** Equipment costing $29,000, with a scrap value of $5,000 was purchased on January 1, by Global Communications, Inc. The estimated useful life of the equipment was four years and it was expected to generate 80,000 finished units of production. Units actually produced were 14,000 in Year 1 and 20,000 in Year 2.

Required

Complete the following table. Can the selection of a depreciation method affect a company's asset replacement policy (i.e., the timing of its asset replacement)? If so, how?

Depreciation Method	Depreciation Expense		Net Book Value	
	Year 1	Year 2	Year 1 year-end	Year 2 year-end
Straight-line	_____	_____	_____	_____
Double-declining-balance	_____	_____	_____	_____
Units-of-production	_____	_____	_____	_____

P7.31 **Successful Efforts versus Full Cost Method.** Barrett Oil and Gas Company was about to embark on a 50-well exploration program in Texas and Louisiana. The CEO estimated that the average cost to drill a well would run $800,000 per well, with a resulting success ratio of 60 percent (30 wells were expected to yield commercially viable quantities of oil while 20 wells were expected to be commercially unproductive). In aggregate, the CEO estimated that the 30 successful wells would yield ten million barrels of oil, to be extracted at the following rates.

Year	Production (in barrels)	Estimated Per Barrel	
		Selling Price	Lifting Cost
2011	1,000,000	$30	$5
2012	1,500,000	30	5
2013	1,500,000	35	6
2014	2,500,000	40	7
2015	3,500,000	45	8
	10,000,000		

The CEO of Barrett Oil and Gas Company was concerned about how the accounting for the exploration project would affect the firm's overall reported results. The exploration program would be financed with a $40 million bank loan at an interest rate of 10 percent per year on the balance of the loan outstanding as of the beginning of the year. The loan would be repaid in four installments of $10 million per year, with the first payment occurring on December 31, 2012.

Required

Assume that this is the company's only exploration project. Prepare the firm's income statements and balance sheets for 2011 through 2015 assuming the use of:

1. The full cost method
2. The successful efforts method

P7.32 **Impairment of Long-Lived Assets: Goodwill.** Dean Foods Company is a food and beverage company that operates in two segments, Fresh Diary Direct and WhiteWave-Alpro. The company was founded in 1925 and is headquartered in Dallas, Texas. Consistent with U.S. GAAP, Dean Foods performed an impairment test of its existing goodwill at year-end 2011 and, on the basis of this test, concluded that:

> "Based on the results of analysis, we recorded a $2.1 billion, non-cash charge ($1.6 billion net of tax), during 2011. This impairment charge did not impact our operations, compliance with our debt covenants or our cash flows." They concluded the implied fair value of our Fresh Dairy Direct goodwill was $87 million.

Required

1. What are the financial effects on Dean Food's financial statements (income statement, balance sheet, statement of cash flow) associated with its goodwill impairment write-off?
2. Assume that Dean Food had substantial borrowings secured by its U.S. assets and under these credit agreements, the company is subject to a number of debt covenants that required a certain level of debt to total assets. How would the goodwill impairment and related write-off affect the company's ability to meet its debt covenants?

P7.33 **Intangible Assets: Deferred Subscriber Acquisition Costs.** **The ADT Corporation** provides electronic security, interactive home and business automation, and related monitoring services in the United States and Canada. Clients typically lease the monitoring system and ADT retains ownership of the security system. The company reports:

> "For transactions in which the Company retains ownership of the security system asset, referred to as subscriber system assets, non-refundable fees (referred to as deferred subscriber acquisition revenue) received in connection with the initiation of a monitoring contract, along with associated direct and incremental selling costs (referred to as deferred subscriber acquisition costs), are deferred and amortized over the estimated life of the customer relationship."

Selected information from ADT's 2012 annual report is presented below:

THE ADT CORPORATION
Consolidated Balance Sheets
As of Sept. 28, 2012 and September 30, 2011

(in millions)	2012	2011
Deferred subscriber acquisition costs, net.	$ 464	$ 417
Total assets.	9,260	8,739

THE ADT CORPORATION
Consolidated Statements of Operations
For the Years Ended Sept. 28, 2012 and September 30, 2011

(in millions)	2012	2011
Revenue	$3,228	$3,110
Cost of revenue	1,374	1,341
Selling, general, and administrative expenses	1,125	1,076
Other operating expenses	7	0
Operating income	722	693
Interest income.	1	1
Interest expense.	(93)	(90)
Income before taxes	630	604
Income tax expense	(236)	(228)
Net income	$ 394	$ 376

THE ADT CORPORATION
Consolidated Statements of Cash Flows
For the Years Ended Sept. 28, 2012 and September 30, 2011

(in millions)	2012	2011
Cash flows from operating activities:		
Net income.	$ 394	$ 376
Amortization of deferred subscriber acquisition costs.	111	102
Deferred subscriber acquisition costs	(147)	(131)
Net cash provided by operating activities	1,493	1,439

Required
1. How much did ADT record as the expenditure of cash for deferred subscriber acquisition costs in 2012?
2. How much would the company's total assets be at September 28, 2012, if the company had always expensed its subscriber acquisition costs?
3. If ADT had always expensed its expenditures for subscriber acquisition costs in its financial statements to shareholders, would the cash flow from operations be higher, the same, or lower? Why?
4. What would the company's income before income taxes be in 2012 if ADT had always expensed its expenditures for subscriber acquisition costs?

CORPORATE ANALYSIS

CA7.34 **The Procter & Gamble Company.**   The 2012 annual report of **The Procter & Gamble Company** (P&G) is available at http://annualreport.pg.com/annualreport2012/index.shtml . After reviewing P&G's annual report, respond to the following questions:

   a.   What percentage of P&G's total assets is represented by its net property, plant and equipment? What percentage of P&G's total assets is represented by its net goodwill and other intangible assets? Which category of noncurrent assets is larger? Calculate the capital intensity ratio. (Recall that in Chapter Four, the capital intensity ratio was defined as the sum of fixed assets plus intangible assets divided by total assets.) Is P&G a capital-intensive company?

   b.   Calculate the fixed asset turnover ratio and the intangible asset turnover ratio. What do these ratios tell you about P&G's operations?

   c.   How much depreciation expense and amortization expense was taken in 2011 and 2012? What depreciation method does P&G use? What is the relative age of P&G's fixed assets (what percentage of the assets has been used up and what percentage remains available)?

   d.   How much in impairment charges related to goodwill and indefinite lived intangible assets did P&G incur in 2012 and 2011?

CA7.35 **Internet-based Analysis.**   Consider a publicly-held company whose products you are familiar with. Some examples might include:

Company	Product	Corporate Website
• **Johnson & Johnson Company**........	• Band-Aids	• www.jnj.com
• **Microsoft Corporation**...............	• Windows XP software	• www.microsoft.com
• **Nokia Corporation**	• Cellular phones	• www.nokia.com
• **Intel Corporation**	• Pentium processors	• www.intel.com
• **Kimberly-Clark Corporation**..........	• Kleenex	• www.kimberly-clark.com

Access the company's public website and search for its most recent annual report. (Note: Some companies provide access to their financial data through an "investor relations" link, while others provide a direct link to their "annual reports.") After locating your company's most recent annual report, open the file and review its contents. After reviewing the annual report for your selected company, prepare answers to the following questions:

   a.   How does the company depreciate its property, plant and equipment (P, P&E)? Calculate the ratio of the accumulated depreciation divided by gross P, P&E for the past two years. How old are the company's P, P&E assets? What percentage of their useful life remains?

   b.   Does the company have any intangible assets? If so, what are they? What percentage of total assets do they represent?

   c.   Did the company invest in new P, P&E or new intangible assets during the past two years? If so, in what amount?

   d.   Calculate the total asset turnover, the P, P&E turnover, and the intangible asset turnover for each of the past two years. Are these turnover ratios increasing or decreasing? What might explain these trends?

CA7.36 **IFRS Financial Statements.**   The 2012 financial statements of **LVMH Moet Hennessey-Louis Vuitton S.A.** are presented in Appendix C of this book. LVMH is a Paris-based holding company and one of the world's largest and best-known luxury goods companies. As a member-nation, French companies are required to prepare their consolidated (group) financial statements using International Financial Reporting Standards (IFRS). In LVMH's Notes to the Consolidated Financial Statements (not presented in Appendix C), the company discloses its accounting policy regarding brand and trade names, an important asset for a luxury goods company:

> Only acquired brands and trade names that are well known and individually identifiable are recorded as assets at their values calculated on their dates of acquisition. Costs incurred in creating a new brand or developing an existing brand are expensed. Brands, trade names and other intangible assets with finite useful lives are amortized over their useful lives. Any impairment expense of brands and trade names and , in some cases, amortization expense, are recognized within "Other operating income and expenses".

Consider the following questions:
  a. Describe the key components of LVMH's accounting policy for brand names.
  b. How might LVMH determine whether a brand name had a finite or infinite useful life?

SOLUTION TO REVIEW PROBLEM

Solution
a. Depreciation schedule

	Straight-Line Method	Double-Declining-Balance Method
Year 1	$ 5,000,000	$10,666,667
Year 2	5,000,000	7,111,111
Year 3	5,000,000	4,740,741
Year 4	5,000,000	3,160,494
Year 5	5,000,000	2,160,494
Year 6	5,000,000	2,160,493
Total	$30,000,000	$30,000,000
Book value	$ 2,000,000	$ 2,000,000

b. If The Arcadia Company earns net income, exclusive of depreciation expense, of $6 million per year, its net income after depreciation expense but before income taxes would be as follows:

	Straight-Line Method	Double-Declining-Balance Method
Year 1	$1,000,000	$(4,666,667)
Year 2	1,000,000	(1,111,111)
Year 3	1,000,000	1,259,259
Year 4	1,000,000	2,839,506
Year 5	1,000,000	3,839,506
Year 6	1,000,000	3,839,507
Total	$6,000,000	$ 6,000,000

The analysis reveals that The Arcadia Company will report substantial losses in Years 1 and 2 under the double-declining-balance method, turning profitable in Year 3 and thereafter, effectively rear-end loading the firm's profitability into Year 3 through Year 6. The straight-line method, however, enables the company to report a smooth earnings stream throughout the six-year period. Unless the CEO has some reason to rear-end load the company's earnings, perhaps to create an earnings reserve in anticipation of lower future operating results, the CEO is likely to prefer the stable earnings under the straight-line method for the company's financial reports to shareholders.

When you complete this chapter you should be able to:

1. Explain why companies acquire ownership interests in other businesses.

2. Describe how to account for investments in debt and equity securities, including the application of the equity method and consolidation accounting.

3. Explain the accounting for joint ventures and special purposes entities.

4. Describe the foreign currency issues that arise with investments in foreign companies.

Investing In
Other Entities

The acquisition of the corporate equity of one company by another is usually strategic in purpose and can be very complex. **BHP Billiton**'s (BHP) proposed 2010 acquisition of **Potash Corp.** of Saskatchewan, Canada, is one example. BHP is the

BHP BILLITON

world's largest natural resources company, and its many diversified businesses produce aluminum, copper, coal, iron ore, gold, lead, silver, and diamonds. Its operations span the globe, with the heaviest concentration in Asia and Europe. The company has an employee and contractor base totaling about 100,000 individuals. Revenues exceed $50 billion, and its market capitalization approximates $150 billion.

In late 2010, BHP launched a $40 billion hostile takeover bid for Potash, a premium of 20 percent over Potash's then market capitalization. Potash was the world's largest fertilizer company and the largest producer of potash, with an estimated 11 percent of global production and 20 percent of global capacity. The acquisition was squarely aimed at meeting BHP's strategy of becoming a leading miner of potash, a complement to its existing natural resource portfolio. The deal would involve a buyout of Potash shareholders, and to finance the acquisition, BHP planned to use cash plus debt. Analysts expected approximately $30 billion of new debt would need to be issued; they further expected goodwill on BHP's balance sheet to increase by over $20 billion on a post-acquisition basis. The deal was expected to be immediately accretive to BHP's earnings per share.

The BHP offer, however, was quickly rejected by the Potash board of directors as both too low and not in the best interest of the company's numerous stakeholders, especially its Canadian investors. Because so many Canadian citizens would be affected by the purchase, the Canadian government noted that any final approval of the deal must not result in any major economic shifts in the region. The line of those opposed to the deal did not stop there. Other stakeholders opposed to the acquisition included the Chinese government, whose concern centered around the acquisition's impact on the pricing and world-wide supply of fertilizers, a critical element of the agricultural growth of that country.

Rejection of the initial offer did not deter BHP's management. The company commenced a newspaper advertisement campaign targeting existing Potash shareholders and the community, and eventually raised its offer price. To assuage the fears of the Canadian people, BHP hailed the numerous benefits of the acquisition. The company publicly announced it was committed to being a strong corporate citizen in Saskatchewan. It would keep its President and management in the region, maintain current employment levels, and proposed a Canadian nominee to stand for election to the BHP board. Further, any planned capital programs of Potash would be maintained, and any spending commitments on community programs would be honored. In the end BHP was unsuccessful. The Canadian government ultimately blocked the deal, citing that it would not be a "net benefit" for Canada. Even though BHP was within its rights to fight this decision, it abandoned the deal.

In this chapter, the investment decisions of companies like BHP are examined in closer detail. Specifically, we will see that companies invest in other companies for a variety of reasons, and from those diverse reasons comes financial reporting that is diverse in its application. Further, we will see that the accounting for investments is driven largely by the size of the ownership interest acquired.

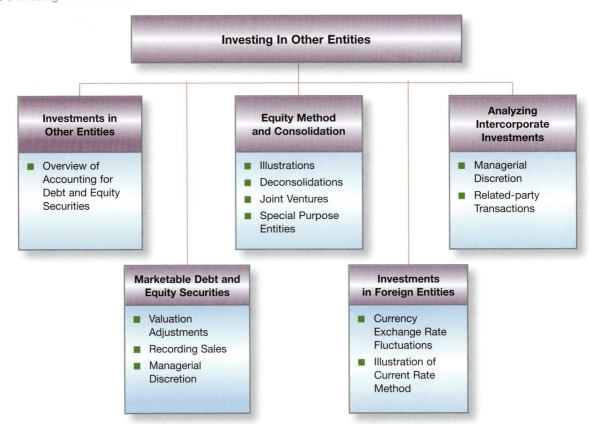

INVESTMENTS IN OTHER ENTITIES

Transactions such as BHP's proposed acquisition of Potash, even though unsuccessful, are a regular part of corporate life as companies frequently buy and sell the shares of other businesses. The amount of equity shares acquired varies from relatively small amounts to 100 percent of the outstanding shares, as in the case of the proposed Potash takeover. When a company acquires a relatively small percentage of the outstanding shares of another entity (defined as less than 20 percent under U.S. GAAP guidelines), it usually indicates an expectation that the investment will provide an acceptable rate of return on idle corporate funds, and also that the investor-company does not intend to take an active role in the management and operations of the investee.

When a company acquires a significant stake in another company—ownership interests of 20 percent or more—it is usually because the investor-company desires to take an active and influential role in the investee's business activities. Gaining control of the business affairs of another company may be of considerable economic value to an investor. It may enable an investor to generate incremental operating profit from cost savings and/or operating revenue enhancements. Operating cost/revenue synergies may be created by eliminating excess productive capacity, dropping unprofitable products, or generating incremental product sales. The investment might, for instance, be in a company that is vertically integrated within a product's manufacturing process, such as a supplier, thus enabling more control over the investor's value chain. An investor-company may also acquire a significant stake in an investee in order to oust an inefficient management team or because the investor believes that the investee's shares are temporarily undervalued and present an opportunity to profit from the capital market mispricing of the investee's shares. The combination of two companies may also be justified on financing grounds—one or both firms may have unused debt capacity capable of providing low-cost financing for growth of the combined entity. Finally, an investor-company may acquire shares in an investee to gain access to various skills, technology, or resources that would be more expensive to obtain in other ways.

Overview of Accounting for Debt and Equity Securities

The accounting for corporate investments can be quite diverse as there are a variety of different accounting methods that may be required. The selection of which method to use depends on (i) the degree of ownership control obtained in the target company, and, (ii) when an investment is for less than 20 percent voting control, the intent of the company making the investment. Exhibit 8.1 summarizes the general considerations that determine which investment accounting to apply. The last line of the exhibit illustrates there are potentially five different accounting methods that may come into play. It further identifies the factors that must be considered when selecting the appropriate accounting, such as whether the investment involves debt or equity, the percent of voting control acquired, and the investment "intent" of the investor-company.

EXHIBIT 8.1 Determining Which Investment Accounting Method to Apply

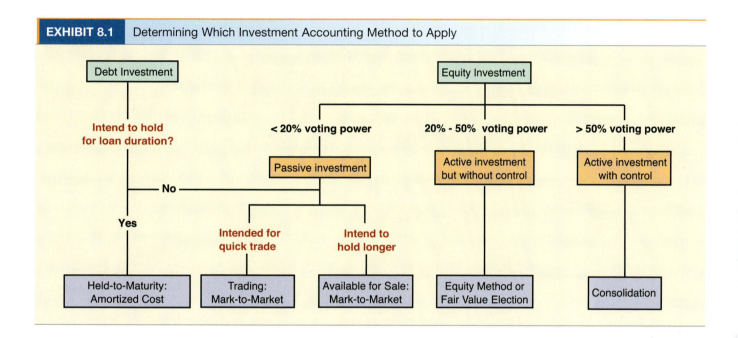

Exhibit 8.2 summarizes the three broad categories of investment categories. These are defined by the ownership level acquired in the investee-company and the amount of control assumed. The first category is for investments in which the ownership level is relatively small—less than 20 percent of the outstanding voting shares— and are referred to as **marketable securities**. These securities can take the form of debt securities (e.g., corporate bonds) or equity securities (e.g., preferred stock or common stock). Provided that a ready market exists for trading these securities—such as the New York Stock Exchange or the NASDAQ—there exists a special accounting treatment known as **mark-to-market accounting**. This is quite different from the accounting approach taken for most other assets on the balance sheet. For most assets, GAAP requires that a company carry its assets at their historical cost, with reductions for such issues as value impairments and depreciation. The general argument in these cases is that while the resulting historical cost number may lack a degree of relevance, it is reliably measured. Mark-to-market accounting is an exception to this generally accepted practice and allows assets to be written up or down to their current market value. This accounting is permitted because a ready resale market exists such that an investment's current value can be reliably ascertained.

Marketable debt and equity securities that are held with the intent to be sold at any time to take advantage of price changes are called **trading securities**. As summarized in Exhibit 8.2, these investments are valued at their market value on the balance sheet, with any unrealized gain (loss) in a security's value included directly in the investor's net income. An **unrealized gain (loss)** is an increase (decrease) in the value of an asset that has not yet been sold. When the asset is sold, the gain (loss) is said to be "realized."

Alternatively, investments in debt and equity securities that management intends to hold for the long term but which, under the right circumstances management might liquidate are referred to as **available-for-sale securities**. As described in Exhibit 8.2, these investments are also valued on the balance sheet at their market value but for these investments, any unrealized gain (loss) in value is reported in a separate shareholders' equity account on the balance sheet. For companies using U.S. GAAP, the unrealized gains (losses) on available-for-sale securities are considered to be part of **Accumulated Other Comprehensive Income**, often called "AOCI" for short, a category of yet-to-be-realized wealth increases or decreases disclosed in the shareholders' equity section of the balance sheet. We will have more to say about Accumulated Other Comprehensive Income in Chapter 11.

EXHIBIT 8.2	Overview of Accounting for Debt and Equity Securities	
Ownership Interest	**Equity Securities**	**Debt Securities**
Less than 20 percent	**Marketable Equity Securities** **Trading securities** • Valued at market value on balance sheet • Unrealized gain/loss included in income • Dividends included in income **Available-for-sale** • Valued at market value on balance sheet • Unrealized gain/loss included as a component of shareholders' equity on balance sheet • Dividends included in income	**Marketable Debt Securities** **Trading securities** • Valued at market value on balance sheet • Unrealized gain/loss included in income • Interest revenue included in income **Available-for-sale** • Valued at market value on balance sheet • Unrealized gain/loss included as a component of shareholders' equity on balance sheet • Interest revenue included in income
Between 20 and 50 percent	**Equity Method** • Investment in Equity Affiliate valued at cost plus share of earnings less share of dividends on balance sheet • Proportionate share of affiliate's earnings included in income of investor-company	

Greater than 50 percent	**Consolidation Accounting**
	• On parent-company books, investment is accounted for using the equity method.
	• Upon consolidation:
	  • Assets and liabilities of subsidiary are added to those of parent, with Investment in Equity Affiliate eliminated and noncontrolling interest shown on balance sheet
	  • Transactions between parent and subsidiary are netted out
	  • Revenue and expenses of subsidiary are combined with those of parent-company, with noncontrolling interest in subsidiary's income deducted from consolidated earnings
		Held-to-maturity
		• Valued at amortized cost on balance sheet
		• Interest revenue included in income

Debt securities that management intends to hold until maturity are referred to as **held-to-maturity debt securities**. These investments are valued at their **amortized cost**—that is, the original purchase price of the debt plus (minus) the amortization of any purchase discount (premium). We will have more to say about the amortization of purchase discounts (premiums) on debt instruments in Chapter 9.

The second investment category summarized in Exhibit 8.2 is for investments in equity securities wherein the investor-company can exercise significant influence over an investee-company's operating policies but that are not sufficiently large to represent voting control—between 20 and 50 percent of the outstanding voting shares. Investments in this category are by definition equity investments, as debt carries no voting control, and these investments are accounted for using the **equity method**. Under the equity method (see Exhibit 8.2), the Investment in Equity Affiliate account on the balance sheet is reported at its original cost plus a proportionate share of the affiliate's net earnings less a proportionate share of any dividends paid by the affiliate. The investor-company is also required to report the proportionate share of the affiliate's net earnings as part of its own income, and frequently you will see this separately classified on the income statement in an account called **equity in the earnings (loss) of an unconsolidated affiliate**.

Finally, investments in equity securities in which an investor-company establishes voting control over an affiliate—over 50 percent ownership—are accounted for using **consolidation accounting**. Under consolidation accounting, the operating results of the affiliated company are combined with those of the investor. Thus, shareholders in the investor-company receive a single set of combined financial statements representing both the investor and affiliate-company financial results. Affiliate companies in which an investor-company owns more than 50 percent of the outstanding voting shares are often referred to as "subsidiaries."

> When preparing a statement of cash flow for an investor-company, it is necessary to (1) subtract (add) the "equity in the earnings (loss) of an unconsolidated affiliate" and (2) subtract (add) any unrealized gains (losses) on trading securities from net income when calculating the cash flow from operations. All cash flows related to non-consolidated investments are captured in the investing section of the statement of cash flow.

ILLUSTRATION OF ACCOUNTING FOR MARKETABLE DEBT AND EQUITY SECURITIES—PASSIVE INVESTMENTS

To illustrate the accounting for, and the financial statement disclosures associated with, passive investments in marketable debt and equity securities, we refer to the investing activities of The New South Wales Trading Company, Inc. (NSWT). Assume that NSWT raised $50 million in cash in Year 1 from an initial public offering of its common shares. The company planned to use most of the cash to establish a chain of fast food restaurants specializing in Australian cuisine. Since the company's planned capital investments would take place over a three-year period, NSWT decided to temporarily invest some of its cash in debt and equity securities having a high degree of liquidity. The company settled on three investments:

Investment	Acquisition Date	Acquisition Cost	Classification	Market Value at Year-End
(1) Qantas Inc. 10% Notes due in Year 6	September	$10.0 million	Held-to-maturity	$9.8 million
(2) 100,000 shares of JWS Inc. common stock	November	6.1 million	Trading	6.8 million
(3) 200,000 shares of Coles Inc. common stock . . .	December	8.4 million	Available-for-sale	8.2 million

In September Year 1, NSWT invested $10 million in Qantas Inc. 10 percent notes. The company planned to hold the notes until Year 6 when they matured and the principal of $10 million is repaid. The notes paid $1 million in interest income (10 percent of $10 million) on December 31 each year. The notes were classified by NSWT's chief financial officer (CFO) as **held-to-maturity debt securities**.

In November, NSWT invested $6.1 million in 100,000 shares of JWS Inc. common stock at $61 per share. Since JWS was a growth company, it paid no dividends to its shareholders. NSWT's CFO thought the shares were substantially undervalued, and consequently, placed an order to sell the JWS shares when they hit $80 per share. JWS's shares were classified by the CFO as **trading securities**.

In December, NSWT purchased 200,000 shares of Coles Inc. common stock at $42 per share for a total cost of $8.4 million. Like JWS, Coles had a policy of paying no dividends. The NSWT CFO thought the shares were fairly valued but that NSWT would sell them in the unlikely event that the Coles shares traded above $50 per share. The Coles shares were classified as **available-for-sale securities**.

The accounting for the acquisition of the three securities in Year 1 is illustrated in the spreadsheet in Exhibit 8.3. The investment in Qantas Inc. notes reduces cash by $10 million and increases held-to-maturity debt securities by $10 million. The investments in JWS and Coles common shares reduce cash by $6.1 and $8.4 million, respectively, and increase trading equity securities and available-for-sale equity securities by $6.1 and $8.4, respectively.

EXHIBIT 8.3	Accounting for Marketable Debt and Equity Securities: The New South Wales Trading Company

(in $ thousands)	Sept. IPO Common Shares	Sept. Quantas Debt Investment	Nov. JWS Stock Investment	Dec. Coles Stock Investment	Dec. 31 Quantas Interest Receipt	Dec. 31 Adjust JWS Value	Dec. 31 Adjust Coles Value	Year 1 End. Bal. (summary)
Assets								
Cash.	50,000	(10,000)	(6,100)	(8,400)	1,000			26,500
: :								
Held-to-maturity debt securities		10,000						10,000
Trading securities.			6,100			700		6,800
Available-for-sale securities				8,400			(200)	8,200
Total assets.								**51,500**
Shareholders' Equity								
Common stock.	50,000							50,000
Retained earnings								1,700
Interest income.					1,000			
Unrealized gain—trading.						700		
Accumulated other comprehensive inc.								(200)
Unrealized gain (loss)—available-for-sale. . . .							(200)	
Total liabilities and shareholders' equity								**51,500**

Valuation Adjustments

At year-end, NSWT must consider several important events concerning its investments. These are shown as the last three transactions in Exhibit 8.3. First, NSWT received an interest payment of $1 million on the Qantas Notes, increasing cash and retained earnings (interest income) by $1 million. Second, the market values at year-end of NSWT's investments differed from their acquisition costs.

Since the Qantas notes are held-to-maturity securities, they are valued at their acquisition cost, requiring no downward adjustment to their market value of $9.8 million. NSWT's trading securities (JWS shares), however, must be valued at their market value with any unrealized gain (loss) in value taken into income. NSWT's trading securities have a market value of $6.8 million versus an acquisition cost of $6.1 million. Thus, the trading equity securities account is increased by $700,000 to reflect its market value of $6.8 million and retained earnings is increased by $700,000 to reflect the unrealized gain includable as current income.

The market value of the Coles shares, however, is just $8.2 million versus an acquisition cost of $8.4 million; consequently, this investment must be written down to market value with the unrealized loss reported as an AOCI component of shareholders' equity. Specifically, recording the unrealized loss reduces available-for-sale securities by $200,000 and reduces the shareholders' equity account Unrealized Gain (loss) on Available-for-Sale-Securities by $200,000. The shareholders' equity account Unrealized Gain (loss) on Available-for-Sale Securities is classified as a component of Accumulated Other Comprehensive Income under U.S. GAAP.

Following these end-of-year adjustments, NSWT's balance sheet at year-end is presented in Exhibit 8.4. The balance sheet shows NSWT's investment in held-to-maturity debt securities at cost and its investments in trading and available-for-sale securities at their market value. Shareholders' equity reflects the unrealized loss on available-for-sale securities and the unrealized gain on the trading securities. NSWT's partial income statement for the year is also presented in Exhibit 8.4. It shows the interest income of $1 million and the $700,000 of unrealized gain on trading securities.

Recording the Sale of Investment Securities

The sale of investment securities, similar to other assets, requires recording the amount received from the sale and removing the balance sheet values of the securities sold. The gain or loss on the transaction

EXHIBIT 8.4	Financial Statement Summary, Year 1: Marketable Debt and Equity Securities

THE NEW SOUTH WALES TRADING COMPANY, INC.
Balance Sheet

($ thousands)	Dec. 31
Cash.	$26,500
Investments	
Held-to-maturity debt securities.	10,000
Trading equity securities.	6,800
Available-for-sale equity securities.	8,200
Total assets.	$51,500
Shareholders' Equity	
Common stock.	$50,000
Retained earnings.	1,700
Accumulated other comprehensive income	
Unrealized loss on available-for-sale securities	(200)
Shareholders' equity	$51,500

THE NEW SOUTH WALES TRADING COMPANY, INC.
Partial Income Statement

($ thousands)	Dec. 31
Interest income.	$ 1,000
Unrealized gain on trading equity securities	700
Net income.	$ 1,700

is, therefore, the difference between the amounts received and the book values of the items sold. This fundamental accounting treatment results in one further important distinction between securities classified as trading and those classified as available-for-sale. For trading securities, because the unrealized market value changes have been recorded as income each period as they occur, when a security is sold only the gain or loss attributable to the period of sale is recorded for that period. For available-for-sale securities, however, when a security is sold the *entire* gain or loss since the year of acquisition is recorded as income. This difference is a direct result of deferring all prior period unrealized changes in market values under available-for-sale accounting, and because these amounts have been previously reflected in the AOCI account on the balance sheet.

    To illustrate, assume that during Year 2 NWST liquidated both equity investments in its portfolio, selling the JWS shares for $64 per share and the Coles shares for $47 per share. To record the gain (or loss) related to each sale, the sale proceeds received are netted against the book value of the securities held. Because both investments are recorded at market value at each balance sheet date, the book values are the last recorded market value. For JWS, the loss recorded as income amounts to $400,000, representing the decline of $4 per share from the prior year ($68 − $64) times the number of shares sold (100,000). For Coles Inc. it is not that simple. Because the security was classified as available-for-sale, the prior period change in market value that was recorded in AOCI must also be removed from the balance sheet. This has the desired effect of recording that value in current income, as it was deferred from income in the prior year. To help you see the accounting a bit clearer, A summary of the total gain realized on each security from acquisition to sale, and how that gain was allocated to the income statement over the two periods, is provided below. Note that the total realized gain for the JWS shares is $300,000 (calculated as ($64 − $61) × 100,000 shares), recorded as a $700,000 gain in year 1 and a $400,000 loss in year 2. The Cole shares, on the other hand, were sold for a total realized gain of $1,000,000 (calculated as ($47 − $42) × 200,000 shares), and all of this amount was recorded in the income statement in the year of sale. Exhibit 8.5 summarizes the transaction effects and the final balance sheet for the two investment sales.

Summary Calculation of Gain (Loss) from Securities Sales		
($ thousands)	JWS Inc.	Coles Inc.
Total income statement gain from sale in Year 2:		
Proceeds received	$6,400	$9,400
less: Investment on balance sheet	6,800	8,200
plus: AOCI previously not recognized as income	n/a	(200)
Total year 2 income statement gain (loss)	$ (400)	$1,000
Total realized gain (loss) from acquisition to sale:		
Proceeds received	$6,400	$9,400
less: Acquisition cost	6,100	8,400
Total realized gain (loss)	$ 300	$1,000
Recorded as income by year:		
Year 1	$ 700	$ —
Year 2	(400)	1,000
Total	$ 300	$1,000

EXHIBIT 8.5	Accounting for Sales of JWS and Cole Securities: The New South Wales Trading Company

	Year 1 End. Bal.	Sale of JWS Shares	Sale of Coles Shares	Balance Sheet after Sales
Assets				
Cash	$26,500	$6,400	$9,400	$42,300
: :				
Held-to-maturity debt securities	10,000			10,000
Trading securities	6,800	(6,800)		—
Available-for-sale securities	8,200		(8,200)	—
Total assets	$51,500			$52,300
Shareholders' Equity				
Common stock	$50,000			$50,000
Retained earnings	1,700			2,300
Gain (loss) on sales of securities		(400)	1,000	
Accumulated other comprehensive income	(200)			—
Unrealized gain—available-for-sale			200	
Total liabilities and shareholders' equity	$51,500			$52,300

Managerial Discretion

One might question why there is an inconsistent treatment of unrealized gains and losses between trading and available-for-sale securities. The difference in treatment coincides with the expected length of the holding period for the two investment categories—a relatively short holding period for trading securities and an uncertain holding period for available-for-sale securities. It could be argued that unrealized gains and losses should never be included in current income since the amount ultimately realized on a sale could be much different than the amount recognized in the current period. In fact, large swings in market values, over which management has no control, may distort current period performance as measured by net income. This argument is the principal reason why unrealized gains and losses for available-for-sale securities are classified as Accumulated Other Comprehensive Income on the balance sheet rather than as current period income on the income statement. Trading securities, on the other hand, are expected to be sold within a relatively short time frame. Hence, large changes in market value are much less likely to occur; and consequently, recognizing these unrealized gains and losses on the income statement in the current period is considered justifiable.

Fair Market Value Estimates

Companies reporting under U.S. GAAP are required to provide a set of comprehensive disclosures related to their estimates of fair market value. The objective is to help users of the financial statements understand both the composition of the investment portfolio and the degree of certainty regarding the measurement of fair value. Not all investments have readily available fair market values, so the FASB established a hierarchy of evidence that must be used when disclosing these estimates. Companies must classify their fair value estimates along three dimensions:

Level 1—quoted market prices for identical items in active markets.
Level 2—inputs to valuation that are directly or indirectly observable with reference to existing data.
Level 3—unobservable inputs, requiring management judgment through estimates or assumptions.

These disclosure requirements were established in 2007, coinciding with the U.S. financial crisis that began around the same time. The timing of the new requirements was significant as many companies were invested in highly risky assets, for instance collaterized debt obligations (CDOs) and other mortgage-backed securities.

The fair value disclosures highlighted to a greater degree the extent to which measurement risk was embedded in a company's investment portfolio. Level 1 provides the greatest confidence as to the accurate measurement of fair value. As a company has more of its portfolio categorized as level 3, arguably there is greater uncertainty and greater risk related to those investments.

Below is an illustrative excerpt from the 2011 annual report of **The Chubb Corporation**. Chubb is a property and casualty insurance company based in Warren, New Jersey. Notice that the predominant amount of the company's $38.7 billion investment portfolio is comprised of level 2 assets; and, only a very small portion is allocated to level 3, which would provide investors some comfort. About four percent ($1.504 billion) of the Chubb portfolio involve traded securities in active markets, and then only stock equity investments.

The fair value hierarchy prioritizes the inputs to valuation techniques used to measure fair value into three broad levels as follows:

Level 1—Unadjusted quoted prices in active markets for identical assets.

Level 2—Other inputs that are observable for the asset, either directly or indirectly.

Level 3—Inputs that are unobservable.

The fair value of fixed maturities and equity securities categorized based upon the lowest level of input that was significant to the fair value measurement was as follows:

	Level 1	Level 2	Level 3	Total
		December 31, 2011		
		(in millions)		
Fixed maturities				
Tax exempt	$ —	$20,203	$ 8	$20,211
Taxable				
U.S. government and government agency and authority obligations	—	868	—	868
Corporate bonds	—	6,313	152	6,465
Foreign government and government agency obligations	—	6,820	3	6,823
Residential mortgage-backed securities	—	845	10	855
Commercial mortgage-backed securities	—	1,962	—	1,962
	—	16,808	165	16,973
Total fixed maturities	—	37,011	173	37,184
Equity securities	1,504	—	8	1,512
	$1,504	$37,011	$181	$38,696

By classifying the shares of JWS Inc. as trading securities rather than as available-for-sale, the unrealized gain of $700,000 in the first year is included in NSWT's earnings rather than as a component of shareholders' equity on the balance sheet. Similarly during that year, classifying the shares in Coles Inc. as available-for-sale rather than as trading securities causes the unrealized loss of $200,000 to be included in shareholders' equity and not in NSWT's current earnings. Perhaps NSWT's CFO anticipated this situation and strategically classified these securities to cause the most favorable impact on reported firm performance. Such a conclusion implies that the CFO has an ability to forecast future share prices, a talent that might lead him to resign his current position and become a professional stock picker. Yet, such strategic decision-making is more plausible in the CFO's decision to sell securities. If a boost in earnings is required for a given year, perhaps because operating profit has fallen short of expectations, a company's CFO could simply choose to sell the available-for-sale securities, enabling an otherwise unrealized gain that would flow to shareholders' equity to manifest itself as a realized gain in current earnings. In some circles, such behavior is known as "cherry picking"—that is, selectively selling securities to include realized gains but not losses in a firm's current earnings. According to U.S. regulators, the **Federal National Mortgage Association** (also known as Fannie Mae), a publicly-held company chartered by the U.S. Congress to provide financing for home mortgages, did just that. The Office of Federal Housing Enterprises Oversight charged in 2005 that Fannie Mae violated GAAP by pursuing an accounting policy that allowed it to keep the best mortgage-backed securities and to sell less attractive ones to investors, a practice that became known as "keep the best, sell the rest."[1]

EQUITY METHOD AND CONSOLIDATION ACCOUNTING

The threshold of 20 percent voting power is presumed to be the tipping point of significant influence, although amounts less than 20 percent can qualify as well. For instance, even with less than 20 percent ownership when the board of directors of the investee is controlled by the investor, or there are key patents that the investor controls, these may be considered in the determination of whether significant influence exists.

When an investor-company acquires enough shares such that it can exert significant influence over the investee, generally 20 percent or more, the accounting requirements for these investments change radically from the mark-to-market accounting described above. To illustrate the accounting for the acquisition of a significant shareholding—20 to 100 percent of a company's shares—we examine three scenarios involving the finan-

EXHIBIT 8.6	Summary Financial Data for Savanna Inc. and Waterloo Inc.

Pre-Investment Balance Sheet
As of January 1

($ millions)	Savanna Inc.	Waterloo Inc.
Cash	$ 50	$ 20
Inventory	100	80
Total assets	$150	$100
Long-term debt	$ 50	$ 80
Common stock	100	20
Liabilities & shareholders' equity	$150	$100

Income Statement
Year Ending December 31

($ millions)	Savanna Inc.	Waterloo Inc.
Revenue	$200	$100
Expenses	170	90
Net income	$ 30	$ 10
Dividend	$ 0	$ 5

---

[1] *The Wall Street Journal*, "Fannie Mae Accused of Rule Breaking," April 7, 2005.

cial statement disclosures of Savanna Inc. and Waterloo Inc. Summary financial information for the two companies is provided in Exhibit 8.6. Savanna Inc. is the larger company in terms of assets—$150 million for Savanna versus $100 million for Waterloo—and has twice the revenue.

To simplify the illustration, we assume that (1) all revenue, expenses, and dividends are paid in cash; (2) there are no income taxes; (3) interest on long-term debt is ignored; (4) neither company initially holds debt or equity securities

> Consolidation accounting requires that prior to the combination of financial results, any profits on intercompany sales between related companies be eliminated. This requirement stems from the accounting principle that only profit from **arms-length transactions** be included in the income statement; that is, it is inappropriate to include the profit on a sale between two divisions of the same company in the consolidated results. In some circumstances, the profit on transactions between a parent-company and an *unconsolidated* affiliate may be included in the consolidated income statement, but this situation (if material) must be disclosed in the footnotes to the consolidated financial statements as a **related-party transaction**.

in the other; and, (5) Savanna pays no dividend during the year while Waterloo pays a $5 million cash dividend. Finally, we assume that there are no intercompany sales between the two companies.

Case 1. Savanna Inc. acquires 40 percent of the common shares of Waterloo Inc. for $8 million on January 2; the fair market value of Waterloo's net assets equals their book value of $20 million ($100 million in assets minus $80 million in liabilities).

Since Savanna's investment of $8 million is equal to 40 percent of the fair market value of Waterloo's net assets (40 percent of $20 million), there is no goodwill associated with the Waterloo investment. **Goodwill** is the excess of total consideration paid for an equity interest over the fair market value of the acquired net assets. The size of Savanna's investment in Waterloo's shares (40 percent) indicates that Savanna desires a significant but not controlling interest in Waterloo's operating decisions. As a consequence, Savanna should use the equity method to account for its investment in Waterloo. Savanna's accounting for its investment under the equity method is summarized below and is displayed in the spreadsheet in Exhibit 8.7:

1. On January 2, Savanna decreases Cash by $8 million for its investment in Waterloo and also increases the Investment in Equity Affiliate account by $8 million.

2. During the year, Savanna reports its earnings as an increase in Cash of $30 million and an increase in Retained Earnings of $30.

> There are many reasons why an acquiring company will pay an amount in excess of the fair value of an acquiree's identifiable assets, thus requiring an amount to be recorded as goodwill. The acquiring firm may believe that there are synergies that can be realized upon the acquisition, or alternatively, that certain "unidentified assets" such as technological know-how or managerial talent may be present in the acquired firm. Consequently, it should not be concluded that the existence of goodwill in an acquisition implies that the acquiring firm simply erroneously paid too much for an acquiree.

3. During the year, Savanna reports its 40 percent share of Waterloo's earnings, or $4 million (40 percent of $10 million), as an increase in the asset account Investment in Equity Affiliate of $4 million and as an increase in Retained Earnings of $4 million (equity in the earnings of an unconsolidated affiliate). Under the equity method, Savanna reports a portion of Waterloo's earnings as both a source of earnings on its own income statement and as an increase in its investment in Waterloo on its balance sheet. If Waterloo had reported a loss instead of a profit, Savanna would report its ownership share of Waterloo's loss on its income statement and as a reduction in the investment account on its balance sheet.

4. During the year, Savanna reports its 40 percent share of Waterloo's cash dividend, or $2 million (40 percent of $5 million), by increasing Cash by $2 million and decreasing the Investment in Equity Affiliate by $2 million. Under the equity method, the payment of a dividend by an affiliate is treated as a reduction in (or liquidation of) the investment and not as a source of earnings. In effect, the affiliate's dividend is accounted for by the parent company (Savanna) as a return of investment, not a return on investment.

The balance sheet for Savanna on January 2 after the initial investment in Waterloo's common shares and at the end of the year is shown in

> A dividend that is considered to be a return of capital, rather than a return on capital, is often called a **liquidating dividend**.

Exhibit 8.8. Savanna's Investment in Equity Affiliate increases from $8 million at the time of the investment to $10 million at the end of the year. The income statement for Savanna is also shown in Exhibit 8.8 and reveals that Savanna's earnings include not only its own net earnings of $30 million, but also Savanna's 40 percent share of Waterloo's earnings ($4 million).

EXHIBIT 8.7	Accounting for Investments Using the Equity Method: Case 1

($ millions)	Beginning Balance Sheet	Acquire Waterloo Shares	Savanna's Earnings for Year	40% of Waterloo Earnings	40% of Waterloo Dividends	Ending Balance Sheet
Assets						
Cash.	$ 50	$(8)	$30		$ 2	$ 74
Inventory.	100					100
Investment in equity affiliate.		8		$4	(2)	10
Total assets.	**$150**					**$184**
Liabilities						
Long-term debt	$ 50					$ 50
Shareholders' Equity						
Common stock.	100					100
Retained earnings						34
Savanna's earnings for the year			30			
Equity in earnings of unconsolidated affiliate				4		
Total liabilities and shareholders' equity	**$150**					**$184**

EXHIBIT 8.8	Financial Statement Disclosures: Case 1

SAVANNA, INC.
Balance Sheet

($ millions)	January 2	December 31
Cash.	$ 42	$ 74
Inventory.	100	100
Investment in equity affiliate.	8	10
Total assets.	$150	$184
Long-term debt	$ 50	$ 50
Common stock.	100	100
Retained earnings	0	34
Liabilities & shareholders' equity	$150	$184

SAVANNA, INC.
Income Statement

($ millions)	December 31
Revenue.	$200
Expenses	170
Operating income.	30
Equity in the earnings of unconsolidated affiliate.	4
Net income.	$ 34

It may appear strange at first to see Savanna increasing its investment account for a portion of Waterloo's earnings, even if they are not received, and then decreasing the investment account for any dividends actually received. There is, however, logic behind this accounting treatment. Savanna's investment account represents its percentage ownership interest in Waterloo's shareholders' equity. Savanna initially paid an amount exactly equal to its percentage share of Waterloo's equity, so the investment account equaled 40 percent of $20 million or $8 million. During the year Waterloo reported net income of $10 million and paid dividends of $5 million. These amounts increase Waterloo's shareholders' equity (retained earnings) by $10 million and decrease its retained earnings by $5 million. Correspondingly, Savanna's investment account was increased by 40 percent of these amounts, $4 million minus $2 million, or $2 million. At year-end, Waterloo's shareholders' equity totals $25 million and Savanna's investment account is 40 percent of this amount, or $10 million. You may wish to try to replicate this reconciliation between Savanna's investment account and Waterloo's shareholders' equity for Case 2.

Finally, worth noting is that one important exception exists to the use of the equity method by U.S. companies. GAAP allows an investor to elect to use a fair value option rather than the equity method for minority ownership investments that exceed a 20% ownership interest. The fair value option, if elected, is irrevocable. Under this option, an investor reports its investments in a manner consistent with the treatment of trading securities, with any unrealized gains and losses resulting from changes in an investment's fair value reported on the income statement. Under the fair value option, the investor does not recognize its proportionate share of the investee's net income, but does report any dividends from the investee as dividend income. The fair value election is similar to the accounting provided under international accounting standards and reflects the continuing effort of the FASB to harmonize U.S. GAAP with IFRS.

Case 2.   Savanna acquires 80 percent of Waterloo's common shares for $16 million; the fair market value of Waterloo Inc.'s net assets equals their book value of $20 million.

Since the total consideration paid of $16 million is equal to 80 percent of the fair market value of Waterloo's net assets (80 percent of $20 million), no goodwill is associated with the Waterloo investment. The size of Savanna's investment indicates that it has acquired a controlling interest

Although it is generally true that when a company acquires a majority shareholding in another, the investor will report its financial results with those of the subsidiary on a consolidated basis, the presentation of consolidated financial statements is not required in every country (such as India). Consolidated financial statements are intended to help investors avoid the problem of **information overload** (giving investors too much financial information to comprehend).

In Practice 8.1 *Equity in the earnings of an unconsolidated affiliate*   Care should be exercised when analyzing the income statements of investor-firms reporting affiliate earnings under the equity method since these earnings are often not received in cash. An analysis of public-company filings in 2008 found many companies reported earnings from affiliate-companies in excess of the cash dividends received from these affiliates. Moreover, in several cases, the affiliate-company earnings accounted for most of the investor-firms' reported net income:

Company	Unremitted portion of unconsolidated affiliate-company earnings as reported under equity method ($ millions)	Consolidated income before extraordinary items and discontinued operations ($ millions)
Acadia Realty Trust.	$ 19.91	$ 19.90
Alliance Bernstein Holding LP	278.64	244.73
Alumina Ltd.	169.41	117.31
American Homepatient Inc.	6.20	0.70
Bell Aliant Regional Comm. FD	255.60	251.70
Canfor Pulp Income Fund	23.28	20.20
Cresud Sacifya.	12.73	7.60
Dow Chemical	787.00	579.00
Electrolux AB	87.72	46.46
Enbridge Energy Mgmt LLC.	51.80	24.20
First Natl. Finl. Income FD	13.42	11.82
Frozen Food Express Inds.	0.88	0.61
Gencor Industries Inc.	15.62	15.25
Kinder Morgan Management LLC	142.20	83.20
Macerich Co.	93.83	85.29
Minas Buenaventura SA.	340.93	153.28
Mission West Properties Inc.	19.62	10.13
Northern Tech. Intl.	4.52	2.55
Noven Pharmaceuticals Inc..	45.64	21.41
Nustar Gp. Holdings LLC.	69.62	66.30
Orbital Corp. LTD	2.25	0.45
Scientific Games Corp.	58.57	8.49
TC Pipelines LP	122.60	107.70
US Cellular Corp.	91.98	32.99
Warwick Valley Telephone Co.	10.36	6.07
Williams Pipeline Partners	54.38	51.88
Yahoo Inc..	596.98	424.30

Source: Standard & Poor's Compustat

in Waterloo's business, and therefore, Savanna should consolidate Waterloo's financial results. Savanna will initially account for its investment in Waterloo using the equity method on its *unconsolidated* financial statements and then prepare consolidated financial statements at the end of the fiscal period by making various consolidating adjustments. We follow that approach in this illustration. Savanna's initial accounting for its investment under the equity method is summarized below and in the spreadsheet in Exhibit 8.9:

1. On January 2, Savanna decreases Cash by $16 million for its cash investment in Waterloo and increases the Investment in Equity Affiliate account by $16 million.
2. During the year, Savanna reports its earnings as an increase in Cash of $30 million and an increase in Retained Earnings of $30 million.
3. During the year, Savanna reports its 80 percent share of Waterloo's earnings, or $8 million, as an increase in the Investment in Equity Affiliate by $8 million and an increase in Retained Earnings by $8 million (equity in the earnings of unconsolidated affiliate).
4. During the year, Savanna reports its 80 percent share of Waterloo's cash dividend, or $4 million, by increasing Cash by $4 million and decreasing the Investment in Equity Affiliate by $4 million.

EXHIBIT 8.9　Accounting for Investments Using the Equity Method: Case 2

($ millions)	Beginning Balance Sheet	Acquire Waterloo Shares	Savanna's Earnings for Year	80% of Waterloo Earnings	80% of Waterloo Dividends	Ending Balance Sheet
Assets						
Cash. . . .	$ 50	$(16)	$30		$ 4	$ 68
Inventory. . . .	100					100
Investment in equity affiliate. . . .		$ 16		$8	$(4)	20
Total assets. . . .	**$150**					**$188**
Liabilities						
Long-term debt	$ 50					$ 50
Shareholders' Equity						
Common stock. . . .	100					100
Retained earnings						38
Savanna's earnings for the year			$30			
Equity in earnings of unconsolidated affiliate				$8		
Total liabilities and shareholders' equity	**$150**					**$188**

The financial statements for Savanna and Waterloo at December 31 are shown in Exhibit 8.10. Waterloo's assets of $105 million reflect its beginning assets of $100 million plus earnings for the year of $10 million less the dividends paid to its shareholders of $5 million. Since Savanna owns 80 percent of Waterloo's common shares, it must report its financial results and those of Waterloo on a consolidated basis. Thus, Waterloo's assets of $105 million are added to Savanna's assets. Similarly, Waterloo's $80 million of long-term debt is added to Savanna's liabilities. However, to avoid overstating the total consolidated assets and liabilities, certain adjusting (eliminating) entries are required. First, the Investment in Equity Affiliate ($20 million) must be removed from the consolidated balance sheet to avoid double-counting some of Waterloo's assets. This amount is offset against Waterloo's common stock and retained earnings. Second, the 20 percent of Waterloo's common stock and retained earnings not legally owned by Savanna belong to another group of shareholders whose claim on Waterloo's net assets, valued at $5 million (20 percent of $20 million plus 20 percent of $5 million), is known as the **noncontrolling interest** since Savanna is the controlling or majority shareholder. Noncontrolling interest refers to the portion of a subsidiary's net assets not owned, but still consolidated, by the parent-company. Under consolidation accounting, 100 percent of an affiliate's assets and liabilities are consolidated with those of the parent-company (Savanna) even though legal ownership may be less than 100 percent. The process of consolidating all of a subsidiary's

The **noncontrolling interest** account was formerly called the "minority interest" account and is disclosed on the consolidated balance sheet as a component of shareholders' equity because it represents an ownership interest in the consolidated entity. For purposes of financial statement analysis, however, many financial analysts regard this account as a component of debt for purposes of calculating such ratios as the debt-to-equity ratio and the total debt-to-total assets ratio.

assets and liabilities even though legal ownership is less than 100 percent is known as **full consolidation**.

By adding across the left three columns, we arrive at Savanna's consolidated balance sheet in Exhibit 8.10, Panel A. The consolidated balance sheet shows that the net assets of $143 million ($273 million in assets less $130 million in long-term debt) are equal to the $138 million of Savanna's pre-consolidated equity claims ($188 of assets less $50 of long-term debt) plus the $5 million in claims by the minority share-holders. In essence, Savanna's $20 million Investment in Equity Affiliate account has been replaced with the assets and liabilities of Waterloo, less the 20% adjustment for noncontrolling interests.

Savanna's consolidated income statement is shown in Exhibit 8.10, Panel B. All of Waterloo's operating revenue and operating expenses are added to those of Savanna despite the fact that Savanna legally owns only 80 percent of Waterloo. To avoid double-counting Waterloo's earnings, it is necessary to eliminate the $8 million of Equity in the Earnings of Unconsolidated Affiliate and to subtract the 20 percent share of Waterloo's earnings, or $2 million (20 percent of $10 million), attributable to the claims of the minority or noncontrolling shareholders. Savanna's consolidated financial statements in Exhibit 8.10 reflect what is commonly referred to as the **acquisition method**.

EXHIBIT 8.10	Financial Statement Disclosures: Case 2			
Panel A: Balance Sheet ($ millions)	**Equity Method Savanna Inc. December 31**	**Waterloo Inc. December 31**	**Consolidating Adjustments**	**Consolidated Savanna Inc. December 31**
Cash.	$ 68	$ 25		$ 93
Inventory.	100	80		180
Investment in equity affiliate.	20	0	$(20)	0
Total assets.	**$188**	**$105**	**$(20)**	**$273**
Long-term debt	$ 50	$ 80		$130
Common stock.	100	20	$(20)	100
Noncontrolling interest in consolidated subsidiary			5	5
Retained earnings	38	5	(5)	38
Liabilities and shareholders' equity	**$188**	**$105**	**$(20)**	**$273**
Panel B: Income Statement ($ millions)	**Equity Method Savanna Inc. December 31**	**Waterloo Inc. December 31**	**Consolidating Adjustments**	**Consolidated Savanna Inc. December 31**
Revenue.	$200	$100		$300
Expenses	(170)	(90)		(260)
Operating income.	30	10		40
Equity in the earnings of unconsolidated affiliate.	8	—	$ (8)	
Noncontrolling interest in the earnings of consolidated subsidiary . . .	—	—	(2)	(2)
Net income	**$ 38**	**$ 10**	**$(10)**	**$ 38**

Notice in Panel B of Exhibit 8.10 that the $38 million of net income reported by Savanna under the equity method is the same as the consolidated net income reported under consolidated accounting. This illustrates that consolidation accounting and the equity method produce similar income statement results. This is not true, however, for the balance sheet: Total assets and long-term debt are higher under consolidation accounting than under the equity method. In fact, Savanna would report a long-term debt-to-equity ratio of 0.94 ($130 million divided by $138 million) under the acquisition method of consolidation accounting but a ratio of only 0.36 ($50 million divided by $138 million) under the equity method.

The equity method enables a parent-company to engage in what is commonly referred to as **off-balance-sheet financing**—that is, avoiding the disclosure of a subsidiary's debt on the parent-company balance sheet. By maintaining an equity holding of 50 percent or less, a company is permitted to use the equity method to account for its intercorporate investments. Under U.S. GAAP, and that of many coun-tries, parent-companies are required to disclose the aggregate assets, liabilities, revenue, and expenses of equity affiliates in the parent-company footnotes. Does it matter if a subsidiary's debt is disclosed in the footnotes rather than reported on the parent's balance sheet? If investors are reasonably astute they should be able to make the necessary adjustments to the parent's unconsolidated balance sheet to derive "as if" consolidated financial statements that reflect the debt of the subsidiary. Nevertheless, some managers go to great lengths to keep debt off the consolidated balance sheet, presumably under the belief that financial statement users don't make full and complete adjustments for off-balance-sheet debt. By keeping such debt off the balance sheet, these managers hope to make their companies appear less risky, and thus, positively impact the company's credit rating and the share price of the company's stock.

Case 3.   Savanna acquires 100 percent of Waterloo's common shares for $25 million; the book value of Waterloo's assets and liabilities equal their fair market value except inventory, which has a current value of $82 million versus a book value of $80 million. Thus, the fair market value of Waterloo's net assets is $22 million ($20 million plus $2 million representing the understatement of inventory).

Savanna's acquisition of 100 percent of Waterloo's shares indicates that Savanna should prepare consolidated financial statements. Further, since Savanna paid a total consideration of $25 million for net assets having a fair market value of $22 million, goodwill in the amount of $3 million is present in the Waterloo acquisition. Finally, since Waterloo's inventory has a fair value of $82 million but a book value of only $80 million, Savanna must increase, or "step-up," the value of Waterloo's inventory by $2 million before the consolidated balance sheet is prepared. Under the acquisition method of consolidation accounting, all of the assets and liabilities of the acquiree are written up (or down) to their fair market value prior to the preparation of the consolidated financial statements.

As in Case 2, Savanna will initially account for its investment in Waterloo using the equity method, and at the end of the fiscal period, prepare consolidated financial statements. Savanna's equity method accounting for its investment in Waterloo is summarized below and in the Exhibit 8.11 transaction summary:

1. On January 2, Savanna increases the Investment in Equity Affiliate account by $25 million and decreases Cash for an equivalent amount.

2. During the year, Savanna reports its earnings for the year as an increase in Cash of $30 million and an increase in Retained Earnings of $30 million.

3. During the year, Savanna reports its 100 percent share of Waterloo's earnings, or $10 million, as an increase in the Investment in Equity Affiliate account and as an increase in Retained Earnings of $10 million (equity in the earnings of unconsolidated affiliate).

4. During the year, Savanna reports its 100 percent share of Waterloo's cash dividend, or $5 million, by increasing Cash by $5 million and decreasing the Investment in Equity Affiliate by $5 million.

EXHIBIT 8.11	Accounting for Investments Using the Equity Method: Case 3						
($ millions)	Beginning Balance Sheet	Acquire Waterloo Shares	Savanna's Earnings for Year	100% of Waterloo Earnings	100% of Waterloo Dividends	Ending Balance Sheet
Assets						
Cash..	$ 50	$(25)	$30		$ 5	$ 60
Inventory....................................	100					100
Investment in equity affiliate..............		$ 25		$10	$(5)	30
Total assets..............................	**$150**					**$190**
Liabilities						
Long-term debt	$ 50					$ 50
Shareholders' Equity						
Common stock............................	100					100
Retained earnings						40
Savanna's earnings for the year			$30			
Equity in earnings of unconsolidated affiliate				$10		
Total liabilities and shareholders' equity	**$150**					**$190**

The balance sheets for Savanna and Waterloo at December 31 are shown in Exhibit 8.12, Panel A. The purchase price of $25 million exceeds the fair value of Waterloo's net assets of $20 million, with the excess of $5 million represented by a $2 million step-up in the value of Waterloo's inventory and goodwill in the amount of $3 million. As before, the Investment in Equity Affiliate of $30 million is eliminated against Waterloo's common stock of $20 million, retained earnings of $5 million, the creation of goodwill for $3 million and the inventory write-up of $2 million. Consolidated financial statements are presented in Exhibit 8.12.

EXHIBIT 8.12	Financial Statement Disclosures: Case 3			
Panel A: Balance Sheet ($ millions)	**Equity Method Savanna, Inc. December 31**	**Waterloo Inc. December 31**	**Consolidating Adjustments**	**Consolidated Savanna, Inc. December 31**
Cash..	$ 60	$ 25		$ 85
Inventory..	100	80	$ 2	182
Investment in equity affiliate......................	30	0	(30)	0
Goodwill...	—	—	3	3
Total assets..	$190	$105	$(25)	$270
Long-term debt	$ 50	$ 80	—	$130
Common stock..	100	20	$(20)	100
Retained earnings	40	5	(5)	40
Liabilities & shareholders' equity	$190	$105	$(25)	$270

Panel B: Income Statement ($ millions)	**Equity Method Savanna, Inc. December 31**	**Waterloo Inc. December 31**	**Consolidating Adjustments**	**Consolidated Savanna, Inc. December 31**
Revenue...	$200	$100		$300
Expenses..	170	90		260
Operating income......................................	30	10		40
Equity in earnings of unconsolidated affiliate....	10	—	$(10)	—
Net income...	$ 40	$ 10	$(10)	$ 40

Deconsolidation

Just as firms consolidate the financial statements of their majority-owned subsidiaries, they must reverse this process when their ownership interest falls below 50 percent. The **deconsolidation** process most commonly occurs when a parent company sells a business division or distributes its ownership shares to its existing shareholders. The distribution of ownership of a business division from a company to its shareholders is called a **spin-off** and is usually executed as a tax-free distribution.

Consider, for example, the 1998 spin-off of Associates First Financial by the **Ford Motor Company**. Ford distributed its 81 percent ownership stake in Associates First Financial to its Ford Class A and Class B shareholders. The spin-off reduced Ford's net worth by one-third (the book value of the net assets transferred to the newly-formed Associates Company), and Ford's share price declined from $65.50 per share prior to the spin-off to $43.75 post–spin-off. The decline in Ford's share price ($21.75) represented the opening fair market value of the distributed shares of the new Associates Company. Following the spin-off, the Associates Company, a consumer-finance company, was able to be exchange-traded as a separate corporate entity from Ford. Following the announcement of the spin-off, Ford's share price rose 18 percent, suggesting that the equity market perceived the transaction to be a value-enhancing decision for Ford Company shareholders. Spin-offs are a mechanism by which companies, like the Ford Motor Company, can unlock value for their shareholders when the consolidated entity is undervalued by the capital market. Examples of more recent high profile spin-offs are **Time Warner**'s of **AOL** in 2009, **Verizon**'s of **Frontier Communications** in 2010, and **ADT** by **Tyco International** in 2012. Conglomerates like these, which are made up of a variety of businesses, often trade at a discount from the sum of their stand-alone fair market values. This discount is known as the **conglomerate discount**.

The accounting for a spin-off is executed like a reverse consolidation—that is, the book value of the division's assets and liabilities are removed from the consolidated balance sheet and placed on a new, separate unconsolidated balance sheet representing the new corporate entity. Parent-company shareholders receive shares in the spun-off entity in proportion to their ownership interest in the parent, and subsequently, can trade the shares of the newly created corporate entity separately from the parent-company.

BUSINESS PERSPECTIVE

The first footnote to the financial statements typically is a summary of significant accounting policies adopted by a company. Certainly for any company engaged in large investments, understanding the accounting policies for those investments would be critical. As an example below, **Foster's Group LTD** disclosed the following information in "Note 1—Summary of significant accounting policies," in its 2011 annual report:

Principles of consolidation

The consolidated financial statements have been prepared for the consolidated entity (also referred to as the 'Group') comprising Foster's Group Limited (FGL) as the parent entity, and all its controlled entities. Controlled entities are listed in note 33. Where control of an entity is obtained during a financial year, its results are included in the income statement from the date on which control commences. Where control of an entity ceases during a financial year its results are included for that part of the year during which control existed. The financial reports of the subsidiaries are prepared for the same reporting period as the parent company, using consistent accounting policies.

Investments in controlled entities

Investments in controlled entities are accounted for using the purchase method. Under this method, the cost of an acquisition is measured at fair value of the assets given up, shares issued or liabilities undertaken at the date of acquisition. The excess of the cost of acquisition over the fair value of the net assets of the subsidiary acquired is recorded as goodwill. If the cost of acquisition is less than the fair value of the net assets of the subsidiary acquired, the difference is recognised directly in the income statement.

Investments in associates and joint ventures

In the consolidated financial statements, investments in associates, which includes partnerships, are accounted for using the equity method of accounting and are initially recognised at cost. Under this method, the Group's share of profits or losses are recognised in the income statement and its share of movements in reserves are recognised in the Group's consolidated other comprehensive income. The cumulative post acquisition changes in the Group's share of net assets of the associate, less any impairment losses, are adjusted against the cost of the investment. When the Group's share of losses in an associate equals or exceeds its interest in the associate, the Group does not recognise any further losses, unless it has an obligation on behalf of the associate. Where there has been a change recognised directly in the associate's equity, the Group recognises its share of any changes and disclose, this when applicable, in the consolidated Statement of comprehensive income. Associates are those entities over which the Group has significant influence, but not control and which is neither a subsidiary nor a joint venture. Unrealised gains and losses in transactions between the Group and its associates are eliminated to the extent of the Group's interest in the associates.

Financial assets

Financial assets are classified as either financial assets at fair value through profit or loss, loans and receivables, held-to-maturity investments, or available-for-sale investments, as appropriate. When financial assets are recognised initially, they are measured at fair value, plus, in the case of investments not at fair value through profit or loss, directly attributable transactions costs. The Group determines the classification of its financial assets after initial recognition and, when allowed and appropriate, re-evaluates this designation at each financial year-end.

Accounting for Joint Ventures

In some cases, a business may establish a **joint venture** with another company to produce a product or provide a service. These ventures are often quite effective because each company typically has some unique skill, knowledge, or resource that makes it more efficient to partner with another company than to attempt the undertaking alone. These partnering arrangements are often established as separate corporate entities in which each partner owns 50 percent of the venture's equity, although owning exactly 50 percent is not a necessary condition to establish a joint venture. When each partner owns half of the joint venture's equity, these ventures are accounted for using the equity method.

For example, the **Starbucks Coffee Company** disclosed in its 2012 annual report that it had ongoing joint ventures to produce and distribute Starbucks-branded products across the globe. Two such ventures were The North American Coffee Partnership, a 50/50 joint venture with the **Pepsi-Cola Company** to produce and distribute bottled Frappuccino coffee, and another with **Shanghai President Coffee Company, Ltd.** wherein the two companies would jointly open retail operations in China. Starbucks accounts for these investments using the equity method. The asset section of Starbucks' balance sheet is presented in Exhibit 8.13, and shows the company's investment in its joint ventures, called Equity and Cost Investments, as a line item in the noncurrent assets section (see **bolded** area in Exhibit 8.13). The data reveal that the value of Starbucks's joint ventures, plus any other equity method investments, increased from 2011 to 2012 by $87.6 million ($459.9 million − $372.3 million). This account would capture Starbucks' original investment, its 50 percent ownership interests in the joint venture's net income, less its 50 percent interest in any dividends paid by the joint ventures to their parent companies.

EXHIBIT 8.13	Financial Statement Disclosures: Joint Ventures

STARBUCKS CORPORATION
Consolidated Balance Sheet

Fiscal Year Ended (in millions)	Sept. 30, 2012	Oct. 2, 2011
Cash and cash equivalents	$1,188.6	$1,148.1
Short-term investments	848.4	902.6
Accounts receivable, net	485.9	386.5
Inventories	1,241.5	965.8
Prepaid expenses and other current assets	196.5	161.5
Deferred income taxes, net	238.7	230.4
Total current assets	4,199.6	3,794.9
Long-term investments—available-for-sale securities	116.0	107.0
Equity and cost investments	**459.9**	**372.3**
Property, plant and equipment, net	2,658.9	2,355.0
Other assets	385.7	409.6
Goodwill	399.1	321.6
Total assets	$8,219.2	$7,360.4

Accounting for Special Purpose Entities

Special purpose entities (SPEs) or **special purpose vehicles** (SPVs) refer to separate legal entities created by a parent company along with other independent investors for a legitimate business purpose. Under U.S. GAAP, an SPE or SPV need not be consolidated by a parent company if certain conditions are met. The reporting rules governing these entities have recently been revised, including a new label for this type of entity, **variable interest entity** or VIE.

Unfortunately, the accounting rules that permitted majority-owned SPEs to remain unconsolidated were integral to several high-profile corporate scandals, most notably the Enron Corporation case a decade ago. It is now known that Enron made extensive use of SPEs, largely as an off-balance-sheet financing tool. An examination of Enron's footnotes concerning its unconsolidated equity affiliates reveals that Enron had extensive off-balance-sheet debt (see Business Perspective on page 276). What was not revealed in Enron's footnotes, however, was the extent to which Enron was contingently liable for much of the debt of its unconsolidated SPEs. The alleged abuses of SPEs led the FASB to revisit the reporting rules governing these entities. The FASB had trouble defining an SPE and instead defined a broader category of entity called a variable interest entity, or VIE. Many former SPEs that previously escaped consolidation are now required to be consolidated under the new accounting rules. Specifically, a VIE must be consolidated with the sponsoring parent-company if the VIE is not independent from the sponsoring company and does not have sufficient capital to operate separately from the sponsoring company. If there is more than one sponsoring company, the VIE should be consolidated with the sponsoring company that will absorb the majority of the VIE's expected losses or receive a majority of the VIE's expected residual returns.

BUSINESS PERSPECTIVE

SPE Disclosures

Enron's abbreviated balance sheet at December 31, 2000, is presented below. The balance sheet reveals that Enron disclosed $8.55 billion of long-term debt and $5.294 billion of Investments in and Advances to Unconsolidated Equity Affiliates at year-end 2000. The use of this latter account indicates that Enron used the equity method to account for its unconsolidated SPEs (see **bolded** area).

ENRON CORPORATION Abbreviated Balance Sheet		
December 31 ($ millions)	**2000**	**1999**
Assets		
Current assets		
Total current assets	$30,381	$ 7,255
Investments & other assets		
Investments in & advances to unconsolidated equity affiliates	**5,294**	**5,036**
Assets from price risk management activities	8,988	2,929
Goodwill	3,638	2,799
Other.	5,459	4,681
Total investments & other assets	23,379	15,445
Property, plant & equipment (net).	11,743	10,681
Total assets.	$65,503	$33,381
Liabilities & shareholders' equity		
Total current liabilities.	$28,406	$ 6,759
Long-term debt.	**8,550**	**7,151**
Total deferred credits & other liabilities	13,759	6,471
Minority interests*.	2,414	2,430
Company-obligated preferred securities of subsidiaries	904	1,000
Total shareholders' equity	11,470	9,570
Total liabilities & shareholders' equity	$65,503	$33,381

* Enron used the label minority interests to refer to its noncontrolling interest. Minority interest was the correct label for noncontrolling interests at the time these statements were prepared.

Enron's footnotes provided summary balance sheet information about its unconsolidated SPEs and revealed that its SPEs held $9.717 billion of related long-term debt. In simple terms, consolidating Enron's SPEs would have added another $9.717 billion of assets and long-term debt to Enron's consolidated balance sheet and consequently, increased Enron's reported debt-to-equity ratio from 0.75 ($8,550/$11,470) to 1.59 ($8,550 + $9,717)/$11,470—an increase of more than 100 percent! As is now known, an important objective in Enron's use of the equity method to account for its many SPEs was to keep the massive debt held by its unconsolidated SPEs off its consolidated balance sheet so that investors and investment professionals would perceive Enron to be less risky than it really was. Even such knowledgeable risk-rating agencies as Moody's and Standard & Poor's failed to correctly identify the financial risk inherent in Enron's financial arrangements. Enron filed for its much publicized bankruptcy in late 2001.

Companies that sell goods or services on credit, for example, often create an SPE to buy outstanding accounts receivable from the parent company. In essence, the SPE acts like a financial services company, borrowing from the investment community to then buy accounts receivable from the parent company. The following are excerpts related to one such transaction from the 2012 annual report of Marriott International. These excerpts highlight how Marriott was required under new accounting rules to consolidate certain VIEs related to timeshare notes receivable that were in place during the year 2010.

Note 1: **Adoption of New Accounting Standards Resulting in Consolidation of Special Purpose Entities** On January 2, 2010, the first day of the 2010 fiscal year, we adopted the new Transfers of Financial Assets and Consolidation standards (which were originally known as Financial Accounting Standards Nos. 166 and 167). Prior to the spin-off date, our former Timeshare segment used certain special purpose entities to securitize Timeshare segment notes receivables, which prior to our adoption of these new standards we treated as off-balance sheet entities. Our former Timeshare segment retained the servicing rights and varying subordinated interests in the securitized notes. Pursuant to GAAP in effect prior to the 2010 fiscal year, we did not consolidate these special purpose entities in our financial statements because the securitization transactions qualified as sales of financial assets. As a result of adopting the new Transfers of Financial Assets and Consolidation standards on the first day of 2010, we consolidated 13 existing qualifying special purpose entities associated with past securitization transactions.

Note 20: **Variable Interest Entities** In accordance with the applicable accounting guidance for the consolidation of variable interest entities, we analyze our variable interests, including loans, guarantees, and equity investments, to determine if an entity in which we have a variable interest is a variable interest entity. Our analysis includes both quantitative and qualitative reviews. We base our quantitative analysis on the forecasted cash flows of the entity, and our qualitative analysis on our review of the design of the entity, its organizational structure including decision-making ability, and relevant financial agreements. We also use our qualitative analyses to determine if we must consolidate a variable interest entity as its primary beneficiary.

INVESTMENT ACCOUNTING UNDER INTERNATIONAL FINANCIAL REPORTING STANDARDS

The accounting for investments across U.S. GAAP and IFRS are on the whole quite similar. Passive investments are accounted for at mark-to-market, and the equity method is required for non-consolidated investments with significant influence. The most stark difference relates to the requirement of when consolidation must take place. Consolidation accounting is required under U.S. GAAP only when a firm acquires more than a majority shareholding (greater than 50 percent) in another entity. Under IFRS, however, consolidation accounting may be required when a firm's ownership interest is less than 50 percent but where it effectively controls another entity. This situation may arise when a firm owns a substantial ownership interest, for example 40 percent or more, and the entity's remaining ownership shares are widely held. Evidence of de facto control may be provided by membership of an acquirer's CEO or other executives on the board of directors of an acquiree. In essence, IFRS requires that considerable judgment be used in determining whether consolidation accounting is warranted or not in situations where ownership is significant but less than a majority.

Although investment accounting in U.S. GAAP and IFRS have few differences, across the globe the practicalities of financial markets influence the ways in which investments are reported. In lesser developed countries where there are not actively traded markets for debt and equity securities, and thus not readily available or reliable market prices, the valuation of marketable debt and equity securities is often at the original **cost** of the investment. In some developed countries, a variant of the market value approach called **lower-of-cost-or-market** is used. Under the lower-of-cost-or-market method, a security is valued at the lower of two values—its current market value or its original cost. When a security's market value falls below its cost, the security is written down to the lower amount and the unrealized loss is reported in current income.

ACCOUNTING FOR INVESTMENTS IN FOREIGN ENTITIES

With increasing globalization, even small companies now consider manufacturing and/or selling their goods and services abroad. Many U.S. companies, for example, have located manufacturing plants as far away as Asia to take advantage of large pools of skilled but relatively inexpensive labor. But another reason that companies locate their operations in other countries is to take advantage of natural currency hedges that exist when receipts from product sales and outlays for production costs are denominated in the same currency. A **currency hedge** is an attempt by a company to avoid the potential losses that may accompany an exchange rate movement between two currencies.

Currency Exchange Rate Fluctuations

A company may locate a sales office in a foreign country or it may establish an entire subsidiary that operates relatively autonomously from the parent-company. One of the issues that must be addressed when locating a production and/or sales organization in another country is the resulting exposure to currency exchange rate fluctuations. If, for instance, a manufacturing facility is built in Mexico by a U.S. company, the value of the Mexico-based business to the U.S. parent company will rise and fall as the exchange rate between the U.S. dollar and the Mexican peso rises and falls. Currency exchange rate problems do not exist between countries in which the currencies are pegged to one another, as for example between the United States and Guatemala or Panama. But they are very real risks to companies that operate in countries with no such agreements, including doing business in all countries of the Euro-zone.

Before any consolidated financial statements that include the results of foreign-based subsidiaries can be prepared, the financial results of any foreign subsidiary must first be converted from its local currency into the currency of the parent-company. Under U.S. GAAP and the GAAP of most countries, the **current rate method** is used to translate the foreign-currency denominated financial statements of foreign subsidiaries that are self-contained business units.

> The financial results of foreign subsidiaries that are not self-contained are usually translated using the **temporal method**. Under the temporal method, monetary assets and liabilities are translated at the current or closing exchange rate, whereas nonmonetary assets and liabilities are translated at historical exchange rates.

Under the current rate method, a foreign subsidiary's assets and liabilities are translated at the current or closing exchange rate as of the balance sheet date while shareholders' equity is translated at the historical exchange rate when the subsidiary was established. Income statement items, on the other hand, are translated at the average exchange rate for the fiscal period. Any foreign currency translation gains/losses—that is, any changes in the translated value of the foreign subsidiary assets and liabilities over the fiscal period—are reported as a component of shareholders' equity and do not flow through to the income statement. Foreign currency translation gains (losses) represent unrealized wealth changes, much like the unrealized gains (losses) on available-for-sale securities. And, as a consequence, the accumulated balance of any foreign currency translation gains (losses) are reported on the balance sheet as a component of Accumulated Other Comprehensive Income under U.S. GAAP.[2]

Illustration of Current Rate Method

Jimbo Inc., is a U.S. manufacturer and distributor of food preparation equipment. To take advantage of growth opportunities outside the United States, the company established a self-contained operating subsidiary in Mexico. The Mexican subsidiary—Jimbo de Mexico SA de CV—was established on January 1 when the exchange rate was 10 pesos (P) to $1. At the inception of the Mexican subsidiary, its balance sheet appeared as follows:

JIMBO DE MEXICO
Balance Sheet
January 1

(P millions)

Cash	P1,500	Long-term debt	P 900
Accounts receivable	300	Common stock	900
Total assets	P1,800	Liabilities & shareholders' equity	P1,800

How would Jimbo de Mexico report its balance sheet in U.S. dollars on January 1? Exhibit 8.14, Panel A, shows Jimbo de Mexico's balance sheet in Mexican pesos and in U.S. dollars. The company's assets and liabilities are translated at the current exchange rate of 10 pesos per dollar while shareholders' equity is translated at the historical exchange rate, which in this instance is also 10 pesos per dollar.

---

[2] This is the same account that is used to reflect the unrealized holding gains or losses on available-for-sale securities discussed earlier in this chapter.

EXHIBIT 8.14	Translating Balance Sheets: Current Rate Method

Panel A. Pre-devaluation

JIMBO DE MEXICO
Balance Sheet

(in millions)	January 1 (Mexican pesos)	Exchange Rate (pesos per $1)	January 1 (U.S. dollars)
Cash..	P1,500	10	$150
Accounts receivable..............................	300	10	30
Total assets	P1,800		$180
Long-term debt	P 900	10	$ 90
Common stock	900	10	90
Cumulative foreign currency translation adjustment	0		0
Liabilities & shareholders' equity	P1,800		$180

Panel B. Post-devaluation

JIMBO DE MEXICO
Balance Sheet

(in millions)	January 2 (Mexican pesos)	Exchange Rate (pesos per $1)	January 2 (U.S. dollars)
Cash..	P1,500	15	$100
Accounts receivable..............................	300	15	20
Total assets....................................	P1,800		$120
Long-term debt	P 900	15	$ 60
Common stock..................................	900	10	90
Cumulative foreign currency translation adjustment	0		(30)
Liabilities & shareholders' equity	P1,800		$120

Now assume that on January 2, the Mexican peso depreciated to an exchange rate of 15 pesos per U.S. dollar. How would Jimbo de Mexico report its balance sheet in U.S. dollars following the devaluation? Jimbo de Mexico's post-devaluation balance sheet in U.S. dollars is shown in Exhibit 8.14, Panel B. After the devaluation, the company's assets and liabilities are translated at the new current exchange rate of 15 pesos per U.S. dollar while shareholders' equity is translated at the historical rate of 10 pesos per U.S. dollar. The **cumulative foreign currency translation adjustment** (CTA) of negative $30 million is required to ensure that the translated balance sheet actually balances. The CTA represents the exposure that Jimbo's shareholders suffered from the currency devaluation on their investment in Jimbo de Mexico. The $30 million unrealized loss is equal to the equity investment in Jimbo de Mexico times the change in the exchange rate [900 million pesos × (1/10 − 1/15)].

The foreign currency translation account may carry either a negative (net unrealized loss) or positive (net unrealized gain) balance. The account balance will increase or decrease each period in response to the changing exchange rate between the currency of the country of the parent and the currency of the country of the subsidiary. The balance at any point in time represents the gain (loss) that could be realized by the parent-company if the foreign subsidiary were sold for a price equivalent to its current book value, with the net proceeds from the sale repatriated back to the parent's currency.

ANALYZING INTERCORPORATE INVESTMENTS

The analysis of intercorporate investments—that is, an investment by one corporate entity in the equity of a second corporate entity—presents analytical challenges for financial statement users at several different levels. First, the managerial discretion that is required in the designation of marketable securities as being either trading securities or available-for-sale securities presents a significant opportunity for earnings' management. If, for example, the manager of an investor-company anticipates that an investee-company is likely to sustain operating losses that might adversely affect its market value, he or she might selectively classify the investment as available-for-sale to avoid the potential negative income statement effect associated with an unrealized loss if the investment were classified as a trading security. Similarly, if an upward share price movement in the value of an investee-company were anticipated by the investor-company manager, he or she might selectively designate the investment as a trading security to enable any unrealized gain to flow through to the investor-company's income statement and positively impact its reported earnings. The manager might also selectively use investment sales transactions merely to influence the timing of reported gains and losses. In each of these cases, financial statement users would be wise to recall the definition of sustainable earnings from Chapter 3—sustainable earnings exclude any one-time or nonoperating events such as an unrealized gain on a trading security.

Second, with respect to equity-method-accounted intercorporate investments, which include an investment in an unconsolidated affiliate, joint venture, or special purpose entity, some investment professionals regard the equity method as a form of off-balance-sheet financing. Under the equity method, an investor-company adjusts its carrying value for an investee-company for its proportionate share of the investee's operating earnings, losses, and dividends paid; but, the investor-company is not required to account for its implicit ownership interest in any changes in the level of debt financing of the investee. As a consequence, an investee may significantly increase its use of leverage, often for the express purpose of transferring the borrowed funds to the investor-company, but the investor is not required to reflect the increased investee borrowing on its own financial statements. The favorable accounting treatment associated with the debt of an equity-method-accounted investee was at the root of Enron Corporation's extensive use of off-balance-sheet special purpose entities.

TAX PERSPECTIVE

Investment Accounting Under U.S. Tax Law

The accounting for investments in other entities outlined in Chapter 8 highlights a diverse set of income measurement rules dependent on the level of ownership. In most respects the income measurement principles followed by the IRS are more straightforward than U.S. GAAP. Here we review some of the highlights.

Recall that under U.S. GAAP, some unrealized losses (gains) are included as income (i.e., trading securities); however, no such treatment is allowed for tax reporting. For investments, the IRS follows an "ability to pay" approach wherein gains or losses are not taxed as income until the asset is sold and the cash has been received by the selling company. Likewise equity income in affiliates is not taxable income as those earnings have been taxed once at the affiliate level and are not required to be taxed again at the investor level. Only at the point of sale is the gain or loss on the investment taxable, and then on an investment account value that has not been increased or decreased by the earnings of the affiliate.

Dividends received by a corporation are also treated differently for tax purposes relative to GAAP. Recall that the treatment of dividends varied under GAAP as follows: (i) if the investment was less than 20 percent ownership, dividends were treated as income, (ii) if the equity method applied, the dividends were not income but rather a return of capital that lowered the investment account value, and (iii) dividends were eliminated between companies if the two were consolidated. For tax purposes most, but not all, of the dividends received from other corporations are not subject to tax. The logic here is to avoid what would effectively be triple taxation once the dollars finally made their way to the individual shareholders of the receiving corporation. The amount of the dividend received that is excludable from taxable income depends on the level of ownership in the company, but ranges from 70 percent for the smallest ownership levels to 100 percent if the subsidiary is wholly-owned.

Finally, we observed that companies that own over 50 percent of another entity are required under U.S. GAAP to consolidate their financial statements. No such requirement exists under the IRC. Each individual entity is expected to file its own separate tax return but with one exception: an affiliated group of corporations may elect, but is not required, to file a single consolidated tax return. "Affiliation" for these purposes is met when one corporation owns at least 80 percent of the voting stock of another.

A final consideration in the analysis of intercorporate investments is the issue of related-party transactions—that is, the profit or loss generated by transactions between two entities that are related by virtue of existing cross-firm equity investments. Although the elimination of any intercompany transactions among consolidated entities is required under existing GAAP, the financial effects of any intercompany transactions between an investor-company and an unconsolidated affiliate company are permitted to be included in the consolidated financial statements. Where such intercompany transactions are material in amount, details of the transactions must be disclosed in the footnotes to the financial statements. With this information, financial statement users are empowered to decide whether (or not) to restate the consolidated financial statements to eliminate the financial effects of these related-party transactions prior to assessing the value of a firm.

REVIEW PROBLEM

The Arcadia Company made an offer to purchase all of the outstanding shares of The Claremont Company at a price of $10 per share, or an aggregate of $22 million. Immediately prior to the purchase offer, the balance sheets of the two companies appeared as follows:

	The Arcadia Company	The Claremont Company
Assets		
Cash.	$ 26,000,000	$ 2,000,000
Inventory.	12,000,000	7,000,000
Fixed assets, net	50,000,000	15,000,000
Intangible assets	30,000,000	18,000,000
Total Assets	$118,000,000	$42,000,000
Liabilities		
Accounts payable.	$ 7,000,000	$ 4,000,000
Bonds payable	25,000,000	19,000,000
Total	32,000,000	23,000,000
Shareholders' Equity		
Capital stock	56,000,000	14,000,000
Retained earnings	30,000,000	5,000,000
Total	86,000,000	19,000,000
Total liabilities and shareholders' equity.	$118,000,000	$42,000,000

During its due diligence review, Arcadia determined that while the liabilities of The Claremont Company were fairly valued, the reported value of Claremont's inventory was understated by $1,000,000 as a consequence of using the LIFO method, and the intangible assets of The Claremont Company were overstated by $4,000,000 because an impairment in the value of certain intangible assets had not yet been recorded in the company's financial statements.

Required

a. Calculate the value of the goodwill implicit in the offer price of $22 million.
b. Prepare the unconsolidated balance sheet of The Arcadia Company immediately following a successful acquisition of 100 percent of the outstanding shares of The Claremont Company.
c. Prepare the consolidated balance sheet for The Arcadia-Claremont Company assuming a successful acquisition offer.

The solution is on pages 295–296.

EXECUTIVE SUMMARY

This chapter examined the accounting for investments in other corporate entities. We considered why such investments are made and how they are accounted for. In general, small equity investments (0 to 20 percent) are accounted for at their current market value. Investments representing 20 to 50 percent of the outstanding equity are accounted for using the equity method, as are most joint ventures and special purpose entities; and, investments involving a controlling equity interest (greater than 50 percent) are accounted for using consolidated accounting.

As a validation of your understanding of the content of this chapter, you should now be able to:

- Explain why companies acquire ownership interests in other businesses.
- Understand how to account for investments in debt and equity securities, including the application of the equity method and consolidation accounting.
- Understand the accounting for joint ventures and special purposes entities.
- Understand the foreign currency issues that arise with investments in foreign companies.

In Chapter 9, we begin an exploration of corporate financing decisions, specifically how companies finance their operations and capital investments using debt.

KEY CONCEPTS AND TERMS

Accumulated Other Comprehensive Income (AOCI), 260
Acquisition method, 271
Amortized cost, 260
Arms-length transactions, 267
Available-for-sale securities, 259, 261
Conglomerate discount, 273
Consolidation accounting, 261
Cumulative foreign currency translation adjustment, 279
Currency hedge, 278
Current rate method, 278

Deconsolidation, 273
Equity in the earnings (loss) of an unconsolidated affiliate, 260
Equity method, 260
Full consolidation, 271
Goodwill, 267
Held-to-maturity debt securities, 260, 261
Information overload, 269
Joint venture, 274
Liquidating dividend, 267
Marketable debt and equity securities, 259

Mark-to-market accounting, 259
Noncontrolling interest, 270
Off-balance-sheet financing, 271
Related-party transaction, 267
Special purpose entities (SPE), 275
Special purpose vehicles (SPV), 275
Spin-off, 273
Temporal method, 278
Trading securities, 259, 261
Unrealized gain (loss), 259
Variable interest entity (VIE), 275

QUESTIONS

Q8.1 **Accounting for Marketable Securities.** Marketable securities are classified under U.S. GAAP as either trading securities or available-for-sale securities. Regardless of their classification, marketable securities are accounted for at their current market value using mark-to-market accounting. Discuss why mark-to-market accounting is superior to accounting for marketable securities at their historical cost. Should mark-to-market accounting be adopted to account for all assets on the balance sheet? Why or why not?

Q8.2 **Equity Method versus Consolidated Reporting.** The equity method is often described as a "one-line consolidation." Discuss the similarities of the equity method and consolidated reporting. Discuss how these methods differ in their financial statement presentation.

Q8.3 **Noncontrolling Interest.** The noncontrolling interest account arises on the consolidated balance sheet and is reported as a component of shareholders' equity. Many financial analysts, however, regard the account as a component of a firm's debt for purposes of financial statement analysis. Discuss whether the noncontrolling interest account on the balance sheet constitutes a component of debt or shareholders' equity.

Q8.4 **Accumulated Other Comprehensive Income.** Accumulated Other Comprehensive Income (AOCI) appears as a subsection of shareholders' equity on the balance sheet. Discuss the components of AOCI. What information does the AOCI convey to financial statement users about the financial health of a business?

Q8.5 **Cumulative Foreign Currency Translation Adjustment.** The cumulative foreign currency translation adjustment (CTA) account appears on the balance sheet as a component of Other Comprehensive Income. The CTA account may have either a positive (credit) or negative (debit) balance. Discuss the financial implications when the CTA account balance is negative and when it is positive.

Q8.6   **Goodwill.** In 1989, **PepsiCo Inc.** acquired three international franchise-food operations—Pizza Hut, Taco Bell, and Kentucky Fried Chicken. PepsiCo paid an aggregate of $3.4 billion for the three businesses, which had been valued by investment professionals to be worth, in aggregate, $400 million. As a consequence, PepsiCo recorded $3.0 billion of goodwill on its consolidated balance sheet associated with the acquisitions. Discuss why PepsiCo may have been willing to pay so much above the fair market value of the three businesses.

Q8.7   **Negative Goodwill.**   Negative goodwill is said to arise in an acquisition transaction when an acquiror pays less than the acquiree's book value to purchase the company. Discuss the circumstances that might lead to the presence of negative goodwill in an acquisition transaction.

Q8.8   **Accounting for Long-term Investments.**   In 2006, **CKX, Inc.**, a New York sports entertainment company, paid $50 million for an 80 percent ownership interest in G.O.A.T. LLC. (G.O.A.T. stands for "Greatest of All Time" and is a business that licenses the name and image of former boxing champion Muhammad Ali.) The remaining 20 percent of G.O.A.T. LLC is owned by the Ali Trust. Recent financial statements reveal that the gross revenue of G.O.A.T. averages $5 million annually, giving the LLC an estimated fair market value of $30 million. Discuss how CKX's investment in G.O.A.T. LLC should be accounted for. How should the Ali Trust account for its 20 percent ownership interest in G.O.A.T.?

Q8.9   **Mergers, Acquisitions, and Share Price.**   In 2006, **Danaher, Inc.** announced its intent to acquire Sybron Dental Specialties, Inc., a manufacturer of dental products. Danaher indicated that it had agreed to pay $47 per share for all of Sybron's outstanding shares. The cash tender offer, which included the assumption of $200 million of Sybron debt, was valued at $2 billion. In response to the acquisition announcement, Danaher's shares increased by 1.3 percent. Discuss how the capital market responds to merger and acquisition announcements, and specifically, the message implied by the market's response to Danaher's announcement of its planned acquisition of Sybron. What was the equity value of Sybron implicit in the transaction?

Q8.10   **Acquisition Bidding and the Winner's Curse.**   **Aztar Corporation** is an operator of casinos and hotels. The company's flagship properties are the Tropicana Hotel & Casino located in Las Vegas, Nevada, and in Atlantic City, New Jersey. In early 2006, Aztar's common shares were trading at $29 per share. On March 12, 2006, Pinnacle Entertainment Inc. made a tender offer to buy all of Aztar's outstanding common shares for $38 per share, a premium of 31 percent above Aztar's market price. Two weeks later, Ameristar Casinos, Inc. made a competing tender offer to buy Aztar's outstanding shares at a price of $43 per share. On April 15, 2006, Columbia Sussex Corporation made an unsolicited offer to buy Aztar at $47 per share, a premium of over 62 percent above Aztar's share price before the bidding competition began. Then, on April 28, 2006, Pinnacle raised its bid to $48 per share, followed immediately by a $50 per share bid by Columbia Sussex. Finally, on May 10, 2006, Pinnacle again raised its bid for Aztar to $51 per share, only to again be outbid by Columbia, which offered $53 per share. Some industry analysts described the bidding war for Aztar as an example of "The Winner's Curse," a situation in auction-like settings in which the winner is the entity that most overvalues the item being bid on, and thus, winning the final bid actually signals that the winner has lost as a consequence of overpaying for the item.

Discuss whether you think the Aztar bidding war is an example of The Winner's Curse. Does the significantly higher bid by Columbia Sussex of $53 per share indicate that the market for Aztar's common stock prior to the bidding war was inefficient? Why would Columbia Sussex be willing to pay such a significant premium ($24 per share) for Aztar's shares?

Q8.11   **Goodwill Impairment.**   On November 9, 2011, **Dean Foods** a Dallas Texas-based food and beverage company, announced that it would write off $1.6 billion, net of tax, in goodwill associated with its Fresh Dairy Direct acquisition. Discuss how Dean Foods will account for the write-off and why the company decided to make this adjustment to its goodwill account. How do you think the capital market reacted to this news announcement, and why?

Q8.12   **Divesting Long-term Investments.**   **BAE Systems**, Europe's largest defense company, announced that it was selling its 20 percent shareholding in Airbus, Europe's largest aircraft manufacturer, to EADS, the Franco-German aerospace company that already owned 80 percent of Airbus. The CEO of BAE Systems stated that Airbus had been an excellent investment but "we believe that now is the right time for us to divest our Airbus shareholding to allow us to concentrate on our core strategy." BAE's cost basis of its investment in Airbus was believed to be $4.3 billion, with a current market value of approximately $7.8 billion. Prior to 2001, at which time BAE and EADS purchased their shareholdings in Airbus, the passenger aircraft manufacturer had been structured as a "consortium" whose assets were held by national companies in the United Kingdom, France, Germany, and Spain. Discuss how Airbus might have been accounted for prior to 2001. Following the sale of Airbus to BAE and EADS in 2004, how would each firm's investment in Airbus have been accounted for? Estimate BAE's gain on the divestiture of its Airbus shareholding.

Q8.13   **De-Merger and Share Prices.**   In early 2006, Henry Silverman, chairman and CEO of Cendant Corporation, announced that the company's board of directors had approved the de-merger of Cendant into four operating companies—Avis Budget (a vehicle rental company composed of Avis, Budget, and Budget Truck), Wyndham Worldwide (a lodging company composed of such hotels and resort chains as Wyndham Resorts, Ramada Inn,

Howard Johnson, and others), Realogy (a real estate franchise company composed of Century 21, Coldwell Banker, and Sotheby's, among others), and Travel Distribution (a travel company composed of Orbitz.com, CheapTickets.com, and RatesToGo.com, among others). Under the split-up plan, Wyndham Worldwide and Realogy would be de-merged by a public offering of shares, whereas Avis Budget and Travel Distribution would be spun off to existing Cendant shareholders.

The reason for the de-merger, according to Silverman, was that Cendant's earnings were not being properly reflected in its share price. "We were among the 100 most profitable companies in America in 2004, yet we were somewhere in the 300s in terms of market value." Discuss the reasons why Cendant's share price in 2004 may not have reflected its earnings in 2004. If the de-merger is successful, what should happen to the share price of the four operating companies? Why?

Q8.14 **Poison-Pill Defense.** Following a series of hostile acquisitions in the global steel industry, **Nippon Steel Corporation** announced the implementation of a "poison-pill" plan designed to fend off any hostile takeover bids for the Japanese steel company. Under the plan, if a hostile buyer attempts to acquire a stake of 15 percent or more in the company, the steelmaker's shareholders would be allowed to double the number of shares they own for a nominal amount. Executives of Nippon Steel indicated that adoption of the plan was aimed at fending off potential acquirers who might damage the firm's corporate value. Market analysts expressed concern that the poison-pill defense would adversely affect the firm's share price. Discuss how Nippon's poison-pill defense could prevent an unwanted takeover bid and why the plan might actually hurt the company's share price.

Q8.15 **Goodwill Impairment and Debt Covenants.** The October 12, 2006, edition of *The Wall Street Journal* carried an article entitled "Expedia Might Trip Debt Covenant." The article revealed that the share price of **Expedia Inc.**, an online travel company, had recently declined by 33 percent following the company's spin-off from its parent company IAC/InterActive Corporation. IAC/InterActive had acquired Expedia several years earlier in an acquisition that involved $5.9 billion in goodwill.

When Expedia was spun off by its parent, the $5.9 billion in goodwill associated with the acquisition was downloaded from the consolidated balance sheet to Expedia's balance sheet. Further, a provision in Expedia's $1 billion borrowing arrangement required that the company maintain a shareholders' equity of $5.4 billion. With the decline in its share price to $16 per share, the company's market capitalization had dropped to just $5.2 billion. The company's book value at the time was just $5.8 billion. Discuss what action the company should take with respect to its $5.9 billion in acquisition goodwill. What are the consequences of those actions?

Q8.16 **(Ethics Perspective) Whistle-Blowing.** Whistle-blowers often question themselves as to whether they are doing the "right thing." Terms such as "snitch" and "tattletale" are often associated with an individual who exposes wrongdoing. Do you believe that it is ethical to report questionable activity as an anonymous whistle-blower, especially if you do not completely understand the events you are reporting?

Assignments with the ✓ logo in the margin are available in BusinessCourse.
See the Preface of the book for details.
CHECK FIGURE indicates that check figures are available on the book's Website.

EXERCISES

E8.17 **Accounting for Short-term Investments.** The Claremont Corporation invests its excess cash in low-risk, dividend-paying equity securities until such funds are needed to support operations. At the beginning of the year, the company's portfolio consisted of the following securities:

Company	Cost Basis
Bristol-Myers Squibb (BMS)	$ 75,000
Johnson & Johnson (JNJ)	55,000
Pfizer, Inc. (PFE)	110,000
Total	$240,000

At year-end, the market values of the three securities were as follows: BMS $82,000; JNJ $53,000; and PFE $100,000. Calculate the income statement effect of the company's short-term investments assuming: (a) all securities are classified as trading; (b) all securities are classified as available-for-sale; (c) BMS and JNJ are classified as trading, while PFE is classified as available-for-sale. Does the classification of a security as trading versus available-for-sale affect a company's reported earnings? Will it affect the value of a company's share price? Will it affect the amount of income taxes that a company pays to the Internal Revenue Service?

E8.18   **Accumulated Other Comprehensive Income.**   The following financial data is taken from the annual report of The Carlton Company:

(in thousands)	Year 1	Year 2	Year 3
Net income...	$20,493	$21,450	$21,846
Accumulated other comprehensive income (loss)			
Net unrealized gain (loss) on available-for-sale securities	(138)	219	33
Cumulative foreign currency translation adjustment	630	(549)	(96)
Total accumulated other comprehensive income.................	$20,985	$21,120	$21,783

Explain (a) what "accumulated other comprehensive income" is and how it differs from net income, (b) what happened to the value of The Carlton Company's available-for-sale securities each year, and (c) what caused the cumulative foreign currency translation adjustment to increase or decrease each year. Explain why The Carlton Company will pay income taxes on its net income but not its accumulated other comprehensive income.

E8.19   **Available-for-Sale Securities.**   The annual report of the Bristol-Myers Squibb (BMS) Company reveals that the company maintains a large investment in marketable securities:

CHECK
FIGURE

(in millions)	Year 1	Year 2
Marketable securities...	$3,794	$2,749

The footnotes to the company's financial statements report:

> The Company accounts for marketable securities in accordance with "Accounting for Certain Investments in Debt and Equity Securities." The Company determined the appropriate classification of all marketable securities was "available-for-sale" at the time of purchase.

Further, the company's statement of cash flow reveals that sales of marketable securities in Year 2 produced a positive cash flow of $1,043. Did the company's remaining portfolio of marketable securities experience a gain or loss in value in Year 2, and in what amount? How did the company account for that gain or loss? Was the gain (loss) taxable (tax deductible) in Year 2?

E8.20   **Available-for-Sale Securities.**   The annual report of Pfizer, Inc. (PFE) reveals that the company maintains a significant investment in short-term investments:

(in millions)	Year 1	Year 2
Short-term investments	$18,085	$19,979

During the year, the company purchased short-term investments (net of sales of short-term investments) totaling $1,261. Did the company's portfolio of short-term investments experience a gain or a loss during Year 2, and in what amount? Assuming all of Pfizer's short-term investments are classified as available-for-sale securities, how did the company account for the gain or loss in Year 2? Was the gain (loss) taxable (tax deductible) in Year 2?

E8.21   **Long-term Equity Investments.**   The annual report of the Bristol-Myers Squibb (BMS) Company discloses the following amounts on its consolidated statement of earnings:

(in millions)	Year 1	Year 2	Year 3
Equity in net income of affiliates..............................	$151	$273	$334

On the company's statement of cash flow, the following amounts appear as a subtraction from net earnings under the Cash Flow from Operating Activities:

(in millions)	Year 1	Year 2	Year 3
Undistributed income of affiliates.	$66	$7	$50

Calculate the amount of cash dividends received by BMS from its affiliates in Year 1, Year 2, and Year 3. Assume that BMS neither sold nor purchased any equity interest in its affiliates in Year 1, Year 2, and Year 3. What happened to the balance sheet value of the "investment in equity affiliates" account in Year 1, Year 2, and Year 3?

CHECK FIGURE ✓ **E8.22** **Long-term Equity Investments.** The annual report of The Arcadia Company discloses the following amounts on its consolidated statement of income:

	Year 1	Year 2	Year 3
Equity in earnings of unconsolidated affiliates.	$350	$415	$520

Further, on Arcadia's consolidated balance sheet, it reports the following amounts for its investment in its unconsolidated affiliates:

	Year 1	Year 2	Year 3
Investment in unconsolidated affiliates	$10,500	$10,715	$10,950

Calculate the amount of cash dividends received by The Arcadia Company from its unconsolidated affiliates in Year 2 and Year 3. Calculate the adjustment to net income that appears on Arcadia's statement of cash flow in Year 2 and Year 3 for "undistributed earnings of unconsolidated affiliates."

✓ **E8.23** **Equity Method.** The balance sheet of The Miller Corporation disclosed a long-term investment in the common shares of The Mann Corporation valued at $350,000 as of December 31, 2012. The investment had been purchased by The Miller Corporation in January, 2009. Further, the following financial information from The Mann Corporation is available:

Year	Net Income (loss)	Dividends Paid
2009	$ (30,000)	$ –0
2010	120,000	50,000
2011	150,000	60,000
2012	200,000	80,000

Determine how much The Miller Corporation paid for its investment in Mann common shares in January 2009 assuming that the investment represents a 25 percent ownership interest.

CHECK FIGURE ✓ **E8.24** **Equity Method.** On January 1, 2011, The Miller Corporation purchased 300,000 shares of The Mayfair Corporation for $5.7 million. The investment represented 25 percent of The Mayfair Corporation's outstanding common shares. During 2011, Mayfair reported net earnings of $2.25 million and paid a cash dividend of $0.15 per share. During 2012, Mayfair reported a net loss of $180,000 and again paid a dividend of $0.15 per share. Calculate the book value of Miller's investment in Mayfair as of December 31, 2011, and December 31, 2012.

✓ **E8.25** **Equity Method.** On January 2, 2011, Winstead & Company purchased 1,000,000 shares of the Secrest Company for $32.0 million. The investment represented 40 percent of the outstanding common shares of The Secrest Company. During 2011, Secrest reported net earnings of $1.05 per share and paid a cash dividend of $0.35 per share. During 2012, Secrest reported net earnings of $1.50 per share and paid a cash dividend $0.40 per share. Calculate the book value of Winstead's investment in Secrest as of December 31, 2011, and December 31, 2012.

✓ **E8.26** **Accounting for Joint Ventures.** **Starbucks Corporation** and **PepsiCo** formed a joint venture to produce and distribute Starbucks' bottled Frappuccino coffee drink throughout North America. Assume that the 50/50 joint venture had a book value on the consolidated balance sheet of Starbucks Corporation of $90 million and $70 million at year-end 2012 and 2011, respectively. Further, assume that on Starbucks' 2012 statement of cash flow, the company disclosed an adjustment to net income for the PepsiCo joint venture as follows:

	2012
Equity in income of joint venture	$(22,000,000)

Calculate the joint venture's total earnings and total cash dividends for 2012.

PROBLEMS

P8.27   Accounting for Marketable Equity Securities.   Tim Propp, CFO of Thunderbird, Inc., invested some of the firm's excess cash in the common shares of what he thought were three undervalued securities. At year-end, he reviewed how the portfolio of securities had done.

Security Name	Cost Basis	Market Value at Year-End	Classification
Microsoft Corporation.................	$100,000	$122,000	Trading security
Pfizer, Inc..............................	75,000	73,000	Trading security
Boeing, Inc.	50,000	48,000	Available-for-sale security
	$225,000	$243,000	

Required

1. Calculate the value that would be assigned to the portfolio of securities on Thunderbird's balance sheet at year-end.
2. Calculate the income statement effect of the portfolio of securities at year-end.
3. Calculate the income statement effect of the portfolio of securities at year-end assuming all securities are classified as available-for-sale.
4. Are the company's reported earnings impacted by whether the portfolio of securities are classified as trading versus available-for-sale? Will the company's share price be impacted by the particular classification adopted? Will the company's income taxes be impacted?

P8.28   Accounting for Marketable Equity Securities.   Among the various responsibilities of the Chief Financial Officer (CFO) of the Amphlett Corporation was the management and oversight of the firm's cash reserves. During the year, the CFO had invested some of the firm's excess cash in what she thought were three undervalued stocks. All of the securities were classified as available-for-sale. At year-end, she reviewed how the portfolio of investments had done.

Investment	Cost Basis	Market Value at Year-End
Bristol-Myers Squibb, Inc.	$ 50,000	$ 42,000
Titanium Metals, Corp.	50,000	55,000
Zila, Inc.	50,000	80,000
	$150,000	$177,000

Required

1. Calculate the value that would be assigned to the portfolio of marketable equity securities on the balance sheet of The Amphlett Corporation at year-end under each of the following approaches:
    a. Cost
    b. Lower-of-cost-or-market
    c. Market value
2. How will the disclosure on the year-end balance sheet change if the entire portfolio is classified as "trading securities" versus "available-for-sale securities"?

P8.29   Equity Method.   At midyear, National Steel Fabricators, Inc. purchased a 35 percent ownership interest in Keystone Consolidated, Inc. for $40 million. At year-end, Keystone reported an operating loss of $6 million, of which only $2 million related to the second half of the year. Despite the operating loss, Keystone paid its regular quarterly dividend of $1 million in both the third and fourth quarters.
CHECK FIGURE

Required

1. Calculate the income statement effect for National Steel at year-end associated with its investment in Keystone.
2. Calculate the book value that National Steel should record on its balance sheet for its investment in Keystone at year-end.

 P8.30   **Consolidation Accounting.**   ABC Inc. purchased all of the outstanding common shares of XYZ Inc. for $100 million. At the time of the acquisition, the fair value of XYZ was $80 million. Presented below are the condensed balance sheets for ABC and XYZ immediately prior to the acquisition:

(in millions)	ABC Inc.	XYZ Inc.
Assets..	$150	$100
Liabilities.....................................	$ 30	$ 20
Shareholders' equity	120	80
Total	$150	$100

Required

Prepare ABC's (a) unconsolidated balance sheet immediately after making the equity investment in XYZ and (b) the consolidated balance sheet immediately following the acquisition.

CHECK FIGURE **P8.31**   **Consolidation Accounting.**   MTF, Inc., acquired all of the outstanding shares of KMF, Inc., by means of a share exchange valued at $50 million. At the time of the acquisition, the fair market value of KMF was $40 million. Presented below are the condensed balance sheets for MTF, Inc. and KMF, Inc. immediately prior to the acquisition:

Balance Sheet	KMF, Inc.	MTF, Inc.
Assets...	$50 million	$70 million
Liabilities....................................	$10 million	$20 million
Shareholders' equity	40 million	50 million
Total	$50 million	$70 million

Required

1. Prepare the unconsolidated balance sheet for MTF immediately after making the investment in KMF.
2. Prepare the MTF-KMF consolidated balance sheet following the acquisition.

P8.32   **Consolidation Accounting.**   Graham Inc. acquired all of the outstanding shares of Mahoney Inc. through an exchange of common shares. The aggregate market value of the Graham shares distributed to the Mahoney shareholders was $400,000. Further, at the time of the exchange, the fair value of Mahoney's net assets was equal to their book value, except for Mahoney's property and equipment, which was appraised at $540,000. Presented below are the pre-acquisition balance sheets of the two companies:

Pre-acquisition Balance Sheets	Graham Inc.	Mahoney Inc.
Cash...	$ 60,000	$ 10,000
Accounts receivable (net).....................	140,000	80,000
Inventory (FIFO)	220,000	120,000
Property and equipment (net)..................	800,000	500,000
Other assets..................................	40,000	20,000
	$1,260,000	$730,000
Accounts payable..............................	$ 100,000	$ 25,000
Other current liabilities	100,000	15,000
Bonds payable	240,000	350,000
Common stock (no par value)	500,000	250,000
Retained earnings	320,000	90,000
	$1,260,000	$730,000

Required

Prepare the consolidated balance sheet for the new company immediately following the transaction using purchase accounting.

P8.33 **Consolidation Accounting.** After an intense period of negotiation, Global Enterprises Corporation agreed to purchase all of the outstanding common shares of The Carlton Corporation. The agreed-upon price was $294 million, payable in Global Enterprise shares. According to the agreement, Global Enterprises would issue one share of its common stock in exchange for each share of The Carlton Corporation. Following the exchange, The Carlton Corporation would become a wholly-owned subsidiary of Global Enterprises. At the time of the negotiations, the market price of Global Enterprises' shares was $24.50 per share. Presented below are the pre-acquisition balance sheets of Global Enterprises and The Carlton Corporation:

Pre-acquisition Balance Sheets	Global Enterprises Corporation	The Carlton Corporation
Assets		
Cash	$ 80,000,000	$ 25,000,000
Short-term investments	50,000,000	35,000,000
Accounts receivable (net)	75,000,000	50,000,000
Inventory (LIFO)	190,000,000	95,000,000
Property & equipment (net)	380,000,000	230,000,000
Other assets	45,000,000	15,000,000
Total assets	$820,000,000	$450,000,000
Liabilities & Shareholders' Equity		
Accounts payable	$ 95,000,000	$ 75,000,000
Other current liabilities	40,000,000	30,000,000
Bonds payable	110,000,000	—
Other long-term debt	75,000,000	125,000,000
Common stock ($10 par)	120,000,000	—
Common stock ($5 par)	—	60,000,000
Capital in excess of par value	70,000,000	20,000,000
Retained earnings	310,000,000	140,000,000
Total liabilities & shareholders' equity	$820,000,000	$450,000,000

As part of Global Enterprises' due diligence, the company determined that while the liabilities of The Carlton Corporation were fairly valued, some of the company's assets were not fairly valued. The fair value of Carlton's assets were as follows:

Asset	Fair Market Value	Under/(Over) Statement
Cash	$ 25,000,000	$ 0
Short-term investments	45,000,000	10,000,000
Accounts receivable (net)	35,000,000	(15,000,000)
Inventory (LIFO)	130,000,000	35,000,000
Property & equipment (net)	280,000,000	50,000,000
Other assets	0	(15,000,000)
Total	$515,000,000	$65,000,000

Required

Prepare the consolidated balance sheet immediately following the acquisition using consolidation accounting.

P8.34 **Equity Investments: International.** Aussie Steaks Inc. operates a chain of steak restaurants in the United States. On January 1, 2011, the company had $500 million in assets.

On January 1, 2011, the company acquired 25 percent of the shares of Sun Devil Burgers, a hamburger chain of 200 outlets, for $10 million in cash. At the time of the acquisition, Sun Devil had total assets of $100 million and total liabilities of $60 million. In 2011, Sun Devil reported net income of $12 million and paid cash dividends of $4 million.

On March 6, 2012, the company established Zaijian Burgers, a wholly-owned self-sustaining Chinese subsidiary, with cash of RMB24 million. The Chinese RMB (renmimbi) is the functional currency for Zaijian Burgers. The exchange rate at the time the subsidiary was established was RMB8 per $1. Immediately after the subsidiary was established the exchange rate changed to RMB12 per $1. Aussie Steaks and its affiliates have a December 31 year-end.

Required

1. What amount will Aussie Steaks Inc. report on its January 1, 2011, balance sheet with regard to its investment in Sun Devil Burgers following the acquisition?
2. What amount will Aussie Steaks Inc. report on its December 31, 2011, balance sheet with regard to its investment in Sun Devil Burgers?
3. What is the amount of total assets that Zaijian Burgers will show on its balance sheet in U.S. dollars on March 6, 2012?
4. What is the amount of the cumulative foreign currency translation adjustment that Aussie Steaks will report on its consolidated balance sheet on March 6, 2012, following the exchange rate change?

 P8.35 **Equity Investments: International.** On January 1, 2011, Tradiciones, Inc., established Tradiciones de Mexico, a wholly-owned, self-sustaining Mexican subsidiary with assets valued at 48 million pesos. The peso (P) is the functional currency for Tradiciones de Mexico. The exchange rate at the time that the subsidiary was established was Ps8 per $1. On January 2, 2011, after the subsidiary was established, the exchange rate changed to Ps6 per $1.

Required

1. What is the amount of total assets that Tradiciones de Mexico will show on its balance sheet in U.S. dollars on January 1, 2011 (before the exchange rate change)?
2. What is the amount of the cumulative foreign currency translation adjustment that Tradiciones, Inc. will report on its balance sheet on January 2, 2011, after the exchange rate change?
3. At December 31, 2011, Tradiciones de Mexico reported the information below. Did the Mexican peso appreciate, remain unchanged, or depreciate against the U.S. dollar?

In millions of dollars	Common Stock	Accumulated Other Comprehensive Income	Retained Earnings	Total
Net income.			100	100
Accumulated other comprehensive income-foreign currency translation adjustment		(5)		(5)

P8.36 **Consolidated versus Unconsolidated Reporting.** Global Enterprises Corporation (GE) is a manufacturing company whose principal products are microwave ovens, refrigerators, and conventional ovens. The company had a long history of selling high-quality, high-priced home appliances; however, recent reductions in the price of competitor products forced GE to consider ways to provide assistance to its customers to help them buy its products. As a consequence, GE started its own finance subsidiary, the GE Acceptance Corporation (GEAC), to assist customers in financing their purchases.

GE Corporation is also associated with three other companies. It holds an 80 percent interest in Scrub-All, a company that makes automatic dishwashers. GE purchased the interest in Scrub-All because the company's product line complemented its own items and the products were a quality that GE would have had difficulty duplicating. Further, to ensure a steady supply of chrome parts for its appliances, GE obtained a 10 percent interest in the common stock of Acme Chrome Company. Well over 50 percent of Acme's sales were attributed to purchases by GE and Scrub-All. Further, to compete in the low-end market for various appliances, GE formed a joint venture (Spotless Appliance) with Whirlwind Products Co. to produce low-cost appliances. The following is a summary of GE's subsidiaries, affiliates, and equity investments:

GE Acceptance Corporation. GEAC is a wholly-owned subsidiary that purchases consumer notes from its parent, GE Corporation. GEAC borrows funds from several banking institutions on a medium- and long-term basis and uses the margins between the short-term interest rates on the consumer notes and the rates on its medium- and long-term liabilities to cover its overhead costs. The parent company (GE) guarantees all of the borrowings of GEAC.

Scrub-All Company. With an ownership interest of 80 percent of the common stock of Scrub-All, GE controls the strategic policies of Scrub-All Company through an interlocking board of directors. Scrub-All, like GE, sells its consumer notes to GEAC.

Acme Chrome Company. To guarantee a steady supply of chrome parts, GE purchased a 10 percent interest in Acme Chrome Company. Over the years, a strong relationship had developed between GE and Acme. For example, Acme schedules the production run of its other customers around the production needs of GE and Scrub-All.

Spotless Appliance Company. Both GE Corporation and Whirlwind Products Company (an otherwise unrelated company) contributed half of the funds necessary to start Spotless Appliance Company. Spotless Appliance Company makes low-end appliance models that are sold under the Spotless trade name or are labeled with various department store names.

GE CORPORATION Consolidated Statement of Financial Position December 31	
Assets	
Current assets	$ 37,500,000
Notes receivable	58,000,000
Investment in Spotless Appliance at equity (50%)	1,750,000
Investment in Acme Chrome Company (10%) at market	5,600,000
Other assets	101,500,000
Goodwill	3,200,000
Total assets	$207,550,000
Liabilities and Shareholders' Equity	
Current liabilities	$ 31,500,000
Long-term liabilities	102,100,000
Common stock	15,000,000
Retained earnings	51,450,000
Noncontrolling interest	7,500,000
Total liabilities and shareholders' equity	$207,550,000

SCRUB-ALL COMPANY Statement of Financial Position December 31	
Assets	
Current assets	$16,400,000
Other assets	52,600,000
Total assets	$69,000,000
Liabilities and Shareholders' Equity	
Current liabilities	$13,350,000
Long-term liabilities	18,150,000
Common stock	12,000,000
Retained earnings	25,500,000
Total liabilities and shareholders' equity	$69,000,000

ACME CHROME COMPANY
Statement of Financial Position
December 31

Assets

Current assets	$14,750,000
Other assets	36,250,000
Total assets	$51,000,000

Liabilities and Shareholders' Equity

Current liabilities	$ 5,000,000
Long-term liabilities	15,000,000
Common stock	18,750,000
Retained earnings	12,250,000
Total liabilities and shareholders' equity	$51,000,000

GE ACCEPTANCE CORPORATION
Statement of Financial Position
December 31

Assets

Current assets	$ 8,000,000
Notes receivable	58,000,000
Other assets	6,500,000
Total assets	$72,500,000

Liabilities and Shareholders' Equity

Current liabilities	$ 5,000,000*
Long-term debt	47,100,000
Common stock ($1 par)	10,000,000
Retained earnings	10,400,000
Total liabilities and shareholders' equity	$72,500,000

*$3,000,000 of the current liabilities is a promissory note to GE Corporation. GE Corporation accounts for this as a long-term receivable in other assets.

SPOTLESS APPLIANCE COMPANY
Statement of Financial Position
December 31

Assets

Current assets	$ 8,500,000
Other assets	16,000,000
Total assets	$24,500,000

Liabilities and Shareholders' Equity

Current liabilities	$ 3,000,000
Long-term debt	18,000,000
Common stock ($1 par)	6,000,000
Retained earnings	(2,500,000)
Total liabilities and shareholders' equity	$24,500,000

Required

1. Why are the investments in Acme Chrome and Spotless Appliance Companies shown on the GE Corporation consolidated balance sheet while the investments in Scrub-All and GEAC are omitted?
2. What is meant by the carrying value "at equity" for the investment in Spotless Appliance Company on GE's consolidated balance sheet?
3. Why is the investment in Acme Chrome Company shown "at market"?
4. Explain the Goodwill account on GE's consolidated balance sheet. To what company is this account related?

5. What is meant by "noncontrolling interest" on GE's consolidated balance sheet? To which company is this account related? Is this a liability or a shareholders' equity account?
6. What are GE Corporation's current ratio, total debt to equity ratio, and total debt to total asset ratio? Are these ratios correct?

CORPORATE ANALYSIS

CA8.37 The Procter and Gamble Company.   The 2012 annual report of **The Procter & Gamble Company** (P&G) is available at http://annualreport.pg.com/annualreport2012/index.shtml. After reviewing P&G's annual report, respond to the following questions:

P&G's consolidated balance sheet reveals that the company has $53.773 ($57.562) billion in goodwill as of June 30, 2012 (2011). What percentage of total assets does goodwill represent in 2012 and 2011? Does P&G amortize its goodwill? If so, over what period? If not, why not? Did P&G recognize an impairment in its goodwill in either 2012 or 2011?

CA8.38 General Electric Company.   The consolidated financial statements of **General Electric Company** (GE) combine the industrial manufacturing and services businesses of GE with the financial services businesses of General Electric Capital Corporation (GECC). GE is the parent-company of GECC. Because of the diverse nature of the businesses reflected in the operations of GE and GECC, GE presents its financial statements in two formats—a fully consolidated format (including the results of GE, GECC, and all other majority-owned entities) and a partially consolidated format (excluding the results of GECC). In GE's partially-consolidated financial statements, the investment in GECC is accounted for using the Equity Method.

 a. Presented below are the partially consolidated income statements and balance sheets for GE and GECC for 2012. Do you think the fully 2012 consolidated statements for GE would include all of the amounts provided in each account presented?
 b. Go to www.ge.com and review the company's 2012 consolidated statements. What significant differences do you notice about GE's financial statements on a partially consolidated basis versus a fully consolidated basis?

Statement of Earnings		
For the years ended December 31		
($ millions)	**GE 2012**	**GECC 2012**
Revenues		
Sales of goods	$ 73,304	$ 119
Sales of services	27,571	0
Other income	2,657	0
GECC earnings from continuing operations	7,401	0
GECC revenues from services	0	45,920
Total revenues	110,933	46,039
Costs and Expenses		
Costs of goods sold	57,118	99
Cost of services sold	17,938	0
Interest and other financial charges	1,353	11,697
Investment contracts, insurances losses and insurance annuity benefits	0	2,984
Provision for losses on financing receivables	0	3,891
Other costs and expenses	17,672	19,413
Total costs and expenses	94,081	38,084
Earnings from continuing operations before income taxes and accounting changes	**16,852**	**7,955**
Provision for income taxes	(2,013)	(491)
Earnings from continuing operations before accounting changes	**14,839**	**7,464**
Earning (loss) from discontinued operations, net of taxes	(1,038)	(1,186)
Net earnings	**$ 13,801**	**$ 6,278**

Statement of Financial Position **At December 31**		
($ millions)	**GE** **2012**	**GECC** **2012**
Assets		
Cash and equivalents..	$ 15,509	$ 61,941
Investment securities...	74	48,439
Current receivables	10,872	0
Inventories	15,295	79
Financing receivables—net	0	268,951
Other GECC receivables	0	13,988
Property, plant and equipment—net	16,033	53,673
Investment in GECC...	77,930	0
Goodwill..	46,143	27,304
Intangible assets—net	10,700	1,294
All other assets..	37,936	62,217
Assets of businesses held for sale......................................	0	211
Assets of discontinued operations......................................	9	1,126
Total assets...	$230,501	$539,223
Liabilities and Shareholders' Equity		
Short-term borrowings..	$ 6,041	$ 95,940
Accounts payable, principally trade accounts............................	14,259	6,277
Progress collections and price adjustment accrued	10,877	0
Dividends payable	1,980	0
Other GE current liabilities	14,896	0
Non-recourse borrowings of consolidated securitization entities	0	30,123
Bank deposits	0	46,461
Long-term borrowings	11,428	224,776
Investment contracts, insurance liabilities and insurance annuity benefits......	0	28,696
All other liabilities	53,093	16,050
Deferred income taxes..	(5,946)	5,871
Liabilities of businesses held for sale...................................	0	157
Liabilities of discontinued operations...................................	70	2,275
Total liabilities	106,698	456,626
Common stock (10,405,625,000 shares outstanding at year-end 2012)........	702	0
Accumulated gains (losses)—net		
Investment securities	677	673
Currency translation adjustments...................................	412	(131)
Cash flow hedges...	(722)	(746)
Minimum pension liabilities..	(20,597)	(736)
Other capital..	33,070	31,586
Retained earnings	144,055	51,244
Less common stock held in treasury	(34,571)	0
Total shareholders' equity..	123,026	81,890
Noncontrolling interests...	777	707
Total equity	123,803	82,597
Total liabilities and shareholders' equity................................	$230,501	$539,223

CA8.39 **Internet-based Analysis.** Consider a publicly held company whose products you are familiar with. Some examples might include:

Company	Product	Corporate Website
• Johnson & Johnson Company....	• Band-Aids	• www.jnj.com
• Microsoft Corporation...........	• Windows XP software	• www.microsoft.com
• Nokia Corporation..............	• Cellular phones	• www.nokia.com
• Intel Corporation	• Pentium processors	• www.intel.com
• Kimberly-Clark Corporation......	• Kleenex	• www.kimberly-clark.com

Access the company's public website and search for its most recent annual report. (Note: Some companies provide access to their financial data through an "investor relations" link, while others provide a direct link to their "annual reports.") After locating your company's most recent annual report, open the file and review its contents. After reviewing the annual report for your selected company, prepare answers to the following questions:

a. Does the company have any short-term investments or marketable securities? If so, are they trading securities or available-for-sale securities? Over the past year, did the company experience any unrealized gain or losses on its marketable securities? If so, in what amount?

b. Does the company have any unconsolidated affiliates or joint ventures? If so, how are they accounted for? Did the unconsolidated affiliates or joint ventures produce a profit or loss last year?

c. Does the company have any consolidated subsidiaries? If so, how many? Does the company own 100 percent of all of its consolidated subsidiaries? How were you able to determine this?

d. Does the company have any goodwill from prior acquisitions? How does the company account for its goodwill? Has the goodwill been impaired in either of the last two years? If so, what amount was the impairment?

CA8.40 **IFRS Financial Statements.** The 2012 financial statements of **LVMH Moet Hennessey-Louis Vuitton S.A.** are presented in Appendix C of this book. LVMH is a Paris-based holding company and one of the world's largest and best-known luxury goods companies. As a member-nation of the European Union, French companies are required to prepare their consolidated (group) financial statements using International Financial Reporting Standards (IFRS). In LVMH's Notes to the Consolidated Financial Statements (not presented in Appendix C), the company discloses its method of consolidation:

> The subsidiaries in which the Group holds a direct or indirect de facto or de jure controlling interest are fully consolidated. Jointly controlled companies are consolidated on a proportionate basis. For distribution subsidiaries operating in accordance with the contractual distribution arrangements with the Diageo group, only the portion of assets and liabilities and results of operations relating to the LVMH group's activities is included in the consolidated financial statements. Companies where the Group has significant influence but no controlling interest are accounted for using the equity method.

How does LVMH's consolidation policy differ from U.S. GAAP?

SOLUTION TO REVIEW PROBLEM

Solution

a. Goodwill

Purchase price...		$22,000,000
Less: Fair market value		
Book value...	$19,000,000	
Add: Inventory understatement	1,000,000	
Less: Intangible asset impairment	(4,000,000)	
		(16,000,000)
Goodwill..		$ 6,000,000

b. Unconsolidated balance sheet

THE ARCADIA COMPANY				
Unconsolidated Balance Sheet				
Assets		**Liabilities & Shareholders' Equity**		
Cash.....................	$ 4,000,000*	Accounts payable.................	$ 7,000,000	
Inventory.................	12,000,000	Bonds payable	25,000,000	
Investment in Claremont Co. . .	22,000,000	Total	32,000,000	
Fixed assets, net	50,000,000	Shareholders' equity		
Intangible assets	30,000,000	Capital stock	56,000,000	
		Retained earnings	30,000,000	
Total	$118,000,000	Total liabilities & equity............	$118,000,000	

* Cash: $26,000,000 − $22,000,000 = $4,000,000

c. Consolidated balance sheet

THE ARCADIA COMPANY				
Consolidated Balance Sheet				
Assets		**Liabilities & Shareholders' Equity**		
Cash.....................	$ 6,000,000	Accounts payable.................	$ 11,000,000	
Inventory.................	20,000,000	Bonds payable	44,000,000	
Investment in Claremont Co. . .	0	Total	55,000,000	
Fixed assets, net	65,000,000	Shareholders' equity		
Intangible assets	44,000,000	Capital stock	56,000,000	
Goodwill..................	6,000,000	Retained earnings	30,000,000	
		Total	86,000,000	
Total	$141,000,000	Total liabilities & equity............	$141,000,000	

When you complete this chapter you should be able to:

1. Explain how bonds and notes are valued and reported in financial statements.

2. Describe how companies account for debt when it is retired before its maturity.

3. Explain the difference between a capital lease and an operating lease and how each is reported in financial statements.

4. Discuss how and why companies manage the amount of debt reported on their balance sheets.

Debt Financing: Bonds, Notes, and Leases

John W. Nordstrom used his stake from the Alaska gold rush to open a small shoe store in Seattle, Washington, in 1901. This small store has since grown into an upscale U.S. apparel and shoe retail chain with 115 Nordstrom department stores and 110 outlet stores (Nordstrom Rack) across 30 states. It also has a strong presence in both the catalog and internet retail markets. The company is perhaps best known for its legendary reputation for top-rate customer service. In addition to its reputation for pleasing the customer, the company has also garnered attention for its treatment of its employees. **Nordstrom** is a Hall of Fame member of *Fortune* magazine's "100 Best Companies to Work For."

NORDSTROM

An examination of Nordstrom's balance sheet reveals that the company's largest single asset is its investment in land, buildings and equipment, valued at nearly $2.5 billion, 29 percent of total assets, as of fiscal year-end January 2012. Nordstrom financed these assets, along with other major assets such as over $1.1 billion of inventory, with a combination of debt and equity. The company's balance sheet reports long-term debt totaling almost $3.7 billion and shareholders' equity of over $1.9 billion, representing a total debt-to-equity ratio of just under 2.0.

Does the Nordstrom balance sheet portray a complete picture of the company's use of financing? Many investment professionals would say "no," and that to better understand how Nordstrom finances its assets, financial statement users need to dig into the footnotes to the financial statements. In particular, it is important to understand Nordstrom's use of off-balance-sheet financing. Nordstrom entered into various operating leases for the land and buildings for many of its 225 stores. Generally accepted accounting principles allow Nordstrom to omit this form of financing, along with the corresponding leased assets, from its corporate balance sheet. The company's footnotes reveal that it is committed to approximately $1.1 billion in future lease payments associated with these leases as of January 2012. Failing to include these leased assets and lease liabilities in an analysis of the company's financial statements, however, can cause serious distortion to such important financial indicators as the debt-to-equity ratio and return-on-assets.

In this chapter, we consider various debt financing strategies and products, including the use of lease financing, available to companies like Nordstrom. In addition, we discuss a methodology that can aid in the analysis of corporate financial statements that rely on off-balance-sheet debt financing.

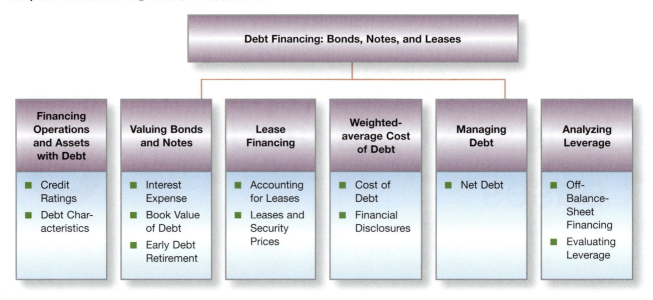

FINANCING OPERATIONS AND ASSETS WITH DEBT: BONDS AND NOTES

Most businesses finance at least a part of their operations with debt. One of the reasons for this is that debt financing is almost always a less expensive form of financing than equity. Since creditors assume less risk than equity investors, it is appropriate that the expected rate of return to be earned by creditors should be less than that expected by shareholders. Remember that shareholders likely will lose all of their invested capital if a business fails, whereas creditors are likely to lose only part, if any, because they have first claim on any remaining assets of the business. Debt also carries the advantage that it is anti-dilutive to the shareholder. That is, if a firm raises needed funds through debt financing, the existing ownership percentage in the company is unchanged. If those funds are raised through a stock issue to new shareholders, then the percentage ownership in the company to shareholders prior to the stock issue will fall.

The specific source of debt financing available to a borrower will depend on the desired length of the borrowing period, the amount of the borrowing, and the riskiness of the borrower. Small firms as borrowers, for example, are considered to be riskier than larger, established firms. A sustained history of operating performance makes lenders more comfortable with a firm's ability to repay debt, and small firms tend to lack a history of operating experience. Further, small firms tend to borrow smaller amounts, and since investment bankers are unlikely to engage in public debt offerings of less than $100 million, small borrowings are typically sourced from a single, private lender. Thus, most small firms have access to only a limited set of lenders—local financial institutions, business development companies, the Small Business Administration, friends and family, and in some cases, private equity and venture capital firms.

Larger, established firms, on the other hand, have many borrowing options, including financial institutions, insurance companies, pension funds, as well as the public debt market. Just which lending segment is likely to be accessed is a function of the desired length of the borrowing period, also called the loan **duration**. Banks and similar financial institutions prefer to limit their risk exposure to loans involving durations of one day to five years, whereas the public debt market is typically the source for borrowings of 5 to 20 years. Finally, borrowings involving durations greater than 20 years tend to be sourced from insurance companies and pension funds, which have the capacity and desire to place funds with borrowers for extended periods of time.

The public debt market is composed of two similar lending products (among others)—bonds and notes. **Bonds** are publicly issued financial instruments that promise to pay the bondholder periodic payments over the life of the investment, usually 10 to 20 years, and then make a lump-sum principal repayment at maturity. **Notes** are similar instruments but have shorter maturities, usually one to ten years, and are frequently privately placed with large institutional investors or financial institutions. Therefore, as long-term liabilities of the company bonds and notes have the same basic structure: the company receives cash up front and then agrees to repay that cash with an interest return to the lender. Bonds and notes also often have the following notable common features:

- No voting rights at the annual shareholders' meeting.

- An **indenture agreement** that specifies covenants, often based on accounting ratios, which may restrict the borrower's ability to pay dividends, issue additional debt, undertake mergers and acquisitions, or sell assets.

- A **trustee**, such as a bank or trust company, which administers the provisions of the indenture agreement and acts as an independent party to protect the interests of the lenders.

- Priority in receiving interest and principal repayments over any payments to common and preferred shareholders, such as dividends or payments in liquidation.

A number of additional features may be included with bonds and notes. For instance, bonds and notes may be **secured**—that is, the lender has a priority claim on specific assets of the borrower in the event of default—or **unsecured** (having no claim on specific assets in the event of a default). Unsecured debt, also known as **debentures**, may be **subordinated**—that is, the claim of the unsecured debtholder has a lower priority, or is "junior" to, the claims of secured creditors. **Unsubordinated** or senior debt has a priority claim equivalent to that of suppliers who hold the accounts payable of a firm, and thus, typically hold a claim against specific operating assets (such as inventory) of a business.

Bonds and notes may also be **convertible** into the common shares of the borrower. Convertible bonds and notes carry a share conversion ratio indicating the number of common shares to be received in the event of conversion, and are convertible at the option of the debtholder (usually, however, only after some portion of the debt duration has expired). Some bonds and notes are **callable** at the option of the borrower. A callable bond or note is one that may be mandatorily redeemed or retired prior to maturity. Callable bonds or notes are also often convertible to provide debtholders with an option to either (i) accept cash if the bond or note is called, or (ii) convert the bond or note into the common shares of the borrower. Finally, some bonds are commodity-based in which the principal repayment is indexed to the price of a commodity like gold, silver, or oil, often with an option to receive the commodity instead of cash at maturity.

Evident from this discussion is that the potential features of bonds and notes are many. They exist though for the simple reason that lenders require some compensation for the risk they will bear relative to their expected return on a company loan. While these features may affect the appeal of the bond or note to the lender, and ultimately its value, the accounting for these debt instruments remains generally unaffected by these features. As we will see the liability on the borrowing company's books is valued at its present value, and interest expense is charged on that liability each period.

Credit Ratings and the Cost of Debt

The interest on debt that is earned by the lender and paid by the company, often labeled the **cost of debt**, is dependent on many factors. These include the inherent riskiness of the lending company, the current economic and political environments, the set of alternative investments available to the lender, and the many features that may attach to the bonds or notes, as described above. One important additional item that affects the cost of debt for publicly issued bonds and notes is the **credit-risk rating**. This rating is a "score" that indicates the likelihood that the borrower will make all interest and principal payments on a timely basis. (Nonpublic debt is often unrated.) Credit rating agencies such as *Moody's* and *Standard & Poor's* make a qualitative assessment of the probability of default of a bond or note using a letter rating system as follows:

Credit Risk	Moody's	Standard & Poor's
Investment Grade.............	Aaa1, Aaa2, Aaa3	AAA+, AAA, AAA−
	Aa1, Aa2, Aa3	AA+, AA, AA−
	A1, A2, A3	A+, A, A−
	Baa1, Baa2, Baa3	BBB+, BBB, BBB−
Junk	Ba1, Ba2, Ba3	BB+, BB, BB−
	B1, B2, B3	B+, B, B−
	Caa1, Caa2, Caa3	CCC+, CCC, CCC−
	Ca1, Ca2, Ca3	CC+, CC, CC−
	C1, C2, C3	C+, C, C−
	D	D

Recall that there is a positive relationship between risk and reward—that is, the higher the credit risk associated with a debt contract, the higher the expected return. Thus, bonds and notes rated Aaa1 or AAA+ will carry a low interest rate because available evidence indicates that there is a very low probability of default by these investment-grade borrowers. Junk bonds and notes (especially ones rated D, which are in default), on the other hand, should be avoided by investors who have a low tolerance for risk. **Junk bonds**, also known as high-yield bonds, have a significantly higher probability of default, and thus, carry higher rates of interest. Nordstrom has provided information on its credit rating in its annual report footnote describing the company's long-term debt. The company reported that certain debt can be cancelled and renewal denied if the company's debt rating falls below Standard & Poor's BB+ rating or Moody's Ba1 rating. The company was rated A− by Standard & Poor's and Baa1 by Moody's as of year-end 2012.

Credit rating agencies are not without fault and have recently been subject to much criticism related to their roles in the 2007-2009 financial crisis. The U.S. **Securities and Exchange Commission (SEC)** cited 10 rating agencies with "apparent failures" during the crisis ranging from not following proscribed methodologies to not managing potential conflicts of interest. The biggest cost to the financial markets arose when many agencies assigned 'AAA' ratings to structured mortgage backed credit instruments (e.g., CDOs) that subsequently defaulted.

Credit rating agencies perform a valuable service to the debt investor community by serving as independent analysts of a company's credit worthiness. Their ratings have significant influence directly on the company's cash flows, as a lower credit rating or a downgrade virtually guarantees higher borrowing costs, and therefore lower cash flows. How do *Moody's* and *Standard & Poor's* arrive at a borrower's credit rating? The process is lengthy but the financial statement analysis skills discussed in Chapter 4 are an integral part of the process. Additionally, these organizations use proprietary bankruptcy prediction models, such as the Z-score and Zeta Analysis, to help identify a borrower's probability of default.[1]

VALUING BONDS AND NOTES

Under U.S. GAAP, and the GAAP of most other developed countries, liabilities are generally valued at their **present value**. (See the appendix at the end of this book for a review of present value concepts.) Exceptions to this rule include such current liabilities as accounts payable, accrued expenses and dividends payable, and such long-term liabilities as deferred income tax liabilities, which will be discussed in Chapter 10. Since the present value of an account payable due in 30, 60, or 90 days is extremely close to its maturity value, discounting of these short-term obligations is not required on practical grounds—that is, there is very little difference between the present value and the future value of a liability payable in 30, 60, or 90 days. For long-term obligations, however, there can be a substantial difference between the present value of the debt—that is, how much cash would be required to pay the obligation off today—and its future settlement value. Consider, for instance, Jacob De Haven's $450,000 loan to the revolutionary army of General George Washington in 1777 (see the appendix at the end of this book). At five percent interest, the settlement or **maturity value** of the De Haven loan would cost the U.S. government over $42 billion today!

To calculate the present value of a bond or note, it is necessary to know the following facts:

- The maturity value and maturity date of the debt
- The coupon, or stated, rate of interest on the debt
- The number of interest payment, or compounding, periods
- The yield, or effective, rate of interest on the debt

The **coupon rate** is the cash rate of interest on a debt instrument whereas the **yield rate** is the effective, or market, rate of interest. The coupon rate is used only to determine the periodic cash flow paid as interest to the bondholder or noteholder. The yield rate, on the other hand, is used to discount both the periodic cash interest payments and the lump-sum repayment of principal at maturity. These two rates are rarely the same, and it is important to understand their different uses to understand bond and note accounting. Think of the coupon rate as a pre-specified, agreed upon numerical value, between the lender and borrower, that defines

---

[1] E. Altman, "Financial Ratios, Discriminant Analysis and the Prediction of Corporate Bankruptcy," *Journal of Finance*, September 1968; E. Altman, R. Haldeman, and P. Narayanan, "Zeta Analysis: A New Model to Identify Bankruptcy Risk of Corporation," *Journal of Banking and Finance,* 1977.

how much cash will be paid each period over the life of the loan. This value technically can be anything, including zero. The coupon rate though is normally fixed over the maturity period of the bond or note. Once the cash payment structure has been defined by the coupon rate, then the value of those cash payments are determined by how much those receiving that cash desire to earn as their investment return. This rate of return is the yield, or effective rate. It can fluctuate markedly over time, as general economic conditions change, or as the financial condition of the company making the cash payments changes.

To illustrate the valuation of, and accounting for, bonds and notes, consider the following scenario:

> On January 1, 2013, **Midwestern Airlines Inc.** issued $100 million face value (maturity value) of mortgage notes with an annual coupon rate of eight percent and a maturity of ten years. The notes pay interest on June 30 and December 31 of each year. The company was considered a high risk investment at the time the notes were issued, and the market yield rate of interest demanded by investors on equivalent risk-rated notes was ten percent. Five years later, on December 31, 2017, the market yield rate of interest on equivalent-risk-rated notes increased to twelve percent.

Ignoring any transaction costs associated with selling the notes to the investing public, the Midwestern Airlines notes would generate proceeds of $87.548 million when issued to the investing public. But how was this value calculated? There are two cash flow streams associated with a bond or note—a lump-sum payment of principal at maturity and the periodic payment of interest. In the case of the Midwestern Airlines' notes, the payment of $100 million in principal will occur in ten years, or 20 compounding periods, on December 31, 2022. Further, with an annual coupon rate of eight percent and interest paid semiannually on June 30 and December 31, noteholders will receive an annuity of 20 payments of $4 million each [($100 million × 8 percent)/2].

> Transaction costs associated with selling bonds or notes to the investing public can be quite significant, averaging one to three percent of the value of the issued debt.

Thus, the present value of the Midwestern notes on the date of issuance is the sum of (1) the present value of $100 million to be paid in ten years, compounded semiannually, discounted at five percent per period (½ of ten percent) and (2) the present value of a 20-period annuity of $4 million per period, also discounted at five percent. Hence:

Present value of $100 million in 20 periods @ 5%: $100 million × 0.377	=	$37.700 million
+ Present value of $4 million per period for 20 periods @ 5%: $4 million × 12.462	=	49.848 million
Present value of notes		$87.548 million

The present value factors of 0.377 and 12.462 were obtained from Tables 1 and 2 in the appendix at the end of this book (n = 20; i = 0.05).

Since the Midwestern Airlines notes carried a coupon rate of only four percent per period (one-half of eight percent) while investors were expecting five percent (one-half of ten percent), perhaps to compensate investors for the higher credit risk associated with the airline company, the notes would, of necessity, be sold at a discount from their face value of $100 million. If the selling price of the notes were not discounted (or lowered), investors would be unwilling to buy the notes and would instead seek out other higher yielding investments. The **discount** of $12.452 million ($100 million − $87.548 million) equals the amount of additional income demanded by investors to earn an effective rate of return of five percent per period over the twenty periods. If investors hold the notes until maturity, they will receive the $12.452 million as part of the lump-sum payment of the $100 million maturity value. Thus, over the life of the notes, investors will receive a total of $180 million—that is, $87.548 million as a return *of* investment and $92.452 million in interest income ($80.0 million + $12.452 million) as a return *on* their investment. From Midwestern's perspective the same holds true, although they will be charging $92.452 in *interest expense* over the life of the loan. The following time-line representation of these cash flows should make this more clear:

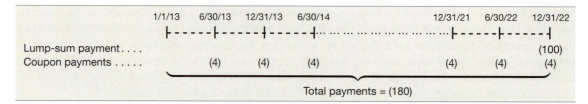

Summary of cash payments over the life of the notes:

On January 1, 2013, when the $100 million face value of notes are sold, Midwestern Airlines will show an increase in cash of $87.548 million, an increase in notes payable for the future value of the debt of $100 million, and an increase in the **note discount** account in the amount of $12.452 million (see the first column of Midwestern's transaction analysis in Exhibit 9.2; we will have more to say about the other transactions later in the chapter). The note discount account is a **contra-liability** account; it is subtracted from the notes payable account to arrive at the book value of the debt. It is rare to see the note discount account on the face of a corporate balance sheet because these amounts are typically netted out against the maturity value of the debt.

Since bond investors demanded an annual rate of return of ten percent but the Midwestern Airlines' notes were offering only eight percent, why didn't Midwestern just change the coupon rate to enable the notes to be sold at their full face value of $100 million? Before any debt or equity securities can be sold in the U.S. capital market, the issuing company must register the securities with the U.S. Securities and Exchange Commission. This requirement is intended to protect investors by insuring that all publicly issued securities meet certain disclosure standards. As part of the registration statement for the debt securities, called a prospectus, the issuing company must contractually establish certain characteristics of the security—the amount to be borrowed, the length of the borrowing period, the purpose of the borrowing, the method of repayment, and the coupon rate, among other things. Thus, once registered, an issuing company is unable to change its coupon rate, or any other security features reported in the filing, even if the goal is to meet or satisfy investor expectations. As the registration statement becomes the equivalent of a binding contract, the only characteristic of the debt instrument that can be altered to meet changing investor expectations is the security's actual selling price, which is not part of the firm's registration statement.

In the case of the Midwestern Airlines' notes, the selling price of the notes was lowered—that is, the notes were sold at a **discount** from their face value—to enable investors to earn the higher expected rate of return. If, on the other hand, investors had demanded only a six percent annual rate of return (or three percent per compounding period), the Midwestern Airlines' notes would have been sold at a price above their face value—that is, the notes would have been sold at a **premium**.[2] Finally, in that rare instance in which the rate of return demanded by investors is exactly equal to the coupon rate provided by a bond or note, the debt instruments will sell at a price exactly equal to their **par** or **face value**.

> As a general rule, companies issuing debt set the offered coupon rate slightly below the expected market yield rate so that the bonds or notes will sell at a small discount from their face value. This practice is undertaken principally for marketing purposes.

Interest Expense

On June 30, 2013, Midwestern Airlines will make its first cash payment of $4 million to its noteholders. But how much interest expense did Midwestern incur during this first six-month period? Interest expense, or the cost of debt financing, is a reflection of the lenders charge for the use of their cash during a given

---

[2] With a coupon rate of eight percent, a yield rate of six percent, and semiannual compounding, the Midwestern Airlines' notes would sell for $114.908 million, a premium of $14.908 million. Can you verify this calculation using Tables 1 and 2 in the appendix to this book?

period. Thus, very similar to how interest on a home mortgage or credit card would be computed, as the loan amount outstanding times the interest rate charged, the same holds true with GAAP financial statements. For Midwestern Airlines, interest expense for the first half of 2013 is calculated by simply multiplying the yield rate on the debt (five percent in this case) times the book value of the debt as of the beginning of the fiscal period; hence,

$$\text{Interest expense} = 5\% \times \$87.548 \text{ million} = \$4.3774 \text{ million}$$

Midwestern's interest expense of $4.3774 million exceeds its actual cash payment of $4.0 million by $0.3774 million. The excess of $0.3774 million represents the portion of the $12.45 million note discount that is allocated to the period January 1, 2013, to June 30, 2013. The $12.45 million to be paid to noteholders on December 31, 2022, represents the additional interest necessary to enable the investors to earn a ten percent rate of return on the Midwestern notes and must be allocated over the twenty interest payment periods. It would be inappropriate and distortive to the financial statements to consider the entire $12.45 million portion of the payment as all interest expense in the year paid (2022).

The process of allocating a bond discount (or bond premium) over the various interest compounding periods is called **amortization**. Amortizing a discount (or premium) using the present value tables from the appendix to this book is called the **effective interest method**. Discounts and premiums may also be amortized in a straight-line fashion, but only if this method does not differ materially from the effective interest method. The straight-line method is not widely used among public companies; and, in any case, straight-line amortization of discounts (premiums) is not recognized as economically meaningful in modern financial theory.

Exhibit 9.1 presents an **amortization schedule** for the Midwestern Airlines' notes. It details the periodic cash interest payments of $4 million (Column 1), Midwestern's interest expense on a period-by-period basis (Column 2), the amortization of the note discount on a period-by-period basis (Column 3), the remaining balance of the note discount (Column 4), the face value of the notes (Column 5), and the book value of the notes (Column 6). Observe that Column 6 is equal to Column 5, the face value of the notes, minus Column 4, the unamortized note discount.

EXHIBIT 9.1	Note Amortization Schedule (in millions)*							
(Principal = $100; Coupon rate = 8%; Yield rate = 10%)								
Date	Period	Cash Flow (1)	Interest Expense[1] (2)	Amortized Note Discount[2] (3)	Note Discount[3] (4)	Face Value of Notes (5)	Book Value of Notes (6)	Market Value of Notes
01/01/13	0	$ 87.55			$12.45	$100.00	$ 87.55	
06/30/13	1	4.00	$4.38	0.38	12.08	100.00	87.93	
12/31/13	2	4.00	4.40	0.40	11.68	100.00	88.32	
06/30/14	3	4.00	4.42	0.42	11.26	100.00	88.74	
12/31/14	4	4.00	4.44	0.44	10.82	100.00	89.18	
06/30/15	5	4.00	4.46	0.46	10.38	100.00	89.62	
12/31/15	6	4.00	4.48	0.48	9.90	100.00	90.10	
06/30/16	7	4.00	4.51	0.51	9.39	100.00	90.61	
12/31/16	8	4.00	4.53	0.53	8.86	100.00	91.14	
06/30/17	9	4.00	4.56	0.56	8.31	100.00	91.69	
12/31/17	10	4.00	4.58	0.58	7.72	100.00	92.28	$ 85.24
06/30/18	11	4.00	4.61	0.61	7.11	100.00	92.89	
12/31/18	12	4.00	4.64	0.64	6.46	100.00	93.54	
06/30/19	13	4.00	4.68	0.68	5.79	100.00	94.21	
12/31/19	14	4.00	4.71	0.71	5.08	100.00	94.92	
06/30/20	15	4.00	4.75	0.75	4.33	100.00	95.67	
12/31/20	16	4.00	4.78	0.78	3.55	100.00	96.45	
06/30/21	17	4.00	4.82	0.82	2.72	100.00	97.28	
12/31/21	18	4.00	4.86	0.86	1.86	100.00	98.14	
06/30/22	19	4.00	4.91	0.91	0.95	100.00	99.05	
12/31/22	20	4.00	4.95	0.95	0.00	100.00	100.00	100.00
12/31/22	20	100.00						

*Figures are rounded to two decimal places.
[1] Column 2 = Column 6_{t-1} × 5 percent
[2] Column 3 = Column 2 − Column 1
[3] Column 4 = Column 4_{t-1} − Column 3_t

On December 31, 2013, Midwestern Airlines must make its second cash payment of $4 million to its noteholders. But how much interest expense did Midwestern incur from June 30 to December 31, 2013? Using the formula to calculate the periodic interest expense (Interest expense = Yield rate × Book value of debt as of the beginning of the period), Midwestern's interest expense for the second compounding period is calculated as follows:

$$\text{Interest expense} = 5\% \times \$87.9254 \text{ million} = \$4.3963 \text{ million}$$

Be sure to observe that on June 30, the book value of the notes is now $87.9254 million ($100 − $12.452 + $0.3774), and thus, the interest expense for the second interest payment period is $4.3963 million. The cash interest payment of $4 million is unchanged, and thus, the discount amortization for the second period is $0.3963 million. After considering the discount amortization, the book value of the Midwestern notes at December 31, 2013, is $88.3217 million (see **bolded** area in Exhibit 9.1), or $87.9254 million plus $0.3963 million.

While the amortization schedule in Exhibit 9.1 is highly mechanical and very descriptive of the entire note liability, there is one very important simplifying feature worth re-emphasizing that is important to understanding the financial statements themselves. Recall we stated that at any balance sheet date long-term liabilities are generally valued at present value. Column (6) of the table identifies the book value of the Midwestern Airlines notes, measurable as the face value less the unamortized note discount account. It is this book value that will be reported on Midwestern's balance sheet at each date specified in the amortization table. For any period referenced in the table, however, net book value is computable directly by calculating the present value of the remaining cash flows to be paid on the note as of a given date. For instance, the net book value on December 31, 2017, of $92.28 million, is the present value of a $4 million annuity paid for the remaining *10 periods*, plus the present value of the lump-sum paid in 10 periods, both at 5 percent (try this on your own to verify). Once this number is computed, the current period discount is known ($100 − $92.28) and the next period's interest can be computed ($92.28 × 5%). The importance of recognizing this feature is that you need not perform a complete amortization table to understand how to measure and understand the amounts reported as long-term liabilities at any balance sheet date.

Market Rates of Interest and the Book Value of Debt

Implicit in the Midwestern Airlines illustration is the assumption that the book value of the notes equals their present value and that the yield rate of interest on the Midwestern notes remains constant over time. In reality, market yield rates are constantly changing in the public debt market to reflect changing investors' expectations regarding the economic and political conditions of the local, national, and global economy. For financial statement purposes, however, the changing market perceptions and related changing market yield rates are generally ignored. On the financial statements of Midwestern, the $100 million notes are reported as if the yield rate on the notes remains a constant ten percent.

What will happen to the actual market value of the Midwestern notes if the market rate of interest demanded by investors increases to, say, twelve percent on December 31, 2012 (with ten interest payment periods remaining)? Using the formula to calculate the present value of a debt instrument, the market value of the Midwestern notes would be $85.24 million, calculated as follows:

Present value of $100 million in 10 periods @ 6%: $100 million × 0.558................... =	$55.80 million
+ Present value of $4 million per period for 10 periods @ 6%: $4 million × 7.360 .... =	29.44 million
Market value of notes	$85.24 million

The book value of the notes on Midwestern's balance sheet, however, remains at $92.28 million, reflecting the assumption that the company's cost of debt is unchanged at ten percent (see **bolded** area in Exhibit 9.1).

The new market value of the Midwestern notes ($85.24 million) demonstrates an important relationship between the market value of fixed interest rate debt instruments and market rates of interest: As market rates of interest increase (decrease), the fair value of debt instruments with a fixed rate of return will decline (increase) to compensate investors for the changing time value of money. Since the coupon

---

BUSINESS PERSPECTIVE

Fair Values of Liabilities on the Balance Sheet

There is one important exception to the requirement of using the interest rate in place when long-term debt is first issued for all of the future accounting associated with that long-term debt. Beginning in 2007, GAAP now allows firms to elect to use the fair values of liabilities as of the balance sheet date in lieu of its amortized value. This still can be viewed as recording long-term liabilities at their present value, however the current market yield, rather than the yield when issued, is used to value the debt. Very few companies have adopted the fair value option due the increased financial statement volatility that might occur. But some have adopted, including many of the major Wall Street banks.

Under the original GAAP rules, if the fair value option for liabilities was adopted by a company any changes in the market value of liabilities from period to period due to fluctuating market interest rates were reportable as income. In the first quarter of 2012, falling interest rates caused a spike in the value of **Morgan Stanley**'s long-term debt on the balance sheet. A quarterly loss of $78 million was reported by the company, rather than what would have been income of $1.4 billion. Volatility of earnings became the norm, as Morgan Stanley's valuation adjustments swung from $216 million in the fourth quarter of 2011 to a $1.5 billion loss the next quarter. Further whipsawing earnings, while most major banks reported approximately $4 billion total valuation gains during 2011 from liability fair value adjustments, in 2012 that total was expected to reverse as interest rates fell. **Bank of America** and **Citigroup** were expected to record losses in excess of $2 billion alone.

Reacting to this important accounting issue, in late 2012 the FASB tentatively agreed to remove the requirement that companies adopting a fair value accounting approach for liabilities report any changes in value as income. Any valuation adjustments would bypass net income and be reportable as a component of "Accumulated Other Comprehensive Income" (see chapter 11 for a discussion of this shareholder's equity account). It remains to be seen how many companies will now decide to adopt the fair value option for liabilities, given the risk of volatility to earnings has been removed.

---

rate of interest on the Midwestern notes must remain fixed at four percent per period, but investors are now demanding a yield rate of six percent per period (one-half of twelve percent), the market price of the notes must decline to enable investors to earn the higher expected market rate of return. If the market price of the Midwestern notes did not adjust downward to enable investors to earn their expected rate of return, other investors would be unwilling to buy the notes.

Early Debt Retirement

Businesses sometimes find that they no longer need their existing debt financing, perhaps because the business has been successful at generating operating cash flow or because their current debt is at a higher rate than current market rates and refinancing can lower the firm's cost of debt financing. When this situation arises, firms will sometimes repurchase, or retire, their outstanding interest-bearing debt. When this occurs, because the book value removed from the balance sheet rarely equals the cash paid to retire the debt, a gain or loss will result:

Book value of debt − Cash paid to repurchase or retire debt = Gain (loss) on debt retirement

Returning to the Midwestern Airlines illustration, assume that the company decides to retire all of its outstanding eight percent notes on December 31, 2017. As indicated above, the market value of the notes is $85.24 million assuming a prevailing market yield rate of twelve percent, whereas the book value is $92.28 million (see **bolded** area in Exhibit 9.1). Ignoring transaction costs that may be necessary to facilitate the note repurchase, Midwestern will pay $85.24 million to retire the debt early. Thus, the company's cash will decline by $85.24 million, notes payable will decline by $100 million, the note discount account will decrease by $7.72 million ($100 million − $92.28 million), and retained earnings will increase by $7.04 million ($92.28 million − $85.24 million). By retiring the notes early, Midwestern will record a gain on early debt retirement of $7.04 million (see the Midwestern spreadsheet in Exhibit 9.2), largely as a consequence of the increase in the market rate of interest from ten to twelve percent.

EXHIBIT 9.2	Accounting for Bonds and Notes: Midwestern Airlines, Inc.				
($ millions)	Jan.1, 2013 Issue Notes	June 30, 2013 Pay Coupon	Dec. 31, 2013 Pay Coupon	... ...	Dec. 31, 2017 Retire Notes
Assets					
Cash	87.548	(4.000)	(4.000)		(85.240)
Liabilities					
Notes payable	100.000				(100.000)
Note discount	(12.452)	0.377	0.396		7.720
Shareholders' Equity					
Retained earnings:					
Interest expense		(4.377)	(4.396)		
Gain on early retirement					7.040

Gains and losses on financing transactions like the early retirement of bonds or notes require special consideration when analyzing a company's income statement. These one-time gains or losses should not be considered as part of a firm's recurring or sustainable earnings. If material in amount, the gains or losses should be separately disclosed on the income statement; however, if immaterial, the gains or losses will need to be identified by financial statement users through a review of the footnotes and then removed from any estimate of sustainable earnings. During the preparation of a statement of cash flow, it is necessary to remove any gains or losses from financing transactions (such as the early retirement of debt) from the cash flow from operations, and report the cash outflow to retire the debt as part of the cash flow from financing.

Zero-Coupon Bonds and Notes

The public market for bonds and notes is made up of many investors and institutions with diverse risk preferences. Some investors prefer debt instruments that pay regular and routine payments, whereas others are willing to forego the regular receipt of cash in exchange for a higher rate of return. Zero-coupon bonds and notes are designed with this latter group of investors in mind.

As the name implies, **zero-coupon bonds** and notes have no coupon rate, and thus, pay no periodic cash interest payment. Instead, the regular but unpaid interest is added to the principal value of the bond (or note) and is paid as a lump sum at maturity. Zero-coupon bonds are important financing tools for companies with limited current cash flow since the issuing company is not required to pay the regular debt servicing associated with traditional interest-bearing bonds or notes.

Zero-coupon bonds and notes pay no regular interest payments to investors, and thus, are considered to be riskier investments than interest-bearing bonds and notes. As a consequence, zero-coupon debt may carry returns as much as 200 basis points (i.e., 2 percent) higher than interest-bearing debt. The higher returns reflect the opportunity cost that must be borne by investors who purchase zero-coupon debt.

To illustrate the valuation of, and accounting for, zero-coupon bonds and notes, consider the following scenario:

On January 1, 2013, **Midwestern Airlines, Inc.** issued $100 million face value of zero-coupon mortgage notes with a maturity of ten years (in 2022), with semiannual compounding. At the time of issuance, the market yield rate on equivalent risk-rated debt instruments was twelve percent.

Assuming no transaction costs, how much would Midwestern Airlines receive from the sale of the notes? Unlike interest-bearing notes, the Midwestern zero-coupon notes have only one cash flow stream to discount, namely the lump-sum payment of principal in 2022. Using the present value formula, the proceeds from the sale of the notes would be $31.2 million, calculated as follows:

Present value of $100 million in 20 periods @ 6%: $100 million × 0.312   = $31.2 million

Thus, the Midwestern zero-coupon notes would be sold at a discount of $68.8 million ($100 million − $31.2 million). The discount of $68.8 million represents the total periodic cash interest payment to be paid to an investor at maturity, assuming a six percent return per period compounded over 20 periods.

Although Midwestern will not make any payment until 2022, the company will still accrue interest expense on its mortgage notes on its income statement. On June 30, 2013, for example, the company's effective cost of borrowing is $1.872 million, or six percent times $31.2 million. Although the interest is unpaid, it is added to the book value of the notes. Thus, the zero-coupon notes are said to be valued at their **accreted value**—that is, the original issue price plus any accrued, but unpaid, interest. On June 30, 2013, for example, the accreted value of the zero-coupon notes is $33.072 million ($31.2 million + $1.872 million).

For the next six-month period ended December 31, 2013, Midwestern's cost of borrowing on the notes is $1.984 million ($33.072 million × 6 percent), and this amount would also be reported as interest expense on Midwestern's income statement. Therefore, total interest expense on the notes for the year 2013 would be $3.856 million ($1.872 + $1.984). Further, the accreted value of the notes at year-end 2013 will be reported as $35.056 million ($33.072 million + $1.984 million) on the airline's balance sheet.

BUSINESS PERSPECTIVE

Century Bonds

In 1996, **International Business Machines Corporation (IBM)** made financing history in the U.S. debt market by launching the largest ever issue of 100-year debentures, or what are now known as **century bonds**. Prior to the IBM debt placement, 21 companies had issued century bonds in the U.S. capital market but none were as large as the $850 million IBM offering. The development of the century bond was patterned after the 1894 sale of $87.3 million (U.S. dollar equivalent) of gold bonds by the Imperial Government of Russia. A unique feature of the Russian gold bonds was that redemption was only by lottery drawing, conducted at the pleasure of the Russian government, causing some pundits to refer to the bonds as "perpetuity bonds" or "permanent debt."

IBM's century bond placement was possible because of the low, stable interest rate environment that characterized the U.S. debt market, as well as the significant demand for very long-term investment products by pension funds and insurance companies. The yield on the IBM century bonds was only 10 to 20 basis points higher than the yields on comparable 30-year bonds. (Note: One hundred basis points equal one percentage point of interest.) One adverse aspect of the IBM bonds was that the U.S. Treasury Department had threatened to rule that the bonds were a form of "permanent capital," and consequently, disallow the tax-deductibility of interest charges on grounds that the interest payments were equivalent to dividend payments, which are not tax deductible under U.S. tax statutes. In 1997, the U.S. Treasury Department enacted tax regulations that eliminated the tax-deductibility of any interest payments on debt instruments after 40 years (such as during the last 60 years of the IBM century bonds).

TAX PERSPECTIVE

Zero Coupon Bonds and Taxes

In general, the tax treatment of zero-coupon bonds and notes follows the GAAP accounting treatment—that is, the accrued interest on the debt is tax-deductible in the period incurred, not when paid at maturity. Thus, zero-coupon bonds have two cash flow advantages: (1) the periodic interest cost remains unpaid until maturity, and (2) the unpaid periodic interest cost is currently tax-deductible, providing an immediate interest tax shield to the issuing company.

From the perspective of the IRS, the tax effect of zero-coupon bonds is essentially tax-neutral. The unpaid interest expense is tax-deductible to the issuing firm but is taxable income to the buyer of the bonds in the period in which the interest is effectively earned, not the period when it is received.

LEASE FINANCING

A lease is a contract that conveys usage rights from an owner of property, the lessor, to a user of that property, the lessee. Leasing has become one of the most frequently utilized financing strategies for acquiring access to business assets. Office buildings, equipment, airplanes, trucks—almost any business asset—can be leased.

Companies lease assets for a variety of reasons. Some firms lease because they lack sufficient cash to purchase an asset outright—bank financing, for example, often requires a substantial down payment. Other firms lease because they have a poor credit rating and are too risky to secure bank financing. Financially healthy companies, on the other hand, often lease because they have better alternatives for investing their cash. And, some companies lease to avoid the risks that come with full ownership, such as with technology that may soon become outdated. Finally, some firms lease to take advantage of the special accounting treatment accorded certain types of leases. Leasing, however, is not without certain disadvantages. For instance, the interest rates implicit in some leases may be higher than typical long-term borrowing rates, and because ownership has not transferred there are often restrictions on asset use. The bottom line, however, is that the decision to lease an asset is a strategic financing decision with both pros and cons.

Accounting for Leases

Leasing is a vehicle for financing the short- or long-term use of an operating asset. The financial reporting issue faced by companies engaged in lease contracts is whether sufficient property rights have been transferred from the lessor to the lessee such that the recording of those rights is warranted. In most countries, this determination is made by reference to the terms of the contract and then, depending on those terms, leases are classified into one of two categories—capital leases and operating leases. A **capital lease** is treated as an asset purchase agreement involving a deferred payment plan; and, as such, the operating asset acquired under a capital lease and the related obligation to make lease payments are capitalized to the lessee's balance sheet. (The lessor accounts for the leased asset as if it has been sold to the lessee.) An **operating lease**, on the other hand, represents a straightforward contractual relationship wherein the lessor is deemed to provide only temporary access to the leased asset to the lessee. Because access to the leased asset under an operating lease is conditional (it is contingent on its future availability), accounting standards do not require that the leased asset or the related obligation to make lease payments be capitalized to the lessee's balance sheet. Critics of the accounting for operating leases contend that this accounting treatment effectively provides a form of **off-balance-sheet financing** in that the lessee gains access to the productive capacity of the leased asset but is not required to report the future payments needed to finance that access on its balance sheet. Critics also observe that the accounting for operating leases effectively understates a lessee's true debt position, possibly leading to inefficiencies in the public and private debt markets. A U.S. Securities and Exchange Commission study found that of 200 publicly held companies analyzed, 77 percent had off-balance-sheet operating leases, valued at approximately $1.25 billion.

The criteria used to identify when a lease is a capital lease varies from country to country. Under current lease accounting rules in the United States, a lease must be reported as a capital lease if *any* of the following conditions apply to the lease:

- The lease agreement transfers legal ownership of the leased asset to the lessee by the end of the lease term.

- The lease agreement contains a "bargain purchase" option—that is, the lessee has the right to buy the leased asset at a price less than its fair market value.

- The lease term is 75 percent or more of the leased asset's remaining economic life.

- The present value of the minimum contractual lease payments is equal to or greater than 90 percent of the leased asset's fair market value.[3]

---

[3] Many leases contain "escalation clauses" linking the actual lease payment to the level of revenues generated by the leased asset. Thus, while the minimum contractual lease payment is known at the time of lease signing, the actual lease payment cannot be known until the level of future revenue is determined.

In Practice 9.1 *Long-Term Leases: A Glimpse of a Sample of Fortune 1000 Companies*   The following table identifies the types of leases disclosed by a sample of 600 *Fortune 1000* companies. The data reveal that 53 percent of the surveyed firms use operating leases exclusively:

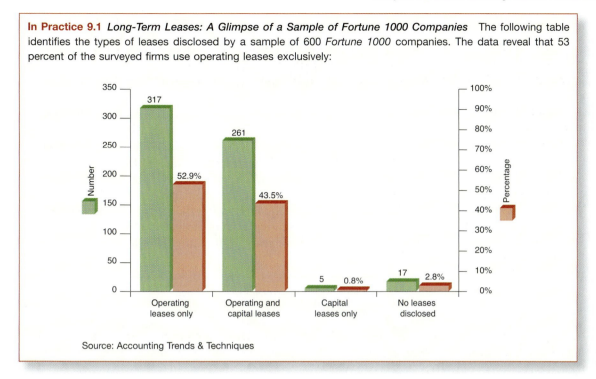

Source: Accounting Trends & Techniques

The evaluation as to whether a lease is a capital or operating lease is made at the inception of a lease. If a lease is determined to be a purchase contract (a capital lease), capitalization of both the leased asset and a lease liability ensues. Otherwise, the lease is accounted for as a **contingent liability**, and the existence, key terms, and characteristics of the operating lease agreement are disclosed in the footnotes to the financial statements but not on the face of the balance sheet. We will have more to say about contingent liabilities in Chapter 10.

On the lessee's income statement, the cost of an operating lease is reported as lease expense (or rent expense), whereas for a capital lease, the income statement effect is reported as depreciation on the capitalized leased asset and interest expense on the capitalized lease liability. It is rare that the lease expense under an operating lease will equal the sum of the depreciation expense plus the interest expense under a capital lease in any given year largely as a consequence of the allocation assumption inherent in most depreciation methods. Over the duration of the entire lease period, however, the total expense will be the same regardless of how a lease is accounted for. On the statement of cash flow, the total cash flow effect of the two lease forms is identical each year because the cash paid, the lease payment, is equivalent under both lease forms.[4]

To illustrate the similarities and differences between an operating lease and a capital lease, consider the case of Midwestern Airlines Inc., which entered into a ten-year lease agreement for flight equipment having a fair market value of $100 million and an implicit interest rate of ten percent per year. The annual lease payments are $16.27 million and are paid annually at the end of each year.[5] The leased equipment had an expected remaining useful life of 13 years.

Capital Lease.   Although the Midwestern Airlines' lease agreement does not provide for a transfer of ownership at any time during the life of the lease or provide the lessee with a bargain purchase option, there are two reasons why this lease should be accounted for as a capital lease. First, the length of the lease period (ten years) exceeds 75 percent of the leased asset's remaining economic life of 13 years (75 percent × 13 years = 9.75 years). Second, the present value of the minimum contractual lease payments is greater than 90 percent of the equipment's fair market value. In fact, the present value of the lease payments is $100 million, which is exactly 100 percent of the equipment's fair market value. (Can you verify that the present value of ten payments of $16.27 million at ten percent interest is $100 million?)

---

[4] There are differences between operating and capital leases in the classification of cash flows across operating, investing and financing activities. Cash payments under capital leases are split between interest (operating) and principal (financing). Cash payments under operating leases are classified entirely as operating cash flows.

[5] A constant set of payments made at the end of each period is referred to as an **ordinary annuity** or an **annuity-in-arrears**.

When discounting the future minimum lease payments under a capital lease, the appropriate discount rate is the interest rate implicit in the lease agreement. The rate implicit in a lease is not always known, however, and thus, it is accepted practice to use a firm's incremental cost of borrowing (the rate at which the firm could borrow an equivalent amount of money given its existing debt structure) to discount the lease payments. When the incremental cost of debt is unknown, a firm's weighted-average cost of debt or an inferred rate based upon a firm's credit rating (if known) can be used.

Assuming treatment as a capital lease, the value of the leased flight equipment will be capitalized to Midwestern's balance sheet as a long-term asset at its present value of $100 million, with a lease liability for the same amount also reflected on the balance sheet. This information is illustrated in Midwestern Airlines' transaction summary in Exhibit 9.3. At the end of the first year of the lease, a cash payment for $16.27 million is made, reducing cash by $16.27 million, the lease liability by $6.27 million, and retained earnings by $10 million representing interest expense on the outstanding lease liability ($100 million × 10 percent). In addition, depreciation expense on the capitalized asset must be recorded. Assuming the use of the straight-line method, a useful life of ten years (the life of the lease agreement), and a zero residual value since the leased asset reverts to the lessor at the end of the lease period, the depreciation expense would amount to $10 million per year ($100 million/10 years).

EXHIBIT 9.3 | Capital Lease Accounting Transaction Summary: Midwestern Airlines

(in $ millions)	Year 1				Year 2		
	Lease Signing	Lease Payment	Recognize Depreciation Expense	Balance Sheet Year 1	Lease Payment	Recognize Depreciation Expense	Balance Sheet Year 2
Assets							
Cash		(16.27)		(16.27)	(16.27)		(32.54)
::							
Equipment	100.00			100.00			100.00
Accumulated depreciation			(10.00)	(10.00)		(10.00)	(20.00)
Total assets				**73.73**			**47.46**
Liabilities							
Lease liability	100.00	(6.27)		93.73	(6.90)		86.83
Shareholders' Equity							
Retained earnings				(20.00)			(39.37)
Depreciation expense			(10.00)			(10.00)	
Interest expense		(10.00)			(9.37)		
Total liabilities and shareholders' equity				**73.73**			**47.46**

A lease **amortization schedule** for Midwestern Airlines is presented in Exhibit 9.4. Consider, for example, Year 2 of the Midwestern equipment lease (see **bolded** area in Exhibit 9.4). According to the amortization schedule, Midwestern's lease payment of $16.27 million in Year 2 will reduce the lease liability by $6.9 million, with the remainder of the payment ($9.37 million) applied as interest expense ($93.73 million × 10 percent). This information is recorded in Midwestern's transaction summary in Exhibit 9.3.

Operating Lease. If the Midwestern Airlines' equipment lease is accounted for as an operating lease, no asset or liability is capitalized to the company's balance sheet. The annual lease payment of $16.27 million is recorded on the income statement as a lease expense and as a reduction in cash on the balance sheet. This is shown in Midwestern's transaction summary in Exhibit 9.5.

As Exhibit 9.4 highlights, the total cash outflow for the Midwestern Airlines' lease is $162.75 million over the ten-year life of the lease, regardless of whether the lease is accounted for as an operating lease or as a capital lease. The total expenses deducted against revenues over the life of the lease are also equivalent ($162.75 million) under either lease accounting treatment. The key financial statement difference between the two types of leases involves the balance sheet disclosure—capital leases are reported on Midwestern's balance sheet as an asset and as a form of debt, whereas operating leases are not.

EXHIBIT 9.4	Lease Amortization Schedule

Ten-year lease with implicit interest rate of 10 percent per year; straight-line depreciation of leased asset

Year	Lease Balance[1] (1)	Interest Expense[2] (2)	Principal Reduction[3] (3)	Lease Payment (4)	Asset Depreciation (5)	Total Expenses Under	
						Operating Lease	Capital Lease
0	$100.00						
1	93.73	$10.00	$ 6.27	$ 16.27	$ 10.00	$ 16.27	$ 20.00
2	86.82	9.37	6.90	16.27	10.00	16.27	19.37
3	79.23	8.68	7.59	16.27	10.00	16.27	18.68
4	70.88	7.92	8.35	16.27	10.00	16.27	17.92
5	61.69	7.09	9.19	16.27	10.00	16.27	17.09
6	51.59	6.17	10.10	16.27	10.00	16.27	16.17
7	40.48	5.16	11.11	16.27	10.00	16.27	15.16
8	28.25	4.05	12.23	16.27	10.00	16.27	14.05
9	14.80	2.82	13.45	16.27	10.00	16.27	12.82
10	0.00	1.48	14.80	16.27	10.00	16.27	11.48
Total		$62.75	$100.00[4]	$162.75	$100.00	$162.75	$162.75

Both methods yield the same total expenses.

[1] Column 1 = Column 1_{t-1} − Column 3
[2] Column 2_t = Column 1_{t-1} × 10%
[3] Column 3_t = Column 4 − Column 2
[4] Your calculation of these numbers may differ slightly due to rounding differences.

EXHIBIT 9.5	Operating Lease Accounting Transaction Summary: Midwestern Airlines

(in $ millions)	Lease Payment	Balance Sheet Year 1	Lease Payment	Balance Sheet Year 2
Assets				
Cash...	(16.27)	(16.27)	(16.27)	(32.54)
::				
Total assets..		(16.27)		(32.54)
Liabilities				
Lease liability		—		—
Shareholders' Equity				
Retained earnings		(16.27)		(32.54)
Lease expense	(16.27)		(16.27)	
Total liabilities and shareholders' equity		(16.27)		(32.54)

Lease Accounting, Disclosures and Security Prices

Although the annual cash outflow of $16.27 million for Midwestern Airlines is the same under each lease treatment, the periodic balance sheet and income statement effects differ. Under the operating lease, Midwestern's lease expense totals $16.27 million each year, whereas under a capital lease the lease-related expenses total $20 million in Year 1 and $19.37 million in Year 2, respectively. On the balance sheet, a capital lease requires the creation of an asset and liability, whereas the operating lease does not. Do the financial statement differences associated with the accounting for operating leases and capital leases affect the perceived riskiness of a firm? And, do the financial statement differences between the two lease forms affect security prices? Available empirical research suggests that investors *do* include the financial

Lease Accounting Under U.S. Tax Law

Throughout this text we have highlighted critical differences between the accounting rules required under GAAP and those required for under U.S. tax law. Although the primary focus of this book is on the former, in any successful organization the financially astute executive must be aware of both perspectives when those differences are material. While understanding the financial statement implications for external reporting under GAAP is important to meet the needs of stakeholders such as creditors and investors, the tax regulation perspective is critical as it can have substantial impact on cash flow in a current period (i.e. taxes paid or saved). Lease accounting is one such area that requires special attention.

Under U.S. GAAP we have described how leases are characterized as operating leases or capital leases, depending on whether any of the four criteria for meeting a capital lease have been satisfied. The characterization has far reaching effects on what is reported on corporate balance sheets as assets and liabilities, and on income statements as expense line items. This important reporting issue exists solely because under lease contracts there is often no clear line drawn as to whether "ownership" has actually transferred to the lessee from the lessor.

A similar reporting issue faces the tax authorities as they enforce the rules that govern the taxation of leases. Has ownership transferred? If so, the payments made under the lease contract would be deemed repayments of a loan (i.e., interest and principal), and depreciation would be allowable based on the value of the leased asset. If not, then rent expense would be charged as each lease payment is made. The difference with GAAP, however, lies in the criteria the IRS uses to determine lease classification. The IRS classifies each lease as either a "True Tax Lease", wherein the lessor has retained ownership, or a "Non-Tax Lease", wherein ownership has deemed to have transferred. A lease is not considered a True Tax Lease by the IRS if any of the following are satisfied:

- A part of the lease payment is applied to an equity position in the asset,
- The lessee will acquire ownership (title) of the asset based upon the payment terms,
- The total amount paid is an exceedingly large proportion of the amount required to outright buy the asset,
- The lease payments exceed the current fair rental value,
- The title to the asset may be acquired for an exceedingly small purchase option price in relation to its actual value, or
- Any portion of the lease payments are specifically designated as interest.

You may note with these criteria that they sound very similar to those under GAAP, but the IRS is focused more on the substance, rather than the form, of the lease contract. GAAP rules are more restrictive and definitive, and most tax professionals will note that a leased asset classified as an operating lease under GAAP will virtually always be classified as a True Tax Lease by the IRS. The reverse is not true, however, as many True Tax Leases are not classified as operating for financial reporting purposes. Unlike under GAAP where there typically exist strong incentives to keep a leased asset "off the books" (i.e., an operating lease), for tax purposes a company generally will benefit from treatment as a "Non-Tax Lease" by the IRS. This is because many purchased assets qualify for accelerated depreciation and sometimes even full expensing in the year acquired, and thus there can be huge early tax savings if a leased asset is classifiable as owned rather than rented.

risk associated with off-balance-sheet operating leases in their assessment of share prices, indicating that investors are not misled by the differing accounting treatment of the two lease forms.[6] Stated alternatively, investors see the two lease forms as economically equivalent forms of asset financing.

One reason that investors are not misled by the difference in accounting treatment for leases no doubt relates to the required footnote disclosure for these items. Accounting standards setters recognized that balance sheets can look drastically different under operating lease accounting, so companies are required to disclose the schedule of expected minimum lease payments that exist under the contracts for both types. Exhibit 9.6 provides an illustrative disclosure extracted from Nordstrom's 2012

---

[6] K. Ely, "Operating Lease Accounting and the Market's Assessment of Equity Risk," *Journal of Accounting Research* (1995).

annual report. The minimum lease payments must be disclosed in tabular form for the five years subsequent to the balance sheet date, and then a cumulative total for amounts thereafter. For Nordstrom, note that the total cash flows to be paid for operating leases swamp those for capital leases, $1,063 million versus $13 million. This indicates that Nordstrom's balance sheet reports very little of the actual lease obligations (only $10 million in 2012), even though the company is committed contractually to pay much more. Providing this detail to financial statement users enables analysts to estimate the amount of off-balance sheet financing related to leases. The estimation techniques that are used vary, but in general the present value of the operating lease cash flows is estimated using a discount rate appropriate for the debt level assumed. Key leverage ratios such as debt-to-equity, and assets-to-equity, thus become more comparable across companies.

EXHIBIT 9.6   Excerpts from Nordstrom, Inc. Lease Footnote

We lease the land or the land and buildings at many of our stores. Additionally, we lease office facilities, warehouses and equipment. Most of these leases are classified as operating leases and they expire at various dates through 2080. The majority of our fixed, non-cancelable lease terms are 15 to 30 years for Nordstrom full-line stores and 10 to 15 years for Nordstrom Rack stores. Many of our leases include options that allow us to extend the lease term beyond the initial commitment period, subject to terms agreed to at lease inception. Most of our leases also provide for payment of operating expenses, such as common area charges, real estate taxes and other executory costs, and some leases require additional payments based on sales, referred to as "percentage rent."

Future minimum lease payments as of January 28, 2012 are as follows:

Fiscal year	Capital Leases	Operating Leases
2012	$2	$ 122
2013	2	118
2014	2	111
2015	2	106
2016	2	100
Thereafter	3	506
Total minimum lease payments	13	$1,063
Less: amount representing interest	(3)	
Present value of net minimum lease payments	$10	

Concerned about the financial statement effect of the accounting for leases on some companies' reported debt, as of 2013 the FASB is exploring whether all noncancelable leases should be accounted for as capital leases. A proposed standard that would require recording all leases on the balance sheet is under review. To illustrate the basis for the FASB's concern, In Practice 9.2 presents data for eight publicly held retail businesses that rely extensively on operating leases to finance their businesses. The data reveals, for example, that **Office Depot** has estimated off-balance-sheet operating lease liabilities over two times its total market capitalization, and over 50% of its total asset value (the estimated off-balance sheet lease liabilities were valued at $2.4 billion as of 2010). Consequently, failure to consider Office Depot's operating leases when valuing the company would cause a serious distortion of the firm's share price.

In Practice 9.2 *Off-Balance-Sheet Lease Liabilities*
The following table presents select estimates of off-balance sheet liabilities related to operating leases, as a percent of market capitalization and total assets. Data are for the year 2010, and based on *Credit Suisse* estimates.

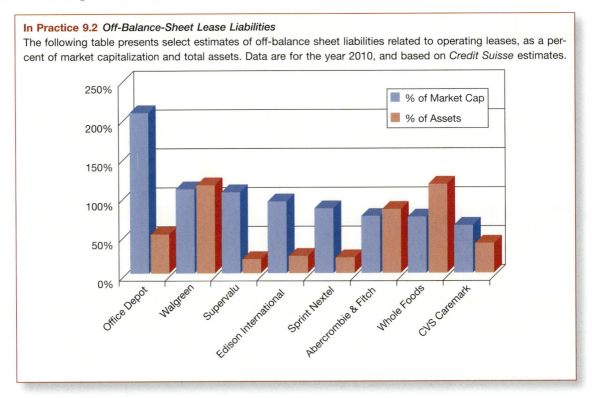

CALCULATING THE WEIGHTED-AVERAGE COST OF DEBT

A firm's cost of borrowing will vary with the amount to be borrowed, the duration of the borrowing, the purpose of the borrowing, the firm's existing debt structure, and whether or not the debt is secured. In general, short-term debt is less costly than longer-term debt as the risk of non-payment increases with the duration of a borrowing. Similarly, a highly leveraged firm will find it increasingly more costly to add additional debt than a less highly leveraged firm (due to existing credit risk). Finally, the larger the proposed borrowing amount, the higher the cost as the amount of risk assumed by a lender is greater.

To help investment professionals and managers estimate the cost of any new debt financing, it is accepted practice in many countries to disclose in the footnotes to the financial statements a firm's **weighted-average cost of debt** for both its short-term and long-term debt. The weighted-average cost of debt is calculated by averaging a firm's various interest rates, weighted by the amount of debt outstanding at the various rates.

To illustrate, consider data for The Claremont Company Inc. presented in Exhibit 9.7. The company has five debt issuances outstanding, with effective interest rates ranging from six percent to nine and one-

EXHIBIT 9.7	Calculating the Weighted-Average Cost of Debt	
THE CLAREMONT COMPANY INC.		
Amount of Borrowing	**Interest Rate**	**Interest Expense**
$100.00	7.50%	$ 7.500
75.00	6.30%	4.725
50.00	6.00%	3.000
200.00	8.00%	16.000
500.00	9.50%	47.500
$925.00		$78.725
Simple average of interest rates....................................		7.46%
Weighted average (78.725/925)......................................		8.51%

half percent. The simple average of the five interest rates is 7.46 percent, but the weighted average is 8.51 percent. If The Claremont Company needed to finance its future growth with debt, at what rate would the company most likely to be able to borrow the needed funds?

Although the company's borrowing rate would be contingent on the length of the borrowing and whether it was secured, a good estimate of The Claremont Company's cost of future borrowing would be its weighted-average cost of existing debt (8.51 percent), which reflects the firm's existing capital structure.

MANAGING REPORTED DEBT

One of the metrics used to measure a firm's solvency, and hence, its credit risk, is the amount of a firm's net debt. **Net debt** is the amount of debt outstanding after subtracting the value of any liquid assets immediately available to repay a firm's debt. Thus, net debt is the amount of debt that a firm expects to repay from future operating cash flows, asset sales, equity issuances, or debt refinancing, and is calculated as follows:

$$\text{Net debt} = \text{Total debt} - \text{Liquid assets}$$

Because of the importance of net debt as an indicator of financial health, especially business solvency, some firms have attempted to manage the level of their reported net debt. Consider, for example, the case of **Parmalat SpA**, an Italian dairy company. In late 2003, the company filed for bankruptcy after revealing that it had massively underreported its outstanding net debt. The accounting fraud had apparently been executed over a decade, without detection by the firm's external auditors, **Grant Thorton**. According to the company's investigative auditor, **PricewaterhouseCoopers**, Parmalat underreported its net debt position by approximately $16 billion. The underreporting was achieved by overstating the amount of liquid assets on its balance sheet, specifically by overstating the amount of cash on hand and retaining worthless accounts receivable on the company's balance sheet.

Another way that some companies manage the amount of debt disclosed on their balance sheet is through the use of off-balance-sheet financing. **Off-balance-sheet financing** refers to the various ways that a company can gain access to productive operating assets while not disclosing the obligation to pay for that access on its balance sheet. Examples of off-balance-financing discussed thus far include the use of operating leases to finance operating assets and the use of the equity method to account for unconsolidated affiliates, joint ventures, and special purpose entities. We will have more to say about other forms of off-balance-sheet debt in Chapter 10.

ANALYZING A COMPANY'S USE OF LEVERAGE

The first thing that a financial statement user should consider when analyzing a firm's debt financing is whether the reported financial statement numbers accurately reflect the firm's use of leverage. As discussed in this chapter, GAAP provides business managers with the opportunity to finance the acquisition of a firm's operating assets with leases and avoid any balance sheet recognition of the lease liability, provided that the lease qualifies as an operating lease. As a consequence, GAAP provides managers with a perverse incentive to structure their company's lease financing to satisfy the criteria for operating-lease accounting. This does not preclude the financial statement user, however, from undertaking various financial statement adjustments to place these obligations on the balance sheet, especially where it is determined that the amount of debt involved is material. U.S. GAAP requires that a company financing its assets with operating leases disclose sufficient information in the footnotes to permit a financial statement user to value the off-balance-sheet debt and to capitalize any lease obligations, along with the corresponding leased assets, on a firm's balance sheet.

Operating lease obligations, however, are only one of several off-balance-sheet financing arrangements that should be considered as part of any financial statement due diligence. In Chapter 8, for example, we examined how the use of the equity method enables parent-companies to report only the net assets of an affiliate company, rather than fully reporting the affiliate's assets and liabilities. We also learned that the equity method was principally used to account for joint ventures and variable interest entities (VIEs), enabling the parent-company of such entities to keep any debt off the parent's balance sheet. In Chapter 10, additional off-balance-sheet liabilities, such as commitments and contingencies, are examined. We will see that, like operating lease obligations, the key elements of these potential obligations are disclosed in the footnotes to the financial statements; and consequently, it is possible for financial statement users to determine whether to include this risk-related information in any assessment of a firm's use of leverage.

BUSINESS PERSPECTIVE

AMR Lease Disclosures Under Bankruptcy

AMR Corporation is the parent company of American Airlines and the regional carrier American Eagle. On November 29, 2011, AMR filed Chapter 11 bankruptcy, an event that required the company to begin operations as a "debtor-in-possession" under the jurisdiction of the bankruptcy courts. As a debtor-in-possession the company is allowed to continue to operate as an ongoing business but may not engage in transactions outside the ordinary course of business without the prior approval of the bankruptcy court. The following is the lease disclosure made by AMR in their fiscal year 2011 annual report. It highlights an important facet of the significant debt-load that was carried by the company.

AMR's subsidiaries lease various types of equipment and property, primarily aircraft and airport facilities. As allowed under Section 365 and other relevant sections of the Bankruptcy Code, the Debtors may assume, assume and assign, or reject certain executory contracts and unexpired leases. Consequently, the company anticipates that its liabilities pertaining to leases will change significantly in the future.

The future minimum lease payments required under capital leases, together with the present value of such payments, and future minimum lease payments required under operating leases that have initial or remaining non-cancelable lease terms in excess of one year as of December 31, 2011, were (in millions):

	Capital Leases Subject to Compromise	Operating Leases
Year ended December 31:		
2012	$ 167	$ 1,176
2013	149	1,091
2014	129	942
2015	118	779
2016	78	685
2017 and thereafter	477	5,940
	$1,118	$10,613
Less amount representing interest.	439	
Present value of net minimum lease payments	$ 679	

AMR's abbreviated balance sheet is presented below and reveals that the company has $11.434 billion ($11.041 billion + $0.393 billion) invested in equipment and property as of year-end 2011, of which $0.393 billion was financed using capital leases. This total fails to include, however, the $10.613 billion that AMR expects to pay in the future for equipment and property financed using operating leases. AMR's lease disclosures reveal that the company relies extensively on operating leases as a form of financing. Interestingly, look what happens to the liability accounts during 2011, the year in which AMR entered Chapter 11 bankruptcy. In 2010 there was only $0.604 billion ($0.497 billion + $0.107 billion) reported by AMR as lease-related debt, a small amount relative to its total lease commitments and total long-term debt, but by 2011 these amounts had dropped to zero. The "Liabilities subject to compromise" explains this change, as under the bankruptcy many of the company's debt obligations ($4,843 to be exact), including those under capital leases, are subject to being restructured as the company attempts to exit bankruptcy.

continued

continued from previous page

(in millions)	2011	2010
AMR CORPORATION		
Debtors and Debtors-in-Possession		
Consolidated Balance Sheets		
Current assets	$ 6,757	$ 6,838
Equipment and property, net	11,041	12,264
Equipment and property under capital leases.	841	824
Less accumulated depreciation	(448)	(580)
	393	244
Other assets	5,657	5,742
Total assets	$23,848	$25,088
Current liabilities	$ 8,630	$ 8,780
Long-term debt, less current maturities	6,702	8,756
Obligations under capital leases, less current obligations		
($0 and $107 in 2011 and 2010, respectively)	—	497
Other liabilities and credits	10,784	11,000
Liabilities subject to compromise	4,843	—
Shareholders' equity	(7,111)	(3,945)
Total liabilities and shareholders' equity	$23,848	$25,088

As lawyers and judges work through the terms of AMR's bankruptcy, one question certainly being addressed is how to deal with the company's $10.613 billion of commitments under operating leases. Financial analysts and investors often ask these questions as well, but rather as "What would be the financial impact on the financial statements if the company's operating leases were accounted for as capital leases (the leased assets and lease liabilities were capitalized to the balance sheet)?" To see this type of computation we will apply the analysis to AMR's lease disclosures as reported above. If we assume that the interest rate implicit in AMR's operating leases is ten percent, the present value of the company's minimum lease payments under its operating leases is $6.025 billion, calculated as follows:

Year	Future Minimum Lease Payments Under Operating Leases (billions)	Present Value Factor (10%)	Present Value of Minimum Lease Payments (billions)
2012 . . .	$ 1.176	0.909	$1.069
2013 . . .	1.091	0.826	0.901
2014 . . .	0.942	0.751	0.707
2015 . . .	0.779	0.683	0.532
2016 . . .	0.685	0.621	0.425
2017 . . .	0.685	0.564	0.386
2018 . . .	0.685	0.513	0.351
2019 . . .	0.685	0.467	0.320
2020 . . .	0.685	0.424	0.290
2021 . . .	0.685	0.386	0.265
2022 . . .	0.685	0.350	0.240
2023 . . .	0.685	0.319	0.219
2024 . . .	0.685	0.290	0.199
2025 . . .	0.460	0.263	0.121
Total . . .	$10.613		$6.025

The footnote information reports the first five years of minimum lease payments (through 2016) along with a summation of the minimum lease payments for all years following the fifth year. In order to compute the present value of the future lease payments, we assume that the minimum lease payment after 2016 remains constant (years 2017 through 2025 in this example) with any remainder to be paid in the final year.

continued

continued from previous page

BUSINESS PERSPECTIVE

Excluding AMR's operating leases, the company's total liabilities at year-end 2011 totaled $30.959 billion ($23.848 billion plus $7.111 billion). Including the present value of AMR's operating leases on the company's balance sheet brings the company's total liability position to $36.984 billion ($30.959 billion + $6.025 billion). These figures reveal the extent to which AMR relies on the use of operating leases as a form of debt financing, but also the extent to which the company uses off-balance-sheet financing to gain access to its operating assets. Over 19 percent ($6.025 billion ÷ $30.959) of AMR's liabilities are carried off-balance-sheet! As a consequence, failure to consider AMR's operating leases as a form of debt financing materially understates the firm's total use of leverage.

In Chapter 4, we examined several financial ratios that can prove useful when evaluating a firm's use of leverage, to include the long-term debt to total assets ratio and the long-term debt to shareholders' equity ratio. Both of these ratios provide information regarding a firm's use of debt financing relative to its use of equity financing. As a general rule, debt financing can be used to enhance shareholder returns so long as the firm is able to earn a return on its borrowed funds that exceeds its cost of borrowing the funds; thus, for most firms, the use of debt financing provides a good approach to build shareholder value. For some firms, however, increasing levels of debt financing will destroy shareholder value, especially when excessive debt levels impair management's operational flexibility. A final ratio that can help assess whether a firm has excessive levels of debt is the interest coverage ratio. By comparing a firm's current level of debt service charges with its operating earnings, the financial statement user can develop an informed opinion regarding a firm's liquidity and its solvency.

ETHICS PERSPECTIVE

Numerous reasons were cited in this chapter as to why some firms use leasing as a financing approach for acquiring capital assets. One reason is the managerial desire to avoid disclosing the operating lease liability on a company's balance sheet. It can be argued that there should not be any difference to financial statement users whether a lease obligation appears on the face of the balance sheet or is disclosed in the footnotes to the financial statements. As demonstrated in this chapter, it is a simple procedure for financial statement users to adjust the balance sheet for this type of off-balance-sheet debt. Nonetheless, many managers behave as if they believe that financial statement users will not undertake the necessary financial statement adjustments to develop a complete assessment of a firm's debt exposure. Available evidence, however, indicates that financial markets are not fooled by off-balance-sheet financing, and instead, market participants appear to incorporate this information in their assessments of the risk premium associated with public companies utilizing off-balance-sheet financing.

REVIEW PROBLEM

The Arcadia Company issued $50 million of five-year bonds on January 2. The bonds carried an annual coupon rate of six percent, with interest paid semiannually, and were issued at a time when similar risk-rated securities were yielding eight percent. Within twelve months of the debt issuance, however, market yield rates had risen to ten percent.

Required

a. Calculate the proceeds from the five-year debt offering on January 2.

b. Calculate the interest expense for the Arcadia Company on June 30 and on December 31.

c. Calculate the market value of the five-year bonds on December 31.

d. If the Arcadia Company elects to retire the bonds on December 31, how much gain (loss) would the company recognize?

e. Is the decision to retire the bonds on December 31 a good decision?

The solution is on page 331.

EXECUTIVE SUMMARY

This chapter investigated the strategic financing decision of companies, specifically how companies finance their operations and asset purchases with bonds, leases, and notes. We saw that most liabilities were valued at their present value. We also examined how and why some firms lease their long-term revenue-producing assets. Finally, we illustrated how to calculate the weighted-average cost of debt of a company. In Chapter 10, our investigation of debt financing continues with a consideration of commitments and contingent liabilities, retirement obligations, deferred income tax liabilities, and financial instruments and derivatives.

As a validation of your understanding of the content of this chapter, you should now be able to:

- ■ Explain how bonds and notes are valued and reported in corporate financial statements.
- ■ Explain how a company accounts for debt when it is retired before its maturity.
- ■ Explain the difference between a capital lease and an operating lease and how each is reported in the financial statements.
- ■ Explain how and why companies manage the amount of debt reported on their corporate balance sheets.

KEY CONCEPTS AND TERMS

Accreted value, 309	Credit-risk rating, 301	Operating lease, 310
Amortization, 305	Debentures, 301	Ordinary annuity, 311
Amortization schedule, 305, 312	Discount, 303, 304	Par value, 304
Annuity-in-arrears, 311	Duration, 300	Premium, 304
Bonds, 300	Effective interest method, 305	Present value, 302
Callable, 301	Face value, 304	Secured, 301
Capital lease, 310	Indenture agreement, 301	Subordinated, 301
Century bonds, 309	Junk bonds, 302	Trustee, 301
Contingent liability, 311	Maturity value, 302	Unsecured, 301
Contra-liability, 304	Net debt, 317	Unsubordinated, 301
Convertible, 301	Note discount, 304	Weighted-average cost of debt, 316
Cost of debt, 301	Notes, 300	Yield rate, 302
Coupon rate, 302	Off-balance-sheet financing, 310, 317	Zero-coupon bonds, 308

QUESTIONS

Q9.1 **Financing with Debt versus Equity.** It is commonly understood that the cost of financing a business's asset purchases with debt is cheaper than financing those purchases with equity. Discuss why debt financing is cheaper than equity financing. Is there a set of circumstances when the cost of debt financing would exceed the cost of equity financing? If so, when?

Q9.2 **Credit Ratings.** In 2005, The **General Motors Corporation** (GM) reported a net loss of $10.6 billion. Moreover, the automobile manufacturer had been losing U.S. market share to increasing competition from Japanese automakers. In response, Standard & Poor's rating service indicated that it was reviewing whether to lower GM's debt rating from its current B rating (five levels below investment grade status). Standard & Poor's also reported that it was "putting GM's debt on its CreditWatch list with negative implications" because the automaker disclosed that as much as $3 billion in lease obligations could be subject to possible covenant violations that might cause an acceleration of debt repayment. The credit-rating agency also expressed concern that the company's recent disappointing performance might affect the firm's access to its $5.6 billion standby credit facility. Discuss why credit ratings are important to a company like GM. Discuss the consequences to a company when it violates its existing debt covenants. (GM filed for Chapter 11 bankruptcy in 2009.)

Q9.3 **Credit Ratings.** In early 2006, The **General Motors Corporation** (GM) took significant steps to improve its deteriorating financial condition. Besides downsizing its workforce and closing certain inefficient plants, the company also sold its ownership interest in several of its subsidiaries. For instance, GM sold its equity stake in Japan's Isusu Motors for $300 million and sold a majority shareholding in its financing subsidiary, General Motors Acceptance Corporation (GMAC), for $14 billion. In response to these GM actions, U.S. credit-rating agencies took the following actions:

- Fitch, Inc. revised its outlook on GMAC's bonds to "positive."
- Standard & Poor's reported that it might raise the ratings on GMAC's bonds from BB to BB+.
- Moody's indicated that it might downgrade the GMAC bonds.

Discuss why a favorable credit rating is important to a company like GM. Do you agree with Moody's response (a possible credit-rating downgrade) to the GM actions? Why?

Q9.4 **Long-Term Debt Disclosures.** The **Johnson & Johnson Company** reported the following borrowings in note 7 of its 2011 its annual report:

7. Borrowings

The components of long-term debt are as follows:

(Dollars in Millions)	2011	Effective Rate %
5.15% Debentures due 2012	$599	5.18%
0.70% Notes due 2013	500	0.75
3.80% Debentures due 2013	500	3.82
3 month LIBOR+0% FRN due 2013	500	0.46
3 month LIBOR+0.09% FRN due 2014	750	0.55
1.20% Notes due 2014	999	1.24
2.15 Notes due 2016	898	2.22
5.55% Debentures due 2017	1,000	5.55
5.15% Debentures due 2018	898	5.15
4.75% Notes due 2019 (1B Euro 1.2892)/(1B Euro 1.3268)	1,282[2]	5.35
3% Zero Coupon Convertible Subordinated Debentures due 2020	199	3.00
2.95% Debentures due 2020	541	3.15
3.55% Notes due 2021	446	3.67
6.73% Debentures due 2023	250	6.73
5.50% Notes due 2024 (500MM GBP 1.5421)/(500MM GBP 1.5403)	765[2]	5.71
6.95% Notes due 2029	294	7.14
4.95% Debentures due 2033	500	4.95
5.95% Notes due 2037	995	5.99
5.85% Debentures due 2038	700	5.86
4.50% Debentures due 2040	539	4.63
4.85% Notes due 2041	298	4.89
Other	132	
	13,585[4]	4.08[1]
Less current portion	616	
	$12,969	

Discuss the difference between a "note" and a "debenture." Of Johnson & Johnson's (J&J) total long-term borrowings of $13,585, what amount will appear as a current liability and what amount will appear as a non-current liability? Were the 3.80% debentures, due 2013, originally sold at a discount, at their par value, or at a premium? Why? Were the 6.95% notes, due 2029, originally sold at a discount, at their par value, or at a premium? Why? Which of J&J's borrowings were sold at their par value? How do you know this?

Q9.5 **Selling Bonds at a Discount, at Par, and at a Premium.** It is widely accepted that bonds may sell at a discount from their par value, at their par value, or at a premium above their par value. Discuss why, and under what circumstances, a bond would sell at a discount, at its par value, and at a premium.

Q9.6 **Accounting for Bonds at a Constant Yield Rate.** When bonds are sold by a company, they are recorded on the issuing firm's financial statements at their selling price. This price reflects the yield rate on the date of sale for equivalent risk-rated debt instruments. Although the market yield rate for a given bond may fluctuate widely in the debt market, the changing market rate is ignored for accounting purposes; and instead, the debt instrument remains on the financial statements of the issuing company at the yield rate prevailing at the time of sale. Discuss the implications of this accounting treatment. Do you believe that bond values should be periodically revised to reflect a changing interest-rate environment? Why or why not?

Q9.7 **Why Do Companies Lease?** Leasing is a common form of asset financing. Discuss why leasing is such a popular form of financing for many businesses.

Q9.8 **Operating Leases and Market Efficiency.** Many businesses use operating leases as a method to finance their operating assets. One of the frequently stated reasons for the popularity of operating leases (as opposed to capital leases) is that operating leases are carried off-balance-sheet—that is, operating leases are a form of off-balance-sheet financing. Discuss whether you think the capital market is "efficient" with respect to operating leases. Stated alternatively, discuss whether you believe that the capital market treats operating leases as off-balance-sheet debt or as on-balance-sheet debt. Be prepared to justify your answer.

Q9.9 **Zero-Coupon Convertible Debentures.** In 2000, ALZA Corporation, a wholly owned subsidiary of the **Johnson & Johnson** (J&J) Company, sold zero-coupon convertible debentures at a price of $551.26 per $1,000 principal amount at maturity. The twenty-year debentures were also convertible into J&J shares. Discuss the reasons why ALZA might issue zero-coupon convertible debentures. Estimate the yield to maturity on the debentures.

Q9.10 **Converting Notes Payable into Common Stock.** In 2006, **US Airways Group** announced that more than 99 percent of its convertible senior notes had been converted into the airline's common stock. The $112 million of 7.5 percent notes, due 2009, had been called for redemption and noteholders had been given six weeks to either convert the notes into common stock or redeem the notes for approximately $1,050 in cash per $1,000 of notes. The notes were convertible into 34.376 shares of US Airways stock, which had recently been trading at $36 per share. Why did the US Airways noteholders convert their notes into the airline's common stock? Why hadn't they converted their notes earlier? Explain how a conversion of debt into common stock might benefit US Airways Group.

Q9.11 **Collateralized Debt Obligations.** Collateralized debt obligations (CDOs) are bonds issued by a bank, real estate investment trust, or financial institution, which are backed by loans collateralized by commercial real estate (such as shopping malls, hotels, office buildings). In short, CDOs represent an interest in a pool of real estate loans and mortgages. Discuss why a bank, real estate investment trust, or financial institution would sell CDOs instead of issuing debentures backed by the firm's credit rating.

Q9.12 **Debt-for-Equity Exchange.** The May 9, 2006, edition of the *Wall Street Journal* carried the following headline:

Accounting Gain Masks UAL Loss of $306 Million

The related article explained that **UAL Corporation**, parent company of United Airlines, reported first quarter net income of almost $23 billion thanks to a $24 billion gain from "discharging its obligations to unsecured creditors in exchange for giving them 115 million UAL common shares." Without the noncash gain, UAL would have reported a net loss of $306 million. UAL emerged from bankruptcy in February 2006. UAL common shares traded at $39 per share prior to the May 9, 2006, announcement. Discuss the financial effects of UAL's exchange of its stock for its unsecured debt. What was the market value of the UAL stock given to creditors? What was the book value of the UAL debt?

Q9.13 **(Ethics Perspective) Avoiding the Recording of Leases on Balance Sheet.** Why do you suppose that managers desire to keep debt off the balance sheet even when they know that the obligation will be fully disclosed in the footnotes? Do you feel that it is ethical to choose to lease an asset rather than to purchase the asset if the only reason for the accounting policy choice is to avoid the balance sheet recognition of the lease obligation?

Assignments with the ✅ logo in the margin are available in BusinessCourse.
See the Preface of the book for details.
CHECK FIGURE indicates that check figures are available on the book's Website.

EXERCISES

E9.14 **Coupon Rates, Yield Rates, and Bond Issuance Prices.** The relation between a bond's coupon rate and yield rate is known to influence a bond's issuance price. Presented below are coupon rates and yield rates for a selection of corporate bonds. Identity whether each bond was sold at a discount, at its par value, or at a premium, and explain why.

Bond	Coupon Rate	Yield Rate
A	7.5%	7.55%
B	8.1	8.0
C	6.0	6.0
D	4.5	4.4
E	9.0	9.15

E9.15   **Calculating Bond Issuance Prices.**   Presented below are annual coupon rates, yield rates, and expected duration for a series of debentures. Calculate the issuance price for each debenture assuming that the face value of each bond is $1,000 and that interest is paid semiannually.

Bond	Coupon Rate	Yield Rate	Duration
A.....................	4.0%	6.0%	5 years
B.....................	10.0	8.0	6 years
C.....................	6.0	6.0	10 years
D.....................	0.0	8.0	15 years
E.....................	8.0	10.0	10 years

E9.16   **Bond Discounts and Effective Interest Rates.**   During 2008, the Mayfield Corporation issued $400 million of zero-coupon debentures, due in 2018. The proceeds of the bond sale totaled approximately $182.56 million. Assuming semi-annual compounding, estimate the effective interest rate on the zero-coupon debentures. Calculate the interest expense incurred by the Mayfield Corporation during the first year that the debt was outstanding.

E9.17   **Calculating the Fair Value of Debt.**   The Longo Corporation issued $50 million maturity value in notes, carrying a coupon rate of six percent, with interest paid semiannually. At the time of the note issue, equivalent risk-rated debt instruments carried yield rates of eight percent. The notes matured in five years.

Calculate the proceeds that Longo Corporation will receive from the sale of the notes. How will the notes be disclosed on Longo's balance sheet immediately following the sale? Calculate the interest expense for Longo Corporation for the first year that the notes are outstanding. Calculate the balance sheet value of the notes at the end of the first year.

E9.18   **Building a Note Amortization Table.**   Valcor Inc. issued $100 million maturity value of three-year notes, which carried a coupon rate of four percent and which paid interest semiannually. At the time of the note sale, equivalent risk-rated debt instruments carried a yield rate of six percent. Develop a note amortization table for Valcor's four percent, three-year notes.

E9.19   **Accounting for Bonds Sold at a Discount.**   The Biltmore National Bank raised capital through the sale of $100 million face value of eight percent coupon rate, ten-year bonds. The bonds paid interest semiannually and were sold at a time when equivalent risk-rated bonds carried a yield rate of ten percent.

Calculate the proceeds that The Biltmore National Bank received from the sale of the eight percent bonds. How will the bonds be disclosed on Biltmore's balance sheet immediately following the sale? Calculate the interest expense on the bonds for the first year that the bonds are outstanding. Calculate the book value of the bonds at the end of the first year.

E9.20   **Market Yield Rates and Bond Values.**   Smith & Company issued $80 million maturity value of five-year bonds, which carried a coupon rate of six percent, with interest paid semiannually. At the time of the debt offering, equivalent risk-rated bonds were yielding eight percent. One year after the five-year bond offering, yield rates had risen to ten percent; but, by the second anniversary of the bond sale, the yield rate on similarly risk-rated debt instruments had dropped to only four percent.

Calculate the proceeds from the sale of the six percent, five-year bonds. Calculate the book value of the bonds after one year and after two years. Calculate the market value of the bonds after one year and after two years. What is the relationship between market yield rates and bond values?

E9.21   **Accounting for Notes Issues at a Premium.**   The Longo Corporation issued $50 million maturity value of eight percent coupon rate notes, with interest paid semiannually. At the time of the note issuance, equivalent risk-rated debt instruments carried a yield rate of six percent. The notes matured in five years.

Calculate the proceeds that the Longo Corporation would receive from the sale of the notes. How will the notes be reported on Longo's balance sheet immediately following the sale? Calculate the interest expense on the notes for the first year. Calculate the book value of the notes at the end of the first year.

E9.22   **Issuing Zero-Coupon Bonds.**   On July 28, 2000, ALZA Corporation completed a private placement of zero-coupon convertible subordinated debentures. The zero-coupon debentures were issued at a price of $551.26 per $1,000 principal amount at maturity. Although the zero-coupon bonds paid no periodic interest payments, interest was assumed to be compounded semiannually. The bonds mature in 2020.

Estimate the yield rate on the zero-coupon bonds at the time of issuance. Why would ALZA Corporation issue non-interest-bearing bonds? Why would ALZA attach a conversion feature to the zero-coupon bonds? Calculate ALZA's implicit interest expense for the first year.

E9.23   **Retiring Debt Early.**   Smith & Company issued $80 million maturity value of five-year bonds, which carried a coupon rate of six percent and paid interest semiannually. At the time of the offering, the yield rate for equivalent risk-rated securities was eight percent. Two years later, market yield rates had risen to ten percent, and since the company no longer needed the debt financing, executives at Smith & Company decided to retire the debt.

Calculate the gain or loss that Smith & Company will incur as a consequence of retiring the debt early. Is the early retirement of the debt a good decision? What factors should be considered in making this decision?

E9.24 **Operating Leases.** The Johnson & Johnson Company disclosed in its annual report that it leases various vehicles and machinery using operating lease agreements. According to its footnotes the minimum payments required under the noncancelable operating lease agreements were as follows:

Year Ending ($ millions)	Operating Leases
2006	$162
2007	142
2008	119
2009	103
2010	88
After 2010	151
Total	$765

If the interest rate implicit in each of the lease agreements is eight percent, what is the present value of the company's noncancelable lease payments? Johnson & Johnson's long-term debt-to-equity ratio at year-end was 8.1 percent ($2,565/$31,813). If the company's operating leases were accounted for as capital leases instead of operating leases, how would the firm's long-term debt-to-equity ratio change?

E9.25 **Capitalizing Operating Leases.** The following information is taken from the 2012 annual report of Delta Air Lines, Inc.:

Total assets.	$44,550
Total liabilities	$46,681
Stockholders' deficit.	$ (2,131)

Operating Leases

Years Ending December 31, (in millions)	Delta Lease Payments	Contract Carrier Aircraft Lease Payments	Total
2013	$ 1,005	$ 502	$ 1,507
2014	949	484	1,433
2015	859	473	1,332
2016	736	423	1,159
2017	627	373	1,000
Thereafter	6,414	1,001	7,415
Total minimum lease payments	$10,590	$3,256	$13,846

Assume that the cost of debt implicit in the company's operating leases is five percent. Calculate the present value of Delta's operating leases at year-end. Calculate the company's total liabilities to total assets ratio for the year (a) with and (b) without considering the company's operating leases. Does the presence of operating leases impact a firm's financial risk?

PROBLEMS

P9.26 **Debt Valuation: Interest-Bearing Debentures.** At the beginning of the year, Global Minds Inc. issued $100 million (maturity value) of 20-year debentures. The debentures carried a four percent per period coupon rate, were subject to semiannual compounding, and had been issued at a time when the yield rate was six percent per period.

Required

1. Calculate the proceeds received by Global Minds when the bonds were sold.
2. Explain why the Global Minds bonds were sold at a discount.
3. Calculate the market value of the bonds if, after ten years, the market yield rate is ten percent per period.
4. Calculate the cost of retiring the Global Minds bonds after 15 years assuming that the market yield rate is ten percent per period at the time of retirement. Does the retirement result in a gain or loss? If so, where will the gain/loss be reported on the company's statement of cash flows?

P9.27   Debt Valuation: Zero-Coupon Debentures.   At the beginning of the year, KMF Inc. issued $100 million (maturity value) of 15-year, zero-coupon debentures, at a time when the yield rate was six percent per period. The KMF, Inc. bonds would be subject to semiannual compounding.

Required

1. Calculate the proceeds to be received by KMF Inc. when the bonds are sold.
2. Calculate the cost to repurchase and retire the bonds after five years assuming that the market yield rate at that time is eight percent per period. Is the early retirement of debt a good decision in this set of circumstances? What factors did you consider in reaching your decision?
3. Under what circumstances would a company consider issuing zero-coupon debentures instead of regular interest-bearing debentures?

 P9.28   Debt Retirement.   MTF Inc. is a manufacturer of electronic components for facsimile equipment. The company financed the expansion of its production facilities by issuing $100 million of ten-year bonds carrying a coupon rate of eight percent with interest payable annually on December 31. The bonds had been issued on January 1. At the time of the issuance, the market rate of interest on similar risk-rated instruments was six percent.

Two years later, the market rate of interest on comparable debt instruments had climbed to twelve percent. The CEO of MTF realized that this might be an opportune time to repurchase the bonds, particularly because an unexpected surplus of cash made the outstanding debt no longer necessary.

Required

1. Calculate the proceeds received by the company when the debt was initially sold.
2. Calculate the interest expense for each of the two years that the bonds were outstanding.
3. Calculate the amount of cash needed to retire the debt after two years assuming a market yield rate of twelve percent. Does the retirement result in a gain or loss? If so, where will the gain/loss be reported on the company's statement of cash flow?

CHECK FIGURE   **P9.29   Note Valuation.   Microsoft Corporation** reported the following information on its long-term debt in its 2012 annual report:

Due Date	Face Value (In millions)	Stated Interest Rate	Effective Interest Rate	Interest Record Date	Interest Pay Date	Interest Record Date	Interest Pay Date
Notes							
September 27, 2013....	$ 1,000	0.875%	1.000%	March 15	March 27	September 15	September 27
June 1, 2014.........	2,000	2.950%	3.049%	May 15	June 1	November 15	December 1
September 25, 2015....	1,750	1.625%	1.795%	March 15	March 25	September 15	September 25
February 8, 2016	750	2.500%	2.642%	February 1	February 8	August 1	August 8
June 1, 2019.........	1,000	4.200%	4.379%	May 15	June 1	November 15	December 1
October 1, 2020.......	1,000	3.000%	3.137%	March 15	April 1	September 15	October 1
February 8, 2021	500	4.000%	4.082%	February 1	February 8	August 1	August 8
June 1, 2039.........	750	5.200%	5.240%	May 15	June 1	November 15	December 1
October 1, 2040.......	1,000	4.500%	4.567%	March 15	April 1	September 15	October 1
February 8, 2041	1,000	5.300%	5.361%	February 1	February 8	August 1	August 8
Total	$10,750						

Required

1. Were the June 1, 2014 notes sold at a discount, a premium, or at par? Why?
2. How much would the June 1, 2019 notes have been sold for if the market rate of interest at the time of sale had been six percent per year? Assume the bonds originally had a 10-year (20 interest payment) term.

3. Assume Moody's reports that the October 1, 2020 notes were rated as Aaa3.
   a. If the rating had been Aa1 instead, would the yield rate on the notes have been lower, higher, or the same?
   b. If the notes had been secured, would the yield rate have been lower, higher, or the same?
4. Assume the company reported that the fair market value of the company's September 25, 2015 notes was $1,850 million on June 30, 2012. If the company repurchased all of the Notes on June 30, 2012, would a gain or loss have been recorded?

P9.30 **Note Valuation.** The Jefferson Company is a multinational manufacturer of electrical equipment and components. Selected financial information is as follows:

Consolidated Statements of Income			
For Period Ended (In millions)	2012	2011	2010
Net sales.	$9,682.00	$9,597.60	$7,819.00
Operating income.	$ 523.20	$1,089.40	$1,079.70
Interest expense	(253.00)	(255.30)	(183.50)
Other income (expense), net.	(6.80)	35.80	3.10
Noncontrolling interests	(20.10)	(39.30)	(29.10)
Earnings before income taxes	243.30	830.60	870.20
(Benefit) provision for income taxes	(2.90)	284.40	307.10
Earnings from continuing operations	246.20	546.20	563.10
Discontinued operations (net of tax)	—	123.20	28.00
Net earnings.	$ 246.20	$ 669.40	$ 591.10

Abbreviated Consolidated Balance Sheet		
(in millions)	2012	2011
Total assets.	$11,063.70	$11,052.60
Long-term debt	$ 2,900.70	$ 1,540.40
Shareholders' equity	$ 3,916.60	$ 3,481.20
Total liabilities and stockholders' equity.	$11,063.70	$11,052.60

Note 8–Long-Term Debt and Credit Facilities		
(in millions)	2012	2011
5.75% Notes Due 2007.	$ 600.00	$ 0
Total long-term debt.	$2,900.70	$1,540.40

Required

1. The company reported that on February 1, 2012, the company issued $600 million of 5.75 percent secured notes due February 1, 2014.
   a. Were the notes sold at a discount, a premium, or at par value?
   b. How much interest expense did the company record on August 1, 2012, assuming semiannual compounding?
   c. How much would the company have raised through the sale of the notes if the market rate of interest had been six percent per year?

2. Moody's reports that the notes were rated **A3**.
    a. If the rating had been A1 instead, would the yield rate have been higher, lower, or the same?
    b. If the notes had been unsecured, would the yield rate have been higher, lower, or the same?
    c. The company reports that the fair market value of the company's long-term debt at December 31, 2012, was $2,996.70. If the company repurchased all of the outstanding long-term debt on December 31, 2012, how much gain (loss) would be recognized?
    d. Assume Moody's only used the long-term debt to equity ratio and the interest coverage ratio in making its rating decision. Would the rating on the 5.75 percent notes have been higher, the same, or lower if the notes had been issued in 2011 instead of 2012?

P9.31   **Valuing a Lease.**   On January 1, the president of KMF Inc. signed an eight-year lease agreement for retail space at a lease rate of $50,000 per year. During the negotiations, the president had learned that the lessor had built an implicit borrowing cost of ten percent per year into the lease contract. The agreement called for the lease payments to be made annually at the beginning of each year. Hence, the first payment of $50,000 was made immediately after the lease agreement was signed on January 1.

Required
1. Assume that the lease agreement is to be accounted for as a capital lease by KMF. How will the lease commitment be reflected on the company's financial statements? At what value?
2. At the beginning of the second year of the lease, what financial effects will be recorded in the financial statements of KMF? At the beginning of the third year?
3. Which lease accounting treatment—operating lease versus capital lease—provides the most preferred income tax treatment (i.e., provides the greatest income tax benefits) to the company?

CHECK
FIGURE
P9.32   **Lease Accounting.**   On January 1, Durant Inc. entered into a noncancelable ten-year lease for cooking equipment with a fair value of $100 million and requiring annual year-end lease payments. The company's year-end is December 31.

Required
1. If the implicit interest rate on the lease is eight percent, what is the annual lease payment?
2. Assuming that the lease is accounted for as a capital lease, what financial effects will be recorded in the financial statements with regard to the lease on January 1?
3. Assuming that the lease is accounted for as a capital lease, what financial effects will be recorded with regard to the lease on December 31 (at the end of the first year)?
4. What are the total expenses associated with the lease in the second year if it is accounted for as an operating lease? As a capital lease?

P9.33   **Lease Accounting.**   On January 1, Longo Inc. entered into a noncancelable 15-year lease for cooking equipment with a fair value of $150 million and requiring annual year-end lease payments. The company's year-end is December 31.

Required
1. If the implicit interest rate on the lease is twelve percent, what is the annual lease payment?
2. Assuming that the lease is accounted for as a capital lease, what financial effects will be recorded in the financial statements with regard to the lease on January 1?
3. Assuming that the lease is accounted for as a capital lease, what financial effects will be recorded with regard to the lease on December 31 (at the end of the first year)?
4. What are the total expenses associated with the lease in the second year if it is accounted for as an operating lease? As a capital lease?

P9.34   **Capitalizing Operating Leases.**   **McDonald's Corp.** was the lessee at 14,139 restaurant locations through ground leases at December 31, 2011. The lease terms are generally for 20 years. The company is also the lessee under noncancelable leases covering certain offices and vehicles. The company's footnotes also revealed that at year-end 2011, the minimum lease commitments under noncancelable operating leases were:

In millions	Restaurant	Other	Total
2012	$ 1,172.6	$ 74.4	$ 1,247.0
2013	1,104.8	62.8	1,167.6
2014	1,019.5	55.4	1,074.9
2015	921.9	43.1	965.0
2016	813.9	37.9	851.8
Thereafter	6,039.1	208.8	6,247.9
Total minimum payments	$11,071.8	$482.4	$11,554.2

The following represents a condensed balance sheet for McDonalds for 2011:

MCDONALD'S CORPORATION Consolidated Balance Sheet	
($ millions)	**2011**
Assets	
Current assets	$ 4,403.0
Noncurrent assets	28,586.9
Total assets.	$32,989.9
Liabilities and Shareholders' equity	
Current liabilities.	$ 3,509.2
Long-term debt	12,133.8
Other noncurrent liabilities	2,956.7
Shareholders' equity	14,390.2
Total liabilities and shareholders' equity.	$32,989.9

Required

1. Calculate the present value of the company's operating leases assuming an interest rate of 6 percent.
2. Restate the company's balance sheet assuming that all operating leases are capitalized.
3. Calculate the:
   a. Long-term debt to shareholders' equity ratio, both with and without capitalization of operating leases.
   b. Total debt to total assets ratio, both with and without the capitalization of the operating leases.

   How would the company's debt rating be affected if all leases (both capital and operating) were capitalized to the balance sheet?

CORPORATE ANALYSIS

CA9.35   **The Procter & Gamble Company.**   The 2012 annual report of the **Procter & Gamble Company** (P&G) is available at http://annualreport.pg.com/annualreport2012/index.shtml. After reviewing P&G's annual report, respond to the following questions.

a. Calculate P&G's total debt to total assets ratio for 2011 and 2012. Is the company principally debt or equity financed? What is the trend in P&G's use of debt financing? What was P&G's short-term and long-term weighted-average cost of debt? What is the trend in P&G's cost of borrowing?

b. Calculate P&G's return on assets for 2011 and 2012. Is the company's financing strategy sound? What is P&G's short-term and long-term credit rating? Does P&G have an "investment grade" rating or a "junk grade" rating?

c. P&G's "total debt" in 2012 was $29.778 billion. What is the composition of P&G's "total debt"? Why would P&G issue notes denominated in British pounds, EU euros, Japanese yen, as well as in U.S. dollars? Is P&G subject to any debt covenants under its various borrowings? If so, what are the covenants and is the company satisfying the covenants?

d. Does P&G use operating leases to finance any of its operating assets? If so, what are the future minimum operating lease payments for 2013, 2014, 2015, 2016, 2017, and thereafter? Calculate the present value of P&G's operating leases assuming an implicit cost of borrowing of four percent. Is P&G's use of operating leases material?

CA9.36 **Internet-based Analysis.** Consider a publicly held company whose products you are familiar with. Some examples might include:

Company	Product	Corporate Website
• Johnson & Johnson Company.......	• Band-Aids	• www.jnj.com
• Microsoft Corporation..............	• Windows XP software	• www.microsoft.com
• Nokia Corporation.................	• Cellular phones	• www.nokia.com
• Intel Corporation	• Pentium processors	• www.intel.com
• Kimberly-Clark Corporation.........	• Kleenex	• www.kimberly-clark.com

Access the company's public website and search for its most recent annual report. (Some companies provide access to their financial data through an "investor relations" link, while others provide a direct link to their "annual reports.") After locating your company's most recent annual report, open the file and review its contents. After reviewing the annual report for your selected company, prepare answers to the following questions:

a. Calculate the total debt to total assets ratio for the past two years. Is the company principally debt-financed or equity-financed? Do you agree with this strategic decision?

b. Review the company's long-term debt footnote. What kinds of debt –bonds, notes, zero-coupon bonds— does the company have outstanding? Are the debt instruments denominated in U.S. dollars? If not, why not?

c. What is the company's weighted-average cost of debt? What is the company's return on assets? Can the company use leverage effectively?

d. Does the company use leases to finance any of its assets? If so, what kind of leases—operating or capital—does the company use?

e. Calculate the company's interest coverage ratio for the past two years. What is the trend in this ratio? Why? What is your assessment of the company's liquidity and solvency? What did you base your opinion on?

CA9.37 **IFRS Financial Statements.** The 2012 financial statements of **LVMH Moet Hennessey-Louis Vuitton S.A.** are presented in Appendix C of this book. LVMH is a Paris-based holding company and one of the world's largest and best-known luxury goods company. As a member-nation of the European Union, French companies are required to prepare their consolidated (group) financial statements using International Financial Reporting Standards (IFRS).

Review the company's IFRS financial statements. Is the company principally debt or equity financed? Calculate the company's long-term borrowings to total equity ratio for 2011 and 2012. Is the company's use of debt financing increasing or decreasing over the two-year period?

SOLUTION TO REVIEW PROBLEM

Solution

a. Proceeds of debt offering:

Present value of $50 million in 10 periods @ 4%: $50,000,000 × 0.676	=	$33,800,000
+ Present value of $1,500,000 per period for 10 periods @ 4%: $1,500,000 × 8.111	=	12,166,500
Proceeds		$45,966,500

b. Interest expense:

June 30: $45,966,500 × .04	=	$1,838,660
December 31: ($45,966,500 + $338,660) × .04	=	$1,852,206

c. Market value:

Present value of $50 million in 8 periods @ 5%: $50,000,000 × 0.677	=	$33,850,000
+ Present value of $1,500,000 per period for 8 periods @ 5%: $1,500,000 × 6.463	=	9,694,500
Market value		$43,544,500

d. Gain on retirement:

Book value of bonds	$45,966,500
Discount amortization (06/30)	338,660
Discount amortization (12/31)	352,206
Book value (12/31)	46,657,366
Less: Market value	(43,544,500)
Gain on early retirement	$ 3,112,866

e. The Arcadia Company will recognize a gain of $3,112,866 on the debt retirement as a consequence of the decline in the market value of the bonds, associated with the market interest rate increase from eight to ten percent. Thus, if the debt is no longer needed to finance the operations of the company, the decision would be a good decision.

When you complete this chapter you should be able to:

1. Explain the difference between a commitment and a contingent liability.

2. Describe deferred income tax and how this account increases and decreases.

3. Explain how employee retirement obligations are reported and disclosed.

4. Describe how financial instruments and derivatives are valued and reported in corporate financial statements.

CHAPTER

10

Commitments and Contingent Liabilities, Deferred Tax Liabilities, and Retirement Obligations

Wal-Mart Stores Inc., with its motto of "Low prices, always," has used its low-price strategy to fuel tremendous growth. Sam Walton, the company founder, opened the first Wal-Mart store in 1962 (called Walmart Discount City) and incorporated the business as *Wal-Mart Stores Inc.* in 1969, by which time it had expanded to 38 stores. As of January 2012, Wal-Mart was the world's largest retailer with over 9,000 stores in 67 countries.

WAL-MART STORES INC.

The company refers to its over 2.2 million employees as "associates." In addition, Wal-Mart stores in the United States and Canada have designated "greeters," whose role is to welcome shoppers at the store entrance and play a role in inventory loss prevention. It has been reported that 80 percent of U.S. residents shop at Wal-Mart at least once a year. Each week, about 200 million customers visit a Wal-Mart store and sales for fiscal year 2012 topped $440 billion. The company sells its goods in retail outlets, online and through mobile phone apps. In late 2012 Wal-Mart launched its first mail subscription service, Goodies, allowing customers to find and order new foods for a flat $7 monthly fee.

While Wal-Mart may be cheered by consumers for its low prices, others are more critical of the company. Wal-Mart has been criticized and sued by community groups, trade unions, and environmental groups for, among other things, its extensive foreign product sourcing, treatment of employees and product suppliers, environmental policies, use of public subsidies, and store impacts on local communities and businesses. One such lawsuit alleges that female employees were discriminated against in pay and promotions. The following description of the lawsuit appeared in the company's 2011 annual report:

Gender Discrimination Class Action: The Company is a defendant in *Dukes v. Wal-Mart Stores, Inc.*, a class-action lawsuit commenced in June 2001 in the United States District Court for the Northern District of California. The complaint alleges that the Company has engaged in a pattern and practice of discriminating against women in promotions, pay, training and job assignments. The complaint seeks, among other things, injunctive relief, front pay, back pay, punitive damages and attorneys' fees. On June 21, 2004, the district court issued an order granting in part and denying in part the plaintiffs' motion for class certification. The class, which was certified by the district court for purposes of liability, injunctive and declaratory relief, punitive damages and lost pay, subject to certain exceptions, includes all women employed at any Wal-Mart domestic retail store at any time since December 26, 1998, who have been or may be subjected to the pay and management track promotions policies and practices challenged by the plaintiffs.

If the Company is not successful in its appeal of class certification, or an appellate court issues a ruling that allows for the certification of a class or classes with a different size or scope, and if there is a subsequent adverse verdict on the merits from which there is no successful appeal, or in the event of a negotiated settlement of the litigation, the resulting liability could be material to the Company's financial condition or results of operations. The plaintiffs also seek punitive damages which, if awarded, could result in the payment of additional amounts material to the Company's financial condition or results of operations. However, because of the uncertainty of the outcome of the appeal, because of the uncertainty of the balance of the proceedings contemplated by the district court, and because the Company's liability, if any, arising from the litigation, including the size of any damages awarded if plaintiffs are successful in the litigation or any negotiated settlement, could vary widely, the Company cannot reasonably estimate the possible loss or range of loss that may arise from the litigation.

(continued on next page)

(continued from previous page)

Presented below is the liabilities section of Wal-Mart's 2011 balance sheet. Where does Wal-Mart disclose the potentially massive legal liability associated with the class-action lawsuit?

Liabilities and Shareholders' Equity (amounts in millions)	
Short-term borrowings.	$ 1,031
Accounts payable.	33,557
Accrued liabilities.	18,701
Accrued income taxes.	157
Long-term debt due within one year.	4,655
Obligations under capital leases due within one year.	336
Current liabilities of discontinued operations.	47
Total current liabilities.	58,484
Long-term debt.	40,692
Long-term obligations under capital leases.	3,150
Deferred income taxes and other.	6,682
Redeemable noncontrolling interest.	408
Commitments and contingencies.	—

If you guessed that the lawsuit is disclosed under "commitments and contingencies" with a zero balance, you are correct. Under U.S. GAAP, a company is required to record its potential litigation exposure only if the company concludes that it is highly probable that it will lose the ruling and if the amount of any potential award can be reasonably estimated. As noted above, Wal-Mart is unable to reasonably estimate the possible loss from this lawsuit, and consequently, the company is not required to record a liability for its potential loss.

In this chapter, we examine the important category of potential liabilities called commitments and contingencies, along with two other corporate obligations, deferred income tax liabilities and employee retirement obligations. In Appendix 10B we examine another potential obligation—financial instruments and derivatives.

EXECUTIVE OUTLINE

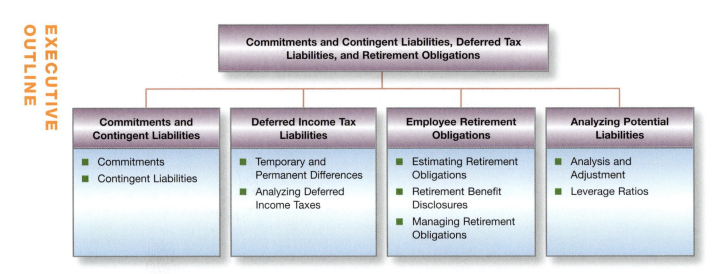

COMMITMENTS AND CONTINGENT LIABILITIES

In the day-to-day running of most businesses, it is common for the managers of a company to engage in **executory contracts** on behalf of the business. An executory contract is an agreement that calls for some form of future performance by both parties to the agreement, often involving an exchange of assets. For example, we reviewed a most basic type of executory contract in Chapter 9—a short-term rental agreement. A company signs a contract agreeing to pay a fixed rent, and in exchange the property owner explicitly agrees to provide the use of the property (i.e., an operating lease). As another example of an executory contract, management may sign a **purchase commitment** with one of a company's key suppliers, committing the firm to buy certain quantities of raw materials in the future. Since financial statements portray "what is" or "what has been" and not "what will be," executory contracts and the related future obligation to perform are not reported in the financial statements, although they are frequently described in the footnotes to the financial statements.

In accounting language, executory contracts are referred to as **commitments**—that is, an unexecuted contract in which the amount of the pending obligation is *relatively certain*. Examples include bank lines of credit, operating leases, purchase commitments, and take-or-pay contracts. In the case of a bank **line of credit**, when a borrower draws down on a credit line, the executory component of the contract is executed—the lender has provided cash and the borrower is now obligated to pay—and the amount of the borrowing must be reported on the borrower's balance sheet along with the amount of borrowed cash. Similarly, in the case of a purchase agreement, as soon as the promised product is delivered, a contractual obligation to pay the supplier is created and must be recorded on the face of the purchaser's balance sheet, along with the newly acquired inventory. Until those events occur, however, the obligation to buy the goods at some point in the future or the obligation to repay unborrowed funds under a line of credit need only be disclosed in the footnotes to the financial statements.

> A **line of credit** is a guaranteed loan, which may be used by a borrower in whole or in part. The borrower pays a fee to gain access to the line of credit and pays interest on any borrowed amounts.

Closely related to commitments are **contingent liabilities**—that is, an obligation contingent upon the occurrence of some future event in which the amount of the pending obligation is *relatively uncertain*. Examples include the financial settlement of a pending lawsuit, environmental clean-up responsibilities, loan guarantees, and the potential reimbursement associated with accounts receivable sold with recourse. In the case of an **account receivable sold with recourse**, the seller of an account receivable is uncertain what its future reimbursement obligation to a factor will be until the factor tries, and fails, to collect on a specific account receivable. Similarly, in the case of a pending lawsuit, until a court verdict is rendered in which the defendant-firm is judged to have damaged the plaintiff and an award to the plaintiff is assessed, there is uncertainty as to whether an award will occur and how large the award will be.

> A "factor" is a third party that purchases accounts receivable from companies at a discount. The factor will then attempt to collect the receivables from the original customer. When receivables are factored without recourse, the transaction is treated as a sale of the receivables by the company. When sold with recourse, if the recourse provision cannot be valued at the transaction date, the transaction is treated as a loan to the company with the accounts receivable the collateral.

GLOBAL PERSPECTIVE

The accounting for some executory contracts under U.S. GAAP and IFRS differs significantly. For example, under U.S. GAAP, purchase commitments are not reported on the balance sheet but instead are disclosed in the footnotes to the financial statements. These executory contracts fail to meet the definition of an accounting liability under U.S. GAAP, although it is widely acknowledged that they represent economic liabilities to an entity. Under IFRS, however, purchase commitments are disclosed on the balance sheet when a company has a clear and demonstrable commitment to another entity. In effect, IFRS is more effective in restricting the incidence of off-balance-sheet debt than is U.S. GAAP.

How and where contingencies are disclosed in corporate financial statements is determined based on the probability of occurrence of the future event and whether an amount can be reliably estimated. **Gain contingencies**, such as the expectation of winning a financial settlement in a lawsuit, are almost never accrued on the financial statements and are rarely even disclosed in the footnotes. Instead, under the **conservatism principle** (see Chapter 6), gain contingencies are normally only recognized when they are realized (i.e., when the event occurs). Liabilities from **loss contingencies**, on the other hand, are commonly disclosed and sometimes must be accrued on the financial statements if certain conditions are met. Specifically, if a loss contingency is both *probable* and can be *reliably estimated*, then it must be accrued as a liability on the balance sheet, with the corresponding loss recorded on the income statement and as a reduction to retained earnings. If, however, a loss contingency is probable but the amount cannot be reliably estimated, or the probability of occurrence is only *reasonably possible*, the contingency must be disclosed via the footnotes but not accrued on the financial statements. The lawsuit against Wal-Mart described in the vignette at the beginning of this chapter falls under this category, and therefore, Wal-Mart elected to disclose but not accrue for this loss contingency. Finally, if the probability of occurrence of a loss is deemed to be only *remote*, then it can be ignored (i.e., not recorded on the balance sheet and not disclosed in the footnotes). It should be noted that existing accounting standards do not provide

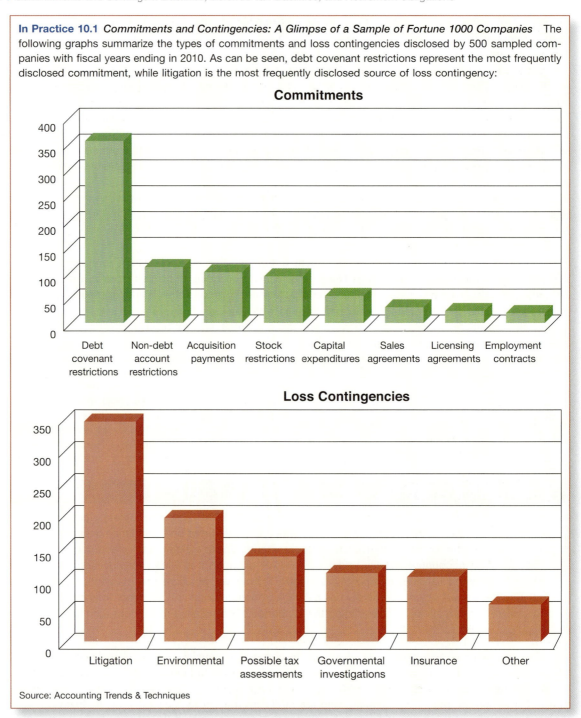

In Practice 10.1 *Commitments and Contingencies: A Glimpse of a Sample of Fortune 1000 Companies*   The following graphs summarize the types of commitments and loss contingencies disclosed by 500 sampled companies with fiscal years ending in 2010. As can be seen, debt covenant restrictions represent the most frequently disclosed commitment, while litigation is the most frequently disclosed source of loss contingency:

Source: Accounting Trends & Techniques

detailed definitions as to what level of probability is considered probable, reasonably possible, or remote. Therefore, a company's management team has considerable discretion as to which contingencies are accrued, which are disclosed, and which are simply ignored. Often legal considerations and risk management figure into the financial statement disclosure decision—management may feel it is safer to disclose a loss contingency in the footnotes even if they truly believe that the contingency is remote.

The commonality of commitments and contingent liabilities is that if and when a specific future event occurs, the firm will face an economic obligation, in most cases involving the payment of cash. Commitments and contingent liabilities are most commonly disclosed in the footnotes to the financial statements, especially if they are material in amount. They constitute an important source of information about a firm's future credit risk and cash flow obligations, and they should be carefully considered by investors and shareholders as they evaluate the future financial well-being of a company.

BUSINESS PERSPECTIVE

Microsoft Corporation

In 1998, the European Union's Commission on Competition began an investigation of **Microsoft Corporation** alleging that the firm failed to disclose information that would enable competitors to fully connect with Microsoft products, the firm engaged in discriminatory product pricing, and the firm improperly bundled certain products to forestall competition. According to Microsoft's footnotes to its 2003 annual report, the Commission could impose "fines in an amount as large as ten percent of worldwide annual revenue" if the company was found guilty of the allegations. Microsoft's 2003 financial statement disclosures illustrate the contingent nature of this potential loss, which could have reached as much as $3.2 billion based on 2003 sales. At the time of Microsoft's 2003 annual report preparation, the EU Commission had not reached a decision on the case. Microsoft's management must have felt that any potential award was either not highly probable or could not be reliably estimated; hence, the potential liability for the fines was carried off-balance-sheet in Microsoft's footnotes. In early 2004, the EU Competition Commission found against Microsoft and fined the company 497.2 million euros ($611 million). Thereafter, Microsoft carried a provision for future litigation settlement on its balance sheet as a liability pending its appeal of the EU commission decision and related fine. (Microsoft subsequently lost its appeal in 2004 and paid the fine that year. In 2006, the EU Commission fined the company another 280 million euros [$450 million] for failing to comply with the original court ruling.)

DEFERRED INCOME TAX LIABILITIES

One frequently hears that firms "keep more than one set of books." This statement is often erroneously interpreted to indicate that a firm is doing something unethical, illegal, or at best, "shady." Quite the contrary, most firms are forced to maintain at least two sets of accounting records since the rules governing financial accounting, as determined by GAAP, differ in many respects from the rules governing the calculation of **taxable income**, as determined in the United States by the Internal Revenue Code (IRC). It should not be surprising that there are significant differences between the measurement of net income under GAAP and the measurement of taxable income under IRC tax regulations. Throughout prior chapters, where appropriate, we have highlighted many of the more important key differences. The motivation for developing effective account-

U.S. corporate income tax rates vary as a function of the level of taxable income. For 2012, those rates were as follows:

Taxable Income	Tax Rate %
0 to $50,000	15
$50,001 to $75,000	25
$75,001 to $100,000	34
$100,001 to $335,000	39
$335,001 to $10,000,000	34
$10,000,001 to $15,000,000	35
$15,000,001 to $18,333,333	38
Over $18,333,333	35

ing standards differs from that associated with legislating tax policies. The goal of the FASB and the IASB, for example, is to develop accounting practices that enable firms to measure and report their financial performance for investors and lenders in a "fair" manner. In essence, accounting standards are designed to help users adequately assess current or potential future investments. Tax regulations, on the other hand, are enacted by elected and appointed governmental officials. Their goal is to raise revenues to help achieve various public policy objectives, such as providing for social services, encouraging investment in R&D, or funding the military. In most cases, the differences in pretax net income created by differing financial accounting practices and income tax regulations are only temporary, and over time, the financial effects of any differences will be eliminated. To appreciate this, consider that over the life of a business the amount of income taxes actually paid to the taxation authority should (and in most cases, does) equal the aggregate income tax expense reported on the income statements for financial statement purposes.

The question that then arises is "What amount should be reported as the income tax expense on a firm's income statement?" Should it be the amount of tax appearing on the firm's income tax return based on taxable income, or should it be the estimated tax expense based on net earnings calculated under GAAP? It is the latter. U.S. GAAP requires that a firm compute its accounting income tax expense based on its GAAP earnings so as to properly *match* its reported income tax expense with its revenues from the same period. Unfortunately, this creates some confusion because the reported financial accounting tax expense for a given period is unlikely to equal the firm's income tax liability for that same period according to the Internal Revenue Service (IRS). But understanding why this inequality occurs is important. The focus of GAAP on the accrual concept requires recording a tax charge (or benefit) for those amounts included in GAAP net income for that period. The actual timing of when that expense is paid may be what is currently due, or may be what is *deferred* to a future period.

The discrepancy between GAAP net income and taxable net income can arise from two types of policy differences—permanent and temporary differences. **Permanent differences** are those that never reconcile. Examples of permanent differences include the interest from municipal bonds, which is included in GAAP net income but excluded from IRC taxable income. The payment of fines on illegal activities is another example, as these amounts are not deductible for income tax purposes but are recorded as a business expense on a firm's corporate income statement. **Temporary differences**, on the other hand, are timing differences between GAAP and taxable income that reverse over time, and hence, eventually fully reconcile. An example of a temporary difference is the income difference created by using straight-line depreciation for accounting purposes and MACRS depreciation for income tax purposes (see Chapter 7).

The **deferred income tax** account is used to reconcile the temporary timing differences between a firm's tax expense based on its GAAP earnings and the taxes actually paid to the U.S. Department of Treasury and other tax authorities (i.e., state and international government tax authorities). It can take the form of either an asset (i.e., amounts to be recovered in the future from tax timing differences) or a liability (i.e., amounts to be paid in the future from tax timing differences). Whether the deferred income tax account is an asset or a liability depends on the nature of the timing differences, but in all cases those timing differences must be temporary. The deferred income tax account does not reconcile the permanent GAAP-Internal Revenue Code differences that exist between a firm's accounting and taxable earnings because, as the name implies, "permanent differences" will persist indefinitely. Thus, the deferred tax asset or liability would never be received or paid. Recall also from Chapter 2 that one of the disciplines imposed on the balance sheet is that it must always balance, and the deferred income tax account helps satisfy this requirement. The Deferred Income Tax account is the cumulative, after-tax effect of the difference between a firm's income tax expense reported in its income statement and the income taxes actually paid that result from the accounting/tax policy differentials that arise in the measurement of net income for some businesses. Examples of these accounting/tax policy differentials include the following:

Income Statement Item	Example Accounting and Tax Policy Differences	
	Common Accounting Policy	**Required Tax Policy**
• Revenue	• Percentage-of-completion	• Completed contract
• Bad debt expense	• Expense estimated using an aging schedule	• Estimates not permitted; tax deduction based on actual receivable write-offs.
• Depreciation expense	• Straight-line method	• Modified accelerated cost recovery system (MACRS)
• Warranty expense	• Expense estimated based on historical experience	• Estimates not permitted; tax deduction based on actual payments for warranty repairs.
• Gain (loss) in value of trading marketable securities	• Unrealized gain (loss) recognized under mark-to-market accounting	• Unrealized gains (losses) not recognized until gain (loss) is realized

To illustrate how *temporary* differences between a firm's accounting income tax expense and the income taxes actually paid may arise, consider the case of Arcadia Inc. Arcadia purchased a piece of equipment costing $100,000, having an expected useful life of eight years, but with an uncertain residual value at retirement. Under the **Modified Accelerated Cost Recovery System (MACRS)** used to depreciate all business assets for U.S. income tax purposes, depreciable assets are first classified into a "life category" (such as a three-year asset, a five-year asset, etc). Each asset life category then specifies how much depreciation may be taken on the asset in any year. If we assume that Arcadia's equipment qualified for depreciation as a five-year asset,[1] it would be depreciated at the following established MACRS rates:

MACRS Depreciation	
Five-Year Asset	**Depreciation Percentage**
1st Year.	20.00%
2nd Year	32.00
3rd Year	19.20
4th Year	11.52
5th Year	11.52
Residual value	5.76
	100.00%

If Arcadia depreciates the asset using the straight-line method for financial statement purposes over its expected useful life of eight years, and assuming no salvage value at retirement, the depreciation expense for GAAP financial accounting and income tax purposes would be as follows:

	Depreciation Expense			
	GAAP Books: Straight-line	**Tax Books: MACRS**	**Temporary Difference**	**Cumulative Temporary Difference**
1st Year.	$ 12,500	$ 20,000	$ 7,500	$ 7,500
2nd Year	12,500	32,000	19,500	27,000
3rd Year	12,500	19,200	6,700	33,700
4th Year	12,500	11,520	(980)	32,720
5th Year	12,500	11,520	(980)	31,740
6th Year	12,500	5,760	(6,740)	25,000
7th Year	12,500	0	(12,500)	12,500
8th Year	12,500	0	(12,500)	0
	$100,000	$100,000	$ 0	

Notice that the depreciation expense taken under the MACRS system for income tax purposes exceeds the straight-line depreciation charge for accounting purposes in Years 1 through 3; but, beginning in Year 4, the depreciation expense for accounting purposes exceeds the MACRS depreciation deduction. Over the life of the asset, the total depreciation expense reported for accounting and tax purposes is the same ($100,000), but the amount reported in any given year differs—and hence, the notion of a temporary difference. Exhibit 10.1 presents a graphical comparison of Arcadia's depreciation expense for GAAP and income tax purposes. The shaded area in Exhibit 10.1 represents the temporary difference between the GAAP and tax depreciation expense that will arise over the life of the asset as a consequence of the differing depreciation treatments.

Assuming Arcadia's pretax income before depreciation expense is $60,000 each year, the company's pretax income after depreciation and its subsequent income tax expense, assuming a 25 percent tax rate, for GAAP and tax purposes is presented in Exhibit 10.2. At the end of Year 1, Arcadia Inc. will make a cash payment of $10,000 to the IRS for its current year income taxes and will report an income statement deduction for its current tax expense of $11,875. To bring the financial statements into balance, it is necessary to create a deferred income tax liability of $1,875 on the company's balance sheet. Thus, Arcadia's **deferred income tax liability** represents the future taxes *to be paid* on the incremental income ($47,500 − $40,000 = $7,500) that has been reported to the shareholders of the company *but not yet* reported to the taxation authorities.

At the end of Year 2, Arcadia will make a cash payment of $7,000 to the IRS for its current income taxes. On the other hand, Arcadia will report an income statement deduction for its current period income tax expense of $11,875. To bring Arcadia's financial statements into balance, it is necessary to increase the deferred income tax liability by $4,875, for a cumulative total of $6,750 (see **bolded** value in Exhibit 10.2). By the end of Year 2, Arcadia has disclosed $27,000 ($7,500 + $19,500) in incremental net income to its shareholders that has not yet been reported to the IRS.

---

[1] Although the expected useful life of Arcadia's asset was eight years, for MACRS purposes it qualified as a five-year asset. This is not unusual as the rapid write-off of assets for income tax purposes has been found to be an effective economic stimulus technique used for promoting business investment in new capital assets.

At the end of Year 3, Arcadia will make a cash payment of $10,200 for its current income taxes, while reporting an income statement deduction for its income tax expense of $11,875. To bring its financial statements into balance, Arcadia will increase its Deferred Income Tax liability by $1,675, for a total cumulative deferred income tax liability at the end of Year 3 of $8,425. By the end of Year 3, Arcadia has reported $33,700 in additional net income to its shareholders that has not yet been reported to the IRS for which it will eventually pay future taxes of $8,425 ($33,700 × 25 percent).

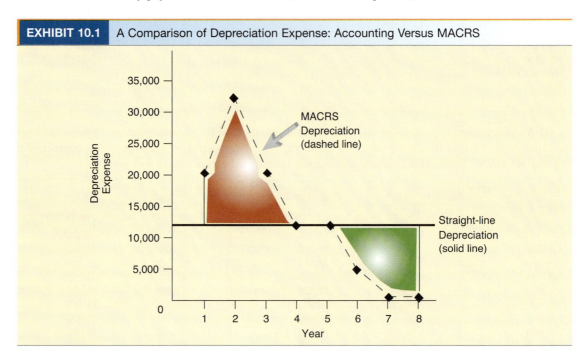

| EXHIBIT 10.1 | A Comparison of Depreciation Expense: Accounting Versus MACRS |

| EXHIBIT 10.2 | Calculating the Deferred Income Tax Liability |

| | Pretax Income* After Depreciation | | GAAP | IRS | Deferred Income Tax |
	GAAP	Tax	(Tax Expense)	(Tax Due)	Liability
1st Year.	$ 47,500	$ 40,000	$11,875	$10,000	$1,875
2nd Year	47,500	28,000	11,875	7,000	**6,750**
3rd Year	47,500	40,800	11,875	10,200	8,425
4th Year	47,500	48,480	11,875	12,120	8,180
5th Year	47,500	48,480	11,875	12,120	7,935
6th Year	47,500	54,240	11,875	13,560	6,250
7th Year	47,500	60,000	11,875	15,000	3,125
8th Year	47,500	60,000	11,875	15,000	0
	$380,000	$380,000	$95,000	$95,000	

*Pretax net income before depreciation is $60,000 annually. Assumed 25% tax rate.

At the end of Year 4, the temporary differences created in Years 1, 2 and 3 begin to reverse. (Observe in Exhibit 10.1, for example, that the MACRS line dips below the straight-line depreciation line.) Arcadia will make a cash payment of $12,120 to the IRS for its current period income taxes, but will show an income statement deduction for its income tax expense of only $11,875. As a consequence, the Deferred Income Tax liability account is reduced by $245, and thus, the cumulative deferred income tax liability at the end of Year 4 declines to $8,180. These financial effects are summarized in Arcadia's spreadsheet in Exhibit 10.3 (see **bolded** values). At the end of Year 4, the amount of income reported to Arcadia's shareholders but not yet reported to the IRS declines to $32,720.

The decline in the Deferred Income Tax liability account continues in Years 5, 6, 7, and 8 as the cash income taxes paid to the IRS grow relative to the income tax expense reported on Arcadia's income statement. This result occurs because the MACRS depreciation is heavily loaded into Years 1, 2, and 3 of the asset's life, and then dramatically declines to zero in Years 7 and 8, causing increasing amounts of

Arcadia's net income to be exposed to income taxes in Years 4 through 8. In essence, MACRS provides a **depreciation tax shield** in the early years of the asset's life, and thereafter, increasingly exposes the company's income to taxation (see shaded areas in Exhibit 10.1).

By the end of Year 8, Arcadia's cumulative income reported to shareholders and to the IRS will total $380,000; and, the cumulative income taxes actually paid and the aggregate accounting tax expense will total $95,000 (see Exhibit 10.2). Thus, over the life of Arcadia's equipment, the differences in taxable income caused by using different depreciation approaches for income tax and accounting purposes are eliminated, reflecting their temporary nature.

EXHIBIT 10.3	Accounting for Deferred Income Taxes								
Year:	**1**	**2**	**3**	**4**	**5**	**6**	**7**	**8**	**Totals**
Assets									
Cash	(10,000)	(7,000)	(10,200)	**(12,120)**	(12,120)	(13,560)	(15,000)	(15,000)	(95,000)
Liabilites									
Deferred income tax	1,875	4,875	1,675	**(245)**	(245)	(1,685)	(3,125)	(3,125)	—
Shareholders' Equity									
Retained earnings:									(95,000)
Tax expense	(11,875)	(11,875)	(11,875)	**(11,875)**	(11,875)	(11,875)	(11,875)	(11,875)	

A = L + SE

Analyzing Deferred Income Taxes

The Arcadia Inc. illustration shows how one policy differential involving the depreciation of equipment affects not only a company's income statement but its balance sheet as well. These policy differences do not, however, affect the statement of cash flow as the amount of cash paid for income taxes is unchanged (it is based on the actual income taxes paid to the IRS).

Deferred income taxes can result from many accounting and tax policy differences, thus potentially creating both deferred income tax liabilities, as illustrated above, and **deferred income tax assets**. In general, the existence of a large deferred income tax liability is often viewed favorably by investment professionals who recognize that the balance of the deferred income tax liability effectively represents an interest-free loan from the tax authorities. Financing a business with interest-free debt creates considerable shareholder value.

Deferred income tax liabilities are common on the financial statements of many U.S. corporations. In fact, a recent study by the U.S. General Accounting Office of the income taxes actually paid by U.S. corporations for the period 1989 to 2000, revealed that 63 percent of the companies paid no income taxes at all![2] Thus, for the majority of U.S. firms, most (and sometimes all) of the income tax expense reported on corporate income statements is effectively deferred, creating a substantial future obligation, as well as considerable interest-free financing from the U.S. Department of Treasury.

TAX PERSPECTIVE

Net Operating Losses
When a company experiences a net operating loss (NOL) during a period, IRS regulations allow the company to carry such losses back up to two years to offset any previously taxed income and obtain a refund of any previously paid income taxes. In the event that the operating loss is large enough to more than offset taxable earnings of the previous two years, the excess operating loss may be carried forward up to 20 years to reduce future income taxes. **NOL carryforwards** and **NOL carrybacks** are found in the tax provisions of most countries; however, the length of the carryback/carryforward period varies dramatically between countries.

The potential future tax savings associated with NOL carryforwards are usually disclosed in the footnotes to the financial statements because of their importance in estimating future operating cash flows. Also recognize that NOL carryforwards will create a *deferred tax asset* for a company. This is because under the matching concept the GAAP net operating loss reported will require an accrued tax benefit on the income statement, but the realization of that benefit for IRS purposes will be deferred to a future year. The tax authorities therefore "owe" the company.

---

[2] *Wall Street Journal,* April 7, 2004.

BUSINESS PERSPECTIVE

General Electric and Corporate Taxes

General Electric (GE) is not only one of the most successful U.S. companies of all time, it also happens to be very adept at minimizing the amount of corporate taxes it pays to the U.S. government. In early 2011 the financial press stoked a controversy when it was reported that GE earned worldwide profit of $14.2 billion—but paid no taxes. In fact, the company claimed a tax benefit of $3.2 billion! While this made for some bad press for the company, minimizing the tax bill was nothing new for GE. The company had long mixed a combination of skilled tax accountants, aggressive tax strategies, and rigorous lobbying to gain a tax advantage and help boost bottom line profits. A historical analysis by one trade group concluded that GE paid an average tax rate of just 2.3 percent over the decade ending in 2011, a far cry from the required 35 percent tax rate expected for companies of GE's size and profitability.* So how does the company pull this off? The reasons are many and complex, but most have concluded that GE's heavy push for favorable changes in the tax law, credits for such things as "green energy" initiatives undertaken by the company, and its vast overseas operations that are minimally taxed as long as the profits remain overseas, have all led to a tax burden much smaller proportionally than for other U.S. companies.

* New York Times, March 24, 2011

Unlike most long-term corporate debt, accounting rules require that deferred income tax liabilities are not discounted; instead, they are valued at their future expected settlement value and not their present value. It also would not be possible to use the present value approach to value these liabilities since the exact date of their payment is unknown (payment of a deferred income tax liability depends upon the future performance of the firm, which of course, is unknown).

GLOBAL PERSPECTIVE

The amount of deferred income tax reported on the balance sheets of multinational corporations varies dramatically from country to country. In the United States, the U.K., and Canada, where significant accounting/tax policy differentials exist, the deferred income tax obligation of large, mature companies can be substantial. However, in Germany and Japan, the amount of permitted accounting/tax policy differentials is constrained, and as a consequence, the deferred income tax obligation of companies from these countries is frequently immaterial in amount.

Some analysts use the information contained in a company's income tax footnote to gain insight into the degree of discretion that management has used in its financial reporting. One measure of the degree of how aggressive a company's accounting policy choices have been is the **conservatism ratio**, defined as:

Conservatism ratio = Net income before taxes/Taxable income

The theory behind this ratio is that firms will choose to delay paying their income taxes as long as it is legally possible and will, therefore, make accounting policy choices that accelerate expenses and defer revenues in reporting taxable income, the denominator of the ratio. Thus, the more the ratio exceeds one, the more aggressive a firm's financial reporting can be assumed to be.

Pretax net income, the numerator in the conservatism ratio, can be taken directly from a company's income statement. Taxable income, on the other hand, must be computed from information contained in the income tax footnote, as follows:

Taxable income = Current year tax liability/Effective tax rate

Utilizing data from **Kohl's** fiscal year 2011 footnote disclosures, (see upcoming Business Perspective) we see that the current year income tax liability is $557 million ($497 million + $60 million) and the effective tax rate is 37.2 percent. The estimate of taxable income is, consequently, $1,497 million ($557 million/ 37.2 percent). Since pretax net income on the income statement is reported to be $1,859 million, Kohl's conservatism ratio is 1.24 ($1,859 million/$1,497 million). Given that Kohl's conservatism ratio is only slightly above 1, we can infer that Kohl's financial versus tax reporting is fairly neutral, or at worst only mildly aggressive.

BUSINESS PERSPECTIVE

Deferred Income Tax Disclosures

Kohl's Corporation operates approximately 1,100 specialty department stores throughout the United States. The company's consolidated balance sheets for the years ended 2011 and 2010 are presented below. The balance sheets reveal that Kohl's reports deferred income taxes both as an asset and as a liability (see **bolded** areas). Combining the deferred income tax asset and the deferred income tax liability reveals that Kohl's had a net deferred income tax liability of $314 million ($386 million − $72 million) and $179 million ($256 million − $77 million), respectively, in 2011 and 2010. These amounts are clearly material in amount, representing approximately three percent of Kohl's outstanding obligations.

KOHL'S CORPORATION Consolidated Balance Sheets		
($ millions)	Jan. 28, 2012	Jan. 29, 2011
Current assets		
Cash and cash equivalents.	$ 1,205	$ 2,277
Merchandise inventories.	3,199	3,036
Deferred income taxes	**72**	**77**
Other.	299	252
Total current assets.	4,775	5,642
Property and equipment, net	8,905	8,692
Long-term investments	153	277
Other assets.	261	238
Total assets.	$14,094	$14,849
Liabilities and Shareholders' Equity		
Current liabilities		
Accounts payable.	$ 1,233	$ 1,138
Accrued liabilities	1,130	1,030
Income taxes payable.	133	127
Current portion of long-term debt	0	400
Current portion of capital lease and financing obligations.	94	86
Total current liabilities	2,590	2,781
Long-term debt	2,141	1,494
Capital lease and financing obligations	2,009	2,018
Deferred income taxes	**386**	**256**
Other long-term liabilities.	460	450
Shareholders' equity		
Common stock—358 and 355 million shares issued	4	4
Paid-in capital.	2,339	2,225
Treasury stock, at cost, 111 and 64 million shares.	(5,977)	(3,643)
Accumulated other comprehensive loss	(53)	(37)
Retained earnings.	10,195	9,301
Total shareholders' equity	6,508	7,850
Total liabilities and shareholders' equity.	$14,094	$14,849

continued

BUSINESS PERSPECTIVE

KOHL'S CORPORATION
Consolidated Income Statements

($ millions)	2011	2010	2009
Net sales.	$18,804	$18,391	$17,178
Cost of merchandise sold (exclusive of depreciation shown separately below) . . .	11,625	11,359	10,680
Gross margin	7,179	7,032	6,498
Operating expenses			
Selling, general, and administrative	4,243	4,190	3,951
Depreciation and amortization	778	750	688
Operating income.	2,158	2,092	1,859
Other expense (income)			
Interest expense	303	313	311
Interest income.	(4)	(9)	(10)
Income before income taxes.	**1,859**	1,788	1,558
Provision for income taxes	**692**	**668**	**585**
Net income.	$ 1,167	$ 1,120	$ 973

Income Tax Note

Deferred income taxes consist of the following:

($ millions)	Jan. 28, 2012	Feb. 29, 2011
Deferred tax liabilities		
Property and equipment.	$1,480	$1,336
Deferred tax assets		
Merchandise inventories.	19	27
Accrued and other liabilities, including stock options	213	216
Capital lease and financing obligations	823	821
Accrued step rent liability	78	69
Unrealized loss on investments	15	24
Unrealized loss on interest rate swap.	18	—
	1,166	1,157
	$ 314	$ 179

The components of the provision for income taxes are as follows:

($ millions)	2011	2010	2009
Current federal	**$497**	$561	$480
Current state.	**60**	69	59
Deferred federal	124	35	42
Deferred state.	11	3	4
	$692	$668	$585

The provision for income taxes differs from the amount that would be provided by applying the statutory U.S. corporate tax rate due to the following items:

Fiscal Year	2011	2010	2009
Provision at statutory rate	35.0%	35.0%	35.0%
State income taxes, net of federal tax benefit	2.7	2.7	2.8
Tax-exempt interest income.	—	(0.3)	(0.3)
Federal HIRE Act tax credits	(0.4)	—	—
Other federal tax credits.	(0.1)	—	—
Provision for income taxes.	**37.2%**	37.4%	37.5%

continued

continued from previus page

> **BUSINESS PERSPECTIVE**
>
> The footnotes to Kohl's financial statements reveal the sources of the company's net deferred tax liability. The income tax footnote data reveals that Kohl's accounting/tax policy differential involving depreciation on its property and equipment resulted in a deferred income tax *liability* of $1,480 million as of fiscal year 2011; however, this is offset by its accounting/tax policy differentials involving such items as inventory, accrued expenses, and capital leases that resulted in a deferred income tax *asset* of $1,166 million as of fiscal year 2011. In essence, Kohl's tax treatment of inventory and accrued expenses was less tax-advantaged than was its tax treatment of depreciation.
>
> Kohl's income statement reports a fiscal year 2011 provision for income taxes—income tax expense—of $692 million on pretax income of $1,859 million. The increase in the net deferred income tax liability of $135 million ($314 million − $179 million) from fiscal year 2010 to fiscal year 2011 represents the amount of Kohl's current period income tax expense that will be paid at a later date. Kohl's income tax expense of $692 million on pretax income of $1,859 million yields an effective income tax rate of 37.2 percent, which differs from the U.S. statutory income tax rate of 35 percent rate largely as a consequence of state income taxes.

EMPLOYEE RETIREMENT OBLIGATIONS

An important employment benefit offered by many businesses to attract and retain qualified employees is the availability of retirement benefits. Foremost among retirement benefits is a pension plan wherein an employee receives a continuous stream of income after retirement from active employment. There are two types of retirement benefit plans—**defined contribution plans** and **defined benefit plans**. Under both types of plans, funds contributed to a retirement plan are managed by an independent **trustee** who invests the funds on behalf of the employee. At retirement, the employee gains access to any contributed funds and earnings thereon, to be used as retirement income or to pay for dental, health, or life insurance during the post-employment period. Any funds contributed by an employer to a retirement trust account are considered to be owned by the employee and not the contributing company. Thus, these retirement plan payments are not carried on the balance sheet of the contributing firm as an asset under U.S. GAAP.

> In the event that an employer overfunds a retirement plan, the firm retains the right to revert the overfunded assets back to the contributing firm. Reverted retirement plan assets, however, are subject to significant income and excise taxes at the time of reversion, which effectively discourages firms from reclaiming any surplus contributions.

In some businesses, the cost of retirement benefits is paid in full by the employer, whereas in others, employees pay the cost in whole or in part. A plan in which an employer pays for all benefits is called **noncontributory**; a plan in which the employee pays some or all of the cost is called **contributory**. Our focus is on those noncontributory or partial-contributory retirement plans in which the employer pays all or part of the cost of the plan, and thus, may retain some obligation to its employees upon their retirement.

Under a defined contribution plan, an employer commits to pay a specified amount into a retirement plan on behalf of each employee. The employer makes no guarantees regarding the ultimate benefit the employee will receive upon retirement; the only guarantee is the amount contributed into the plan. The employee, therefore, assumes all of the risk under this type of plan in which the final payout will be largely determined by how much the pension funds contributed by the employer earn while invested. The accounting for a defined contribution plan is straightforward. The employer simply reduces cash and records a pension expense when a contribution is made. Defined contribution plans are often supplemented by other retirement programs, such as a 401(k) plan, that permit the employee to make tax-deferred contributions to their own retirement plans.

Under a defined benefit plan, an employer commits to provide each employee with a specific level of future income or compensation upon retirement based on a pension formula. The formula is usually based on years of service and the salary the employee is earning at the time of retirement. Since retirement benefits are linked directly to an employee's current employment, the cost associated with the future retirement benefit is considered to be part of an employee's total compensation, and thus, part of a business's current wage expense. However, since the retirement benefit may not be paid for many years, it is necessary to estimate the future cost of the benefit and then discount the estimated future cost to its present value. It is the present value of the future retirement cost that must be funded by a firm, and if unfunded, reported on the firm's balance sheet as an obligation. Unfortunately, the estimation of a firm's future retirement obligation, and correspondingly, its current expense, is much more complex with defined benefit plans. Consider that, at a minimum, the calculation involves estimates of (1) the length of service for the employee until retirement, (2) the employee's future salary at retirement, (3) the number of years the employee will live beyond retirement to collect benefits, (4) the amount of earnings that will be earned by contributions made to the plan, and (5) an appropriate interest rate to discount these amounts to a present value. This is no small task and usually requires the assistance of outside experts such as actuaries. A key difference between the defined contribution plan and the defined benefit plan is the shift of risk from the employee to the employer. Whereas under the defined contribution plan the employer simply agrees to make certain contributions but does not guarantee any future payout, under the defined benefit plan the employer agrees to provide a certain level of future benefits. Largely due to this future uncertainty and the increased costs of defined benefit plans, many employers are abandoning defined benefit plans. In fact, in 2012 only one in ten large U.S. companies offered new employees a pension plan, compared to about nine in ten a generation earlier.

For many years, employers were not required to contribute funds to fund the estimated pension obligation of a defined benefit plan. In fact, some firms intentionally underfunded their plans and subsequently went out of business, leaving the employees without their promised benefits. The government enacted the Employee Retirement Income Securities Act (ERISA) in 1974 to prevent these abuses. ERISA mandates certain minimum levels of funding; however, it is quite common that a defined benefit plan can be underfunded at any point in time and still be within compliance with ERISA funding requirements. In addition to the minimum funding requirements mandated by ERISA, additional employee protection is provided by the Pension Benefit Guarantee Corporation (PBGC), which provides federal insurance for defined benefit plans and assumes funding responsibility for pension plans of insolvent employers.

Estimating Retirement Obligations and Their Cost

Under U.S. GAAP, and that of many other countries, the cost of any currently earned retirement benefits must be expensed and funded in the period in which those benefits are earned. The amount that should be expensed is the present value of the future benefit. The primary pension plan components that need to be calculated to estimate the pension obligation and the related pension expense include:

- The **service cost**, which represents the increase in the pension obligation from an additional year of employee service.
- The **interest cost**, which represents the increase in the pension obligation from an additional year of accrued interest. This cost results from the discounting process in which the present value of the pension obligation increases since it is now one year closer to the date on which an employee is expected to retire and begin receiving benefits.
- The **investment return**, which is the increase in the pension assets earned by the fund trustee on any contributed funds.

In the past, nearly all pension reporting occurred off-balance-sheet in the footnotes to the financial statements. This changed in 2007 with the introduction of FASB pension accounting guidance, which requires the recording of the actual funding status of a pension plan on the corporate balance sheet. In addition to the actual funding status, required disclosures consist of details regarding the pension obligation and the fair value of the plan assets. The difference between these two figures represents the **funding status** of the pension plan.[3]

Retirement Benefit Disclosures

To understand the financial statement disclosures relating to retirement benefits, it is necessary to understand several key concepts:

---

[3] A complete discussion of pension accounting is beyond the scope of this textbook. This topic is covered in more detail in intermediate accounting texts.

- **Plan assets at fair value**—the market value of the retirement plan assets held by the retirement plan trustee. The balance of this account is increased (decreased) by investment gains (losses), increased by new contributions, and decreased by any benefits paid to retirees.

- **Projected benefit obligation (PBO)**—the present value of the future retirement plan benefits earned by employees assuming some rate of future salary increase. The balance of the PBO is increased by service costs and interest costs and decreased by benefits paid to retirees. The balance may also be changed for plan amendments and actuarial adjustments.

- **Benefit cost**—the current period matching of the increase in compensation expense attributed to the pension plan with the service provided by employees in the current period. This cost is increased by service and interest costs and decreased by the expected return on plan investments. The expense is also adjusted for the amortization of deferred amounts that were not currently recognized in earnings of prior periods. Note that GAAP allows the use of expected rather than actual investment earnings in the calculation of benefit cost. The rationale behind this choice is to prevent large swings in current income resulting from investment return volatility.

An illustration of the typical corporate pension plan disclosures, as reported by the Procter & Gamble Company, is presented in the following Business Perspective.

BUSINESS PERSPECTIVE

Retirement Obligation Disclosures

According to the financial statement footnote disclosures of the **Procter & Gamble Company (P&G)**, the company's retirement obligation at year-end 2012 totaled $19.579 billion, composed of $6.006 billion of retirement benefits-other-than pensions and $13.573 billion of pension benefits. With respect to the funding status of P&G's retirement plans, the footnotes reveal that the company has failed to fund $8.892 billion ($5.599 billion + $3.293 billion) of its total retirement obligation (pension plus other benefits) as of year-end 2012 (see **bolded** area).

THE PROCTER & GAMBLE COMPANY				
	Pension Benefits		Other Retiree Benefits	
Years Ended June 30 ($ millions)	2012	2011	2012	2011
Change in benefit obligation				
Benefit obligation at beginning of year.	$12,229	$11,245	$4,886	$4,778
Service cost	267	270	142	146
Interest cost	611	588	276	270
Participant's contributions	22	21	68	67
Amendments	(44)	93	—	7
Actuarial loss/(gain)	1,911	(633)	957	(235)
Acquisitions (divestitures).	(17)	—	—	—
Special termination benefits.	—	—	27	3
Currency translation and other.	(847)	1,137	(95)	89
Benefit payments	(559)	(492)	(255)	(239)
Benefit obligation at end of year.	**$13,573**	**$12,229**	**$6,006**	**$4,886**
Change in plan assets				
Fair value of plan assets at beginning of year	$ 7,962	$ 6,562	$2,975	$2,843
Actual return on plan assets.	459	685	(126)	253
Employer contributions	485	555	24	29
Participants' contributions	22	21	68	67
Currency translation and other.	(395)	631	—	2
ESOP debt impacts (4).	—	—	27	20
Benefit payments	(559)	(492)	(255)	(239)
Fair value of plan assets at end of year	7,974	7,962	2,713	2,975
Funded status.	**$ (5,599)**	**$(4,267)**	**$(3,293)**	**$(1,911)**

continued

BUSINESS PERSPECTIVE

P&G's pension footnote information reveals that the company has recognized the full $8.892 billion in pension underfunding as a component of its other noncurrent liabilities on its consolidated balance sheet.

THE PROCTOR & GAMBLE COMPANY				
	Pension Benefits		Other Retiree Benefits	
Years Ended June 30 ($ millions)	2012	2011	2012	2011
Classification of net amount recognized				
Noncurrent assets	$ 128	$ 168	$ —	$ —
Current liability	(43)	(47)	(23)	(24)
Noncurrent liability	(5,684)	(4,388)	(3,270)	(1,887)
Net amount recognized	$(5,599)	$(4,267)	$(3,293)	$(1,911)

In addition to disclosure of the funding status of the retirement plans, P&G's footnote disclosures also detail the net benefit expense for 2012 that is a component of P&G's 2012 net income. The primary components of this expense are service and interest costs, partially offset by the expected return on plan assets. Note that P&G follows GAAP rules and uses expected returns rather than actual returns so as to avoid large annual swings in investment earnings.

THE PROCTOR & GAMBLE COMPANY						
	Pension Benefits			Other Retiree Benefits		
Years Ended June 30 ($ millions)	2012	2011	2010	2012	2011	2010
Service cost	$ 267	$ 270	$ 218	$ 142	$ 146	$ 103
Interest cost	611	588	579	276	270	253
Expected return on plan assets	(573)	(492)	(437)	(434)	(431)	(429)
Prior service cost /(credit) amortization	21	18	15	(20)	(18)	(21)
Net actuarial loss amortization	102	154	91	99	96	20
Curtailments, settlements and other	6	—	3	27	3	14
Gross benefit cost/(credit)	434	538	469	90	66	(60)
Dividends on ESOP preferred stock	—	—	—	(74)	(79)	(83)
Net periodic benefit cost/(credit)	$ 434	$ 538	$ 469	$ 16	$ (13)	$(143)

GAAP requires that the major assumptions used in the above calculations be fully disclosed in the footnotes. These assumptions include discount rates, expected rates of return on plan assets, and the anticipated annual increases in employee compensation rates. Observe that P&G changed a number of its pension assumptions from 2011 to 2012. In general, a decrease in the discount rate will increase the magnitude of plan underfunding, while an increase in the expected return on plan assets will have the opposite effect.

THE PROCTOR & GAMBLE COMPANY				
	Pension Benefits		Other Retiree Benefits	
Years Ended June 30 ($ millions)	2012	2011	2012	2011
Assumptions used to determine benefit obligations				
Discount rate	4.2%	5.3%	4.3%	5.7%
Rate of compensation increase	3.3%	3.5%	—	—
Assumptions used to determine net periodic benefit cost				
Discount rate	5.3%	5.0%	5.7%	5.4%
Expected return on plan assets	7.4%	7.0%	9.2%	9.2%
Rate of compensation increase	3.5%	3.5%	—	—

Managing Retirement Obligations

Companies have resorted to two discretionary actions in an effort to minimize the magnitude of their reported retirement obligations disclosed in corporate financial statements:

■   Use a higher-than-justified discount rate to measure the present value of their retirement benefits (a higher discount rate lowers the present value of the benefit).

■   Use a higher-than-justified rate of return to estimate the future return on plan assets (a higher assumed rate of return lowers the amount of future funding required to meet a plan's obligations).

BUSINESS PERSPECTIVE

General Motors Offers a Buyout

Over the years General Motors (GM) had affectionately become known as "Generous Motors", in large part because of its very generous pension plan offered to most of the company's 118,000 white-collar retirees. In early 2012, years of pressure from unions, competitors, and a weak economy, had taken its toll; the company had a pension plan underfunded by a whopping $25 billion. To help reduce this future burden, GM first transferred $26 billion of its worldwide $134 billion pension obligation to Prudential. This "annuitized" a large block of pensions and had the effect of transferring the future monthly obligation for retiree payments to Prudential, thus enhancing GM's future financial flexibility. A second offer was made to approximately 42,000 management retirees: accept a single lump-sum payout, or continue receiving monthly payouts that were at risk perhaps of one day being reduced if the underfunding became worse. Of course, the amounts offered varied from person-to-person, but each retiree was faced with a financial decision wherein they had to factor in assumptions about their own morbidity and their expected investment returns. About 30 percent of those offered the deal took the lump-sum payout. GM's pension payout technique was widely expected to be followed by other companies in similar underfunded positions.

The effect of these two actions is to lower the size of any funding insufficiency, and thus, to lower the retirement obligation to be reported on a firm's balance sheet. A higher discount rate, however, will have an undetermined effect on the benefit expense through the interest cost component. A higher discount rate will result in a smaller obligation being multiplied by a higher interest rate; and, the ultimate effect could be a higher or lower interest cost.

Consider, for example, **IBM Corporation**, one of the largest computer equipment manufacturers in the world. In 2000, IBM raised the assumed rate of return on its pension plan assets from 9.5 to 10.0 percent. This increase lowered its pension expense in 2001 and 2002 by five percent, causing an equal increase in pretax net income. Was the rate of return increase justified? Apparently not in that the U.S. Securities and Exchange Commission warned U.S. companies in 2002 that, based on historical returns on equity and debt securities, it would challenge companies that used rate of return assumptions above nine percent. As a consequence, the rate of return assumptions utilized by U.S. corporations (such as IBM) to forecast the returns on their plan assets fell to an average 8.4 percent in 2003.[4]

Appendix 10A to this chapter contains an illustration of the computations needed to compute the funding status and the benefit cost of a hypothetical defined benefit pension plan.

ANALYZING OTHER POTENTIAL LIABILITIES

In this chapter, we examined several potential liabilities. As was noted in Chapter 9, it is the responsibility of financial statement users to first determine whether a company's balance sheet adequately portrays the extent of a firm's use of leverage; and, if not, whether any financial statement adjustments should be undertaken.

GAAP provides corporate managers with considerable discretion regarding the balance sheet presentation of contingent liabilities. While these potential liabilities may not appear on the balance sheet, they are usually disclosed in the footnotes to the financial statements. Consequently, financial statement users must use their judgment as to whether a balance sheet adjustment is needed to provide a better portrayal of a firm's debt exposure to these potential liabilities. At a minimum the user should be aware

---

[4] "Pumped-up Pension Plays," *BusinessWeek*, October, 25, 2004.

that the potential exists for additional future claims on resources should uncertainty around future events be resolved in ways not in the firm's favor.

Deferred income taxes, on the other hand, while often appearing as a liability on the balance sheet, require additional consideration because this, unlike a more traditional accounting liability, does not represent an amount actually owed at a specific time. Because it is simply a reconciling item between the income taxes payable to the tax authorities based on taxable income and the income tax provision based on GAAP income appearing on a company's income statement, the item that caused the deferred tax (e.g., depreciation differences) must actually reverse for the liability to be removed from the balance sheet. Assuming that a firm is a going concern and continues to replace items such as its depreciable assets, it is quite likely that a firm's deferred income tax liability will remain outstanding long into the future. As a consequence, many investment professionals feel that the proper value to assign to any deferred income tax liability is zero, since the present value of an indefinitely deferred amount is close to zero.

Finally, prior to the recently enacted FASB accounting guidance on employee retirement obligations, most pension liabilities appeared off-balance-sheet; and consequently, extensive footnote disclosures were required to aid financial statement users in assessing a firm's debt exposure to its employees. Beginning in 2007, this type of footnote due diligence became unnecessary as the new FASB accounting guidance on pension reporting requires that the full extent of pension plan under- or overfunding be recognized on the balance sheet. Nonetheless, when conducting a financial review of fiscal years prior to 2007, some pension footnote due diligence is required to evaluate a firm's pension liability exposure under the prior pension plan accounting rules. In addition, it is prudent for financial statement users to consider whether the pension assumptions reported in the footnotes, including the discount rate, the estimated rate of wage increase, and the expected return on plan assets, are reasonable.

Chapter 9 discussed three ratios that are helpful when analyzing a firm's use of leverage. Those ratios include the long-term debt to total assets ratio, the long-term debt to shareholders' equity ratio, and the interest coverage ratio. These ratios can be useful for assessing a firm's solvency, with the caveat that it may be necessary to modify the level of reported debt for any material off-balance-sheet obligations reported in the footnotes.

ETHICS PERSPECTIVE

Different Sets of Books

Many firms maintain multiple sets of financial data for income tax purposes and for financial reporting purposes because of different rules governing GAAP-based financial reporting and income tax reporting governed by the U.S. Internal Revenue Code. No one should question a firm's ethical standards for maintaining these multiple sets of books since the firms are simply complying with external reporting requirements. In addition to the record keeping required for GAAP financial reporting and tax reporting, firms sometimes keep a third set of books for their own internal decision making. This supplemental financial reporting is often used for internal decision-making and for incentive compensation contracts. Unlike GAAP reporting and income tax reporting, the assumptions used for internal reporting purposes are rarely, if ever, disclosed to individuals outside the firm to protect a firm's competitive market position.

REVIEW PROBLEM

The Glendale Water Company is a retailer of water-softening equipment used principally in residential facilities. An entire system costs $3,600 including installation. The Glendale Water Company requires a down payment of $1,200 for those customers deciding to pay for the system over 24 months (in equal monthly installments of $100). Approximately one-half of the company's customers pay for the system in full at the time of installation. For accounting purposes, Glendale recognizes the revenue from the sale of a system when installation of the system is complete, regardless of whether a customer pays in full or over 24 months. For income tax purposes, however, Glendale uses the installment basis to recognize the revenue from the sale of a system. The revenue streams for accounting and income tax purposes for a single system sold on January 1 appear as follows. The cost of a complete system, including installation is $900.

	Accounting	Income Tax
Year 1	$3,600	$2,400
Year 2	0	1,200
Total	$3,600	$3,600

Required

Assume that The Glendale Water Company has an effective tax rate of 30 percent. Illustrate the accounting for the sale of a system using a spreadsheet approach. Your spreadsheet should assume that the system is financed over a 24-month period; hence, remember to consider the deferred income tax effect.

The solution is on page 368.

EXECUTIVE SUMMARY

This chapter concludes our investigation of corporate liabilities. Specifically, we examined the valuation and financial statement disclosure of such potential obligations as commitments and contingent liabilities, deferred income tax liabilities, unfunded retirement obligations, and financial derivatives (see Appendix 10B). In Chapter 11, we consider the shareholders' equity section of the balance sheet and examine how companies raise capital through the sale of equity instruments.

As a validation of your understanding of the content of this chapter, you should now be able to:

- Explain the difference between a commitment and a contingent liability.
- Explain deferred income tax liabilities and why this account increases and decreases.
- Explain how employee retirement obligations are valued and disclosed.
- Explain how financial instruments and derivatives are valued and reported in corporate financial statements (see Appendix 10B).

KEY CONCEPTS AND TERMS

Account receivable sold with recourse, 335
Benefit cost, 347
Commitments, 335
Conservatism ratio, 342
Contingent liabilities, 335
Contributory, 345
Counterparties, 354
Deferred income tax, 338
Deferred income tax assets, 341
Deferred income tax liability, 339
Defined benefit plans, 345
Defined contribution plans, 345

Depreciation tax shield, 341
Derivative financial instruments, 354
Executory contracts, 334
Financial instruments, 354
Funding status, 346, 354
Gain contingencies, 335
Interest cost, 346, 352
Interest rate swap, 354
Investment return, 346
Line of credit, 335
Loss contingencies, 335
Modified Accelerated Cost Recovery System (MACRS), 338

Noncontributory, 345
Permanent differences, 338
Plan assets at fair value, 347
Projected benefit obligation (PBO), 347
Purchase commitment, 334
Repo agreement, 354
Service cost, 346, 352
Taxable income, 337
Temporary differences, 338
Trustee, 345
Zero-sum game, 354

APPENDIX 10A: Illustration of Pension Accounting

George is the only employee of Solo Inc. George is getting older and has decided to work for Solo because of the defined benefit pension plan he was offered as part of his compensation package. He has agreed to work for five years before he retires. Solo determined from a medical examination that George took for employment purposes that he will only live for five years after retirement. The pension plan guarantees that for each year he works for Solo, George will receive $1,000 at the end of each year during his retirement. In other words, if George works five years, he will receive $5,000 a year during each year of his retirement. Solo discounts its future obligations at six percent to compute a present value. Further, Solo estimates that it will be able to earn a rate of return of twelve percent on its pension plan assets. Finally, Solo has decided to contribute $3,315 at the end of each year that George works for Solo.

Service cost represents the pension cost attributable to the company service that George provides each year that he works for Solo. Service cost is computed as the present value of each future benefit attributed to the current year's service. For George, this will amount to $1,000 for each of five years following retirement. The service cost computation is illustrated in the diagram below:

Service Cost Computation									
Year of Service					Year of Retirement				
1	2	3	4	5	1	2	3	4	5
$3,337					$1,000	$1,000	$1,000	$1,000	$1,000
	$3,537				1,000	1,000	1,000	1,000	1,000
		$3,749			1,000	1,000	1,000	1,000	1,000
			$3,974		1,000	1,000	1,000	1,000	1,000
				$4,212	1,000	1,000	1,000	1,000	1,000

The diagram shows that the service cost for the first year of George's employment is $3,337. This represents the present value of an annuity of $1,000 for five years starting five years from the present. The service cost increases each year because the present value calculation is computed using an annuity starting date one year sooner.

The projected benefit obligation (PBO) represents the present value of the entire amount of future benefits, not just the benefits from one year of service. Therefore, the PBO calculation considers not just the current year's service, but also all prior years' service that has been performed. To take the prior years' service into account, Solo calculates an **interest cost** on each year's prior service.

Since the pension benefit obligation is computed following each year of service, there isn't any interest cost the first year. For the second year, the interest cost is computed as the prior year's accumulated service cost multiplied by the interest rate. For Solo, this will be $200 calculated as $3,337 × .06. For the third year, the interest cost will be $424 calculated as $212 for year one service [($3,337 + $200) × .06] and $212 for year two service ($3,537 × .06). In a similar manner, year four interest cost will be $675 calculated as $225 for year one service [($3,337 + $200 + $212) × .06] plus $225 for year two service [($3,537 + $212) × .06] plus $225 for year three service ($3,749 × .06). The computation of the interest cost is illustrated in the diagram below:

Interest Cost Computation					
	Interest Cost For Year				
Cost attributed to year	1	2	3	4	5
1..		$200	$212	$225	$238
2..			212	225	238
3..				225	238
4..					238
Total..	$0	$200	$424	$675	$954*

*Amounts are rounded.

For our simple defined benefit plan, the projected benefit obligation at the end of each year is simply the prior year ending balance plus the sum of the service and interest costs for the current year, as shown below:

Projected Benefit Obligation					
	Year of Service				
	1	2	3	4	5
Beginning balance...............................	$ 0	$3,337	$ 7,074	$11,247	$15,896
Service cost.....................................	3,337	3,537	3,749	3,974	4,212
Interest cost.....................................	0	200	424	675	954
Total...	$3,337	$7,074	$11,247	$15,896	$21,062

Solo elects to contribute to the pension plan $3,315 at the end of each year of George's employment. Solo expected to earn twelve percent each year on the invested funds; however, things did not go so well, with actual earnings of only eight percent. This leads to a total of $19,448 for the fair value of the plan assets at the end of George's five-year employment. The details of the plan assets are shown below:

Plan Assets At Fair Value					
	Year of Service				
	1	2	3	4	5
Beginning balance	$ 0	$3,315	$ 6,895	$10,762	$14,938
Contribution	3,315	3,315	3,315	3,315	3,315
Earnings	0	265	552	861	1,195
Total	$3,315	$6,895	$10,762	$14,938	$19,448

The actual funding status of the pension plan is simply the difference between the projected benefit obligation and the fair value of plan assets. If the plan assets at fair value exceed the projected benefit obligation, the pension fund is overfunded; otherwise, it is underfunded. Solo is underfunded for each year of George's employment, and is $1,614 underfunded at the beginning of George's retirement as shown below:

Pension Plan Funding Status					
	Year of Service				
	1	2	3	4	5
Plan assets at fair value	$3,315	$6,895	$10,762	$14,938	$19,448
Projected benefit obligation	3,337	7,074	11,247	15,896	21,062
Funding status	$ (22)	$ (179)	$ (485)	$ (958)	$ (1,614)

Under current GAAP, effective in 2007, Solo is required to record the funded status of the plan on its balance sheet. Because the PBO exceeds plan assets, a liability is recorded.

To determine the amount of expense to be recognized on the income statement, three components must be considered. The first two components are the service costs and interest costs described above. The third component is the *expected* plan earnings using the expected rate of twelve percent. These amounts are shown below.

Pension Benefit Cost					
	Year of Service				
	1	2	3	4	5
Service cost	$3,337	$3,537	$3,749	$3,974	$4,212
Interest cost	0	200	424	675	954
Expected return	(0)	(398)	(827)	(1,291)	(1,793)
Total	$3,337	$3,339	$3,346	$3,357*	$3,374*

*Amounts are rounded.

Note that the expected rate of twelve percent is different than the actual rate of eight percent, yielding lower total expense for the five years of George's employment.

Solo would then recognize a net liability as the recognized expense less the cash contributed. This is shown below in spreadsheet format:

Year	Assets	=	Liabilities	+	Equity	
	Cash		Pension Liability		Retained Earnings	
1	(3,315)		22		(3,337)	Pension expense
2	(3,315)		24		(3,339)	Pension expense
3	(3,315)		31		(3,346)	Pension expense
4	(3,315)		42		(3,357)	Pension expense
5	(3,315)		59		(3,374)	Pension expense
Totals	(16,575)		178		(16,753)	

Actual Versus Recognized Net Pension Obligation					
	Year of Service				
	1	2	3	4	5
Actual funding status	$(22)	$(179)	$(485)	$(958)	$(1,614)
Recognized net obligation	(22)	(46)	(77)	(119)	(178)
Difference	$ 0	$(133)	$(408)	$(839)	$(1,436)

In the case of Solo's pension, the reason for the difference between the actual **funding status** and the recognized pension obligation is due to the lower-than-expected actual returns on plan assets. The actual returns are used to compute the actual funding status since the actual returns are what are included in the fair value of plan assets. In contrast, the expected returns are used to calculate the recognized benefit cost, and hence the recognized net obligation. For more complex pensions, many other items can cause a difference between recognized and actual funding status. It is not at all unusual for the recognized net obligation to be much smaller than the actual funding status even though the firm is complying with GAAP. For example, Ford Motor Company recognized a net asset on its 2005 balance sheet for its pensions of approximately $5.5 billion even though Ford's pensions were underfunded by nearly $11 billion! For this reason, it is quite important for a reader of the financial statements to go beyond the actual statements and carefully review the footnotes, where the details regarding a company's pension plans are disclosed.

New pension accounting rules, however, require that the actual funding status of a pension plan appear as either an asset, if overfunded, or a liability, if underfunded, on a company's balance sheet. The corresponding adjustment required to keep the balance sheet in balance is to Accumulated Other Comprehensive Income in the shareholders' equity section of the balance sheet. The income statement presentation does not change under the new pension accounting.

APPENDIX 10B: Financial Instruments and Derivatives

As businesses have come under increasing pressure from shareholders to maximize firm value, more and more firms have begun utilizing exotic financial contracts to minimize the risk of business losses and maximize the likelihood of business gains. Examples of such contracts include financial instruments and derivative securities.

Financial instruments are financial contracts that impose an obligation on a business that uses these instruments to exchange cash (or some other financial asset) under potentially unfavorable conditions. (Not all financial instruments are obligations; some are assets. We restrict our consideration to those financial instruments that impact a firm's credit risk.) Examples include repurchase or repo agreements, forward purchase agreements for securities or commodities, and various hybrids of these instruments. For example, a business with excess cash, desiring to maximize its return on its excess cash, might purchase a portfolio of bonds from a brokerage firm under a repurchase agreement. During the term of the **repo agreement**, often six months to one year, the business receives interest income from its investment in the portfolio of bonds. However, at the end of the agreement, the business is obligated to sell the portfolio of bonds back to the brokerage firm at their original purchase price; and, as a consequence, the buyer is protected from any loss due to a decline in the principal value of the bond investment. Both parties to the repo agreement, however, are exposed to market risk—that is, the risk that the market value of the portfolio of bonds could be greater than or less than the amount that the purchaser originally paid for them. If the bond portfolio declines in value because of an increase in market interest rates, the brokerage firm loses while the purchaser gains. On the other hand, if the portfolio gains in value, the brokerage firm gains and the purchaser loses. A repo agreement is, in effect, a **zero-sum game**—one party gains what the other party loses! Why would a company engage in a repo arrangement? In an attempt to maximize the return on its excess cash, and thus, maximize shareholder value.

Derivative financial instruments are financial contracts that derive their value from some other asset or index. Examples include options, forward contracts, futures contracts, and interest rate swaps. For example, to illustrate the mechanics of an **interest rate swap**, assume that Firm A has an outstanding note payable with a face value of $100,000 that bears interest at the rate of 7 percent, payable annually on December 31. Firm A has the option of repaying the note anytime prior to its maturity in five years; however, the amount of the repayment will be determined based on the market value of the note at the time of repayment. Firm A is worried that interest rates may fall and cause the value of the note to increase. Firm Z also has an outstanding note payable with a face value of $100,000 with payments due annually on December 31. In contrast to the Firm A note, Firm Z's note has a variable interest rate based on the prime lending rate. Firm Z is concerned that its cash flow will be harmed if interest rates increase, causing its interest payments to increase. To mitigate these risks, Firm Z may negotiate a contract to swap or exchange its interest payments with Firm A. This is typically accomplished through a swap dealer such as a bank that serves as an intermediary to bring together the two **counterparties** to the swap transaction. Under a swap arrangement, Firm A assumes responsibility for the payment of Firm Z's variable rate interest payment, whereas Firm Z assumes responsibility for the payment of Firm A's fixed rate interest payment. As a consequence of the swap, Firm Z locks in a fixed rate to protect its cash flow and Firm A will have a variable rate interest payment whose cash flow changes will be offset by the change in the fair value of its outstanding note. To illustrate the financial effects of an interest rate swap, assume that Companies A and Z agree to swap interest expense payments over a three-year period. Each firm has an outstanding loan obligation in the amount of $100,000, and while Company Z pays a variable rate equivalent to the London InterBank Offering Rate (LIBOR) as of the beginning of the year, Company A pays a fixed rate of 8 percent per year. At the beginning of the swap period, the LIBOR rate is also 8 percent, and hence, for the first year of the agreement, both firms pay interest charges of $8,000. At the beginning of the second year, however, the LIBOR rate rises to 10 percent; and, as a consequence, at year-end, Company A will make a variable payment of $10,000 while Company Z continues to pay $8,000 based on the fixed rate that it assumed in the swap. If, at the beginning of the third year, LIBOR resets to 12 percent, Company A's annual payment will amount to $12,000 while Company Z's payment remains fixed at $8,000. Over the three-year swap period, Company Z will have paid a total of $24,000 while Company A paid $30,000, $6,000 more than it would have paid had it not entered into the swap agreement. Company Z, on the other hand, saved $6,000 by entering into the swap agreement. Interest rate swaps are derivative instruments because they derive their value from movements in the general corporate borrowing rate. Like repo agreements, interest rate swaps are a zero-sum game in which one party gains while the other party loses.

Financial instruments such as repurchase agreements and derivative financial instruments such as interest rate swaps may constitute significant obligations for a company. Under U.S. GAAP, the accounting for these instruments depends upon a firm's intent in utilizing the instrument. Gains and losses on speculative hedge instruments that do not attempt to mitigate a business-related risk are reported in the income statement, whereas gains and losses on business-related hedges that qualify for hedge accounting treatment are matched with the corresponding gain or loss on the hedged item. If the gain (loss) on the hedged item is reported in current income, the loss (gain) on the related hedge instrument is likewise reported as part of current income. If, however, the gain (loss) on the hedged item is deferred to a later fiscal period, the loss (gain) from the related hedge instrument is reported in Other Comprehensive Income as a component of shareholders' equity. We will have more to say about unrealized gains and losses on derivative securities in Chapter 11. Under IASB GAAP, however, the unrealized gain (loss) on financial instruments is reported on the income statement rather than on the balance sheet as under U.S. GAAP. This divergence in practice between U.S. and IASB GAAP reflects the IASB's commitment to the use of market-value based accounting.

QUESTIONS

Q10.1 **Contingent Liability Accounting.** In 2006, **Merck & Company** was sued by the survivors of a plaintiff who had died of a heart attack while taking Merck's painkiller drug Vioxx. A jury found the company guilty and awarded the plaintiff's estate $4.5 million in damages. In a similar case, Merck was found not liable by the courts for a second plaintiff's death. By mid-2006, more than 9,600 Vioxx-related cases were pending in the U.S. courts. According to *CFO Magazine,* Merck's potential Vioxx-related liability was somewhere between $5 billion and $50 billion. Discuss how Merck should disclose the $4.5 lawsuit award and the 9,600 pending Vioxx-related cases in its 2006 annual report.

Q10.2 **Debt Covenants and Going-Concern Exceptions.** The May 2, 2006, edition of *The Financial Times* carried the following leading story headline:

Auditors to Warn over Sea Containers

The related article reported that **Sea Containers Ltd.**, a Bermuda-based container leasing and passenger transport company, remained unable to file its 2005 financial statements with the U.S. Securities and Exchange Commission. The company reported that while it expected to receive an unqualified auditor's opinion on its 2005 financial report, it also "anticipated that there would be a paragraph (in the auditor's report) raising substantial doubt about (the company's) ability to continue as a going concern." When issuing an audit opinion, an audit firm may note one or more concerns that it has regarding a firm's reported results or its ability to continue to operate as a going concern. In March of 2006, Sea Containers disclosed to the public that it had violated some of its debt covenants when it wrote off $500 million of its leasing business, causing the firm's net worth to drop below required covenant minimums. Discuss why a violation of an existing debt covenant might cause an auditor to issue a going-concern exception about Sea Containers.

Q10.3 **Pension Accounting and Debt Covenants.** In 2006, the Financial Accounting Standards Board adopted new pension accounting guidance which required that, effective year-end 2007, pension and retirement-benefit plan surplus and deficit funding be disclosed on corporate balance sheets as an asset or liability, respectively. The new accounting, however, might adversely affect the ability of some businesses to satisfy their debt covenants on existing loan agreements. Consider, for example, **Electronic Data Systems** (EDS), which faced a debt covenant of a required minimum level of $6.42 billion in shareholders' equity. (EDS's shareholders' equity was $7.5 billion.) Under the new FASB pension accounting, EDS would be required to add $1.08 billion to its liabilities due to a pension plan funding deficit and also reduce its shareholders' equity to exactly the covenant minimum of $6.42 billion. Discuss how EDS should respond to the new pension accounting with respect to its creditors.

Q10.4 **Accounting for Pending Lawsuits.** On April 13, 2006, **Bausch & Lomb Inc.** pulled its ReNu contact lens solution from suppliers' shelves over mounting concerns that the product was linked to over 100 cases of a rare fungal eye infection (Fusarium Keratitis) that could lead to corneal damage and required corneal transplant. In a statement released on April 14, 2006, the Federal Food and Drug Administration indicated its support for the product recall/removal while the Center for Disease Control investigated Bausch & Lomb's production facilities for possible contamination. On May 9, 2006, the law firm of Weitz & Luxenberg filed a lawsuit against Bausch & Lomb on behalf of a Philadelphia client who was diagnosed with Fusarium Keratitis after using the ReNu product. Discuss how Bausch & Lomb should disclose the pending lawsuit in its 2006 annual report. Discuss the financial effects to Bausch & Lomb's financial statements associated with the ReNu product recall/removal.

Q10.5 **Interpreting Deferred Income Tax Assets.** The following information was taken from the annual report of **Microsoft Inc.**:

($ millions)	Year 1	Year 2
Current assets		
Deferred income taxes	$1,701	$2,097
Noncurrent assets		
Deferred income taxes	3,621	3,808
Total	$5,322	$5,905

A review of the footnotes to Microsoft's annual report reveals that the two major accounting policies affecting its deferred income taxes were (1) the accounting for unearned revenue and (2) the accounting for its portfolio of trading securities. When Microsoft sells a software product, it defers a portion of the revenue received to cover the cost of future technical service and free upgrades that may be provided during the warranty period. Discuss how Microsoft's accounting for unearned revenue and its accounting for its portfolio of trading securities could result in the creation of a deferred income tax asset. Discuss the difference between a current deferred income tax asset and a noncurrent deferred income tax asset.

Q10.6 **Interpreting Deferred Income Tax Liabilities.** The following information is taken from the annual report of **Coca-Cola Enterprises, Inc.**:

($ millions)	Year 1	Year 2
Long-term Deferred Income Tax Liability	$5,338	$5,106

The footnotes to the company's annual report reveal that the primary contributor to its deferred income tax liability was its accounting for franchise licenses. According to Coca-Cola Enterprises' Summary of Significant Accounting Policies:

> We do not amortize our goodwill and franchise license intangible assets. Instead, we test these assets for impairment annually.

Discuss why and how the company's accounting for franchise licenses results in a deferred income tax liability. The long-term deferred income tax liability declined by $232 million from Year 1 to Year 2; what does this decline suggest?

Q10.7 **Analyzing the Funding Status of a Pension Plan.** The following information is taken from the annual report of **Coca-Cola Enterprises, Inc.**:

Pension Plans ($ millions)	Year 2	Year 1
Benefit obligations (at end of year)	$2,904	$2,576
Fair value of plan assets	2,221	1,810

Discuss whether Coca-Cola Enterprises' (CCE) pension plans are fully funded at year-end of Year 1 and Year 2. Did the company's funding improve from Year 1 to Year 2? The footnotes reveal that CCE changed the discount rate that it used to discount its benefit obligations from 5.8 percent in Year 1 to 5.4 percent in Year 2; how would this change likely impact the value of CCE's benefit obligation?

Q10.8   **Changing Pension Plan Assumptions.**   The annual report of The **Johnson & Johnson Company** (J&J) disclosed the following information:

U.S. Retirement Plans	Year 1	Year 2	Year 3	Year 4
Discount rate	6.75%	6.00%	5.75%	5.75%
Expected long-term rate of return on plan assets	9.00	9.00	9.00	9.00
Rate of increase in compensation levels	4.50	4.50	4.50	4.50

Between Year 1 and Year 4, J&J lowered the discount rate used to calculate the present value of its projected benefit obligation from 6.75 percent to 5.75 percent, while it maintained the expected rate of return on plan assets at nine percent. Discuss how a lowering of the assumed discount rate while maintaining the expected rate of return on plan assets would impact J&J's pension obligations. Why would J&J lower the discount rate on its projected benefit obligation?

Q10.9   **Discounting Deferred Income Tax Liabilities.**   Deferred income tax liabilities arise because of differences in the policies used to account for revenue and expenses for financial reporting purposes versus the policies utilized to report revenue and expenses for income tax purposes. For instance, revenue might be recognized for financial reporting purposes at the point of sale, whereas for income tax purposes, revenue might be recognized at the point of cash collection using the installment method. It is generally accepted practice to discount liabilities to their present value for purposes of presentation on the balance sheet. Discuss why deferred income tax liabilities are not valued on corporate balance sheets at their present value.

Q10.10   **(Appendix B) Interest Rate Swaps.**   The 2011 annual report of **The Home Depot Inc.** revealed the following information regarding its derivative securities:

> In March 2011, we entered into an interest rate swap that expires on March 1, 2016, with a notional amount of $500 million, accounted for as a fair value hedge, that swaps fixed rate interest on our 5.40% Senior Notes due March 1, 2016 for variable interest equal to LIBOR plus 300 basis points. At January 29, 2012, the approximate fair value of this agreement was an asset of $39 million, which is the estimated amount we would have received to settle the agreement.

Describe the financial effects of the swap for Home Depot. At what LIBOR rate does Home Depot benefit from the swap? At what LIBOR rate does Home Depot lose from the swap? Discuss what is meant by a "zero-sum game."

Q10.11   **Underfunded Retirement Obligations and Firm Valuation.**   In its annual report, The **Johnson & Johnson Company** disclosed that its employee retirement obligations were underfunded by $2.063 billion at year-end. And, of this amount, only $475 million was reported on the company's balance sheet, leaving the remainder ($1.588 billion) as an off-balance-sheet liability. Discuss whether the off-balance-sheet portion of J&J's underfunded retirement obligation should be considered when calculating the value of Johnson & Johnson's capital stock.

Q10.12   **(Ethics Perspective) Multiple Sets of Books.**   As noted in the ethics perspective at the end of this chapter, firms routinely maintain separate sets of books for their financial reporting and their tax reporting. Can you think of any reason why a firm would be justified in keeping a third, internal set of books? Do you feel that it is ethically acceptable to not fully disclose to shareholders how a company's internal books differ from those used for external reporting purposes?

Assignments with the logo in the margin are available in BusinessCourse.
See the Preface of the book for details.
CHECK FIGURE indicates that check figures are available on the book's Website.

EXERCISES

 E10.13   Calculating Deferred Income Taxes.   The Sample Corporation prepared the following income statements and income tax returns for Year 1 through Year 4.

Income Statement	Year 1	Year 2	Year 3	Year 4
Sales.	$1,000	$1,000	$1,000	$1,000
Operating expenses	650	650	650	650
Pretax net income	350	350	350	350
Provisions for income taxes	140	140	140	140
Net income.	$ 210	$ 210	$ 210	$ 210

Income Tax Return	Year 1	Year 2	Year 3	Year 4
Sales.	$1,000	$1,000	$1,000	$1,000
Operating expenses	900	900	400	400
Taxable income	100	100	600	600
Income tax payable	40	40	240	240
After-tax net income.	$ 60	$ 60	$ 360	$ 360

Calculate the balance in the company's deferred income tax liability account at the end of each year. Assume that the time value of money is ten percent per year; calculate the implicit value of the company's tax deferral strategy. Explain what a growing balance in the deferred income tax liability is likely to indicate about a company's net income relative to its taxable income. Why might investment professionals view this situation positively? Negatively?

CHECK FIGURE **E10.14   Deferred Income Taxes and Changing Tax Rates.**   The Waterloo Company uses straight-line depreciation accounting in its corporate financial reports but MACRS depreciation accounting for income tax purposes. At the end of the year, Waterloo reported taxable income to the IRS totaling $130,000 and pretax net income to its shareholders of $160,000. MACRS depreciation expense for the year totaled $70,000, while straight-line depreciation was only $40,000. Assume an effective tax rate of 35 percent; calculate Waterloo's deferred income taxes for the year. Is the company's deferred income tax effect an asset or a liability? If the income tax rate was lowered to 30 percent, how much will the company's deferred income taxes change? Explain the change in deferred income taxes.

 E10.15   Reporting the Provision for Income Taxes.   Smith & Sons Company presented the following information in the income tax footnote in its annual report:

Note 13. Income Taxes   Provision for income taxes includes the following (in thousands)

	End-of-year
Current payable	
U.S.	$4,028
Foreign	438
Deferred	
U.S.	2,880
Foreign	(174)
Total	$7,172

How much tax expense did Smith & Sons report on its income statement for the year? How much of the reported income tax expense was paid currently and how much was deferred to a future period for payment? What is implied by the negative foreign deferred income taxes of $174?

E10.16 **Analyzing Retirement Fund Obligations.** The following information is taken from the annual report of The **Johnson & Johnson Company** (J&J):

($ millions)	Year 2	Year 1
Projected benefit obligation	$10,171	$8,941
Plan assets at fair value	8,108	7,125
Net amount recognized in the company's balance sheet (as a liability).	475	288

Calculate the amount that J&J's retirement fund obligations are underfunded as of each year-end. How much of the underfunding is reported on the company's balance sheet? Is the unreported portion of the underfunded pension obligation an example of an off-balance-sheet liability? If so, how might you restate J&J's balance sheet to fully reflect its pension debt as is now required under current pension accounting?

E10.17 **Analyzing Retirement Fund Obligations.** The following information is taken from the annual report of the **Intel Corporation**:

CHECK FIGURE

($ millions)	Year 2	Year 1
Projected benefit obligation	$903	$546
Plan assets at fair value	568	283
Net amount recognized in the company's balance sheet (as a liability).	190	219

Calculate the amount that Intel's retirement fund obligations are underfunded as of each year-end. How much of the underfunding is reported on Intel's balance sheet? Is the unreported portion of the underfunded pension obligation an example of an off-balance-sheet liability? If so, how would you restate Intel's balance sheet to fully reflect its pension debt as is now required under current pension accounting?"

E10.18 **(Appendix 10B) Analyzing Foreign Currency Hedges.** The Arizona Company, a U.S.-based manufacturer, ordered a piece of equipment from Sonora Inc., a Mexico-based supplier, agreeing to pay 200,000 Mexican pesos upon delivery of the equipment in three months time. At the time of the contract signing, the exchange rate between the U.S. dollar and the Mexican peso was 10P:$1. With concerns about a weakening U.S. dollar, The Arizona Company decided to hedge its currency exposure by purchasing a forward foreign exchange contract from a local bank. The forward contract committed The Arizona Company to pay $20,300 in three months in exchange for 200,000 pesos.

What was the forward foreign exchange rate implicit in the contract (assuming no transaction costs)? If the foreign exchange rate in three months was 9.5P:$1, how much did The Arizona Company save by purchasing the currency hedge? If the foreign exchange rate in 3 months was 9.0P:$1, how much did the company save by purchasing the currency hedge? Was the decision to hedge the foreign exchange exposure a good decision?

E10.19 **(Appendix 10B) Analyzing Interest Rate Swaps.** The Phoenix Company purchases a piece of equipment from the Anthem Company by issuing a three-year note with a face value of $100,000. The two companies agree that the interest rate on the note will be pegged to LIBOR (London InterBank Offering Rate), which was currently eight percent, and would be reset at the end of each year for the following year.

Because of concerns about rising interest rates, The Phoenix Company arranged an interest rate swap with its local bank. Under the swap agreement, The Phoenix Company agreed to pay the bank eight percent annually for the three-year period, thus swapping its potentially variable-rate interest payment for a fixed-rate payment. Calculate the value of The Phoenix Company's loss over the three-year swap assuming that LIBOR drops to six percent at the end of the first year and remains there until the end of the swap agreement. Calculate the value of The Phoenix Company's gain over the three-year swap assuming that LIBOR goes to ten percent at the end of the first year and remains there until the end of the swap agreement.

E10.20 **(Appendix 10B) Analyzing Forward Commodity Contracts.** The Portet Wine Company holds 20,000 gallons of wine in inventory at year-end. The company expects to age the wine for another six months before selling it as bulk wine. Given uncertainties surrounding the economic conditions in six months, Portet Wine Company decided to purchase a forward commodity contract in which it promised to sell the 20,000 gallons of wine in six months at a total fixed price of $3.2 million.

Ignoring transaction costs, what was the forward price per gallon of wine implicit in the commodity contract? If the purchase price per gallon of bulk wine in six months is $170 per gallon, was the decision to purchase a forward commodity contract a good decision? If so, why? If not, why not?

PROBLEMS

P10.21 **Legal Proceedings: Patent Infringement.** Bristol-Myers Squibb Company (BMS) engages in the discovery, development, license, manufacture, marketing, distribution, and sale of pharmaceutical and other health care products. Selected financial information for the company is as follows:

	2004	2003
Revenue	$19.4 billion	$20.9 billion
Net income	2.4 billion	3.1 billion
Total assets	30.4 billion	27.5 billion
Total liabilities	20.2 billion	17.7 billion

BMS's 2004 annual report disclosed the following information in its footnotes:

Legal Proceedings and Contingencies Various lawsuits, claims, proceedings, and investigations are pending against the Company and certain of its subsidiaries. In accordance with SFAS No. 5, *Accounting for Contingencies,* the Company records accruals for such contingencies when it is probable that a liability will be incurred and the amount of loss can be reasonably estimated. These matters involve antitrust, securities, patent infringements, the Employee Retirement Income Security Act of 1974, as amended (ERISA), pricing, sales and marketing practices, environmental, health and safety matters, product liability and insurance coverage. The most significant of these matters are described on the next page.

Plavix Litigation The Company's U.S. territory partnership under its alliance with Sanofi is a plaintiff in three pending patent infringement lawsuits instituted in the U.S. District Court for the Southern District of New York. Plaintiffs' infringement position is based on defendants' filing of their Abbreviated New Drug Application (ANDA) with the FDA, seeking approval to sell generic clopidogrel bisulfate prior to the expiration of the composition of matter patent in 2011. Plavix is currently the Company's largest product ranked by net sales. Net sales of Plavix were approximately $3.3 billion and $2.5 billion for the years ended December 31, 2004 and 2003, respectively. Loss of market exclusivity of Plavix and the subsequent development of generic competition would be material to the Company's sales of Plavix and results of operations and cash flows and could be material to its financial condition and liquidity.

Required
1. Historically, the loss of patent protection on a brand name pharmaceutical product has resulted in a 70 percent decline in product sales. Assuming that (a) BMS's patent protection on Plavix is lost as of the beginning of 2005, (b) revenue and earnings for 2005 would, in the absence of the loss of patent protection, have equaled those of 2004, and (c) the after-tax margin on Plavix is 60 percent, estimate BMS's revenue and earnings for 2005. How material are these financial effects?
2. BMS's Plavix patent is carried on its balance as an intangible asset valued at $120 million. In the event of patent protection loss, how should the company reflect this in its financial statements?
3. How should the capital market react to (a) the disclosure that a patent infringement suit involving Plavix had been filed against BMS and (b) the disclosure that the suit had been lost (won)?

P10.22 **Loss Contingency: Lawsuit Award.** Microsoft Corporation is a leading designer and retailer of PC software applications. In its 2012 annual report, the company disclosed that the European Union Competition Commission had opened an investigation concerning a commitment to make browser choice selection easier in the company's Windows operating system:

Government Competition Law Matters

In December 2009, the European Commission adopted a decision that rendered legally binding commitments offered by Microsoft to address the Commission's concerns about the inclusion of Web browsing software in Windows. Among other things, Microsoft committed to display a "Browser Choice Screen" on Windows-based PCs in Europe where Internet Explorer is set as the default browser. Due to a technical error, we failed to deliver the requisite software to enable that display to PCs that came preinstalled with a version of Windows 7 called Windows 7 Service Pack 1. We did deliver the requisite software to PCs running the original version of Windows 7 and earlier editions of Windows. Following notification by the Commission of reports that some PCs were not receiving the update, we promptly fixed the error and advised the Commission of what we had discovered. PCs that come preinstalled with Windows 7 Service Pack are now receiving the Browser Choice Screen software, as intended. On July 17, 2012, the Commission announced that it had opened proceedings to investigate whether Microsoft had failed to comply with this commitment. The Commission stated that if a company is found to have breached a legally binding commitment, the company may be fined up to 10% of its worldwide annual revenue.

In March 2013 the European Union fined Microsoft $731 million for its failure to provide Windows PC users a Web browser choice screen.

Required

1. How should Microsoft account for the EU Competition Commission investigation in its 2012 annual report? Why?
2. How should Microsoft account for the potential fine of up to 10% of its worldwide annual revenue? Why?
3. How would the capital markets react to an announced investigation like that filed by the EU Competition Commission in 2012? How would the capital markets react to the announcement that a fine of $731 million was imposed?

P10.23 **Deferred Income Taxes: Bad Debt Expense Policy.**   Claremont Enterprises, Inc. started operations in early 2011. During the first year of operations, Claremont generated sales of $3.2 million, and at year-end, had $350,000 in outstanding accounts receivable. Using collection estimates provided by its controller, the company estimated that its bad debt expense for 2011 would be $10,925.

CHECK
FIGURE

During its second year of operations, Claremont generated sales of $5.3 million, and at year-end, had $800,000 in outstanding accounts receivable. Using an aging schedule, the controller estimated that Claremont's bad debt expense for 2012 would be $22,500. In June of 2012, Claremont received confirmation that one of its outstanding accounts receivable in the amount of $11,500 had gone into bankruptcy, and thus would not be collected.

In discussions with the firm's independent auditor, the CFO of Claremont Enterprises learned that while an estimate of expected uncollectible accounts was permitted for purposes of preparing its U.S. GAAP-based annual report, the U.S. Treasury Department only allowed firms to deduct actual, known uncollectible accounts for purposes of preparing their income tax returns.

Required

Prepare a schedule showing the company's income tax expense, its income tax payable, and its deferred income tax balance for 2011 and 2012. Assume an effective tax rate of 30 percent and that Claremont has no other expenses other than the bad debt expense. Do you agree with the tax policy of the U.S. Treasury Department regarding the treatment of bad debts? Why or why not?

P10.24 **Deferred Income Taxes: Depreciation Accounting Policy.**   At the start of business, the Miller Company acquired a $100,000 piece of equipment that was to be depreciated on a straight-line method basis for financial statement purposes but on an accelerated depreciation basis for income tax purposes. The Miller Company employed a half-year convention under which only one-half of the first year's depreciation expense would be taken regardless of when an asset was purchased and placed in service. The company also followed the accounting practice that if the level of accelerated depreciation charges fell below the level of straight-line depreciation charges (such as in Year 4 in the schedule below), the company would switch from accelerated depreciation to a straight-line approach. The company's CFO prepared the following depreciation schedule for financial statement and income tax purposes.

	Straight-Line Depreciation	Accelerated Depreciation
Year 1	$ 8,333	$ 16,667
Year 2	16,666	27,778
Year 3	16,667	18,519
Year 4	16,667	12,347
Year 5	16,667	8,230
Year 6	16,667	8,230
Year 7	8,333	8,229
	$100,000	$100,000

Required

Assuming a 30 percent effective tax rate, prepare a schedule illustrating the deferred income tax effects for Year 1 through Year 7 associated with this asset. Which are more likely to be favorably viewed by the capital markets—deferred income tax assets or deferred income tax liabilities?

 P10.25 **Deferred Income Taxes: Natural Resource Accounting Policy.** The Herberger Oil & Gas Company explored for and developed oil and gas wells in Texas, Louisiana, and Oklahoma. Presented below are the company's income statements for a five-year period under the successful efforts method and the full cost method. Herberger Oil & Gas used the successful efforts method for purposes of preparing its income tax return but the full cost method for purposes of preparing its audited financial statements for its equity investors.

Income Statement Under the Successful Efforts Method						
($ millions)	Year 1	Year 2	Year 3	Year 4	Year 5	Total
Revenues	$30.0	$45.0	$52.5	$100.0	$157.5	$385.0
Less						
Lifting costs	5.0	7.5	9.0	17.5	28.0	67.0
Exploration costs	16.0	0.0	0.0	0.0	0.0	16.0
Interest expense	4.0	4.0	3.0	2.0	1.0	14.0
Depletion expense	2.4	3.6	3.6	6.0	8.4	24.0
Income before tax	$ 2.6	$29.9	$36.9	$ 74.5	$120.1	$264.0

Income Statement Under the Full Cost Method						
($ millions)	Year 1	Year 2	Year 3	Year 4	Year 5	Total
Revenues	$30.0	$45.0	$52.5	$100.0	$157.5	$385.0
Less						
Lifting costs	5.0	7.5	9.0	17.5	28.0	67.0
Exploration costs	0.0	0.0	0.0	0.0	0.0	0.0
Interest expense	4.0	4.0	3.0	2.0	1.0	14.0
Depletion expense	4.0	6.0	6.0	10.0	14.0	40.0
Income before tax	$17.0	$27.5	$34.5	$ 70.5	$114.5	$264.0

Required

Assuming an effective tax rate of 30 percent, calculate the deferred income tax effect for Herberger Oil & Gas Company for the five-year period Year 1 through Year 6.

CHECK FIGURE **P10.26** **(Appendix 10B) Interest Rate Swaps.** Global Enterprises (GE) acquired MNC Inc. As part of the acquisition, GE assumed responsibility for MNC's $150 million of eight percent, senior notes. Global Enterprises subsequently guaranteed the senior notes to avoid having them called by the lender (the sale of MNC triggered an immediate redemption covenant in the note indenture). To hedge its interest rate risk associated with the senior note guarantee, Global Enterprises entered into the following three-year reverse swap arrangement:

The Company entered into a three-year reverse interest rate swap beginning June 1, 2012, and ending June 1, 2015. Under the terms of the swap, the Company receives a fixed interest payment of 4.9 percent and pays six-month LIBOR* for the prior six months on $150 million. The effect of the swap is to convert the first three years of the eight percent senior notes from a fixed rate obligation to a floating rate obligation (composed of a fixed payment of 3.1 percent plus a floating payment based on six-month LIBOR for the prior six months). The swap agreement increased the company's interest expense by $1 million in 2013 and reduced its interest expense by $1.2 million in 2012. *(LIBOR = London InterBank Offered Rate)

Required

1. Describe the financial effects of the reverse swap for Global Enterprises.
2. Under what LIBOR rate does Global Enterprises gain from the swap? Under what LIBOR rate does Global Enterprises lose?
3. How should GE account for this interest rate swap on its financial statements?

P10.27 **(Appendix 10B) Foreign Exchange Contracts.** The financial statements of **MNE Corporation** revealed the following:

The Company operates internationally and is exposed to fluctuations in currency values. The fluctuations can increase the costs of financing and operating the business.

The Company manages this risk to acceptable limits through the use of derivatives to create offsetting positions in foreign currency markets. The Company views derivative financial instruments as risk management tools and is not party to any leveraged derivatives.

The notional amounts of derivative contracts do not represent the amounts exchanged by the parties, and thus are not a measure of the exposure of the Company through its use of derivatives. The amounts exchanged by the parties are normally based on the notional amounts and other terms of the derivatives, which relate to exchange rates. The value of derivatives is derived from those underlying parameters and changes in the relevant rates.

At December 31, Year 1, the Company had $139 million notional principal amount of outstanding currency swap contracts to hedge its foreign net assets, which were terminated in Year 2.

Foreign currency commitment and transaction exposures are managed at the operating unit level as an integral part of the business and residual exposures that cannot be offset to an insignificant amount are hedged. Hedged items include foreign currency denominated receivables and payables on the balance sheet, firm purchase orders, and firm sales commitments.

At December 31, the Company had the following amounts related to foreign exchange contracts hedging foreign currency transaction and firm commitments:

($ millions)	Year 2	Year 1
Notional amount		
Buy contracts..	$1,747	$1,928
Sell contracts..	1,062	780
Gains and losses explicitly deferred as a result of hedging firm commitment		
Gains deferred...	$ 14	$ 14
Losses deferred..	(69)	(14)
	$ (55)	$ 0

Required

1. Why does MNE Corporation use foreign exchange derivatives? What is the likely form of these derivatives?
2. What is the "notional amount" of a derivative?
3. How are the gains/losses on MNE's foreign exchange derivatives accounted for?

P10.28 **(Appendix 10B) Interest Rate Swaps.** The **Procter & Gamble Company** is a U.S.-based multinational enterprise that manufactures and markets a range of consumer products worldwide. The company's annual report discloses that:

> The Company is exposed to market risk, including changes in interest rates, currency exchange rates and commodity prices. To manage the volatility relating to these exposures, the Company nets the exposures to take advantage of natural offsets and enters into various derivative transactions for the remaining exposures. The Company does not hold or issue derivative financial instruments for trading purposes.
>
> **Interest rate management** The Company's policy is to manage interest cost using a mix of fixed and variable rate debt. To manage this mix in a cost-efficient manner, the Company enters into interest rate swaps in which the Company agrees to exchange, at specified intervals, the difference between fixed and variable interest amounts calculated by reference to an agreed-upon notional principal amount. These swaps are designed to hedge underlying debt obligations. For qualifying hedges, the interest rate differential is reflected as an adjustment to interest expense over the life of the swaps. The following table presents information for all interest rate instruments. The notional amount does not necessarily represent amounts exchanged by the parties, and, therefore, is not a direct measure of the Company's exposure to credit risk. The fair value approximates the cost to settle the outstanding contracts. The carrying value includes the net amount due to counterparties under swap contracts, currency translation associated with currency interest rate swaps, and any marked-to-market value adjustments of instruments.

June 30	Year 2	Year 1
Notional amount	$2,149	$1,488
Fair value	7	(54)
Carrying value	28	(28)
Unrecognized loss	$ (21)	$ (26)

> Although derivatives are an important component of the Company's interest rate management program, their incremental effect on interest expense for Year 2 and Year 1 was not material. *(The company's interest charges for Year 2 totaled about $550 million.)*

Required

1. Describe Procter & Gamble's strategy involving its use of interest rate swaps.
2. Identify the notional amount, carrying value, and fair value of the company's swap contracts as of year-end Year 2. What is the difference between these values?
3. Was the company's use of interest rate swaps effective in Year 1 and Year 2?
4. How does the company account for its unrecognized loss of $26 million in Year 1 and $21 million in Year 2 on its swap contracts?

CHECK FIGURE

P10.29 **Retirement Obligations: Funding Status.** Global Enterprises Inc. (GE) is a multinational company based in the United States. The company maintains private pension plans for its employees worldwide. Presented below is information from GE's annual report regarding its U.S. pension plans.

U.S. Plans ($ millions)	Plan Assets Exceed Accumulated Benefits		Accumulated Benefits Exceed Plan Assets	
	Year 2	Year 1	Year 2	Year 1
Actuarial present value of benefit obligations				
Vested..	$(468)	$(452)	$(2)	$(14)
Nonvested...	(10)	(18)	—	4
Accumulated benefit obligation...........................	(478)	(470)	(2)	(10)
Effect of projected future compensation levels..................	(59)	(61)	—	(12)
Projected benefit obligation..............................	(537)	(531)	(2)	(22)
Plan assets at fair value.................................	803	645	—	5
Plan assets in excess of (less than) projected benefit obligation......	266	114	(2)	(17)
Unrecognized net loss (gain)..........................	(255)	(60)	(1)	—
Unrecognized prior service cost.......................	20	14	—	11
Unrecognized net transition obligation..................	3	8	—	(2)
Post September 30 contributions......................	—	1	—	—
(Accrued) prepaid pension cost at December 31.................	$ 34	$ 77	$(3)	$ (8)

During Year 2, GE's total pension expense was $10 million and was fully funded. In addition, the company earned $200 million on its plan assets due to a strong U.S. stock market.

Required

1. Identify the following values for Year 2:
   a. Total projected benefit obligation (PBO)
   b. Total pension plan assets
   Using the PBO as a standard, was GE's U.S. pension plan over- or underfunded as of year-end? If overfunded, where do the excess pension plan assets appear on GE's financial statements?
2. How much cash was paid by the pension plan to GE's former employees in Year 2?
3. How much is GE's "minimum pension liability" for Year 2? Where is the minimum pension liability disclosed on GE's balance sheet? Do you agree with this disclosure? Why?
4. What adjustments to GE's balance sheet would be necessary to bring the company's pension accounting disclosures into compliance with the new pension accounting?

P10.30   **Retirement Obligations Funding Status.**   **MNC Inc.** is a worldwide manufacturer of plastic parts. The company's pension disclosures from its annual report were as follows:

Employee Benefit Plans   The Company has defined benefit and defined contribution retirement plans for its employees. The defined benefit pension plans pay benefits to employees at retirement using formulas based on a participant's years of service and compensation. The funded status of the defined benefit plans is as follows:

($ thousands)	Year 2	Year 1
Assets available for benefits..............................	$287,482	$247,783
Projected benefit obligation		
Vested...	(244,050)	(182,005)
Nonvested.....................................	(17,938)	(12,696)
Total accumulated benefit obligation..........................	(261,988)	(194,701)
Effect of projected future compensation increases..............	(45,164)	(30,203)
Total actuarial projected benefit obligation......................	(307,152)	(224,904)
Assets (less than) in excess of projected obligation...............	$ (19,670)	$ 22,879

continued

continued from previous page

($ thousands)	Year 2	Year 1
Consisting of amounts to be offset against (charged to) future pension costs		
Remaining assets in excess of obligation existing at adoption of SFAS 87 in 1986	$ 5,598	$ 6,777
Unrecognized actuarial (loss) gain due to differences in assumptions and actual experience	(15,977)	8,974
Unrecognized prior service cost	6,262	7,199
Accrued pension costs	(15,553)	(71)
	$ (19,670)	$ 22,879

The actuarial present value of the accumulated benefit obligation and the projected benefit obligation was calculated using a discount rate of 7.25 percent in Year 2 and 8.0 percent in Year 1, and the rate of increase in future compensation levels used was 5.5 percent each year. The expected long-term rate of return on assets was 10.0 percent in Year 2 and 9.0 percent in Year 1. The plan invests primarily in marketable securities and time deposits.

Required

1. Identify the following values of Year 1 and Year 2:
   a. Projected benefit obligation (PBO)
   b. Pension plan assets
   Is MNC's defined benefit plan over- or underfunded relative to its PBO? What financial statement adjustment would be required to fully reflect MNC's pension asset/debt position on its balance sheet?

2. What was the financial effect on MNC's PBO in Year 2 when it lowered its discount rate from 8.00 percent in Year 1 to 7.25 percent in Year 2? What was the financial effect on MNC's plan assets in Year 2 when it raised its expected long-term rate of return from 9 percent in Year 1 to 10 percent in Year 2? Do you agree with these changes?

CORPORATE ANALYSIS

CA10.31 The Procter & Gamble Company. The 2012 annual report of The Procter & Gamble Company (P&G) is available at http://annualreport.pg.com/annualreport2012/index.shtml. After reviewing P&G's annual report, respond to the following questions.

a. Describe P&G's outstanding commitments and contingencies as of June 30, 2012. Does the company consider these commitments and contingencies to be material?

b. What was the company's effective tax rate for 2012? How much of the 2012 tax expense was deferred? P&G discloses deferred income taxes as a current asset and deferred income taxes as a noncurrent liability on its balance sheet. What is the difference between these two accounts (what do they represent)?

c. Describe some of P&G's financial instruments and derivatives that it uses to manage its various business risks.

d. Describe P&G's postretirement benefit plans for its employees. Evaluate the funding status of the company's defined benefit pension plan in 2012. Is the plan fully funded relative to the benefit obligation (BO)? If not, how underfunded is this plan relative to the BO? How much of the underfunding is reported on P&G's balance sheet and how much is carried off-balance-sheet?

CA10.32 Internet-based Analysis. Consider a publicly held company whose products you are familiar with. Some examples might include:

Company	Product	Corporate Website
• Johnson & Johnson Company....	• Band-Aids	• www.jnj.com
• Microsoft Corporation...........	• Windows XP software	• www.microsoft.com
• Nokia Corporation..............	• Cellular phones	• www.nokia.com
• Intel Corporation	• Pentium processors	• www.intel.com
• Kimberly-Clark Corporation......	• Kleenex	• www.kimberly-clark.com

Access the company's public website and search for its most recent annual report. (Some companies provide access to their financial data through an "investor relations" link, while others provide a direct link to their "annual reports.") After locating your company's most recent annual report, open the file and review its contents. After reviewing the annual report for your selected company, prepare answers to the following questions:

1. Review the company's commitments and contingent liabilities footnote. Describe the company's existing commitments. Is the company involved in any litigation? If so, what kind?

2. Does the company have any pension or retirement plans for its employees? If so, are they defined benefit plans or defined contribution plans? Are the plans underfunded or overfunded? If so, by what amount?

3. Does the company use derivatives to hedge its business risks? If so, what kinds of derivatives does it use and what kinds of business risks are being hedged?

4. Does the company have any deferred income taxes on its balance sheet? If so, are the deferred income taxes an asset or a liability? Is the amount of the deferred income tax asset or liability increasing or decreasing? What might explain this increase or decrease?

CA10.33 IFRS Financial Statements. The 2012 financial statements of **LVMH Moet Hennessey-Louis Vuitton S.A.** are presented in Appendix C of this book. LVMH is a Paris-based holding company and one of the world's largest and best-known luxury goods companies. As a member-nation of the European Union, French companies are required to prepare their consolidated (group) financial statements using International Financial Reporting Standards (IFRS). In LVMH's Notes to the Consolidated Financial Statements (not presented in Appendix C), the company discloses its off-balance-sheet commitments as purchase commitments (for grapes), operating leases (for retail space), pending litigation regarding brand rights and intellectual property rights, and various financial guarantees on outstanding loans. The undiscounted value of these off balance-sheet commitments was approximately 7.5 billion euros.

Consider the following:

1. Relative to LVMH's on-balance-sheet debt, is the aggregate value of the company's off-balance-sheet commitments material?

2. To evaluate the company's debt exposure, should the value of these commitments be considered as part of the company's outstanding debt? If so, describe how you might determine the current or present value of these commitments.

SOLUTION TO REVIEW PROBLEM

Solution

	Jan 1	Jan 1	Jan 1	Feb 1	....	repeat	....	Dec 1	Dec 31	Account Summary Year 1	Jan 1	Feb 1	....	repeat	....	Dec 1	Dec 31	Account Summary Year 2
Assets																		
Cash..................	1,200		100	100	....	....	....	100	(540)	1,860	100	100	....	....	....	100	(270)	2,790
Accounts receivable.......	2,400		(100)	(100)	....	....	....	(100)		1,200	(100)	(100)	....	....	....	(100)		-
Inventory..............		(900)								(900)								(900)
Total assets.............										2,160								1,890
Liabilities																		
Deferred income tax.......									270	270							(270)	-
Shareholders' Equity																		
Retained Earnings:										1,890								1,890
Revenue	3,600																	
Cost of goods sold		(900)																
Income tax expense									(810)									
Total liabilities and shareholders' equity....										2,160								1,890

1. Calculation of the Deferred Income Tax Liability for Year 1:

	Accounting	Income Tax	Deferred Income Tax
Revenue	$3,600	$2,400	
Less: Cost of goods sold	900	600	
Pretax income	2,700	1,800	
Income tax (30%).............................	810	540	$270
Net income..................................	$1,890	$1,260	

2. Calculation of the Deferred Income Tax Liability for Year 2:

	Accounting	Income Tax	Deferred Income Tax
Revenue	$0	$1,200	
Less: Cost of goods sold	0	300	
Pretax income	0	900	
Income tax (30%).............................	0	270	−$270
Net income..................................	$0	$ 630	$ 0

When you complete this chapter you should be able to:

1. Explain the accounting for share issuances and repurchases.

2. Describe why companies issue stock dividends and how they account for them.

3. Explain the motivation behind forward and reverse stock splits.

4. Describe the components of other comprehensive income as reported on the balance sheet.

Equity Financing and Shareholders' Equity

Microsoft Corporation was founded to develop and sell BASIC interpreters for the Altair 8800 computer. Under the guidance of its former CEO and current Chairman Bill Gates, the company eventually grew to a position of dominance in the computer software industry. Microsoft is now a multinational company with global revenue of $70 billion and 90,000 full-time employees in over 100 countries. Although best known for its Windows operating system and Office productivity suite, Microsoft also sells a wide range of other software. In addition to software, the company markets such home entertainment products as the Xbox, music devices such as Zune, and computer accessories like the Microsoft mouse. Microsoft is also involved in other endeavors, including a number of cloud-based services and mobile platforms in partnership with Nokia.

MICROSOFT CORPORATION

Microsoft went public in 1986 at a price of $21 per share. Since then, the stock has split nine times such that if you held one of the original IPO shares, you would now own 288 shares of the company. As of early 2013, Microsoft stock was trading at $27 per share, making an original $21 investment worth over $7,800, an annual share price appreciation rate in excess of 25 percent.

While Microsoft's share price has performed beyond the expectations of even the most optimistic investor, the company's recent share price performance has lagged since its peak in 1999. But despite the mediocre share price performance in recent years, the same cannot be said of Microsoft's financial performance. Microsoft reported record net income of nearly $17 billion and cash flow from operations in excess of $31 billion for its fiscal year ending June 30, 2012. The company is also nearing completion of a stock repurchase program announced in 2008, over four years earlier. The following news release on Cnet News.com accompanied that announcement:

> **Microsoft on Thursday reported earnings that were just ahead of analysts' expectations, as the company announced a plan to buy back as much as an extra $40 billion worth of its stock.** *The company disclosed that its board of directors had authorized the company to buy back up to $40 billion worth of stock through September 2013. "With our share repurchase programs announcement today, we reaffirm our confidence and optimism in the long-term future of the company and continue to execute on our strategy of returning capital to shareholders," Microsoft Chief Financial Officer said in a statement.*

By mid-2012 Microsoft had completed about 83 percent of the planned stock repurchase, using over $33 billion of its available cash. But why is the company buying back its shares? The following explanation appeared on Fool.com: "When a profitable company generates excess cash flow, one of the best ways to return that cash to shareholders is through a share buyback. If a company knows its shares are undervalued, and who else is in a better position to know whether a company's shares are undervalued, repurchasing shares is a surefire way for the company to create value. And even if a company thinks its shares are overvalued, a share buyback is almost always preferable to a cash dividend considering that dividends are taxed at the marginal individual income tax rate, which can be 30 percent or higher."

continued

(continued from previous page)

Many possible reasons exist for a company's share repurchases in addition to sending a signal to the market that management believes that the company's shares are undervalued. One reason, for example, is to acquire shares to be distributed to employees when they exercise their employee stock options. Buying back shares on the open market rather than issuing new shares to these employees prevents existing outstanding shares from being diluted.

In this chapter, we discuss the various types of corporate equity transactions, including share issuances and repurchases, dividends, stock splits, and employee stock options.

EXECUTIVE OUTLINE

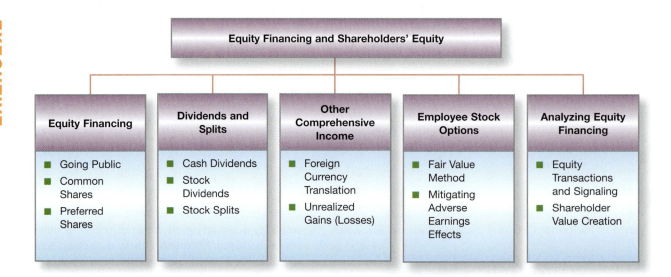

EQUITY FINANCING

Going Public

Small businesses start and grow for many years utilizing financing provided by the business's owners, family and friends, and from such external sources as the Small Business Administration, a business development company, a regional bank, or a local "incubator." After a history of operating performance has been established, a small business might find equity funding available through an "angel" investor or possibly a venture capital firm. Only after a firm's business model has been vetted and refined, and a history of operating earnings and cash flow established, will the firm be ready to "go public" through an **initial public offering** (IPO) of its shares. Taking a company public provides the original founders and investors, angel investors, and venture capital investors with an "exit strategy"—that is, a means to gain liquidity by selling some or all of their shareholdings in the business.

Because most businesses do not have direct access to the many individual investors and mutual funds that comprise the capital market (see Chapter 1), companies desiring to go public typically hire an investment banker to assist with the public offering of their shares. Investment bankers have direct access to many potential investors who are their clients. Prior to an IPO, the executives of a firm, along with the lead investment banker for the IPO, will typically go on a "road show" visiting investment professionals, portfolio managers, and other investment bankers in key financial centers around the country. The purpose of the road show is to provide an opportunity for a company to explain and market the firm's business plan and future prospects to financial advisors and investment professionals in hopes that they, in turn, will recommend adding the firm's shares to their clients' investment portfolios.

For a fee, investment bankers advise companies about the appropriate IPO share price, the number of shares to offer for sale, and ultimately, help execute the sale of the firm's shares. Most commonly, IPOs are executed on a **best efforts basis** in which the investment bank attempts to place (sell) all of the shares available for sale but does not guarantee the sale of all available shares. On some occasions, an IPO may be handled on a **firm commitment basis** in which the investment bank agrees to purchase any shares that remain unsold following an IPO. The investment banker's fees for a firm commitment IPO are considerably higher than the fees for a best efforts IPO because the investment banker bears the market risk associated with any unsold shares.

BUSINESS PERSPECTIVE

Why Become a Public Company?

The increased need for capital or the desire of the original investors to gain liquidity often means the small, privately-held company will transform and become "public." By definition, a public company is one whose securities are traded on an open exchange and, therefore, subject to the reporting, disclosure, and other requirements of the federal securities laws. Thus, there are increased demands on the firm to provide financial information to those outside the organization. But why else would a private company ever choose to become public and thus open its records to intense scrutiny? The advantages and disadvantages are many. Some of those are summarized below:

Advantages of Becoming a Public Company	
Raise Growth Capital	At the IPO the company raises cash through a stock equity offering. Often the funds generated are larger but at lower costs than other financing sources.
Enhances Future Access to Capital	The company may return to the markets to raise additional cash in what are called "seasoned equity" offerings.
Established Market Value	Private companies are frequently valued significantly lower given illiquidity costs. The enhanced information flow associated with an established market value also often results in lower borrowing costs.
Stock as Currency	The ability to use stock as a "currency" facilitates mergers and acquisitions. In rapidly changing markets this can offer a substantial advantage over private competitors. Stock compensation plans are also measurable forms of compensation and benefits.
Liquidity	Liquidity results in the shareholders' ability to have relatively easy and unrestricted trading in the company's securities.
Perceived Stability and Stature	By being public the corporate image and perceived stability is frequently higher, helping to strengthen the competitive position. For instance, private companies sometimes encounter more questions from potential vendors about the firm's long-term stability. "Free" advertising from public markets also helps boost name recognition.

Disadvantages of Becoming a Public Company	
Management Distraction	Significant senior management time and attention are necessary for successful completion of a security offering.
Offering Expenses	The total aggregate costs of an equity offering may range from 10-15% of the gross offering proceeds.
Short-term Orientation	Because important strategic decisions will be subjected to public scrutiny, frequently management will face the choice between long-term goals and short-term financial results (e.g., quarter earnings releases and the pressure to "meet or beat" market expectations).
Voluminous Disclosures	Public companies are required to disclose volumes of information at both the IPO and on an ongoing basis.
Increased Litigation Risk	Given the requisite public disclosures, lawsuits against public companies claiming violations of securities laws have become commonplace.
Ongoing expense and effort	Taking a company public can be quite costly. In-house personnel additions often include a Chief Financial Officer (CFO), an investor relations department and related increases in staffing. External advisors and consultants are required. Routine decision making becomes more cumbersome and time consuming. There are also increased costs for such matters as premiums for directors and officers liability insurance, printing and distribution expenses associated with securities law compliance.

Adapted from: Aronson, Donald H., *Raising Capital for the Emerging Business: A Primer for Entrepreneurs*, Greenberg Traurig, LLP, Fourth Edition (2001).

Issuances and Repurchases of Equity

There are two basic forms of equity capital—common (or ordinary) shares and preferred (or preference) shares.

Common Shares   **Common shares** are the purest form of equity capital and all corporations must have at least one common shareholder. But common shares are also the riskiest form of capital because in the event the firm liquidates, common shareholders are only paid if there is anything left after paying off all of the other investors in the firm. Thus common shareholders have a **residual interest** in the firm's net assets. With this high risk, however, comes the right to vote for the firm's board of directors and on key corporate governance issues. In most companies, for instance, only common shareholders may vote on such corporate governance matters as the selection of a firm's independent auditors, increasing or decreasing the firm's outstanding equity, whether to offer or amend an executive stock bonus plan, and whether to approve a proposed merger or acquisition. The total number of common shares that may be sold by a company is specified in the firm's **charter of incorporation** and is referred to as the **authorized** shares of a firm. When shares are sold, they are said to be **issued**; and, when shares are held by investors they are said to be **outstanding**.

When shares are **repurchased** by a company with the intent of reissuing them for some future corporate purpose they are called **treasury shares**, and while these shares are no longer outstanding they are still considered to be issued. Hence, the total number of shares issued is equal to the number of shares outstanding plus any shares held in treasury. Under International Financial Reporting Standards (IFRS) and U.S. GAAP, treasury shares are reported on the balance sheet as a contra-shareholders' equity account; that is, the repurchase cost of any treasury shares is reported as a negative value in total shareholders' equity. In addition, IFRS and U.S. GAAP precludes the recognition of any gain or loss by a company from share transactions involving its own equity. In contrast, some countries such as France and Japan allow treasury shares to be reported on the asset side of the balance sheet as an investment in marketable securities. Under IFRS and U.S. GAAP, treasury shares do not satisfy the definition of an asset, and therefore, cannot be reported as marketable securities. Instead, treasury shares are considered to be equivalent to authorized-but-unissued common shares, which have no value until sold to the investing public. A summary of the relation between authorized, issued, repurchased, and outstanding shares is provided below:

> Shares which are repurchased without the intent to reissue them are canceled, reducing both the number of shares issued and shares outstanding.

Authorized shares	Shares specified as available for issue in the company's charter of incorporation.
↓	
Issued shares	Shares sold to investors, and not since retired, over the life of the company. These shares are accounted for in the "common (or preferred) stock" and "paid in capital" accounts.
↓	
Repurchased shares	Shares that have been issued but then subsequently repurchased by the company. These shares are accounted for in the "treasury" stock account.
↓	
Outstanding shares	Shares currently held by investors in the firm. Outstanding shares can be computed as issued shares less repurchased shares.

There are several reasons why firms buy back their own shares. Companies that repurchase their own outstanding shares often do so as a means to take advantages of the stock market's undervaluation of its shares. (In some countries, share buybacks are illegal because they are viewed as a form of price manipulation.) This not only allows the company to benefit if and when the share price ultimately rises, but it also sends a positive signal to the financial markets about the company's prospects. The $40 billion Microsoft stock buyback program referenced at the introduction of this chapter is perhaps an example of such a corporate objective. Important to note is that any "gain" or "loss" from the repurchasing shares at one price and reselling at a different price is never reflected on the income statement as profit or loss. Rather the difference is captured in the additional paid-in capital accounts on the balance sheet. In this way the firm can show the economic benefits from the repurchase and resale transactions within stockholders' equity, but it does not report earnings from such transactions.

Other reasons for share repurchases relate to strategic benefits at both the shareholder and company levels. The profits on shares sold back to the company by investors are often taxed at lower capital gains

BUSINESS PERSPECTIVE

IPOs Around the World

Historically, the U.S. stock exchanges have attracted the vast majority of the world's initial public offerings (IPOs). Recently, however, as world economies and financial markets have grown, stock exchanges around the world have become attractive alternatives. The tables below from a recent Ernst & Young study confirm this fact; they summarize the top 10 worldwide IPOs for 2011 by the number of deals and by cumulative size. While the New York Stock Exchange (NYSE) still leads the way in terms of total dollars of new capital, China's Shenzen stock exchange had the greatest number of new deals, and was a close second in dollars of IPO capital. The NYSE and NASDAQ combined had just under 10 percent of the world's 2011 IPOs.

2011 Global IPOs by Stock Exchange					
Top 10 Exchanges by Number of Deals			**Top 10 Exchanges by Capital Raised**		
Exchange	**No. of Deals**	**% of Global Total**	**Exchange**	**Capital Raised ($ mill.)**	**% of Global Total**
Shenzen	243	19.84%	New York	$ 30,502	17.96%
Warsaw-NewConnect	123	10.04%	Shenzen	27,809	16.37%
Australian	100	8.16%	Hong Kong	25,296	14.89%
Hong Kong	68	5.55%	Shanghai	15,075	8.88%
New York	67	5.47%	London	13,915	8.19%
NASDAQ.	54	4.41%	NASDAQ.	9,614	5.66%
KOSDAQ	53	4.33%	Singapore	7,257	4.27%
Toronto-Venture	47	3.84%	Madrid	5,300	3.12%
Bombay	39	3.18%	Sao Paulo	4,412	2.60%
Shanghai	37	3.02%	Warsaw.	2,775	1.64%
All other exchanges	394	32.16%	All other exchanges	27,895	16.42%
Total	1,225	100.00%	Total	$169,850	100.00%

Source: "Global IPO Trends 2012," Ernst & Young

Even though the U.S. is still the world's leading capital market, IPOs in the United States have dropped precipitously over the last two decades. The accompanying graph from a recent finance study confirms this trend. The graph stratifies the IPOs by large firms (sales greater than $50 million, adjusted to 2009 dollars) and small firms (sales less than $50 million). One reason asserted to explain the declining popularity of the U.S. markets is the high regulatory costs imposed by the Sarbanes-Oxley Act (SOX). For example, in 2006 the largest IPO in history by the **Commercial and Industrial Bank of China**, scrapped plans to go public in New York citing the high costs of SOX, and instead raised $18.4 billion in Hong Kong. But researchers studying the systematic evidence more carefully generally conclude that SOX is not the only explanation. Other factors include the increasing quality of foreign stock exchanges as well as changes in the profiles of firms raising capital. The 2012 study by Gao, Ritter and Zhu, from which the graph below is based, concludes that many smaller firms have found that there are greater and quicker advantages to selling out to a larger firm, rather than take the company public.

Number of U.S. IPOs by Large and Small Firms, 1992-2011

Source: Gao, X., J. R. Ritter, and Z. Zhu, "Where Have All the IPOs Gone?", working paper, December 17, 2012.

rates than the rate of taxation on ordinary income. At the corporate level, some companies repurchase their shares in order to have a sufficient number available to execute an acquisition through a share exchange, or to meet the demand for new shares when employees exercise their stock options. Alternatively, some companies repurchase as a takeover defense, for example, when the company's share price is below its intrinsic value per share and outsiders have been accumulating the shares. Finally, some companies repurchase their own shares as a means to build shareholder value—the firm has excess cash and a share repurchase is judged to create greater shareholder value than alternative discretionary managerial actions.

Depending upon the securities laws of the state or province of incorporation, a firm will issue either **no-par value** shares or **par value** shares. Par value, sometimes referred to as **stated value**, is an outdated legal concept that was developed when security markets were largely unregulated and there was a required protected value for a firm's common or preferred shares. It represented the amount of equity capital that cannot be impaired by management (such as paid out in the form of dividends to shareholders) unless a firm was legally restructuring or liquidating itself. In the United States, most shares are now issued without par, or because there are no statutes specifying the dollar amount of a firm's par value, it is not uncommon to see par values as low as $0.01 or $.001 per share. The assignment of a value to par often differs across countries, however. In Japan, for instance, all common shares carry a statutory par value of 50 yen.

In Practice 11.1 *Stock Repurchases versus Dividends*

Stock repurchases were relatively rare in the United States until the 1980s, but have mushroomed in recent years, from about $5 billion in 1980 to over $400 billion by 2011. In fact, share repurchases have become so popular that they now account for over half of all cash distributions to shareholders.

This means that on an annual basis, firms pay more to shareholders for stock repurchases than they do for dividends. The accompanying graph shows the total amount of operating income, dividends and stock repurchases for the S&P 500 by quarter from 2007 through 2011. You will note how dividends remained relatively constant throughout the economic downturn spanning 2007 and 2008, and how repurchases follow the company's ability to fund those repurchases with income.

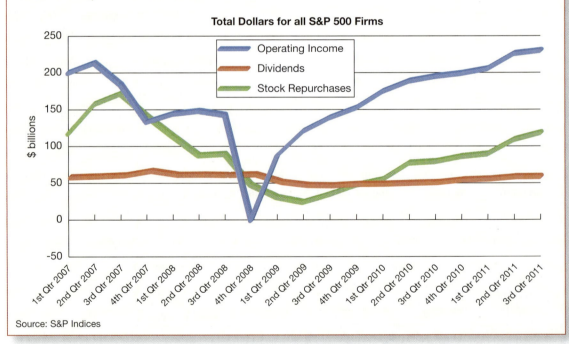

Source: S&P Indices

When common shares are issued, they are rarely sold at their par value, but instead for some greater amount reflecting the intrinsic value of the firm. **Intrinsic value** refers to the underlying economic value of a business as a going concern—that is, the value that a business could be sold for in an efficient market, and as such investors acquiring a company's shares will typically pay an amount that reflects this intrinsic value. Because intrinsic value is a market-based value, it almost always differs from a firm's **book value**, which is based on the accounting-based balance sheet value of shareholders' equity.

When shares are sold for an amount greater than their par value, any payment in excess of the par value is placed in a shareholders' equity account called **additional paid-in-capital**. The total **contributed**

capital of a firm for shares issued, therefore, is the sum of the par value account and the additional paid-in-capital account. When common shares are issued without a par value, there is no additional paid-in-capital account, and hence, all proceeds from the sale of stock are placed in the common or capital stock account.

> While additional paid-in-capital, or APIC for short, is the commonly used name for the excess above par, other commonly used names for this account are **capital in excess of par value**, **capital surplus**, or **share premium**.

In some companies, there may be multiple classes of common shares, often labeled Class A, Class B, Class C, etc. These categories refer either to the **voting rights** of the shares or to the fact that one or more classes of shares represent **tracking shares**. Class A shares are often the shares issued to the original capital providers of a company (such as the founders of the business, angel investors, and venture capital investors) and may carry voting rights as much as ten to one hundred times greater than the voting rights of Class B shares. In the case of tracking shares, any dividends paid on these shares and their market value are linked to the earnings of a particular operating division of a company—that is, the value of the shares is said to "track" the performance of a specific business unit or division. For example, during the 1990s, General Motors had three classes of common shares outstanding—GM, GM-E, and GM-H. The value of the GM common shares was linked to the overall performance of the consolidated company, whereas GM-E and GM-H were tracking shares whose market values were tied to the earnings performance of the EDS and Hughes Aircraft divisions, respectively, of General Motors.

> An extreme example of Class A voting power is the **Adolph Coors Company**. The founding Coors' family (and trusts) own 100 percent of the Class A shares of the Adolph Coors Company, whose value is just 3.5 percent of the firm's total market capitalization. Coors Company Class B shares, owned by the public and representing 96.5 percent of firm value, have no voting rights except in the case of a merger; all other issues are decided by the Class A shareholders.

GLOBAL PERSPECTIVE

In some countries, when common shares carry a letter class designation, it is in reference to who may purchase the shares (a citizen of the country or a noncitizen). For instance, in China for many years, Class A shares could only be purchased by Chinese citizens whereas (until 2001) only noncitizens could purchase Class B shares. In 2003, as China began liberalizing its capital markets to facilitate increased foreign investment, its securities laws were relaxed to permit the sale of H shares in Hong Kong, L shares in London, N shares in New York, and S shares in Singapore.

To illustrate the accounting for share issuances and repurchases, consider the following equity transactions for the Ito Company. The Ito Company share transactions are displayed in the Exhibit 11.1 transaction summary below.

1. Ito Company issues 100 shares of $1 par value common stock at an initial market price of $10 per share.
2. The market value of the Ito common shares increases to $12 per share.
3. Ito repurchases 30 shares of its common stock at $12 per share.
4. The market value of the Ito common shares increases to $13 per share.
5. Ito reissues 10 shares of its treasury common shares at $13 per share.

EXHIBIT 11.1   Share Issue and Repurchase Transactions

THE ITO COMPANY

| | Transaction | | | | | Balance Sheet Totals |
	1	2	3	4	5	
Assets						
Cash...............................	$1,000		$(360)		$130	$770
		No Entry		No Entry		
Shareholders' equity						
Common stock ($1 par).....................	100					100
Additional paid-in-capital...................	$ 900				10	910
Treasury stock			$(360)		$120	(240)
Total shareholders' equity..................						$770

Several items should be noted regarding the accounting for these equity transactions. As illustrated in the first transaction, the recognition of the initial issuance of the $1 par value common stock increases cash by the total proceeds of $1,000 ($10 × 100 shares), increases the common stock account by $100 ($1 par value × 100 shares), and increases the additional paid-in-capital on common stock account by $900, which equals the issuance price per share minus the par value per share times the number of shares issued [($10 − $1) × 100 shares]. Transactions two and four indicate that the Ito Company does not record the changes in the market value of its stock because these changes do not directly impact the firm (although they do impact the firm's shareholders). Transaction three illustrates that treasury stock is recorded in a contra-shareholders' equity account that reduces shareholders' equity by $360 ($12 × 30 shares) and reduces cash by $360. GAAP allows two different methods to record treasury stock. The method presented here is called the "cost method," and its use is far more widespread than the alternate "stated value method." The stated value method, also known as the "par value method," is described in advanced courses.

Finally, transaction five reports that the reissuance of the treasury stock increases cash by the proceeds of $130, removes the 10 treasury shares from the treasury stock account at the price for which they were initially purchased ($12 × 10 shares), and increases additional paid-in-capital by $10, which equals the difference between the reissuance price per share minus the original purchase price per share times the number of shares reissued [($13 − $12) × 10 shares]. After the five transactions, the cumulative effect on the three shareholders' equity accounts total $770, the amount of net cash proceeds received by The Ito Company.

If The Ito Company eventually reissues the rest of its treasury stock and the reissuance price is below its cost of $12 per share, the company first reduces the additional paid-in-capital account for the difference between the reissuance price and the cost per share, and if the balance in the additional paid-in-capital account is insufficient to absorb the difference, Ito then reduces retained earnings for the remaining amount. For example, if Ito reissues the remaining 20 treasury shares for $9 per share, the transaction increases cash by $180 ($9 × 20 shares), eliminates the remaining balance of $240 ($12 × 20 shares) in the treasury stock account, and reduces additional paid-in-capital by the remaining $60 ($240 − $180). If the additional-paid-in-capital account were less than $60, the difference would reduce retained earnings.

Preferred Shares. **Preferred shares**, or preference shares, take their name from the fact that this form of equity is legally entitled to receive dividends before any dividends are paid on the common stock. Unlike common stock, preferred stock receives a periodic fixed dividend, and in the event that the firm liquidates, is paid before the common shareholders. These "preferences" come at a cost, however, in that preferred shares rarely carry the right to vote at shareholder meetings. Further, since the market value of preferred shares is more closely linked to the amount of their fixed dividend payments than to the financial performance of the issuing company, preferred shares rarely experience the share price appreciation that characterizes common shares. For these reasons, investment professionals frequently treat preferred shares as a quasi-form of debt, often as part of a firm's **mezzanine financing**.

> Preferred shares are frequently referred to as **mezzanine financing** along with the subordinated debt of a business. The concept of mezzanine financing takes its name from the fact that this type of financing is less risky than pure equity financing but is more risky than secured debt financing (bank debt)—that is, mezzanine financing falls somewhere in the middle of the risk continuum. Although accounted for as shareholders' equity on the balance sheet, many investment professionals consider preferred stock to be equivalent to debt for financial analysis purposes.

Preferred shares may also have a number of economically important investment features, most of which are designed to make the preferred shares more attractive to investors. For example, some preferred shares are **convertible** into common shares at a predetermined share conversion ratio. This enables the preferred shareholder to share in the success of the company, as reflected in any appreciation of the common shares. Preferred shares may also be **participating**, in which case if a company declares a special dividend for the common shareholders, the participating preferred shareholder will share in the special dividend. Some preferred shares are **cumulative**, in which case if a regular dividend is not paid, the company will maintain a record of any unpaid dividends and the cumulative preferred shareholder must be paid the previously unpaid dividends before any new regular dividends can be distributed. An unpaid cumulative dividend is called a **dividend-in-arrears** and represents a contingent liability to the firm that is disclosed in the footnotes to the financial statements. Finally, some preferred shares are **callable**. A callable preferred share is one that can be

> The share **conversion ratio** of convertible preferred shares (or convertible bonds and notes) into common shares is established at the time the securities are originally issued. The ratio, however, may be subsequently changed in the event that a firm undergoes a stock split. Changing the share conversion ratio following a forward stock split, for instance, protects the convertible preferred shareholder against the dilutive effect of the split.

mandatorily redeemed, or "called," by the issuing company. Companies that issue callable preferred shares often attach a conversion feature to the shares, creating callable convertible preferred stock, to enable preferred shareholders to convert their shares into a company's common shares in the event that the preferred shares are called by the issuing company.

DIVIDENDS

Cash Dividends

As a mechanism to provide an immediate cash return to a shareholder, as well as a means to attract investor interest in a company, some companies pay a **regular dividend** on their equity shares. In the case of preferred shares, regular dividends are paid at a fixed rate, much like interest on a bond. In the case of common shares, however, the dividend rate may change over time as a company's performance and operating cash flows increase or decrease. Dividend-paying companies are frequently evaluated by investors on the basis of their **dividend yield**—that is, the dividend paid per share divided by the market price per share. It is noteworthy that dividends on equity shares are never guaranteed; they must be formally approved and declared each fiscal period by a company's board of directors. In addition, dividends are not a liability of the firm until such time as they are declared by the board of directors.

Once a dividend has been declared, a **record date** and a **distribution date** are established. To receive a dividend, a shareholder must own the shares on the record date, which is typically four to six weeks after a dividend has been declared by the board of directors. Subsequent to the record date, a stock is said to be "ex-dividend;" that is, the stock is sold without the right to receive the latest declared dividend.

In Practice 11.2 *Dividend Payout and Dividend Yield for the S&P 500*   The **dividend payout ratio** is a measure of the amount of dividends paid by a firm relative to its current net income (dividend per share divided by earnings per share). As of early 2013 the average dividend payout for S&P 500 firms approximated 37%, well below its historical 50-year average of 53%. A related ratio is the dividend yield, calculated as follows: Dividend paid per share/Market price per share. A common misperception is that dividend-paying companies attempt to maintain a stable payout ratio. In reality, dividend-paying companies determine the dividend to be paid on the basis of their sustainable discretionary cash flow, and not net income. Below is a graph of the average dividend payout for S&P 500 firms since 1980, along with a list of the current highest dividend yielding stocks in the S&P 500 as of October 2012 (data source: Bloomberg).

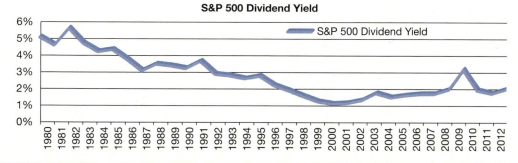

S&P 500 Dividend Yield

Ten Highest Dividend Yields for the S&P 500—October 2012				
Company	**Stock Price**	**Est. Annual Dividend**	**Dividend Yield**	**Dividend Payout**
Pitney Bowes Inc.............................	$14.52	$1.52	10.47%	85.1%
Windstream Corp.............................	9.66	1.00	10.35	308.0
RR Donnelley & Sons.......................	10.13	1.04	10.27	52.9
Frontier Communications...................	4.74	0.40	8.44	498.9
CenturyLink Inc.	38.30	2.88	7.52	269.6
Cliffs Natural Resources...................	36.20	2.48	6.85	7.3
Avon Products Inc...........................	15.46	0.92	5.95	76.3
Exelon Corp.	35.81	2.12	5.92	69.9
Reynolds American Inc.	41.26	2.36	5.72	89.5
Altria Group Inc.	31.77	1.76	5.54	96.3

The distribution date—that is, the date on which any dividend is actually paid—is approximately two weeks following the record date.

Since the payment of a cash dividend can affect the market price of a stock, dividend changes are approached cautiously by the board of directors. Dividend increases, for example, are rarely observed unless a firm's projected discretionary cash flow is sufficient to sustain the dividend increase for the foreseeable future. Dividend decreases, on the other hand, are received poorly by equity investors, often interpreted as a negative "signal" about a firm's future prospects. An announced reduction in a firm's dividend is typically accompanied by a dramatic drop in share price, and thus, dividend reductions are avoided by most firms.

As a general rule, companies that are considered to be "growth companies" rarely pay dividends on their common shares. Instead, these companies use their available operating cash flow to fund their growth. As the rate of revenue growth declines, companies will often begin to pay dividends as a means to retain their shareholders. Companies that pay large amounts of their earnings out as dividends are often referred to as "mature companies," having little or no revenue growth opportunities other than that caused by inflation or normal market expansion.

Dividend increases, on the other hand, are typically accompanied by only modest increases in share price. Since growth companies rarely pay dividends—that is, growth companies reinvest all available cash to fuel continued growth—an increase in a firm's dividend could be interpreted by the equity market as a negative signal about a firm's future prospects. For example, an increase in a firm's dividend may signal that a firm is no longer a growth company or that its industry is no longer a growth industry. To many investors, a dividend increase is a signal from management that they believe that shareholders have investment opportunities superior to those of the company (such as because of slowing industry or firm growth). Hence, under this scenario, a dividend increase is intended to maximize shareholder wealth by distributing cash directly to investors and enabling them to invest in their superior return-generating opportunities.

BUSINESS PERSPECTIVE

Shareholders' Equity Disclosures

The shareholders' equity section of the balance sheet of Ford Motor Company is below:

December 31 ($ millions)	2011	2010
Shareholders' equity		
Capital stock (Note 24)		
Common stock, par value $0.01 per share		
(3,745 million shares issued of 6 billion authorized)	$ 37	$ 37
Class B stock, par value $0.01 per share		
(71 million shares issued of 530 million authorized)	1	1
Capital in excess of par value of stock	20,905	20,803
Retained earnings/(accumulated deficit)	12,985	(7,038)
Accumulated other comprehensive income/(loss)	(18,374)	(14,313)
Treasury stock (15 million common shares)	(166)	(163)
Total equity/(deficit) attributable to Ford Motor Company	15,028	(673)
Equity/(deficit) attributable to noncontrolling interests	43	31
Total equity/(deficit)	15,071	(642)
Total liabilities and equity	$178,348	$164,687

Ford's shareholders' equity section reveals that, at year end 2011, the company had 3.73 billion shares of Class A common stock outstanding (3,745 − 15 million) and 71 million shares of outstanding Class B common stock. Ford's total net contributed capital in 2011 amounted to $20.777 billion ($20,905 million + $37 million + $1 million − $166 million), whereas its earned capital (retained earnings + accumulated other comprehensive income) amounted to negative $5.389 billion. $43 million of shareholders' equity belongs to noncontrolling interests in consolidated affiliates. The company's book value, or shareholders' equity, of $15.071 billion, is well short of its end of year 2011 market value, or market capitalization, of $45 billion. The difference between these two amounts emphasizes the distinction between a company's book value and its market capitalization—the former reflects the company's past performance whereas the latter reflects the market's expectations regarding the firm's future performance. It is clear from the disparity of these two amounts that the market expects a bright future for Ford.

Occasionally, a firm facing a limited investment opportunity set, but with large amounts of available cash on hand, will pay its shareholders a **special dividend**. A special dividend is a one-time distribution of cash unrelated to a stock's regular dividend. A special dividend may be distributed to avoid an unwanted takeover bid or to maximize shareholder value when management believes that shareholders have superior investment opportunities. For example, by 1998 the **Ford Motor Company** had accumulated over $22 billion in cash on its balance sheet. With few acquisition opportunities available—Ford had already acquired Jaguar, Volvo, and Land Rover—and since any further automotive acquisitions would likely have encountered antitrust opposition from both the U.S. Federal Trade Commission and the EU Competition Commission, Ford distributed its excess cash to shareholders as a special dividend of $21.09 per share.

When a company pays a dividend, the share price of the dividend-paying company typically falls by an amount approximately equal to the value of the dividend. For example, in late 2012 **AOL Inc.** paid its shareholders a special dividend of $5.15 per share. On the day prior to the ex-dividend date, the shares of AOL closed at $37.52 per share. On the ex-dividend date, the price of the shares dropped to a close of $31.90, a decline of $5.62 per share. Most of this decline, $5.15 to be exact, is attributable to the dividend now due to shareholders owning AOL shares on the prior date. The remainder of the decline can be attributed to other market movements. Importantly though, the share price of a firm will decline following the announcement of a special dividend when the market perceives the payout as being so large as to impede the firm's future performance.

Regular or special cash dividends are a distribution of earned income that is accounted for by reducing both the cash account and retained earnings on the balance sheet. Although interest, the cost of debt financing, is considered to be an expense, dividends, or the cost of equity financing, are not. This differential treatment of the cost of debt and the cost of equity financing reflects the fact that the income statement is prepared from the perspective of a company's shareholders, before any distributions of earnings are made to shareholders.

BUSINESS PERSPECTIVE

All in the Family

The equity ownership structure of U.S. and U.K. public companies is characterized by small diffuse investors, each of whom owns only a small fraction of the firm. But the ownership structure of public companies in most of the rest of the world is strikingly different, and is characterized by the presence of a large investor who holds a controlling interest in the company's stock. These large owners usually consist of families who are typically directly involved in managing the company's operations. The accompanying graph reports the percentage of public companies in seven East Asian countries that are controlled by families. It indicates that more than fifty percent of the public companies in each country are controlled by families and that South Korea has the highest with nearly 80 percent.

Percent of Corporations in East Asian Economies that Are Family Controlled

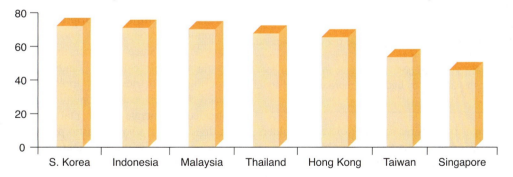

This difference in ownership structure means that public companies in the United States and U.K. have a somewhat different "agency" problem than companies in the rest of the world. While the agency problem for U.S. and U.K. firms involves conflicts of interest between the managers and outside owners, the agency problem in the rest of the world involves conflicts between the large insider-owners and the small minority shareholders.

Source: Fan, J., and Wong, T. J., 2002. Corporate ownership structure and the informativeness of accounting earnings in East Asia. *Journal of Accounting and Economics*.

Free Share Distributions

Investors in publicly held corporations may obtain their ownership interest by purchasing shares of stock through a firm's initial public offering, a secondary public offering, or by buying the shares from another investor on the open market. Sometimes a company will distribute additional shares of stock to its existing shareholders via a **free share distribution**. Free share distributions occur in two forms—a stock dividend or a stock split. Free share distributions take their name from the fact that investors receive the additional shares without having to pay for them.

BUSINESS PERSPECTIVE

Dividends, or the Lack Thereof, at Apple Inc.

Apple Inc. is unquestionably one of the most successful and innovative companies of the last quarter century. The company is a global corporate icon, best known today for its popular set of consumer electronics: the Mac line of personal computers, and the iPod, iPad and iPhone handheld devices, among others. With the Apple platform, one of its original founders, Steve Jobs (deceased 2011), single-handedly is credited with revolutionizing the personal computer, the electronics, and the media distribution industries. Jobs' success at Apple has brought the company and its shareholders unprecedented financial success. It was the world's second largest corporation in terms of value as of early 2013 (market capitalization of approximately $450 billion), and during the calendar year 2012 Apple earned over $40 billion in profits alone.

Despite Apple's innovative research focus, the company is surprisingly known to be overly conservative financially. The company carried little debt, and had accumulated a cash hoard of over $137 billion as of February 2013. Less than a year earlier, the company had initiated a $2.65 per share quarterly dividend, and with just under 950 million shares outstanding this approximated a total dividend payment to shareholders of $10 billion annually ($2.65 per share × 4 quarters × 950 million shares). While this may seem like a healthy payout, Apple's shareholders were not pleased given its under-utilized cash balance. One of Apple's largest shareholders, Greenlight Capital, even threatened a lawsuit against the company for its poor "capital allocation strategy." With rates of return below 2 percent on most cash holdings, the arguments were sound—that this cash would be better served in the hands of shareholders, either through a new preferred stock issue that paid a dividend, a special cash dividend on the common stock, or a stock buyback. Apple management, as it always had before, said it was "considering all such options." Stay tuned.

Stock Dividends

Cash dividends—that is, a distribution of a firm's earned income—commonly occur as a regular or special dividend to shareholders. Occasionally, a business may distribute a **property dividend** to its shareholders by giving them the product (or a coupon for the product) that the firm produces. For example, **McDonald's Holdings Company (Japan) Ltd.** gives its shareholders a coupon book good for several free "Big Macs." Since customers at a McDonald's restaurant rarely eat just a sandwich, often also ordering french fries and a drink, it may be surmised that McDonald's property dividend is also intended to generate incremental food sales.

> The **William Wrigley Company**, the world's largest bubble gum manufacturer, sends its shareholders twenty free packs of gum around Christmas each year. Companies that distribute property dividends generally believe that this encourages their shareholders to retain their shares by becoming more informed about the company's products.

When a firm desires to reward its shareholders with a dividend but also desires to preserve its operating cash, it may resort to the distribution of a **stock dividend**—that is, the distribution of additional shares of common stock in proportion to the shares already owned by shareholders. For instance, if a firm declares a ten percent stock dividend, the number of new shares to be distributed to shareholders is equal to ten percent of the shares outstanding prior to the free share distribution.

It is important to observe that a firm is not transferring anything of value to the shareholders in a "free" share distribution. While the shareholders hold a larger number of shares after receiving a stock dividend, the value of the shareholders' investment is unchanged. There is some variation in the accounting for stock dividends, but the most common treatment is to reduce retained earnings by the market value of the distributed shares, increase the common stock account by the par value of the distributed shares, and increase the additional paid-in-capital account by the excess of market value above par value.

For example, consider the case of the Julius Company, with ten million shares outstanding, a par value of $1 per share, and a market value of $12 per share. If Julius declares a ten percent stock dividend it will issue an additional 1 million shares to its shareholders (10 percent times 10 million shares). To account for this stock dividend Julius decreases the retained earnings account by $12 million (1 million shares times $12 market value per share), increases the common stock account by $1 million (1 million shares times $1 par value), and increases the additional paid-in-capital account by $11 million, which equals the difference between the decrease in the retained earnings account and the increase in the par value account ($12 million minus $1 million). Thus, following a stock dividend, Julius's total shareholders' equity balance remains unchanged, while its retained earnings account declines by the fair value of the distributed shares and the paid-in-capital accounts (common stock at par value plus additional paid-in-capital) increase by the same amount. By transferring the market value of the distributed shares from retained earnings to paid-in capital, the accounting treatment for stock dividends permanently capitalizes a portion of Julius's retained earnings.

Because nothing of value is transferred to the shareholders, the stock's price per share following a stock dividend should fall exactly proportionately to the size of the stock dividend. Empirical evidence indicates, however, that the announcement of a stock dividend results in an increase in share price. One explanation for this increase in shareholder value is that by permanently capitalizing a portion of retained earnings, stock dividends signal to the market that managers expect greater future growth.[1]

An exception to the accounting described above for stock dividends does exist. When stock dividends are proportionally quite large—that is, when the quantity of the distributed shares is 25 percent or more of the existing number of outstanding shares—it is the standing policy of the New York Stock Exchange (and other stock exchanges) that the stock dividend be accounted for in the same way as a stock split, to which we now turn.

Stock Splits

Stock splits are used to both increase and decrease the number of outstanding shares, and hence, the market price per share. A **forward stock split**, for example, increases the number of outstanding shares, whereas a **reverse stock split** reduces the number of outstanding shares.

A forward stock split is used principally to lower the market value of a stock. For example, in January 2003, **Microsoft Corporation** announced a two-for-one split of its common stock. Prior to the split, the firm's shares traded at $48.30 per share. Immediately following the split, the stock traded at $24.96 per share, almost exactly one-half of its prior market value (see **bolded** area in Exhibit 11.2). Previously, Microsoft had split its stock on eight other occasions. Thus, an original IPO investor in Microsoft with one share of common stock would now own the equivalent of 288 post-split shares, having an aggregate market value in excess of $7,800. (Microsoft originally went public in 1986 at $21.00 per share, with a par value of $.01).

EXHIBIT 11.2	Microsoft's History of Forward Stock Splits			
	Stock Split	Par Value	Share Price	
Date of Forward Stock Split	Ratio	After Split	Before Split	After Split
September, 1987	2:1	$0.005	$114.50	$53.50
April, 1990	2:1	0.0025	120.75	60.75
June, 1991	3:2	0.0016667	100.75	68.00
June, 1992	3:2	0.00111111	112.50	75.75
May, 1994	2:1	0.0005556	97.75	50.63
December, 1996	2:1	0.00025*	152.88	81.75
February, 1998	2:1	0.00025**	155.13	81.63
March, 1999	2:1	0.000125	178.13	92.38
February, 2003	**2:1**	**0.0000625**	**48.30**	**24.96**

* Rounded from 0.000277
** Stock split effected as a stock dividend

At $7,800 per share (Microsoft's pre-split value per share), only institutional and wealthy investors could afford to buy Microsoft's stock. Thus, the purpose of a forward split is to lower a firm's share price

---

[1] G. Rankine and K. Stice, "Accounting Rules and the Signaling Properties of 20% Stock Dividends," *The Accounting Review*, (1997).

to a price range affordable by most investors. Most stock exchanges charge the lowest transaction fees when shares are purchased or sold in "round lots"—that is, in lots of 100 shares. Thus, to receive the lowest transaction cost per share, a Microsoft investor would need to be able to invest $780,000 in the company's shares if they were trading at $7,800 per share, an amount beyond the means of most individual investors.

BUSINESS PERSPECTIVE

Berkshire Hathaway

A contrary example to those firms that use forward stock splits as a means to lower a firm's share price to a trading range affordable by most investors is **Berkshire Hathaway**. As of early 2013, the company's Class A common stock trades on the NYSE at approximately $145,000 per share and may be the most expensive price for a single share of stock worldwide. The company's CEO, Warren Buffett, does not believe in the notion of stock splits or stock dividends; however, to make the Berkshire Hathaway shares affordable to small investors, the company issued a Class B share, with unit values and fewer voting rights than the company's Class A common shares. The Class B shares trade at approximately $95 per share, this after a 2010, Class B stock split of 50-for-1 as part of Berkshire's takeover of **Burlington Northern Santa Fe Corporation**. After the split the relative value of Class B shares are 1/1,500 of Class A shares, but with only 1/10,000 of the voting rights.

The traditional accounting for a forward stock split is to proportionally lower the par value of the stock to compensate for the increase in the quantity of shares outstanding. Hence, if a company executes a two-for-one stock split when its par value is $.01, the number of shares outstanding will double and its par value will halve to $.005 per share. Following a stock split, the total par value of the firm is unchanged although the market value of the firm, and of a share of stock, may actually increase. Forward stock splits, like stock dividends, are frequently viewed by the market as a favorable signal about a firm's future operating prospects, and thus, the post-split share price tends to drift upward in anticipation of subsequent favorable corporate news.[2]

A reverse stock split, on the other hand, is used principally to raise the market value of a company's common stock. Consider, for example, the case of **Titanium Metals Corporation**. Titanium Metals Corporation was an integrated manufacturer of titanium sponge, the basic form of titanium metal used in processed titanium products. A major use of titanium metal is in the construction of aircraft. Prior to the terrorist attack on the New York City World Trade Center in September 2001, Titanium Metals' shares traded at approximately $15. In the days following September 11, 2001, Titanium Metals' share price fell to less than $3 per share, eventually falling to less than $1, as the demand for commercial aircraft, and hence titanium, declined. In early 2003, Titanium Metals announced a one-for-ten reverse split. Earlier the company had been informed by the New York Stock Exchange that since its share price had traded below $1 per share for more than 30 consecutive days, its shares were in danger of being de-listed. Hence, one reason why some firms attempt to raise their share price is to avoid stock exchange de-listing. When a company's shares are de-listed, shareholders face a liquidity crisis in that it is extremely difficult to find buyers for unlisted shares.

> Most stock exchanges maintain a minimum listing price. In the event that a firm's share price falls below the minimum listing price for a consecutive period of time, usually 30 days or more, the shares may be de-listed. Exchange de-listed shares may, and usually do, trade in the over-the-counter market.

Another reason that some firms attempt to raise their share price through a reverse stock split involves the stock "screens" used by many institutional investors and mutual fund managers. There are over 20,000 publicly traded companies in the United States, and thus, portfolio managers need an approach to narrow the universe of companies that they consider for their portfolio selections. One way that mutual fund managers constrain the set of firms they evaluate is by the use of "screens," and one such screen is a minimum share price.

Many institutional investors and mutual fund managers do not consider companies as potential investments whose share price is consistently below $5 per share (unless, of course, the mutual fund specializes in "low-price" stocks). To be sure that mutual fund managers consider a firm's shares for possible purchase and inclusion in their portfolio, some companies execute a reverse split to get their share price above the $5 screen threshold. Stocks whose share price is below the price threshold don't attract institutional investors whose buying in large blocks often drives up share prices. A recent high profile example of a reverse stock split for

---

[2] R.M. Conroy and R.S. Harris, "Stock Splits and Information: The Role of Share Price," *Financial Management*, 1999.

these purposes is **Citigroup, Inc.** Following the financial crisis beginning 2008, Citigroup saw its stock price fall from a high of over $50 per share to at one point under $2 per share. After over a year lingering below the $5 level, Citigroup engaged in a reverse split of one-for-ten. From the day before the split to the day after the traded per share value of the stock was changed from approximately $4.50 per share to $45.00 per share.

In Practice 11.3 *Stock Splits: A Glimpse of a Sample of Fortune 1000 Companies*   The following chart identifies the stock split ratios disclosed by a sample of 600 *Fortune 1000* companies. The most commonly executed split is a 2-for-1 split:

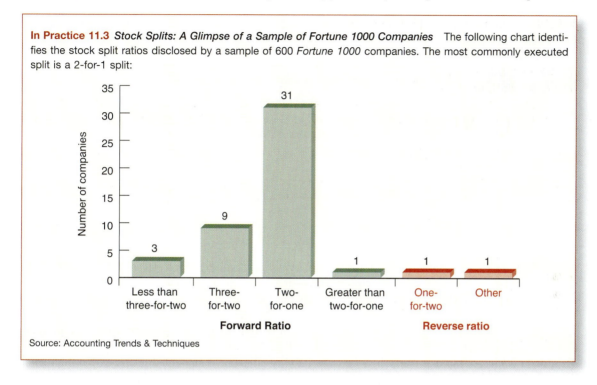

Source: Accounting Trends & Techniques

OTHER COMPREHENSIVE INCOME

Under U.S. GAAP, companies are required to report various increases and decreases in shareholder wealth that have not yet been realized, and thus, not yet reported on the income statement, as a component of shareholders' equity on the balance sheet called **other comprehensive income**. Examples of such wealth changes, which are not reportable as income include:

■ Foreign currency translation adjustments

■ Employee benefit adjustments

■ Unrealized gains (losses) on available-for-sale marketable securities

■ Unrealized gains (losses) on financial derivatives

Collectively these items represent changes in shareholders' equity, unrelated to amounts contributed by or distributed to shareholders, that are part of company performance but not recorded as income in the current period. Items of other comprehensive income taken together with reported net income will yield *total* "**comprehensive income**." The notion of comprehensive income is thus a more inclusive view of how well a company has performed. Note also that while retained earnings accumulates all recorded income statement earnings, less dividends paid, the account "**accumulated other comprehensive income**" (often labeled AOCI for short) serves as the repository for differences between net income and comprehensive income. Below we provide some background into some of the more common components of other comprehensive income.

As discussed in Chapter 8, when a firm maintains operations in a foreign country, the translated value of those foreign operations will fluctuate as the exchange rate between the currencies of the two countries fluctuates. These unrealized changes in value of the foreign operations are accumulated in a shareholders' equity account on the consolidated balance sheet called the **cumulative foreign currency translation adjustment** account, or more commonly, the CTA. To illustrate, consider the case of **General Electric Company (GE)**, a U.S.-based manufacturing and financial services company with global operations. As of year-end 2010, the value of GE's overseas operations had decreased by $86 million as compared to the cost basis of its original investment due to currency fluctuations (see **bolded** area in Exhibit 11.3). By year-end

2011, the total unrealized gain in value was $133 million, a reversal of the 2010 loss position. Thus, from 2010 to 2011, as a consequence of the decrease in the U.S. dollar relative to the foreign currencies of the countries in which GE maintained overseas operations, the value of GE's foreign operations increased by $219 million. If GE were to liquidate those foreign investments at exchange rates characteristic of year-end 2011 and repatriate those monies back to the United States, the firm could expect to realize a gain of as much as $219 million. Until that unlikely event (until the loss is actually realized), GE is required to disclose the magnitude of the potential wealth decline on its balance sheet as part of its Other Comprehensive Income.

EXHIBIT 11.3	Other Comprehensive Income Disclosures			
GENERAL ELECTRIC COMPANY				
December 31 ($ millions)		**2011**	**2010**	**Change**
Accumulated other comprehensive income, net				
Investment securities		$ (30)	$ 636	$ 606
Currency translation adjustments		133	(86)	219
Cash flow hedges		(1,176)	(1,280)	104
Benefit plans		(22,901)	(15,853)	(7,048)
Total accumulated other comprehensive income, net		$(23,974)	$(17,855)	$(6,119)

In Chapter 10, the accounting for retirement obligations was discussed. It was noted that, under U.S. GAAP, companies with underfunded pension plans—that is, a retirement plan in which the present value of the future employee retirement benefits exceeds the value of the pension plan assets—are required to record a liability for the amount of the underfunding. In some instances, the offsetting balance sheet effect to the pension liability is the creation of a contra-shareholders' equity account called the **pension liability adjustment**. (GE refers to this account as Benefit Plans in Exhibit 11.3.) In the case of GE, Exhibit 11.3 reveals that the company's pension liability adjustment amounted to $22.901 billion as of year-end 2011, having increased by $7.048 billion from 2010 to 2011. These amounts represent unrealized wealth declines for GE because the disclosed amount has not yet been paid into the GE pension fund nor expensed against the firm's earnings. In essence, the wealth decline remains unrealized until GE satisfies its pension obligation by actually contributing the cash to its pension fund.

GLOBAL PERSPECTIVE

There exist a number of significant differences between U.S. GAAP and IFRS with respect to the reporting of shareholders' equity. First, under U.S. GAAP, shareholders' equity includes the investment of both common and preferred shareholders, whereas under IFRS, equity includes only the investment of the common (or ordinary) shareholders. Under IFRS, preferred equity is considered to be a component of debt financing; however, this difference is under review by the joint FASB/IASB convergence project. Second, under U.S. GAAP, the financing component of the balance sheet is segmented into three categories—debt, mezzanine financing, and shareholders' equity. Under IFRS, this section of the balance is segmented into just two components—debt and equity. Under U.S. GAAP, the mezzanine financing section is the repository of those accounts which are neither debt nor equity. Finally, there exist a number of significant terminology differences under the two systems:

U.S. GAAP	IFRS
Common stock	Share capital
Additional paid-in-capital	Share premium
Retained earnings	Retained profits
Accumulated other comprehensive income	Other reserve accounts

In Chapter 8, the accounting for marketable securities was discussed. At that time it was noted that under U.S. GAAP, equity investments classified as "available-for-sale" are valued at their fair market value, with any increase (decrease) in value reflected as part of Other Comprehensive Income as long as the securities remain unsold, and hence, the wealth gain (loss) unrealized. Exhibit 11.3 reveals that GE investment securities classified as "available-for-sale" are in a $30 million net loss position, significantly worse than the $636 million gain position in 2010.

Finally, in Appendix 10B, the accounting for financial instruments and derivatives was discussed. It was noted that such instruments should be valued at their fair market value and that any increase (decrease) in their market value above their original cost should be reported on the balance sheet as part of other comprehensive income. As long as the financial instruments remain outstanding, no gain or loss need be reported on the income statement until such time as the instrument expires or is eliminated. GE's accumulated other comprehensive income disclosure reveals that the company had cash flow derivative hedge positions with cumulative net losses of $1.176 billion as of the end of 2011, a $104 million improvement over the prior year.

In aggregate, Exhibit 11.3 reveals that GE's unrealized losses exceeded its unrealized gains by $6.119 billion during 2011. If all of GE's unrealized gains and losses disclosed as other comprehensive income in Exhibit 11.3 were realized, GE's 2011 pre-tax net income would decline by a massive $23.974 billion.

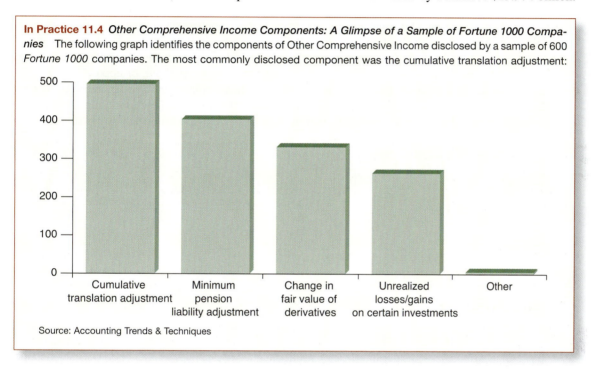

In Practice 11.4 *Other Comprehensive Income Components: A Glimpse of a Sample of Fortune 1000 Companies* The following graph identifies the components of Other Comprehensive Income disclosed by a sample of 600 *Fortune 1000* companies. The most commonly disclosed component was the cumulative translation adjustment:

Source: Accounting Trends & Techniques

EMPLOYEE STOCK OPTIONS

An important component of the compensation of many corporate employees is the annual stock option grant.[3] **Stock options** grant employees the right to buy a company's common shares at a fixed price (the **strike price** or **exercise price**) within a specified period of time. A typical employee stock option does not vest—that is, it is not exercisable by the employee—for a number of years, often as long as five to ten years, cannot be sold or transferred, and is ultimately valuable only if the firm's common share price rises above the option strike price.

During the 1990s, stock options became an integral part of employee compensation packages in the United States as companies tried to more closely align the shareholder goal of share price maximization with the employee goal of increased compensation. And, since option exercise prices are typically set at the share's market price at the time of granting, an option is worthless to an employee unless their efforts are successful in raising the company's share price above its strike price. Because most employee stock options have no immediate or **intrinsic value** (they are issued "at the money"), and in any case, can't be exercised for years, the traditional accounting treatment was to ignore the options for financial statement purposes—that is, the options were described in the footnotes to the financial statements but were not actually reflected in the financial statements. This accounting approach, called the intrinsic value method, was quite controversial since it was believed by many investment professionals that stock options have

---

[3] As one extreme example, in 2011 **Apple Computer** CEO Tim Cook received a salary of $900,000, but on top of that he also received stock options valued at nearly $377 million.

a **fair value** at the time of granting since there is an expected value associated with the possibility that the options will be exercisable at a profit in the future when, and if, the share price increases. The FASB concluded that stock options represented a real employee compensation cost to the firm and proposed that the options be expensed in the period in which they were granted. This proposal met with stiff opposition from the business community, and consequently, the proposal was defeated (recall the discussion from Chapter 1). The topic of expensing employee stock options resurfaced, however, following the accounting scandals at Enron and WorldCom, where some attributed the fraudulent activity of management at least in part to the earnings' management incentives provided by their stock options.

BUSINESS PERSPECTIVE

Controversy Over Employee Stock Options

The impact on the income statement of expensing stock options can be quite significant. To illustrate, consider the case of **Cisco Systems, Inc.**, a worldwide leader in networking hardware and software for the internet. The following table presents Cisco's 2000 to 2003 earnings per share both with and without the cost associated with issuing employee stock options. The cost of employee stock options represents as much as $0.15 to $0.24 per share of the firm's total net income per share, or approximately 42 to 65 percent of Cisco's net earnings. Thus, it is clear that Cisco's employee stock options had a material impact on the firm's reported performance. For the period 2000 to 2003, Cisco reported the financial impact of its employee stock options in its footnotes but not as an expense on its income statement.

| | Net Income Per Share | | |
Effect of Stock Options on Reported Net Income (Fiscal Year)	As Reported	After Stock Option Expense	Difference
2000	$ 0.36	$ 0.21	(0.15)
2001	(0.14)	(0.38)	(0.24)
2002	0.25	0.05	(0.20)
2003	0.50	0.32	(0.18)

Source: U.S. Securities and Exchange filings

Stock options like those issued by Cisco must now be expensed, but controversy remains over how to measure an option's fair value. Two widely used approaches to estimate the value of employee stock options are the **Black-Scholes model** and the **binomial model**. Although easier to apply, the Black-Scholes model does not consider the likelihood that changes in a stock's market price will influence the timing of when employees exercise their options. As a consequence, the binomial model is becoming more widely used. Consider, for example, the **American International Group, Inc.** (AIG). AIG disclosed that in 2002, it changed the method it used to value its employee stock options from the Black-Scholes approach to the binomial approach. By switching methods, AIG was able to lower its option expense by $30 million in 2000 and by $18 million in 2001. In 2002, the company deducted $140 million as its cost of granting options under the binomial method, a savings of $30 million as compared to the Black-Scholes method. In 2007, the U.S. Securities and Exchange Commission approved a new approach to value employee stock options called ESOARS, or employee stock option appreciation rights securities. ESOARS use an auction process to assign value to employee stock options. Recently, **Google Inc.** announced that it would use an online auction process to enable its employees to trade, and hence value, their stock options granted by the company.

In the response to the requirement that the cost of employee stock options be immediately expensed, a study by **New Constructs** research firm found that many firms affected by the new accounting requirement attempted to mitigate the adverse earnings effect of the new accounting by altering the projected volatility assumptions used in their option pricing models. The research study found that over 20 percent of the Russell 1,000 companies changed their model volatility assumptions to reduce the adverse earnings effect associated with recognizing the cost of employee stock options. The volatility assumption change refers to the degree to which the price of a company's shares fluctuate in the capital market. For some companies, the effect of the volatility assumption change reduced the negative earnings effect of expensing employee stock options by as much as 50 percent.

BUSINESS PERSPECTIVE

Statement of Shareholders' Equity

The fourth basic financial statement is the statement of shareholders' equity. This statement summarizes the changes during the year of each component of the shareholders' equity section of the balance sheet. Presented below is **Ford Motor Company**'s 2011 statement of shareholders' equity, which reveals the 2011, 2010, and 2009 change in the balance of each of Ford's shareholders' equity components—capital stock, capital in excess of par value of stock, retained earnings, treasury stock, accumulated other comprehensive income, and equity attributable to noncontrolling interests. Ford's total shareholders' equity increased by $30.442 billion from a negative balance of $15.371 billion to start 2009 to a positive $15.071 billion to end 2011. Quite a turnaround! This $30.442 billion increase is shown in the statement of shareholders' equity to be related to a number of components, but principally to the net income reported in each of those three years (and recorded as part of retained earnings). In 2011 net income was $20.213 billion, accounting for the biggest contributor to the increase in equity. Note the purpose of the statement of shareholders' equity—to convey detail that is important to understanding Ford's shareholder equity accounts that might not be found elsewhere in the financial statements.

FORD MOTOR COMPANY and Subsidiaries
Consolidated Statement of Shareholders' Equity
For Years Ended December 31, 2011, 2010, and 2009

(in millions)	Capital Stock	Capital in Excess of Par Value	Retained Earnings (Accum. Deficit)	Accum. Other Compr. Income (Loss)	Treasury Stock	Total	Equity Attributable to Non-Controlling Interests	Total Equity (Deficit)
Year Ended December 31, 2009								
Balance at beginning of year	$24	$10,875	$(16,316)	$(10,123)	$(181)	$(15,721)	$350	$(15,371)
Comprehensive income/(loss)								
Net income/(loss)	—	—	2,717	—	—	2,717	—	2,717
Foreign curr. translation (net of $65 of tax)	—	—	—	2,235	—	2,235	—	2,235
Net gain/(loss) on derivative instruments (net of $0 of tax)	—	—	—	(127)	—	(127)	—	(127)
Employee benefit related (net of $302 of tax benefit & other)	—	—	—	(2,851)	—	(2,851)	—	(2,851)
Net holding gain/(loss) (net of $0 of tax)	—	—	—	2	—	2	—	2
Comprehensive income/(loss)						1,976	—	1,976
Common Stock issued	10	5,911	—	—	—	5,921	—	5,921
Impact of deconsolidation of AutoAlliance International, Inc.	—	—	—	—	—	—	(269)	(269)
Treasury stock/other	—	—	—	—	4	4	(40)	(36)
Cash dividends declared	—	—	—	—	—	—	(3)	(3)
Balance at end of year	$34	$16,786	$(13,599)	$(10,864)	$(177)	$(7,820)	$ 38	$ (7,782)
Year Ended December 31, 2010								
Balance at beginning of year	$34	$16,786	$(13,599)	$(10,864)	$(177)	$(7,820)	$ 38	$ (7,782)
Comprehensive income/(loss)								
Net income/(loss)	—	—	6,561	—	—	6,561	(4)	6,557
Foreign curr. translation (net of $2 of tax benefit)	—	—	—	(2,233)	—	(2,233)	(1)	(2,234)
Net gain/(loss) on derivative instruments (net of $0 of tax)	—	—	—	(24)	—	(24)	—	(24)
Employee benefit related (net of $222 of tax benefit & other)	—	—	—	(1,190)	—	(1,190)	—	(1,190)
Net holding gain/(loss) (net of $0 of tax)	—	—	—	(2)	—	(2)	—	(2)
Comprehensive income/(loss)						3,112	(5)	3,107
Common Stock issued	4	4,017	—	—	—	4,021	—	4,021
Treasury stock/other	—	—	—	—	14	14	—	14
Cash dividends declared	—	—	—	—	—	—	(2)	(2)
Balance at end of year	$38	$20,803	$(7,038)	$(14,313)	$(163)	$(673)	$ 31	$ (642)
Year Ended December 31, 2011								
Balance at beginning of year	$38	$20,803	$(7,038)	$(14,313)	$(163)	$(673)	$ 31	$ (642)
Comprehensive income/(loss)								
Net income/(loss)	—	—	20,213	—	—	20,213	9	20,222
Foreign curr. translation (net of $2 of tax benefit)	—	—	—	(718)	—	(718)	(2)	(720)
Net gain/(loss) on derivative instruments (net of $67 of tax benefit)	—	—	—	(152)	—	(152)	—	(152)
Employee benefit related (net of $1,560 of tax benefit & other)	—	—	—	(3,553)	—	(3,553)	—	(3,553)
Net holding gain/(loss) (net of $0 tax)	—	—	—	2	—	2	—	2
Comprehensive income/(loss)						15,792	7	15,799
Common Stock issued	—	102	—	—	—	102	—	102
Treasury stock/other	—	—	—	—	(3)	(3)	5	2
Cash dividends declared	—	—	(190)	—	—	(190)	—	(190)
Balance at end of year	$38	$20,905	$12,985	$(18,734)	$(166)	$15,028	$ 43	$ 15,071

Stock Options Under the U.S. Tax Law

Under U.S. GAAP a company must record compensation expense over the vesting period of stock options granted to all employees. However, the tax deductibility of those same options under U.S. tax law follows a different set of rules. First, some stock options, specifically *incentive* stock options (ISOs), are not deductible at all for tax purposes. This restriction exists because with ISOs the employee is able to avoid ordinary income tax when the option is exercised, as long as he or she meets certain holding period restrictions (e.g., the stock is held at least 1 year, among others). There are a number of other restrictive criteria and administrative burdens on companies that issue ISOs. These are too complex and many for our purposes here, but note that when these added costs are coupled with the inability of a company to reduce its taxes through a deduction against income, ISOs have become the less commonly granted type of options.

Any option that does not meet the requirements of being an ISO is by default classified as a *nonqualified* stock option. For IRS tax purposes, a nonqualified option is deductible under IRS rules in the year of exercise. And the measurement of "compensation expense" takes a different form. Whereas under U.S. GAAP the fair value estimate of option value at the date of grant determines total compensation (e.g. under a model such as Black-Scholes), under U.S. tax law the allowable deduction is the difference between (i) the fair market value of the company's stock on the exercise date, and (ii) the exercise price received by the company from the employee. In essence, in the eyes of the IRS the company has "given up" a difference in economic value as of the exercise date equivalent to the acquisition discount received by the employee. In the eyes of FASB, however, the grant date option fair value represents how much effort the employee has provided the company over the vesting period. Since these amounts are "earned" by the employee over the vesting period, they must be matched to revenues in the proper time periods consistent with accrual accounting. Noteworthy is that IRS will typically tax as income to the employee who exercises nonqualified options the same amount that is allowed as a deduction by the corporation, and in the same year.

Because with nonqualified options the IRS allows a tax deduction if and when exercised, nonqualified options can yield temporary timing differences between book and tax income. These timing differences will create a deferred tax asset (see chapter 9) on the company's balance sheet because the options are also expensed under GAAP, but sooner. The deferred tax asset must be eliminated on one of three dates: (i) the date the employee severs employment if before the options have vested, (ii) the vesting date if the options are out-of-the-money, or (iii) the exercise date because it is then that a deductible expense is finally recorded on the tax books.

As you can no doubt see, the accounting for options, both under GAAP and U.S. tax law, is complex and dependent on many different inputs. These complexities mean that managers and executives that grant or receive stock options need be aware of both the financial reporting and tax rules, as they can have large impacts on the company and its employees. This brief review only touched on some of the more general factors to consider, and thus it is important for those affected to research this topic more fully.

The FASB's proposal to expense stock options met with particularly strong opposition from companies in the high-tech industry. High-tech companies are some of the biggest stock option users and executives in this industry argued that expensing stock options would dramatically reduce their profitability. In response to claims that lower reported profits would hurt the competitiveness of U.S. businesses and cost jobs, the House of Representatives passed HR 3574 in 2004, a bill that outlawed the FASB from requiring companies to expense stock options. While the bill ultimately failed to become law, its existence demonstrates the political nature of accounting standard setting.

Internationally, the prevailing view has been that despite the fact that employee stock options are rarely granted "in the money," the options are valuable because they may assume significant future value for an employee if, and when, the share price rises. As a consequence, both the IASB and the FASB now require that companies granting employee stock options must estimate the fair market value of the options at the time of granting and deduct that value as employee compensation expense on a straight-line basis over the vesting period. The offset to the retained earnings from the compensation

BUSINESS PERSPECTIVE

The Backdating Scandal

In 2004, finance Professor Erik Lie at the University of Iowa published research reporting that the option grant dates of many U.S. corporations happened to coincide with the day of the year in which the stock was at its annual low. This research was followed by a series of investigative articles in the *Wall Street Journal* in 2006 that alleged large numbers of U.S. companies were deceptively "backdating" their option grant dates. An example is United Health, a large managed health care company. United Health reported that it granted 250,000 options to its CEO in October 1998 when the stock was selling at $35 per share, and hence assigned a $35 exercise price to the options (see the accompanying graph). With a grant date and exercise price both equaling $35 per share, the options have an intrinsic value of zero, and the proper accounting is to make no adjustments to the books. In 2006, however, the SEC and the Internal Revenue Service launched investigations into allegations that the options were actually granted in December 1999, when the stock was trading at $85 per share. If true, the stock options actually had an intrinsic value of $12.5 million ($85 minus $35, times 250,000 options) and the proper accounting is to increase compensation expense by $12.5 million, an event that also has tax consequences. The SEC opened investigations of more than 130 companies suspected of backdating their executive stock options, including against such high profile companies such as Apple and Dell. In October of 2006, United Heathcare CEO William McGuire agreed to resign his position. In 2007, McGuire settled with the SEC, agreeing to repay $468 million, and under the Sarbanes-Oxley Act, was barred from serving as an officer or director of a public company for ten years.

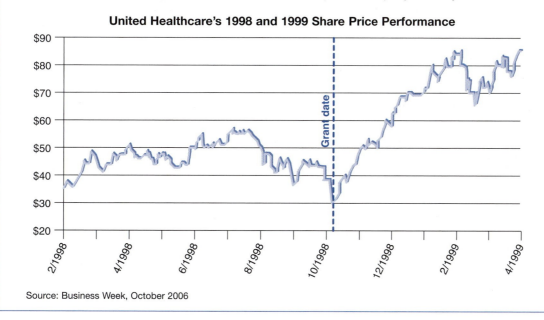

United Healthcare's 1998 and 1999 Share Price Performance

Source: Business Week, October 2006

expense is an increase in the additional paid-in-capital account in shareholders' equity. This accounting method is known as the fair value method.

To illustrate the accounting for stock options under the fair value method, consider the following scenario for the Walsh Company. Assume that certain Walsh employees receive stock options on 200,000 shares of Walsh stock. At the time of grant the stock was trading for $40 per share, the options were issued at the money (i.e., the strike price is $40), and the options would vest in 4 years. The controller for Walsh estimated that the value of all the options on the date of grant equaled $10 million. Suppose further that five years after the options were granted the stock price of Walsh had risen to $75 per share, and during that fifth year all employees exercised their right to purchase shares at $40 per share. The 200,000 shares of stock were then issued, and they carried a par value of $1 per share. The yearly Walsh Company transactions related to their stock options are summarized in Exhibit 11.4 below (for purposes of this illustration taxes are ignored):

EXHIBIT 11.4	Summary Transactions for Stock Option Grant and Exercise

THE WALSH COMPANY
Summary Transactions for Stock Option Grant and Exercise

Transaction ($ thousands):	Year 1: Options Granted	Year 2	Year 3	Year 4: Options Vest	Year 5: Options Exercised	Balance Sheet Totals
Assets						
Cash.					$8,000	**$8,000**
Shareholders' Equity						
Common stock ($1 par)					200	200
Additional paid-in-capital.	2,500	2,500	2,500	2,500	7,800	17,800
Retained earnings						(10,000)
Stock compensation expense.	(2,500)	(2,500)	(2,500)	(2,500)		
Total shareholders' equity						**$ 8,000**

Note from the summary transactions the systematic allocation (i.e., amortization) of the option fair value across each year prior to vesting. Stock compensation is recorded each year, but since no cash has changed hands, and since the company has no obligation to pay employees, the excess-paid-in-capital account must be increased by the amount of expense recorded each year. This treatment in effect records the compensation as-if the employee has contributed to the company as a shareowner. By the fourth year the entire $10 million of compensation has been recorded. When the option is exercised, Walsh Company simply treats the transaction as it would the issue of any new stock. Cash is received in the amount of $8 million, the common stock account is increased for the par value of $0.2 million (200,000 shares × $1 par), and additional-paid-in-capital balances the transaction ($7.8 million). Note if the stock price of Walsh Company never reached a value for which the options would be exercised, then this last transaction would not occur, but the prior expensing of the fair value would remain.

ANALYZING EQUITY FINANCING AND SHAREHOLDERS' EQUITY

The analysis of equity transactions requires a substantial amount of judgment on the part of financial statement users. As discussed in this chapter, there are multiple reasons why a firm may elect to engage in transactions such as issuing shares, share buybacks, or dividend payments. Companies issue shares usually because there exists a need for capital. The accounts that reflect a share issuance are recorded at historical cost as of the date of the stock issue, and thus financial statement users need to interpret those accounts with that in mind. Both share repurchases and dividend increases are often considered to be shareholder-value increasing events because they signal the market about management's optimistic beliefs regarding a firm's future prospects. For example, share repurchases often signal that management feels that the current share price undervalues a firm's intrinsic value, while increases in a firm's dividend payout signal that management believes that future operating cash flow will be more than adequate to support the larger dividend payments. Unfortunately, negative signals can also be associated with each of these events. Both share repurchases and dividend increases are sometimes interpreted by the capital market as indicating that a firm no longer has high revenue growth prospects.

Shareholder value creation can arise in two ways—share price appreciation and dividend payments. Two measures of the latter include the dividend payout ratio and the dividend yield. The dividend payout ratio compares the amount of dividends paid to shareholders relative to a firm's net income, while the dividend yield computes dividends paid relative to a firm's share price. According to modern financial theory, in the absence of income taxes, it should not matter to shareholders whether or not a firm chooses to pay dividends since any dividend paid would cause an equivalent decrease in share price. Still, many investment professionals pay close attention to the dividend policy adopted by a firm because many shareholders prefer a steady, dependable dividend to the uncertainty of share price appreciation.

As noted in prior chapters, it is the responsibility of the financial statement user to not only analyze the numbers that appear in a company's financial statements, but also to adjust the financial

In Practice 11.5 *Title of the Shareholders' Equity Section on the Balance Sheet: A Glimpse of a Sample of Fortune 1000 Companies*   The following chart identifies the title used on the balance sheet for the shareholders' equity section by a sample of 600 *Fortune 1000* companies. Over 50 percent of the surveyed firms used the label "stockholders' equity:"

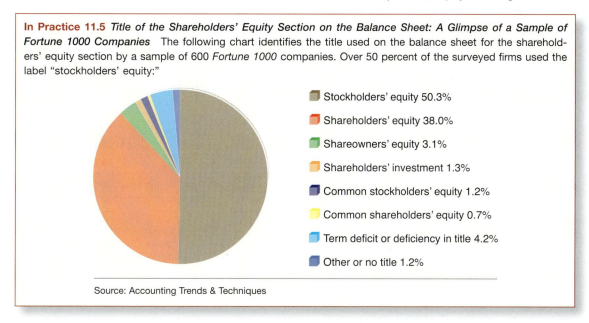

- Stockholders' equity 50.3%
- Shareholders' equity 38.0%
- Shareowners' equity 3.1%
- Shareholders' investment 1.3%
- Common stockholders' equity 1.2%
- Common shareholders' equity 0.7%
- Term deficit or deficiency in title 4.2%
- Other or no title 1.2%

Source: Accounting Trends & Techniques

statements for any business risks (such as operating leases and pending lawsuits) that they feel are not adequately reflected in the financial data. Examples of the latter that are discussed in this chapter include dividends-in-arrears and employee stock option expense (for financial statements prior to 2007). Dividends-in-arrears result from the failure of a firm to pay dividends on its cumulative preferred stock. Since dividends are not recorded as liabilities until they are actually declared by the board of directors, dividends-in-arrears represent a contingent liability and thus require only footnote disclosure. The presence of dividends-in-arrears, however, serves as a red flag to financial statement users that a firm is (or at least, was) in financial distress, and consequently, has been forced to conserve its operating cash flow by not paying its preferred stock dividends.

Prior to 2007 managers had considerable discretion as to how they reported the cost of employee stock options in corporate financial statements. Most managers elected to simply disclose this cost in the financial statement footnotes rather than reporting the expense as a deduction against earnings on the income statement. Beginning in 2007, however, firms were required to expense employee stock option costs as an operating expense on the income statement. Nonetheless, if an analysis of a firm includes prior years (2006 and before), it is important to consider the earnings impact of the employee stock option expense that can be found in a firm's footnotes.

Finally, the financial statement user should pay careful attention to items that appear in the Accumulated Other Comprehensive Income section of shareholders' equity. The items reported in this section of the balance sheet represent unrealized wealth changes to a firm that bypass the income statement, at least temporarily. The financial statement user should, at a minimum, consider whether their inclusion is warranted in any analysis of a firm's future cash flow and sustainable earnings.

ETHICS PERSPECTIVE

One of the basic tenets of modern financial theory is that the primary goal of a public corporation is to maximize shareholder value. The rationale underlying this argument is that the shareholders are the owners of the corporation, and as the residual claimants, they bear all of the risks and rewards of ownership. Further, economic theory dating from the teachings of Adam Smith argues that capital will flow to those firms that provide the best returns and that this flow of capital will benefit society as a whole. The construct of shareholder value maximization, however, is not universally embraced. Some would call "stakeholder theory" a competing theory of the firm. Under stakeholder theory, shareholders are but one of the many stakeholders of the corporation, with other stakeholders being a company's employees, customers, suppliers, the government, the surrounding community, and the environment. Stakeholder theory proponents believe that it is the obligation of the corporation to balance the needs of each of its stakeholder groups, rather than to focus solely on shareholder maximization. Some have gone so far as to equate the doctrine of shareholder maximization with corporate greed.

REVIEW PROBLEM

The Arcadia Company began operations on January 1, by issuing 500,000 shares of $1 par value common stock at a price of $10.00 per share. During the first year of operations, the company generated revenue of $2 million and incurred expenses totaling $800,000. (Assume all transactions are in cash.) During its second year of operations, the company executed the following events in the sequence listed:

a. Declared a 2-for-1 forward stock split.
b. Repurchased 10,000 shares of its common stock for cash at a price of $15 per share.
c. Declared and distributed a ten percent stock dividend on the outstanding shares at a time when the market price per common share was $18 per share.
d. Paid a cash dividend of $.10 per share on all outstanding common shares.
e. Generated revenue of $3 million and incurred expenses of $1.2 million.

Required

Using a spreadsheet approach, record the transactions for Years 1 and 2 for The Arcadia Company. Using the account balances at the end of Year 2, prepare the shareholders' equity section of the balance sheet for The Arcadia Company.

The solution is on page 406.

EXECUTIVE SUMMARY

This chapter investigated the shareholders' equity section of the balance sheet. Specifically, we considered how companies raise equity capital through the sale of common and preferred shares, and how and why they sometimes execute free share distributions through stock dividends and stock splits. Finally, we examined the Other Comprehensive Income section of the shareholders' equity section of the balance sheet, and the accounting for, and disclosure of, employee stock options.

As a validation of your understanding of the content of this chapter, you should now be able to:

- Explain the accounting for share issuances and repurchases.
- Explain why companies issue stock dividends and how they account for them.
- Explain the motivation behind forward and reverse stock splits.
- Explain the various components of the Other Comprehensive Income section of shareholders' equity on the balance sheet.

In the next and final chapter, we illustrate the discounted cash flow approach and the residual income approach to firm valuation.

KEY CONCEPTS AND TERMS

Additional paid-in-capital, 376
Authorized, 374
Best efforts basis, 372
Binomial model, 388
Black-Sholes model, 388
Book value, 376
Callable, 378
Capital in excess of par value, 377
Capital surplus, 377
Charter of incorporation, 374
Common shares, 374
Contributed capital, 376
Conversion ratio, 378
Convertible, 378
Cumulative, 378
Cumulative foreign currency
    translation adjustment, 385
Distribution date, 379

Dividend-in-arrears, 378
Dividend payout ratio, 379
Dividend yield, 379
Exercise price, 387
Fair value, 388
Firm commitment basis, 372
Forward stock split, 383
Free share distribution, 382
Initial public offering, 372
Intrinsic value, 376, 387
Issued, 374
Mezzanine financing, 378
No-par value, 376
Other comprehensive income, 385
Outstanding, 374
Participating, 378
Par value, 376
Pension liability adjustment, 386

Preferred shares, 378
Property dividend, 382
Record date, 379
Regular dividend, 379
Repurchased, 374
Residual interest, 374
Reverse stock split, 383
Share premium, 377
Special dividend, 381
Stated value, 376
Stock dividend, 382
Stock options, 387
Stock splits, 383
Strike price, 387
Tracking shares, 377
Treasury shares, 374
Voting rights, 377

QUESTIONS

Q11.1   **Book Value versus Market Capitalization.**   Home Depot Inc. reports has a book value of approximately $18 billion in its 2011 annual report, however its market capitalization exceeds $105 billion (almost six times its book value). Discuss why Home Depot's book value is so much less than its market capitalization. Describe the circumstances in which a company's book value might exceed its market capitalization.

Q11.2   **Free Share Distributions.**   Stock dividends and stock splits are often referred to as "free share distributions." Discuss why the use of the label "free share distribution" is an appropriate description of these shareholders' equity transactions.

Q11.3   **Dividend-in-Arrears.**   When dividends are unpaid on a cumulative preferred stock, they are referred to as a dividend-in-arrears. Discuss why dividends-in-arrears are disclosed as a contingent liability in the footnotes to the financial statements and not as a liability on the balance sheet. What message do dividends-in-arrears convey about the financial health of a business?

Q11.4   **Multiple Classes of Voting Rights.**   During 2006 *The Wall Street Journal* carried the following headline and lead paragraph:

> **New York Times Faces Share Class Challenge**   The *New York Times Co.* became the latest newspaper company to come under fire from some of its restive investors, this time for its use of two classes of shares with unequal voting power. Morgan Stanley's money-management division, which holds more than 5% of the New York Times Class A shares, pressed the company to eliminate its Class B stock.

The Times' Class B shares, which are primarily owned by the family of Chairman Arthur Sulzberger, carry significantly more voting power than the newspaper company's Class A shares. Discuss why Morgan Stanley would want to see the two-class share structure eliminated. Why would the family of Chairman Sulzberger prefer to maintain a two-class share structure?

Q11.5   **Oversubscribed Initial Public Offering.**   In early 2006, India's Reliance Petroleum announced that it would hold an initial public offering (IPO) of its common shares. The announced IPO was for 1.8 million shares at an estimated price range of 57 to 62 rupees per share, or approximately $2.5 billion to $2.7 billion. Because of exceptionally strong investor interest worldwide for Indian company shares, and especially for oil and gas company shares, the Reliance Petroleum IPO was oversubscribed by 7.5 times (the total number of shares sought by investors was 13.5 million). Discuss what strategies Reliance Petroleum might adopt in response to this dramatic oversubscription of its initial public offering. If Reliance's outstanding shares total 7.2 million shares following the IPO, what is the implicit value of the entire company? (Reliance Petroleum's remaining outstanding shares were held by its parent company Reliance Industries.)

Q11.6   **Stock Splits and Share Prices.**   The Loews Corporation, a property and casualty insurance company, announced that its board of directors had approved a 3-for-1 forward stock split. At the time of the stock split announcement, Loews' common shares were trading at $99 per share but gained nearly $2 per share in after-hours trading following the announcement. In the year prior to the split announcement, the Loews shares had steadily increased in price from $70 per share to its current price of $99 per share, an increase of nearly 42 percent in just one year. Discuss why the board of directors might have approved the stock split. Is the announcement of a stock split "positive news" to the market? If so, why?

Q11.7   **Dividend Reduction.**   The Mills Corporation announced that it would cut its dividend payment to shareholders from $0.63 per share to just $0.25 per share. In response to the announcement, Mills' share price rose about $4 per share, or approximately 13 percent. Over the past year, Mills' share price had fallen about 53 percent, from $64 per share to $30 per share, after the real estate investment trust (REIT) company had revealed to its shareholders that it was incurring significant operating losses on a number of its real estate projects. Analysts had been predicting a dividend cut since Mills had been unable to cover its dividend payout through its ongoing operating cash flow. REITs are usually reluctant to cut their dividend because the dividend yield on such investments is one of the principal attractions for investors. Discuss how the equity market is likely to react to news of a dividend cut. Discuss how companies set their dividend policy and under what conditions they are likely to increase or decrease a dividend.

Q11.8   **Dividend Payout Ratio.**   The dividend payout ratio, or the percentage of net income paid out to shareholders in the form of a dividend (Dividends paid/Net income), is used by some investors to identify securities to add to their portfolio of investments. For example, in recent years, the dividend payout ratio for the **Procter & Gamble Company** averaged 37.6 percent, the **Johnson & Johnson Company** averaged 36.4 percent, and for **Pfizer, Inc.** averaged 68.7 percent. Discuss whether having a high payout ratio (such as Pfizer, Inc.) is a good strategy for a company. What type of investor would prefer a high payout ratio versus a low (or zero) payout ratio? What does a high payout ratio suggest about a company's future growth prospects?

Q11.9   **Cost of Employee Stock Options.**   The April 19, 2006, edition of *The Wall Street Journal* carried the following headline: "**Yahoo**'s Net Declines 22% After Accounting Change." The article explained that while the internet company's revenue had increased by 30 percent over the same period one year earlier, its profit had fallen 22 percent as a consequence of the mandatory adoption of a new accounting standard regarding the accounting for employee stock options. Without the adoption of the accounting change, Yahoo's first quarter earnings would have been $231 million, or $0.15 per share. Including the cost of employee stock options issued to Yahoo employees during the first quarter caused Yahoo's earnings to fall $71 million, or $0.04 per share, to just $160 million, or $0.11 per share. Yahoo's share price rose six percent in response to the news announcement while the S&P 500 index closed slightly down for the day. Discuss why the capital market may have responded positively to Yahoo's earnings announcement. Do you agree that the cost of employee stock options should be expensed in the period in which they are granted?

Q11.10   **Directors' Compensation.**   In 2006, the **Coca-Cola Company** announced a major change in company policy regarding the compensation of its board of directors. Under the new director compensation plan, nonexecutive directors would be paid an annual director's fee of $175,000 only if the soft drink company met its target of eight percent compounded annual earnings growth over a three-year period. If the target was missed, directors would receive nothing. Coca-Cola director Warren Buffett hailed the program as "pioneering," noting that the new policy would align the interests of the board of directors and Coke's shareholders more closely than in any other large company. Discuss whether you think Coke's new director compensation scheme will achieve its intended goal.

Q11.11   **Special Dividends: Return on Capital or Return of Capital.**   On April 24, 2006, **Cablevision Systems Corporation** paid its shareholders a special dividend of $10 per share. At the time that the special dividend was announced, the company's share price was trading at $27 per share. Following the dividend distribution, the company's share price dropped to $18 per share. Special dividends that represent a return *on* capital are taxed at regular dividend tax rates (currently 15 percent), whereas special dividends that represent a return *of* capital are not subject to any income tax. Discuss under what circumstances a special dividend would be considered a return of capital versus a return on capital. Describe the financial performance of a company that might justify classification of a special dividend as a return of capital.

Q11.12   **(Ethics Perspective) Stakeholder Theory and Shareholder Wealth Maximization.**   To whom do you feel corporate managers owe their responsibility? Do you feel that shareholder wealth maximization and stakeholder theory are necessarily competing theories? If you feel that managers owe a responsibility to more than just shareholders, how should they resolve the ethical dilemma of the competing needs of each group (such as profits for shareholders, quality and fair prices for customers, good wages for employees, etc.)?

Assignments with the ✓ logo in the margin are available in **BusinessCourse**.
See the Preface of the book for details.
CHECK FIGURE indicates that check figures are available on the book's Website.

EXERCISES

 E11.13   **Shareholders' Equity Transactions.**   The following transactions occurred during the year for The Niagara Company:

1. Generated net income of $2.5 million.
2. Sold common stock having a par value of $0.01 for $22 per share.
3. Paid a cash dividend of $2 per share to its preferred shareholders.
4. Issued a ten percent stock dividend on its outstanding common stock.
5. Repurchased 10,000 shares of common stock at $18 per share.
6. Declared a 2-for-1 forward stock split on its common stock.

Identify whether the above transactions increased, decreased, or had no effect on total shareholders' equity. Identify the specific shareholders' equity accounts affected by each transaction and indicate whether the accounts increased, decreased, or remained unchanged. How is the capital market likely to react to the ten percent stock dividend, the repurchase of 10,000 shares of common stock, and the 2-for-1 forward stock split? Why?

E11.14   **Accounting for Shareholders' Equity Transactions.**   The shareholders' equity section of the balance sheet of The Claremont Company appeared as follows at the end of the first year of operations:

Common stock, $0.10 par value	$ 600,000
Additional paid-in-capital.	89,400,000
Retained earnings	32,000,000
Treasury stock	(7,500,000)
Shareholders' equity	$114,500,000

During the second year of operations, the following transactions occurred:

1. Generated net income of $6 million.
2. Paid a cash dividend of $1.5 million.
3. Purchased 100,000 shares of common stock at $9.50 per share.
4. Executed a 1-for-2 reverse stock split.

Prepare the shareholders' equity section of the balance sheet of Claremont Company at the end of the second year of operations.

E11.15   **Accounting for Shareholders' Equity Transactions.**   The shareholders' equity section of the consolidated balance sheet of **The Tortuga Rum Cake Company** appeared as follows at the beginning of the year.

Common stock, $1.00 par value	$ 100,000
Additional paid-in-capital.	1,200,000
Convertible preferred stock, no par value	800,000
Retained deficit	(600,000)
Treasury stock	(250,000)
Shareholders' equity	$1,250,000

The following transactions occurred during the year:

1. Generated net income of $80,000.
2. Paid cash dividends of $220,000.
3. Issued a ten percent common stock dividend; the fair value of the stock was $10 per share at this time.
4. Declared and issued a 2-for-1 forward stock split.
5. Converted 10,000 shares of convertible preferred stock with a book value of $300,000 into 30,000 shares of common stock.

Prepare the shareholders' equity section of the balance sheet of Tortuga Rum Cake Company at year-end. How is the capital market likely to react to the conversion of convertible preferred stock into common stock? Why?

E11.16   **Dividend Yield and Dividend Payout.**   The following information is available for West Texas Waste Management Inc. (WTWM).

	Year 1	Year 2	Year 3
Dividends per share	$ 0.04	$ 0.08	$ 0.16
Earnings per share.	1.07	1.28	1.41
Market price per share.	16.00	19.00	21.00

Calculate WTWM's dividend payout ratio and dividend yield for Year 1 through Year 3. Describe the trend in WTWM's dividend payout and dividend yield. Which factor—dividends or earnings—seems to be driving WTWM's share price movement?

E11.17   Accounting for Stock Dividends and Stock Splits.   The Irvine Corporation reported the following data at year-end:

Common stock, par value $1	$ 100,000
Additional paid-in-capital	300,000
Retained earnings	1,400,000
Treasury shares	(600,000)
Other comprehensive income	200,000
Total shareholders' equity	$1,400,000

The following transactions occurred during the year in the following sequence:

1. Declared and distributed a ten percent stock dividend on the outstanding common shares at a time when the common shares were selling for $15 per share.
2. Declared a 3-for-2 forward stock split on the outstanding common shares.
3. Declared and issued a 20 percent stock dividend on the outstanding common shares at a time when the shares were selling for $30 per share.
4. Declared a 2-for-1 forward stock split on the outstanding common shares.

Calculate the par value per share and number of shares outstanding at year-end. Prepare the shareholders' equity section of the balance sheet for the Irvine Corporation at year-end.

E11.18   Interpreting the Foreign Currency Translation Adjustment Account.   The following information is taken from the annual report of **Home Depot Inc.**:

Other Comprehensive Income (in millions)	Year 1	Year 2	Year 3
Foreign currency translation adjustment account	$(124)	$109	$172

Discuss why the Foreign Currency Translation Adjustment account was negative for Home Depot in Year 1. Explain why the account balance became positive in Year 2 and grew larger in amount in Year 3. Are the changes in this account reported on the income statement or in the statement of cash flow for Home Depot? Why or why not? Why are changes in a company's "other comprehensive income" not subject to income taxation?

E11.19   Analyzing the Net Unrealized Gain on Available-for-Sale Securities.   The following information is taken from the annual report of Smith & Sons Inc. :

Other Comprehensive Income (in millions)	Year 1	Year 2	Year 3
Net unrealized gain (loss) on available-for-sale securities	$(9,324)	$47,230	$19,238

Explain why the net unrealized gain on available-for-sale securities was negative in Year 1. Explain why the account balance became positive in Year 2 but then declined in Year 3. Are the changes in this account reported on the company's income statement? Would this account appear on Smith & Sons' statement of cash flow? Why or why not?

E11.20   Adjusting Conversion Ratios for Stock Splits and Stock Dividends.   R.J. Miller & Company has the following securities outstanding:

- Common stock, $0.10 par value
- Convertible preferred stock
- Convertible debentures

The convertible preferred stock carried a conversion ratio of 3-to-1 (each share of preferred stock may be converted into three shares of common stock), whereas the convertible debentures carried a conversion ratio of 46-to-1 (each debenture may be converted into 46 shares of common stock). During the year, R.J. Miller & Company declared and issued a ten percent common stock dividend, followed by a 2-for-1 forward common stock split. Calculate the new conversion ratios for the convertible preferred stock and convertible debentures following the common stock dividend and common stock split. Why is it appropriate to adjust the conversion ratios of the convertible preferred stock and the convertible debentures following the stock dividend and stock split?

E11.21 **Contrasting the Contributed Capital of a Firm with Treasury Stock.** The following information is taken from the annual reports of **Cisco Systems Inc.**, **Intel Inc.**, and **Microsoft Inc.**:

Shareholders' Equity (amounts in millions)	Cisco Systems	Intel	Microsoft
Contributed capital..................................	$27,096	$ 7,698	$62,150
Retained earnings	22,957	38,994	(5,978)
Treasury stock	(27,153)	(10,637)	(8,057)
Other comprehensive income	274	127	0
	$23,174	$36,182	$48,115

For each company, calculate the ratio of treasury stock divided by contributed capital. What does this ratio tell you about each of the three companies?

E11.22 **Analyzing Shareholders' Equity.** Presented below is the consolidated statement of shareholders' equity for **The Johnson & Johnson Company** (J&J) at year-end:

(in millions)	Total	Compre-hensive Income	Retained Earnings	Notes Receivable From ESOP	Accumulated Other Comprehensive Income	Common Stock	Treasury Stock
Beginning balance	$31,813		$35,223	$(11)	$(515)	$3,120	$(6,004)
Net earnings.........................	10,411	$10,411	10,411				
Cash dividends paid..................	(3,793)		(3,793)				
Employee stock compensation and stock option plans	1,017		(441)				1,458
Conversion of subordinated debentures ...	369		(132)				501
Repurchase of common stock...........	(1,717)		203				(1,920)
Other comprehensive income, net of tax ...							
Currency translation adjustment	(415)	(415)			(415)		
Unrealized losses on securities	(16)	(16)			(16)		
Pension liability adjustment	26	26			26		
Gains on derivatives & hedges...........	165	165			165		
Reclassification adjustment		(15)					
Total comprehensive income		$10,156					
Note receivable from ESOP	11			11			
Ending balance.......................	$37,871		$41,471	$—	$(755)	$3,120	$(5,965)

Based on your review of this data, consider the following questions:

1. How much cash dividends did J&J pay during the year?
2. What was the value of the common stock distributed to employees under J&J's stock compensation plan and stock option plan? Where did J&J get the shares to distribute to its employees?
3. What was the value of the convertible subordinated debentures converted into common stock during the year? Where did J&J get the shares to give to the debentureholders?
4. What was the value of the treasury stock repurchase during the year?
5. What happened to J&J's currency translation adjustment account? Did the U.S. dollar appreciate, depreciate, or remain unchanged during the year?

E11.23   **Analyzing Shareholders' Equity.**   Presented below is the Shareholders' Equity section of the consolidated balance sheet of **Pfizer Inc.** The data is taken from the company's annual report:

(in millions)	Year 2	Year 1
Convertible preferred stock (no par)	$ 169	$ 193
Common stock, $0.05 par value	439	438
Additional paid-in-capital	67,622	67,098
Employee benefit trust	(923)	(1,229)
Treasury stock, at cost	(39,767)	(35,992)
Retained earnings	37,608	35,492
Other comprehensive income	479	2,278
Total shareholders' equity	$65,627	$68,278

Based on your review of this data, develop an explanation as to why each of the account balances changed from Year 1 to Year 2.

PROBLEMS

P11.24   **Accounting for Share Transactions.**   At the beginning of the year, The Mann Corporation, a private entity, decided to go public. A charter of incorporation was constructed which authorized the sale of ten million shares of $1 par value common stock, 100,000 shares of $100 par value, eight percent preferred stock, and 200,000 shares of $5 no-par-value convertible preferred stock. The following shares were sold as part of the firm's initial public offering:

- 1,000,000 shares of common stock at $10 per share.
- 100,000 shares of $100 par value, eight percent preferred stock at $105 per share.
- 100,000 shares of $5 convertible, no-par preferred stock at $55 per share.

At year-end, the full dividend was declared and paid on both preferred stock offerings.

Required

Using a spreadsheet, record the financial effects of the shareholders' equity transactions for The Mann Corporation for the year.

P11.25   **Accounting for Share Transactions.**   The Mayfair Corporation went public on January 1, 2012, with an initial public offering of 10,000,000 common shares, $1 par value, at a market price of $3 per share. Since then, the following equity transactions had occurred:

1. In 2013, a ten percent stock dividend was issued. At the time, the Mayfair common shares were trading at $6 per share.
2. In 2014, a three-for-one forward stock split was executed. At the time, the Mayfair common shares were trading at $12 per share.
3. In 2015, 500,000 common shares were repurchased on the open market at a price of $15 per share.
4. On December 31, 2015, the company declared and paid its first cash dividend of $0.10 per share on all outstanding common shares.

Required

1. Calculate the par value per share and the number of shares outstanding for the Mayfair Corporation on December 31, 2015.
2. Prepare a spreadsheet to illustrate the financial effects of each of the above share transactions.

P11.26   **Accounting for Share Transactions.**   The shareholders' equity section of the consolidated balance sheet of **CompX International** appeared as follows at the beginning of the year:

Shareholders' Equity	
Class A common stock, $.01 par value; 20,000,000 shares authorized;	
6,100,000 shares issued	$ 61,000
Additional paid-in-capital	118,127,000
Retained earnings	14,270,000
Currency translation adjustment	(2,412,000)
Total equity	$130,046,000

The following events occurred sequentially during the year:

1. A 2-for-1 forward stock split was executed.
2. A ten percent stock dividend was distributed when the CompX share price was $20 per share.
3. Treasury stock valued at $3,000,000 was repurchased when the CompX share price was $15 per share.

Required

1. How many Class A common shares are outstanding following the above events?
2. What is the par value per share of the Class A common stock following the above events?
3. Identify the financial effects associated with the above three share transactions.
4. Calculate the total value of shareholders' equity following the above events.
5. How is the capital market likely to react to the forward stock split, the stock dividend, and the treasury stock purchase? Why?

P11.27 **Stock Dividends.** Mic Dundee, President of Aussie Steaks Inc., is contemplating issuing a stock dividend that would lower the company's share price to the $24 to $25 per share range. Aussie Steaks' share price is currently trading at $30 per share. The shareholders' equity section of Aussie Steaks' balance sheet at year-end is as follows:

Common stock ($1 par)	$ 500,000
Additional paid-in-capital	2,000,000
Retained earnings	3,100,000
Total shareholders' equity	$5,600,000

For the past several years, Aussie Steaks has paid annual cash dividends of $0.80 per share. Mic would like to maintain this level of cash dividends after the stock dividend is issued. Mic expects net income for the next few years to average $300,000 per year. Some members of Aussie Steaks' board of directors want a 20 percent stock dividend; others want a 25 percent stock dividend.

Required

1. Identify the financial effects associated with a 25 percent stock dividend.
2. Identify the financial effects associated with a 20 percent stock dividend.
3. Is there any reason why the Aussie Steaks' shareholders would prefer a small stock dividend to a large stock dividend?
4. Should Aussie Steaks declare a 20 percent stock dividend or a 25 percent stock dividend? Why?
5. What event must have occurred if the shareholders' equity section of Aussie Steaks' balance sheet at January 1of the following year was reported as follows:

Common stock ($1 par)	$1,000,000
Additional paid-in-capital	1,500,000
Retained earnings	3,100,000
Total shareholders' equity	$5,600,000

P11.28 **Convertible Preferred Stock: A Redemption.** The *Financial Times* and the *Wall Street Journal* carried a legal notice entitled "**The Thomas Regout Company** has called for the redemption of all of its €3.50 Convertible Preferred Stock." According to the notice Thomas Regout, a Dutch company, had decided to exercise the redemption feature on its outstanding preferred stock and to redeem all of the outstanding shares at a price of €52.45 per share plus accrued dividends of €0.16 per share, for a total of €52.61, on August 31. The Thomas Regout preferred stock also carried a conversion feature that would permit the owner to convert the preferred stock into 1.9608 shares of common stock (par value of €1). The market price of the common stock on August 13 was €32.625 per share. The legal notice of redemption emphasized that the conversion feature of the preferred stock expired on August 27.

Required

1. Assume that Thomas Regout has 1 million shares of preferred stock outstanding and that its par value is €5. How would the company account for (1) the redemption of all of the preferred shares and (2) the conversion of all of the preferred shares?
2. If you held 100 shares of Thomas Regout preferred stock, which alternative (conversion or redemption) would you choose, and why?
3. If you were the CEO of Thomas Regout, which alternative (conversion or redemption) would you prefer, and why?

P11.29   **Analyzing Shareholders' Equity.**   **Microsoft Corporation** is one of the world's leading developers and retailers of PC software. Presented below are excerpts from Microsoft's 2012 annual report regarding its shareholders' equity:

Shareholders' Equity Statements			
(In millions) **Year Ended June 30,**	**2012**	**2011**	**2010**
Common stock and paid-in capital			
Balance, beginning of period	$63,415	$ 62,856	$62,382
Common stock issued	1,924	2,422	2,311
Common stock repurchased	(1,714)	(3,738)	(3,113)
Stock-based compensation expense	2,244	2,166	1,891
Stock-based compensation income tax deficiencies	(75)	(292)	(647)
Other, net	3	1	32
Balance, end of period	65,797	63,415	62,856
Retained earnings (deficit)			
Balance, beginning of period	(6,332)	(16,681)	(22,824)
Net income	16,978	23,150	18,760
Other comprehensive income:			
Net unrealized gains (losses) on derivatives	255	(627)	27
Net unrealized gains (losses) on investments	(390)	1,054	265
Translation adjustments and other	(306)	381	(206)
Comprehensive income	16,537	23,958	18,846
Common stock cash dividends	(6,721)	(5,394)	(4,547)
Common stock repurchased	(2,918)	(8,215)	(8,156)
Balance, end of period	566	(6,332)	(16,681)
Total stockholders' equity	$66,363	$57,083	$46,175

Required

Prepare a list of the key events and their financial effects that impacted Microsoft's shareholders' equity in 2012. Where possible, explain why these transactions occurred. You may wish to access Microsoft's 2012 annual report at www.microsoft.com to assist you with your answer.

P11.30   **Other Comprehensive Income: Calculating the Cumulative Foreign Currency Translation Adjustment.**   Graham International Ltd., an Australian Company, is a wholly owned but financially independent operating subsidiary of its U.S.-parent company and reports its financial results in Australian dollars. As of January 1, Graham International had a balance of $(10,780) U.S. in its cumulative foreign currency translation adjustment account (see translated balance sheet). During the year, the exchange rates between the Australian and U.S. dollars were as follows:

January 1:	0.75	($1A = $0.75 U.S.)
December 31:	0.78	($1A = $0.78 U.S.)
Average for year:	0.76	

Graham International Ltd.'s balance sheet as of January 1 was as follows:

January 1	$A	Exchange Rate	$US
Assets			
Cash	$ 28,000	0.75	$ 21,000
Accounts receivable	84,000	0.75	63,000
Inventory	98,000	0.75	73,500
Property and equipment, net	476,700	0.75	357,525
Total	$686,700		$515,025
Liabilities	$434,700	0.75	$326,025
Common stock	42,000	H *	25,830
Retained earnings	210,000	H *	173,950
Translation adjustment	—		(10,780)
Total	$686,700		$515,025

*H = the historical exchange rate in effect at the time the account balance was created.

At the end of the year Graham International's income statement and balance sheet appeared as follows:

Income Statement (Australian Dollars)	
Sales.	$1,148,000
Less: Operating expenses	(781,200)
Net income before taxes	366,800
Income tax expense.	(186,200)
Net income.	$ 180,600

Balance Sheet: Year-End (Australian Dollars)	
Assets	
Cash.	$ 63,000
Accounts receivable.	103,600
Inventory.	140,000
Property and equipment, net.	462,000
Total	$768,600
Liabilities.	$336,000
Common stock.	42,000
Retained earnings	390,600
Total	$768,600

Required

1. Translate Graham International's income statement using the average exchange rate for the year.
2. Translate Graham International's year-end balance sheet using the current rate method (all assets and liabilities are translated at the end-of-year exchange rate).
3. Explain the change in Graham's cumulative foreign currency translation adjustment from $(10,780) at the beginning of the year to $392 at year-end. Why did the currency translation adjustment increase from an unrealized loss to an unrealized gain? When will this unrealized gain be realized?

P11.31 Analyzing Shareholders' Equity. Wal-Mart Stores Inc. is the world's largest retailer as measured by total revenues. As of September 2012, the company operated approximately 10,130 retail units under 69 banners in 27 countries. Wal-Mart Stores Inc. was founded in 1945 and is based in Bentonville, Arkansas. Presented below are selected parts of Wal-Mart's 2011 10-K report:

WAL-MART STORES INC. Consolidated Balance Sheet (selected)		
(in millions)	**Jan. 31, 2012**	**Jan. 31, 2011**
Equity:		
Preferred stock ($0.10 par value; 100 shares authorized, non issued).	—	—
Common stock ($0.10 par value; 11,000 shares authorized, 3,418 and 3,516 issued and outstanding at January 31, 2012 and 2011 respectively).	342	352
Capital in excess of par value.	3,692	3,577
Retained earnings.	68,691	63,967
Accumulated other comprehensive income (loss)	(1,410)	646
Total Walmart shareholder's equity.	71,315	68,542
Noncontrolling interest	4,446	2,705
Total equity	75,761	71,247

WAL-MART STORES INC.
Consolidated Statements of Stockholders' Equity

(Amounts in millions, except per share data)	Common Stock Shares	Common Stock Amount	Capital in Excess of Par Value	Retained Earnings	Accumulated Other Comprehensive Income (Loss)	Total Walmart Shareholder's Equity	Noncontrolling Interest	Total Equity
Balances—February 1, 2009	3,925	$393	$3,920	$63,344	$(2,688)	$64,969	$1,794	$66,763
Consolidated net income (excludes redeemable noncontrolling interest)	—	—	—	14,370	—	14,370	499	14,869
Other comprehensive income	—	—	—	—	2,618	2,618	64	2,682
Cash dividends ($1.09 per share).	—	—	—	(4,217)	—	(4,217)	—	(4,217)
Purchase of Company stock	(145)	(15)	(246)	(7,136)	—	(7,397)	—	(7,397)
Purchase of redeemable noncontrolling interest	—	—	(288)	—	—	(288)	—	(288)
Other.	6	—	417	(4)	—	413	(177)	236
Balances—January 31, 2010	3,786	378	3,803	66,357	(70)	70,468	2,180	72,648
Consolidated net income (excludes redeemable noncotrolling interest)	—	—	—	16,389	—	16,389	584	16,973
Other comprehensive income	—	—	—	—	716	716	162	878
Cash dividends ($1.21 per share).	—	—	—	(4,437)	—	(4,437)	—	(4,437)
Purchase of Company stock	(280)	(28)	(487)	(14,319)	—	(14,834)	—	(14,834)
Other.	10	2	261	(23)	—	240	(221)	19
Balances—January 31, 2011	3,516	352	3,577	63,967	646	68,542	2,705	71,247
Consolidated net income (excludes redeemable noncontrolling interest). . .	—	—	—	15,699	—	15,699	627	16,326
Other comprehensive loss.	—	—	—	—	(2,056)	(2,056)	(660)	(2,716)
Cash dividends ($1.46 per share)	—	—	—	(5,048)	—	(5,048)	—	(5,048)
Purchase of Company stock	(113)	(11)	(229)	(5,930)	—	(6,170)	—	(6,170)
Noncontrolling interest of acquired entity	—	—	—	—	—	—	1,988	1,988
Other	15	1	344	3	—	348	(214)	134
Balances—January 31, 2012	3,418	$342	$3,692	$68,691	$(1,410)	$71,315	$4,446	$75,761

Required

1. During fiscal year 2011, Wal-Mart repurchased some of its outstanding shares. What was the average price paid for the repurchased treasury shares?

2. Wal-Mart reports a noncontrolling interest account on its consolidated balance sheet. What does the existence of this account reveal about Wal-Mart's investments in its subsidiaries?

3. Wal-Mart uses the current rate method to account for its foreign subsidiaries. During fiscal year 2011, did the U.S. dollar appreciate, remain unchanged, or depreciate relative to the currencies of the countries in which these subsidiaries operate? Assume other comprehensive loss applies to foreign currency translation.

4. On March 4, 1999, the Company announced a two-for-one forward stock split in the form of a 100 percent stock dividend. Prior to the announcement, the company's stock price was $89 3/8 per share. What was the target share price that the company achieved with the March 1999 forward stock split?

5. On March 4, 1998, Wal-Mart's share price was $48 per share. Why did Wal-Mart split its stock in 1999?

6. How much would retained earnings change if Wal-Mart had declared a 20 percent stock dividend instead of a 100 percent stock dividend? The two-for-one stock split added 2,224 shares.

CORPORATE ANALYSIS

CA11.32 The Procter & Gamble Company.   The 2012 annual report of **The Procter & Gamble Company (P&G)** is available at http://annualreport.pg.com/annualreport2012/index.shtml. After reviewing P&G's annual report, respond to the following questions.

a.   What types of equity securities does P&G have outstanding? What is their par or stated value, how many shares are authorized, and how many shares are outstanding at year-end 2011 and 2012?

b.   What percentage of P&G's assets are debt-financed versus equity-financed in 2011 and 2012? Why do you think the company has followed this strategic financing policy? What is P&G's cost of debt in 2012?

c.   How many common shares did P&G repurchase in 2012 and at what aggregate price?

d.   How many common shares were issued in 2012 to employees under P&G's employee stock option plan? If P&G had utilized the fair value method to account for its employee stock options, what would have been the effect on P&G's basic and diluted EPS for 2012?

CA11.33 Internet-based Analysis.   Consider a publicly held company whose products you are familiar with. Some examples might include:

Company	Product	Corporate Website
• **Johnson & Johnson Company**....	• Band-Aids	• www.jnj.com
• **Microsoft Corporation**...........	• Windows XP software	• www.microsoft.com
• **Nokia Corporation**	• Cellular phones	• www.nokia.com
• **Intel Corporation**	• Pentium processors	• www.intel.com
• **Kimberly-Clark Corporation**......	• Kleenex	• www.kimberly-clark.com

Access the company's public website and search for its most recent annual report. (Some companies provide access to their financial data through an "investor relations" link, while others provide a direct link to their "annual reports.") After locating your company's most recent annual report, open the file and review its contents. After reviewing the annual report for your selected company, prepare answers to the following questions:

a.   How many common shares are authorized, issued, and outstanding? What is the par (or stated) value of the common stock? What is the company's market capitalization?

b.   Does the company have any preferred stock issued and outstanding? If so, what is its par (or stated) value and what is the amount of the annual dividend? Is the preferred stock callable, convertible, or participating?

c.   Has the company repurchased any of its common shares in the last two years? If so, how much was spent on treasury stock in each of the last two years?

d.   Does the company give stock options to its management team? If so, how many shares might be issued if all of the outstanding stock options are exercised? What would happen to the company's earnings per share if the options are exercised?

e.   Does the company pay dividends on its common stock? If so, what is the company's dividend payout ratio? What is the company's dividend yield? Is the company a "growth" company?

CA11.34 IFRS Financial Statements.   The 2012 financial statements of **LVMH Moet Hennessey-Louis Vuitton S.A.** are presented in Appendix C of this book. LVMH is a Paris-based holding company and one of the world's largest and best-known luxury goods companies. As a member-nation of the European Union, French companies are required to prepare their consolidated (group) financial statements using International Financial Reporting Standards (IFRS). After reviewing LVMH's consolidated statement of changes in equity in Appendix C, prepare answers to the following questions:

a.   LVMH lists eight equity accounts—Share capital, Share premium account, Treasury shares and LVMH-share settled derivatives, Revaluation reserves, Cumulative translation adjustment, Net profit-group share and other reserves, and Minority interests. Briefly describe each of these accounts using equivalent U.S. GAAP account titles.

b.   At year-end 2012, LVMH reports that its Revaluation reserve totaled 2,819 million euros. If LVMH used a spreadsheet based on the balance sheet equation (A = L + SE), what other account(s) would likely have been impacted by the recording of 818 million euros in the Revaluation reserve?

SOLUTION TO REVIEW PROBLEM

Solution

THE ARCADIA COMPANY					a.	b.	c.	d.	e.	e.	
	Issue Stock	Generate Revenue	Incur Expenses	EOY 1 Balance Sheet	2:1 Stock Split	Repurch. Shares	10% Stock Dividend	Cash Dividend	Generate Revenue	Incur Expenses	EOY 2 Balance Sheet
Assets											
Cash	$5,000,000	$2,000,000	$(800,000)	$6,200,000		$(150,000)		$(108,900)	$3,000,000	$(1,200,000)	$7,741,100
Total assets				6,200,000	no entry						7,741,100
					::						
Shareholders' Equity					::						
Common stock ($1 par).	500,000			500,000	reduce		$49,500[1]				549,500
Additional paid-in-capital . . .	$4,500,000			4,500,000	par		1,732,500				6,232,500
Retained earnings				1,200,000	to		$(1,782,000)[1]	$(108,900)[2]			1,109,100
Revenues		$2,000,000			$0.50				$3,000,000		
Expenses			$(800,000)		::					$(1,200,000)	
Treasury stock				—		$(150,000)					(150,000)
Total shareholders' equity . .				$6,200,000							$7,741,100

1.   990,000 outstanding shares × 10% × $0.50 par value = $49,500.   990,000 outstanding shares × 10% × $18 per share = $1,782,000.
2.   1,089,000 outstanding shares × $0.10 = $108,900.

THE ARCADIA COMPANY Partial Balance Sheet	
Shareholders' equity	
Common stock, $0.50 par value 1,099,000 shares issued; 1,089,000 shares outstanding	$ 549,500
Additional paid-in-capital	6,232,500
Retained earnings	1,109,100
Treasury stock	(150,000)
Total shareholders' equity	$7,741,100

When you complete this chapter you should be able to:

1. Construct pro forma financial statements.

2. Estimate the value of a company using the discounted cash flow approach.

3. Estimate the value of a company using the residual income approach.

4. Estimate the value of a company using price-earnings multiples.

Using Accounting Information in Equity Valuation

12

WHOLE FOODS MARKET

John Mackey, along with two other Austin, Texas, investors, decided that the natural foods industry was ready for a super-market format. In 1980 they opened the first **Whole Foods Market** with a staff of only 19 people. The company is now the world's leading retailer of natural and organic foods, with 335 stores in the U.S., Canada, and the United Kingdom. For the fiscal year ended September 30, 2012, sales reached $11.7 billion, an astounding 26 percent compounded growth rate over the prior 21 years.

Whole Foods Market is a mission driven company with a strong belief in a "virtuous circle," including the food chain, people, and the planet. The company motto is "Whole Foods, Whole People, Whole Planet." It is consistently honored for its commitment to corporate social responsibility, ranking among "The Top 50 Best Corporate Citizens" by *Business Ethics* magazine and among "The Top 10 Companies To Work For" by *Fortune* magazine.

Whole Foods Market is also customer driven. The company strives to provide a high level of customer satisfaction and believes that by "offering the highest quality food available, we are helping to transform the diet of America, helping people live longer, healthier, more pleasurable lives while responding positively to the challenge of environmental sustainability." It has been recognized consistently for these efforts, and is ranked among the most socially responsible businesses by the U.S. Environmental Protection Agency.

Whole Foods Market understands that profits are an essential ingredient if they wish to be a responsible corporate citizen and provide benefits to their many stakeholders. As the company states, profits are "the 'seed corn' for next year's crop. We are the stewards of our shareholders' investments and we are committed to increasing long-term shareholder value." The company utilizes Economic Value Added (EVA), a variation of the residual income method discussed in this chapter, to help evaluate the firm's progress in reaching this goal.

What does it mean to increase long-term shareholder value? Shareholder value is increased when the return on the shareholders' investment in a business enterprise is increased through a combination of dividend distributions and share price appreciation. To determine whether this goal is attained requires that a value be calculated as to what an enterprise is worth. In this chapter, we examine various methodologies that allow a financial statement user to estimate the value of a company like Whole Foods Market.

EXECUTIVE
OUTLINE

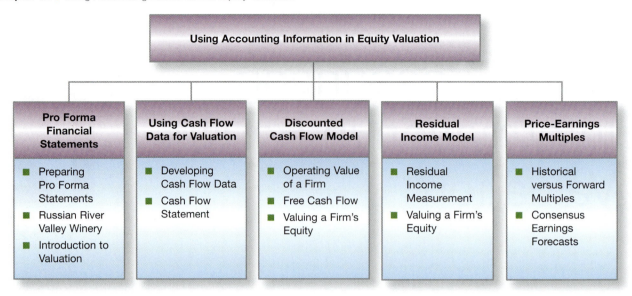

PRO FORMA FINANCIAL STATEMENTS

We first considered pro forma financial statements in Appendix 4B. At that time, we observed that investment professionals, managers, and shareholders are often interested in knowing how a firm might perform in the future under various economic scenarios. Pro forma financial statements are a good source of information to address these kinds of questions, particularly with respect to equity valuation. Indeed, a complete set of forecasted financial statements yield most inputs needed in a variety of valuation models, such as dividends, book values, earnings, and cash flows. An added advantage of pro-forma financial statements is that they necessitate consideration of all possible financial aspects of the business. Examples include the required capital structure, the cash-generating ability of the company, solvency risk assessments, and sources of growth. In this chapter, we continue our exploration of pro forma financial statements as they relate to valuing the shareholders' equity of a business. As we will soon see, pro forma statements provide the raw data to develop an assessment of the fair value of a business.[1]

To facilitate the calculations necessary to develop pro forma financial statements, we recommend utilizing an electronic spreadsheet. To illustrate the process of setting up such a spreadsheet, we again turn to the financial data of the Russian River Valley Winery, Inc. developed in Chapter 2. In Chapter 2, we prepared a forecast of the firm's first year of operations in conjunction with the winery's request for bank financing. The winery's first-year results (here assumed to be 2012) were stronger than predicted as the firm was able to sell more wine than its owners initially forecasted (sales of $1.9 million were forecasted while actual sales of $2.2 million were achieved). In addition, cost of goods sold comprised only 15 percent of sales rather than the predicted 20 percent. This positive turn of events lead to a higher than expected net income for the first year ($317,000 forecasted net income versus $521,000 actual net income). The second year of operations (2013) proved to be even better than the first, with an additional ten percent increase in sales (actual sales of $2.42 million). We now turn our attention to forecasting the next five years of performance for the winery to estimate the value of Matt's and Kate's investment in the business.

Exhibit 12.1 presents a spreadsheet summary for the winery, reflecting both its historical and forecasted financial performance. Columns two and three, for example, display the two years of actual performance data for the winery (2012 and 2013). This historical performance data, along with our knowledge of the operating environment of the winery, provides the necessary data for forecasting the winery's future financial performance. Our goal is to develop pro forma financial statements for the period 2014 through 2018.

---

[1] The term "pro forma" in Latin means "as a matter of form." In business this has come to mean financial statements prepared in advance of a planned transaction, investment, or period. The pro forma statements take the "form", therefore, of an anticipated set of results that summarize the future.

EXHIBIT 12.1	Pro Forma Financial Statements: Russian River Valley Winery, Inc.

Panel A Income Statement

	Actual		Forecast					Terminal
($ thousands)	2012	2013	2014	2015	2016	2017	2018	Year
Sales (net).	$2,200	$2,420	$2,662	$2,928	$3,221	$3,543	$3,897	$4,092
Cost of goods sold.	(330)	(363)	(399)	(439)	(483)	(531)	(585)	(614)
Gross profit.	1,870	2,057	2,263	2,489	2,738	3,012	3,312	3,478
SG&A expense	(506)	(557)	(612)	(673)	(741)	(815)	(896)	(941)
Depreciation and amortization	(275)	(275)	(275)	(275)	(275)	(275)	(275)	(289)
Interest expense	(288)	(230)	(202)	(173)	(144)	(115)	(86)	(91)
Income before income taxes	801	995	1,174	1,368	1,578	1,807	2,055	2,158*
Income taxes	(280)	(348)	(411)	(479)	(552)	(632)	(719)	(755)
Net income.	$ 521	$ 647	$ 763	$ 889	$1,026	$1,174*	$1,336	$1,403

Panel B Balance Sheet

	Actual		Forecast					Terminal
($ thousands)	2012	2013	2014	2015	2016	2017	2018	Year
Cash	$ 860	$ 726	$ 799	$ 878	$ 966	$ 1,063	$ 1,169	$ 1,228
Other current assets	1,180	968	1,065	1,171	1,288	1,417	1,559	1,637
Total current assets	2,040	1,694	1,864	2,050*	2,254	2,480	2,728	2,865
PP&E (net)	9,275	9,275	9,275	9,275	9,275	9,275	9,275	9,739
Intangibles	50	0	0	0	0	0	0	0
Total assets.	$11,365	$10,969	$11,139	$11,325	$11,529	$11,755	$12,003	$12,603*
Current debt	$ 480	$ 480	$ 480	$ 480	$ 480	$ 480	$ 480	$ 504
Other current liabilities	384	605	666	732	805	886	974	1,023
Total current liabilities	864	1,085	1,146	1,212	1,285	1,366	1,454	1,527
Long-term debt	3,840	3,360	2,880	2,400	1,920	1,440	960	1,008
Total liabilities	4,704	4,445	4,026	3,612	3,205	2,806	2,414	2,535
Paid-in-capital	6,400	6,400	6,400	6,400	6,400	6,400	6,400	6,720
Retained earnings	261	124	713	1,313	1,924	2,549	3,189	3,348
Total shareholders' equity	6,661	6,524	7,113	7,713	8,324	8,949	9,589	10,068
Total liabilities and shareholders' equity.	$11,365	$10,969	$11,139	$11,325	$11,529	$11,755	$12,003	$12,603

Panel C Statement of Retained Earnings

	Actual		Forecast					Terminal
($ thousands)	2012	2013	2014	2015	2016	2017	2018	Year
Beg. retained earnings	$ 0	$261	$124	$ 713	$1,313	$1,924	$2,549	$3,189
+ Net income	521	647	763	889	1,026	1,174	1,336	1,403
− Dividends	(260)	(784)	(174)	(289)	(414)	(549)	(696)	(1,243)
= End. retained earnings	$261	$124	$713	$1,313	$1,924*	$2,549	$3,189	$3,348*

*minor rounding difference

continued next page

To begin, the single most important assumption when developing pro forma financial statements is the forecast of future sales revenue. The forecasting process begins with projected sales because, as you might expect, future assets and liabilities frequently arise directly from the revenue activities of a firm. A number of income statement costs follow directly from the sales activity forecasted as well. Recurring costs—such as cost of goods sold and selling, general, and administrative expenses (SG&A)—are usually incurred to generate sales, and thus are typically some reasonable function of predicted sales. Because so many of the income statement and balance sheet accounts are dependent on a firm's future sales, a poor forecast with this line item is very likely to result in a poorly constructed set of pro forma financial statements, and hence, an incorrect estimate of firm value. Consequently, it is essential to utilize whatever data may be available, such as a firm's prior operating history, the expected demand for new products, demographic trends, and inflation to make the sales forecast as accurate as possible.

continued from previous page

EXHIBIT 12.1	Pro Forma Financial Statements: Russian River Valley Winery, Inc.

Panel D Statement of Cash Flow

($ thousands)	Actual		Forecast					Terminal
	2012	2013	2014	2015	2016	2017	2018	Year
Operating activities								
Net income.	$ 521	$ 647	$ 763	$ 889	$1,026	$1,174	$1,336	$1,403
+ Depreciation and amortization	275	275	275	275	275	275	275	289
− Increase in other current assets	(1,180)	212	(97)	(106)	(117)	(129)	(142)	(78)
+ Increase in other current liabilities.	384	221	61	66	73	81	88	49
= Cash from operations	(0)	1,355	1,002	1,124	1,257	1,401	1,557	1,663
Investing activities								
− Capital expenditures.	(9,550)	(225)	(275)	(275)	(275)	(275)	(275)	(753)
− Purchases of intangibles.	(50)	0	0	0	0	0	0	0
= Cash from investing	(9,600)	(225)	(275)	(275)	(275)	(275)	(275)	(753)
Financing activities								
+ Increase in debt.	4,320	(480)	(480)	(480)	(480)	(480)	(480)	72
− Dividends	(260)	(784)	(174)	(289)	(414)	(549)	(696)	(1,243)
Issuance of common stock	6,400	0	0	0	0	0	0	320
= Cash from financing	10,460	(1,264)	(654)	(769)	(894)	(1,029)	(1,176)	(851)
Change in cash.	$ 860	$ (134)	$ 73	$ 80	$ 88	$ 97	$ 106	$ 59
+ Beg. cash	0	860	726	799	878	966	1,063	1,169
Ending cash balance	$ 860	$ 726	$ 799	$ 878*	$ 966	$1,063	$1,169	$1,228

*minor rounding difference

The process of preparing pro forma financial statements typically progresses with the following set of steps:

1. Forecast sales revenue.
2. Forecast the cost of goods sold, gross profit, and other operating expenses on the income statement as a function of forecasted sales, using the historical common-size percentages for those accounts (as a percentage of sales) where a linear relationship with sales is evident.
3. Forecast the balance sheet working capital accounts such as cash, accounts receivable, inventory, and accounts payable needed to support the forecasted sales, using such historical relationships as revealed by the receivable, inventory, and payable turnover ratios.
4. Forecast the property, plant and equipment and intangible assets needed to support the forecasted level of sales, using such historical relationships as revealed by the fixed asset turnover and intangible asset turnover ratios.
5. Forecast depreciation and amortization expense as a function of forecasted property, plant, and equipment and intangible assets. (Investment professionals frequently adopt a half-year convention when forecasting the depreciation and amortization expense associated with these capital investments to compensate for the uncertainty regarding the timing of such investments.)
6. Forecast the level of debt financing based on such strategic factors as the desired capital structure and the forecasted growth in sales.
7. Forecast interest expense based on the level of forecasted debt.
8. Forecast any remaining items on the income statement (e.g., investment income and non-recurring items) and then forecast the income tax expense based on forecasted earnings before tax and the firm's effective tax rate.
9. Forecast the statement of retained earnings based on the forecasted income statement, including any expected dividend payments.
10. Prepare the pro forma statement of cash flow from the forecasted income statement and forecasted balance sheets using the indirect method (see Chapter 3).

11. Determine a **terminal year growth rate** for the pro forma terminal year. Practically speaking, it is unreasonable to continue to forecast indefinitely. The terminal year is the year following the final forecast period (2018 for the Russian River Valley Winery) wherein it is assumed that the firm has reached a steady state and constant growth will persist in perpetuity. More on the terminal year a bit later.

The above steps illustrate one approach to preparing pro forma financial statements. Other approaches also exist. For example, while accounts receivable, inventory, and accounts payable may be forecasted based on their respective turnover ratios, some investment professionals instead use the historical common-size balance sheet percentages to forecast these operating assets. And, some will use a combination of ratios and common-size percentages to develop their pro forma estimates. As a consequence of the alternative approaches that may be used to forecast the individual balance sheet accounts, it is not unusual for a pro forma balance sheet to be out-of-balance. When this occurs, it is common to create a plug figure to achieve the necessary equality demanded by the balance sheet equation. Possible plug figures include cash and marketable securities when a plug figure is needed to balance the asset side of the balance sheet, and short-term debt or a line of credit when a plug figure is needed to balance the liability side of the balance sheet.[2]

Exhibit 12.2 presents the various assumptions that were used to construct the pro forma financial statements for the Russian River Valley Winery that appear in the forecast columns (2014 through 2018) of Exhibit 12.1. As detailed in Exhibit 12.2, the following assumptions were utilized:

- Sales are expected to grow by ten percent per year for five years and by five percent annually thereafter. As mentioned above, in practice a number of economic, industry and company specific factors would need to be evaluated to determine the appropriate level of expected sales.

- Cost of goods sold will remain a constant fifteen percent of sales. This assumption equates to an expected 85% gross margin. As cost of sales relates directly to the purchase and distribution of wine products, any changes in expected margins should be considered and included in the forecast.

- Selling, general, and administrative (SG&A) expenses will remain a constant 23 percent of sales. Without any information to the contrary, the historical relation between these costs and sales is a reasonable approximation. The forecaster should be careful to incorporate any known fixed costs into the assumed relation if known. That is, if for example $0.5 million of Russian River Valley Winery's SG&A related to management salary and were known beforehand to be fixed, then the forecast should include a smaller percentage of SG&A that would be predicted to vary with the level of sales. The $0.5 million would be treated as a constant fixed cost.

- Since Russian River Valley Winery has sufficient capacity to produce enough wine to satisfy projected sales for the next five years without any new capital investment, PP&E is expected to remain constant for the next five years. As a consequence, depreciation will remain constant at the 2013 level. In practice, any known additional PP&E required to support a level of sales would be included in the forecast. The only capital outlay in the present case will be an amount equal to the annual depreciation expense.

- Interest expense will be six percent of the outstanding beginning-of-year balance of bank debt. This rate should always be the assumed borrowing rate required for the level of bank debt carried by the company.

- Income taxes will be 35 percent of earnings before income taxes. This is typical of most tax rate assumptions, as 35 percent is the base U.S. corporate tax rate (see Chapter 10). To the extent the winery does business and earns profits in other tax jurisdictions (e.g., internationally, or within certain states), then these different tax rates should be what drive the tax rate assumption used in the forecast.

- Cash will be maintained at thirty percent of sales. Companies typically require a certain level of liquidity, and as the company grows, so often also does the cash balance.

---

[2] Care must be taken, however, when choosing a plug figure account as there are many interdependencies in the financial statements. For example, if debt is used as a plug figure to balance the liability side of the balance sheet, then interest expense on the income statement will need to be recomputed each time that the level of debt changes. This will alter net income, and therefore retained earnings, forcing another change to debt. While such situations can be resolved with more advanced mathematical techniques, it is often easier to use an account that has fewer dependencies (such as cash). It is also possible to solve these "circular reference" situations with the iteration function within Excel.

- Other current assets will be maintained at forty percent of sales, and other current liabilities will remain a constant 25 percent of sales. As is often the case with cash, a required level of working capital is often needed to support ongoing sales.

- The current debt will continue to be paid down at a constant rate ($480,000 per year) for five years. After 2018, debt will grow at a rate equal to sales growth. The forecast should always include any known reductions in debt, as well as new borrowings.

- Dividend payments are forecasted as a plug figure to balance retained earnings on the balance sheet. Dividends here are considered a discretionary cash outlay after the other remaining needs of the business have been satisfied. This assumption also helps serve as the final balancing amount for the balance sheet.

The spreadsheet summary in Exhibit 12.1 reveals that based upon the above set of assumptions, the Russian River Valley Winery will likely have both increasing profits and increasing cash flow from operations throughout the forecast period and beyond. Therefore, our assumptions regarding the need for debt and continuing dividend payments appear reasonable. One advantage of the electronic spreadsheet approach is that it is possible to conduct "what if" analyses—that is, to evaluate how the winery's financial performance would be affected if, for instance, sales growth is reduced to, say, five percent or if gross profit percentages are increased to reflect the realization of economies of scale that come with greater levels of output. In the next section, we will see how the pro forma financial statements can be used to help assess the equity value of a firm.

EXHIBIT 12.2	Pro Forma Assumptions used for Russian River Valley Winery
Item	**Assumption**
Sales.	Grows annually at 10% until terminal year
Cost of goods sold.	15% of sales
SG&A expense.	23% of sales
Depreciation.	Constant until terminal year
Interest expense.	6% of outstanding debt
Income taxes	35% of earnings before taxes
Cash.	30% of sales
Other current assets.	40% of sales
PP&E	Constant net PP&E until terminal year
Debt	Constant payments of $480 until terminal year
Other current liabilities	25% of sales
Dividends	Plug figure to balance the balance sheet
All items	Terminal 5% annual growth

Introduction to Equity Valuation

How much is the Russian River Valley Winery worth? Recall from Chapter 2 that Matt and Kate sold 200,000 shares of the winery's common stock to an outside investor for $2 per share. How could that outside investor determine if this was a reasonable price to pay for the Russian River Valley Winery shares? An important role for accounting information is its use in valuing a business. To answer the question of what a share of stock in the Russian River Valley Winery is worth, it is first necessary to select a valuation framework to estimate the company's value. There are several valuation models that are widely used. If done correctly and under the same set of forecasting assumptions, each model will yield an identical estimate of firm value since they are based on the same fundamental theory of economic risk and reward. Which model is used is usually determined by individual investor preference, or practical considerations such as data availability.

The two models that we will illustrate are the discounted cash flow model, which is based on a firm's free cash flow, and the residual income model, which is based on a firm's accrual-based earnings. We also explore the popular price-earnings multiple model—a model whose popularity can be traced to its ease of use and ease in understanding.

USING CASH FLOW DATA TO VALUE A COMPANY

A fundamental tenet of modern financial theory is that the value of an asset or a bundle of assets (such as an entire company), is equal to the present value of the future cash flows that accrue from ownership. Thus, this tenet suggests that the primary source of firm value is a firm's operating cash flows that are not required to reinvest back into the company to keep it viable and growing. This excess cash flow is the lifeblood of the valuation process. Hence, the first task that investment professionals, equity investors, and managers face when trying to value a company is to forecast a firm's future cash flows freely available to distribute back to the owners, using pro forma financial statements, and to then value those projected future cash flows into today's dollar equivalent using an appropriate discount rate. This valuation framework is called the **discounted cash flow approach**.

Developing Cash Flow Data

Use of the discounted cash flow approach to firm valuation assumes an understanding of, and capability of, developing cash flow data. As indicated above, pro forma cash flow data is extracted from the pro forma income statements and balance sheets using the indirect method format. In Chapter 3, we illustrated a five-step process for preparing a statement of cash flow using the indirect method. That illustration was, of necessity, highly simplistic. We now return to that five-step process and consider a more sophisticated cash flow example that integrates some of the accounting measurement concepts and approaches discussed in Chapters 5 through 11. Specifically, we now consider how the accounting for zero-coupon bonds (Chapter 9), the use of the equity method to account for unconsolidated affiliates, joint ventures or special purpose entities (Chapter 8), and the accounting for a gain or loss on the sale or retirement of a long-lived asset (Chapter 7) affect the cash flow of a business.

Our illustration for this purpose involves the Arctic Sea Oil & Gas Company Ltd., a Canadian energy company. Financial information for the company for 2012 and 2013 is presented in Panels A and B of Exhibit 12.3. As discussed in Chapter 3, the five-step process to prepare a statement of cash flow using the indirect method format is as follows:

1. Measure the change in all balance sheet accounts by subtracting the beginning balance from the ending balance. Recall that the increase or decrease in the cash and cash equivalents account is the check figure for the cash flow statement.

2. Classify each of the balance sheet accounts into one of the three cash flow activity categories: Operating, Investing, or Financing.

3. Prepare a *preliminary* statement of cash flow using the values from Step 1 and the activity classifications from Step 2. Remember that the signs of the changes of the asset accounts are reversed, but the signs of the changes of the liability and shareholders' equity accounts are not.

4. Integrate the income statement data (such as depreciation and amortization expense) into the preliminary statement of cash flow, remembering that it is necessary to always balance to the change in cash.

5. Make any necessary refinements to the cash flow from operations (CFFO) to identify the sustainable operating cash flow of the business by removing any nonrecurring, nonoperating gains or losses.

Panel A of Exhibit 12.3 presents the results of Steps 1 and 2 of our five-step process; and, Panel C presents the results of Step 3—Arctic's preliminary statement of cash flow using only the company's balance sheet data. As required, Arctic's preliminary statement of cash flow balances to the change in cash on Arctic's balance sheet of negative $10.183 million. Can you replicate Arctic's preliminary statement of cash flow in Panel C using the data from Panel A of Exhibit 12.3?

Step 4 involves the introduction of Arctic's income statement data presented in Panel B of Exhibit 12.3. The adjustments (in thousands) to the preliminary statement of cash flow required at this step include the following:

1. Replace Arctic's change in retained earnings of $22,668 with net income of $46,168 in the operating activities section. The difference of $23,500 ($46,168 – $22,668) is also shown as a cash outflow for dividends paid to shareholders in the financing activities section.

2. Depreciation and depletion expense of $24,800, a noncash expense, is added back to accrual net income in the operating activities section and also subtracted from the change in the oil and gas properties (net) in the investing activities section.

3. Amortization expense of $750, a noncash expense, is added back to accrual net income in the operating activities section and subtracted from the change in intangible assets in the investing activities section.

4. Zero-coupon interest expense of $4,757, a noncash expense, is added back to accrual net income in the operating activities section and subtracted from the change in zero-coupon debenture issuance in the financing activities section.

5. The equity in the earnings of unconsolidated affiliates of $36,650, representing Arctic's ownership interest in the earnings of its affiliates that it does not control (and thus which remain unconsolidated), is subtracted from accrual net income in the operating activities section and added to the change in the Investment in Affiliated Companies in the investing activities section.

6. The gain on the sale of property and equipment of $1,000, a nonrecurring and nonoperating event, is subtracted from net income in the operating activities section and added to the change in oil and gas properties (net) in the investing activities section.

EXHIBIT 12.3	Financial Data: Arctic Sea Oil & Gas Company Ltd.				
Panel A Consolidated Balance Sheet (in thousands)		**2013**	**2012**	**Change**	**Category**
Assets					
Current assets					
Cash..		$100,067	$110,250	$ (10,183)	Check Fig.
Accounts receivable..........................		69,100	53,200	15,900	O
Inventory		58,950	46,800	12,150	O
Prepaid expenses		11,108	13,850	(2,742)	O
		239,225	224,100		
Investments					
In affiliated companies........................		159,000	151,000	8,000	I
Marketable equity securities		2,500	0	2,500	I
Long-term assets					
Oil & Gas properties, equipment (net)		237,850	246,900	(9,050)	I/O
Intangible assets		3,000	3,750	(750)	I/O
Total assets.................................		$641,575	$625,750	$ 15,825	
Liabilities and Shareholders' Equity					
Current liabilities					
Accounts payable		$ 1,650	$ 8,000	$ (6,350)	O
Income taxes payable		4,750	3,250	1,500	O
Long-term liabilities					
Zero-coupon debentures.......................		53,507	0	53,507	F
Deferred income taxes........................		46,000	40,000	6,000	O
Employee retirement benefits		62,500	60,000	2,500	O
Total liabilities..............................		168,407	111,250		
Shareholders' equity					
Common shares at par		103,000	75,000	28,000	F
Capital in excess of par.......................		157,500	150,000	7,500	F
Preferred shares, no par		0	100,000	(100,000)	F
Retained earnings		212,168	189,500	22,668	O/F
Other comprehensive income Unrealized gain on available-for-sale securities		500	0	500	I
Total liabilities and shareholders' equity................		$641,575	$625,750	$ 15,825	

continued

continued from previous page

EXHIBIT 12.3	Financial Data: Arctic Sea Oil & Gas Company Ltd.

Panel B Consolidated Income Statements

(in thousands)	2013
Revenue	$483,135
Costs and expenses	
Cost of goods sold	345,920
Depreciation and depletion expense	24,800
Selling and general expenses	54,215
Amortization expense	750
Operating income	57,450
Other (expense) income	
Interest expense	(4,757)
Equity in earnings of unconsolidated affiliates	36,650
Gain on sale of property and equipment	1,000
Income before income taxes	90,343
Less: Income tax provision	(44,175)
Net income	$ 46,168

Panel C Preliminary Statement of Cash Flow

(in thousands)	2013
Operating activities	
Retained earnings	$ 22,668
Accounts receivable	(15,900)
Inventory	(12,150)
Prepaid expenses	2,742
Accounts payable	(6,350)
Income tax payable	1,500
Deferred income taxes	6,000
Employee retirement benefits	2,500
Cash flow from operations	1,010
Investing activities	
Investment in affiliated companies	(8,000)
Marketable equity securities	(2,500)
Unrealized gain on long-term marketable securities	500
Oil and gas properties, equipment (net)	9,050
Intangible assets	750
Cash flow for investing	(200)
Financing activities	
Zero-coupon debenture issuance	53,507
Common stock issuance	35,500
Preferred share retirement	(100,000)
Cash flow for financing	(10,993)
Change in cash	(10,183)
Beginning cash	110,250
Ending cash	$100,067

Following the set of six adjustments, it is now possible to develop Arctic's final statement of cash flow using the indirect method format, and this final statement is presented in Exhibit 12.4. Arctic's statement of cash flow in Exhibit 12.4 reveals that the company's cash flow from operations is $17.167 million, its cash flow from investing is $11.9 million, and its cash flow for financing is negative $39.25 million, aggregating to a decrease in cash of $10.183 million. Now that you have a more complete understanding of how to construct a complex statement of cash flow, let's consider how this data can be used to value a company using the discounted cash flow approach.

EXHIBIT 12.4	Statement of Cash Flow: Arctic Sea Oil & Gas Company Ltd.

Consolidated Statement of Cash Flow

(in thousands)	2013
Operating activities	
Net income	$ 46,168
Accounts receivable	(15,900)
Inventory	(12,150)
Prepaid expenses	2,742
Accounts payable	(6,350)
Income tax payable	1,500
Deferred income taxes	6,000
Employee retirement benefits	2,500
Depreciation and depletion expense	24,800
Amortization expense	750
Zero-coupon interest expense	4,757
Equity in earnings of unconsolidated affiliates	(36,650)
Gain on sale of property and equipment	(1,000)
Cash flow from operations	17,167
Investing activities	
Investment in affiliated companies	28,650
Marketable equity securities	(2,000)
Oil and gas properties, equipment (net)	(14,750)
Cash flow for investing	11,900
Financing activities	
Zero-coupon debenture issuance	48,750
Common stock issuance	35,500
Preferred share retirement	(100,000)
Dividend paid	(23,500)
Cash flow for financing	(39,250)
Change in cash	(10,183)
Beginning cash	110,250
Ending cash	$100,067

VALUATION USING THE DISCOUNTED CASH FLOW MODEL

The Operating Value of a Firm

One of the well-documented limitations of humans is an inability to forecast the future. Meteorologists routinely forecast the temperature and weather conditions for days, and sometimes even weeks in advance with considerable accuracy; but, they rarely attempt to forecast weather conditions years in advance because they lack the skill to do so. This same situation confronts financial analysts, investment professionals, and managers as they try to estimate the value of a business. Since firm value depends on events that will occur well into the future, it is necessary to forecast the unknown, or at least some part of the unknown.

In general, most investment professionals and managers feel comfortable forecasting a firm's performance for the coming year, at least for most industries. But, that confidence quickly erodes as they attempt to forecast beyond one or two years. Fortunately, as a consequence of the discounting process, the value of near-term forecasts is far more important when assessing firm value than are longer-term forecasts (since the value of $1 in one year is considerably greater than the value of $1 in ten years).

Because of our inability to accurately forecast far into the future, we dichotomize a company's future into two time periods—a specific forecast period (the pro forma statement preparation period) and the period thereafter. The pro forma forecast period is that period of time for which investment professionals, managers and shareholders feel confident in their ability to prepare specific pro forma financial statements, and thereafter is all periods in which they feel unable to do so. Using this simple dichotomy, we define the **operating value** of a business as follows:

$$\begin{array}{ccc} \textbf{Operating Value} & \textbf{Present Value of Operating Cash Flows} & \textbf{Present Value of Operating} \\ \textbf{of a Business} = & \textbf{During the Specific Forecast Period} + & \textbf{Cash Flows Thereafter} \end{array}$$

The second component of operating value is commonly referred to as the **continuing value** of a business, or alternatively, as its **terminal value** (TV). It is the value of a business from the end of the specific forecast period (the pro forma statement preparation period) until the business is sold or otherwise terminated. Thus, we can refine the definition of firm operating value as follows:

$$\begin{array}{ccc} \textbf{Operating Value} & \textbf{Present Value of Operating Cash Flows} & \textbf{Present Value of} \\ \textbf{of a Business} = & \textbf{During the Specific Forecast Period} + & \textbf{a Firm's TV} \end{array}$$

We will have more to say about computing terminal values shortly.

Free Cash Flow

As noted earlier, the primary source of a firm's value is its **operating cash flow**—that is, the cash generated from its sustainable, recurring operations. There are two approaches to discounting the operating cash flow to value a company. One approach is to utilize a measure of the cash flow to all capital providers, both creditors and equity investors. This approach leads to a value for the entire enterprise. To obtain a value for just the equity of a business—that is, the value of a business's common shares—it is necessary to obtain a separate value for the firm's debt (as discussed in Chapter 9). The value of a firm's debt is then subtracted from the enterprise's total value to yield its equity value.[3] In this chapter, we illustrate a second discounted cash flow approach that is used to directly value the equity of a firm.

To be a going concern, a business must constantly reinvest in itself, replacing those assets consumed by its operations each period. As discussed in Chapter 3, a firm's **free cash flow** (FCF) is defined as the cash flow from operations (CFFO) available to capital contributors (debtholders and shareholders) less the capital expenditures necessary to enable a firm to maintain itself as a going concern (to replace or replenish any assets consumed).[4] A variant of a firm's FCF is its **free cash flow to equity**, which is nothing more than the net cash distributions to common shareholders.[5] Free cash flow to equity can be measured in multiple ways; however, all definitions are equivalent and must yield the same result. Exhibit 12.5 illustrates the computation of free cash flow to equity for the Russian River Valley Winery utilizing the financial statement data from Exhibit 12.1.[6]

The first definition of free cash flow to equity in Panel A is perhaps the simplest and most straightforward. It merely looks to the financing section of the statement of cash flow and identifies the two items that are cash flow transactions involving the common shareholders. For the Russian River Valley Winery in 2014, projected dividend payments are $174,000, but there are no other forecasted cash flows to or from shareholders, such as no sales or repurchases of common shares. Therefore, the free cash flow to equity is $174,000.

The second definition of free cash flow to equity, illustrated in Panel B of Exhibit 12.5, uses the statement of cash flow and backs into the amount of cash flow to equity by removing all other cash flows. This definition starts with the CFFO and subtracts any increase in the cash account (if the cash account increased, this would suggest that the cash was not paid to shareholders). Next, any cash from investing is added if it is positive and subtracted if it is negative. Finally, any cash received from borrowings is added and any cash paid to a firm's creditors is subtracted. What remains is the free cash flow to equity since the cash retained by the firm, used to purchase assets, or used to retire debt has been removed. For the Russian River Valley Winery in 2014, projected cash flow from operations is $1,002,000; however, the company retained $73,000 of this amount. From this net cash of $929,000 ($1,002,000 − $73,000), $275,000 was invested in long-term assets and $480,000 was used to retire debt, yielding a cash flow to equity of $174,000 ($929,000 − $480,000 − $275,000).

---

[3] For an example of this first approach, see the News Corp. Business Perspective illustration on pages 422–423.
[4] Recall from Chapter 3 that we defined a firm's free cash flows (FCF) as: FCF = CFFO – Capital expenditures.
[5] We will refer to free cash flow to common equity as simply "free cash flow to equity" under the assumption that a firm does not have any preferred shareholders.
[6] Valuation computations for the Russian River Valley Winery were done with the aid of the spreadsheet program eVal. See Russel Lundholm and Richard Sloan, *Equity Valuation and Analysis with eVal*. McGraw-Hill, 2004.

| EXHIBIT 12.5 | Free Cash Flow to Equity Computation: Russian River Valley Winery | | | | | |

Year of Forecast (in 000's) Panel A	2014	2015	2016	2017	2018	Terminal Year
Financing flows						
Dividends paid........................	$ 174	$ 289	$ 414	$ 549	$ 696	$1,243
− Net issuance of common stock...........	0	0	0	0	0	(320)
Free cash flow to equity	**$ 174**	**$ 289**	**$ 414**	**$ 549**	**$ 696**	**$ 923**
Panel B						
Cash flow from operations.................	$1,002	$1,124	$1,257	$1,401	$1,557	$1,663
− Increase in operating cash..............	(73)	(80)	(88)	(97)	(106)	(59)
+ Cash from investing....................	(275)	(275)	(275)	(275)	(275)	(753)
+ Increase in debt......................	(480)	(480)	(480)	(480)	(480)	72
Free cash flow to equity	**$ 174**	**$ 289**	**$ 414**	**$ 549**	**$ 696**	**$ 923**
Panel C						
Net income............................	$ 763	$ 889	$1,026	$1,174	$1,336	$1,403
− Increase in common equity	(589)	(600)	(611)	(625)	(640)	(479)
Free cash flow to equity	**$ 174**	**$ 289**	**$ 414***	**$ 549**	**$ 696**	**$ 923**

* rounding error

The final definition of free cash flow to equity uses only the income statement and the balance sheet. As noted in Panel C, the free cash flow to equity is simply net income less any increase in common shareholders' equity. For the Russian River Valley Winery in 2014, projected net income is $763,000 and the only change in common equity is an increase of $589,000 in retained earnings. Therefore, the free cash flow to equity is again computed to be $174,000 ($763,000 − $589,000).

Russian River Valley's free cash flows for years 2015 through 2018, along with the terminal year forecast, are calculated in a similar fashion and are presented in Exhibit 12.5. Having determined the free cash flow to equity for the winery, we now turn to the valuation of the firm's equity.

Valuing a Firm's Equity

The first step in valuing any asset, such as a piece of equipment or a whole company, is to realize that the payoffs received from ownership of the asset are worth less the longer it takes to receive the payoffs. This economic fact is referred to as the time value of money. (See Appendix A at the end of this book for a discussion of the time value of money.) In essence, $1 received in ten years is worth much less than $1 received immediately. In fact, $1 received in ten years would be worth only $0.39 if you could earn ten percent per year by putting your money in an investment elsewhere. Thus, if you were offered a deal in which you had to pay a sum of money today to receive $1 in ten years, the most you should be willing to pay is $0.39. The value today—$0.39—is called the present value of $1 to be received in ten years with a rate of return of ten percent per year. The ten percent per year is the opportunity cost or required rate of return on your investment. The opportunity cost is also known as the **discount rate** for the investment.

Financial theory postulates that the value of any financial asset is simply the sum of the future cash flows to be received from the asset, discounted at an appropriate risk-adjusted rate. In Chapter 9, we saw that the value of a bond could be calculated by discounting each of the future interest payments along with the final principal payment. While the same definition applies to the valuation of a firm's equity, several factors make the calculation more complex. The first complexity involves the degree of uncertainty associated with the future cash flows. We incorporate this uncertainty into our valuation analysis through the use of a discount rate based on the firm's cost of equity capital, an amount that is commonly several percentage points greater than a firm's cost of debt.

A widely accepted tenet of modern financial theory is that the appropriate rate to discount a stream of cash is that rate which best reflects the riskiness of the flows. In the case of a business's free cash flow to equity, since the cash flows are net of the interest expense paid to debtholders, the valuation model discounts these payoffs—that is, finds their present value—at the rate of return required by the firm's shareholders, or what is commonly referred to as the firm's **cost of common equity** (r_e). This topic is covered extensively in basic finance courses but the idea is simple. Finance professionals use the **capital asset pricing model** (CAPM) to establish the point that there is a linear relationship between a company's risk (β) and the expected return required by equity investors (r_e). The model says that if investors can earn the risk-free rate of return (r_f) by investing in government securities, the expected return on a risky investment should be the risk-free (r_f) rate *plus* a risk premium that is proportional to the company's risk. That is, $r_e = r_f + \beta*$risk premium, where β is the company's **beta**. (See Appendix C to Chapter 4 for additional information on CAPM.)

> Beta is a measure of the historical volatility of a company's share price relative to the capital market as a whole. Betas can be found in Standard & Poor's publications, Yahoo!Finance, or in ValueLine publications, among others.

To facilitate our illustration, assume that: (1) the beta for the Russian River Valley Winery is 0.8, compared to 1.0 for the U.S. stock market as a whole (such as the Standard & Poor's 500 index); (2) the yield rate on ten-year U.S. Treasury Bonds, a long-term risk-free rate of interest, is 2.8 percent; and (3) the historical risk premium of 9.0 percent is estimated as the average difference between the annual returns on U.S. Treasury Bonds and an index of common stocks over a long period of time. (The calculation of an appropriate risk premium is a hotly debated topic in financial circles; a full discussion of this issue is beyond the scope of this book.) Under these assumptions, the cost of equity (r_e) for the Russian River Valley Winery is 10.0 percent (2.8% + 0.8*9.0%).

The second complexity involves the timing and duration of the future cash flows associated with a business. When finding the value of a bond in Chapter 9, we knew when and for how long the various cash flows associated with the bond would be received. The same cannot be said for a firm's equity. In fact, we assume in most cases that a firm will continue indefinitely. Since the value of the equity requires us to discount to the present all future cash flows, we are presented with a dilemma. Fortunately, there is an accepted shortcut that allows us to forecast a relatively small number of years (such as five years for Russian River Valley Winery) and then create a terminal year forecast to reflect the cash flows for all years thereafter.

Because we assume that a business is a going concern, the terminal value is an aggregate measure of a business's free cash flows for all periods beyond the specific forecast period; it is a proxy measure for the future free cash flow of a business that an analyst is unable to forecast on a period-by-period basis using pro forma financial statements. As a practical matter, the longer the forecast period, the smaller will be the terminal value (TV). For short forecast periods (such as five years for the Russian River Valley Winery), the TV may constitute the majority of a business's total operating value.

A widely used approach to estimate a firm's TV is the **perpetuity growth formula**. Under the perpetuity growth formula, a business is assumed to grow at some constant annual rate, g, in perpetuity. Since g is likely to be unknown, it is common practice to set g equal to the expected rate of inflation. Under this formula, a firm's TV is estimated as follows:

$$TV = FCF/(r_e - g)$$

where FCF is the firm's free cash flow to equity in the terminal year and r_e is the firm's cost of equity capital, which can be calculated using the CAPM.

Valuing the Russian River Valley Winery Shares

Exhibit 12.6 presents a discounted cash flow analysis of the Russian River Valley Winery's operating cash flow assuming a five-year forecast horizon. The free cash flow to equity values were obtained from Exhibit 12.5. Each of these cash flows for the five-year forecast horizon is discounted to the present using the firm's ten percent cost of equity. The sum of these present values is shown to be $1.516 million.

EXHIBIT 12.6	Discounted Cash Flow Valuation of Russian River Valley Winery						
Year of Forecast (in 000's)		2014	2015	2016	2017	2018	Terminal Year
Free cash flow to common equity		$ 174	$289	$414	$549	$696	$923
Present value of FCF		158	239	311	375	432	
Present value of first 5 years		$ 1,516*					
Present value beyond 5 years		$11,463					
Value attributable to common equity		$12,979					
÷ Common shares outstanding...............		6,200					
= **Forecast price per share**		**$ 2.09**					

* rounding error

The terminal year FCF of $923,000 produces a terminal value of $18.460 million ($923,000/0.05) using the perpetuity growth formula and assuming a growth rate of five percent and a cost of equity of ten percent. This value, discounted back to the present, equals $11.463 million.

$$PV(TV) = \frac{FCF}{(r_e - g)}/(1 + 0.10)^5$$

$$= \frac{\$923}{(0.10 - 0.05)}/(1 + 0.10)^5$$

$$= \$18,460/(1 + 0.10)^5$$

$$= \$11,463$$

The $12.979 million value of Russian River Valley equity is the sum of these two amounts ($1.516 million + $11.463 million), or $2.09 per share when divided by the 6.2 million shares outstanding. Obviously, this value is highly dependent on the reasonableness of the assumptions that were used to build the winery's pro forma financial statements in Exhibit 12.1. An error in any of the key assumptions, such as the growth rate of revenue, could result in a material error in the discounted cash flow estimate of firm value. Thus, considerable effort should be expended developing reasonable assumptions, and hence, generating reliable pro forma data.

In the next section, an accounting-based valuation model, the residual income (RI) model, is illustrated. This model uses accounting variables that are found in a company's basic financial statements to assess firm value. Following a discussion of RI valuation, valuation using price-earnings multiples is considered.

BUSINESS PERSPECTIVE

Needham and Company Valuation of News Corp.

As we have described throughout this chapter, investors can use many different models in their valuation of a company. Analysts on Wall Street are no exception, and frequently in their research reports on a company's stock they will present more than one approach to support their buy, sell or hold recommendation. This is part of the analyst's due diligence, but it also serves to reassure potential investors that their quantitative analysis was not dependent on a single selected valuation approach. As an illustrative example of the application of discounted cash flow, Laura Martin prepared a report on June 27, 2012 recommending the purchase of News Corp. Martin is Managing Director and Senior Analyst at **Needham and Company**, an investment bank and asset management firm headquartered in New York City. **News Corp.** (ticker NWSA) is a diversified mass media company controlled by Rupert Murdoch. The company owns a number of popular U.S. media outlets such as *Fox News*, *The Wall Street Journal*, and *Twentieth Century Fox*. In 2011, Murdoch and his company received much unwanted press when staff at the *News of the World* (in Great Britain) were charged with hacking the phones and voicemails of private citizens. After the ensuing scandal News Corp. stock languished for about a year.

Laura Martin's June 2012 research report and recommendation were driven by new information that News Corp. would be spinning off its publishing net assets into a separate entity. Martin placed a "Buy" recommendation on the stock, citing (i) how the spinoff would create $5 per share of additional value,

continued

continued from previous page

BUSINESS PERSPECTIVE

(ii) how the spinoff would simplify the company, and (iii) how projections for earnings were already just too low. Below are two excerpts from Martin's 20 page research report. The first is from the opening page, specifying the overall research conclusion and key quantitative facts. She provides her main conclusions, the "Buy" recommendation, and a $27.00 price target relative to a current value of only $21.76 per share.

News Corporation (NWSA) - Buy
NWSA: Upgrading to Buy with Target Price of $27

Rating Change

We are upgrading NWSA based on the following analytical building blocks:

➤ A potential spin-off would add more than $5/share of value to NWSA, in our view.
➤ We believe that NWSA earnings estimates are too low for FY13 owing to higher affiliate fees tied to recent negotiations. We are introducing a FY13E EPS estimate of $1.72, above consensus.
➤ Over the past year NWSA has been aggressively dealing with its non-consolidated assets, which simplifies valuations, raises EBITDA, and should drive multiple expansion.

We upgrade NWSA from Hold to BUY, with a 12-month target price of $27 per share.

Market Data	
Price (06/26/12)	$21.76
12-Month Price Target	$27.00
52-Week range	$21.76-13.62
Shares Out. (MM)	2,620.0
Market cap (MM)	$57,011.6
Avg. daily volume (000)	16,454.5

Financial Data	
Total Debt/Cap.	34.8%
Price/LTM Rev.	1.6x
Tangible BVPS	$2.08
Net Cash Per Share	($1.93)

The second excerpt below comes from Table 5 of the report. Here you see the conclusions of a DCF model as applied by Martin. The analysis has slightly more components than our summary valuation in Exhibit 12.6, not a surprise given News Corp. is a bit more complex than the Russian River Valley Winery, but the similarities should be apparent. First, note the forecast period spans 10 years (2013E-2022E, "E" means "estimate") and the conclusions for the "value of operations" are an almost even split between the present value of the FCF over the first 10 years ($35.174 billion) and the present value of the terminal value ($33.917 million). The DCF analysis performed then discounts the FCF values using a "WACC", an acronym for "**weighted average cost of capital**", which is a blend between the cost of borrowing and the cost of common equity. To this value Martin adds certain other "non-operating" items of value that are not reflected in her estimates of FCF. And because she uses a WACC approach rather than the cost of equity, long-term debt and interest bearing capital leases are later subtracted from the total enterprise value calculated, yielding a total common equity value of $67.803 billion. Dividing this amount by shares outstanding (2.509 billion) yields an estimated stock price of $27.02 per year, a 24% upside relative to the current stock price on June 27, 2012. Interestingly, to the right of the analysis is provided the analyst's view of the strengths and weaknesses of the general DCF model.

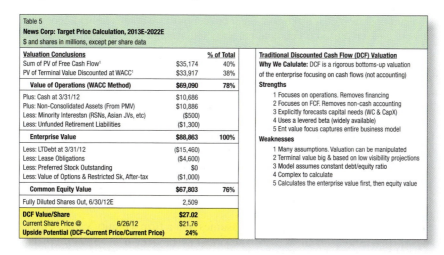

Table 5
News Corp: Target Price Calculation, 2013E-2022E
$ and shares in millions, except per share data

Valuation Conclusions		% of Total
Sum of PV of Free Cash Flow[1]	$35,174	40%
PV of Terminal Value Discounted at WACC[1]	$33,917	38%
Value of Operations (WACC Method)	**$69,090**	**78%**
Plus: Cash at 3/31/12	$10,686	
Plus: Non-Consolidated Assets (From PMV)	$10,886	
Less: Minority Interestsn (RSNs, Asian JVs, etc)	($500)	
Less: Unfunded Retirement Liabilities	($1,300)	
Enterprise Value	**$88,863**	**100%**
Less: LTDebt at 3/31/12	($15,460)	
Less: Lease Obligations	($4,600)	
Less: Preferred Stock Outstanding	$0	
Less: Value of Options & Restricted Sk, After-tax	($1,000)	
Common Equity Value	**$67,803**	**76%**
Fully Diluted Shares Out, 6/30/12E	2,509	
DCF Value/Share	**$27.02**	
Current Share Price @ 6/26/12	$21.76	
Upside Potential (DCF-Current Price/Current Price)	**24%**	

Traditional Discounted Cash Flow (DCF) Valuation
Why We Calulate: DCF is a rigorous bottoms-up valuation of the enterprise focusing on cash flows (not accounting)
Strengths

1 Focuses on operations. Removes financing
2 Focuses on FCF. Removes non-cash accounting
3 Explicitly forecasts capital needs (WC & CapX)
4 Uses a levered beta (widely available)
5 Ent value focus captures entire business model

Weaknesses

1 Many assumptions. Valuation can be manipulated
2 Terminal value big & based on low visibility projections
3 Model assumes constant debt/equity ratio
4 Complex to calculate
5 Calculates the enterprise value first, then equity value

Source: Martin, L. and D. Medina. "*News Corporation (NWSA)—Buy—Upgrading to Buy with Target Price of $27*", June 27, 2012. Needham and Company, LLC.

VALUATION USING THE RESIDUAL INCOME MODEL

Unlike the free cash flow model, the **residual income** model (RI) focuses on accounting variables rather than cash flows.[7] Residual income is derived from the basic financial tenet that a firm only adds value to its shareholders if it is able to earn a return greater than its cost of capital. As with the free cash flow to equity valuation model just discussed, the cost of capital is simply the firm's cost of equity (r_e). More formally, residual income, also known as **excess earnings**, is defined as the firm's net income, or **normal earnings**, less the opportunity cost associated with common shareholders' equity:

$$RI_t = NI_t - r_e CE_{t-1}$$

The opportunity cost associated with shareholders' equity, $r_e CE_{t-1}$, is defined as the firm's cost of equity times it's beginning-of-period common shareholders' equity. In other words, residual income is the amount of net income the firm earns above the amount that could have been earned by the shareholders if they had invested their money elsewhere at their required rate of return. This is best illustrated by thinking of a savings account that pays five percent interest in which you deposit $1,000 at the beginning of the year. Your opportunity cost of withdrawing your savings and investing elsewhere is the foregone interest you would no longer earn—$50 in this case. If you took your savings and invested in a project that earned eight percent, the residual income would be the excess earning of three percent (eight percent less five percent) times your investment of $1,000—$30 in this example ($80 − $50). Further, since this project can earn a rate of return in excess of the cost of capital, it will be popular with other investors. These other investors, in an effort to also earn the higher rate of return, will try to acquire ownership shares in the project, and in so doing, will bid up the price of the project so that your investment will be worth more than its original $1,000. In other words, by earning residual income, the project will be able to add value and this additional value is equal to the present value of all expected future residual income.

BUSINESS PERSPECTIVE

Whole Foods Market and EVA

As mentioned in the vignette at the beginning of this chapter, Whole Foods Market utilized a variation of the residual income method known as **Economic Value Added**. The company described its usage of this valuation approach in its 2012 annual report as follows:

> Most of our stores are located in high-traffic shopping areas on premier real estate sites and are either freestanding or in strip centers. We also have a number of urban stores located in high-density, mixed-use developments. In selecting store locations, we use an internally developed model to analyze potential sites based on various criteria such as education levels, population density and income levels within certain drive times. After we have selected a target site, our development group does a comprehensive site study and sales projection and works with our regional teams to develop construction and operating cost estimates. Each project must meet an internal Economic Value Added ("EVA") hurdle return, based on our internal weighted average cost of capital, which for new stores generally is expected to be cumulative positive EVA in five years or less. In its simplest definition, EVA is equivalent to net operating profits after taxes minus a charge on the cost of invested capital necessary to generate those profits. Our current internal weighted average cost of capital metric is 8%.

Under the RI approach, the value of a firm's equity (E_t)—that is, the value of its outstanding common shares—is equal to the book value of shareholders' equity (CE_{t-1}) from the balance sheet plus the sum of future residual income (RI_t) over the life of the firm, all discounted at the cost of equity (r_e):

$$E_0 = CE_{t-1} + \Sigma RI_t/(1 + r_e)^t$$

Stated alternatively, the residual income model assumes that a firm's equity value (E_0) is equal to the current book value of shareholders' equity (CE_{t-1}) plus the present value of the firm's expected future residual income (future earnings less normal earnings).

---

[7] For a complete discourse on the residual income valuation model, see S. Penman, *Financial Statement Analysis and Security Valuation,* 5th edition, McGraw-Hill International (2012).

A natural question to ask is how a firm's equity can be valued as the present value of its future free cash flow to equity, a measure based on cash flows, and also as the present value of its future residual income, a measure based on earnings, and come to the same valuation result. You may even be wondering how it is even possible to perform a valuation using earnings given all the myriad of accounting policy choices and estimates present under the GAAP framework. How can a consistent valuation be achieved when so many different earnings numbers are possible depending upon which accounting policy choices and estimates are made? These are good questions and luckily there is a good answer for each.

First, it can be demonstrated mathematically that the present value of free cash flow and of residual income over the life of a firm are identical. Likewise, with some algebra, it can also be demonstrated that operating cash flow and residual income valuation will lead to the exact same valuation result. Therefore, which method is used comes down to practical issues such as data availability and one's ability to forecast earnings versus cash flows.[8]

It can also be shown with some algebra that the types of accounting policy choices and estimates made by managers will not affect the ultimate equity valuation.[9] The reason behind this resides in the way that the balance sheet and the income statement work together, along with the way that the residual income computation is discounted. For example, if a firm's assets are depreciated using the double-declining-balance method, then net income will be lower in the early years. At the same time, the common equity account (through retained earnings) will also be lower, leading to a lower charge against net income to compute residual income. These offsetting amounts, when discounted at the cost of equity, exactly cancel each other out and lead to the same valuation result regardless of the accounting policy choices and estimates.

Valuing the Russian River Valley Winery Shares

Exhibit 12.7 illustrates the valuation of the Russian River Valley common equity using the residual income method. We first compute the residual income for the five-year forecast period, along with the terminal year. The computation begins with net income, which we obtain from Panel A of Exhibit 12.1. We then subtract the opportunity cost of the shareholders' investment, defined as beginning-of-year common equity (obtained from Panel B of Exhibit 12.1) multiplied by the firm's ten percent cost of equity capital (such as in 2014, 10 percent × $6.524 million = $652,000). For 2014, this yields residual income of $111,000 ($763,000 − $652,000). We next discount the future residual income values back to the present using the firm's ten percent cost of equity capital. The present values of the five years of forecasted residual income are then aggregated to $946,000. As we did with the free cash flow valuation, the terminal year residual income is first divided by the difference between the cost of equity capital (ten percent) and the assumed growth rate (five percent), and this amount is then discounted to the present at the cost of equity, yielding $5.509 million. These two amounts are combined with the initial common equity of $6.524 million to yield a $12.979 million valuation of common equity. When divided by the outstanding shares of 6.2 million, we get a value of $2.09 per share, exactly as with the free cash flow to equity valuation.

EXHIBIT 12.7	Residual Income Valuation of Russian River Valley Winery					
Year of Forecast (in 000's)	2014	2015	2016	2017	2018	Terminal Year
Net income.	$ 763	$ 889	$1,026	$1,174	$1,336	$1,403
Common equity at beginning of year.	6,524	7,113	7,713	8,324	8,949	9,589
Residual income.	111	178	254*	342	441	444
Present value of residual income	101	147	191	233*	274	
Present value of first 5 years	$ 946					
Present value beyond 5 years	$ 5,509					
Common equity as of 2014	$ 6,524					
Value attributable to common equity	$12,979					
÷ Common shares outstanding	6,200					
= Forecast price per share	$ 2.09					

*rounded

[8] Ohlson, James A.,"Earnings, book value, and dividends in equity valuations," 1995. *Contemporary Accounting Research*, 11, pp. 661–687.
[9] R. Lundholm and R. Sloan, *Equity Valuation and Analysis with eVal*. 3rd ed. McGraw-Hill, 2013.

It is instructive to compare the results of the two valuations methods. While each yields the same $12.979 million valuation estimate for equity, the component parts of the valuation analysis are much different. The discounted cash flow approach attributes far more of the firm's value to the firm's terminal value—$11.463 million compared to $5.509 million—than does the residual income approach. In contrast, the residual income approach attributes far more of the firm's value to the first five years of forecasted operations—$7.470 million compared to $1.516 million. Why is this?

These differences are a consequence of how each approach considers value creation. The residual income approach considers the existing investment to have value—$6.524 million in this case—and then considers future excess earnings above the firm's cost of capital as incremental value. The discounted cash flow approach, in contrast, only considers future cash flows as value-relevant, and therefore, places a greater percentage of the equity's value on the firm's future cash flows.

VALUATION USING PRICE-EARNINGS MULTIPLES

Both the free cash flow to equity and the residual income valuation approaches are premised on the basic financial concept that the value of any asset is simply the present value of the future returns generated by the asset. Unfortunately, while these valuation methods are widely accepted as theoretically sound, they are not easy to apply. Each requires forecasted pro forma financial statements and each is subject to the various uncertainties inherent in forecasting the future. Academic research indicates that investment professionals often use a much simpler approach based on comparable firms to value a company, although they often later supplement this simple approach with one of the two approaches discussed.[10]

This simplified approach is based on the concept that equally risky financial assets that provide similar payouts should sell for prices that are similar. One of the most common forms of the comparable firms approach is price-earnings (P/E) multiples valuation. The P/E multiple—or the market price per share divided by the earnings per share—indicates the relative amount that investors are willing to pay for $1 of sustainable corporate earnings. Thus, a P/E multiple of 20 indicates that investors are willing to pay $20 for each dollar of future recurring income earned by a company.

Earnings multiples can be calculated for a variety of earnings-based metrics but are most often calculated for earnings after taxes (P/E), earnings before interest and taxes (P/EBIT), and earnings before interest, taxes, depreciation, and amortization (P/EBITDA). The two most popular earnings multiples are P/E and P/EBITDA, the latter largely because of its close proximity to a firm's cash flow from operations.

Earnings multiples can also be calculated for a variety of time periods. A **trailing multiple**, for example, is obtained by dividing a company's recent closing share price by its *historical* earnings per share (EPS) for the most recently completed fiscal period (quarter or year). (Most analysts use basic EPS but some use diluted EPS.) A **forward multiple**, on the other hand, is a company's current closing share price divided by *forecasted* earnings per share. Since a firm's share price is thought to be a function of future earnings, forward multiples are conceptually superior to historical multiples.

Most businesses routinely develop budgeted (or pro forma) financial statements for internal planning purposes; hence, forecasted EPS values are readily available to managers to assess a firm's value. These internal forecasts of profitability are rarely externally publicized, however; and thus, investment professionals and shareholders must develop their own forecasts of EPS, or alternatively subscribe to such data services as *Zacks Investment Research*, *Institutional Brokers' Estimate System*, or *First Call/Thomson Reuters* which provide consensus earnings forecasts for most publicly held companies. **Consensus earnings forecasts** are the average forecast of future earnings from a group of professional analysts that routinely follow a particular company's performance.

Perhaps the most difficult aspect of the comparable companies approach is to actually find the comparable companies. While most professionals simply look at similar-size firms in the same industry, care must be taken to consider such factors as firm risk, accounting policy differences, and growth options. Each of these factors should be value relevant and result in different P/E multiples. Once a group of comparable firms is determined, the P/E multiples approach is quite easy to implement. This process is best illustrated by way of an example.

To value the common equity of the Russian River Valley Winery, Kate and Matt found four wineries that appeared to be comparable. The earnings per share and share price, along with the computed P/E ratio of each winery, are presented in Exhibit 12.8.

---

[10] Demirakos, N. Strong, and M Waller, "What Valuation Models Do Analysts Use," *Accounting Horizons*, December, 2004.

EXHIBIT 12.8	Comparable Price-Earnings Ratios			
Winery		**EPS**	**Share Price**	**P/E Ratio**
A...		$0.50	$ 9.00	18
B...		$0.06	$ 1.32	22
C...		$1.25	$20.00	16
D...		$0.60	$14.40	24
Average				20

Russian River Valley's 2013 net income was $647,000. Since the outstanding number of shares was 6.2 million, the winery's EPS for 2013 is $0.104. Using an average P/E multiple of 20, based on the identified comparable firms (see Exhibit 12.8), yields a share price of $2.08 ($0.104 × 20) for the Russian River Valley Winery.

BUSINESS PERSPECTIVE

Johnson & Johnson Inc.

To illustrate the use of P/E multiple valuation, consider the case of Johnson & Johnson Inc. (J&J), a leading pharmaceutical and consumer products' company. J&J reported EPS (adjusted for nonrecurring items) for the year ending December 30, 2012 of $5.10 per share and had a closing share price of $70.10 per share. Hence, the company's trailing P/E multiple was 13.7 times earnings:

$$\text{Trailing P/E Multiple} = \$70.10/\$5.10 = 13.7$$

The consensus EPS forecast of a survey of 18 professional analysts that tracked the company was $5.41 for the following fiscal year, yielding a forward P/E multiple of:

$$\text{Forward P/E Multiple} = \$70.10/\$5.41 = 13.0$$

Presumably, J&J's year-end price of $70.10 reflects the consensus earnings estimate, and thus, conceptually, the forward multiple of 13.0 would more accurately reflect the market's consensus of the value of the firm.

How can the forward multiple be used to value J&J? As new information is obtained, such as actual first quarter earnings for the following year, the multiple can be used to calculate whether the firm's current share price is undervalued (a buy), overvalued (a sell), or fairly valued (a hold). For instance, if J&J reports first quarter earnings of $1.50 per share, the annualized earnings would equal $6.00 per share (4 × $1.50). On the basis of its annualized earnings and a forward P/E multiple of 13.0, J&J's shares would be fairly priced at $78 per share. If J&J's share price is below (above) $78, it would be considered undervalued (overvalued) using the P/E multiple framework.

ETHICS PERSPECTIVE

Historically, there have been three approaches to developing and teaching ethics. Utilitarianism, which is closely associated with John Stuart Mill, teaches that ethical behavior leads to the best consequences. Deontology, associated with Immanuel Kant, teaches that ethics is a matter of finding the right rule. Finally, a virtue-based approach to ethics states that ethics is a matter of acquiring and putting into practice the relevant "virtue." Which of the three approaches do you feel most accurately describes your personal philosophy of ethics?

EXECUTIVE SUMMARY

Accounting information can be used to benchmark a firm's performance, to help managers make important operating decisions, and to help assess the value of a firm. The focus of this final chapter was firm valuation. Using the discounted cash flow framework, we saw that it was possible to value a firm by discounting the various operating cash flows expected to be generated by the firm. We also saw that it was possible to value a firm using its book value and its residual income. Finally, we saw that some professionals value a firm by reference to earnings multiples.

As a validation of your understanding of the content of this chapter, you should now be able to:

■ Develop pro forma financial statements.
■ Estimate the value of a company using the discounted cash flow approach.
■ Estimate the value of a company using the residual income approach.
■ Estimate the value of a company using price-earnings multiples.

KEY CONCEPTS AND TERMS

Beta, 421
Capital asset pricing model, 421
Consensus earnings forecasts, 426
Continuing value, 419
Cost of common equity, 421
Discounted cash flow approach, 415
Discount rate, 420
Economic Value Added, 424

Excess earnings, 424
Forward multiple, 426
Free cash flow, 419
Free cash flow to common
   equity, 419
Normal earnings, 424
Operating cash flows, 419

Operating value, 418
Perpetuity growth formula, 421
Residual income, 424
Terminal value, 419
Terminal year growth rate, 413
Trailing multiple, 426
Weighted average cost of capital, 423

QUESTIONS

Q12.1 **Discounted Cash Flow versus Residual Income Valuation.** Describe the general steps followed to value the common equity of a business using (a) the discounted cash flow method and (b) the residual income method. Discuss what circumstances will yield equivalent valuation results under the two approaches.

Q12.2 **Pro Forma Financial Statements.** Describe the basic steps to be followed in developing pro forma financial statements. Discuss why it is unnecessary to make a separate set of pro forma assumptions for the statement of cash flow. Discuss why it is necessary to develop a terminal year projection.

Q12.3 **Free Cash Flow versus Residual Income.** Discuss how (a) the free cash flow and (b) the residual income of a business are calculated. Describe how these two measures are related.

Q12.4 **Capital Asset Pricing Model and Beta.** Explain the Capital Asset Pricing Model. What does it mean if a company has a beta of 1.3? What does it mean if a company has a beta of 1.0?

Q12.5 **Analyzing and Reporting Operating Loss Carryforwards.** The following information is taken from the annual report of **Coca-Cola Enterprises**:

> As of December 31, 2012, we had $6,494 million of loss carryforwards available to reduce future taxable income. Loss carryforwards of $279 million must be utilized within the next five years, and the remainder can be utilized over a period greater than five years.

Discuss how the existence of operating-loss carryforwards affects firm value. Discuss how the financial effects of operating-loss carryforwards are reflected in the calculation of firm value using (a) the discounted cash flow model and (b) the residual income model.

Q12.6 **Forecasting the Cost of Goods Sold: Economies and Diseconomies of Scale.** Many investment professionals forecast the cost of goods sold on the pro forma income statement using recent historical common-size percentages. Common-size percentages, however, may be significantly impacted by economies of scale or diseconomies of scale. Discuss what an economy of scale is and how it can impact the historical relation of the cost of goods sold divided by sales. Discuss what a diseconomy of scale is; under what circumstances can diseconomies of scale arise?

Q12.7 **Unlevering Cash Flow from Operations.** Some investment professionals "unlever" the cash flow from operations by adding the following term $i(1-t_x)$ to the cash flow from operations (CFFO). Discuss why these professionals might modify the CFFO in this fashion. How does unlevering change the CFFO?

Q12.8 **Discounting Cash Flows and Earnings.** Under the residual income approach and the discounted cash flow approach to firm valuation, earnings and cash flows, respectively, are discounted using a firm's cost of equity. Discuss why the cost of equity is the appropriate discount rate to use to discount a firm's earnings and cash flows. Why is the cost of debt inappropriate to use to discount a firm's earnings or cash flows?

Q12.9 **(Ethics Perspective) Virtue-based Approach to Ethics.** The virtue-based approach to ethics asks the following questions—What role should an individual occupy in an organization? What good traits (or virtues) are needed to succeed at that role? And, how should someone with those virtues act when confronted with ethical dilemmas? Discuss the role that accountants are meant to occupy. Discuss the traits or virtues that an accountant should have to succeed in that role. Discuss how an accountant should act when faced with an ethical dilemma.

Assignments with the logo in the margin are available in BusinessCourse.
See the Preface of the book for details.
CHECK FIGURE indicates that check figures are available on the book's Website.

EXERCISES

E12.10 **Calculating the Cost of Equity.** Assume that the Coffman Company has a beta of 1.2 and that the risk-free rate of return is five percent. If the equity-risk premium is six percent, calculate the cost of equity for the Coffman Company using the capital asset pricing model.

E12.11 **Calculating the Cost of Equity.** Assume that The Jackson Company has a beta of 0.8 and the risk-free rate of return is 4.5 percent. If the equity-risk premium is seven percent, calculate the cost of equity for The Jackson Company using the capital asset pricing model.   **CHECK FIGURE**

E12.12 **Valuation Using Price-Earnings Multiples.** The Claremont Company is planning an initial public offering (IPO) and management would like to have an idea of an appropriate price to charge for a share of its stock. The company plans to issue 100,000 shares. The Claremont Company's most recent earnings per share (EPS) are $1.25; however, the consensus forecast among analysts who follow the company is for EPS to be $1.50. The EPS and share price of four comparable firms are shown below:

Firm	EPS	Share Price	P/E ratio
A	$ 1.00	$ 18.00	18
B	0.60	13.20	22
C	10.00	140.00	14
D	2.20	57.20	26

Compute the value of a share of Claremont Company stock using the price-earnings multiples method.

E12.13 **Calculating Terminal Values.** Scripps Inc. is projected to generate free cash flow (FCF) of $950,000 in its terminal year, at which point it is forecasted to have a four percent growth rate. The firm's cost of equity is estimated to be twelve percent. Calculate the terminal value of Scripps Inc.

E12.14 **Calculating Free Cash Flow.** Below are data from the financial statements of Sand and Glass Audio:

Net income.	$ 900
Common stock issued (net)	200
Cash from operations (net).	1,150
Cash from investing (net)	(400)
Change in debt (net).	(475)
Dividends paid	300
Change in operating cash (net)	175
Change in common equity (net).	800

Compute the company's free cash flow to equity using three different methods. (Each method should yield the same answer.)

E12.15 **Calculating Free Cash Flow.** Below are data from the financial statements of Ann A. Logg Audio.

Net income.	$1,800
Common stock issued (net)	400
Cash from operations (net).	2,300
Cash from investing (net)	(800)
Change in debt (net).	(950)
Dividends paid	600
Change in operating cash (net)	350
Change in common equity (net)	1,600

Compute the company's free cash flow to equity using three different methods. (Each method should yield the same answer.)

E12.16 **Discounted Cash Flow Valuation.** Presented below are data for Boso Audio:

	Forecast Year					
	1	**2**	**3**	**4**	**5**	**Terminal**
No. of outstanding shares	500	500	500	500	500	500
Terminal year growth rate						5%
Cost of common equity	10%	10%	10%	10%	10%	10%
Net income.	$ 79	$ 94	$111	$130	$150	$157
Beginning of year common equity	$649	$683	$720	$758	$797	$839
Free cash flow to common equity	$ 44	$ 58	$ 73	$ 90	$108	$115

Compute the value of a share of Boso common stock using the discounted cash flow method.

E12.17 **Residual Income Valuation.** Presented below are data for Boso Audio:

	Forecast Year					
	1	**2**	**3**	**4**	**5**	**Terminal**
No. of outstanding shares	500	500	500	500	500	500
Terminal year growth rate						5%
Cost of common equity	10%	10%	10%	10%	10%	10%
Net income.	$ 79	$ 94	$111	$130	$150	$157
Beginning of year common equity	$649	$683	$720	$758	$797	$839
Free cash flow to common equity	$ 44	$ 58	$ 73	$ 90	$108	$115

Compute the value of a share of Boso common stock using the residual income method.

E12.18 **Residual Income Valuation.** Presented below are data for Hero Cable:

	Forecast Year					
	1	**2**	**3**	**4**	**5**	**Terminal**
No. of outstanding shares	1,000	1,000	1,000	1,000	1,000	1,000
Terminal year growth rate						4%
Cost of common equity	12%	12%	12%	12%	12%	12%
Net income.	$128	$148	$170	$194	$221	$230
Beginning of year common equity	$698	$738	$780	$824	$870	$919
Free cash flow to common equity	$ 88	$106	$126	$148	$172	$193

Compute the value of a share of Hero common stock using the residual income method method.

E12.19   Price-Earnings Multiple Valuation.   General Electric Company (GE) is one of the world's leading infrastructure and financial services company. On March 8, 2013 the company's trailing (twelve months) earnings per share was $1.29, and with a market price per share of $23.77, indicated a trailing price-earnings multiple of 18.40.

Required

1. According to Thomson Financial, the consensus forward price-earnings multiple is 12.85. What is the consensus forecasted earnings-per-share?

2. Using your consensus forecast of future earnings-per-share from part one, and the current trailing price-earnings multiple of 18.40, what should GE's target share price be? According to Thomson Financial, GE's one-year target price was $25 per share. How does the Thomson Financial one-year target price compare to your target price?

E12.20   Pro Forma Income Statements.   Presented below is the consolidated statement of earnings for Mann & Miller, Inc.

MANN & MILLER, INC. Consolidated Statement of Earnings			
($ millions)	2012	2011	2010
Sales to customers.	$36,298	$32,317	$29,172
Cost of goods sold.	10,447	9,581	8,957
Gross profit.	25,851	22,736	20,215
Selling, marketing & administrative expense	12,216	11,260	10,495
Research expense	3,957	3,591	3,105
Purchased in-process research & development	189	105	66
Interest income.	(256)	(456)	(429)
Interest expense, net of portion capitalized.	160	153	204
Other (income) expense, net	294	185	(94)
	16,560	14,838	13,347
Earnings before provision for income taxes.	9,291	7,898	6,868
Provision for income taxes.	2,694	2,230	1,915
Net earnings.	$ 6,597	$ 5,668	$ 4,953
Basic net earnings per share	$2.20	$1.87	$1.65
Diluted net earnings per share.	$2.16	$1.84	$1.61

Using the Mann & Miller Inc. (M&M) consolidated statement of earnings as your base year, prepare pro forma income statements for M&M for 2013 and 2014 using an EXCEL spreadsheet. Relevant assumptions that you should use include:

• Sales growth is twelve percent per year.
• Gross profit margin is 70 percent.
• Effective income tax rate is 29 percent.
• All expenses, except interest expense, vary as a function of sales.
• Interest expense is eight percent of the beginning balance of long-term debt.

PROBLEMS

P12.21   Generating Cash Flow Information.   Presented below are recent financial statements for The Gamble Company.

THE GAMBLE COMPANY Consolidated Balance Sheet		
	2012	**2011**
Assets		
Cash & cash equivalents	$ 1,549	$ 2,350
Marketable securities.	857	760
Trade receivables.	2,781	2,738
Inventories	3,284	3,087
Prepaid expenses	1,511	1,190
Total current assets	9,982	10,125
Property, plant & equipment (net)	12,180	11,376
Intangible assets (net)	7,011	3,949
Other noncurrent assets	1,198	1,433
Total assets	$30,371	$26,883
Liabilities & Shareholders' Equity		
Accounts payable	$ 2,051	$ 2,203
Accrued expenses & other liabilities	3,942	3,802
Taxes payable	976	944
Debt due within one year.	2,281	849
Current liabilities	9,250	7,798
Long-term debt	5,765	4,143
Deferred income taxes.	(167)	(102)
Other noncurrent liabilities	3,287	2,998
Shareholders' equity		
Capital stock (at par)	3,158	3,210
Additional paid-in-capital.	907	559
Retained earnings	11,144	10,730
Cumulative translation adjustment account	(2,973)	(2,453)
Total liabilities & shareholders' equity	$30,371	$26,883

THE GAMBLE COMPANY Consolidated Statement of Earnings		
	2012	**2011**
Net sales.	$37,154	$35,764
Cost of goods sold*	(21,064)	(20,510)
Marketing research & administrative expenses**	(10,035)	(9,766)
Operating income.	6,055	5,488
Interest expense.	(548)	(457)
Other income (net)†	201	218
Earnings before income taxes	5,708	5,249
Income taxes	(1,928)	(1,834)
Net earnings.	$ 3,780	$ 3,415

* Includes depreciation on plant & equipment of 1,480 in 2012 and 1,387 in 2011.
** includes amortization of intangible assets of 118 in 2012 and 1000 in 2011.
† includes one-time gains of 150 in 2012 and 125 in 2011 from the sale of equipment.

Required
Prepare a statement of cash flow using the indirect method. What does the company's statement of cash flow reveal about the company's financial health?

P12.22   **Generating Cash Flow Information.**   Presented below are recent financial data for the Coca-Cola Company.

THE COCA-COLA COMPANY Consolidated Balance Sheet	Year 9	Year 8
Assets		
Cash & cash equivalents	$ 1,611	$ 1,648
Marketable securities	201	159
Trade accounts receivable (net)	1,798	1,666
Inventories	1,076	890
Prepaid expenses & other current	1,794	2,017
Total current assets	6,480	6,380
Equity investment in affiliated companies	6,792	6,686
Marketable securities	2,124	1,863
Property, plant & equipment (net)	4,267	3,669
Goodwill & other intangibles (net)	1,960	547
Total assets	$21,623	$19,145
Liabilities & Shareholders' Equity		
Accounts payable & accrued expenses	$ 3,714	$ 3,141
Loans & notes payable	5,112	4,459
Current maturities of long-term debt	261	3
Accrued income taxes	769	1,037
Total current liabilities	9,856	8,640
Long-term debt	854	687
Long-term pension liabilities	902	991
Deferred income taxes	498	424
Shareholders' equity		
Common stock @ par	867	865
Additional paid-in-capital	2,584	2,195
Reinvested earnings	20,773	19,922
Cumulated currency translation adjustment	(1,551)	(1,434)
Treasury stock	(13,160)	(13,145)
Total liabilities & shareholders' equity	$21,623	$19,145

THE COCA-COLA COMPANY Consolidated Statement of Income	Year 9
Net operating revenues	$19,805
Less: Cost of goods sold [1]	6,009
Gross profit	13,796
Less: Selling and administrative expenses [2]	9,001
Other operating charges	813
Operating income	3,982
Interest expense (net of income)	(77)
Equity income (loss)	(184)
Other income (net)	68
Gains on issues of stock by equity investors	30
Income before income taxes	3,819
Income taxes	1,388
Net income	$ 2,431

[1] Includes depreciation on property & equipment of $528.
[2] Includes amortization of intangible assets of $264.

Required

Prepare a statement of cash flow for Year 9 using the indirect method format. What does the company's statement of cash flow reveal about the company's financial health?

P12.23 **Generating Cash Flow Information: International.** China Yuchai International Ltd. is a Bermuda holding company that owns 76.4 percent of the outstanding common shares of Guangxi Yuchai Machinery Company Ltd. Guangxi Yuchai is one of the leading manufacturers of diesel engines in China. Presented below are recent financial statements for China Yuchai International:

CHINA YUCHAI INTERNATIONAL LTD. Consolidated Statement of Income		
	Year 3	Year 4
Assets		
Current assets		
Cash.	173,038	285,831
Inventories	301,366	292,192
Receivable from related company	98,270	60,263
Trade receivables (net)	548,128	475,254
Prepaid expenses	69,343	84,252
Investments	—	800
Total current assets	1,190,145	1,198,592
Noncurrent assets		
Property, plant, & equipment (net)	1,136,242	1,082,976
Investments	99,446	50,063
Goodwill (net)	263,211	246,353
Deferred income tax	21,703	22,322
Total assets	2,710,747	2,600,306
Liabilities & Shareholders' Equity		
Current liabilities		
Short-term bank loans	128,016	90,000
Current maturities of long-term loans	183,800	294,800
Trade accounts payable	209,954	134,696
Income taxes payable	559	1,057
Accrued expenses payable	138,374	138,472
Total current liabilities	660,703	659,025
Long-term bank loans	208,800	60,000
Total liabilities	869,503	719,025
Minority interest	358,589	354,926
Shareholders' equity		
Common stock	30,349	30,349
Contributed surplus	1,486,934	1,486,934
Statutory reserves	98,868	108,095
Accumulated deficit	(133,496)	(99,023)
Total liabilities & shareholders' equity	2,710,747	2,600,306

CHINA YUCHAI INTERNATIONAL LTD. Consolidated Statement of Operations	
	Year 4
Net sales	1,270,337
Cost of goods sold	828,865[1]
Gross profit	441,472
Selling, general & administrative expenses	309,995
Amortization of goodwill	16,859
Impairment of plant & equipment	4,449
Operating income	110,169
Interest expense	36,602
Income before income taxes & minority interest	73,567
Income tax expense	11,217
Income before minority interest	62,350
Minority interest in income of consolidated subsidiaries	(18,650)
Net income	43,700

[1] Includes depreciation expense of $127,892

Required

Prepare a statement of cash flow using the indirect method. What does the company's statement of cash flow reveal about the company's financial health?

P12.24   **Statement of Cash Flow: International.**   Presented below are the financial statements of the Wacoal Corporation, a leading manufacturer of women's apparel in Japan. Wacoal's footnotes and other supplementary data revealed the following additional information:

1. Depreciation and amortization on property, plant, and equipment taken in Year 2 amounted to ¥3,265 million.
2. Effective April 1, Year 2, Wacoal changed its method of accounting for employee retirement benefits. As a result of this change in accounting principle, net income for Year 2 decreased by ¥1,429 million, **including** the cumulative effect of the change as of the beginning of the year of ¥1,286 million.
3. The consolidated statement of shareholders' equity revealed that cash dividends paid in Year 2 were ¥2,544 million, and that treasury stock in the amount of ¥2,803 million had been repurchased and had been deducted against retained earnings.

WACOAL CORPORATION Consolidated Balance Sheet		
(in millions of Yen)	**Year 2**	**Year 1**
Assets		
Cash....................................	¥ 7,634	¥ 9,403
Time deposits & certificates of deposit................................	33,562	40,486
Total cash & cash equivalents..................................	41,196	49,889
Marketable securities..........................	34,499	24,178
Notes & accounts receivable		
Trade notes	2,651	2,902
Trade accounts	22,049	21,851
Allowance for returns & doubtful receivables	(2,869)	(2,633)
Inventories..	25,601	25,515
Deferred income taxes.............................	4,647	4,142
Other current assets	1,734	1,890
Total current assets	129,508	127,734
Property, plant & equipment		
Land..	25,284	25,247
Buildings	55,197	54,784
Machinery & equipment............................	11,530	11,148
Total...	92,011	91,179
Accumulated depreciation...........................	(33,367)	(31,189)
Net property, plant, & equipment.....................	58,644	59,990
Other assets		
Investments in affiliates	8,670	7,305
Investments	28,877	37,327
Lease deposits & other	6,563	5,365
Total other assets.................................	44,110	49,997
Total	¥232,262	¥237,721
Liabilities and Shareholders' Equity		
Short-term bank loan.............................	¥ 8,088	¥ 8,125
Trade notes	8,513	7,391
Trade accounts	7,214	6,769
Accrued payroll & bonuses	7,743	8,053
Income taxes payable	3,093	3,033
Other current liabilities............................	6,281	4,340
Current portion of long-term debt	517	779
Total current liabilities	41,449	38,490
Long-term liabilities		
Long-term debt	892	1,369
Liability for termination & retirement benefits	6,709	11,734
Deferred income taxes.............................	8,957	10,675
Total long-term liabilities	16,558	23,778
Minority interests	1,697	1,841

continued

continued from previous page

WACOAL CORPORATION
Consolidated Balance Sheet

(in millions of Yen)	Year 2	Year 1
Shareholders' equity		
Common stock par value of ¥50 per share-authorized, 237 million &		
240 million shares in Year 2 & Year 1; issued & outstanding 151,116,685		
and 154,116,685 shares in Year 2 & Year 1	13,260	13,260
Additional paid-in-capital.	25,242	25,242
Retained earnings	132,322	126,780
Accumulated other comprehensive income (loss)		
Foreign currency translation adjustments	(2,418)	(3,231)
Unrealized gain on securities.	4,152	11,561
Total	1,734	8,330
Total shareholders' equity	172,558	173,612
Total	¥232,262	¥237,721

WACOAL CORPORATION
Consolidated Statement of Income

(in millions of Yen)	Year 2
Net sales.	¥162,023
Operating costs and expenses	
Cost of sales	87,493
Selling, general & administrative expense.	64,906
Total operating costs and expenses	152,399
Operating income.	9,624
Other income and expenses	
Interest income	395
Interest expense	(333)
Dividend income	268
Equity in net income of affiliated companies.	1,271
Gain (loss) on sale, transfer or exchange of investments	11,025
Other (net)	(850)
Total other income and expenses	11,776
Income before income taxes, minority interests and cumulative effect of accounting change. . .	21,400
Income taxes	
Current.	5,181
Deferred.	3,877
Total income taxes.	9,058
Income before minority interests and cumulative effect of accounting change.	12,342
Minority interests	(167)
Income before cumulative effect of accounting change	12,175
Cumulative effect of accounting change	(1,286)
Net income.	¥ 10,889

Required

Prepare a statement of cash flow for Year 2 using the indirect method format. What does the company's statement of cash flow reveal about the company's financial health?

P12.25   **Firm Valuation: Discounted Cash Flow.**   The Mann Corporation is a small manufacturer of office products. Until recently, the company was all equity-financed (shareholders' equity totaled $20 million), having a cost of equity of twelve percent. The company decided to expand its productive capacity by investing in new plant and equipment at a cost of $12 million. Executives at Mann decided to finance the capital investment with lower-costing debt financing that carried an interest rate of only eight percent. The CEO of The Mann Corporation wondered what the company was now worth following the plant expansion; consequently, the CEO instructed the company's CFO to prepare a forecast of the firm's free cash flows. The CFO's forecast was as follows:

(in thousands)	Year 1	Year 2	Year 3	Year 4
Free cash flow	$2,500	$4,675	$5,573	$ 5,930
Terminal value				30,000

Required

1. Calculate the value of The Mann Corporation.
2. Is the company's decision to invest in new plant and equipment a good operating decision? Why?

P12.26   **Pro Forma Financial Statements.**   The venture capital division of a major U.S. financial institution has elected to fund an investment in an oil and gas exploration and production company that will operate both onshore and offshore in Texas and Louisiana in the United States. The initial financing commitment from the bank is for $40 million.

The company's strategic plan calls for an aggressive drilling program to be carried out during 2009. Hofstedt Oil & Gas estimates that it will drill 50 wells at an average cost of $800,000 per well and that 30 of those wells will yield aggregate crude oil reserves of approximately 10 million barrels. The remaining 20 wells are expected to be dry or commercially unproductive. These forecasts were based on the expert opinion of geologists familiar with the properties and were confirmed by petroleum engineers employed directly by the bank.

The company's production plan calls for a maximum exploration effort to earn the highest financial return. Tom Hofstedt, president of the company, developed the following production scenario:

Year	Number of Barrels to Be Produced	Estimated Selling Price per Barrel	Estimated Lifting Cost per Barrel
2009	1,000,000	$30	$5
2010	1,500,000	30	5
2011	1,500,000	35	6
2012	2,500,000	40	7
2013	3,500,000	45	8

Hofstedt Oil & Gas is concerned about the impact of this operation on its financial statements and on the company's stock price. Consequently, any available accounting policy choices loom as very important in the overall evaluation of the investment. As a result, Hofstedt sent a terse memo to the company's controller, the closing line of which stated, "Prepare pro forma statements showing the alternative accounting effects on cash flow, income before tax, and financial position if we elect to use the successful efforts method or the full-cost method." Under the full-cost method, the cost of all wells—successful and unsuccessful—are capitalized to the balance sheet and then depleted over the expected productive life of the successful wells. Under the successful efforts method, only the cost of the successful wells are capitalized (the cost of any unsuccessful wells are immediately expensed) to be depleted over their expected productive life.

Required

For purposes of pro forma statement preparation, assume that the $40 million loan agreement will be repaid as follows: (1) $10 million principal repayment per year to be paid on December 31 beginning on December 31, 2010; and (2) interest payments of 10 percent per year on the balance of the loan outstanding as of the beginning of the year. Ignore income taxes and all other operations. Based on your pro forma cash flows, income statements, and balance sheets for the period 2009 through 2013, what accounting method (successful efforts or full cost) recommendation would you make to Hofstedt, and why?

P12.27   **Pro Forma Financial Statements.**   Handy Dan, Inc., operates warehouse-style stores, selling a variety of home building products and lawn and garden supplies. Presented below are Handy Dan's historical financial statements for Year 1 and Year 2:

HANDY DAN, INC. Statement of Income	
($ millions)	Year 2
Sales.	$980
Cost of goods sold.	(727)
Gross profit.	253
Depreciation expense.	(8)
Other operating expenses	(217)
Operating income.	28
Interest expense.	(21)
Income before taxes.	7
Income tax expense.	(2)
Net income.	$ 5

HANDY DAN, INC. Balance Sheets					
($ millions)	Year 1	Year 2		Year 1	Year 2
Assets			**Equities**		
Cash.	$ 10	$ 14	Accounts payable.	$ 74	$104
Accounts receivable (net).	27	38	Short-term loans payable.	10	29
Inventory.	153	214	Long-term debt	207	289
Total current assets	190	266	Total liabilities	291	422
Property & equipment (cost).	199	279	Contributed capital.	50	62
Accumulated depreciation	(9)	(17)	Retained earnings	39	44
Net property & equipment	190	262	Total shareholders' equity	89	106
Total assets.	$380	$528	Total equities	$380	$528

HANDY DAN, INC. Statement of Retained Earnings	
($ millions)	Year 2
Retained earnings (Year 1)	$39
Add: Net income	5
Less: Dividends	0
Retained earnings (Year 2)	$44

HANDY DAN, INC. Statement of Cash Flow	
($ millions)	Year 2
Operations	
Net income...	$ 5
Depreciation expense	8
Accounts receivable (net).................................	(11)
Inventory	(61)
Accounts payable	30
Cash flow from operations................................	(29)
Investing	
Purchase of property & equipment	(80)
Cash flow from investing..................................	(80)
Financing	
Short-term borrowing	19
Long-term borrowing.......................................	82
Stock sales	12
Dividend payment	0
Cash flow from financing..................................	113
Change in cash..	4
Beginning cash..	10
Ending cash	$ 14

Required

Using the following set of assumptions, prepare pro forma financial statements for Handy Dan, Inc., for Year 3:

- Sales are projected to grow by 40 percent.
- Cash is expected to increase at the same rate as sales.
- Assume the following ratios to forecast the identified accounts:

Account	Financial Ratio		
Accounts receivable.....................................	Receivable turnover	=	25.9
Inventory..	Inventory turnover	=	3.39
Property & equipment	Fixed asset turnover	=	3.52
Cost of goods sold.....................................	Gross profit margin %	=	25.9%
Operating expenses....................................	Operating expenses/sales	=	22.1%
Accounts payable.......................................	Payable turnover	=	7.55

- Depreciation expense is based on a 30-year expected life with no salvage value; any property and equipment acquired during the year is depreciated for only one-half year.
- Interest expense is based on a six percent short-term cost of debt and eight percent long-term cost of debt; only one-half year of interest is charged on loans taken out during the year.
- Effective income tax rate is 33.33 percent.
- The mix of short-term loans payable, long-term debt and contributed is set to satisfy an existing debt covenant that requires the company to maintain a current ratio of 2.0 (or greater) and a total debt-to-total assets ratio of 80 percent (or less).

P12.28   **Residual Income Valuation.**   **Lowe's Companies Inc.** is the second largest retailer of home improvement products in the world, with a specific emphasis on retail do-it-yourself (DIY) and commercial business customers. Lowe's specializes in offering products and services for home improvement, home decor, home maintenance, home repair and remodeling, and maintenance of commercial buildings.

Required

On July 8, Year 6, Lowe's stock price closed at $45.30 per share. Lehman Brothers set a price target of $52 per share based on an EPS forecast of $2.22 per share for fiscal Year 6. Assume that the company's cost of equity is 14 percent. Using the Residenual Income valuation model to calculate the equity value of the Lowe's Companies. [As a base case, a company whose expected ROE is 25 percent per year, whose cost of equity is 14 percent, and whose growth in book value is expected to be 20 percent per year for the first ten years and five percent per year thereafter, would have an intrinsic value of 4.015 times current book value.] Do you think Lowe's is worth $52 per share? Why?

LOWE'S COMPANIES INC. Consolidated Balance Sheet		
($ millions)	Year 5	Year 4
Assets		
Cash and cash equivalents	$ 853	$ 799
Short-term investments	273	54
Accounts receivable—net	172	166
Merchandise inventory	3,968	3,611
Deferred income taxes	58	93
Other current assets	244	197
Total current assets	5,568	4,920
Property, less accumulated depreciation	10,352	8,653
Long-term investments	29	22
Other assets	160	141
Total assets	$16,109	$13,736
Liabilities		
Short-term borrowings	$ 50	$ 100
Current maturities of long-term debt	29	59
Accounts payable	1,943	1,715
Employee retirement plans	88	126
Accrued salaries and wages	306	221
Other current liabilities	1,162	796
Total current liabilities	3,578	3,017
Long-term debt, excluding current maturities	3,736	3,734
Deferred income taxes	478	305
Other long-term liabilities	15	6
Total liabilities	7,807	7,062
Shareholders' Equity		
Preferred stock—$5 par value, none issued	—	—
Common stock—$.50 par value; shares issued and outstanding Year 5, 782; Year 4, 776	391	388
Capital in excess of par value	2,023	1,803
Retained earnings	5,887	4,482
Accumulated other comprehensive income	1	1
Total shareholders' equity	8,302	6,674
Total liabilities and shareholders' equity	$16,109	$13,736

LOWE'S COMPANIES INC. Consolidated Statements of Income			
($ millions except per share amounts for period ended)	Year 5	Year 4	Year 3
Net sales	$26,491	$22,111	$18,779
Cost of sales	18,465	15,743	13,488
Gross margin	8,026	6,368	5,291
Expenses:			
Selling, general and administrative	4,730	3,913	3,348
Store opening costs	129	140	132
Depreciation	626	517	409
Interest	182	174	121
Total expenses	5,667	4,744	4,010
Pretax earnings	2,359	1,624	1,281
Income tax provision	888	601	471
Net earnings	$ 1,471	$ 1,023	$ 810
Basic earnings per share	$ 1.89	$ 1.33	$ 1.06
Diluted earnings per share	1.85	1.30	1.05
Cash dividends per share	0.09	0.08	0.07

Selected Financial Data for Lowe's					
Lowe's Companies	**Year 5**	**Year 4**	**Year 3**	**Year 2**	**Year 1**
Net sales.....................................	$26,491	$22,111	$18,779	$15,906	$13,331
Growth in net sales (%)	19.8%	17.7%	18.1%	19.3%	—
Net earnings................................	1,471	1,023	810	673	500
Total assets................................	16,109	13,736	11,358	9,007	7,087
Shareholders' equity	8,302	6,674	5,494	4,695	3,620
Growth in shareholders' equity (%)	24.4%	21.5%	17.0%	29.7%	—
ROE Analysis					
ROE (net earnings/beginning shareholder's equity)......................	22.04%	18.62%	17.25%	18.59%	—
Return on sales (net earnings/net sales)	5.55%	4.63%	4.31%	4.23%	3.75%
Asset turnover (net sales/total assets)	1.64	1.61	1.65	1.77	1.88
Leverage (total assets/beginning shareholders' equity)......................	2.41	2.50	2.42	2.49	—

P12.29   **Integrative Case Analysis.   CSK Auto Corp.** is the largest retailer of automotive parts and accessories in the Western United States and one of the largest retailers of such products in the United States based on the number of stores. As of February 4, 2001, the company operated 1,152 stores as one fully integrated company under three brand names: Checker Auto Parts, Schuck's Auto Supply, and Kragen Auto Parts. Presented below is selected information from CSK Auto Corp.'s 2001 10-K report. Assume an effective tax rate of 40 percent.

Required

1. On March 17, 1998, the Company completed an initial public offering (IPO). What was the average price (net of underwriting fees) that CSK sold its shares for?

2. In 1999, CSK Auto spent $260.221 million on investing activities. How did the company finance this investment?

3. On February 4, 2001, the company's share price was $6.10 per share. The Board of Directors believes that the company's share price is too low and has recommended a share buyback program. What would be the financial effect of a share buyback, and what accounts would be affected if the company repurchased ten percent of its outstanding shares?

4. On March 1, 2000, the company participated in the formation of a new joint venture, PartsAmerica.com (PA) by acquiring 37 percent of the outstanding equity of PA. The company accounted for its investment in PA under the equity method.
   a. What financial effects did the company record to reflect its investment in PartsAmerica on its financial statements?
   b. During fiscal 2000, the company recognized its proportionate share of PA's net loss and wrote off the remaining investment in the joint venture. What did the company record to reflect these events in its financial statements?

5. CSK Auto reports that included in property and equipment (net) are assets under capital leases (net of accumulated amortization) of $38.067 million and $35.676 million on February 4, 2001 and January 30, 2000, respectively. Consider the information on leases provided in the financial statements and footnotes.
   a. What cash payment is CSK Auto expecting to make for operating leases for the year ending February 4, 2002?
   b. What financial effects will CSK Auto record for its capital leases for the year ending February 4, 2002?

6. CSK Auto recognizes income taxes based on pretax income.
   a. What financial effects did CSK record to recognize income taxes in 2000?
   b. Has CSK Auto reported more or less income to its shareholders cumulatively through February 4, 2001, than to the tax authorities? How much more or less?

7. On February 4, 2001, CSK Auto's share price closed at $6.10 per share. Using the residual income valuation model, calculate the equity value of the company. Assume that the company's cost of equity is approximately 10.4 percent. Top management thinks the share price should be considerably higher. How would you explain the situation to management?

CSK AUTO CORP. Consolidated Balance Sheet		
($ thousands)	02/04/01	01/30/00
Assets		
Cash and cash equivalents	$ 11,131	$ 11,762
Receivables, net of allowances of $4,236 and $3,294, respectively	79,901	69,129
Inventories	621,814	625,480
Deferred income taxes	3,133	—
Assets held for sale	1,497	4,745
Prepaid expenses and other current assets.	19,169	18,471
Total current assets	736,645	729,587
Property and equipment, net	175,358	160,561
Leasehold interests, net	20,244	8,341
Goodwill, net	130,544	124,750
Other assets, net	14,190	12,413
Total assets.	$1,076,981	$1,035,652
Liabilities and Stockholders' Equity		
Accounts payable.	$ 199,483	$ 168,770
Accrued payroll and related expenses.	27,673	38,910
Accrued expenses and other current liabilities	42,448	50,663
Current maturities of amounts due under Senior Credit Facility	54,640	3,340
Current maturities of capital lease obligations.	10,878	9,893
Deferred income taxes	—	1,417
Total current liabilities.	335,122	272,993
Facility	471,840	505,480
Subordinated Notes	81,250	81,250
Obligations under capital leases	29,273	27,170
Deferred income taxes	10,544	5,801
Other.	9,339	8,411
Total noncurrent liabilities.	602,246	628,112
Stockholders' equity		
Common stock, $0.01 par value, 50,000,000 shares authorized, 27,841,178 and 27,834,574 shares issued and outstanding at February 4, 2001, and January 30, 2000, respectively	278	278
Additional paid-in-capital	291,063	291,004
Stockholder receivable.	(745)	(584)
Deferred compensation	(156)	(324)
Accumulated deficit	(150,827)	(155,827)
Total stockholders' equity	139,613	134,547
Total liabilities and stockholders' equity.	$1,076,981	$1,035,652

CSK AUTO CORP. Consolidated Statements of Income			
($ thousands)	2/4/01	1/30/00	1/31/99
Net sales.	$1,452,109	$1,231,455	$1,004,385
Cost of sales.	769,043	636,239	531,073
Gross profit.	683,066	595,216	473,312
Other costs and expenses.	—	—	—
Operating and administrative.	568,873	471,340	391,528
Store closing costs	6,060	4,900	335
Legal settlement	8,800	—	—
Transition and integration expenses	23,818	30,187	3,075
Equity in loss of joint venture.	3,168	—	—
Goodwill amortization	4,799	1,941	—
Write-off of unamortized management fee	—	—	3,643
Secondary stock offering costs.	—	—	770
Operating profit	67,548	86,848	73,961
Interest expense, net	62,355	41,300	30,730
Income before income taxes, extraordinary loss and cumulative effect of change in accounting principle	5,193	45,548	43,231
Income tax expense.	193	17,436	15,746
Income before extraordinary loss and cumulative effect of change in accounting principle	5,000	28,112	27,485
Extraordinary loss, net of $4,236 of income taxes.	—	—	(6,767)
Income before cumulative effect of change in accounting principle.	5,000	28,112	20,718
Cumulative effect of change in accounting principle, net of $468 of income taxes	—	(741)	—
Net income.	$ 5,000	$ 27,371	$ 20,718

CSK AUTO CORP.
Consolidated Statements of Cash Flow

($ thousands)	02/04/01	01/30/00	01/31/99
Cash flows provided by (used in) operating activities			
Net income.	$ 5,000	$ 27,371	$ 20,718
Adjustments to reconcile net income to net cash provided by			
(used in) operating activities	—	—	—
Depreciation and amortization of property and equipment	33,120	26,066	20,930
Amortization of goodwill.	4,799	1,941	—
Amortization of leasehold interests	1,841	761	919
Amortization of other deferred charges	1,067	607	563
Amortization of deferred financing costs	2,224	1,406	1,016
Tax benefit relating to stock option exercises	—	393	184
Equity in loss of joint venture	3,168	—	—
Extraordinary loss on early retirement of debt, net of income taxes	—	—	6,767
Cumulative effect of change in accounting principle, net of income taxes	—	741	—
Write-off of unamortized deferred charge	—	—	3,643
Deferred income taxes	193	15,637	15,542
Change in operating assets and liabilities, net of effects of acquisitions	—	—	—
Receivables	(11,915)	(5,812)	(21,056)
Inventories	(7,577)	(93,567)	(45,848)
Prepaid expenses and other current assets	(208)	7,240	(200)
Accounts payable	25,172	11,203	7,925
Accrued payroll, accrued expenses and other current liabilities.	(23,332)	2,793	(947)
Other operating activities.	(1,083)	(811)	(6,753)
Net cash provided by (used in) operating activities	32,469	(4,031)	3,403
Cash flows provided by (used in) investing activities			
Business acquisitions, net of cash acquired	(1,182)	(218,201)	(892)
Capital expenditures	(32,080)	(41,358)	(37,846)
Expenditures for assets held for sale.	(5)	(7,400)	(19,144)
Proceeds from sale of property and equipment and assets held for sale	5,029	8,760	21,650
Investment in joint venture	(3,168)	—	—
Due to affiliate	—	—	(1,000)
Other investing activities	(3,136)	(2,022)	(292)
Net cash used in investing activities	(34,542)	(260,221)	(37,524)
Cash flows provided by (used in) financing activities			
Borrowings under Senior Credit Facility.	309,500	502,000	126,000
Payments under Senior Credit Facility.	(291,840)	(218,340)	(87,065)
Issuance of common stock in initial public offering.	—	—	172,482
Underwriter's discount and other IPO costs	—	—	(13,859)
Premiums paid upon early retirement of debt	—	—	(4,875)
Retirement of 11% Senior Subordinated Notes.	—	—	(43,750)
Retirement of 12% Subordinated Notes	—	—	(50,000)
Payment of Senior Credit Facility with public offering proceeds	—	—	(53,825)
Payment of debt issuance costs	(1,815)	(4,730)	—
Payments on capital lease obligations.	(10,934)	(10,905)	(8,634)
Advances to stockholders	(189)	—	—
Recovery of stockholder receivable.	28	434	150
Exercise of options.	59	791	367
Other financing activities	(3,367)	(726)	(232)
Net cash provided by financing activities.	$ 1,442	$268,524	$ 36,759
Net increase (decrease) in cash and cash equivalents	(631)	4,272	2,638
Cash and cash equivalents, beginning of period.	11,762	7,490	4,852
Cash and cash equivalents, end of period.	$ 11,131	$ 11,762	$ 7,490

CSK AUTO CORP.
Consolidated Statements of Stockholders' Equity (Deficit)

($ thousands)	Common Stock Shares	Common Stock Amount	Additional Paid-in Capital	Shareholder Receivable	Deferred Compensation	Accumulated Deficit	Total Equity (Deficit)
Balances at February 1, 1998	19,113,388	$191	$130,513	−$1,168	−$675	−$203,916	−$ 75,055
Amortization of deferred compensation....					182		182
Recovery of stockholder receivable.......				150			150
Issuance of common stock in initial public offering, net of transaction costs	8,625,000	86	158,537				158,623
Stock compensation			220				220
Exercise of options...................	30,444	1	366				367
Tax benefit of options.................			184				184
Net income.........................						20,718	20,718
Balances at January 31, 1999	27,768,832	278	289,820	−1,018	−493	−183,198	105,389
Amortization of deferred compensation....					169		169
Recovery of stockholder receivable.......				434			434
Exercise of options...................	65,742		791				791
Tax benefit of options.................			393				393
Net income.........................						27,371	27,371
Balances at January 30, 2000	27,834,574	278	291,004	−584	−324	−155,827	134,547
Amortization of deferred compensation....					168		168
Recovery of stockholder receivable.......				28			28
Advances to stockholders				−189			−189
Exercise of options...................	6,604		59				59
Net income.........................						5,000	5,000
Balances at February 4, 2001	27,841,178	$278	$291,063	−$745	−$156	−$150,827	$139,613

Note 8: The Company leases its office and warehouse facilities, all but three of its retail stores, and a majority of its equipment. Generally, store leases provide for minimum rentals and the payment of utilities, maintenance, insurance and taxes. Certain store leases also provide for contingent rentals based upon a percentage of sales in excess of a stipulated minimum. The majority of lease agreements are for base lease periods ranging from 15 to 20 years, with three to five renewal options of five years each.

Operating lease rental expense is as follows (in thousands):

Fiscal Year	2000	1999	1998
Minimum rentals...	$123,298	$97,748	$75,689
Contingent rentals	945	976	1,088
Sublease rentals..	−6,970	−5,395	−5,089
	$117,273	$93,329	$71,688

Future minimum lease obligations under noncancelable leases at February 4, 2001, follows:

For Fiscal Years ($ thousands)	Operating Leases	Capital Leases
2001	$122,985	$14,800
2002	115,549	13,387
2003	103,244	10,002
2004	87,459	6,496
2005	77,683	1,456
Thereafter..	387,218	3,410
	$894,138	49,551
Less amounts representing interest.........................		9,400
Present value of obligations...............................		40,151
Less: current portion		(10,878)
Long-term obligation		$29,273

P12.30 **Financial Statement Analysis and Firm Value.** Weis Markets, Inc., is a Pennsylvania business founded by Harry and Sigmund Weis in 1912. The company is engaged principally in the retail sale of food and pet supplies in Pennsylvania and surrounding states. The Weis family currently owns approximately 62 percent of the outstanding shares. The company's retail food stores sell groceries, dairy products, frozen foods, meats, seafood, fresh produce, floral, prescriptions, deli/bakery products, prepared foods, fuel and general merchandise items, such as health and beauty care and household products.

Required

1. Was Year 3 a good year or a bad year for Weis? Why?
2. What was the company's interest coverage ratio in Year 3 and Year 2? On July 1, Year 3, Weis considered borrowing $100 million of long-term debt at an interest rate of ten percent per year to finance a $100 million investment in additional stores. The new properties would not generate earnings until Year 4. What would the company's interest coverage ratio have been for Year 3 if it had completed the borrowing?
3. Evaluate Weis's profitability in Year 2 and Year 3 using the ROE Model discussed in Chapter 4.
4. On March 31, following Year 3, Weis's share price closed at $29.85 per share. Value Line forecasted sales of $2,050 million and $2,125 million and EPS of $2.00 and $2.10 per share for fiscal Year 4 and Year 5, respectively. The company's cost of equity is approximately nine percent. Using the Residual Income valuation model, calculate the equity value of the company. [As a base case, a company whose expected ROE is twelve percent (14 percent) per year, whose cost of equity is nine percent, and whose growth in book value is expected to be four percent per year for the first ten years and three percent per year thereafter, would have an intrinsic value of 1.54 (1.90) times current book value.] Do you think Weis is worth $29.85 per share? Why?

WEIS MARKETS, INC. Consolidated Balance Sheet		
($ thousands, for period ended)	**Year 3**	**Year 2**
Assets		
Cash.	$ 3,929	$ 3,255
Marketable securities.	43,510	28,675
Accounts receivable, net	30,188	26,530
Inventories	182,832	169,952
Prepaid expenses.	3,980	8,294
Income taxes recoverable	—	3,395
Total current assets	264,439	240,101
Property and equipment, net	428,153	439,977
Intangible and other assets	24,107	24,107
	$716,699	$704,185
Liabilities		
Accounts payable.	$101,917	$ 98,382
Accrued expenses	15,704	11,043
Accrued self-insurance.	16,117	15,040
Payable to employee benefit plans	8,950	8,672
Income taxes payable	6,112	—
Deferred income taxes.	702	4,633
Total current liabilities.	149,502	137,770
Deferred income taxes.	14,765	16,051
Long-term debt	—	25,000
Shareholders' Equity		
Common stock, no par value, 100,800,000 shares authorized, 32,986,337 and 32,978,037 shares issued, respectively.	7,882	7,630
Retained earnings	678,294	648,522
Accumulated other comprehensive income.	4,145	6,479
	690,321	662,631
Treasury stock at cost, 5,792,800 and 5,774,830 shares, respectively	(137,889)	(137,267)
Total shareholders' equity	552,432	525,364
	$716,699	$704,185

WEIS MARKETS, INC.
Consolidated Statements of Income

($ thousands except per share amounts, for period ended)	Year 3	Year 2	Year 1
Net sales.	$1,999,364	$1,971,665	$2,042,329
Cost of sales, including warehousing and distribution expenses.	1,471,479	1,457,002	1,518,136
Gross profit on sales	527,885	514,663	524,193
Operating, general and administrative expenses.	448,478	451,723	444,110
Income from operations.	79,407	62,940	80,083
Investment income.	879	9,860	18,557
Interest expense.	(394)	(1,400)	—
Other income	14,794	10,447	18,172
Income before provision for income taxes.	94,686	81,847	116,812
Provision for income taxes.	35,537	31,792	42,989
Net income.	$ 59,149	$ 50,055	$ 73,823
Cash dividends per share.	$1.08	$1.08	$1.06
Basic and diluted earnings per share.	2.17	1.55	1.77

WEIS MARKETS, INC.
Consolidated Statements of Cash Flow

($ thousands, for period ended)	Year 3	Year 2	Year 1
Cash flows from operating activities			
Net income.	$ 59,149	$ 50,055	$ 73,823
Adjustments to reconcile net income to net cash provided by operating activities			
Depreciation.	41,885	43,755	44,169
Amortization.	5,797	7,222	6,682
(Gain) loss on sale of fixed assets	(3,620)	1,629	(5,913)
Gain on sale of marketable securities	—	(570)	(1,279)
Changes in operating assets and liabilities			
Inventories	(12,880)	(1,411)	(1,395)
Accounts receivable and prepaid expenses	656	(2,923)	8,508
Income taxes recoverable	3,395	(251)	1,194
Accounts payable and other liabilities	9,551	14,993	(2,696)
Income taxes payable	6,112	—	—
Deferred income taxes.	(3,561)	1,381	2,472
Net cash provided by operating activities	106,484	113,880	125,565
Cash flows from investing activities			
Purchase of property and equipment.	(46,056)	(48,046)	(56,331)
Proceeds from the sale of property and equipment.	14,520	86	11,714
Purchase of marketable securities.	(21,754)	(299,064)	(259,574)
Proceeds from maturities of marketable securities	2,929	556,141	108,154
Proceeds from sale of marketable securities.	—	123,660	127,043
Increase in intangible and other assets	(702)	(19)	(13,379)
Net cash provided by (used in) investing activities	(51,063)	332,758	(82,373)
Cash flows from financing activities			
Proceeds (payments) of long-term debt, net	(25,000)	25,000	–0–
Proceeds from issuance of common stock	252	36	35
Dividends paid	(29,377)	(37,202)	(44,191)
Purchase and cancellation of stock.	—	(434,317)	—
Purchase of treasury stock.	(622)	(289)	(199)
Net cash used in financing activities	(54,747)	(446,772)	(44,355)
Net increase (decrease) in cash	$ 674	$ (134)	$ (1,163)

CORPORATE ANALYSIS

CA12.31 The Procter & Gamble Company. The 2012 annual report of **The Procter and Gamble Company (P&G)** is available at http://annualreport.pg.com/annualreport2012/index.shtml. After reviewing P&G's annual report, respond to the following questions:

a. Prepare pro forma income statements for 2010, 2011, and 2012, using the following assumptions. Round all amounts to the nearest million. (*Hint:* You will need to access the 2009 annual report for your historical data accumulation.)

- Sales will grow by 2.5 percent annually.
- Cost of goods sold will remain 49.2 percent of sales.
- Selling, general and administrative expense will amount to 30.4 percent of sales.
- Interest expense will be 3.5 percent times the beginning-of-year "debt due in one year" plus 4.0 percent times the beginning-of-year "long-term debt."
- Other nonoperating income will amount to 0.3 percent of sales.
- The effective tax rate will remain 26.3 percent.
- Net earnings from discontinued opeartions are nonrecurring.

b. Prepare pro forma balance sheets for 2010, 2011, and 2012, using the following assumptions:

Assets:
- Total assets will maintain a turnover rate of 0.59 times.
- Cash and cash equivalents will grow at the same rate as sales.
- Accounts receivable will maintain a turnover rate of 13.45 times.
- Inventories (total) will maintain a turnover rate of 5.65 times.
- Deferred income taxes will remain flat each year.
- Prepaid expenses and other current assets will grow at two percent per year.
- Net property, plant and equipment will maintain a fixed asset turnover of 4.06 times.
- Net goodwill and other intangible assets will maintain an intangible assets turnover of 0.89 times.
- Other current assets will remain constant at $4,348.

Liabilities:
- Total liabilities and shareholders' equity will equal forecasted total assets.
- Accounts payable will maintain a turnover rate of 6.5 times.
- Accrued and other liabilities will remain constant at $8,601.
- Taxes payable will remain a constant 70 percent of the income tax expenses (from the income statement).
- Debt due within one year is a plug figure to balance the total liabilities and total shareholders' equity.
- Long-term debt will remain constant at $20,652 .
- Deferred income taxes will grow by 20 percent of the change in net property, plant and equipment.
- Other noncurrent liabilities will remain constant at $9,429.

Shareholders' equity:
- Convertible preferred stock, common stock (at par), and Additional paid-in-capital will remain constant as the company will finance all growth and operating needs using short-term debt.
- The Reserve for ESOP debt retirement and other comprehensive income will remain constant.
- Treasury stock repurchases will increase at a rate of 7.5 percent per year.
- Ending retained earnings equals beginning retained earnings plus net earnings attributable to P&G less dividends paid.
- Consistent with its past behavior, P&G is assumed to grow its dividend eleven percent annually as follows:

2010	$5,599
2011	$6,125
2012	$6,898

c. Using the pro forma income statements from part (a) and pro forma balance sheets from part (b), prepare pro forma statements of cash flow for 2010, 2011, and 2012.
- Assume that the depreciation and amortization expense equals three percent of the beginning-of-year balance of net property, plant and equipment plus net goodwill and other intangible assets.
- Assume no change in investments.
- Gain on sale of business is assumed to be nonrecurring.
- Proceeds from asset sales are assumed to be nonrecurring.
- Acquisitions, net of cash acquired are assumed to be nonrecurring.

d. Calculate the equity value of Procter & Gamble using the discounted cash flow approach and the following assumptions:
- P&G's cost of equity is six percent.
- Assume that the growth rate (g) of free cash flow is two percent after 2012.

How does your estimate of firm value compare to P&G's current market capitalization?

e. After completing the pro forma financial statements in question b above, return to P&G's website and compare your pro forma results to the company's actual results for the period 2010 through 2012. How well do the pro forma data match up with the company's actual results? Which assumption(s) in part (b) were primarily responsible for any observed variances?

CA12.32 Internet-based Analysis.   Consider a publicly held company whose products you are familiar with. Some examples might include:

Company	Product	Corporate Website
Johnson & Johnson Company	Band-Aids	www.jnj.com
Microsoft Corporation	Windows XP software	www.microsoft.com
Nokia Corporation	Cellular phones	www.nokia.com
Intel Corporation	Pentium processors	www.intel.com
Kimberly-Clark Corporation	Kleenex	www.kimberly-clark.com

Access the company's public website and search for its most recent annual report. (Some companies provide access to their financial data through an "investor relations" link, while others provide a direct link to their "annual reports.") After locating your company's most recent annual report, open the file and review its contents. After reviewing the annual report for your selected company, prepare answers to the following questions:

a. What is the book value of the company? What is the market capitalization of the company? Why are they different?

b. What is the company's current price to book value multiple, price to sales multiple, and price to earnings multiple?

c. Calculate the company's cost of equity, assuming a risk-free rate of 4.5 percent and an equity-risk premium of 7.0 percent. How does the company's cost of equity compare to its ROE? What does the comparison tell you about the company?

d. Calculate the equity value of the company using the residual income model.

The Time Value of Money

In this appendix, we illustrate compounding and the time value of money—important concepts that affect your everyday life. To set the stage, consider the following regarding a loan made by Mr. Jacob DeHaven to General George Washington in 1777:

> The U.S. Supreme Court has upheld a refusal to repay a loan that helped save the American Revolution as George Washington's beleaguered army camped in the snow at Valley Forge. Jacob DeHaven of Philadelphia made the loan of gold, food and other supplies with an estimated value of $450,000 in February 1777. The failure of the United States ever to repay the loan obsesses Hershel Weasenforth, one of DeHaven's descendants. Before he died in 1984 at age 79, his daughter, Thelma Lunaas, promised him she would strive to get the U.S. government to settle the debt . . . DeHaven, a wealthy merchant and wine importer, was one of the patriots who responded to a desperate plea for aid for Washington's army at Valley Forge. . . . His descendants have made periodic efforts to get repayment over the past 215 years. (*Houston Chronicle*, January 29, 1992, p. 13A).

The information is not explicit as to whether Mr. DeHaven and General Washington discussed the interest rate on the loan, and if they did, whether they agreed on a specific interest rate. However, if Mr. DeHaven had written a loan agreement with just a five percent annual rate of interest and the U.S. Supreme Court had upheld the claim, Mr. DeHaven's heirs would be owed an astounding $42.9 billion some 235 years later. This case illustrates that even a modest sum of money invested at a low rate of interest for a long period of time can accumulate to a substantial sum as a consequence of the phenomenon of compounding. **Compounding** is a process in which interest is earned not only on an outstanding loan amount but also on any prior unpaid interest.

The key to understanding the concept of compounding is that the value of invested funds grows over time. Another way to think of this is that having $1 now is not the same as having $1 one year from now. If you have $1 now, you can invest it and have more than $1 in a year because your investment can earn interest. This notion—the **time value of money**—is important when evaluating the attractiveness of any investment.

How did we arrive at the $42.9 billion figure owed to Mr. DeHaven by the U.S. government? If Mr. DeHaven had written a loan for one year at five percent interest, he would expect to receive his original investment of $450,000 plus interest of $22,500 (5 percent of $450,000), or a total of $472,500 at the end of year one. If General Washington had wanted to roll the loan over for a second year, Mr. DeHaven could expect to receive $496,125 ($472,500 plus interest of $23,625 [5 percent of $472,500]) at the end of year two. If we repeated the exercise 233 more times (i.e., until 2012), you arrive at $42.9 billion.

Time	0	1	2	235
	1777	1778	1779	2012
Principal $450,000	$450,000	$472,500		
Interest	22,500	23,625		
Amount owed	$472,500	$496,125		$42.9 billion

An interesting twist to the story is that Jacob DeHaven's relatives actually sued the U.S. government for $100 billion! What rate of interest would yield that amount? You may be surprised to learn that it would only take an interest rate of 5.379 percent compounded annually over 235 years to grow to $100 billion. In fact, at six percent interest, the amount owed would be over $398 billion! A one percent increase in the rate of interest results in almost a ten-fold increase in the future amount, reflecting the power of compounding.

FUTURE VALUE OF A SINGLE AMOUNT

The DeHaven loan example illustrates the concept of **future value**. The future value of an investment is the amount that an initial investment, or a series of payments, will be worth at some point in the future. In the above example, $42.9 billion is the future value of an initial investment of $450,000 earning five percent interest per year for 235 years. The following formula can be used to compute future values:

$$\text{Future Value} = \text{Present Value} \times (1 + r)^n$$

where the present value is the amount currently invested, r is the prevailing rate of interest, and n is the number of periods (e.g., months, quarters, or years) until the cash inflow occurs. For example, if you can earn eight percent on your investment, how much would an investment of $2,000 today be worth in five years? Using the formula above, we see that the future value of your investment is $2,938, calculated as follows:

$$\text{Future Value} = \$2,000(1+.08)^5 = \$2,938.$$

Alternatively, you can use a future value table (see Table 3 at the end of this appendix), which shows that the future value of $1 to be received in 5 years at an interest rate of 8 percent, PV(5, 8%), is equal to 1.469.[1] Hence,

$$FV = \$2,000 \times PV(5,8\%) = \$2,000 \times 1.469 = \$2,938.$$

What if you want to find the future value of more than one deposit? This is not a problem as you simply add the individual future value computations together using the following formula:

$$FV = \sum_{t=1}^{n} CF_t (1 + r)^{n-t}$$

where CF represents the individual deposits.

To illustrate, suppose you deposit $200 today into a savings account, $150 one year from today, and $300 in three years from today. What will all of this be worth in five years, assuming a six percent rate of interest?

Your first deposit will earn interest for five years and therefore will have a future value of $267.60. The future value of your second and third deposit are $189.30 and $337.20, respectively, for a total future value of $794.10. (You should be certain that you can compute these amounts on your own.)

---

[1] In order to use Tables 1 through 4 at the end of this appendix, you simply find the number, called an interest factor, which is at the intersection of the appropriate interest rate column and the period row. Can you find the interest factor of 1.469 in Table 3, at the intersection of row n = 5 and the column i = 8%?

FUTURE VALUE OF AN ANNUITY

Rather than investing a single lump sum, or several deposits of differing value, you might invest a fixed amount on a regular basis. To illustrate this, assume that you plan to deposit $100 in a savings account on January 1st of each year for ten years and that you can earn seven percent interest on your deposits. How much would you have at the end of the tenth year? One way to solve this problem would be to use the future value (FV) formula (or Table 3) and compute the sum of the future value of each of the ten deposits. The first $100 deposit will be able to earn interest for ten years so it will be worth $196.70 at the end of ten years. Similarly, the second $100 deposit will earn interest for nine years and be worth $183.80. If we were to do the same calculations for each of the ten deposits and then sum the results, we would have our answer, $1,381.60. Luckily, there is an easier way to solve this type of problem.

An **annuity** is defined as a stream of equal size payments occurring at equal intervals.[2] Fortunately, a formula has been derived that can shorten the computation of the future value of an annuity:

$$\text{Future Value of an Annuity} = \text{Payment} \times FV_a(n, r\%) = \text{Payment} \times [(1+r)^n - 1]/r$$

Using the above formula, we see that $1,381.60 = \$100 \times [(1.07^{10} - 1) / .07]$. To facilitate this calculation, we can use Table 4 and find the interest factor of 13.816, which when multiplied by the recurring deposit of $100 yields our future value of $1,381.60.

To this point, all of our examples have assumed that the payments and the compounding of interest occur just once per year. This, however, may not be the case in all situations. The only adjustment needed to compute a non-annual compounding is to convert the annual interest rate into a per-period rate of interest and to work with the number of periods rather than the number of years. The per-period interest rate is calculated by dividing the annual interest rate by the number of periods per year (e.g., a twelve percent annual rate would be a one percent monthly rate). In the above example, rather than making one payment per year for ten years, let's compute the future value for ten semiannual payments of $100 with annual interest at eight percent.

We first need to convert the eight percent annual interest rate to a four percent per-period rate. Our formula then becomes $\$100 \times [(1 + .04)^{10} - 1]/.04 = \$1,200.60$. Note that we could also use the interest factor from Table 4 and compute the future value as $\$100 \times 12.006 = \$1,200.60$.

PRESENT VALUE OF A SINGLE AMOUNT

Thus far, we have been focusing on what an amount will be worth in the future. So, let's reverse our thinking and now consider what an amount to be received in the future is worth today. For example, consider a $100 investment today that will pay back $121.90 in ten years. Intuitively, this doesn't seem like a very good investment. It seems like you could do better just putting your money in a money market account at a bank. A common way to evaluate an investment opportunity like this is to compute the **present value** of the $121.90—that is, the amount that you would have to invest now, at a specified rate of interest, that would grow to $121.90 in ten years. In this case, if we assume that the prevailing interest rate is twelve percent, the present value of $121.90 to be received in ten years is $39.25—that is, if you invested $39.25 now at twelve percent annual interest, in ten years your investment would grow to a future value of $121.90.

The present value (PV) of a single amount is computed like this:

$$\text{Present Value} = \text{Future Amount} \times [1/(1+r)^n]$$

where r is the prevailing rate of interest and n is the number of periods (e.g., months, quarters, or years) until the cash inflow occurs. In the example just shown, the present value of the $121.90 would be computed as follows:

$$\text{Present Value} = \$121.90 \times [1/(1 + 0.12)^{10}] = \$39.25$$

Alternatively, you can use a present value table (see Table 1), which shows that the present value of $1 to be received in 10 years at an interest rate of twelve percent, PV(10, 12%), is equal to 0.322. Hence,

---

[2] In this appendix we assume that the deposits (often referred to as payments) occur at the end of each period. This type of annuity is called an ordinary annuity or an annuity-in-arrears. An annuity-in-advance is an annuity in which the payments occur at the beginning of each period.

$$PV = \$121.90 \times PV(10,12\%) = \$121.90 \times 0.322 = \$39.25$$

To help us decide whether to undertake an investment, we can compute the **net present value (NPV)** of the investment as follows:

> **NPV = Present value of cash flows − cost of investment**

An investment is considered to be a good one if the NPV $\geq$ 0—that is, if the present value of the expected cash inflow is greater than the cost of the investment. Conversely, if the NPV $<$ 0, it is considered to be a bad investment. In our case, the NPV of the $100 investment is equal to negative $60.75 ($39.25 − $100) assuming a prevailing interest rate of twelve percent, and, since the NPV of the investment is less than zero, it would be considered a bad investment.[3]

Let's consider another present value example. Anna Amphlett recently learned that in ten years she would receive $1 million from a trust fund established by her uncle when Anna was born. Given that she could earn about eight percent per year, Anna wondered how much her trust fund was currently worth. Using the present value approach, Anna's trust fund would be currently worth $463,000, calculated as follows:

$$PV = \$1,000,000 \times PV(10, 8\%) \text{ [from Table 1, PV(10,8\%) is equal to 0.463]}$$
$$= \$1,000,000 \times 0.463$$
$$= \mathbf{\$463,000}$$

In ten years, with an interest rate of eight percent per year, Anna's trust fund will grow to be worth $1 million, its future value.

PRESENT VALUE OF AN ANNUITY

Investments often involve a series of cash flows rather than a single lump-sum cash payment at the end of the investment. For example, consider a $60,000 investment in an MBA degree that is expected to yield an increment to your salary of $5,000 a year for the next 25 years. Is this a good investment? Unlike the previous example, this education investment pays off each year. One way to compute the present value of the incremental cash flows would be to compute the present value of each of the $5,000 annual salary flows and then add the 25 amounts up as follows:

$$5,000 \times PV(1, 10\%)$$
$$5,000 \times PV(2, 10\%)$$
$$\vdots$$
$$\underline{5,000 \times PV(25, 10\%)}$$
$$\$45,385$$

Fortunately, a formula similar to the future value of an annuity has been derived that can shorten the computation of the present value of an annuity:

Present Value of an Annuity = Payment $\times$ PV$_a$(n, r%) = Payment $\times \{1 - [1/(1 + r)^n]\}/r$

The present value of the 25 years of extra salary, assuming an interest rate of ten percent, is computed as follows:

Present Value of an Annuity = $\$5,000 \times \{1 - [1/(1 + .10)^{25}]\}/.10 = \$45,385$

Alternatively, you can use a present value table (see Table 2), which shows that the present value of $1 to be received every year for 25 years at an interest rate of ten percent, PV$_a$(25, 10%), is equal to 9.077. Hence,

---

[3] You may wonder what interest rate resulted in the deposit of $100.00 growing to $121.90 in ten years. This can be found with the use of Table 1 and the present value formula. Simply rearrange the present value (PV) formula as follows:

$$PV = FV \times PV \text{ factor}$$
$$PV / FV = PV \text{ factor}$$

We can then compute the PV factor as $100.00 / $121.90 = .820. We then search for this PV factor in Table 1 by scanning across the ten-period row until we find this a factor of 0.820 in the two percent column.

Present Value of an Annuity = $5,000 × 9.077 = $45,385

But is this a good investment? Using the formula to calculate the net present value of an investment reveals that the NPV of receiving $5,000 per year for 25 years, with a prevailing interest rate of ten percent, is negative $14,615, calculated as follows:

$$\text{NPV} = \$5,000 \times PV_a(12,10\%) - \$60,000$$
$$= \$5,000 \times 9.077 - \$60,000$$
$$= \$45,385 - \$60,000$$
$$\mathbf{= -\$14{,}615 < 0}$$

In this case, since the NPV of the investment is less than zero, the investment in the MBA degree is a bad one from a financial standpoint.

Consider a final example of an annuity. Josie Walsh recently won the lottery, which will pay her $500,000 every year for the next 20 years. Josie's friend, Paul, offered her $3.5 million now if she will give him the winning ticket. Josie figures that she could always put the money in U.S. government bonds earning twelve percent. Should Josie sell her winning ticket for $3.5 million? Calculating the net present value of 20 payments of $500,000 reveals that the NPV of keeping the ticket is $234,500, calculated as follows:

$$\text{NPV} = \$500,000 \times PV_a(20, 12\%) - \$3,500,000 \text{ [from Table 2, } PV_a(20,12\%) \text{ is equal to 7.469]}$$
$$= \$500,000 \times 7.469 - \$3,500,000$$
$$= \$3,734,500 - \$3,500,000$$
$$= \$234,500 > 0$$

Since the NPV of refusing the offer is $234,500, which is greater than zero, Josie should not accept Paul's offer to buy her winning lottery ticket.

TABLE 1	Present Value of $1											
Period	**1%**	**2%**	**3%**	**4%**	**5%**	**6%**	**7%**	**8%**	**9%**	**10%**	**11%**	**12%**
1	0.990	0.980	0.971	0.962	0.952	0.943	0.935	0.926	0.917	0.909	0.901	0.893
2	0.980	0.961	0.943	0.925	0.907	0.890	0.873	0.857	0.842	0.826	0.812	0.797
3	0.971	0.942	0.915	0.889	0.864	0.840	0.816	0.794	0.772	0.751	0.731	0.712
4	0.961	0.924	0.888	0.855	0.823	0.792	0.763	0.735	0.708	0.683	0.659	0.636
5	0.951	0.906	0.863	0.822	0.784	0.747	0.713	0.681	0.650	0.621	0.593	0.567
6	0.942	0.888	0.837	0.790	0.746	0.705	0.666	0.630	0.596	0.564	0.535	0.507
7	0.933	0.871	0.813	0.760	0.711	0.665	0.623	0.583	0.547	0.513	0.482	0.452
8	0.923	0.853	0.789	0.731	0.677	0.627	0.582	0.540	0.502	0.467	0.434	0.404
9	0.914	0.837	0.766	0.703	0.645	0.592	0.544	0.500	0.460	0.424	0.391	0.361
10	0.905	0.820	0.744	0.676	0.614	0.558	0.508	0.463	0.422	0.386	0.352	0.322
11	0.896	0.804	0.722	0.650	0.585	0.527	0.475	0.429	0.388	0.350	0.317	0.287
12	0.887	0.788	0.701	0.625	0.557	0.497	0.444	0.397	0.356	0.319	0.286	0.257
13	0.879	0.773	0.681	0.601	0.530	0.469	0.415	0.368	0.326	0.290	0.258	0.229
14	0.870	0.758	0.661	0.577	0.505	0.442	0.388	0.340	0.299	0.263	0.232	0.205
15	0.861	0.743	0.642	0.555	0.481	0.417	0.362	0.315	0.275	0.239	0.209	0.183
16	0.853	0.728	0.623	0.534	0.458	0.394	0.339	0.292	0.252	0.218	0.188	0.163
17	0.844	0.714	0.605	0.513	0.436	0.371	0.317	0.270	0.231	0.198	0.170	0.146
18	0.836	0.700	0.587	0.494	0.416	0.350	0.296	0.250	0.212	0.180	0.153	0.130
19	0.828	0.686	0.570	0.475	0.396	0.331	0.277	0.232	0.194	0.164	0.138	0.116
20	0.820	0.673	0.554	0.456	0.377	0.312	0.258	0.215	0.178	0.149	0.124	0.104
25	0.780	0.610	0.478	0.375	0.295	0.233	0.184	0.146	0.116	0.092	0.074	0.059
30	0.742	0.552	0.412	0.308	0.231	0.174	0.131	0.099	0.075	0.057	0.044	0.033
35	0.706	0.500	0.355	0.253	0.181	0.130	0.094	0.068	0.049	0.036	0.026	0.019
40	0.672	0.453	0.307	0.208	0.142	0.097	0.067	0.046	0.032	0.022	0.015	0.011
50	0.608	0.372	0.228	0.141	0.087	0.054	0.034	0.021	0.013	0.009	0.005	0.003

TABLE 2	Present Value of an Ordinary Annuity of $1 per Period											
Period	1%	2%	3%	4%	5%	6%	7%	8%	9%	10%	11%	12%
1	0.990	0.980	0.971	0.962	0.952	0.943	0.935	0.926	0.917	0.909	0.901	0.893
2	1.970	1.942	1.913	1.886	1.859	1.833	1.808	1.783	1.759	1.736	1.713	1.690
3	2.941	2.884	2.829	2.775	2.723	2.673	2.624	2.577	2.531	2.487	2.444	2.402
4	3.902	3.808	3.717	3.630	3.546	3.465	3.387	3.312	3.240	3.170	3.102	3.037
5	4.853	4.713	4.580	4.452	4.329	4.212	4.100	3.993	3.890	3.791	3.696	3.605
6	5.795	5.601	5.417	5.242	5.076	4.917	4.767	4.623	4.486	4.355	4.231	4.111
7	6.728	6.472	6.230	6.002	5.786	5.582	5.389	5.206	5.033	4.868	4.712	4.564
8	7.652	7.325	7.020	6.733	6.463	6.210	5.971	5.747	5.535	5.335	5.146	4.968
9	8.566	8.162	7.786	7.435	7.108	6.802	6.515	6.247	5.995	5.759	5.537	5.328
10	9.471	8.983	8.530	8.111	7.722	7.360	7.024	6.710	6.418	6.145	5.889	5.650
11	10.368	9.787	9.253	8.760	8.306	7.887	7.499	7.139	6.805	6.495	6.207	5.938
12	11.255	10.575	9.954	9.385	8.863	8.384	7.943	7.536	7.161	6.814	6.492	6.194
13	12.134	11.348	10.635	9.986	9.394	8.853	8.358	7.904	7.487	7.103	6.750	6.424
14	13.004	12.106	11.296	10.563	9.899	9.295	8.745	8.244	7.786	7.367	6.982	6.628
15	13.865	12.849	11.938	11.118	10.380	9.712	9.108	8.559	8.061	7.606	7.191	6.811
16	14.718	13.578	12.561	11.652	10.838	10.106	9.447	8.851	8.313	7.824	7.379	6.974
17	15.562	14.292	13.166	12.166	11.274	10.477	9.763	9.122	8.544	8.022	7.549	7.120
18	16.398	14.992	13.754	12.659	11.690	10.828	10.059	9.372	8.756	8.201	7.702	7.250
19	17.226	15.678	14.324	13.134	12.085	11.158	10.336	9.604	8.950	8.365	7.839	7.366
20	18.046	16.351	14.877	13.590	12.462	11.470	10.594	9.818	9.129	8.514	7.963	7.469
25	22.023	19.523	17.413	15.622	14.094	12.783	11.654	10.675	9.823	9.077	8.422	7.843
30	25.808	22.396	19.600	17.292	15.372	13.765	12.409	11.258	10.274	9.427	8.694	8.055
35	29.409	24.999	21.487	18.665	16.374	14.498	12.948	11.655	10.567	9.644	8.855	8.176
40	32.835	27.355	23.115	19.793	17.159	15.046	13.332	11.925	10.757	9.779	8.951	8.244
50	39.196	31.424	25.730	21.482	18.256	15.762	13.801	12.233	10.962	9.915	9.042	8.304

TABLE 3	Future Value of $1											
Period	1%	2%	3%	4%	5%	6%	7%	8%	9%	10%	11%	12%
1	1.010	1.020	1.030	1.040	1.050	1.060	1.070	1.080	1.090	1.100	1.110	1.120
2	1.020	1.040	1.061	1.082	1.103	1.124	1.145	1.166	1.188	1.210	1.232	1.254
3	1.030	1.061	1.093	1.125	1.158	1.191	1.225	1.260	1.295	1.331	1.368	1.405
4	1.041	1.082	1.126	1.170	1.216	1.262	1.311	1.360	1.412	1.464	1.518	1.574
5	1.051	1.104	1.159	1.217	1.276	1.338	1.403	1.469	1.539	1.611	1.685	1.762
6	1.062	1.126	1.194	1.265	1.340	1.419	1.501	1.587	1.677	1.772	1.870	1.974
7	1.072	1.149	1.230	1.316	1.407	1.504	1.606	1.714	1.828	1.949	2.076	2.211
8	1.083	1.172	1.267	1.369	1.477	1.594	1.718	1.851	1.993	2.144	2.305	2.476
9	1.094	1.195	1.305	1.423	1.551	1.689	1.838	1.999	2.172	2.358	2.558	2.773
10	1.105	1.219	1.344	1.480	1.629	1.791	1.967	2.159	2.367	2.594	2.839	3.106
11	1.116	1.243	1.384	1.539	1.710	1.898	2.105	2.332	2.580	2.853	3.152	3.479
12	1.127	1.268	1.426	1.601	1.796	2.012	2.252	2.518	2.813	3.138	3.498	3.896
13	1.138	1.294	1.469	1.665	1.886	2.133	2.410	2.720	3.066	3.452	3.883	4.363
14	1.149	1.319	1.513	1.732	1.980	2.261	2.579	2.937	3.342	3.797	4.310	4.887
15	1.161	1.346	1.558	1.801	2.079	2.397	2.759	3.172	3.642	4.177	4.785	5.474
16	1.173	1.373	1.605	1.873	2.183	2.540	2.952	3.426	3.970	4.595	5.311	6.130
17	1.184	1.400	1.653	1.948	2.292	2.693	3.159	3.700	4.328	5.054	5.895	6.866
18	1.196	1.428	1.702	2.026	2.407	2.854	3.380	3.996	4.717	5.560	6.544	7.690
19	1.208	1.457	1.754	2.107	2.527	3.026	3.617	4.316	5.142	6.116	7.263	8.613
20	1.220	1.486	1.806	2.191	2.653	3.207	3.870	4.661	5.604	6.727	8.062	9.646
25	1.282	1.641	2.094	2.666	3.386	4.292	5.427	6.848	8.623	10.835	13.585	17.000

continued

continued from previous page

TABLE 3	Future Value of $1											
Period	1%	2%	3%	4%	5%	6%	7%	8%	9%	10%	11%	12%
30	1.348	1.811	2.427	3.243	4.322	5.743	7.612	10.063	13.268	17.449	22.892	29.960
35	1.417	2.000	2.814	3.946	5.516	7.686	10.677	14.785	20.414	28.102	38.575	52.800
40	1.489	2.208	3.262	4.801	7.040	10.286	14.974	21.725	31.409	45.259	65.001	93.051
50	1.645	2.692	4.384	7.107	11.467	18.420	29.457	46.902	74.358	117.391	184.565	289.002

TABLE 4	Future Value of an Ordinary Annuity of $1 per Period											
Period	1%	2%	3%	4%	5%	6%	7%	8%	9%	10%	11%	12%
1	1.000	1.000	1.000	1.000	1.000	1.000	1.000	1.000	1.000	1.000	1.000	1.000
2	2.010	2.020	2.030	2.040	2.050	2.060	2.070	2.080	2.090	2.100	2.110	2.120
3	3.030	3.060	3.091	3.122	3.153	3.184	3.215	3.246	3.278	3.310	3.342	3.374
4	4.060	4.122	4.184	4.246	4.310	4.375	4.440	4.506	4.573	4.641	4.710	4.779
5	5.101	5.204	5.309	5.416	5.526	5.637	5.751	5.867	5.985	6.105	6.228	6.353
6	6.152	6.308	6.468	6.633	6.802	6.975	7.153	7.336	7.523	7.716	7.913	8.115
7	7.214	7.434	7.662	7.898	8.142	8.394	8.654	8.923	9.200	9.487	9.783	10.089
8	8.286	8.583	8.892	9.214	9.549	9.897	10.260	10.637	11.028	11.436	11.859	12.300
9	9.369	9.755	10.159	10.583	11.027	11.491	11.978	12.488	13.021	13.579	14.164	14.776
10	10.462	10.950	11.464	12.006	12.578	13.181	13.816	14.487	15.193	15.937	16.722	17.549
11	11.567	12.169	12.808	13.486	14.207	14.972	15.784	16.645	17.560	18.531	19.561	20.655
12	12.683	13.412	14.192	15.026	15.917	16.870	17.888	18.977	20.141	21.384	22.713	24.133
13	13.809	14.680	15.618	16.627	17.713	18.882	20.141	21.495	22.953	24.523	26.212	28.029
14	14.947	15.974	17.086	18.292	19.599	21.015	22.550	24.215	26.019	27.975	30.095	32.393
15	16.097	17.293	18.599	20.024	21.579	23.276	25.129	27.152	29.361	31.772	34.405	37.280
16	17.258	18.639	20.157	21.825	23.657	25.673	27.888	30.324	33.003	35.950	39.190	42.753
17	18.430	20.012	21.762	23.698	25.840	28.213	30.840	33.750	36.974	40.545	44.501	48.884
18	19.615	21.412	23.414	25.645	28.132	30.906	33.999	37.450	41.301	45.599	50.396	55.750
19	20.811	22.841	25.117	27.671	30.539	33.760	37.379	41.446	46.018	51.159	56.939	63.440
20	22.019	24.297	26.870	29.778	33.066	36.786	40.995	45.762	51.160	57.275	64.203	72.052
25	28.243	32.030	36.459	41.646	47.727	54.865	63.249	73.106	84.701	98.347	114.41	133.33
30	34.785	40.568	47.575	56.085	66.439	79.058	94.461	113.28	136.31	164.49	199.02	241.33
35	41.660	49.994	60.462	73.652	90.320	111.43	138.24	172.32	215.71	271.02	341.59	431.66
40	48.886	60.402	75.401	95.026	120.80	154.76	199.64	259.06	337.88	442.59	581.83	767.09
50	64.463	84.579	112.80	152.67	209.35	290.34	406.53	573.77	815.08	1,163.9	1,668.8	2,400.0

Assignments with the ✓ logo in the margin are available in BusinessCourse.
See the Preface of the book for details.

EXERCISES

A.1   Margaret Diver invests $7,000 into her bank account that pays 12 percent, compounded annually. How much
will she have if:
    a. She leaves the money in her account for two years?
    b. She leaves the money in her account for three years?
    c. She leaves the money for two years but the bank's 12 percent annual rate is compounded quarterly?

A.2   Jay Stone invested $3,000 he won in a poker match at 8 percent annual interest for 10 years. At the end of
the 10 years he took all the money out and went on a spending spree. How much can he spend if:
    a. The interest is compounded annually?
    b. The interest is compounded semiannually?
    c. The interest is compounded quarterly?

A.3   Julie Lynch invests $1,000 annually into her bank at the end of each year for five years. Her bank pays inter-
est at the annual rate of 6 percent. How much will she have at the end of the fifth year?

A.4   Murat Borat just opened an Individual Retirement Account (IRA) and plans to contribute $4,000 per year for
30 years at which time he will retire. Assume he funds his IRA at the end of each of the 30 years and he can
earn 12 percent compounded annually. How much will he have at retirement?

A.5   Debra Moore needs $20,000 3 years from now. How much should she invest today in order to reach her
goal if
    a. She can earn 6 percent compounded annually?
    b. She can earn an annual rate of 6 percent compounded semiannually?

A.6   Abe Washington sold some property in Oregon and will receive $40,000 in 5 equal payments of $8,000 at
the end of each year from today. What is the present value of these future payments at an interest rate of 9
percent compounded annually?

A.7   Lucky Lewis won a jackpot that offered him the option of receiving $15,000 immediately or $30,000 20
years from now. Assuming Lucky can earn a rate of 8 percent compounded annually, which option should he
select?

A.8   You have been offered an investment that will pay you a lump sum of $30,000 25 years from today, along with
a payment of $1,000 per year for 25 years starting one year from today. How much are you willing to invest
today to have this investment in your portfolio assuming you wish to earn a rate of 6 percent compounded
annually?

A.9   Jesse would like to have $1 million dollars in 10 years. Jesse will invest $75,000 in a money market account
at the end of each year for the next 10 years. His account will earn an annual rate of 6 percent compounded
annually. Will Jesse reach his goal of becoming a millionaire? If not, how much will his mother have to gift
him at the end of 10 years?

A.10   Muir would like to have $6 million dollars in 20 years. Muir will invest $150,000 in a money market account
at the end of each year for the next 20 years. His account will earn an annual rate of 7 percent compounded
annually. Will Muir reach his goal of accumulating $6 million? He told his business partner that if he exceeds
his goal he will contribute the excess to charity. How large of a contribution, if any, will he make?

B Financial Statement Ratios and Metrics

Asset Management

Accounts receivable turnover
Receivable collection period
Intangible asset turnover
Inventory turnover
Inventory-on-hand period
Fixed asset turnover
Total asset turnover

Cash flow

Cash conversion ratio
Discretionary cash flow
Free cash flow
Free cash flow yield
Operating funds ratio

Profitability

Common equity share of operating earnings
Earnings per share (basic, diluted)
Earnings before interest, income taxes, depreciation and amortization (EBITDA)
Gross profit margin
Pro forma earnings
Return on assets
Return on equity
Return on sales

Liquidity

Accounts payable turnover
Days' payable period
Cash collection period
Cash and marketable securities to total assets
Current ratio
Operating cash flow to current liabilities
Quick ratio

Solvency

Financial leverage
Interest coverage
Long-term debt to equity
Long-term debt to total assets
Total debt to total assets

Miscellaneous

Accumulated depreciation to gross property, plant and equipment
Allowance for uncollectible accounts to gross accounts receivable
Capital intensity
Conservatism ratio
Cost of debt
Cost of equity
Dividend payout
Dividend retention rate
Dividend yield
Inventory reserve
Sustainable growth rate

C IFRS Illustrated: LVMH Moet Hennessey-Louis Vuitton S.A.

In this appendix, the financial statements of **LVMH Moet Hennessey-Louis Vuitton S.A.** (LVMH hereafter) are presented as an illustration of IFRS-based financial statements. LVMH is a French company that was founded in 1987 with the merger of champagne producer Moet et Chandon and the cognac manufacturer Hennessey. The company is one of the world's largest luxury goods conglomerates, owning more than 60 well-recognized luxury brands of wines and spirits, watches and jewelry, fashion and leather goods, retailing, and perfumes and cosmetics. The company's brands include Dom Perignon (wines/spirits), TAG Heuer (watches), Givenchy (fashion and leather goods), DFS (retail), and Parfums Christian Dior (perfumes).

LVMH is Paris-based and is a member of the prestigious CAC 40 index on the Euronext Paris Exchange. The company employs almost 100,000 and operates over 3,000 retail stores worldwide. The company's shares trade in the United States as an American Depository Receipt on the Over-The-Counter (OTC) exchange under the symbol LVMUY. The company prepares its financial statements using IFRS.

LVMH GROUP
Condensed Consolidated Financial Statements
Consolidated Income Statement

(€ millions, except for earnings per share)	Notes	2012	2011	2010
Revenue	23	**28,103**	**23,659**	**20,320**
Cost of sales		(9,917)	(8,092)	(7,184)
Gross margin		**18,186**	**15,567**	**13,136**
Marketing and selling expenses		(10,101)	(8,360)	(7,098)
General and administrative expenses		(2,164)	(1,944)	(1,717)
Profit from recurring operations	23-24	**5,921**	**5,263**	**4,321**
Other operating income and expenses	25	(182)	(109)	(152)
Operating profit		**5,739**	**5,154**	**4,169**
Cost of net financial debt		(140)	(151)	(151)
Other financial income and expenses		126	(91)	763
Net financial income (expense)	26	**(14)**	**(242)**	**612**
Income taxes	27	(1,820)	(1,453)	(1,469)
Income (loss) from investments in associates	7	4	6	7
Net profit before minority interests		**3,909**	**3,465**	**3,319**
Minority interests	17	(485)	(400)	(287)
Net profit—Group share		**3,424**	**3,065**	**3,032**
Basic Group share of net earnings per share *(in €)*	28	**6.86**	**6.27**	**6.36**
Number of shares on which the calculation is based		499,133,643	488,769,286	476,870,920
Diluted Group share of net earnings per share *(in €)*	28	**6.82**	**6.23**	**6.32**
Number of shares on which the calculation is based		502,229,952	492,207,492	479,739,697

LVMH GROUP
Condensed Consolidated Financial Statements
Consolidated Balance Sheet

(€ millions)	Notes	2012	2011	2010
ASSETS				
Brands and other intangible assets	3	11,510	11,482	9,104
Goodwill	4	7,806	6,957	5,027
Property, plant and equipment	6	8,769	8,017	6,733
Investments in associates	7	163	170	223
Non-current available for sale financial assets	8	6,004	5,982	3,891
Other non-current assets	9	524	478	319
Deferred tax		881	716	668
Non-current assets		**35,657**	**33,802**	**25,965**
Inventories and work in progress	10	8,080	7,510	5,991
Trade accounts receivable	11	1,985	1,878	1,565
Income taxes		201	121	96
Other current assets	12	1,811	1,455	1,255
Cash and cash equivalents	14	2,196	2,303	2,292
Current assets		**14,273**	**13,267**	**11,199**
Total assets		**49,930**	**47,069**	**37,164**
LIABILITIES AND EQUITY				
Share capital		152	152	147
Share premium account		3,848	3,801	1,782
Treasury shares and LVMH-share settled derivatives		(414)	(485)	(607)
Cumulative translation adjustment		342	431	230
Revaluation reserves		2,819	2,689	1,244
Other reserves		14,393	12,798	11,370
Group share of net profit		3,424	3,065	3,032
Equity—Group share	15	24,564	22,451	17,198
Minority interests	17	1,102	1,061	1,006
Total equity		**25,666**	**23,512**	**18,204**
Long-term borrowings	18	3,836	4,132	3,432
Provisions	19	1,530	1,400	1,167
Deferred tax		3,960	3,925	3,354
Other non-current liabilities	20	5,456	4,506	3,947
Non-current liabilities		**14,782**	**13,963**	**11,900**
Short-term borrowings	18	2,976	3,134	1,834
Trade accounts payable		3,134	2,952	2,298
Income taxes		442	443	446
Provisions	19	335	349	339
Other current liabilities	21	2,595	2,716	2,143
Current liabilities		**9,482**	**9,594**	**7,060**
Total liabilities and equity		**49,930**	**47,069**	**37,164**

LVMH GROUP
Condensed Consolidated Financial Statements
Consolidated Statement of Changes in Equity

(€ millions)	Share Capital: Number of Shares	Share Capital	Share Premium Account	Treasury Shares and LVMH-Share Settled Derivatives	Cumulative Translation Adjustment	Revaluation Reserves: Available for Sale Financial Assets	Revaluation Reserves: Hedges of Future Foreign Currency Cash Flows	Revaluation Reserves: Vineyard Land	Net Profit and Other Reserves	Total Equity: Group Share	Total Equity: Minority Interests	Total
Notes		15.1		15.2	15.4						17	
As of December 31, 2009	490,405,654	147	1,763	(929)	(495)	213	63	595	12,439	13,796	989	14,785
Gains and losses recognized in equity					725	297	(32)	108		1,098	88	1,186
Net profit.									3,032	3,032	287	3,319
Comprehensive income . . .		—	—	—	725	297	(32)	108	3,032	4,130	375	4,505
Stock option plan and similar expenses.									41	41	3	44
(Acquisition)/disposal of treasury shares and LVMH-share settled derivatives				221					(43)	178	—	178
Exercise of LVMH share subscription options.	2,012,478		120							120	—	120
Retirement of LVMH shares	(1,775,900)		(101)	101	—					—	—	—
Capital increase in subsidiaries										—	1	1
Interim and final dividends paid									(953)	(953)	(158)	(1,111)
Changes in control of consolidated entities										—	(3)	(3)
Acquisition and disposal of minority interests' shares .									(83)	(83)	(104)	(187)
Purchase commitments for minority interests' shares . . .									(31)	(31)	(97)	(128)
As of December 31, 2010 . .	490,642,232	147	1,782	(607)	230	510	31	703	14,402	17,198	1,006	18,204
Gains and losses recognized in equity					201	1,480	(46)	11		1,646	33	1,679
Net profit.									3,065	3,065	400	3,465
Comprehensive income . . .		—	—	—	201	1,480	(46)	11	3,065	4,711	433	5,144
Stock option plan and similar expenses.									49	49	3	52
(Acquisition)/disposal of treasury shares and LVMH-share settled derivatives				15					(8)	7	—	7
Exercise of LVMH share subscription options.	1,395,835		94							94	—	94
Retirement of LVMH shares .	(2,259,454)		(107)	107						—	—	—
Acquisition of a controlling interest in Bulgari	18,037,011	5	2,032	—					201	2,238	772	3,010
Capital increase in subsidiaries										—	4	4
Interim and final dividends paid									(1,069)	(1,069)	(187)	(1,256)
Changes in control of consolidated entities, excluding Bulgari									(5)	(5)	20	15
Acquisition and disposal of minority interests' shares . . .									(681)	(681)	(785)	(1,466)
Purchase commitments for minority interests' shares . . .									(91)	(91)	(205)	(296)
As of December 31, 2011 . .	507,815,624	152	3,801	(485)	431	1,990	(15)	714	15,863	22,451	1,061	23,512

continued next page

continued from previous page

LVMH GROUP
Condensed Consolidated Financial Statements
Consolidated Statement of Changes in Equity

(€ millions)	Share Capital: Number of Shares	Share Capital	Share Premium Account	Treasury Shares and LVMH-Share Settled Derivatives	Cumulative Translation Adjustment	Revaluation Reserves — Available for Sale Financial Assets	Revaluation Reserves — Hedges of Future Foreign Currency Cash Flows	Revaluation Reserves — Vineyard Land	Net Profit and Other Reserves	Total Equity — Group Share	Total Equity — Minority Interests	Total
As of December 31, 2011	507,815,624	152	3,801	(485)	431	1,990	(15)	714	15,863	22,451	1,061	23,512
Gains and losses recognized in equity					(89)	(47)	133	44		41	(3)	38
Net profit									3,424	3,424	485	3,909
Comprehensive income		—	—	—	(89)	(47)	133	44	3,424	3,465	482	3,947
Stock option plan and similar expenses									50	50	3	53
(Acquisition)/disposal of treasury shares and LVMH-share settled derivatives				24					(12)	12	—	12
Exercise of LVMH share subscription options	1,344,975		94							94	—	94
Retirement of LVMH shares	(997,250)		(47)	47						—	—	—
Capital increase in subsidiaries										—	8	8
Interim and final dividends paid									(1,448)	(1,448)	(317)	(1,765)
Changes in control of consolidated entities									(11)	(11)	(11)	(22)
Acquisition and disposal of minority interests' shares									(39)	(39)	(26)	(65)
Purchase commitments for minority interests' shares									(10)	(10)	(98)	(108)
As of December 31, 2012	508,163,349	152	3,848	(414)	342	1,943	118	758	17,817	24,564	1,102	25,666

LVMH GROUP
Condensed Consolidated Financial Statements
Consolidated Cash Flow Statement

(€ millions)	Notes	2012	2011	2010
I. OPERATING ACTIVITIES AND OPERATING INVESTMENTS				
Operating profit		5,739	5,154	4,169
Net increase in depreciation, amortization and provisions		1,299	999	788
Other computed expenses		(62)	(45)	(126)
Dividends received		188	61	20
Other adjustments		(51)	(32)	(3)
Cash from operations before changes in working capital		**7,113**	**6,137**	**4,848**
Cost of net financial debt: interest paid		(154)	(152)	(149)
Income taxes paid		(1,970)	(1,544)	(897)
Net cash from operating activities before changes in working capital		**4,989**	**4,441**	**3,802**
Change in working capital	14.1	(813)	(534)	247
Net cash from operating activities		**4,176**	**3,907**	**4,049**
Operating investments	14.2	**(1,702)**	**(1,730)**	**(976)**
Net cash from operating activities and operating investments (free cash flow)		**2,474**	**2,177**	**3,073**
II. FINANCIAL INVESTMENTS				
Purchase of non-current available for sale financial assets	8	(131)	(518)	(1,724)
Proceeds from sale of non-current available for sale financial assets	8	36	17	70
Impact of purchase and sale of consolidated investments	2	(45)	(785)[a]	(61)
Net cash from (used in) financial investments		**(140)**	**(1,286)**	**(1,715)**
III. TRANSACTIONS RELATING TO EQUITY				
Capital increases of LVMH	15.1	94	94[a]	120
Capital increases of subsidiaries subscribed by minority interests	17	8	3	1
Acquisition and disposals of treasury shares and LVMH-share settled derivatives	15.2	5	2	155
Interim and final dividends paid by LVMH	15.3	(1,447)	(1,069)	(953)
Interim and final dividends paid to minority interests in consolidated subsidiaries	17	(314)	(189)	(158)
Purchase and proceeds from sale of minority interests	2	(206)	(1,413)	(185)
Net cash from (used in) transactions relating to equity		**(1,860)**	**(2,572)**	**(1,020)**
IV. FINANCING ACTIVITIES				
Proceeds from borrowings		1,068	2,659	564
Repayment of borrowings		(1,526)	(1,005)	(1,290)
Purchase and proceeds from sale of current available for sale financial assets	13	(67)	6	(32)
Net cash from (used in) financing activities		**(525)**	**1,660**	**(758)**
V. EFFECT OF EXCHANGE RATE CHANGES		**(42)**	**60**	**188**
NET INCREASE (DECREASE) IN CASH AND CASH EQUIVALENTS (I+II+III+IV+V)		**(93)**	**39**	**(232)**
CASH AND CASH EQUIVALENTS AT BEGINNING OF PERIOD	14	**2,081**	**2,042**	**2,274**
CASH AND CASH EQUIVALENTS AT END OF PERIOD	14	**1,988**	**2,081**	**2,042**
Transactions included in the table above, generating no change in cash:				
- acquisition of assets by means of finance leases		5	3	6

(a) Not including the impact of the amount attributable to the acquisition of Bulgari remunerated by the capital increase of LVMH SA as of June 30, 2011, which did not generate any cash flows.

D Accounting Mechanics

CHAPTER 2: TECHNICAL LANGUAGE OF ACCOUNTING— THE DEBIT AND CREDIT PARADIGM

The spreadsheet approach used in Chapter 2 to analyze the effects of various accounting events on the balance sheet equation is intuitive and closely resembles how modern electronic accounting systems process accounting information. Yet financial professionals often use the technical accounting language of "debit" and "credit" when referring to accounting transactions. To help you understand this technical language, we revisit the accounting events of the Russian River Valley Winery and process them using the debit/credit mechanism and double-entry bookkeeping. But first a little history!

Luca Pacioli, an Italian monk, is credited with being the first to describe double-entry bookkeeping in his book, *Summa de Arithmetica, Geometria, Proportioni et Proportionalita,* published in Latin in 1494. Some claim that Luca didn't really invent double-entry bookkeeping; he just took the time to observe what Italian merchants were doing and then documented his observations. Instead of using pluses and minuses, Luca invented the T-account having two sides. The left side was referred to as the **debit** side—often represented as "Dr"—and the right side he called the **credit** side—or "Cr" for short. The T-account Luca invented looked like this:

T-Account

Debit	Credit
(Dr)	(Cr)

Of course, Luca had to decide which side would be a positive and which would be negative. So, he concluded that an increase in assets would be a debit (the left side) and a decrease in assets would be a credit (the right side). Similarly, an increase in a liability must be a credit and a decrease in a liability a debit. And, since shareholders' equity is on the same side of the balance sheet equation as the liabilities, an increase (decrease) in shareholders' equity would be a credit (debit). The reasons why Luca selected this particular convention have been lost with time. Be careful to note that the words debit and credit are not synonymous with increase and decrease. Instead, they merely identify the left or right side of the T-account. The following diagram summarizes the debit/credit convention described by Luca:

Asset		=	Liability		+	Shareholders' Equity	
Debit	Credit		Debit	Credit		Debit	Credit
(+)	(−)		(−)	(+)		(−)	(+)

The Accounting Cycle

The process of analyzing and recording accounting data for a business is often referred to as the **accounting cycle**. The cycle begins when an accounting event involving a business occurs. The event is analyzed and a determination made as to which of the business's accounts are affected. This analysis is then entered into the firm's accounting system by means of a **journal entry**, which will be illustrated shortly. Immediately after the data is entered into the firm's accounting system, it is transferred, or **posted**, to the appropriate T-accounts. The preparation of journal entries and posting of data to the T-accounts are daily activities at a business.

At the end of each fiscal period, prior to the preparation of any financial statements, a number of data verification checks are undertaken. First, **adjusting entries** are prepared to update various accounts for any new or previously unreported financial information and to correct any observed data errors. Second, a **trial balance** is prepared to insure that the amount of recorded debits equals the amount of recorded credits. Finally, the financial statements are prepared, typically in the following sequence: income statement, statement of shareholders' equity, balance sheet, and statement of cash flow. The preparation sequence reflects the fact that the basic financial statements are interdependent—that is, they articulate with one another.

Prior to the preparation of the statement of shareholders' equity, **closing entries** are prepared. Closing entries transfer the results of a business's operating activities—that is, its revenues, expenses, and dividends—to retained earnings on the statement of shareholders' equity (and hence, the balance sheet). The accounts appearing on the income statement, along with the dividend account, are referred to as temporary accounts because they are closed, or zeroed out, at the end of each accounting period. Each of these accounts will therefore start the next accounting period with a zero balance. This makes intuitive sense since we wish to measure performance over a period of time and thus need to start each period with a blank slate. The accounts appearing on the balance sheet, in contrast, are referred to as permanent accounts because they are not closed out at the end of each accounting period. In fact, the temporary accounts are closed to a permanent account, retained earnings. Again, this makes intuitive sense since it is the purpose of the balance sheet to report a business's financial condition at a point in time, rather than for a period of time. Considered a different way, the various accounts such as cash or accounts payable that exist at the end of the period should still exist at the start of the next period unless all cash is paid out and all accounts payable are paid in full. After the closing entries are executed, the remaining financial statements—the statement of shareholders' equity, the balance sheet, and the statement of cash flow—can be prepared.

To summarize, the various steps in the accounting cycle are:

1. Record the daily accounting events using journal entries.
2. Post the journal entry data to the appropriate T-accounts.
3. At the end of the fiscal period, record any needed adjusting entries.
4. Prepare a trial balance.
5. Record the closing entries for the revenue, expense, and dividend accounts.
6. Prepare the financial statements.

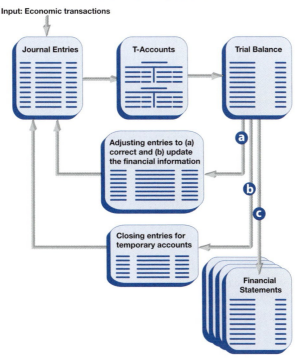

There are three arrows originating from the Trial Balance. Each of these loops represents a different version of the trial balance—(a) pre-adjustment, (b) post-adjustment, and (c) post-closing trial balances. It is the final post-closing trial balance that is used to create the company's financial statements.

To illustrate the accounting cycle, we return to the pre-opening balance sheet for the Russian River Valley Winery presented in Exhibit D.1.

EXHIBIT D.1	

RUSSIAN RIVER VALLEY WINERY, INC. Balance Sheet	
($ thousands)	Pre-Opening
Assets	
Cash..	$ 4,700
Buildings..	2,000
Land...	4,000
Intangible assets	100
Total assets...	$10,800
Liabilities and Shareholders' Equity	
Loan payable	$ 4,800
Shareholders' equity	
Common stock..	6,000
Liabilities and shareholders' equity	$10,800

Step 1—Record the accounting events using journal entries.

The 14 events for the Russian River Valley Winery are recorded below using journal entries and the debit/credit paradigm (see Chapter 2 for a summary of these transactions in spreadsheet form). The convention is to record the debit portion of a journal entry on top and then to record the credit part of the entry below. Care must be exercised that the total of the debit portion of each entry exactly equals the credit portion.

Event	Accounts	Debit	Credit
1(a)	Inventory	380	
	Accounts payable............................		380
1(b)	Accounts payable...............................	360	
	Cash.......................................		360
2	Equipment	1,500	
	Cash.......................................		1,500
3	Equipment	2,000	
	Cash.......................................		2,000
4(a)	Cash...	380	
	Accounts receivable............................	1,520	
	Sales revenue.................................		1,900
4(b)	Cash...	720	
	Accounts receivable...........................		720
5(a)	Wage expense	100	
	Cash.......................................		100
5(b)	Selling & administrative expense	300	
	Cash.......................................		300
6(a)	Loan payable	480	
	Cash.......................................		480
6(b)	Interest expense................................	288	
	Cash.......................................		288
7	Cost of goods sold..............................	380	
	Inventory....................................		380

continued

Event	Accounts	Debit	Credit
8(a)	Depreciation expense—equipment	175	
	Accumulated depreciation		175
8(b)	Depreciation expense—buildings.	50	
	Accumulated depreciation		50
9	Amortization expense.	50	
	Intangible asset		50
10	Cash.	400	
	Common stock.		400
11	(No event is recorded.)		
12	Income tax expense.	240	
	Income taxes payable		96
	Cash.		144
13	Inventory.	60	
	Accounts payable.		60
14	Retained earnings (dividend declared).	260	
	Cash.		260

Step 2—Post the journal entry data to the appropriate T-accounts.

If you examine the T-accounts below, you will see that each of the debits and credits from the journal entries above have been entered into the appropriate T-accounts. Notice that the ending balance[s] for each of the T-accounts exactly correspond to the ending balances obtained using the spreadsheet approach followed in Chapter 2.

Cash

Bal	4,700		
4(a)	380	360	1(b)
4(b)	720	1,500	2
		2,000	3
		100	5(a)
		300	5(b)
		480	6(a)
		288	6(b)
10	400	144	12
		260	14
Bal	768		

Accounts Receivable

Bal	0		
4(a)	1,520		
		720	4(b)
Bal	800		

Inventory

Bal	0		
1(a)	380		
		380	7
13	60		
Bal	60		

Equipment

Bal	0		
2	1,500		
3	2,000		
Bal	3,500		

Accounts Payable

		0	Bal
		380	1(a)
1(b)	360		
		60	13
		80	Bal

Income Taxes Payable

		0	Bal
		96	12
		96	Bal

Loan Payable

		4,800	Bal
6(a)	480		
		4,320	Bal

Common Stock

		6,000	Bal
		400	10
		6,400	Bal

Retained Earnings

		0	Bal
14	260		
Bal	260	317	17
		57	Bal

Income Summary

		1,900	15
16	1,583		
17	317		
		0	Bal

Sales Revenue

		1,900	4(a)
15	1,900		
		0	Bal

Cost of Goods Sold

7	380		
		380	16
Bal	0		

Wage Expense

5(a)	100		
		100	16
Bal	0		

continued

continued from previous page

Buildings		
Bal	2,000	

Accumulated Depreciation		
	0	Bal
	175	8(a)
	50	8(b)
	225	Bal

Land		
Bal	4,000	

Intangible Assets			
Bal	100	50	9
Bal	50		

Depreciation Expense		
8(a)	175	
8(b)	50	
Bal	225	
		225	16
Bal	0	

Selling & Admin Expense		
5(b)	300	
		300	16
Bal	0	

Interest Expense		
6(b)	288	
		288	16
Bal	0	

Amortization Expense		
9	50	
		50	16
Bal	0	

Income Tax Expense		
12	240	
		240	16
Bal	0	

* Entries 15, 16, and 17 in blue font are closing entries from Step 5.

Step 3—At the end of the fiscal period, make any needed adjusting entries.

Accounting events such as the recording of depreciation expense (8(a)) and amortization expense (8(b)) are considered to be adjusting entries. They are often recorded at the end of each fiscal period when a company's accounting staff reviews the business's financial data for completeness. Other examples of adjusting entries include correcting any amounts that were previously incorrectly recorded and estimating and recording the estimated losses associated with any uncollected accounts receivable.

Step 4—Prepare a trial balance.

The trial balance is a listing of the account balances from the company's various T-accounts. Russian River Valley's post-adjustment trial balance is presented in Exhibit D.2. Notice in the winery's post-adjustment trial balance that the total debit balance ($13,021) for the winery's T-accounts equals the total credit balance ($13,021). If the balances were not equal, it would indicate that an error had been made in recording some piece of accounting information.

EXHIBIT D.2

RUSSIAN RIVER VALLEY WINERY, INC.
Post-Adjustment Trial Balance

Account	Debit	Credit
Cash.	$ 768	
Accounts receivable.	800	
Inventory.	60	
Equipment	3,500	
Buildings.	2,000	
Accumulated depreciation		$ 225
Land	4,000	
Intangible assets	50	
Accounts payable.		80
Taxes payable.		96
Loan payable		4,320
Common stock.		6,400
Retained earnings	260	
Sales revenue.		1,900
Cost of goods sold.	380	
Wages expense	100	
Depreciation expense.	225	
Selling & administrative expense	300	
Interest expense.	288	
Amortization expense.	50	
Tax expense	240	
Totals	$13,021	$13,021

Step 5—Record closing entries for the temporary accounts.

Closing entries (events 15, 16, and 17) transfer the ending balances from the revenue and expense T-accounts to an income summary account, and then ultimately to the retained earnings account on the statement of shareholders' equity, and thus, the balance sheet. Closing entries also serve another function—they set the revenue and expense T-accounts equal to zero at the end of each fiscal period (see the closing balances for the T-accounts from Step 2). By doing so, the revenue and expense T-accounts only contain information from the current period, thus facilitating comparisons of net income from one fiscal period to the next.

Event	Account	Debit	Credit
15	Sales revenue.	1,900	
	Income summary		1,900
16	Income summary	1,583	
	Cost of goods sold		380
	Wage expense.		100
	Depreciation expense		225
	Selling & administrative expense.		300
	Interest expense		288
	Amortization expense		50
	Tax expense.		240
17	Income summary	317	
	Retained earnings		317

Exhibit D.3 presents Russian River Valley's post-closing trial balance, reflecting the closing of the company's temporary accounts—that is, the revenue, expense, and dividend accounts.

EXHIBIT D.3

RUSSIAN RIVER VALLEY WINERY, INC.
Post-Closing Trial Balance

Account	Debit	Credit
Cash..	$ 768	
Accounts receivable......................	800	
Inventory..................................	60	
Equipment	3,500	
Buildings..................................	2,000	
Accumulated depreciation		$ 225
Land.......................................	4,000	
Intangible assets	50	
Accounts payable.........................		80
Taxes payable............................		96
Loan payable		4,320
Common stock............................		6,400
Retained earnings		57
Totals	$11,178	$11,178

Step 6—Prepare the financial statements.

The financial statements prepared from data organized using the debit/credit paradigm will be identical to those derived using the spreadsheet approach, as presented in Exhibits 2.2 through 2.5 in the text and reproduced below.

EXHIBIT 2.2   Illustrative Balance Sheets

RUSSIAN RIVER VALLEY WINERY, INC.
Balance Sheets

($ thousands)	Pre-Opening	End of Year 1	Liabilities and shareholders' equity	Pre-Opening	End of Year 1
Assets			**Liabilities and shareholders' equity**		
Current assets			*Current liabilities*		
Cash.........................	$ 4,700	$ 768	Accounts payable.........	$ 0	$ 80
Accounts receivable............	0	800	Taxes payable.............	0	96
Inventory.....................	0	60	Loan payable—current.....	0	480
Total current assets	4,700	1,628	Total current liabilities......	0	656
Noncurrent assets			*Noncurrent liabilities*		
Property, plant & equipment			Loan payable—noncurrent..	4,800	3,840
Equipment	0	3,500	**Total liabilities**	**4,800**	**4,496**
Buildings....................	2,000	2,000			
Land........................	4,000	4,000	*Shareholders' equity*		
	6,000	9,500	Common stock...........	6,000	6,400
Accumulated depreciation	0	(225)	Retained earnings	0	57
Property, plant & equipment (net)..	6,000	9,275	**Total shareholders' equity** .	**6,000**	**6,457**
Intangible assets	100	50	**Total liabilities &**		
			shareholders' equity......	**$10,800**	**$10,953**
Total noncurrent assets	6,100	9,325			
Total assets..................	**$10,800**	**$10,953**			

EXHIBIT 2.3	An Illustrative Income Statement

RUSSIAN RIVER VALLEY WINERY, INC.
Income Statement

($ thousands)	Year 1
Revenues	$1,900
Cost of goods sold	380
Gross profit	1,520
Operating expenses	
Wages and salaries	100
Selling & administrative	300
Depreciation	225
Amortization	50
Total operating expenses	675
Operating income	845
Interest expense	288
Income before income taxes	557
Income taxes	240
Net income	$ 317

EXHIBIT 2.4	An Illustrative Statement of Shareholders' Equity

RUSSIAN RIVER VALLEY WINERY, INC.
Statement of Shareholders' Equity

($ thousands)	Common Stock	Retained Earnings	Total
Balance at beginning of Year 1	$6,000	$ 0	$6,000
Net income		317	317
Dividends paid		(260)	(260)
Sale of common stock	400		400
Balance at end of Year 1	$6,400	$ 57	$6,457

EXHIBIT 2.5	An Illustrative Statement of Cash Flow

RUSSIAN RIVER VALLEY WINERY, INC.
Statement of Cash Flow

($ thousands)	Year 1
Operating activities	
Cash receipts	
Cash sales	$ 380
Cash collections on account	720
Total cash receipts	1,100
Cash disbursements	
Cash payments for inventory	(360)
Cash payments for interest	(288)
Cash payments for wages & salaries	(100)
Cash payments for selling & administrative	(300)
Cash payments for taxes	(144)
Total cash disbursements	(1,192)
Cash flow from operations	**(92)**
Investing activities	
Purchases of property, plant & equipment	(3,500)
Cash flow from investing	**(3,500)**
Financing activities	
Sale of common stock	400
Repayment of loan	(480)
Payment of common stock dividends	(260)
Cash flow from financing	**(340)**
Change in cash	(3,932)
Cash balance, beginning of year	4,700
Cash balance, end of year	**$ 768**

D.1 **Recording Transactions Using the Debit/Credit Paradigm.** Miller & Co. experienced the following six events in its first year of operations:

1. Shareholders contributed $60,000 cash.
2. Purchased land for $40,000 cash.
3. Borrowed $18,000 in cash from a bank.
4. Provided services for $16,000, which will be paid to Miller & Co. next year.
5. Paid $11,000 cash for miscellaneous operating expenses.
6. Paid a $1,000 cash dividend to shareholders.

Required
Prepare journal entries using the debit/credit paradigm to record the above transactions.

D.2 **Recording Transactions Using the Debit/Credit Paradigm.** The following events occurred for The KMF Corporation during 2013:

1. Sales of products totaled $219,000, of which $15,000 remained uncollected at year-end.
2. The cost of goods sold during the year was $56,000.
3. A cash disbursement of $50,000 was made on July 1, 2013, to pay for a 12-month office equipment lease that expires on June 30, 2014.
4. Depreciation expense for the year on the company's warehouse amounted to $7,500.
5. Employee wages for the year totaled $40,000, of which $2,000 was unpaid at year-end.
6. Selling, general, and administrative expenses amounted to $10,000 for the year and were paid in full.
7. A cash payment of $25,000 was made to reduce the balance of accounts payable.
8. Interest expense on long-term debt was $18,000 for the year, of which $4,500 was unpaid at year-end.
9. The company paid income taxes of $25,000 on its earnings.

Required
Prepare journal entries using the debit/credit paradigm to record the above transactions.

CHAPTER 5: RECORDING OPERATING REVENUE AND RECEIVABLES USING THE DEBIT AND CREDIT PARADIGM

In this appendix, the traditional approach to recording accounting transactions—that is, the debit and credit paradigm—is followed to illustrate how the journal entries for the operating revenue and receivables for ProFlight Inc. and for Pan American Enterprises, Inc. would be recorded by these enterprises. The information used in this appendix is taken directly from the content of Chapter 5. To facilitate your understanding of the transactions, asset accounts are labeled with an (A), liability accounts with an (L), shareholders' equity accounts with an (SE), and revenue or expense accounts with an (R) or an (E), respectively.

Revenue Recognition Transactions: ProFlight Inc.

ProFlight Inc., a manufacturer of private corporate jets, signed a contract to build five jets over a two-year period for TransGlobal Airlines. Under the terms of the contract, ProFlight will receive total revenue of $10 million and anticipates that its cost to build the planes will total $8 million. During 2011, ProFlight completed 20 percent of the work, sent an invoice for $1 million to TransGlobal, and received a cash payment of $500,000. During 2012, ProFlight completed the remaining 80 percent of the work on budget, delivered the five planes, sent an invoice for the remaining $9 million to TransGlobal and received a $4.5 million cash payment. In 2013, after completing flight testing of the aircraft, Trans-Global remitted the final $5 million in cash to ProFlight. Journal entries are presented to reflect ProFlight's accounting transactions under the percentage-of-completion method and the completed contract method of revenue recognition.

Percentage-of-Completion Method.   Under the percentage-of-completion approach to revenue recognition, ProFlight will recognize its operating revenue and expenses on the basis of the amount of work actually completed each fiscal period (20 percent in 2011 and 80 percent in 2012). Consequently, the journal entries for ProFlight for the period 2011 through 2013 would appear as follows:

Date	Accounts	Debit	Credit
2011	No entry is required at contact signing		
	Production-in-progress (A).	2,000,000	
	Accounts payable (L).		2,000,000
	To record the acquisition of production material on credit.		
	Accounts receivable (A)	1,000,000	
	Unbilled accounts receivable (A)	1,000,000	
	Revenue (R).		2,000,000
	To recognize revenue based on a 20 percent work completion: *20% × $10,000,000.*		
	Cash (A)	500,000	
	Accounts receivable (A).		500,000
	To record the collection of cash on the billed account receivable.		
	Cost of production (E)	1,600,000	
	Production-in-progress (A)		1,600,000
	To record the consumption of production material—that is, cost of goods sold—related to the revenue recognized, 20 percent of $8 million.		
	Accounts payable (L)	2,000,000	
	Cash (A).		2,000,000
	To record the payment of accounts payable for production materials.		
2012	Production-in-progress (A).	6,000,000	
	Accounts payable (L).		6,000,000
	To record the acquisition of production material on credit to complete the contract.		
	Accounts receivable (A)	9,000,000	
	Unbilled accounts receivable (A).		1,000,000
	Revenue (R).		8,000,000
	To record the completion of the contract, the remaining revenue and final customer billing.		

continued

Date	Accounts	Debit	Credit
2012 cont.	Cash (A)	4,500,000	
	Accounts receivable (A)..		4,500,000
	To record the collection of cash on billed accounts receivable.		
	Cost of production (E)	6,400,000	
	Production-in-progress (A)		6,400,000
	To record the consumption of production material—that is, the cost of goods sold—related to the revenue recognized in 2012, 80 percent of $8 million.		
	Accounts payable (L)	6,000,000	
	Cash (A)..		6,000,000
	To record the payment of accounts payable.		
2013	Cash (A)	5,000,000	
	Accounts receivable (A)..		5,000,000
	To record the collection of cash on billed accounts receivable.		

Completed Contract Method.   Under the Completed Contract approach, ProFlight will defer the recognition of any operating revenue or expenses until the contract is fully satisfied at the end of 2012. Consequently, the journal entries for ProFlight for the period 2011 through 2013 would appear as follows:

Date	Accounts	Debit	Credit
2011	No entry is required at contact signing		
	Production-in-progress (A)......................................	2,000,000	
	Accounts payable (L)...		2,000,000
	To record the acquisition of production materials on credit.		
	Accounts receivable (A)	1,000,000	
	Deferred revenue (L)		1,000,000
	To record progress billing sent to customer.		
	Cash (A)	500,000	
	Accounts receivable (A)..		500,000
	To record cash collected on billed account receivable.		
	Accounts payable (L)	2,000,000	
	Cash (A)..		2,000,000
	To record payment of accounts payable related to production material.		
2012	Production-in-progress (A)......................................	6,000,000	
	Accounts payable (L)...		6,000,000
	To record the acquisition of production material on credit.		
	Accounts receivable (A)	9,000,000	
	Deferred revenue (L)		9,000,000
	To record progress billing sent to customer.		
	Cash (A)	4,500,000	
	Accounts receivable (A)..		4,500,000
	To record cash collection on billed account receivable.		
	Accounts payable (L)	6,000,000	
	Cash (A)..		6,000,000
	To record payment of accounts payable related to production material.		
	Deferred revenue (L)...	10,000,000	
	Revenue (R)...		10,000,000
	To recognize revenue associated with contract completion.		
	Cost of production (E)	8,000,000	
	Production-in-progress (A)		8,000,000
	To recognize the cost of goods sold associated with contract completion.		

continued

Date	Accounts	Debit	Credit
2013	Cash (A)	5,000,000	
	Accounts receivable (A)..		5,000,000
	To record the collection of cash on billed accounts receivable.		

Accounting for Receivables: Pan American Enterprises, Inc.

Pan American Enterprises, Inc. sells its internationally recognized wine on account to bars and restaurants throughout the United States. The company's credit terms require customers to pay their bills within 30 days of a transaction. During 2012 and 2013, Pan American Enterprises experienced the following accounting events:

Year	Credit Sales	Cash Collections	Estimated Bad Debt	Bad Debt Write-Off
2012	$3,200,000	$2,850,000	$10,925	$ —
2013	5,300,000	4,838,500	22,500	11,500

Using the debit/credit paradigm, Pan American Enterprises would record the following journal entries to reflect this accounting information:

Date	Accounts	Debit	Credit
2012	Accounts receivable (A)	3,200,000	
	Sales (R)		3,200,000
	To record credit sales for 2012.		
	Cash (A)	2,850,000	
	Accounts receivable (A)..		2,850,000
	To record collections on credit sales.		
	Bad debt expense (E)..	10,925	
	Allowance for uncollectible accounts (CA)		10,925
	To record the estimated bad debt expense and establish the allowance for future account write-offs.		
2013	Allowance for uncollectible accounts (CA)........................	11,500	
	Accounts receivable (A)..		11,500
	To write off uncollected accounts receivable that have proven to be worthless.		
	Accounts receivable (A)	5,300,000	
	Sales (R)		5,300,000
	To record credit sales for 2013.		
	Cash (A)	4,838,500	
	Accounts receivable (A)..		4,838,500
	To record cash collections on credit sales.		
	Bad debt expense (E)..	23,075	
	Allowance for uncollectible accounts (CA))....................		23,075
	To record the estimated bad debt expense of $22,500 for 2013 and to record the underestimated expense of $575 for 2012.		

To validate your understanding of the above journal entries, create T-accounts for each of the accounts, post the journal entry amounts to the appropriate T-accounts, and create account totals. Your T-account balances should reconcile with the balances reported in the chapter.

D.3   **Recording the Bad Debt Expense Using the Debit/Credit Paradigm.**   Holcombe Inc. uses the aging method to estimate the company's bad debt expense. Travis Holcombe, president of the company, collected information about the company's outstanding accounts receivable and their probability of collection:

Account Age	Amount	Probability of Non-Collection
0–30 days	$725,000	0.5%
31–60 days	275,000	1.5
61–90 days	170,000	2.5
91–120 days	100,000	4.0
Over 120 days	40,000	20.0

Required

Calculate the expected bad debt expense for Holcombe Inc., and prepare the journal entry to record the estimate using the debit/credit paradigm. Assume that one-half of the estimated bad debts prove to be uncollectible. Prepare the journal entry to write off the uncollectible accounts receivable. If $1,000 of the previously written off uncollectible receivables is found to be collectible, what entry would be needed to reinstate the accounts receivable on the books of Holcombe Inc.?

D.4 **Recording Revenue and Expenses Using the Debit/Credit Paradigm.** RJ Miller Company won a contract to build a shopping center at a price of $240 million. The following schedule details the estimated and actual costs of construction and the actual cash collections under the contract:

	Estimated (Actual) Costs of Construction	Cash Collections From Customer
2012	$ 40,000,000	$ 48,000,000
2013	60,000,000	60,000,000
2014	70,000,000	60,000,000
2015	30,000,000	72,000,000
	$200,000,000	$240,000,000

Required

1. Prepare the journal entries to record the revenue and expenses for RJ Miller Company for 2012 through 2015 assuming that the company recognizes revenue under the completed contract method.
2. Prepare the journal entries to record the revenue and expenses for RJ Miller Company for 2012 through 2015 assuming that the company recognizes revenue under the percentage-of-completion method.

CHAPTER 6: RECORDING COST OF GOODS SOLD AND INVENTORY USING THE DEBIT AND CREDIT PARADIGM

In this appendix, the traditional approach to recording accounting transactions—that is, the debit and credit paradigm—is used to illustrate how the journal entries for the cost of goods sold and inventory for the Arizona Ice Cream Company, Inc., would be recorded. Since the journal entries are similar under FIFO, LIFO, and the weighted-average cost method (only the recorded amounts differ), we assume that the company adopts the FIFO method to value its cost of goods sold and ending inventory (see Exhibit 6.3).

Arizona Ice Cream Company, Inc: Recording Inventory Transactions

During the year, Arizona Ice Cream Company, Inc. (AICC), made the following cash purchases of ice cream:

Date	Amount	Cost per Bucket	Total Cost
September 5	1,000	$10	$ 10,000
October 22	2,500	12	30,000
November 15	4,500	13	58,500
December 30	2,000	15	30,000
	10,000		$128,500

AICC also sold 8,000 buckets of ice cream at a retail price of $20 per bucket for total operating revenue of $160,000. All sales were in cash and the sales occurred on the following dates:

Date	Number of Buckets Sold
September 20.	800
November 4	2,600
December 22	3,400
December 31	1,200
	8,000

At year-end, the AICC's CEO determined that the replacement cost of the company's inventory of 2,000 buckets of ice cream was $28,000 ($14 per bucket x 2,000 buckets).

The above financial data would be recorded as follows:

Date	Accounts	Debit	Credit
Sep 5	Inventory (A)	10,000	
	Cash (A)		10,000
	To record the cash purchase of 1,000 buckets.		
Sep 20	Cash (A)	16,000	
	Revenue (R)		16,000
	To record the cash sale of 800 buckets.		
	Cost of Goods Sold (E)	8,000	
	Inventory (A)		8,000
	To record the cost of goods sold on 800 buckets.		
Oct 22	Inventory (A)	30,000	
	Cash (A)		30,000
	To record the cash purchase of 2,500 buckets.		
Nov 4	Cash (A)	52,000	
	Revenue (R)		52,000
	To record the cash sale of 2,600 buckets.		
	Cost of Goods Sold (E)	30,800	
	Inventory (A)		30,800
	To record the cost of goods sold on 2,600 buckets.		
Nov 15	Inventory (A)	58,500	
	Cash (A)		58,500
	To record the cash purchase of 4,500 buckets.		
Dec 22	Cash (A)	68,000	
	Revenue (R)		68,000
	To record the cash sale of 3,400 buckets.		
	Cost of Goods Sold (E)	44,100	
	Inventory (A)		44,100
	To record the cost of goods sold on 3,400 buckets.		
Dec 30	Inventory (A)	30,000	
	Cash (A)		30,000
	To record the cash purchase of 2,000 buckets.		
Dec 31	Cash (A)	24,000	
	Revenue (R)		24,000
	To record the cash sale of 1,200 buckets.		
	Cost of Goods Sold (E)	15,600	
	Inventory (A)		15,600
	To record the cost of goods sold on 1,200 buckets.		
	Cost of Goods Sold (E)	2,000	
	Inventory (A)		2,000
	To record the lower-of-cost-or-market write-down of inventory.		

D.5 **Recording Inventory and the Cost of Goods Sold Using the Debit/Credit Paradigm.** The following information was disclosed in the 2012 annual report of The Claremont Company.

	2012	2011
Beginning inventory	$20,970	$11,560
Purchase of inventory	83,300	42,640
Ending inventories	19,310	20,970
Cost of goods sold	84,960	33,230

Required

Prepare the journal entries to record (1) the purchase of inventory and (2) the cost of goods sold for The Claremont Company for 2011 and 2012.

CHAPTER 7: RECORDING INVESTMENTS IN, AND SALES OF, LONG-LIVED ASSETS USING THE DEBIT AND CREDIT PARADIGM

In this appendix, the traditional approach to recording accounting transactions—that is, the debit and credit paradigm—is used to illustrate the journal entries for the acquisition, depreciation, and retirement of long-lived assets. Data for the current illustration follows the example in the chapter and assumes the use of straight-line depreciation:

A truck having an expected useful life of five years and a resale value of $4,000 upon retirement is purchased for $30,000 cash at the beginning of the year (BOY). At the end of the five-year period, the truck is sold for $4,500. Note: End of the year is represented by (EOY).

Illustrative Journal Entries

Date	Accounts	Debit	Credit
Year 1 (BOY)	Truck (A)	30,000	
	Cash (A)		30,000
	To record the cash purchase of an asset.		
Year 1 (EOY)	Depreciation Expense (E)	5,200	
	Accumulated Depreciation (CA)		5,200
	To record the annual depreciation expense on the truck.		
Year 2 (EOY)	Depreciation Expense (E)	5,200	
	Accumulated Depreciation (CA)		5,200
	To record the annual depreciation expense on the truck.		
Year 3 (EOY)	Depreciation Expense (E)	5,200	
	Accumulated Depreciation (CA)		5,200
	To record the annual depreciation expense on the truck.		
Year 4 (EOY)	Depreciation Expense (E)	5,200	
	Accumulated Depreciation (CA)		5,200
	To record the annual depreciation expense on the truck.		
Year 5 (EOY)	Depreciation Expense (E)	5,200	
	Accumulated Depreciation (CA)		5,200
	To record the annual depreciation expense on the truck.		
	Cash (A)	4,500	
	Accumulated Depreciation (CA)	26,000	
	Gain on Sale of Asset		500
	Truck (A)		30,000
	To record the sale of the truck for $4,500, the gain (G) on sale of $500, and the removal of the truck and related accumulated depreciation from the financial records.		

D.6 **Recording Investments in, and Sales of, Long-lived Assets Using the Debit/Credit Paradigm.** At the beginning of 2011, The Beall Corporation purchased a warehouse for $10 million and immediately made certain necessary renovations to the facility which cost $2 million. The chief financial officer of the company decided to depreciate the new warehouse using the straight- line method over a 20 year expected useful life, assuming no salvage value at the end of the 20 year period. After two years of use, Beall received an offer to sell the warehouse for $17 million and accepted the offer.

Required

Prepare the journal entries to record (1) the purchase and renovation of the warehouse, (2) the depreciation expense on the warehouse for the first two years, and (3) the sale of the warehouse.

CHAPTER 8: RECORDING INVESTMENTS IN OTHER CORPORATE ENTITIES USING THE DEBIT AND CREDIT PARADIGM

In this appendix, the traditional approach to recording accounting transactions—that is, the debit and credit paradigm—is used to illustrate the journal entries associated with the various investments made by The New South Wales Trading Company, Inc. and by Savanna, Inc. Please refer to the content of Chapter 8 for additional information regarding these transactions (see Exhibits 8.3 through 8.12).

Accounting for Marketable Debt and Equity Securities: The New South Wales Company Inc.

In August, The New South Wales Trading Company, Inc. raised $50 million from an initial public offering (IPO) of its common shares. The company decided to temporarily invest some of its IPO cash in various debt and equity securities having a high degree of liquidity. These events are recorded below:

Date	Accounts	Debit	Credit
August	Cash (A)	50,000,000	
	Common Stock (SE)		50,000,000
	To record the sale of common stock for $50 million.		
September	Investment in Qantas Inc. 10% Notes (A)	10,000,000	
	Cash (A)		10,000,000
	To record the purchase of held-to-maturity debt securities.		
November	Investment in BHP, Inc. Common Stock (A)	6,100,000	
	Cash (A)		6,100,000
	To record the investment in trading equity securities.		
December	Investment in Coles Inc. Common Stock (A)	8,400,000	
	Cash (A)		8,400,000
	To record the investment in available-for-sale equity securities.		

At the end of the year, the CFO of The New South Wales Trading Company, Inc. determined that the Qantas notes were worth $9.8 million, the BHP common shares worth $6.8 million, and the Coles Inc. common shares worth $8.2 million. In addition, the CFO observed that Qantas Inc. had made an interest payment of $1 million on its notes on December 31. This information would be recorded as follows:

Date	Accounts	Debit	Credit
December 31	Cash (A)	1,000,000	
	Interest Income (I)		1,000,000
	To record interest income I on the Qantas notes.		
	Investment in BHP Inc. common stock (A)	700,000	
	Unrealized Gain on Trading Securities (G)		700,000
	To record the gain of $700,000 on trading equity securities.		
	Unrealized Loss on Available-For-Sale Securities (SE)	200,000	
	Investment in Coles Inc. Common Stocks (A)		200,000
	To record the decline in market value on available-for-sale securities.		

To verify your understanding of these transactions, create a series of T-accounts for the affected accounts, post the amounts to the T-accounts, and calculate a year-end balance. Your results should reveal the following balances:

Assets		Shareholders' Equity	
Cash...........................	$26,500,000	Common stock....................	$50,000,000
Investments		Retained earnings	1,700,000
Qantas notes	10,000,000	Other Comprehensive Income	
BHP common stock..............	6,800,000	Unrealized loss on available-for-sale	
Coles common stock.............	8,200,000	securities	(200,000)
Total	**$51,500,000**	Total	**$51,500,000**

Equity Method and Consolidated Accounting: Savanna, Inc.

Case 1.   Savanna Inc. acquires 40 percent of the common shares of Waterloo Inc. for $8 million at the beginning of the year. At year-end, Savanna reports cash earnings of $30 million; Waterloo reports cash earnings of $10 million; and, Waterloo pays its shareholders a cash dividend of $5 million. These transactions would be recorded as follows on Savanna's books:

Date	Accounts	Debit	Credit
January	Investment in Waterloo Inc. (A).	8,000,000	
	Cash (A).		8,000,000
	To record the initial investment in Waterloo Inc.		
December	Cash (A)	30,000,000	
	Retained Earnings (SE)		30,000,000
	To record Savanna's cash earnings of $30 million.		
	Investment in Waterloo Inc. (A).	4,000,000	
	Income From Equity Affiliate (I)		4,000,000
	To record Savanna's 40 percent share of Waterloo's $10 million in earnings.		
	Cash (A)	2,000,000	
	Investment in Waterloo Inc. (A)		2,000,000
	To record Savanna's 40 percent share of Waterloo's $5 million dividend payment.		

Case 2.   Savanna Inc. acquires 80 percent of Waterloo's common shares for $16 million in January; the fair market value of Waterloo's net assets equals their book value of $20 million (no goodwill is implicit in the investment). At year-end, Savanna reports cash earnings of $30 million; Waterloo reports cash earnings of $10 million; and, Waterloo pays its shareholders a cash dividend of $5 million. Because of its majority shareholding, Savanna prepares consolidated financial statements at year-end. These transactions would be recorded as follows on Savanna's books:

Date	Accounts	Debit	Credit
January	Investment in Waterloo Inc. (A).	16,000,000	
	Cash (A).		16,000,000
	To record Savanna's acquisition of a 80 percent shareholding in Waterloo Inc.		
December	Cash (A)	30,000,000	
	Retained Earnings (SE)		30,000,000
	To record Savanna's cash earnings of $30 million.		
	Investment in Waterloo Inc. (A).	8,000,000	
	Income From Equity Affiliate (I)		8,000,000
	To record Savanna's 80 percent ownership interest in Waterloo earnings of $10 million.		

continued

Date	Accounts	Debit	Credit
December cont.	Cash (A)	4,000,000	
	Investment in Waterloo (A).		4,000,000
	To record Savanna's 80 percent ownership interest in Waterloo's dividend payment of $5 million.		
	Cash (A)	25,000,000	
	Inventory (A)	80,000,000	
	Investment in Waterloo (A).		20,000,000
	Minority Interest (L/SE)		5,000,000
	Long-Term debt (L)		80,000,000
	To consolidate Waterloo's net assets with those of Savanna and to establish the minority interest account.		

(The journal entries for Case 3 are not presented here. You may wish to create these entries using the contents of Exhibits 8.11 and 8.12)

D.7 **Recording Marketable Equity Securities Transactions Using the Debit/Credit Paradigm.** **Microsoft Inc.** maintains a large investment in marketable securities (principally fixed income securities) valued at approximately $42 billion as of the beginning of the year. During the year, the securities produced investment income (dividends and interest income) totaling $2 billion. At year-end, the portfolio of marketable securities had appreciated to $43.5 billion.

Required

Using journal entries, record (1) Microsoft's purchase of the securities at the beginning of the year, (2) the receipt of $2 billion in investment income during the year, and (3) the appreciation of the portfolio by $1.5 billion at the end of the year. Assume that the entire portfolio is classified as "trading securities."

D.8 **Recording Equity Method Transactions Using the Debit/Credit Paradigm.** On January 1, 2012, The Miller Corporation purchased 300,000 shares of The Mayfair Corporation for $5.7 million. The investment represented 25 percent of The Mayfair Corporation's outstanding common shares. During 2012, Mayfair reported net earnings of $2.25 million and paid a cash dividend of $0.15 per share. During 2013, Mayfair reported a net loss of $180,000 and again paid a dividend of $0.15 per share.

Required

Using journal entries, record (1) The Miller Corporation's initial investment in The Mayfair Corporation and (2) the appropriate entries for 2012 and 2013 assuming that The Miller Corporation uses the equity method to account for its investment in Mayfair.

CHAPTER 9: RECORDING DEBT FINANCING TRANSACTIONS USING THE DEBIT AND CREDIT PARADIGM

In this appendix, the traditional approach to recording accounting transactions—that is, the debit and credit paradigm—is used to illustrate how the journal entries associated with the issuance of various debt instruments by Midwestern Airlines, Inc. would be recorded. Specifically, the accounting for interest-bearing notes, zero-coupon notes, and operating and capital leases is illustrated.

Accounting for Notes

On January 1, 2013, Midwestern Airlines, Inc., issued $100 million face value (maturity value) of mortgage notes with an annual coupon rate of eight percent and a maturity of ten years. The notes pay interest on June 30 and December 31 of each year. At the time the notes were issued, the market yield rate on equivalent risk-rated instruments was ten percent. Five years later, on December 31, 2017, the market yield rate on equivalent risk-rated securities had increased to twelve percent. No longer needing the debt financing, Midwestern Airlines decided to retire all of its outstanding debt on December 31, 2017. (Please refer to the chapter for the calculation of the following values.)

Date	Accounts	Debit	Credit
Jan 1, 2013	Cash (A)	87,548,000	
	Note discount (CL)	12,452,000	
	Notes payable (L).		100,000,000
	To record the issuance of $100 million in notes at a discount.		
Jun 30, 2013	Interest expense (E)	4,377,400	
	Cash (A).		4,000,000
	Note discount (CL).		377,400
	To record the payment of interest on the notes.		
Dec 31, 2013	Interest expense (E)	4,396,300	
	Cash (A).		4,000,000
	Note discount (CL).		396,300
	To record the payment of interest on the notes.		

(Interest payment entries similar to those presented above would be recorded for 2014, 2015, 2016, and 2017. Appropriate values for the entries can be obtained from the Note Amortization Table in Exhibit 9.1)

Date	Accounts	Debit	Credit
Dec 31, 2017	Notes payable (L)	100,000,000	
	Cash (A).		85,240,000
	Note discount (CL).		7,720,000
	Gain on early retirement (G).		7,040,000
	To record the early retirement of the notes at a gain.		

Assume now that on January 1, 2013, Midwestern Airlines, Inc., issued $100 million face value of zero-coupon mortgage notes, having a maturity of ten years with semiannual compounding. At the time of issuance, the yield rate on equivalent risk-rated debt securities was twelve percent. (Please refer to the chapter for the calculation of the following values.)

Date	Accounts	Debit	Credit
Jan 1, 2013	Cash (A)	31,200,000	
	Note discount (CL)	68,800,000	
	Notes payable (L).		100,000,000
	To record the issuance of $100 million in zero-coupon notes.		
Jun 30, 2013	Interest expense (E)	1,872,000	
	Note discount (CL).		1,872,000
	To record the interest expense implicit in the zero-coupon notes.		
Dec 31, 2013	Interest expense (E)	1,984,000	
	Note discount (CL).		1,984,000
	To record the interest expense implicit in the zero-coupon notes.		

Accounting for Leases

Midwestern Airlines entered into a ten-year lease agreement for flight equipment having a fair market value of $100 million and an implicit interest rate of ten percent per year. Annual lease payments of $16.27 million are paid at the end of each year. The leased equipment had an expected remaining useful life of 13 years.

If the lease is accounted for as an operating lease, the following transactions would be recorded:

Date	Accounts	Debit	Credit
Year 1 (BOY)	No entry is recorded at the time of lease signing.		
Year 1 (EOY)	Lease expense (E)	16,270,000	
	Cash (A).		16,270,000
	To record the annual lease payment and lease expense.		
Year 2 (EOY)	Lease expense (E)	16,270,000	
	Cash (A).		16,270,000
	To record the annual lease payment and lease expense.		

(Equivalent journal entries would be recorded each year until the lease agreement expires at the end of ten years.)

If the lease is accounted for as a capital lease, the following transactions would be recorded:

Year 1 (BOY)	Leased equipment (A)	100,000,000	
	Lease liability (L)		100,000,000
	To record the signing of a capital lease agreement.		
Year 1 (EOY)	Interest expense (E)	10,000,000	
	Lease liability (L)...	6,270,000	
	Cash (A)...		16,270,000
	To record annual lease payment, debt reduction, and interest expense.		
	Depreciation expense (E)	10,000,000	
	Accumulated depreciation (CA)............................		10,000,000
	To record the depreciation expense on the leased equipment.		
Year 2 (EOY)	Interest expense (E)	9,370,000	
	Lease liability (L)...	6,900,000	
	Cash (A)...		16,270,000
	To record annual lease payment, debt reduction, and interest expense.		
	Depreciation expense (E)	10,000,000	
	Accumulated depreciation (CA)............................		10,000,000
	To record annual depreciation expense on the leased equipment.		

D.9   **Recording Debt Financing Transactions Using the Debit/Credit Paradigm.** During 2012, the Mayfield Corporation issued $100 million of zero-coupon debentures, due in 2022. The proceeds of the bond sale totaled approximately $45.64 million, assuming the bonds were sold to yield 4 percent per period.

Required

Using journal entries, record (1) the proceeds from the sale of the Mayfield bonds in 2012 and (2) the interest expense to be recognized on the bonds at the end of the first six-month period.

D.10   **Recording Lease Financing Transactions Using the Debit/Credit Paradigm.** Maximum Electronics Inc. is a retail chain of discount electronic stores throughout the southwest United States. Maximum leases a fleet of 200 trucks to deliver purchases to its customers. The annual lease payment per truck totals $5,000 and the interest rate implicit in the lease is eight percent. On January 1, 2013, Maximum renewed its truck fleet lease under the same terms for a five-year period.

Required
1. Assume that the fleet lease should be accounted for as a capital lease. Using journal entries, record the leased assets and lease liability on January 1, 2013.
2. Assume that the trucks will be depreciated on a straight-line basis with no salvage value. Using journal entries, record the depreciation expense on the leased assets and the interest expense and debt payment on the lease liability on December 31, 2013.

CHAPTER 11: RECORDING EQUITY FINANCING TRANSACTIONS USING THE DEBIT AND CREDIT PARADIGM

In this appendix, the traditional approach to recording accounting transactions—that is, the debit and credit paradigm—is used to illustrate the journal entries for various equity financing transactions. For purposes of this appendix, the following illustrative transactions are assumed to have occurred during the year.

- Claremont Company incorporated on January 1, and authorized the issuance of 100,000 shares of $1 par value common stock and 50,000 shares of no-par value preferred stock. The preferred stock had a stated dividend of $5 per share.
- On January 10, Claremont Company sold 25,000 shares of common stock for $500,000 cash and 10,000 shares of preferred stock for $100,000 cash.
- On June 30, the Board of Directors of Claremont Company declared and paid a cash dividend of $0.10 per share on each outstanding common share and $2.50 per share on each outstanding preferred share, or a total of $27,500 in cash dividends ($2,500 + $25,000).

- On September 1, Claremont Company repurchased 5,000 shares of common stock at a cost of $15 per share, or a total outlay of $75,000.
- On December 31, the Board of Directors of Claremont Company declared a 2:1 forward stock split on the issued and outstanding common shares.
- On December 31, the Board of Directors of Claremont Company issued 1,000 treasury shares to company executives who exercised stock options at an exercise price of $10 per share.

The following journal entries would be recorded to reflect the above equity transactions.

Date	Accounts	Debit	Credit
Jan 1	No entry is recorded to reflect the authorization to sell equity shares		
Jan 10	Cash (A)	500,000	
	Common stock, $1 par (SE)		25,000
	Additional paid-in-capital (SE).....................................		475,000
	To record the sale of 25,000 shares of $1 par value common stock.		
	Cash (A)	100,000	
	Preferred stock (SE)...		100,000
	To record the sale of 10,000 shares of no-par value preferred stock.		
Jun 30	Dividends (D)	27,500	
	Cash (A)..		27,500
	To record the declaration and payment of a cash dividend on the outstanding common and preferred shares.		
Sep 1	Treasury Stock (SE)	75,000	
	Cash (A)..		75,000
	To record the repurchase of 5,000 common shares at $15 per share.		
Dec 31	Common Stock, $1 par value..	25,000	
	Common Stock, $0.50 par value....................................		25,000
	To record a reduction in the par value on the common shares from $1.00 to $0.50 per share, and to increase the shares issued and outstanding from 25,000 to 50,000 shares.		
	Retained Earnings (SE)...	5,000	
	Cash (A)	10,000	
	Treasury Shares (SE)..		15,000
	To record the exercise of stock options on 1,000 shares of common stock previously purchased at $15 per share		

To validate your understanding of the above journal entries, create a set of T-accounts and calculate the value of shareholders' equity for Claremont Company at year-end. Your answer should appear as follows:

Shareholders' Equity	
Common stock, $0.50 par value	$ 25,000
Additional paid-in-capital...	475,000
Preferred stock, no par value..	100,000
Retained earnings	(32,500)
Treasury stock	(60,000)
	$507,500

D.11   **Recording Shareholders' Equity Transactions Using the Debit/Credit Paradigm.**   The following transactions occurred during 2013 for The Niagara Company:

1. Sold 10,000 shares of common stock having a par value of $0.01 for $22 per share.
2. Paid a cash dividend of $2 per share to its preferred shareholders when 5,000 shares were outstanding.
3. Issued a ten percent stock dividend on its outstanding common stock when the price was $22 per share.
4. Repurchased 10,000 shares of common stock at $18 per share.
5. Declared a 2-for-1 forward stock split on its common stock.

Required

Using journal entries, record the shareholders' equity transactions for 2013 for The Niagara Company.

D.12   **Recording Shareholders' Equity Transactions Using the Debit/Credit Paradigm.**   During 2013, The Mann Corporation, a private entity, decided to go public. A charter of incorporation was constructed which authorized the sale of ten million shares of $1 par value common stock, 100,000 shares of $100 par value eight percent preferred stock, and 200,000 shares of $5 no-par value convertible preferred stock. The following shares were sold as part of the firm's initial public offering:

- 1,000,000 shares of common stock at $10 per share.
- 100,000 shares of $100 par value, eight percent preferred stock at $105 per share.
- 100,000 shares of $5 convertible, no-par preferred stock at $55 per share.

At the end of 2013, the full dividend was declared and paid on both preferred stock offerings.

Required

Using journal entries, record the financial effects of the shareholders' equity transactions for The Mann Corporation for 2013.

Index

Note: The letter e indicates an exhibit on that page. The letter n indicates footnote.

Note: The letter e indicates an exhibit on that page. The letter n indicates footnote.

Note: The letter e indicates an exhibit on that page. The letter n indicates footnote.

Note: The letter e indicates an exhibit on that page. The letter n indicates footnote.

Note: The letter e indicates an exhibit on that page. The letter n indicates footnote.

Note: The letter e indicates an exhibit on that page. The letter n indicates footnote.

Note: The letter e indicates an exhibit on that page. The letter n indicates footnote.

Note: The letter e indicates an exhibit on that page. The letter n indicates footnote.